MICRO ECONOMICS

SCARCITY, WANTS, AND CHOICES

SEVENTH CANADIAN EDITION

ALSO AVAILABLE FROM McGRAW-HILL RYERSON

MACROECONOMICS: Canada in the Global Economy
Seventh Canadian Edition
by Campbell R. McConnell, Stanley L. Brue, and Thomas P. Barbiero
ISBN 0-07-552614-X

STUDY GUIDE TO ACCOMPANY MICROECONOMICS
Seventh Canadian Edition
by William B. Walstad, Robert C. Bingham, Torben Andersen
ISBN 0-07-552615-8

STUDY GUIDE TO ACCOMPANY MACROECONOMICS
Seventh Canadian Edition
by William B. Walstad, Robert C. Bingham, Torben Andersen
ISBN 0-07-552616-6

MICRO ECONOMICS

SCARCITY, WANTS, AND CHOICES

SEVENTH CANADIAN EDITION

CAMPBELL R. McCONNELL
University of Nebraska, Lincoln

STANLEY L. BRUE
Pacific Lutheran University

THOMAS P. BARBIERO
Ryerson Polytechnic University

McGraw-Hill Ryerson Limited

Toronto New York Auckland Bogotá Caracas
Lisbon London Madrid Mexico Milan New Delhi
San Juan Singapore Sydney Tokyo

MICROECONOMICS: Scarcity, Wants, and Choices
Seventh Canadian Edition

ISBN: 0-07-552613-1

1 2 3 4 5 6 7 8 9 10 BBM 5 4 3 2 1 0 9 8 7 6

Printed and bound in Canada

Care has been taken to trace ownership of copyright material contained in this text. The publishers will gladly take any information that will enable them to rectify any reference or credit in subsequent editions.

SENIOR EDITOR: Jennifer Mix
SUPERVISING EDITOR: Margaret Henderson
DEVELOPMENT EDITOR: Daphne Scriabin
PRODUCTION EDITOR: Wendy Thomas
COVER & TEXT DESIGN: Lisa Kinloch, David Murphy/ArtPlus Limited
PRINTING & BINDING: Best Book Manufacturers

Canadian Cataloguing in Publication Data

McConnell, Campbell R.
      Microeconomics

7th Canadian ed.
Includes index.
ISBN 0-07-552613-1

1. Microeconomics. I. Brue, Stanley, L., 1945–   .
II. Barbiero, Thomas Paul, 1952–   .
III. Title.

HB172.M23 1996   338.5   C95-931814-3

This edition is dedicated to my dear wife, Elsa.

ABOUT THE AUTHORS

Campbell R. McConnell earned his Ph.D. from the University of Iowa after receiving degrees from Cornell College and the University of Illinois. He taught at the University of Nebraska — Lincoln from 1953 until his retirement in 1990. He is also coauthor of **Contemporary Labor Economics,** 4th ed. (McGraw-Hill) and has edited readers for the principles and labour economics courses. He is a recipient of both the University of Nebraska Distinguished Teaching Award and the James A. Lake Academic Freedom Award, and is past-president of the Midwest Economics Association. Professor McConnell was awarded an honorary Doctor of Laws degree from Cornell College in 1973 and received its Distinguished Achievement Award in 1994. His primary areas of interest are labour economics and economic education. He has an extensive collection of jazz recordings and enjoys reading jazz history.

Stanley L. Brue did his undergraduate work at Augustana College (S.D.) and received his Ph.D. from the University of Nebraska — Lincoln. He teaches at Pacific Lutheran University, where he has been honoured as a recipient of the Burlington Northern Faculty Achievement Award. He has also received the national Leavey Award for excellence in economic education. Professor Brue is national President and member of the International Executive Board of Omicron Delta Epsilon International Economics Honorary. He is coauthor of **Economic Scenes,** 5th ed. (Prentice-Hall) and **Contemporary Labor Economics,** 4th ed. (McGraw-Hill) and author of **The Evolution of Economic Thought,** 5th ed. (HB/Dryden). For relaxation, he enjoys boating on Puget Sound and skiing trips with his family.

Thomas P. Barbiero received his Ph.D. from the University of Toronto after completing undergraduate studies at the same university. He has published papers on the role of the agricultural sector in the industrial development of northern Italy in the period 1861–1914. His research interests in the last few years have turned to economic methodology and the application of economic theory to explain social phenomena. Professor Barbiero is presently associate professor of economics at Ryerson Polytechnic University. He spends his summer in Italy with his wife and three children. While there, apart from following his interest in the country's economic history, he assiduously pursues good food and wine.

CONTENTS IN BRIEF

CONTENTS

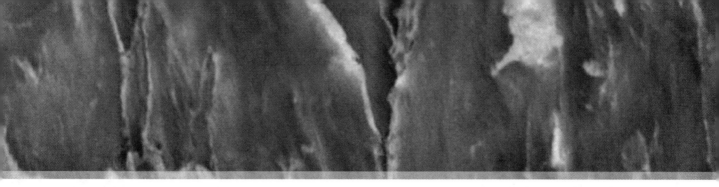

PREFACE

We are pleased to present the seventh Canadian edition of *Macroeconomics* and *Microeconomics*. *Macroeconomics* and *Microeconomics* continue to be leading economics texts in both Canada and the United States. Moreover, the Russian language versions of *Macroeconomics* and *Microeconomics* are the leading economics texts in Russia. More than 1 million Russians have used this book since the fall of communism.

Capitalism in Russia, interest rate hikes, GATT and NAFTA, pollution rights, governments' pursuit of balanced budgets — what a remarkable time for teaching and learning economics! The message of our day is clear: People who comprehend economic principles will have an advantage functioning in, and making sense of, the emerging world. We thank each of you using *Macroeconomics* and *Microeconomics* for granting us a modest role in your efforts to teach or learn this vital subject.

WHAT'S NEW?

This edition has been thoroughly revised, polished, and updated. Many of the changes have been motivated by the comments of nine reviewers. We sincerely thank each of them and acknowledge them by name at the end of this preface.

Here, we strive only for an overview of the changes in the seventh Canadian edition; chapter-by-chapter details are provided in the *Instructor's Resource Manual*.

NEW CHAPTERS

We have added two new chapters for this edition of *Microeconomics*.

• THE PUBLIC SECTOR. Responding to reviewers' suggestions, we have added a chapter on the government sector in the introductory part of the text (Chapter 5). Reviewers rightly pointed out the important role of government in the Canadian economy and that the public sector should be introduced early in the text. The economic functions of government, externalities, and public goods are introduced, and the size of government as measured by expenditures and revenues is discussed. The public sector is then put into the circular flow model introduced in Chapter 2.

• CANADA IN THE GLOBAL ECONOMY. The material of Part I has been condensed and rearranged to allow an early and comprehensive chapter (Chapter 6) on the global economy. This chapter contains not only descriptive material (volume and pattern of world trade), but also essential theory (comparative advantage, exchange rates) and institutional features (trade barriers, GATT, EU, NAFTA). By providing the basics of international trade and finance, the chapter is a springboard for the instructor who wishes to fully integrate micro and macro materials into a global framework.

NEW FEATURES

The seventh edition contains three new "features" — one adding another global dimension to *Macroeconomics* and *Microeconomics*, the other two making the book more interactive.

- **THE BIG PICTURE.**   Responding to reviewers' comments, we have added a box at the beginning of each chapter that connects the material already learned with the new materials still to be covered, to give the reader "The Big Picture." Sometimes students lose the forest for the trees, and this new feature helps them to avoid it.

- **IN THE MEDIA.**   In the sixth edition we introduced "In the Media" boxes — newspaper articles about current economic events. These have been updated and economic analysis has been added. A question at the end of the analysis allows students to test their understanding of the economic theory behind the story.

- **GLOBAL PERSPECTIVES.**   We have added Global Perspective sections — most containing charts — throughout the book to compare the Canadian economy with other nations. To merely state, for example, Canada's rates of inflation, unemployment, or taxes or the size of Canadian farm subsidies without international comparisons denies students the context needed for meaningful comparisons.

- **KEY QUESTIONS (WITH ANSWERS).**   We have designated two to five end-of-chapter questions as "Key Questions," answering them in the back of the text. Many of these questions are quantitative and are designed to help the student work through and understand basic concepts. The reader is alerted within the chapters as to when a particular Key Question is relevant. Students wanting to immediately test their understanding can turn to the specially marked Key Question, checking their answer against the end-of-book answer. Others may want to wait until they have read the full chapter before answering the Key Questions. Either way, the Key Questions make *Macroeconomics* and *Microeconomics* more interactive.

THE ECONOMIC PERSPECTIVE

We have placed greater emphasis on the economic way of thinking. In Chapter 1 we have greatly expanded the section on the economic perspective, discussing scarcity and choice, rational behaviour, and marginal analysis. In Chapter 2 we use the ideas of marginal benefits and marginal costs (Figure 2-2) to determine the optimal position on the production possibilities curve. We then take opportunities to reinforce the economic perspective in the remainder of the book.

CULLING AND TIGHTENING

Our considerable culling and tightening in the sixth edition has been well-received by reviewers and the marketplace. Buoyed by that response, we have again looked for places to delete the archaic, remove redundancy, tighten sentences, and reduce formality. In further economizing on words, we were careful *not* to reduce the thoroughness of our explanations. Where needed, the "extra sentence of explanation" remains a distinguishing characteristic of our textbook.

OTHER NEW TOPICS AND REVISED DISCUSSIONS

Along with the changes just discussed, there are many other revisions worth noting.

- **Part 1.** *Chapter 1:* Reorganization of the "policy" section; new discussion of the correlation-causation fallacy. *Chapter 2:* Clarification of productive vs. allocative efficiency; new application on lumber vs. owls. *Chapter 3:* Expanded discussion of property rights. *Chapter 4:* New examples: Increased demand for broccoli, carrots, guns; reduced supply of haddock.
- **Part 2.** *Chapter 7:* Fuller discussions of cross and income elasticity of demand; a new section on elasticity and the incidence of excise taxes. *Chapter 8:* Clearer delineation of total utility-marginal utility relationship (Figure 8-1); new applications: compact discs, transfers, and gifts. *Chapter 9:* New numerical example of the difference between accounting and economic profits; new examples of scale economies: prices of introductory vs. advanced textbooks and bank mergers. *Chapter 10:* Improved discussion of

economies of scale as an entry barrier (Figure 10-1); new graphical comparison of a single-price monopolist vs. price discriminating monopolist (Figure 11-7). *Chapter 12:* Revised discussion of long-run equilibrium in monopolistic competition; new Figure 12-4 on advertising and economies of scale. *Chapter 13:* Revision of the "causes of oligopoly" section; updating in the case study on autos. *Chapter 14:* New section on the tradeoffs between anti-combines laws and other goals (balance of trade and promoting new technologies); major new section on industrial policy.

- *Part 3.* *Chapter 15:* New applications of the determinants of labour demand: auto workers, fast-food workers, impact of personal computers, contingent workers. *Chapter 16:* Discussions of real wage stagnation and failed pay-for-performance plans. *Chapter 17:* New application: usury laws.
- *Part 4.* *Chapter 19:* Graphical analysis of spillovers. *Chapter 21:* New discussions of rent-seeking in agriculture and environmental impacts of price supports. *Chapter 18:* New discussions on causes of increasing inequality.

APPLYING THE THEORY

These selections serve several purposes: some provide current or historical real-world applications of economic concepts; others reveal "human interest" aspects of economic problems; some present contrasting or "non-mainstream" points of view; and still others present economic concepts or issues in a global context. In the sixth edition these selections were placed in boxes without any heading. Besides unifying these "minireadings" through giving them a heading, we have placed a question about the story at the end of the chapter. Ten of the Applying the Theory boxes are new and others have been revised and updated.

The new topics are: Cuba's declining production possibilities (Chapter 2); the inefficiency of Christmas giving (Chapter 8); creative destruction as a competitive force (Chapter 10); the De Beers diamond monopoly (Chapter 11).

We trust that the outcome of these revision efforts is a text and set of ancillaries superior to their predecessors.

FUNDAMENTAL GOALS

Although the seventh edition bears only a modest resemblance to the first, the basic purpose remains the same — to introduce the beginning economics student to principles essential to an understanding of the economizing problem and the policy alternatives available for dealing with it. We hope that an ability to reason accurately and objectively about economic matters and a lasting interest in economics will be two byproducts of this basic objective. Our intention remains to present the principles and problems of economics in a straightforward, logical fashion. Therefore, we continue to put great stress on clarity of presentation and organization.

ACKNOWLEDGEMENTS

The publication of this seventh edition will extend the life of *Microeconomics* well into its second decade. The acceptance of the parent text, *Economics*, which was generous from the outset, has expanded with each edition. This gracious reception has no doubt been fostered by the many teachers and students who have been kind enough to provide their suggestions and criticisms.

Our colleagues at the University of Nebraska-Lincoln, Pacific Lutheran University, and Ryerson Polytechnical University have generously shared knowledge of their specialties with us and have provided encouragement. We are especially indebted to Ryerson professors John Hughes, David Cape, Dagmar Rajagopal, Gus Zaks, George Carter, Ingrid Bryan, Tom Tushingham, and Mark Lovewell, who have been most helpful in offsetting our comparative ignorance in their areas of specialty.

As indicated, the seventh edition has benefited from a number of perceptive reviews. In both quality and quantity, they provided the richest possible source of suggestions for this revision. We wish to thank the following instructors who participated in the formal review process:

D. Garrie	Georgian College
D. Gray	University of Ottawa
W. Hanna	Humber College
R. Schwindt	Simon Fraser University
J. Shahidi	Kwantlen University College

We also owe a debt of gratitude to all those instructors who contributed in an informal manner their comments and suggestions to authors, editors, and McGraw-Hill Ryerson representatives over the life of the sixth edition. In this connection, I. Hayani of Centennial College, Sage Traveza of the International Centre for Tax Studies, Faculty of Management Studies, University of Toronto, and Torben Andersen of Red Deer College were particularly helpful, and we are grateful to them.

We also wish to thank the following instructors who participated in the formal review process of the sixth edition:

M. Benarroch	University of Winnipeg
E. Black	Brandon University
D. Box	University College of the Fraser Valley
C. Burke	Lethbridge Community College
N. Clegg	Kwantlen College
K. Dawson	Conestoga College
C. Dickhoff	British Columbia Institute of Technology
S. Dodaro	St. Francis Xavier University
S. Fefferman	NAIT
P. Fortura	Algonquin College
B. Gayle-Anyiwe	Seneca College
P. Jacobs	Champlain Regional College
E. Jacobson	NAIT
M. Moy	University College of Cape Breton
V. Nallainayagam	Mount Royal College
A. Nimarko	Vanier College
D. Pepper	British Columbia Institute of Technology
R. Schwindt	Simon Fraser University
L. Smith	University of Waterloo
T. Tushingham	Ryerson Polytechnic University

We are greatly indebted to the many professionals at McGraw-Hill Ryerson — and in particular to Daphne Scriabin, Margaret Henderson, and Gary Bennett — for their expertise in the production and distribution of the book. Wendy Thomas's editing has been invaluable.

With such quality assistance, we see no compelling reason that the authors should assume full responsibility for errors of omission or commission. But we bow to tradition.

Our greatest debt is to Jennifer Mix for her conscientious and imaginative supervision of this revision. Her patience and many positive contributions are gratefully acknowledged.

Campbell R. McConnell
Stanley L. Brue
Thomas P. Barbiero

TO THE STUDENT

Economics is concerned with efficiency — accomplishing goals using the best methods. Therefore, we offer some brief introductory comments on how to improve your efficiency — and your understanding and grade — in studying economics. Several features of this book will aid your learning.

- **APPENDIX ON GRAPHS** Being comfortable with graphical analysis and a few related quantitative concepts will be a big advantage to you in understanding principles of economics. The appendix to Chapter 1 reviews graphing, line slopes, and linear equations. Be sure not to skip it!

- **THE BIG PICTURE** The new Big Picture in each chapter is designed to stimulate interest, state the main objectives, and present an organizational overview of the chapter and its connection with previously covered chapters.

- **TERMINOLOGY** A significant portion of any introductory course is terminology. To designate key terms, we have put them in boldface type, listed them at the end of each chapter, and provided a glossary of definitions at the end of the book.

- **REVIEWS** Important things should be said more than once. You will find a chapter summary at the conclusion of every chapter as well as two or three "Quick Reviews" within each chapter. These review statements will help you focus on the essential ideas of each chapter and also to study for exams. If any of these statements is unclear, you should reread the appropriate section of the text.

- **KEY GRAPHS** We have labelled graphs having special relevance as "Key Graphs." Your instructor may or may not emphasize each of these figures, but pay special attention to those your instructor discusses in class. You can bet there will be exam questions on them!

- **FIGURE LEGENDS** Economics is known for its many graphs. The legends accompanying the diagrams in this book are self-contained analyses of the concepts shown. Study these legends carefully — they are quick synopses of important ideas.

- **GLOBALIZATION** Each nation functions increasingly in a global economy. To gain appreciation of this wider economic environment, be sure to take a look at the "Global Perspectives," which compare Canada to other selected nations.

- **APPLYING THE THEORY** While it is tempting to ignore these boxes, doing so is a mistake. Some "Applying the Theory" boxes are revealing applications of economic concepts; some are short case studies; still others present views that contrast with mainstream thinking. All will deepen and broaden your grasp of economics.

• IN THE MEDIA Interesting stories have been selected from the printed media that show the real-world application of the economic theory just learned. Each of these stories ends with a question to test your understanding of the chapter's materials.

• QUESTIONS A comprehensive list of questions is located at the end of each chapter. The old cliché that you "learn by doing" is very relevant to economics. Use of these questions will enhance your understanding. We designate several of them as "Key Questions" and answer them at the end of the book. You can immediately turn to these particular questions when they are cited in each chapter, or later after you have read the full chapter.

• SOFTWARE Many of the end-of-chapter questions deal with subject matter reinforced by the computerized tutorial, *Concept Master III*, which complements this text. A floppy disk symbol appears in connection with questions whose underlying content correlates to a lesson in the tutorial program.

• STUDY GUIDE We enthusiastically recommend the *Study Guide* accompanying this text. This "portable tutor" contains not only a broad sampling of various kinds of questions, but a host of useful learning aids.

You will find in Chapter 1 that economics involves a special way of thinking — a unique approach to analyzing problems. The overriding goal of this book is to help you acquire that skill. If our co-operative efforts — yours, ours, and your instructor's — are successful, you will be able to comprehend a whole range of economic, social, and political problems that otherwise would have remained murky and elusive.

So much for the pep talk. Let's get on with the show.

Drabble reprinted by permission of United Feature Syndicate, Inc.

AN INTRODUCTION TO ECONOMICS

CHAPTER 1

THE NATURE AND METHOD OF ECONOMICS

Human beings, unfortunate creatures, are plagued with many material wants. The fact is, however, that the total of all our material wants is beyond the productive capacity of all available resources. Thus, scarcity is pervasive in all aspects of our lives. This unyielding fact is the basis of our definition of economics: *Economics is concerned with the efficient use (or management) of limited productive resources to attain the maximum satisfaction of human material wants.* Though it may not be self-evident, all the headline-grabbing issues of the day — inflation, unemployment, the federal budget deficit, poverty and inequality, pollution, government regulation of business — have their roots in the issue of using scarce resources efficiently.

In this chapter, however, we will not plunge into the problem and issues of the moment. Our immediate concern is with some basic preliminary questions:

1. Of what importance or consequence is the study of economics?

2. How should we study economics — what are the proper procedures? What is the methodology of this subject?

3. What specific problems, limitations, and pitfalls might we encounter in studying economics?

4. How do economists think about problems? What is the economic perspective?

BOX 1-1 THE BIG PICTURE

You are about to embark on the study of economics, a discipline that can help you understand a vast array of human issues and problems. Economics is about *scarcity, wants,* and *choices.* Try to think of any goods or services of which there is such an abundance that *everyone* in the world has as much as he or she wants. You will not have much success! Even time must be carefully budgeted because there is less of it than we would like. As George Stigler, a Nobel Prize winner in economics, points out, "Anything that is an object of conscious desire must be scarce: One does not consciously desire the air breathed, or to hear bad jokes. Scarce things are costly. If they weren't, everyone would get so much of each that they would not be scarce anymore. So anything scarce, and worth having, has been costly for someone to obtain."*

The only reason you do not consciously think about breathing is that you have as much oxygen as you could possibly want. If you didn't, you would have to carefully budget even the air you breathe! It is

* G.J. Stigler, *Memoirs of an Unregulated Economist* (New York: Basic Books, 1988).

because economics deals with an issue — scarcity — that pervades our daily lives that its study is relevant to a large spectrum of interests and pursuits.

If we wanted or needed very little in relation to available resources, the scarcity problem would be less pronounced. But because there are so many goods and services we need and want, we must make choices about which goods and services we most desire. Despite often being referred to as the "dismal science," economics is really about getting enjoyment out of life: getting as much enjoyment as possible out of the limited resources available to us; the study of economics may thus be your ticket to "happiness"! More realistically, you may come to better understand and appreciate the ubiquitous problem of scarcity in our daily lives.

You need to understand the scarcity problem if you are to succeed in the study of economics, particularly microeconomics. "The Big Picture" boxes have been written to continuously remind you of the raison d'être of economics, and to put the information in each chapter within the larger context of scarcity, wants, and choices.

THE RELEVANCE OF ECONOMICS

Why should you study economics? Is studying economics worth your time and effort? Half a century ago John Maynard Keynes (1883–1946) — one of the most influential economists of this century — offered a telling response:

> The ideas of economists and political philosophers, both when they are right and when they are wrong, are more powerful than is commonly understood. Indeed the world is ruled by little else. Practical men, who believe themselves to be quite exempt from any intellectual influences, are usually the slaves of some defunct economist.

The ideologies of the modern world have been shaped in substantial measure by the great economists of the past — for example, Adam Smith, David Ricardo, John Stuart Mill, Karl Marx, and John Maynard Keynes. And it is currently common for world leaders to ask for and receive the advice and policy prescriptions of economists.

The Government of Canada has more than a thousand economists in its various ministries and agencies — and the advice of this army of economists is considered essential to the functioning of modern government. The areas economists advise on include unemployment and inflation, economic growth and productivity, taxation and public expenditures, poverty and income maintenance, the balance of payments and the international monetary system, labour-management relations, health care, pollution, immigration, competition, and industrial regulation, among others.

ECONOMICS FOR CITIZENSHIP

A basic understanding of economics is essential if we are to be well-informed citizens. Many of today's problems have important economic aspects, and as informed voters we can influence the decisions of our political leaders in these matters. What are the causes and consequences of the federal budget deficit that is often a main item in the news? What of the depressing stories of homeless people? Are mergers of corporations good or bad? Why is inflation undesirable? What can be done to reduce unemployment? Are existing welfare programs effective and justifiable? Should we continue to subsidize farmers? Do we need further reform of our tax system? Will free trade with the United States and Mexico help or hurt our industries, employment, and incomes?

Since the answers to such questions are determined largely by our elected officials, intelligence in the voting booth depends on a basic working knowledge of economics. Needless to say, a sound grasp of economics is more than helpful to politicians themselves!

PERSONAL APPLICATIONS

Economics is also important in business. An understanding of the overall operation of the economic system puts the business executive in a better position to decide on policies. The executive who understands the causes and consequences of inflation is better equipped, during inflationary periods, to make more intelligent business decisions. Indeed, that is why economists are on the payrolls of most large corporations. Their job is to gather and interpret economic information on which rational business decisions can be made.

Economics also gives the individual as consumer and worker some insights as to how to make wiser buying and employment decisions. How can you "hedge" against the reduction in the purchasing power of the dollar that accompanies inflation? Which occupations pay well; which are most immune to unemployment? Should you buy or lease a car? Should you use a credit card or pay cash? Similarly, an individual who understands, for example, the relationship between budget deficits and security (stock and bond) values will be able to make more enlightened personal financial investment decisions.

METHODOLOGY

Mastering the discipline of economics will be much easier if you understand the methodology used by economists. You will be studying theories of economic relationships that economists have assembled in the last several hundred years. How have they constructed these theories and how can we be sure that these theories adequately describe the workings of a market economy?

The methodology used by economists to arrive at an understanding of economic phenomena is no different than that used in other social sciences and the natural sciences. It is generally referred to as the scientific method. Economists try to formulate economic *theories* (also known as principles, models, or laws) that shed light on economic phenomena, economic *policies* that aim to solve economic *problems*.

The procedures employed by economists to arrive at theories are summarized in Figure 1-1.

1. Sometimes economists begin by gathering facts relevant to a specific economic problem. This task is referred to as *descriptive* or *empirical economics*.
2. From the facts a general principle or **theory** may be derived. A theory seeks to explain the relationship among facts. When theories are distilled from facts we refer to such a derivation as **induction**. The inductive method begins with an accumulation of facts, which are then arranged systematically and analyzed so as to permit a generalization or principle. Induction moves from facts to theory, from the particular to the general. The induction method is represented by the left upward arrow from box 1 to box 2 in Figure 1-1.

Economists also arrive at new theories by drawing on insight, logic, or intuition. We refer to such a process as **deduction**. When a new theory is formed through the deductive method, it is in the first instance tentative until verified by facts. Until the theory is verified by facts, we refer to it as a **hypothesis**. For example, we may conjecture that it is rational for consumers to buy more of a product when price is low than when it is high.

To test the validity of the hypothesis they have deduced, economists must subject it to the systematic and repeated examination of relevant facts. Do data in fact reveal a negative or inverse relationship between price and the amount purchased? This testing process is represented by the right downward arrow from box 2 to box 1 in Figure 1-1.

Deduction and induction are complementary, rather than opposing, techniques of investigation. Hypotheses formulated by deduction provide guidelines

FIGURE 1-1   **The relationship between facts, principles, and policies in economics**

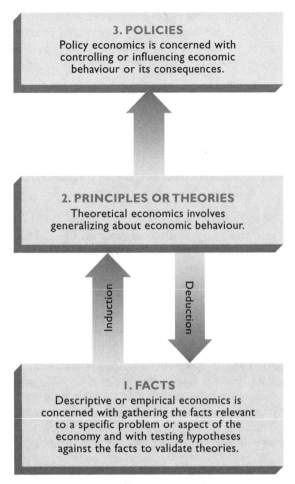

In analyzing problems or aspects of the economy, economists may use the inductive method, whereby they gather, systematically arrange, and generalize on facts. Alternatively, the deductive method develops hypotheses that are then tested against facts. Generalizations derived from either method of inquiry are useful not only in explaining economic behaviour, but also as a basis for formulating economic policies.

for economists as they gather and systematize empirical data. Conversely, some understanding of factual evidence — of the "real world" — is a prerequisite to the formulation of meaningful hypotheses.

The general knowledge of economic behaviour that economic principles provide can then be used in formulating policies for correcting or avoiding the problem

under scrutiny. This aspect of the field is sometimes called "applied economics" or **policy economics** (box 3).

Continuing to use Figure 1-1 as a point of reference, let us now examine the economist's methodology in more detail.

DESCRIPTIVE ECONOMICS

All sciences are empirical. That means all sciences are based on observable and verifiable behaviour of certain data or subject matter. In the physical sciences, the factual data are inorganic. As a social science, economics is concerned with the behaviour of individuals and institutions engaged in the production, exchange, and consumption of goods and services.

The gathering of economic data can be a complex task. Because the world of reality is cluttered with a multitude of interrelated facts, economists must use discretion in gathering them. They must distinguish economic from noneconomic facts and then determine which economic facts are relevant and which are irrelevant for the particular problem under consideration. But even when this sorting process has been completed, the relevant economic facts may appear diverse and unrelated.

ECONOMIC THEORY

Economic theory systematically arranges, interprets, and generalizes on economic data or facts. Principles and theories bring order and meaning to facts by tying them together, determining the relationship to one another, and generalizing on them. But facts in turn serve as a check on the validity of principles already established. Since how individuals and institutions actually behave in producing, exchanging, and consuming goods and services may change with time, it is essential that economists continuously check theories against the changing economic environment.

TERMINOLOGY   Economists talk about "laws," "principles," "theories," and "models." These terms all mean essentially the same thing: generalizations, or statements of regularity, concerning the economic behaviour of individuals and institutions. The term "economic law" is a bit misleading because it implies a high degree of precision, universal application, and even moral rightness. Some people incorrectly assume "theory" has nothing to do with the facts and realities of the world. In truth, theory helps us to understand the facts and realities of the world. The term "model" has much to commend it. A model is a simplified picture of reality, an abstract generalization of how relevant data actually behave.

In this book the four terms (laws, principles, theories, and models) will be used synonymously. The choice of terms in labelling any particular generalization will be governed by custom or convenience. Thus, the relationship between the price of a product and the quantity consumers purchase will be called the "law" of demand, rather than the theory or principle of demand, simply because this is the customary designation.

Several other points regarding the character and derivation of economic principles are in order.

GENERALIZATIONS   Economic principles are **generalizations.** They are frequently stated as averages or statistical probabilities. For example, when economists say that the average Canadian family earned an income of $52,000 in 1994, they are generalizing. It is recognized that some families earned much more and many families earned less. Yet this generalization, properly handled and interpreted, can be very meaningful and useful.

Similarly, economic generalizations are often stated in terms of probabilities. For example, a researcher may tell us that there is a 95% probability that every $1 reduction in personal income taxes will result in a $0.90 increase in consumer spending.

"OTHER THINGS EQUAL" ASSUMPTION   Like other scientists, economists make use of the **ceteris paribus**, or **other things being equal assumption** to construct their generalizations. We assume that all other variables, except those under immediate consideration, are held constant. This simplifies the reasoning process by isolating the relationship under consideration. To illustrate: In considering the relationship between the price of Pepsi and the amount purchased, it is helpful to assume that of all factors that might influence the amount of Pepsi purchased (for example, the prices of other goods, such as Coke, and consumer incomes and preferences), only the price of Pepsi varies. The economist is then able to focus on the "price of Pepsi–purchases of Pepsi" relationship without reasoning being blurred or confused by the intrusion of other variables.

In the natural sciences, controlled experiments usually can be performed where "all other things" are in fact held constant, or virtually so. Thus the scientist can test the assumed relationship between two variables with great precision. But economics is not a laboratory science. The economist's process of empirical verification is based on "real world" data generated by the actual operation of the economy. In this rather bewildering environment, "other things" *do* change. Despite the development of rather complex statistical techniques designed to hold other things equal, such controls are less than perfect. As a result, economic theories are sometimes less certain and less precise in application than those of the laboratory sciences.

ABSTRACTIONS   Economic principles, or theories, are necessarily abstractions. The very process of sorting out noneconomic and irrelevant facts in the fact-gathering process involves abstracting from "reality." Unfortunately, the abstractness of economic theory prompts the uninformed to identify theory as something that is impractical and unrealistic. This is nonsense!

Economic theories are practical, in fact, *because* they are abstractions. Economists theorize in order to give meaning to a maze of facts that would otherwise be confusing and useless, and to put facts into a more usable, practical form. Thus, to generalize is to abstract or purposely simplify; generalization for this purpose is practical, and therefore so is abstraction. An economic theory is a model — a simplified picture or map — for some segment of the economy. This model enables us to better understand reality *because* it avoids confusing details. Theories — *good* theories — are grounded on facts and therefore are realistic. Theories that do not fit the facts are simply not good theories.

MACRO AND MICRO   There are two levels of analysis at which the economist can derive laws concerning economic behaviour. **Macroeconomics** deals with the economy as a whole or with the basic subdivisions or aggregates — such as the household, business, government, and foreign trade sectors — making up the economy. An aggregate is a collection of specific economic units treated *as though* they were one unit. Thus we might find it convenient to lump together the many businesses in our economy and treat them as though they were one huge unit.

Macroeconomics is concerned with obtaining an overview, or general outline, of the structure of the economy and the relationships between the major aggregates that make up the economy. It deals with such magnitudes as *total* output, the *total* level of employment, *total* income, *aggregate* expenditures, and the *general* level of prices, in analyzing various economic problems. Macroeconomics examines the forest, not the trees. It gives us a bird's-eye view of the economy.

Microeconomics deals with *specific* economic units and a *detailed* consideration of the behaviour of these individual units. Here we analyze an individual industry, firm, or household and concentrate on such magnitudes as the output or price of a *specific* product, the number of workers employed by a single firm, the revenue or income of a particular firm or household, and the expenditures of a given firm or family. In microeconomics we examine the trees, not the forest.

Many topics and subdivisions of economics are rooted in both "micro" and "macro." There has been a convergence of macro and micro in important areas in recent years. While the problem of unemployment was once treated as a macroeconomic topic ("unemployment depends on *aggregate* spending"), economists now recognize that decisions made by *individual* workers in searching for jobs and the way specific product and labour markets function are also critical in determining the unemployment rate. (**Key Question 5**)

GRAPHIC EXPRESSION Many of the economic models or principles in this book will be expressed graphically. The most important of these are labelled "**Key Graphs.**" You should read the appendix to this chapter to review graphing and other relevant quantitative relationships.

QUICK REVIEW 1-1

1. Economics is concerned with the efficient management of scarce resources.

2. Induction is the observation of regularities in factual data and drawing generalizations from them; deduction uses logic to create hypotheses that are then tested with factual data.

3. Economic theories ("laws," "principles," or "models") are generalizations, based on facts, concerning the economic behaviour of individuals and institutions.

4. Macroeconomics deals with the economy as a whole; microeconomics focuses on specific units that make up the economy.

DESIGNING ECONOMIC POLICY

Economic theories should provide the basis for *economic policy*. Our understanding of economic principles can be applied in resolving or alleviating specific problems and in furthering the realization of society's overall goals (box 3 of Figure 1-1). Economic principles are valuable as predictive devices. And prediction, even if not completely accurate, is required if we want to alter some event or outcome. If some undesirable event such as unemployment or inflation can be predicted or understood through economic theory, we may then be able to influence or control that event.

FORMULATING ECONOMIC POLICY The creation of policies designed to achieve specific goals is no simple matter. Here's a brief examination of the basic steps in policy formulation.

1. STATING GOALS The first step is to make a clear statement of a goal. If we say that we want "full employment," do we mean that everyone between, say, 16 and 65 years of age should have a job? Or do we mean that everyone who wants to work should have a job? Should we allow for some "normal" unemployment caused by inevitable changes in the structure of industry and workers' voluntarily changing jobs?

2. POLICY OPTIONS Next, we must state and recognize the possible effects of alternative policies designed to achieve the goal. This requires a clear understanding of the economic impact benefits, costs, and political feasibility of alternative programs. For example, economists debate the relative merits and demerits of fiscal policy (which involves changing government spending and taxes) and monetary policy (which entails altering the supply of money) as alternative means of achieving and maintaining full employment.

3. EVALUATION We are obligated to ourselves and future generations to review our experiences with chosen policies and evaluate their effectiveness; it is only through this evaluation that we can hope to improve policy applications. Did a specific change in taxes or the supply of money alter the level of employment to the extent originally predicted? Did deregulation of a particular industry (for example, the airlines) yield the predicted beneficial results? If not why not? (**Key Question 1**)

ECONOMIC GOALS Economic policies are designed to achieve certain economic goals that are widely accepted in our own and many other societies. They include:

1. ECONOMIC GROWTH The production of more and better goods and services, for the purpose of attaining a higher standard of living, is desired.

2. FULL EMPLOYMENT Suitable jobs should be available for all who are willing and able to work.

3. PRICE LEVEL STABILITY Sizable upswings or downswings in the general price level, that is, inflation and deflation, should be avoided.

4. AN EQUITABLE DISTRIBUTION OF INCOME No group of citizens should face stark poverty while other citizens enjoy extreme luxury.

5. BALANCE OF TRADE We seek a reasonable balance in our international trade and financial transactions.

This list of goals provides the basis for several significant points.

1. INTERPRETATION This and any other statement of basic economic goals inevitably results in problems of interpretation. What, for example, is an "equitable" distribution of income? On the other hand, most of us might accept the above goals, but might disagree as to the types of policies needed to attain these goals.

2. COMPLEMENTARY Certain of these goals are complementary in that when one goal is achieved, some other goal or goals will also tend to be realized. For example, growth (goal 1) will help achieve full employment (goal 2).

3. CONFLICTING Some goals *may* be conflicting or mutually exclusive. Thus, there are **trade-offs**, meaning that to achieve one goal we must sacrifice some other goal. Some economists argue that those forces that further the attainment of economic growth and full employment may be the very same forces that cause inflation. In fact, the possible conflict between

goals 2 and 3 has been at the forefront of economic research and debate in recent years. Goals 1 and 4 may also be in conflict. Some economists point out that efforts to achieve greater equality in the distribution of income may weaken incentives to work, invest, innovate, and take business risks, all of which promote rapid economic growth.

4. PRIORITIES When goals do conflict, society must develop a system of priorities for the objectives it seeks. If full employment and price stability are to some extent mutually exclusive, that is, if full employment is accompanied by some inflation *and* price stability entails some unemployment, society must decide on the relative importance of these two goals. There is clearly ample room for disagreement here. But society must assess the trade-offs and make decisions.

POSITIVE AND NORMATIVE As we move from the fact and principles levels (boxes 1 and 2) of Figure 1-1 to the policy level (box 3) we are making a leap from positive to normative economics.

Positive economics attempts to set forth statements about economic behaviour that are devoid of value judgements. Positive statements are verifiable by appealing to facts. In contrast, **normative economics** embodies someone's value judgements. Normative statements cannot be tested against facts to determine whether they are true. Positive economics is concerned with *what* is, while normative economics embodies subjective feelings about *what ought* to be.

Positive economics is concerned with what the economy is actually like; normative economics has to do with whether certain conditions or aspects of the economy are desirable.

Consider the following examples. Positive statement: "Unemployment is 7% of the labour force." Normative statement: "Unemployment ought to be reduced." Positive statement: "Other things being the same, if tuition is increased, enrolment at Informed University (IU) will fall." Normative statement: "Tuition should be lowered at IU so that more students can obtain an education." Indeed, whenever such words as "ought" or "should" appear in a sentence, there is a strong chance that you are dealing with a normative statement. However, it is worth noting that the choice of what positive statement to make may, in itself, be a normative statement. (**Key Question 6**)

PITFALLS TO OBJECTIVE THINKING

You should be aware that there are pitfalls to thinking objectively about economic problems. Avoiding these pitfalls will greatly facilitate your grasp of economic reasoning. The following are pitfalls to objective thinking that you should guard against.

BIAS

In contrast to neophyte physicists or chemists, budding economists often launch into their field of study with a bundle of biases and preconceptions. For example, you might be suspicious of business profits or feel that deficit spending is evil. Biases may cloud your thinking and interfere with objective analysis. Students beginning their studies in economics must be willing to shed biases and preconceptions not warranted by facts.

LOADED TERMINOLOGY

The economic terminology in newspapers and popular magazines is sometimes emotionally loaded. The writer — or the particular interest group represented — may have a cause to further or an axe to grind, and the terms will be slanted to solicit the support of the reader. A governmental flood-control project in the Prairies may be called "creeping socialism" by its opponents and "protecting the national interest" by its proponents. We must be prepared to discount such terminology to objectively understand economic issues.

DEFINITIONS

No scientist is obligated to use immediately understandable definitions of terms. The economists may find it convenient and essential to define terms in such a way that they are at odds with the definitions held by most people in everyday speech. No problem, so long as the economist is explicit and consistent in these definitions. For example, the term "investment" to John Q. Citizen is associated with the buying of bonds and stocks in the securities market. How often have we heard someone talk of investing in Bell Canada stock or government bonds? But to the economist, "investment" means the purchase of real capital assets such as machinery and equipment, or the construction of a new factory building.

FALLACY OF COMPOSITION

Another pitfall in economic thinking is assuming "what is true for the individual or part of a group is *necessarily* true for the group or whole." This is a logical **fallacy of composition**; it is *not* correct. For example, a wage increase for Smith is desirable because, with constant product prices, it increases Smith's purchasing power and standard of living. But if everyone gets a wage increase, product prices will likely rise; that is, inflation will occur. Thus Smith's standard of living may be unchanged as higher prices offset this larger salary.

Second illustration: An *individual* farmer who is fortunate enough to realize a bumper (particularly large) crop is likely to realize a sharp increase in income. But this generalization does not apply to farmers as a *group*. An individual farmer's bumper crop will not influence crop prices because it is such a negligible fraction of the total farm output, but for farmers as a group prices vary inversely with total output. Thus if *all* farmers realize bumper crops, the total output of farm products rises, thereby depressing crop prices. If price declines are relatively greater than the increased output, farm incomes will *fall*.

CAUSATION FALLACIES

Economists often try to discern if economic phenomenon A actually affects economic phenomenon B. Causation, however, is sometimes difficult to discern in economics. Beware of these two fallacies.

POST HOC FALLACY You must be very careful before concluding that because event A precedes event B, A is the cause of B. This kind of faulty reasoning is known as the **post hoc, ergo propter hoc,** or **after this, therefore because of this, fallacy.**

Example: Suppose early each spring the medicine man of a tribe performs his ritual by cavorting around the village in a green costume. A week or so later the trees and grass turn green. Can we conclude that event A, the medicine man's gyrations, has caused event B, the landscape's turning green? Obviously not. The rooster crows before dawn, but this doesn't mean the rooster is responsible for the sunrise!

Informed University hires a new hockey coach and the team's record improves. Is the new coach the cause? Maybe. But perhaps the presence of more experienced players or an easier schedule is the true cause.

CORRELATION VERSUS CAUSATION We must not confuse **correlation** with **causation.** *Correlation* is a technical term indicating that two sets of data are associated in some systematic and dependable way. For example, we may find that when X increases, Y also increases. But this does not necessarily mean that X is the cause of Y. The relationship could be purely coincidental or determined by some other factor, Z, not included in the analysis.

Example: Economists have found a positive correlation between education and income. In general, people with more education earn higher incomes than people with less education. Common sense suggests education is the cause and higher incomes are the effect; more education suggests a more productive worker and such workers receive larger monetary rewards.

But might not causation run the other way? Do people with higher incomes buy more education, just as they buy more automobiles and steaks? Or is the relationship explainable in terms of still other factors? Are education and income positively correlated because the bundle of characteristics — ability, motivation, personal habits — required to succeed in education are the same characteristics required to be a productive and highly paid worker? **(Key Question 9)**

THE ECONOMIC PERSPECTIVE

The methodology used by economists to help them come up with good theories is common to all the natural and social sciences. And all scholars try to avoid the reasoning errors just discussed. Thus, economists do *not* think in a special way. But they *do* think about things from a special perspective.

The **economic perspective** has several critical and closely interrelated features, including scarcity, rational behaviour, and benefit-cost comparisons.

SCARCITY AND CHOICE

Recall that economists view the world from the vantage point of scarcity. Human and property resources are scarce. It follows that outputs of goods and services must be scarce as well. Scarcity limits our options and necessitates choices. If we cannot have it all, what should we choose to have?

At the core of economics is the ever-present reality of scarcity in relation to our material wants, and thus the idea that "there is no free lunch" (no wonder economics is referred to as the "dismal science"!). Someone may treat you to lunch, making it "free" to you. But there is a cost to someone. The lunch requires scarce inputs of farm products and the labour of cooks and waiters. These resources could have been used in alternative productive activities and those activities — those other goods and services — are sacrificed in providing your lunch.

RATIONAL BEHAVIOUR

Economics assumes "rational self-interest." This means that individuals make decisions that yield them the greatest satisfaction or maximum fulfilment of some goal. As consumers, workers, and businesspersons, people have goals and make rational decisions to achieve those objectives. Thus, consumers seek to spend their incomes to get the greatest satisfaction from the goods and services their limited incomes allow them to buy. It is in this sense that consumers are rational.

Rational behaviour does not mean everyone will make similar choices because their circumstances (constraints), preferences, and available information may differ. You may decide that it is in your self-interest to attend college or university before entering the labour force. But a high school classmate decides to forgo additional schooling and take a job. Why the different choices? Your academic abilities, along with your family's income and wealth, may be significantly greater than those of your classmate; or perhaps your job preferences are different from your classmate's. You may also be better informed, realizing for example that college- and university-educated workers earn much higher incomes and are less likely to be unemployed than are workers with just a high school education. Thus, you opt for college or university while your high school classmate with either very different job preferences, or with fewer human and financial resources and less information, chooses a job. Both are rational choices, but based on differing constraints, information, or preferences.

Our example implies that rational decisions may change as circumstances change. Suppose the federal government decides it is in the national interest to increase the supply of college- and university-educated workers. As a result, government policy changes to provide greater financial assistance to post-secondary students. Under these new conditions, your high school classmate may opt for college or university rather than a job after graduating from high school.

Rational self-interest is *not* the same as selfishness. People make personal sacrifices to help family members or friends and contribute to charities because they derive pleasure from doing so. Parents contribute financially to their children's education because they derive satisfaction from that choice.

MARGINAL ANALYSIS: BENEFITS AND COSTS

The economic perspective focuses largely on *marginal analysis* — decisions that compare marginal benefits and marginal costs. Marginal means "extra" or "additional." Most economic choices result in changes to the status quo. When you graduated from high school, you faced the question of whether you should get *additional* education. Similarly, businesses are continuously deciding whether to employ more or fewer workers or to produce more or less output.

In making such choices rationally, we must compare marginal benefits and marginal costs. Because of scarcity, any choice will result in *both* extra benefits and additional costs. Example: Your time is scarce. What to do with, say, two "free" hours on a Saturday afternoon? Option: Watch the Vancouver Canucks play the Montreal Canadiens on television. Marginal benefit: The pleasure of seeing the game. Marginal cost: Any of the other things you sacrifice by spending an extra two hours in front of the tube, including studying (economics, we hope), jogging, or taking a nap. If the marginal benefit exceeds the marginal cost, then it is rational to watch the game. But if you perceive the marginal cost of watching the game to exceed its marginal benefits, then one of the other options will be chosen.

BOX 1-2   APPLYING THE THEORY

The key to understanding economic behaviour is to *constantly* apply the marginal cost-benefit perspective. An illuminating example of its application can be had by economists' response to the automobile safety legislation that ensued in Canada and the United States after Ralph Nader published *Unsafe at Any Speed*, which pointed out the danger to passengers of available car models. Economists predicted that once padded dashboards, seat belts, collapsible steering columns, and other safety enhancement features were introduced, the number of automobile accidents would increase! It is the type of response that would not likely come from a non-economist. Economists reasoned that if drivers felt the threat to being killed in an automobile accident diminished with the new safety features, they would, on average, be less careful.

In 1975 Sam Peltzman of the University of Chicago investigated the impact of the new safety features on automobile accidents. He found that there *were* more accidents, but the number of deaths remained the same as previously, presumably on account of the enhanced safety features on the later-model automobiles.

If you are still in doubt about the applicability of the marginal cost-benefit perspective, consider the comments of Armen Alchian of the University of California at Los Angeles. He was certain the accident rate for automobiles would fall if automobile manufacturers were required to install a spear on the steering wheel aimed directly at the driver's heart! Who could argue with Alchian that drivers would be much more careful with a spear aimed at their heart? The marginal cost could be very high!

Adapted from Steven E. Landsburg, *The Armchair Economist.* (New York: The Free Press, 1993), Chapter 1.

BOX 1-3 APPLYING THE THEORY

FAST-FOOD LINES: AN ECONOMIC PERSPECTIVE

How might the economic perspective help us understand the behaviour of fast-food consumers?

When you enter a fast-food restaurant, which line do you select? What do you do when you are in a long line in the restaurant and a new station opens? Have you ever gone to a fast-food restaurant, only to see long lines, and then leave? Have you ever had someone in front of you in a fast-food line place an order that takes a long time to fill?

The economic perspective is useful in analyzing the behaviour of fast-food customers. These customers are at the restaurant because they expect the marginal benefit or satisfaction from the food they buy to match or exceed its cost. When customers enter the restaurant, they scurry to the shortest line — lest someone else beat them there — in the belief that the shortest line will reduce their time cost of obtaining their food. They are acting purposefully; time is limited and most people would prefer using it in some way other than standing in line.

All lines in the fast-food establishment normally are of roughly equal lengths. If one line is temporarily shorter than other lines, some people will move towards that line. These movers apparently view the time saving associated with the shorter line to exceed the cost of moving from their present line. Line changing normally results in an equilibrium line length. No further movement of customers between lines will occur once all lines are of equal length.

Fast-food customers face another cost-benefit decision when a clerk opens a new station at the counter. Should customers move to the new station or stay put? Those who do shift to the new line decide that the benefit of the time savings from the move exceeds the extra cost of physically moving. In so deciding, customers must also consider just how quickly they can get to the new station compared to others who may be contemplating the same move. (Those who hesitate in this situation are lost!)

Customers at the fast-food establishment select lines without having perfect information. For example, they do not first survey those in the lines to determine what they are ordering before deciding on which line to enter. There are two reasons. First, most customers would tell them "it is none of your business," and therefore no information would be forthcoming. Second, even if they could obtain the information, the amount of time necessary to get it (cost) would most likely exceed any time saving associated with finding the best line (benefit). Because information is costly to obtain, fast-food patrons select lines on the basis of imperfect information. Thus, not all decisions turn out to be as expected. For example, some people may enter a line in which the person in front of them is ordering hamburgers and fries for the 40 people in the Greyhound bus parked out back! Nevertheless, at the time the customer made the decision, he or she thought that it was optimal.

Imperfect information also explains why some people who arrive at a fast-food restaurant and observe long lines decide to leave. These people conclude that the marginal cost (monetary plus time costs) of obtaining the fast food is too large relative to the marginal benefit. They would not have come to the restaurant in the first place had they known the lines were so long. But, getting that information by, say, employing an advance scout with a cellular phone, would cost more than the perceived benefit.

Finally, customers must decide what to order when they arrive at the counter. In making these choices, they again compare marginal costs and marginal benefits in attempting to obtain the greatest personal well-being.

Economists believe that what is true for the behaviour of customers at fast-food restaurants is true for economic behaviour in general. Faced with an array of choices, consumers, workers, and businesses rationally compare marginal costs and benefits in making decisions.

On the national level, government is continuously making decisions involving marginal benefits and costs. More spending on health care means sacrifices on spending on shelter for the homeless, aid for the poor, or military security. Lesson: In a world of scarcity the marginal benefit derived from a given choice also means you incur the marginal cost of forgoing something else. Unfortunately, there's no free lunch.

One of the implications of marginal analysis in a world pervaded by scarcity is that there can be too much of a "good thing." Although certain goods and services seem inherently desirable — education, health care, a clean environment — we can in fact have too much of them. "Too much" occurs when we push their production to some point where their marginal costs (the value of the forgone options) exceeds their marginal benefit. If we choose to produce health care to the extent that its marginal cost exceeds its marginal benefit, we are providing "too much" health care even though health care is a good thing. If the marginal cost of health care is greater than its marginal benefit, then we are sacrificing alternative products (for example, education and pollution reduction) that are more valuable than health care at the margin. (**Key Question 13**)

QUICK REVIEW 1-3

1. Beware of logical errors such as the fallacy of composition and the post hoc fallacy when engaging in economic reasoning.

2. The economic perspective stresses **a** resource scarcity and the necessity of making choices; **b** the assumption of rational behaviour; and **c** marginal analysis.

CHAPTER SUMMARY

1. Economics deals with the efficient use of scarce resources in the production of goods and services to satisfy material wants.

2. A knowledge of economics contributes to effective citizenship and provides useful insights for consumers and businesspersons.

3. The tasks of descriptive or empirical economics are **a** gathering those economic facts relevant to a particular problem or specific segment of the economy, and **b** testing hypotheses against facts to validate theories.

4. Generalizations stated by economists are called "principles," "theories," "laws," or "models." The derivation of these principles is the task of economic theory,

5. Induction distils theories from facts; deduction uses logic to derive hypotheses that are then tested against facts.

6. Some economic principles deal with macroeconomics (the economy as a whole or major aggregates), while others pertain to microeconomics (specific economic units or institutions).

7. Economic principles are valuable as predictive devices; they are the bases for the formulation of economic policy designed to solve problems and control undesirable events.

8. Economic growth, full employment, price level stability, equity in the distribution of income, and a viable balance of payments are widely accepted economic goals in our society. Some of these goals are complementary; others are mutually exclusive.

9. Positive statements deal with facts ("what is"), while normative statements encompass value judgements ("what ought to be").

10. In studying economics the beginner may encounter numerous pitfalls. Some of the more important are **a** biases and preconceptions, **b** terminological difficulties, **c** the fallacy of composition, and **d** the difficulty of establishing clear cause-effect relationships.

11. The economic perspective envisions individuals and institutions making rational decisions based on costs and benefits.

TERMS AND CONCEPTS

ceteris paribus or "other things being equal" assumption (p. 7)

choices (p. 11)

correlation and causation (p. 11)

descriptive economics (p. 6)

economics (p. 3)

economic goals (p. 9)

economic perspective (p. 11)

economic policy (p. 8)

economic theory (p. 6)

fallacy of composition (p. 10)

hypothesis (p. 5)

induction and deduction (p. 5)

macroeconomics and microeconomics (p. 7, p. 8)

normative economics (p. 9)

policy economics (p. 6)

positive and normative economics (p. 9)

post hoc, ergo propter hoc or "after this, therefore because of this" fallacy (p. 10)

principles or generalizations (p. 7)

scarcity (p. 11)

theory (p. 5)

trade-offs (p. 9)

wants (p. 11)

QUESTIONS AND STUDY SUGGESTIONS

1. *Key Question* *Explain in detail the interrelationships between economic facts, theory, and policy. Critically evaluate: "The trouble with economics is that it is not practical. It has too much to say about theory and not enough to say about facts."*

2. Analyze and explain the following quotation:

   Facts are seldom simple and usually complicated; theoretical analysis is needed to unravel the complications and interpret the facts before we can understand them.... The opposition of facts and theory is a false one; the true relationship is complementary. We cannot in practice consider a fact without relating it to other facts, and the relation is a theory. Facts by themselves are dumb; before they will tell us anything we have to arrange them, and the arrangement is a theory. Theory is simply the unavoidable arrangement and interpretation of facts, which gives us generalizations on which we can argue and act, in the place of a mass of disjointed particulars.[1]

3. Of what significance is the fact that economics is not a laboratory science? What problems may be involved in deriving and applying economic principles?

4. Explain each of the following statements:

   a. "Like all scientific laws, economic laws are established in order to make successful prediction of the outcome of human actions."

   b. "Abstraction... is the inevitable price of generality.... Indeed abstraction and generality are virtually synonyms."

   c. "Numbers serve to discipline rhetoric."

---

[1] Henry Clay, *Economics for the General Reader* (New York: The Macmillan Company, 1925), pp. 10-11.

5. *Key Question*   *Indicate whether each of the following statements pertains to microeconomics or macroeconomics:*

   a. The unemployment rate in Canada was 10.3% in 1994.
   b. The Alpo dogfood plant in Bowser, Alberta, laid off 15 workers last month.
   c. An unexpected freeze in central Florida reduced the citrus crop and caused the price of oranges to rise.
   d. Our domestic output, adjusted for inflation, dropped by 1.5% in 1991.
   e. Last week the Bank of Montreal lowered its interest rate on business loans by one-half of a percentage point.
   f. The consumer price index rose by less than 3% in 1994.

6. *Key Question*   *Identify each of the following as either a positive or a normative statement:*

   a. The high temperature today was 33°C.
   b. It was too hot today.
   c. The general price level rose by 4.4% last year.
   d. Inflation greatly eroded living standards last year and should be reduced by government policies.

7. To what extent would you accept the five economic goals stated and described in this chapter? What priorities would you assign to them? It has been said that we seek simply four goals: progress, stability, justice, and freedom. Is this list of goals compatible with that given in the chapter?

8. Analyze each of the following specific goals in terms of the five general goals stated in this chapter, and note points of conflict and compatibility: a. conservation of natural resources and the lessening of environmental pollution; b. increasing leisure; c. protection of Canadian producers from foreign competition. Indicate which of these specific goals you favour, and justify your position.

9. *Key Question*   *Explain and give an illustration of a. the fallacy of composition; b. the "after this, therefore because of this" fallacy. Why are cause-and-effect relationships difficult to isolate in the social sciences?*

10. Suppose empirical studies show that students who study more hours receive higher grades, as suggested by the graph accompanying question 4 in this chapter's appendix. Does this relationship guarantee that any particular student who studies longer will get higher grades?

11. A recent psychiatric study found that there is a positive correlation between the amount of time children and youth spend watching television and mental depression. Speculate on possible cause-effect relationships.

12. "Economists should never be popular; men who afflict the comfortable serve equally as those who comfort the afflicted and one cannot suppose that ... capitalism would prosper without the critics its leaders find such a profound source of annoyance."[2] Interpret and evaluate.

13. *Key Question*   *Use the economic perspective to explain why someone who normally is a light eater at a standard restaurant may become somewhat of a glutton at a buffet-style restaurant that charges a single price for all you can eat.*

14. (Applying the Theory, Box 1-3) Explain how the economic perspective can be used to explain the behaviour of customers in fast-food restaurants.

---

[2] John Kenneth Galbraith, *American Capitalism*, rev. ed. (Boston: Houghton Mifflin Company, 1956), p. 49.

APPENDIX TO CHAPTER 1

GRAPHS AND THEIR MEANING

If you glance quickly through the pages of this text, you will find many graphs. Some seem simple while others appear more formidable. Graphs are employed to help you visualize and understand important economic relationships. They are a way for economists to express their theories or models. Physicists and chemists sometimes illustrate their theories by building arrangements of multicoloured wooden balls that represent protons, neutrons, and so forth, held in proper relation to one another by wires or sticks. Economists often use graphs to illustrate their models. By understanding these "pictures" you can more readily understand what economists are saying.

Most of our models will explain the relationship between just two sets of economic facts, which can be conveniently represented with two-dimensional graphs.

CONSTRUCTING A GRAPH

A graph is a visual representation of the relationship between two variables. Table A1-1 provides a hypothetical illustration that shows the relationship between income and consumption. Without ever having studied economics, you would intuitively expect that high-income people consume more than low-income people. Thus we are not surprised to find in Table A1-1 that consumption increases as income increases.

TABLE A1-1 The relationship between income and consumption

Income (per week)	Consumption (per week)	Point
$ 0	$ 50	a
100	100	b
200	150	c
300	200	d
400	250	e

How can the information in Table A1-1 be expressed graphically? Glance at the graph shown in Figure A1-1. Now look back at the information in Table A1-1 and we will explain how to represent in it a meaningful way by constructing the graph you just examined.

FIGURE A1-1 Graphing the direct relationship between consumption and income

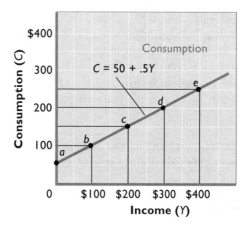

Two sets of data that are positively or directly related, such as consumption and income, graph as an upsloping line. In this case the vertical intercept is $50 and the slope of the line is $+\frac{1}{2}$.

What we are trying to visually show is how consumption changes as income changes. Since income is the determining factor, we represent it on the horizontal axis of the graph as is customary. And, because consumption is dependent on income, we represent it on the vertical axis of the graph, as is also customary. What we are doing is representing the independent variable on the **horizontal axis** and the dependent variable on the **vertical axis**.

Now arrange the vertical and horizontal scales of the graph so that they reflect the range of values of consumption and income. As you can see, the ranges in the graph cover the ranges of values in Table A1-1. The increments on both scales are $100 for each 1 cm.

Next, we locate for each consumption value and the income value a single point that reflects the same information graphically. Our five income–consumption combinations are plotted by drawing perpendiculars from the appropriate points on the two axes. For example, in plotting point c — the $200 income–$150 consumption point — perpendiculars must be drawn up from the horizontal (income) axis at $200 and across from the vertical (consumption) axis at $150. Where these perpendiculars intersect at point c locates this particular income–consumption combination. The other income–consumption combinations shown in Table A1-1 have also been located in Figure A1-1. A line or curve can now be drawn to connect these points.

Using Figure A1-1 as a benchmark, we can make several additional comments.

DIRECT AND INVERSE RELATIONSHIPS

Our upsloping line tells us that there is a **direct relationship** between income and consumption. By a positive or direct relationship, we mean that the two variables change in the *same* direction. An increase in consumption is associated with an increase in income; a decrease in consumption is associated with a decrease in income. When two sets of data are positively or directly related, they will always graph as an *upsloping* line as in Figure A1-1.

In contrast, two sets of data may be inversely related. Consider Table A1-2, which shows the relationship between the price of hockey tickets and game attendance at Informed University (IU). We observe a negative or **inverse relationship** between ticket prices and attendance; these two variables change in *opposite* directions. When ticket prices decrease, attendance increases. When ticket prices increase, attendance decreases. In Figure A1-2 we have plotted the six data points of Table A1-2 following the same procedure outlined above. Observe that an inverse relationship will always graph as a *downsloping* line.

TABLE A1-2 The relationship between ticket prices and attendance

Ticket price	Attendance (thousands)	Point
$25	0	a
20	4	b
15	8	c
10	12	d
5	16	e
0	20	f

DEPENDENT AND INDEPENDENT VARIABLES

Although it is not always easy, economists seek to determine which variable is "cause" and which is "effect," or, more formally, the independent and the dependent variables. By definition, the **dependent variable** is the "effect" or outcome; it changes as a consequence of a change in some other (independent) variable.

The **independent variable** is the "cause"; it causes the change in the dependent variable. In our income–consumption example, income is the independent variable and consumption is the dependent variable. Income causes consumption to be what it is rather than the other way around. Similarly, ticket prices determine attendance at IU

FIGURE A1-2 Graphing the inverse relationship between ticket prices and game attendance

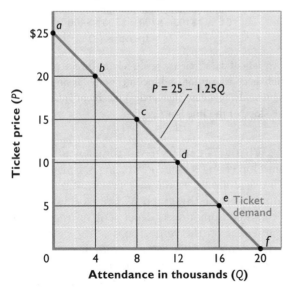

Two sets of data that are negatively or inversely related, such as ticket price and the attendance at basketball games, graph as a downsloping line. The slope of this line is $-1\frac{1}{4}$.

hockey games; attendance does not determine ticket prices. Ticket price is the independent variable, and the quantity purchased is the dependent variable.

You may recall from your high school courses that mathematicians always put the independent variable (cause) on the horizontal axis and the dependent variable (effect) on the vertical axis. Economists are less tidy; their graphing of independent and dependent variables is more arbitrary. Thus their conventional graphing of the income–consumption relationship is consistent with mathematical presentation. But economists put price and cost data on the vertical axis. Hence, the economist's graphing of IU's ticket price–attendance data conflicts with mathematical procedure.

OTHER VARIABLES HELD CONSTANT

Our simple two-variable graphs ignore a variety of other factors that might affect the amount of consumption occurring at each income level or the number of people that attend IU hockey games at each possible ticket price. When we plot the relationship between any two variables, we invoke the *ceteris paribus* or "other things being equal" assumption. Thus in Figure A1-1 all other factors (that is, all factors other than income) that might affect the amount of consumption are presumed to be constant or unchanged. Similarly, in Figure A1-2 all factors other than ticket price that might influence attendance at IU hockey games are assumed constant. In reality, we know "other things" often change, and when they do, the specific relationships presented in our two tables and graphs may change. Specifically, we would expect the lines we have plotted to shift to new locations.

For example, what might happen to the income–consumption relationship if there occurred a stock market crash such as that of October 1987? The expected impact of this dramatic fall in the value of stocks would be to make people feel less wealthy and therefore less willing to consume at each income level. Thus, we would anticipate a downward shift of the consumption line in Figure A1-1. You should plot a new consumption line based on the assumption that consumption is, say, $20 less at each income level. Note that the relationship remains direct, but the line has merely shifted to reflect less consumer spending at each level of income.

Similarly, a variety of factors other than ticket prices might affect IU game attendance. For example, if the provincial government were to abandon its program of student loans, IU enrolment and hence attendance at games might be less at each ticket price. You are urged to redraw Figure A1-2 on the assumption that 2000 fewer students attend IU games at each ticket price. (**Key Appendix Question 2**)

SLOPE OF A LINE

Lines can be described in terms of their slopes. The **slope of a straight line** between any two points is defined as the ratio of the vertical change (the rise or fall) to the horizontal change (the run) involved in moving between those points.

POSITIVE SLOPE   In moving from point *b* to point *c* in Figure A1-1 we find that the rise or vertical change (the change in consumption) is +$50 and the run or horizontal change (the change in income) is +$100. Therefore:

$$\text{Slope } = \frac{\text{vertical change}}{\text{horizontal change}} = \frac{+50}{+100} = +\frac{1}{2}$$

Note that our slope of $\frac{1}{2}$ is positive because consumption and income change in the same direction, that is, consumption and income are directly or positively related.

A slope of $+\frac{1}{2}$ indicates that there will be a $1 increase in consumption for every $2 increase in income. It also indicates that for every $2 decrease in income there will be a $1 decrease in consumption.

NEGATIVE SLOPE   For our ticket price–attendance data, the relationship is negative or inverse, with the result that the slope of Figure A1-2's line is negative. In particular, the vertical change or fall is 5 and the horizontal change or run is 4. Therefore:

$$\text{Slope } = \frac{\text{vertical change}}{\text{horizontal change}} = \frac{-5}{+4} = -1\frac{1}{4}$$

This slope of $\frac{-5}{+4}$ or $-1\frac{1}{4}$ means that lowering the price of a ticket by $5 will increase attendance by 4000 people, which is the same as saying that a $1 price reduction will increase attendance by 800 persons.

THREE ADDENDA   Our discussion of line slopes needs three additional comments.

1. MEASUREMENT UNITS   The slope of a line will be affected by the choice of units for either variable. For example, if in our ticket price illustration we had chosen to measure prices in dimes rather than dollars, then our vertical change for a price cut would be −50 (dimes) instead of −5 (dollars) and the slope would be −12$\frac{1}{2}$ (= 50 ÷ 4) rather than −1. The measurement of slope depends on the way the relevant variables are denominated.

2. MARGINAL ANALYSIS   Economics is largely concerned with *marginal* or incremental changes. Should you work an hour more or an hour less each day on your part-time job? Should you buy one more or one less IU basketball ticket? Should a fast-food restaurant, now employing eight workers, hire an extra or marginal worker?

This is relevant because the slopes of lines measure marginal changes. For example, in Figure A1-1 the slope shows that $50 of extra or marginal consumption is associated with each $100 increase in income. Consumers will spend half of any increase in their income and reduce their consumption by half of any decline in income. The concept of slope is important in economics because it reflects marginal changes.

3. INFINITE AND ZERO SLOPES   Many variables are unrelated or independent of one another. We would not expect the price of bananas to be related to the quantity of wristwatches purchased. If we were to put the price of bananas on the vertical axis and the quantity demanded of watches on the horizontal axis, the absence of a relationship between them would be described by a line parallel to the vertical axis, indicating that changes in the price of bananas have no impact on watch purchases. The slope of such a line is *infinite*. Similarly, if aggregate consumption were completely unrelated to, say, the quantity of rainfall and we were to put consumption on the vertical axis and rainfall on the horizontal axis, this unrelatedness would be represented by a line parallel to the horizontal axis. This line has a slope of *zero*.

INTERCEPT

In addition to its slope, the only other information needed in locating a line on a graph is the vertical intercept. The **vertical intercept** is the point where the line meets the vertical axis. For Figure A1-1 the intercept is $50. This means that, if current income were zero, consumers would still spend $50. How might they manage to consume when they have no current income? Answer: By borrowing or by selling some of their assets. Similarly, the vertical intercept in Figure A1-2 shows us that at a $25 ticket price IU's hockey team would be playing in an empty arena.

EQUATION FORM

With a specific intercept and slope, our consumption line can be succinctly described in equation form. In general, a linear equation is written as $y = a + bx$, where y is the dependent variable, a is the vertical intercept, b is the slope of the line, and x is the independent variable. For our income–consumption example, if C represents consumption (the dependent variable) and Y represents income (the independent variable), we can write $C = a + bY$. By substituting the values of the intercept and the slope for our specific data, we have $C = 50 + .5Y$. This equation allows us to determine consumption at *any* level of income. At the $300 income level (point d in Figure A1-1), our equation predicts that consumption will be $200 [= $50 + (.5 × $300)]. You should confirm that at the $250 income level consumption will be $175.

When economists reverse mathematical convention by putting the independent variable on the vertical axis and the dependent variable on the horizontal axis, in a sense the standard linear equation solves for the independent, rather than the dependent, variable. We noted earlier that this case is relevant for IU ticket price–attendance data. If we let P represent the ticket price and Q represent attendance, our relevant equation is $P = 25 − 1.25Q$, where the vertical intercept is 25 and the slope is −1$\frac{1}{4}$ or −1.25. But knowing the value for P enables us to solve for Q, which is actually our dependent variable. For example, if P = 15, then the values in our equation become: $15 = 25 − 1.25(Q)$, or $1.25Q = 10$, or $Q = 8$. Check this answer against Figure A1-2, and use this equation to predict IU ticket sales when the price is $7.50. **(Key Appendix Question 3)**

SLOPE OF A NONLINEAR CURVE

We now move from the simple world of linear relationships (straight lines) to the more complex world of nonlinear relationships (curves). By defini-

FIGURE A1-3 Determining the slopes of curves

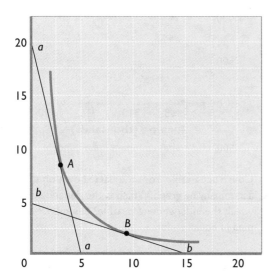

The slope of a nonlinear curve changes as one moves from point to point on the curve. The slope at any point can be determined by drawing a straight line tangent to that point and calculating the slope of that straight line.

tion, the slope of a straight line is constant at every point. The slope of a curve changes as we move from one point to another on the curve.

For example, consider the downsloping curve in Figure A1-3. Although its slope is negative throughout, it diminishes or flattens as we move southeast along the curve. Because the slope is constantly changing, we can measure the slope only at some particular point on the curve.

We begin by drawing a straight line that is tangent to the curve at that point where we want to measure its slope. A line is **tangent** at that point where it touches, but does not intersect, the curve. Thus, line *aa* is tangent to the curve at point A in Figure A1-3. Having done this, we can measure the slope of the curve at point A by measuring the slope of the straight tangent line *aa*. Specifically, in Figure A1-3 the vertical change (fall) in *aa* is –20 and the horizontal change (run) is +5. Thus the slope of the tangent *aa* line is $^{-20}/_{+5}$ or –4 and therefore the slope of the curve at A is also –4.

We can now draw line *bb* tangent to a flatter part of the curve at point B. Following the same procedure, we find the negative slope to be smaller, specifically $^{-5}/_{15}$ or $^{-1}/_3$. Similar analysis applies to upsloping curves. **(Key Appendix Question 6)**

APPENDIX SUMMARY

1. Graphs are a convenient and revealing means of presenting economic relationships or principles.

2. Two variables are positively or directly related when their values change in the same direction. Two directly related variables will plot as an upsloping line on a graph.

3. Two variables are negatively or inversely related when their values change in opposite directions. Two variables that are inversely related will graph as a downsloping line.

4. The value of the dependent variable ("effect") is determined by the value of the independent variable ("cause").

5. When "other factors" that might affect a two-variable relationship are allowed to change, the plotted relationship will likely shift to a new location.

6. The slope of a straight line is the ratio of the vertical change to the horizontal change in moving between any two points. The slope of an upsloping line is positive; the slope of a downsloping line is negative.

7. The slope of a line depends on the choice of units in denominating the variables. The slope of a line is especially relevant for economics because it measures marginal changes.

8. The slope of a horizontal line is zero; the slope of a vertical line is infinite.

9. The vertical (or horizontal) intercept and the slope of a line establish its location and are used in expressing the relationship between two variables as an equation.

10. The slope of a curve at any point is determined by calculating the slope of a straight line drawn tangent to that point.

APPENDIX TERMS AND CONCEPTS

dependent and independent variables (p. 18)
direct and inverse relationships (p. 18)
slope of a straight line (p. 19)
tangent (p. 21)
vertical and horizontal axes (p. 17)
vertical intercept (p. 20)

APPENDIX QUESTIONS AND STUDY SUGGESTIONS

 *1. Briefly explain the use of graphs as a means of presenting economic principles. What is an inverse relationship? How does it graph? What is a direct relationship? How does it graph? Graph and explain the relationships one would expect to find between *a.* the number of centimetres of rainfall per month and the sale of umbrellas; *b.* the amount of tuition and the level of enrolment at a university; *c.* the size of an NHL club's budget for player salaries and the number of games won. In each case, cite and explain how considerations other than those specifically mentioned might upset the expected relationship. Is your second generalization consistent with the fact that historically enrolments and tuition have both increased? If not, explain any difference.

2. *Key Appendix Question   Indicate how each of the following might affect the data shown in Table A1-2 and Figure A1-2 of this appendix: a. IU's athletic director schedules higher quality opponents; b. IU's Fighting Aardvarks experience three losing seasons; c. IU contracts to have all of its home games televised.*

3. *Key Appendix Question   The following table contains data on the relationship between saving and income. Rearrange these data as required, and graph the data on the accompanying grid. What is the slope of the line? The vertical intercept? Interpret the meaning of both the slope and the intercept. Write the equation that represents this line. What would you predict saving to be at the $12,500 level of income?*

Income (per year)	Saving (per year)
$15,000	$1000
0	−500
10,000	500
5,000	0
20,000	1500

* Note to the reader: A floppy disk symbol precedes each of the questions in this appendix. This icon is used throughout the text to indicate that a particular question relates to the content of one of the tutorial programs in the student software that accompanies this book. Please refer to the Preface for more detail about this software.

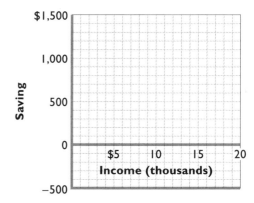

4. Construct a table from the data shown on the accompanying graph. Which is the dependent and which the independent variable? Summarize the data in equation form.

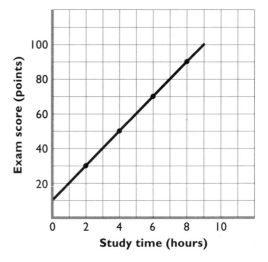

5. Suppose that when the interest rate that must be paid to borrow funds is 16%, businesses find it is unprofitable to invest in machinery and equipment. However, when the interest rate is 14%, $5 billion worth of investment is profitable. At 12%, a total of $10 billion of investment is profitable. Similarly, total investment increases by $5 billion for each successive 2 percentage point decline in the interest rate. Indicate the relevant relationship between the interest rate and investment verbally, tabularly, graphically, and as an equation. Put the interest rate on the vertical axis and investment on the horizontal axis. In your equation use the form $i = a - bI$, where i is the interest rate, a is the vertical intercept, b is the slope of the line, and I is the level of investment. Comment on the advantages and disadvantages of each of these four forms of presentation.

6. *Key Appendix Question* The accompanying diagram shows curve XX and three tangents at points A, B, and C. Calculate the slope of the curve at these three points.

7. In the accompanying diagram is the slope of curve AA' positive or negative? Does the slope increase or decrease as we move from A to A'? Answer the same two questions for curve BB'.

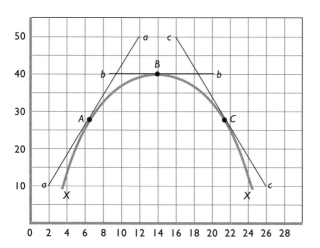

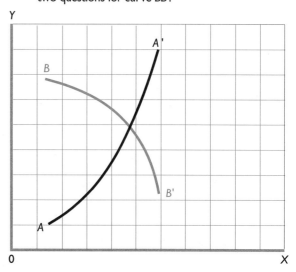

CHAPTER 2

THE ECONOMIZING PROBLEM: SCARCITY, WANTS, AND CHOICES

You make decisions every day that capture the essence of economics. Suppose you have $20 and are deciding how to spend it. Should you buy a new pair of blue jeans? A couple of compact discs? A ticket for a rock concert? Similarly, what to do with your time between three and six o'clock on, say, a Thursday afternoon? Should you work extra hours on your part-time job? Do research on a term project? Prepare for an economics quiz? Watch TV? Take a nap? Money and time are both scarce and making decisions in the context of scarcity implies costs. If you choose the jeans, the cost is the forgone CDs or concert. If you nap or watch TV, the cost might be a low grade on your quiz. Scarcity, wants, choices — these are the building blocks of this chapter.

Here we introduce and explore the fundamentals of economic science. We expand on the definition of economics introduced in Chapter 1 and explore the essence of the economizing problem. We will illustrate, extend, and modify our definition by using production possibilities tables and curves. Next, we will briefly survey different ways by which institutionally and ideologically diverse economies respond to the economizing problem. Finally, we present an overview of the market system in the form of the circular flow model.

BOX 2-1 THE BIG PICTURE

The economizing problem arises from scarcity (or limited) resources and human unlimited wants. As a consequence, individuals and societies must make choices about what they want to produce and consume.

Consider the following scenario. Fall term has just ended and one weekend remains before the Christmas holiday begins. You must study for a final exam but you also need to do your Christmas shopping. Also, it just snowed and you are itching to ski for the first time of the season. Moreover, your friends have invited you to a Christmas party Friday night of the same weekend.

You need to make choices since it would be impossible for you to do all the things you want. And whatever choices you make entails giving something up. That, in short, captures the economizing problem, the result of limited resources and many wants.

As you read this chapter, keep the following points in mind:

- Resources to produce the goods and services we want are limited in relation to our wants.
- Even if a few very wealthy individuals have all the material things they desire, the vast majority of the human race certainly does not.
- In the face of limited resources, choices about what to produce and consume must be made.
- Limited resources imply that choosing more of one good or service means giving up some quantity of another good or service. If you have $50 to spend, a decision to buy a pair of jeans means *not* buying a $50 shirt.

THE FOUNDATION OF ECONOMICS

Two fundamental facts that constitute the **economizing problem** provide a foundation for economics. You must fully understand these two facts, because everything that follows depends directly or indirectly on them:

1. *Society's material wants are virtually unlimited.*
2. *Economic resources — the means for goods and services — are limited or scarce.*

UNLIMITED WANTS

In the first statement, what do we mean by "material wants"? We mean, first, the desires of consumers to obtain and use various *goods and services* that provide **utility**, the economist's term for pleasure or satisfaction.[1] An amazingly wide range of products fills the bill in this respect: houses, automobiles, toothpaste, compact-disc players, pizzas, sweaters, and the like. Innumerable products, sometimes classified as *necessities* (food, shelter, clothing) and *luxuries* (perfumes, yachts, mink coats), are all capable of satisfying human wants. Of course, what is a luxury to Smith may be a necessity to Jones, and what is a common necessity today may have been a luxury a few short years ago.

Services satisfy our wants as much as products. Repair work on our car, the removal of our appendix, a haircut, and legal advice also satisfy human wants. We buy many goods — such as automobiles and washing machines — for the services they render. The differences between goods and services are often less than they first appear.

Businesses and governments also seek to satisfy material wants. Businesses want factory buildings, machinery, communication systems, and so forth, to assist them in realizing their production goals. Government, reflecting the collective wants of its citizenry or goals of its own, seeks highways, schools, hospitals, and military equipment.

As a group, these material wants are *insatiable*, or *unlimited*, meaning that material wants for goods and services cannot be completely satisfied. Our wants for a *particular* good or service can be satisfied. For example, over a short period of time we can get sufficient amounts of toothpaste or beer. Certainly one appendicitis operation is par for the course.

But goods in *general* are another story. We do not, and presumably cannot, get enough. A simple experiment will help verify this. Suppose all members of society are asked to list those goods and services they want. Chances are this list will be impressive!

---

[1] This definition leaves a variety of wants — recognition, status, love, and so forth — for the other social sciences to worry about.

Furthermore, over time, our wants multiply. As we fill some of the wants on the list, we add new ones. The rapid introduction of new products whets our appetites and extensive advertising persuades us that we need countless items we might not otherwise buy. Not long ago, we didn't want personal computers, light beer, video cassette recorders, fax machines, and compact discs because they didn't exist. Furthermore, we often cannot stop with simple satisfaction: the acquisition of an Escort or Geo has been known to whet the appetite for a Porsche or Mercedes.

The overall objective of all economic activity is the attempt to satisfy all these diverse material wants.

SCARCE RESOURCES

In considering the second fundamental fact — **economic resources are limited or scarce** — what do we mean by **economic resources**? In general, we mean all the natural, human, and manufactured resources that go into the production of goods and services. This covers a lot of ground: factory and farm buildings and all sorts of equipment, tools, and machinery used in the production of manufactured goods and agricultural products; transportation and communication facilities; innumerable types of labour; and land and mineral resources of all kinds.

RESOURCE CATEGORIES We need economic resources to produce goods and services to satisfy human wants. Let's divide these various resources into categories so we can get a better understanding of them.

LAND **Land** refers to all natural resources or raw materials — all "gifts of nature" — that are usable in the productive process. Resources such as arable land, forests, mineral and oil deposits, and water resources come under this general classification.

CAPITAL **Capital**, or investment goods, refers to all manufactured aids to production such as tools, machinery, equipment, and factory storage, transportation, and distribution facilities used in producing goods and services and getting them to the consumer. The process of producing and purchasing capital goods is known as **investment**.

Two other points are pertinent. First, *capital goods* ("tools") differ from *consumer* goods in that the latter satisfy wants directly, whereas capital goods do so indirectly by facilitating the production of consumable goods. Second, the term "capital" does *not* refer to money. Business executives and economists often do talk of "money capital," meaning money that is available for use in the purchase of machinery, equipment, and other productive facilities. But money, as such, produces nothing, and therefore is not an economic resource. To re-emphasize, *real capital* — tools, machinery, and other productive equipment — is an economic resource; *money* or *financial capital* is not.

LABOUR **Labour** is a broad term referring to all the physical and mental talents of men and women available and usable in producing goods and services. (This excludes a special set of human talents — entrepreneurial ability — which, because of their special significance in a market economy, we consider separately.) The services of a logger, retail clerk, machinist, teacher, professional football player, and nuclear physicist all fall under the general heading of labour.

ENTREPRENEURIAL ABILITY The final category is **entrepreneurial ability**, or, simply, *enterprise*. The entrepreneur has four related functions:

1. The entrepreneur takes the *initiative* in combining the resources of land, capital, and labour in the production of a good or service. The entrepreneur is at once the driving force behind production and the agent that combines the other resources in what is hoped will be a profitable venture.
2. The entrepreneur undertakes major *business-policy decisions* — that is, those nonroutine decisions that set the course of a business enterprise.
3. The entrepreneur is an *innovator* — the person who attempts to introduce on a commercial basis new products, new productive techniques, or new forms of business organization.
4. The entrepreneur is a *risk taker*. This is apparent from a close examination of the other three entrepreneurial functions. The entrepreneur in a market economy has no guarantee of profit. The reward for his or her time, efforts, and abilities may be profits *or* losses and eventual bankruptcy.

RESOURCE PAYMENTS The income received from supplying property resources — raw materials and capital equipment — is called **rental** and **interest income.** The income to those who supply labour is

BOX 2-2   IN THE MEDIA

DOWN'S TRANSPLANT BID POSES DILEMMA: LUNG RECIPIENTS FACE LONG ODDS

BY ALANNA MITCHELL

CALGARY — Terry Urquhart's request for a new lung has created a moral dilemma for the doctors and ethicists who decide who gets organ transplants.

Mr. Urquhart, 17, who has been placed on a waiting list and who reports for his medical assessment next week, is the first person with Down's syndrome in Canada, perhaps in the world, to be actively considered for a new lung, and the decision to put him on the list has raised an ethical storm that has shaken Alberta.

Some call it a moral victory and others say it is a waste of a scarce resource. To Mr. Urquhart, the medical miracle of a new lung means simply the chance to live out his last few years without gasping for air.

The people who run Canada's transplant programs say that since lung transplants became an option in Canada in the late 1980s, Mr. Urquhart is the first person with Down's to request one, despite the fact that severe lung problems are a common feature of that genetic disorder.

The case poses a problem for those who decide who gets which scarce organs, especially since costly transplant programs need to show success in order to survive. They also have a duty to use the scarce donated lungs in the best way possible.

In all of Canada, just 28 single-lung transplants were performed in 1993, the last year for which statistics are available. Between 20 per cent and 40 per cent of those who await a lung die during the wait.

Those who survive the operation face long odds. Roughly 14 per cent die within 30 days of the operation. About half are alive three years later. Doctors cannot offer recipients a guarantee of longer life, only the possibility of a life of better quality.

SOURCE: *The Globe and Mail*, April 28, 1995, p. A1. Reproduced with permission.

The Story in Brief

Scarcity often causes difficult moral dilemmas. There are not enough human organ donors to satisfy the need for organs. In this story, the issue is whether a person with Down's syndrome should receive one of the "scarce donated lungs."

The Economics Behind the Story

- The number of patients who want a lung transplant is greater than the number of donated lungs.

- A person with Down's syndrome has requested one of the scarce donated lungs. But giving a donated lung to one person necessarily means denying another patient one.

- The "moral" dilemma arises because of scarcity. If there were enough donated lungs to satisfy the demand for them, the "moral" dilemma would be resolved.

- Think of some other examples where "moral dilemmas" could be resolved by having more of any good or service so that painful trade-offs are avoided. Is there a direct relationship between scarcity and moral dilemmas?

called **wages**, which includes salaries and various wage and salary supplements, such as bonuses, commissions, and royalties. Entrepreneurial income is called **profits** (which may be a negative figure — losses).

These four broad categories of economic resources, or **factors of production** as they are often called, leave room for debate when it comes to classifying specific resources. For example, is a dividend on some newly issued Canadian Pacific stock you may own an interest return for the capital equipment the company was able to buy with the money you provided, or a profit that compensates you for the risks involved in purchasing corporate stock? But, although we might quibble about classifying a particular flow of income as wages, rent, interest, or profits, all income can be fitted under one of the general headings.

RELATIVE SCARCITY   All economic resources, or factors of production, have one fundamental characteristic in common: *They are scarce or limited in supply given our unlimited wants.* Our "spaceship earth" contains only limited amounts of resources that can be put to use in the production of goods and services. Quantities of arable land, mineral deposits, capital equipment, and labour (time) are all limited. The scarcity of productive resources and the constraint this scarcity puts on productive activity means output will necessarily be limited. Society will *not* be able to produce and consume all the goods and services it wants.

ECONOMICS: GETTING THE MOST FROM AVAILABLE RESOURCES

Let's restate the basic definition of economics: **Economics is the social science concerned with the problem of fulfilling society's unlimited wants with limited, or scarce, resources.** Thus, economics is about "doing the best we can with what we have." If the available resources are scarce, we cannot satisfy all our unlimited material wants. The next best thing is to satisfy as many of the material wants as possible.

The challenge for economics is to satisfy unlimited wants with limited resources and thus it is concerned with *efficiency:* getting the most output with the resources, or inputs, we have available. The more output from a specific quantity of inputs results in an increase in efficiency.

If a society wants to satisfy as many of its material wants as possible, it needs to have full employment of its available resources and must get the most from them — what we term full production.

FULL EMPLOYMENT: USING ALL AVAILABLE RESOURCES

A society has **full employment** when all available resources are used in the production of goods and services. No worker who is willing and able to work is unemployed, all capital equipment, land, and natural resources known to exist and all entrepreneurial talents are utilized. Note we say all *available* resources must be utilized to achieve full employment. Each society has certain customs and practices that determine what particular resources are available for employment. For example, legislation and custom dictate that children and the very old cannot be employed. Also, it is desirable to "conserve" some resources for future generations.

FULL PRODUCTION: USING AVAILABLE RESOURCES EFFICIENTLY

The employment of all available resources is not sufficient to get the maximum output from them. We also require **full production**: the most efficient use of the available resources. If a society fails to achieve full production, at least some resources are *underemployed*; we are not getting the maximum amount of output those resources are capable of contributing.

Full production requires two kinds of efficiency — allocative and productive efficiency.

ALLOCATIVE EFFICIENCY   **Allocative efficiency** means that resources are being devoted to the production of goods and services most wanted by society. It is attained when we produce the best or optimal output-mix: the combination of goods and services society wants most. For example, society now wants resources allocated to compact discs and cassettes, rather than 45 rpm or long-playing records. We now prefer word processors and personal computers to manual typewriters. Photocopiers are desired, not mimeograph machines.

PRODUCTIVE EFFICIENCY   **Productive efficiency** is achieved when the goods and services society wants most are produced in the least costly ways. Producing in the least costly ways automatically ensures producers use more of the relatively abundant resources and less of the relatively scarce resources. For example, if labour is in short supply compared to capital equipment, labour inputs will be costly compared to machinery. Productive efficiency will be achieved if less labour and more capital equipment are used, resulting in the least costly way of producing a good or service.

The relative costs of labour and capital in the 1990s requires that Tauruses and Grand Ams be produced with computerized and robotized assembly techniques rather than the more primitive and labour-intensive assembly lines of the 1920s. Productive efficiency is not achieved today by farmers picking corn by hand when advanced harvesting equipment will do the job at a much lower cost per bushel.

In summary, society's unlimited material wants in a world of limited resources can best be satisfied if we get the most production from our scarce resources. To achieve this desirable end, all available resources have to be fully employed and we must get full production from them. Full production implies producing the "right" good (allocative efficiency) in the "right" way (productive efficiency). Allocative efficiency occurs when resources are apportioned among firms and industries so that the particular product mix society most desires is produced. Productive efficiency occurs when goods and services in this optimal product mix are produced in the least costly fashion. **(Key Question 5)**

QUICK REVIEW 2-1

1. Human material wants are virtually unlimited.

2. Economic resources — land, capital, labour, and entrepreneurial ability — are scarce or limited.

3. Economics is concerned with the efficient management of these scarce resources to achieve the maximum fulfilment of our material wants.

4. Getting the most output from available resources requires both full employment and full production, the latter necessitating both allocative and productive efficiency.

PRODUCTION POSSIBILITIES TABLE

We can clarify the economizing problem through the use of a **production possibilities table**. This device reveals the core of the economizing problem: *Because resources are scarce, even a full-employment, full-production economy cannot have an unlimited output of goods and services. A society must make choices about which goods and services to produce and which to forgo.*

ASSUMPTIONS   In order to better understand the production possibilities table (Table 2-1), we make several assumptions to set the stage.

1. EFFICIENCY   The economy is operating at full employment and achieving productive efficiency. (We will consider allocative efficiency later.)

2. FIXED RESOURCES   The available supplies of the factors of production are fixed in both quantity and quality. But they can be shifted or reallocated, within limits, among different uses; for example, a relatively skilled labourer can work on a farm, at a fast-food restaurant, or as a gas-station attendant.

3. FIXED TECHNOLOGY   Technology does not change during the course of our analysis.

Assumptions 2 and 3 are another way of saying that we are looking at our economy at some specific point in time. Over a relatively long period, technological advances are possible and resource supplies can vary.

4. TWO PRODUCTS   To further simplify, suppose our economy is producing just two products — industrial robots and pizza — instead of the innumerable goods and services actually produced. Pizza is symbolic of **consumer goods**, those goods that directly satisfy our wants; industrial robots are symbolic of **capital goods**, those goods that satisfy our wants *indirectly* by permitting more efficient production of consumer goods.

NECESSITY OF CHOICE   From our assumptions we see a choice must be made among alternatives since the available resources are limited. Thus, the total amounts of robots and pizza that our economy is capable of producing are limited. *Limited resources result in a limited output.* Since resources are limited in supply and fully employed, any increase in the production of robots will require shifting resources away from the production of pizza. And the reverse holds true: if we choose to step up the production of pizza, needed resources must come at the expense of robot production.

Table 2-1 shows alternative combinations of robots and pizza that our economy might choose. Though the data in this and the following production possibility tables are hypothetical, the points illustrated are of great practical significance. At alternative A, our economy would be devoting all its resources to the production of robots (capital goods). At alternative E, all available resources would be devoted to pizza production (consumer goods).

Both these alternatives are unrealistic extremes: any economy typically strikes a balance in dividing its total output between capital and consumer goods. As we move from alternative A to alternative E, we step up the production of consumer goods (pizza) by shifting resources away from capital good production.

Since consumer goods directly satisfy our wants, any movement towards alternative E looks tempting. In making this move, society increases the current satisfaction of its wants. But there is a cost involved. This shift of resources catches up with society over time as its stock of capital goods dwindles — or at least ceases to expand at the current rate — with the result that the potential for greater future production is impaired. In moving from alternative A towards alternative E, society is in effect choosing "more now" at the expense of "much more later."

In moving from E towards A, society is choosing to forgo current consumption. This sacrifice of current consumption frees resources that can now be used to increase the production of capital goods. By building up its stock of capital, society can anticipate greater production and therefore greater consumption in the future. In moving from E towards A, society is choosing "more later" at the cost of "less now."

TABLE 2-1 Production possibilities of pizza and robots with full employment, 1996

Type of product	Production alternatives				
	A	B	C	D	E
Pizza (in hundred thousands)	0	1	2	3	4
Robots (in thousands)	10	9	7	4	0

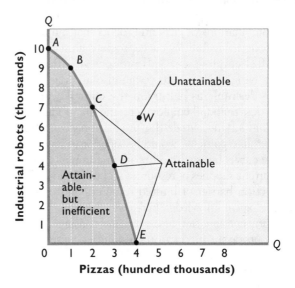

KEY GRAPH

FIGURE 2-1 The production possibilities curve

Each point on the curve represents some maximum combination of any two products that can be achieved if full employment and full production are realized. When operating on the curve, more robots mean less pizza, and vice versa. Limited resources and a fixed technology make any combinations of robots and pizza lying outside the curve, such as W, unattainable. Points inside the curve are attainable, but indicate that full employment and productive efficiency are not being realized.

At any point in time, an economy that is achieving full employment and productive efficiency must sacrifice some of product X *to obtain more of product* Y. *The fact that economic resources are scarce prohibits such an economy from having both X and Y.*

PRODUCTION POSSIBILITIES CURVE

To ensure our understanding of the production possibilities table, let's view these data graphically. We employ a two-dimensional graph, arbitrarily putting the output of robots (capital goods) on the vertical axis and the output of pizza (consumer goods) on the horizontal axis, as in **Figure 2-1 (Key Graph)**. Following the plotting procedure in the appendix to Chapter 1, we can locate the "production possibilities" curve, as shown in Figure 2-1.

Each point on the production possibilities curve represents some maximum output of the two products. Thus the curve is a frontier. To realize the various combinations of pizza and robots that fall *on* the production possibilities curve, society must achieve both full employment and productive efficiency. Points lying *inside* the curve are also attainable, but not as desirable as points on the curve because it means less than full employment and full production.

Points lying *outside* the production possibilities frontier, like point *W*, would be superior to any point on the curve; but such points are unattainable, given the current supplies of resources and technology. The production barrier of limited resources and existing technological knowledge makes it impossible to produce any combination of capital and consumer goods lying outside the production possibilities curve.

LAW OF INCREASING OPPORTUNITY COSTS

The amount of other products that must be forgone or sacrificed to obtain some amount of a specific product is called the opportunity cost of that good. In our case the amount of Y (robots) that must be forgone or given up to get another unit of X (pizza) is the **opportunity cost** of that unit of X.

In moving from possibility A to B in Table 2-1, we find that the cost of 1 additional unit of pizza is 1 less unit of robots. But as we now pursue the concept of cost through the additional production possibilities — B to C, C to D, and D to E — an important economic principle is revealed. The sacrifice or cost of robots involved in getting each additional unit of pizza *increases*. In moving from A to B, just 1 unit of robots is sacrificed for 1 more unit of pizza; but going from B to C sacrifices 2 additional units of robots for 1 more of pizza; then 3 more of robots for 1 more of pizza; and finally 4 to 1. Conversely, you should confirm that in moving from E to A the cost of an additional robot is $1/4$, $1/3$, $1/2$, and 1 unit of pizza respectively for each of the four shifts.

Note two points about this discussion of opportunity costs:

1. The analysis is in *real* or physical terms. We will shift to monetary comparisons in a moment.
2. Our explanation also is in terms of *marginal* (meaning "added" or "extra") cost, rather than cumulative or *total* opportunity cost. For example, the marginal opportunity cost of the third unit of

pizza in Table 2-1 is 3 units of robots (= 7 – 4). But the total opportunity cost of 3 units of pizza is 6 units of robots (= 10 – 4 or 1 + 2 + 3).

CONCAVITY   Graphically, the **law of increasing opportunity costs** is reflected in the shape of the production possibilities curve. The curve is *concave*, or bowed out from the origin. When the economy moves from A towards E, it must give up successively larger amounts of robots (1, 2, 3, 4) to acquire equal increments of pizza (1, 1, 1, 1). The slope of the production possibilities curve becomes steeper as we move from A to E. Such a curve, by definition, is concave as viewed from the origin.

RATIONALE   The rationale for the law of increasing opportunity costs is: *Economic resources are not completely adaptable to alternative uses.* As we attempt to step up pizza production, resources less and less adaptable to making pizza must be induced, or "pushed," into pizza production. As we move from B to C, C to D, and so on, those resources that are highly productive of pizza become increasingly scarce. To get more pizza, resources whose productivity in robots is great in relation to their productivity in pizza will be needed. It will take more and more of such resources — and a greater sacrifice of robots — to achieve each increase of 1 unit in the production of pizza. This lack of perfect interchangeability is behind the law of increasing opportunity costs. **(Key Question 6)**

ALLOCATIVE EFFICIENCY REVISITED

Our analysis has purposely stressed full employment and productive efficiency, both of which allow society to achieve *any point* on its production possibilities curve. We now focus again on allocative efficiency, the question of determining the most-valued or *optimal point* on the production possibilities curve. Of all the attainable combinations of pizza and robots in Figure 2-1, which is optimal or "best"? What quantities of resources should be allocated to pizza and what quantities to robots?

Our discussion of the "economic perspective" in Chapter 1 puts us on the right track. Recall that economic decisions compare marginal benefits and marginal costs. Any economic activity — for example, production or consumption — should be expanded so long as marginal benefits exceed marginal costs.

Consider pizza. We already know from the law of diminishing opportunity costs that the marginal cost (MC) of additional units of pizza will rise as more

FIGURE 2-2   Allocative Efficiency: MB = MC

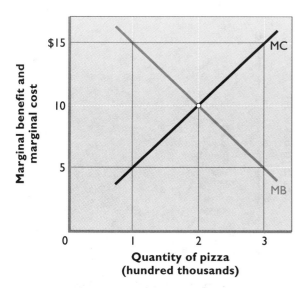

Resources are efficiently allocated to any product when its output is such that marginal benefits equal marginal costs.

units are produced. This is shown by the upsloping MC curve in Figure 2-2. We are also aware that we obtain extra or marginal benefits (MB) from additional units of pizza. However, although material wants *in the aggregate* are insatiable, the consumption of each *particular* product yields less and less extra satisfaction or, in other words, less MB. A consumer can become relatively saturated with a specific product. A second pizza provides less additional utility to you than does the first. And a third will provide even less MB than did the second. So it is for society as a whole. Thus, we can portray the marginal benefits from pizza by the downsloping MB line in Figure 2-2.

The optimal amount of pizza to produce is 200,000 units as indicated by the intersection of the MB and MC curves. Why is this optimal? If only 100,000 pizzas were produced, the MB of pizzas would be greater than their MC. In money terms the MB of a pizza here might be $15 while its MC is only $5. This suggests that society is *underallocating* resources to pizza production.

Why? Because society values an additional pizza at $15, while the alternative products or services the required resources could have produced are valued at $5. Society will benefit — it will be better off in the sense of having a larger total output to enjoy — whenever it can gain something worth $15 by giving up something (alternative goods and services) worth

only $5. A reallocation of resources from other products to pizza means society is using its resources more efficiently. Each additional pizza up to 200,000 provides such gains, indicating that allocative efficiency is improved. But when MB=MC, the value of producing pizza or alternative products with available resources is the same. Allocative efficiency is achieved when MB=MC.

The production of 300,000 pizzas would represent an *overallocation* of resources to their production. Here the MC of pizza is $15 and their MB is only $5. A unit of pizza is worth only $5 to society while the alternative products are valued at $15. By producing 1 less unit, society suffers the loss of a pizza worth $5, but by reallocating the freed resources it gains other products worth $15. Any time society can gain something worth $15 by forgoing something (a pizza) worth only $5, it has realized a net gain. The net gain in this instance is $10 worth of total output. In Figure 2-2 net gains can be realized as long as pizza production is reduced from 300,000 to 200,000. A more valued output from the same aggregate amount of inputs means greater allocative efficiency.

Resources are being efficiently allocated to any product when its output is such that its marginal benefit equals its marginal cost (MB=MC). Suppose that by applying the same analysis to robots we find that 7000 is their optimal or MB=MC output. This means that alternative C on our production possibilities curve — 200,000 pizzas and 7000 robots — results in allocative efficiency for our hypothetical economy. **(Key Question 9)**

QUICK REVIEW 2-2

1. The production possibilities curve illustrates four basic concepts.

   a. Resources are scarce. All combinations of output lying outside the production possibilities curve are unobtainable.

   b. Choices must be made. A society must select among the various attainable combinations of goods lying on (or within) the curve.

   c. The downward slope of the curve implies the notion of opportunity cost — choosing more of one good, an individual or a society has to accept less of another good.

   d. The concavity of the curve reveals increasing opportunity costs.

2. Full employment and productive efficiency must be attained for the economy to operate on its production possibilities curve. A comparison of marginal benefits and marginal costs is needed to determine allocative efficiency — the best or optimal output mix on the curve.

3. A comparison of marginal benefits and marginal costs is needed to determine allocative efficiency — the best or optimal output-mix on the curve.

UNEMPLOYMENT, GROWTH, AND THE FUTURE

Let's now drop the first three assumptions underlying the production possibilities curve to see what happens.

UNEMPLOYMENT AND PRODUCTIVE INEFFICIENCY

The first assumption was that our economy is characterized by full employment and productive efficiency. With unemployment or inefficient production, the economy would be producing less than each alternative shown in the table.

Graphically, a situation of unemployment can be illustrated by a point *inside* the original production possibilities frontier, such as point U in Figure 2-3. Here the economy is falling short of the various maximum combinations of pizza and robots reflected by all the points *on* the production possibilities frontier. The broken arrows in Figure 2-3 indicate three of the possible paths back to full employment and least cost production. A movement towards full employment and productive efficiency will mean a greater output of one or both products.

A GROWING ECONOMY

When we drop the remaining assumptions that the quantity and quality of resources and technology are fixed, the production possibilities curve can shift position and the potential total output of the economy will change. An expanding economy will shift the frontier rightward, while an economy whose potential total output declines will shift the production possibility curve leftward. What are the factors that can increase the potential total output of an economy?

FIGURE 2-3 Unemployment and the production possibilities curve

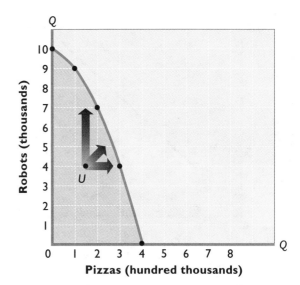

Any point inside the production possibilities curve or frontier, such as U, indicates unemployment or a failure to achieve productive efficiency. By achieving full employment and productive efficiency, the economy can produce more of either or both of the two products, as the arrows indicate.

1. EXPANDING RESOURCE SUPPLIES Let's abandon the assumption that total supplies of land, labour, capital, and entrepreneurial ability are fixed in both quantity and quality. Common sense tells us that over a period of time a nation's growing population will bring about increases in the supplies of labour and entrepreneurial ability.[2] The quality of labour improves over time if the percentage of community college and university graduates rises. Over the long run, a nation with a more skilled and educated labour force and a larger entrepreneurial pool will be able to produce more goods and services.

The stock of capital will affect the capacity of an economy. Those nations that devote a large proportion of their outputs to the production of capital goods achieve high rates of economic growth. The

[2] This is not to say that population growth as such is always desirable. Overpopulation can be a constant drag on the living standards of many less-developed countries. In advanced countries, overpopulation can have adverse effects on the environment and the quality of life.

discovery of new sources of energy and mineral resources will also contribute to increasing output of goods and services.

The net result of these increased supplies of the factors of production will be the ability to produce more of both robots and pizza. Thus in, say, the year 2016, the production possibilities of Table 2-1 (for 1996) may be obsolete, having given way to those in Table 2-2. The greater abundance of resources results in a greater potential output of one or both products at each alternative.

But such a favourable shift in the production possibilities frontier does not guarantee that the economy will actually operate at a point on that new frontier. The economy might fail to realize fully its new potentialities.

2. TECHNOLOGICAL ADVANCE Advancing technology translates into new and better goods *and* improved ways of producing them. For now, let's

think of technological advance as improvements in capital facilities — more efficient machinery and equipment. Such technological advance will alleviate the economizing problem by improving productive efficiency, allowing society to produce more goods with a fixed amount of resources. As with increases in resource supplies, technological advance permits the production of more robots *and* more pizza.

When the supplies of resources increase or an improvement in technology occurs, the frontier shifts outward and to the right, as illustrated by the thin curve in Figure 2-4. **Economic growth** — *the ability to produce a larger total output — is reflected in a rightward shift of the production possibilities frontier; it is the result of increases and the improvement in quality of resource supplies and technological progress.* The consequence of growth is that our full-employment economy can enjoy a greater output of both pizza and robots.

Economic growth does *not* typically translate into proportionate increases in a nation's capacity to produce various products. Note in Figure 2-4 that, while the economy is able to produce twice as much pizza, the increase in robot production is only 40%. You should pencil in two new production possibilities curves: one to show the situation where a better technique for producing robots has been developed, the technology for producing pizza being unchanged, and the other to illustrate an improved technology for pizza, the technology for producing robots being constant.

PRESENT CHOICES AND FUTURE POSSIBILITIES
An economy's current choice on its production possibilities frontier is a basic determinant of the future location of that curve. Let's designate the two axes of the production possibilities frontier as "goods for the future" and "goods for the present," as in Figures 2-5(a) and

FIGURE 2-4 Economic growth and the production possibilities curve

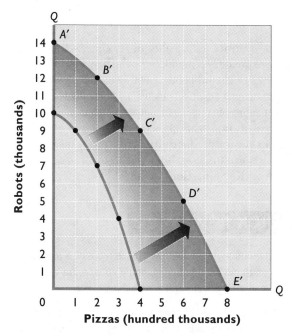

Pizzas (hundred thousands)

The expanding resource supplies and technological advances that characterize a growing economy move the production possibilities curve or frontier outward and to the right. This permits the economy to enjoy larger quantities of both types of goods.

TABLE 2-2 Production possibilities of pizza and robots with full employment, 2016

Type of product	Production alternatives				
	A'	B'	C'	D'	E'
Pizza (in hundred thousands)	0	2	4	6	8
Robots (in thousands)	14	12	9	5	0

FIGURE 2-5

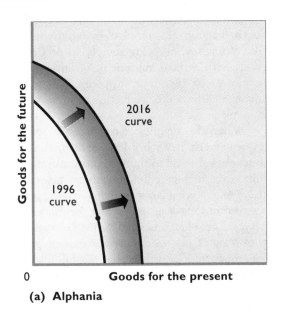

(a) **Alphania**

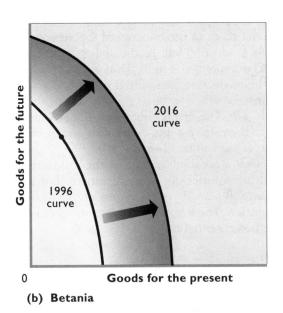

(b) **Betania**

A current choice favouring "present goods," as made by Alphania in (a), will cause a modest rightward shift of the frontier. A current choice favouring "future goods," as made by Betania in (b), will result in a greater rightward outward shift of the frontier.

(b). "Goods for the future" are such things as capital goods, research and education, and preventive medicine, which increase the quantity and quality of resources, enlarge the stock of technological information, and improve the quality of human resources. It is "goods for the future" that are the ingredients of economic growth. "Goods for the present" are pure consumer goods in the form of such things as food, clothing, and automobiles.

Now suppose there are two economies, Alphania and Betania, which are initially identical in every respect except that Alphania's current (1996) choice of position on its production possibilities frontier strongly favours "present goods" as opposed to "future goods." The dot in Figure 2-5(a) indicates this choice. Betania, on the other hand, renders a current (1996) choice that stresses large amounts of "future goods" and lesser amounts of "present goods" as shown by the dot in Figure 2-5 (b).

All other things being the same, we can expect the future (2016) production possibilities frontier of Betania to be farther to the right than Alphania's curve. By currently choosing an output that is more conducive to technological advance and to increases

in the quantity and quality of resources, Betania will achieve greater economic growth than will Alphania. In terms of capital goods, Betania is choosing to make larger current additions to its "national factory" — to invest more of its current output — than is Alphania. The payoff from this choice is more rapid growth — greater future productivity capacity — for Betania. The opportunity cost is fewer consumer goods in the present. **(Key Questions 10 and 11)**

QUICK REVIEW 2-3

1. Unemployment and the failure to realize productive efficiency cause the economy to operate at a point inside its production possibilities curve.

2. Expanding resource supplies, improvements in resource quality, and technological progress cause economic growth, depicted as an outward shift of the production possibilities curve.

3. An economy's present choice of capital and consumer goods output determines the future location of its production possibilities curve.

BOX 2-2 APPLYING THE THEORY

THE DIMINISHING PRODUCTION POSSIBILITIES OF CASTRO'S CUBA

Inefficiencies associated with its command economy, a 30-year trade embargo with the United States, and the recent loss of Soviet aid are causing the Cuban economy to collapse.

The fortieth anniversary in 1993 of Cuba's communist revolution was overshadowed by a collapsing economy. Shortages of essential goods began to appear on the island by mid-1989 and have since become widespread and severe. Long lines are common as consumers attempt to buy rationed goods such as eggs, fish, meat, and soap. Some 50,000 Cubans have been diagnosed as having optic neuritis, a disease causing gradual blindness because of malnutrition and vitamin deficiencies. Energy shortages have closed factories and disrupted construction projects. Shortages of gasoline and spare parts have idled automobiles, buses, and farm tractors. Ox carts are being substituted for tractors in agriculture and hundreds of thousands of bicycles are being imported from China as substitutes for autos and buses.

There are three reasons for the collapse of Fidel Castro's Cuban economy. First, the Cuban economy has suffered increasingly from the central planning problems that brought about the fall of the command economies of Eastern Europe and the former Soviet Union. Central planning has failed to (a) accurately assess consumer wants, (b) provide the market signals needed to minimize production costs, and (c) provide adequate economic incentives for workers and business managers.

The second factor in Cuba's economic decline is the American trade embargo. Although Cuba is only 144 km from the vast American market, that market has been denied to Cuba for some 30 years, causing a substantial decline in and distortion of Cuba's world trade.

Third, Soviet patronage has ended. For decades the Soviet Union heavily subsidized its communist partner in the Western Hemisphere. The Soviets bought Cuban exports (primarily sugar) at inflated prices and sold oil and other goods to Cuba at low prices. Best estimates suggest Soviet economic and military aid averaged about $5 billion per year. The decline of the Soviet economy and the subsequent political breakup of the Soviet Union has brought an end to these subsidies and dealt a damaging blow to the Cuban economy.

Estimates of the decline in Cuba's production possibilities vary. Some suggest that in recent years the domestic output has fallen by one-half; others indicate a three-quarters decline. In either case this decline in output is not simply a temporary move to a point inside Cuba's production possibilities curve, but rather a significant inward shift of the curve itself.

Castro has attempted to rejuvenate the Cuban economy in several ways. First, an effort is being made to revitalize the tourist industry through joint ventures — for example, hotel and resort construction — with foreign firms. Second, Cuba has invited foreign companies to explore the island for oil. Third, Cuba is making a concerted effort to cultivate trade relations with new trading partners such as China and Japan. Whether such efforts will be successful is doubtful and most experts predict the economic crisis in Cuba to spark either widespread reforms towards a market economy or the overthrow of the Castro regime.

APPLICATIONS

Let's consider several applications of the production possibilities curve that highlight scarcity, choice, and opportunity cost.

1. BUDGETING Individuals have limited money incomes. A limited budget means making choices when buying goods and services. The opportunity cost of buying a pair of blue jeans may be the dinner and a rock concert that must be given up. Many students are faced with the problem of allocating a fixed amount of time between studying and working to finance their education. The trade-off is that more hours spent working mean more income, but also less study time and a probable lower grade average.

2. DISCRIMINATION Discrimination based on race, sex, age, or ethnic background is an obstacle to the efficient employment of labour resources and keeps the economy operating at some point inside the production possibilities curve. Discrimination prevents racial minorities, women, and others from obtaining jobs in which society can efficiently utilize their skills and talents. The elimination of discrimination would help to move the economy from some point inside the production possibilities curve towards a point on the curve.

3. PRODUCTIVITY SLOWDOWN

During the 1970s and early 1980s, Canada experienced a decline in the growth of labour productivity, defined as output per worker hour. One cause of this decline is that the rate of increase in the mechanization of labour slowed because of investment in manufacturing. One remedy is an increase in investment as compared with consumption — a D to C type of shift in Figure 2-1. Special tax incentives to make business investment more profitable might be an appropriate policy to facilitate this shift. The restoration of a more rapid rate of productivity growth will accelerate the growth of the economy and shift of the production possibilities curve rightward.

During the mid-1980s the growth of output per hour recovered somewhat. While the reasons for the partial recovery of productivity are complex and controversial, an increase in capital investment contributed to the improvement.

4. LUMBER VERSUS OWLS

The trade-offs portrayed in the production possibilities curve occur regularly in environmental issues. An example is the much-publicized conflict between the logging industry of the U.S. Pacific Northwest and environmentalists. Envision a production possibilities curve with "lumber production" on one axis and "environmental quality" or "biodiversity" on the other. The conflict is centred on the spotted owl, which depends on the mature or old-growth trees of the Pacific Northwest for survival. Increasing the output of lumber limits the owl's habitat, destroys the species, and thus reduces environmental quality. Maintaining the old-growth forests preserves the owl, but destroys thousands of jobs in the logging and lumber industries. The production possibilities curve is an informative context within which to grasp the many difficult environmental decisions confronting society.

5. INTERNATIONAL TRADE ASPECTS

The message of the production possibilities curve is that a nation cannot live beyond its means or production potential. When the possibility of international trade is taken into account, this statement must be modified in two ways.

TRADE AND GROWTH   We will discover in later chapters that a nation can circumvent the output constraint imposed by its domestic production possibilities curve through international specialization and trade. International specialization and trade have the same impact as having more and better resources or discovering improved production techniques. Both have the effect of increasing the quantities of both capital and consumer goods available to society. International specialization and trade are the equivalent of economic growth.

TRADE DEFICITS   Within the context of international trade, a nation can consume a combination of goods outside of its domestic production possibilities curve (such as point W in Figure 2-1) by incurring a *trade deficit*. A nation may buy and receive an amount of imported goods from the rest of the world that exceeds the amount of goods exported to the rest of the world.

This looks like a favourable state of affairs. Unfortunately, there is a catch. To finance its deficit — to pay for its excess of imports over exports — a nation must go into debt to its international trading partners *or* it must give up ownership of some of its assets to those other nations. Analogy: How can you live beyond your current income? Answer: Borrow from your parents, the sellers of goods, or a financial institution. Or sell some of the real assets (your car or stereo) or financial assets (stocks or bonds) you own.

We would find that a major consequence of large and persistent trade deficits is that foreign nationals hold larger portions of our private and public debt and own larger amounts of our business corporations, agricultural land, and real estate. To pay for debts and to repurchase those assets would mean living well *within* a nation's means. A *trade surplus* is required to pay off world debts and reacquire ownership of those assets.

6. GROWTH

The growth impact of a nation's decision on how to divide its domestic output is vividly illustrated by comparing the growth performance of a few advanced industrialized nations. As Global Perspective 2-1 shows, between 1970 and 1990 Japan invested a yearly average of over 30% of its domestic output in productive machinery and

GLOBAL PERSPECTIVE 2-1

Investment and economic growth, selected countries

Nations that invest large proportions of their national outputs achieve high growth rates, measured here by output per person. Additional capital goods make workers more productive and this means greater output per person.

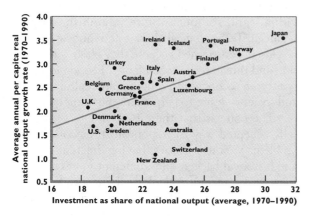

SOURCE: International Monetary Fund data, as reported in the U.S. government publication *Economic Report of the President, 1994*, p. 37.

equipment. Not surprisingly Japan's output growth during the period averaged 3.5% per year. The United States, on the other hand, invested an average of less than 20% of its domestic output and, thus, had a lower growth rate of slightly over 1.5% per year on average. Canada invested an average of slightly over 20% of its domestic output, which translated into an average growth rate of about 2.5% per year.

7. FAMINE IN AFRICA Modern industrial societies take economic growth — more-or-less continuous rightward shifts of the production possibilities curve — for granted. But as the recent catastrophic famines in Somalia and other sub-Saharan nations of Africa indicate, in some circumstances the production possibilities curve may shift leftward. In addition to drought, a cause of African famines is ecological degradation — poor land-use practices. Land has been deforested, overfarmed, and overgrazed, causing the production possibilities of these highly agriculturally oriented countries to diminish. In fact, the per capita domestic output of most of these nations declined in the last decade or so.

THE "ISMS"

A society can use different institutional arrangements and co-ordinating mechanisms to respond to the economizing problem. Generally speaking, the industrially advanced economies of the world differ essentially on two grounds: (1) the ownership of the means of production, and (2) the method of co-ordinating and directing economic activity. Let's examine the main characteristics of the two "polar" types of economic systems.

PURE CAPITALISM

Pure, or **laissez-faire**, **capitalism** is characterized by the private ownership of resources and the use of a system of markets and prices to co-ordinate and direct economic activity. In such a system each participant is motivated by his or her own self-interests. The market system communicates and co-ordinates individual decisions and preferences. Because goods and services are produced and resources are supplied under competitive conditions, there are many independent buyers and sellers of each product and resource. As a result, economic power is widely dispersed. Advocates of pure capitalism argue that such an economy is conducive to efficiency in the use of resources, output and employment stability, and rapid economic growth. Thus there is little or no need for government planning, control, or intervention. The term *laissez-faire* means "let it be": keep the government from interfering with the economy. Interference will disturb the efficient working of the market system. Government's role is therefore limited to the protection of private property and establishing an appropriate legal framework for free markets.

THE COMMAND ECONOMY

The polar alternative to pure capitalism is the **command economy**, characterized by public ownership of virtually all property resources and the rendering of economic decisions through central economic planning. All major decisions concerning the level of resource use, the composition and distribution of output, and the organization of production are determined by a central planning board. Business firms are government-owned and produce according to state directives. Production targets are determined by the planning board for each enterprise and the plan specifies the amounts of resources to be allocated to each enterprise so that it might realize its production goals. The division of output between capital and consumer goods is centrally decided and capital goods are allocated among industries based on the central planning board's long-term priorities.

MIXED SYSTEMS

Most economies fall between the extremes of pure capitalism and the command economy. The Canadian economy leans towards pure capitalism, but with important differences. Government plays an active role in our economy in promoting economic stability and growth, in providing certain goods and services that would be underproduced or not produced at all by the market system, in modifying the distribution of income, and so forth. In contrast to the wide dispersion of economic power among many small units that characterizes pure capitalism, Canadian capitalism has spawned powerful economic organizations in the form of large corporations and labour unions. The ability of these power blocs to manipulate and distort the functioning of the market system to their advantage provides a further reason for governmental involvement in the economy.

While the former Soviet Union historically approximated the command economy, it relied to some extent on market-determined prices and had some vestiges of private ownership. Recent reforms in the former Soviet Union, China, and most of the Eastern European nations are designed to move these command economies towards more market-oriented systems. North Korea and Cuba are the best remaining examples of centrally planned economics.

But private ownership and reliance on the market system do not always go together, nor do public ownership and central planning. For example, the fascism of Hitler's Nazi Germany has been dubbed **authoritarian capitalism** because the economy had a high degree of governmental control and direction, but property was privately owned. In contrast, the former Yugoslavian economy of **market socialism** was characterized by public ownership of resources coupled with considerable reliance on free markets to organize and co-ordinate economic activity. The Swedish economy is also a hybrid system. Although over 90% of business activity is in private hands, government is deeply involved in achieving eco-

nomic stability and in redistributing income. Similarly, the market-oriented Japanese economy entails a great deal of planning and "co-ordination" between government and the business sector.

THE TRADITIONAL ECONOMY

Many of the less developed countries of the world have **traditional** or **customary economies**. Production methods, exchange, and the distribution of income are all sanctioned by custom. Heredity and caste circumscribe the economic roles of individuals and socioeconomic immobility is pronounced. Technological change and innovation may be closely constrained because they clash with tradition and threaten the social fabric. Economic activity is often secondary to religious and cultural values and society's desire to perpetuate the status quo.

The point is that there is no unique or universally accepted way to respond to the economizing problem. Various societies, having different cultural and historical backgrounds, different mores and customs, and contrasting ideological frameworks — not to mention resources that differ both quantitatively and qualitatively — use different institutions in dealing with the reality of relative scarcity. Canada, China, the United States, and Great Britain, for example, are all — in their accepted goals, ideology, technologies, resources, and culture — attempting to achieve efficiency in the use of their resources. The best method for responding to the unlimited wants–scarce resources dilemma in one economy may be inappropriate for another economic system.

THE CIRCULAR FLOW MODEL

Market-oriented systems now dominate the world scene. Thus, our focus in the remainder of this chapter and in the following two chapters is on how nations use markets to respond to the economizing problem. Our goal in this last section is modest; we want to identify the major groups of decision makers and the major markets in the market system. Our point of reference is the circular flow diagram.

RESOURCE AND PRODUCT MARKETS

Figure 2-6 (Key Graph) shows two groups of *decision makers* — households and businesses. (Government will be added as a third decision maker in Chapter

KEY GRAPH

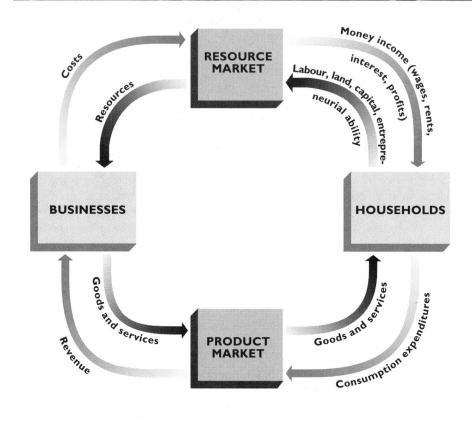

FIGURE 2-6 The circular flow of output and income

The prices paid for the use of land, labour, capital, and entrepreneurial ability are determined in the resource market shown in the upper loop. Businesses are on the demand side and households on the supply side of this market. The prices of finished goods and services are determined in the product market located in the lower loop. Households are on the demand side and businesses on the supply side of this market.

5.) The *co-ordinating mechanism* that brings the decisions of households and businesses into alignment with one another is the market system, in particular resource and product markets.

The upper half of the diagram portrays the **resource market**. Here, households, which directly or indirectly (through their ownership of business corporations) own all economic resources, *supply* these resources to businesses. Businesses will *demand* resources because they are the means by which firms produce goods and services. The interaction of demand and supply for the immense variety of human and property resources establishes the price of each. The payments that businesses make in obtaining resources are costs to businesses, but simultaneously constitute flows of wage, rent, interest, and profit income to the households supplying these resources.

Now consider the **product market** shown in the bottom half of the diagram. The money income received by households from the sale of resources does not, as such, have real value. Consumers cannot eat or wear coins and paper money. Thus,

through the expenditure of money income, households express their *demand* for a vast array of goods and services. Simultaneously, businesses combine the resources they have obtained to produce and *supply* goods and services in these same markets. The interaction of these demand and supply decisions determines product prices (Chapter 4). Note, too, that the flow of consumer expenditures for goods and services constitutes sales revenues or receipts from the viewpoint of businesses.

The **circular flow model** implies a complex, interrelated web of decision making and economic activity. Note that households and businesses participate in both basic markets, but on different sides of each. Businesses are on the buying or demand side of resource markets, and households, as resource owners and suppliers, are on the selling or supply side. In the product market, these positions are reversed; households, as consumers, are on the buying or demand side, and businesses are on the selling or supply side. Each group of economic units both buys and sells.

Furthermore, the spectre of scarcity haunts these transactions. Because households have only limited amounts of resources to supply to businesses, the money incomes of consumers will be limited. This means that each consumer's income will go only so far. A limited number of dollars clearly will not permit the purchase of all the goods and services the consumer might like to buy. Similarly, because resources are scarce, the output of finished goods and services is also necessarily limited. Scarcity and choice permeate our entire discussion.

To summarize: In a monetary economy, households, as resource owners, sell their resources to businesses and, as consumers, spend the money income received buying goods and services. Businesses must buy resources to produce goods and services; their finished products are then sold to households in exchange for consumption expenditures or, as businesses view it, revenues. The net result is a counter-clockwise *real* flow of economic resources and finished goods and services, and a clockwise *money* flow of income and consumption expenditures. These flows are simultaneous and repetitive.

LIMITATIONS

Our model simplifies in many ways. Intrahousehold and intrabusiness transactions are concealed. Government and the "rest of the world" are ignored as decision makers. The model subtly implies constant flows of output and income, while in fact these flows are unstable over time. Nor is the circular flow a perpetual motion machine; production exhausts human energies and absorbs physical resources, the latter giving rise to problems of environmental pollution. Finally, our model does not explain how product and resource prices are actually determined, which is examined in Chapter 4.

CHAPTER SUMMARY

1. Economics centres on two basic facts: first human material wants are virtually unlimited; second, economic resources are scarce.

2. Economic resources may be classified as land, capital, labour, and entrepreneurial ability.

3. Economics is concerned with the problem of administering scarce resources in the production of goods and services to fulfil the material wants of society. Both full employment and full production of available resources are essential if this administration is to be efficient.

4. Full production requires productive efficiency — producing any output in the least costly way — and allocative efficiency — producing the specific output mix most desired by society.

5. An economy that is achieving full employment and productive efficiency — operating *on* its production possibilities curve — must sacrifice the output of some types of goods and services to achieve increased production of others. Because resources are not equally productive in all possible uses, shifting resources from one use to another yields the law of increasing opportunity costs; the production of additional units of product X requires the sacrifice of increasing amounts of product Y.

6. Allocative efficiency means achieving the optimal or most desired point on the production possibilities curve. It is determined by comparing marginal benefits and marginal cost.

7. Over time, technological advance and increases in the quantity and quality of resources permit the economy to produce more of all goods and services. Society's choice as to the composition of current output is a determinant of the future location of the production possibilities curve.

8. The various economic systems of the world differ in their ideologies and also in their responses to the economizing problem. Critical differences centre on **a** private versus public ownership of resources, and **b** the use of the market system versus central planning as a co-ordinating mechanism.

9. An overview of the operation of the market system can be gained through the circular flow of income. This simplified model locates the product and resource markets and presents the major income-expenditure flows and resources-output flows that constitute the lifeblood of the capitalist economy.

TERMS AND CONCEPTS

allocative efficiency (p. 29)	land, capital, labour, and entrepreneurial ability (p. 27)
authoritarian capitalism (p. 40)	law of increasing opportunity costs (p. 32)
capital goods (p. 30)	market socialism (p. 40)
circular flow model (p. 41)	opportunity cost (p. 32)
command economy (p. 39)	production possibilities table (curve) (p. 30)
consumer goods (p. 30)	productive efficiency (p. 29)
economic growth (p. 35)	product market (p. 41)
economizing problem (p. 26)	profits (p. 29)
economic resources (p. 27)	pure or laissez-faire capitalism (p. 39)
factors of production (p. 29)	rental income (p. 27)
full employment (p. 29)	resource market (p. 41)
full production (p. 29)	traditional or customary economies (p. 40)
interest income (p. 27)	utility (p. 26)
investment (p. 27)	wages (p. 29)

QUESTIONS AND STUDY SUGGESTIONS

1. "Economics is the study of the principles governing the allocation of scarce means among competing ends when the objective of the allocation is to maximize the attainment of the ends." Explain.

2. Comment on the following statement from a newspaper article: "Our junior high school serves a splendid hot meal for $1 without costing the taxpayers anything, thanks in part to a government subsidy."

3. Critically analyze: "Wants aren't insatiable. I can prove it. I get all the coffee I want to drink every morning at breakfast." Explain: "Goods and services are scarce because resources are scarce." Analyze: "It is the nature of all economic problems that absolute solutions are denied us."

4. What are economic resources? What are the major functions of the entrepreneur?

5. *Key Question*   *Why is the problem of unemployment a part of the subject matter of economics? Distinguish between allocative efficiency and productive efficiency. Give an illustration of achieving productive, but not allocative, efficiency.*

6. *Key Question*   *The following is a production possibilities table for war goods and civilian goods:*

Type of production	Production alternatives				
	A	B	C	D	E
Automobiles	0	2	4	6	8
Rockets	30	27	21	12	0

   a. *Show these data graphically. On what specific assumptions is this production possibilities curve based?*
   b. *If the economy is at point C, what is the cost of one more automobile? One more rocket? Explain how this curve reflects the law of increasing opportunity costs.*
   c. *What must the economy do to operate at some point on the production possibilities curve?*

7. What is the opportunity cost of attending college or university?

8. Suppose you arrive at a store expecting to pay $100 for an item, but learn that a store three kilometres away is charging $50 for it. Would you drive there and buy it? How does your decision benefit you? What is the opportunity cost of your decision? Now suppose that you arrive at a store expecting to pay $6,000 for an item, but learn that it costs $5,950 at the other store. Do you make the same decision as before? Perhaps surprisingly, you should! Explain why.

9. *Key Question*   *Specify and explain the shape of the marginal benefit and marginal cost curves and use these curves to determine the optimal allocation of resources to a particular product. If current output is such that marginal cost exceeds marginal benefit, should more or fewer resources be allocated to this product? Explain.*

10. *Key Question*   *Label point G inside the production possibilities curve you have drawn in question 6. What does it indicate? Label point H outside the curve. What does this point indicate? What must occur before the economy can attain the level of production indicated by point H?*

11. *Key Question*   *Referring again to question 6, suppose improvement occurs in the technology of producing rockets but not in the production of automobiles. Draw the new production possibilities curve. Now assume that a technological advance occurs in producing automobiles but not in producing rockets. Draw the new production possibilities curve. Finally, draw a production possibilities curve that reflects technological improvement in the production of both products.*

12. Explain how, if at all, each of the following affects the location of the production possibilities curve.

   a. standardized examination scores of high school and college and university students decline
   b. the unemployment rate falls from 11 to 8% of the labour force
   c. defence spending is reduced to allow the government to spend more on education
   d. society decides it wants compact discs rather than long-playing records
   e. a new technique improves the efficiency of extracting copper from ore
   f. a new "baby boom" increases the size of the nation's work force

13. Explain: "Affluence tomorrow requires sacrifice today."

14. Explain how an international trade deficit may permit an economy to acquire a combination of goods in excess of its domestic production potential. Explain why nations try to avoid having trade deficits.

15. Contrast how pure capitalism, market socialism, and a command economy try to cope with economic scarcity.

16. Describe the operation of pure capitalism as portrayed by the circular flow model. Locate resource and product markets and emphasize the fact of scarcity throughout your discussion. Specify the limitations of the circular flow model.

17. (Applying the Theory)   What are the major causes of Cuba's diminishing production possibilities?

CHAPTER 3

OVERVIEW OF THE MARKET SYSTEM

In the past few years the media have inundated us with stories of how Russian and other centrally planned economies are trying to alter their systems in the direction of capitalism, otherwise referred to as the market system or market economy. Precisely what are the features and institutions of a market system that these nations are trying to emulate?

Our initial task is to describe and explain how a pure market system, or laissez-faire capitalism, functions. Although a pure market system has never existed, a description of such an economy provides a useful first approximation of how the economies of Canada and many other industrially advanced nations function. We will modify our model of a pure market economy in later chapters to correspond more closely to the reality of modern economies.

In explaining the operation of a pure market economy we will discuss: (1) the institutional framework and basic assumptions underlying its dynamics; (2) certain institutions and practices common to all modern economies; and (3) how a market system can co-ordinate economic activity and contribute to the efficient use of scarce resources.

BOX 3-1   THE BIG PICTURE

The scarcity problem is confronted by all societies. Each society much choose a co-ordinating system that will determine how much of each product is produced, how it will be produced, and how output is divided among its population. This chapter offers an overview of one way to co-ordinate production and distribution: the market system — sometimes referred to as the capitalist system. A familiarity with the main features of a market system will greatly help you put the materials of this textbook in their proper perspective.

As you read this chapter, keep the following points in mind:

- A market system does not arise automatically; it needs the proper institutions, such as private property.
- The driving force of the market system is "self-interest," not to be confused with selfishness. In a world of limited resources in relation to wants, competition ensues automatically. In competing for the available resources, all participants in a market system — businesses and households — try to do the best they can for themselves.
- The distinguishing characteristics of the market system are *a.* autonomous decision-making by each participant, and *b.* spontaneous co-ordination of production and consumption.

THE MARKET SYSTEM

There is no neat and universally accepted definition of a market system, or, as it is sometimes referred to, capitalism. We must examine in some detail the basic tenets of the market economy to acquire a comprehensive understanding of how it functions. The framework of the market system has the following institutions and assumptions: (1) private property, (2) freedom of enterprise and choice, (3) self-interest as the dominant motive, (4) competition among firms and consumers, (5) reliance on self-regulating markets, and (6) a limited role for government.

PRIVATE PROPERTY

In a pure market system, resources are owned by private individuals and private institutions, not by government. **Private property**, coupled with the freedom to negotiate binding legal contracts, permits private persons or businesses to obtain, control, employ, and dispose of resources as they see fit. The institution of private property is sustained over time by the right of a property owner to designate the recipient of this property at the time of death.

Property rights — rights to own, use, and dispose of property — are significant because they encourage investment, innovation, exchange, and economic growth. Why would anyone build a house, construct a factory, or clear land for farming if some-

one or some institution (for example, government) could confiscate that property for their own benefit?

Property rights also apply to "intellectual property." Patents and copyrights exist and are enforced to encourage individuals to write books, music, and computer programs and to invent new products and production processes without fear that others will expropriate them along with the associated economic rewards.

Another important role of property rights is that they facilitate exchange. A title to an automobile or a deed to a house assures the buyer that the seller is in fact the legitimate owner. Finally, without property rights, people would have to devote a considerable portion of their energy and resources simply to protect and retain the property they have produced or acquired.

Society often imposes broad legal limits to this right to private ownership if such rights can lead to the harming of oneself or others. For example, the use of resources for the production of illicit drugs is prohibited. Nor is public ownership nonexistent. Even in a pure market system, public ownership of certain utilities may be essential to the achievement of efficiency in the use of resources.

FREEDOM OF ENTERPRISE AND CHOICE

Closely related to private ownership of property is freedom of enterprise and choice. The market system imposes on its participants the responsibility of making certain choices. **Freedom of enterprise** means that private business enterprises are free to obtain economic resources, to organize these resources in the production of a good or service of the firm's own choosing, and to sell it in the markets of their choice. No artificial obstacles or restrictions imposed by government or other producers block an entrepreneur's choice to enter or leave a particular industry.

Freedom of choice means that owners of resources can employ or dispose of them as they see fit. It also means that workers are free to enter any of those lines of work for which they are qualified. Consumers are at liberty, within the limits of their money incomes, to buy goods and services that they feel satisfy their wants.

Freedom of *consumer* choice is perhaps the most profound of these freedoms. Recall that economics is about scarcity of resources and unlimited wants, and how to best satisfy those wants within the scarcity constraint. Thus, the consumer is in a particularly strategic position in a market economy for it is consumers collectively that decide to what use the scarce resources will be allocated. In a sense, the consumer is sovereign. The range of free choices for suppliers of resources is circumscribed by the choices of consumers. The consumer ultimately decides what the economy should produce and resource suppliers must make their choices within the constraints delineated. Resource suppliers and businesses are not "free" to produce goods and services consumers do not desire because their production would be unprofitable.

ROLE OF SELF-INTEREST

The primary driving force of a market economy is **self-interest**; each economic unit attempts to do what is best for itself. Note that the assumption of self-interest follows naturally from the universal problem of scarcity and unlimited wants. If there were no scarcities of resources, there would be no reason to behave in a self-interested way. The existence of scarcity means entrepreneurs aim at the maximization of their firms' profits, and owners of resources attempt to get the highest price or rent from these resources. Those who supply labour resources will try to get the highest possible incomes from their employment. Consumers, in purchasing a product, will seek to get it at the lowest price. Specific consumers apportion their expenditures to maximize their satisfaction; they try to fulfil their many wants as best they can within a given income. That means getting the goods they want at the lowest possible price.

The pursuit of economic self-interest must not be confused with selfishness. A stockholder may invest to receive the best available corporate dividends and then may contribute a portion to the United Way or leave bequests to grandchildren. Similarly, a church official may carefully compare price and quality among various brands in buying new pews for the church.

COMPETITION

Freedom of choice exercised in promoting one's own monetary returns provides the basis for **competition**, or economic rivalry, as a fundamental feature of a market economy. Competition requires:

1. Large numbers of independent buyers and sellers operating in the market for any particular product or resource.
2. The freedom of buyers and sellers to enter or leave particular markets.

LARGE NUMBERS The essence of competition is the widespread diffusion of economic power within the two major groups that make up the economy: businesses and households. When many buyers and sellers are present in a particular market, no one buyer or seller will be able to noticeably influence the price. Let's examine this statement in terms of the selling or supply side of the product market.

When a product becomes unusually scarce, its price will rise. An unseasonable frost in Florida may seriously curtail the supply of citrus crops and sharply increase the price of oranges. Similarly, *if a single producer, or a small group of producers together, can somehow control or restrict the total supply of a product, then price can be raised to the seller's advantage. By controlling supply, the producer can "rig the market" on his or her own behalf. The essence of competition is that there are so many independent pure sellers that each, *because he or she is contributing an almost negligible fraction of the total supply,* has virtually no influence over the supply nor, therefore, over product price.

Suppose there are 10,000 farmers, each supplying 100 bushels of wheat in the Winnipeg grain market when the price of wheat is $4 per bushel. Could a single farmer who feels dissatisfied with that price cause an artificial scarcity of wheat and thereby boost the price above $4? No, because Farmer Jones, by restricting output from 100 to 75 bushels, exerts virtually no effect on the total supply of wheat. In fact, the total amount supplied is reduced only from 1,000,000 to 999,975 bushels. Not much of a shortage! Supply is virtually unchanged, and, therefore, the $4 price persists.

Competition means that each seller is providing a drop in the bucket of total supply. Individual sellers can make no noticeable dent in total supply; thus, a seller cannot *as an individual producer* manipulate product price. This is what is meant when it is said that an individual competitive seller is "at the mercy of the market."

The same rationale applies to the demand side of the market. Buyers are plentiful and act independently. Thus single buyers cannot manipulate the market to their advantage. *The widespread diffusion of economic power underlying competition controls the use and limits the potential abuse of that power.*

ENTRY AND EXIT Competition also implies that it is simple for producers to enter or leave a particular industry; there are no artificial legal or institutional obstacles to prohibit expansion or contraction of specific industries. The freedom of an industry to expand or contract provides a competitive economy with the flexibility to remain efficient over time. Freedom of entry and exit is necessary for the economy to adjust appropriately to changes in consumer tastes, technology, or resource supplies.

MARKETS AND PRICES

What co-ordinates production and consumption decisions in a capitalist economy is the market system. *Capitalism is a market economy and markets use price to allocate resources.* Decisions by buyers and sellers of products and resources are made through a system of markets. A **market** is a mechanism or arrangement that brings buyers and sellers of a good or service into contact with one another. A McDonald's, a gas station, a grocery supermarket, a Sotheby's art auction, the Toronto Stock Exchange, and worldwide foreign exchange markets are but a few illustrations. The preferences of sellers and buyers are registered on the supply and demand sides of various markets, and the outcome of these choices is a system of product and resource prices. These prices are guideposts on which resource owners, entrepreneurs, and consumers make and revise their free choices in furthering their self-interests.

Just as competition is the controlling mechanism, so a system of markets and prices is a basic organizing force. Prices relay information about supply and demand conditions in each market. The market system is an elaborate communication system through which innumerable individual free choices are recorded, summarized, and balanced against one another. Those who obey the dictates of the market system are rewarded; those who ignore them are penalized by the system. Through this communication system, society decides what the economy should produce, how it should be produced, and how the fruits of productive endeavour are distributed among the individual economic units that make up a market economy.

Not only is the market system the mechanism through which society decides how it allocates its resources and distributes the resulting output, but it is through the market system that these decisions are carried out.

LIMITED GOVERNMENT

A competitive market economy promotes a high degree of efficiency in the use and allocation of resources. There is allegedly little real need for governmental intervention in the operation of such an economy beyond its role of imposing broad legal limits on the exercise of individual choices and the use of private property. The concept of a pure market system as a self-regulating and self-adjusting economy precludes any extensive economic role for government.

QUICK REVIEW 3-1

1. A pure market economy rests on the private ownership of property and freedom of enterprise and choice.

2. Economic entities — business, resource suppliers, and consumers — seek to further their own self-interests.

3. The co-ordinating mechanism of a market economy is a competitive system of markets that use prices to allocate resources.

4. The efficient functioning of the market system allegedly precludes significant government intervention.

OTHER CHARACTERISTICS

Private property, freedom of enterprise and choice, self-interest as a motivating force, competition, and reliance on a market system are all institutions and assumptions that are associated with a pure market system.

In addition, there are certain institutions and practices characteristic of all modern economies: (1) the use of an advanced technology and large amounts of capital goods, (2) specialization, and (3) the use of money. Specialization and an advanced technology are prerequisites to the efficient employment of any economy's resources. The use of money is a permissive characteristic that allows society more easily to practise and reap the benefits of specialization and of the employment of advanced productive techniques.

EXTENSIVE USE OF CAPITAL GOODS

All modern or "industrially advanced" economies are based on state-of-the-art technology and the extensive use of capital goods. In a market economy it is competition that brings about technological advance. Technological advancement helps a society get more output of goods and services with the same inputs as before, or even fewer inputs, thereby alleviating the scarcity problem. The market is highly effective in harnessing incentives to develop new products and improved techniques of production because the rewards accrue directly to the innovator. A market economy therefore presupposes the extensive use and relatively rapid development of complex capital goods: tools, machinery, large-scale factories, and facilities for storage, transportation, communication, and marketing.

Advanced technology and the use of capital goods is important because the most direct method of producing a product is usually the least efficient. Even Robinson Crusoe avoided the inefficiencies of direct production in favour of **roundabout production**. It would be ridiculous for a farmer — even a backyard farmer — to go at production with bare hands. It pays to create tools of production — capital equipment — to aid in the productive process. There is a better way of getting water out of a well than to dive in after it!

But there is a catch. Recall our discussion of the production possibilities curve and the basic nature of the economizing problem. For any economy operating on its production possibilities curve, resources must be diverted from the production of consumer goods in order to be used in the production of capital goods. We must currently tighten our belts as consumers in order to free resources for the production of capital goods that will allow a greater output of consumer goods at some future date. Greater abundance tomorrow requires sacrifice today. **(Key Question 2)**

SPECIALIZATION AND EFFICIENCY

The extent to which society relies on **specialization** is astounding. The vast majority of consumers produce virtually none of the goods and services they consume. The machine-shop worker who spends a lifetime stamping out parts for jet engines may never "consume" an airline trip. The worker who devotes eight hours a day to the installation of windows in Fords may own a Honda.

Few households seriously consider any extensive production of their own food, shelter, and clothing. Many farmers sell their milk to the local dairy and then buy margarine at the nearest supermarket. Society learned long ago that self-sufficiency breeds inefficiency. The jack-of-all-trades may be a very colourful individual, but is certainly not efficient.

DIVISION OF LABOUR   In what ways might specialization — the **division of labour** — enhance a society's output and lessen the economizing problem?

1. ABILITY DIFFERENCES   Specialization permits individuals to take advantage of existing differences in their abilities and skills. If caveman A is strong, swift afoot, and accurate with a spear, and caveman B is weak and slow, but patient, these talents can be most efficiently used by making A a hunter and B a fisherman.
2. LEARNING BY DOING   Even if the abilities of A and B are identical, specialization may be advantageous. By devoting all one's time to a single task, it is more likely one will develop the appropriate skills and discover improved techniques than when apportioning time among a number of diverse tasks. A person learns to be a good hunter by hunting!
3. SAVING TIME   Specialization also avoids the loss of time shifting from one job to another. For all these reasons, the division of labour results in greater productive efficiency in the use of resources.

GEOGRAPHIC SPECIALIZATION Specialization works on a regional and international basis. Apples could be grown in Saskatchewan, but because of the unsuitability of the land, rainfall, and temperature, the cost would be very high. The Okanagan Valley could achieve some success in the production of wheat, but for similar reasons such production would be relatively costly. Saskatchewan produces those products — wheat in particular — for which its resources are best adapted and the Okanagan does the same, producing apples and other fruit.

In so doing, both produce surpluses of their specialties. Then Saskatchewan and the Okanagan swap some of their surpluses. Specialization permits each area to turn out those goods its resources can most efficiently produce. In this way, both Saskatchewan and the Okanagan can enjoy a larger amount of both wheat and apples than would otherwise be the case.

Similarly, on an international basis we find Canada specializing in such items as the Dash-8 aircraft and communication equipment that it sells abroad in exchange for video cassette recorders from Japan, bananas from Honduras, shoes from Italy, and coffee from Brazil. In short, *specialization is essential to achieve efficiency in the use of scarce resources and thus get the most output from those resources.*

USE OF MONEY

Exchange can, and sometimes does, occur on the basis of **bartering**, that is, swapping goods for goods. But bartering as a means of exchange can pose serious problems for the economy. Exchange by barter requires a **coincidence of wants** between the two transactors. In our example, we assume Saskatchewan had excess wheat to trade and wanted to obtain apples. We also assumed the Okanagan had excess apples to swap and that it wanted to acquire wheat. So exchange occurred. But if this coincidence of wants did not exist, trade would not occur. Let us examine this.

Suppose Saskatchewan does not want any of the Okanagan's apples but is interested in buying potatoes from New Brunswick. Ironically, New Brunswick wants the Okanagan's apples but not Saskatchewan's wheat. And to complicate matters, suppose that the Okanagan wants some of Saskatchewan's wheat but none of New Brunswick's potatoes. The situation is summarized in Figure 3-1.

Specialization requires that people exchange the goods and services they produce for others they lack. In our Saskatchewan-Okanagan example, Saskatchewan must trade or exchange wheat for the Okanagan's apples if both regions are to share in the benefits of specialization. Because consumers want a wide variety of products, without trade they would devote their resources to many diverse types of production. If exchange could not occur or was very inconvenient, Saskatchewan and the Okanagan would be forced to be self-sufficient, denying both the advantages of specialization.

In no case do we find a coincidence of wants. Trade by barter would be difficult. *Thus, a convenient means of exchanging goods is a prerequisite of specialization.*

To overcome such a stalemate, economies use a **medium of exchange**, or **money**, which is convenient for facilitating the exchange of goods and services. Historically cattle, cigarettes, skins, liquor,

---

FIGURE 3-1   Money facilitates trade where wants do not coincide

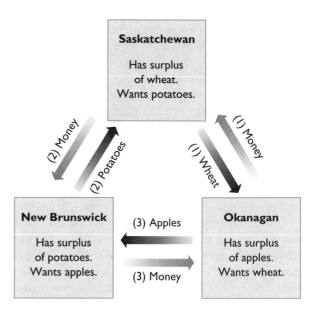

By the use of money as a medium of exchange, trade can be accomplished, as indicated by the arrows, despite a noncoincidence of wants. By facilitating exchange, the use of money permits an economy to realize the efficiencies of specialization.

BOX 3-2 APPLYING THE THEORY

BACK TO BARTER

Despite the advantages of using money, there is evidence that bartering is a "growth industry."

Since money facilitates exchange, it may seem odd that a considerable and growing volume of both domestic and international trade occurs through barter.

Suppose you own a small firm selling equipment to television stations. The economy is in recession; business is slow, your cash flow is down; and your inventories are much higher than desired. What do you do? You approach a local TV station that needs new equipment. But it, too, is feeling the effects of recession. Its advertising revenues are down and it also faces a cash-flow crunch. So a deal is struck. You provide $50,000 worth of equipment in exchange for $50,000 worth of "free" advertising. Advantage to seller: You move unwanted inventory, eliminating warehousing and insurance costs. You also receive valuable advertising time. The TV station gets needed equipment and pays for it with time

slots which would otherwise be unfilled. Both parties gain and no money changes hands.

Internationally, a firm might encounter an obstacle in selling its goods to a nation that does not have "hard" (exchangeable) currencies such as dollars, marks, or yen. Barter circumvents this problem. Example: PepsiCo swaps cola syrup for Russian vodka. Coca-Cola has traded for Egyptian oranges, Turkish tomato paste, Polish beer, and Hungarian soft-drink bottles. Recently, large Canadian companies have negotiated "joint ventures" with Russia based on barter.

Estimates differ on the volume of barter transactions within Canada. One estimate is that 17,500 businesses engaged in barter transactions of almost $100 million in 1990, a fivefold increase in dollar volume since 1980. Other estimates put the dollar value of barter transactions as high as $600 million per year.

playing cards, shells, stones, pieces of metal, and many other diverse commodities have been used with varying degrees of success as a medium for facilitating exchange. To be money, an item needs to pass only one test: *it must be generally acceptable by buyers and sellers in exchange*. Money is socially defined; whatever society accepts as a medium of exchange is money.

Most economies, for reasons made clear in macroeconomics, find it convenient to use paper as money. This is the case with the Saskatchewan-Okanagan-New Brunswick economy; they use pieces of paper called "dollars" as money. Can the use of paper dollars as a medium of exchange overcome the stalemate we have posed?

Yes, with trade occurring as shown in Figure 3-1:

1. The Okanagan can exchange money for some of Saskatchewan's wheat.
2. Saskatchewan uses the money from the sale of wheat and exchanges it for some of New Brunswick's potatoes.

3. New Brunswick can then exchange the money received from the sale of potatoes for some of the Okanagan's surplus apples.

The willingness to accept paper money (or any other kind of money) as a medium of exchange has permitted a three-way trade, which allows each region to specialize in one product and obtain the other product(s) its residents desire, despite the absence of a coincidence of wants between any two of the parties. Barter, resting as it does on a coincidence of wants, would impede this exchange, and thus keep the three regions from specializing. The efficiencies of specialization would then have been lost to those regions.

QUICK REVIEW 3-2

1. Advanced economies achieve greater efficiency in production through the use of large quantities of capital goods.

2. Specialization enhances efficiency and brings about surpluses by having individuals, regions, and nations produce those goods and services for which their resources are best suited.

3. The use of money is necessary to facilitate the exchange of goods that specialization brings about.

THE COMPETITIVE MARKET SYSTEM

There are two primary *decision makers* in a market economy: **households** (consumers) and **firms** (businesses). Households are the ultimate suppliers of all economic resources and simultaneously the major spending group in the economy. Firms provide goods and services to the economy.

Consumers are at liberty to buy what they choose; firms to produce and sell what they choose; and resource suppliers to make their resources available in whatever endeavours or occupations they choose. We may wonder why such an economy does not collapse in chaos. If consumers want breakfast cereal, businesses choose to produce aerobic shoes, and resource suppliers want to offer their services in manufacturing computer software, production would seem to be deadlocked because of the apparent inconsistency of these free choices.

In reality, the millions of decisions made by households and firms are highly consistent with one another. Firms do produce those particular goods and services that consumers want. Households provide the kinds of labour that businesses want to hire. What we want to explain is how a competitive market system constitutes a co-ordinating mechanism that overcomes the potential chaos of freedom of enterprise and choice. The competitive market system is a mechanism both for communicating the decisions of consumers, producers, and resource suppliers to one another and for synchronizing those decisions towards consistent production objectives.

THE FIVE FUNDAMENTAL QUESTIONS

To understand the operation of a market economy we must recognize that there are **Five Fundamental Questions** to which *every* economy must respond:

1. *How much* is to be produced? At what level — to what degree — should available resources be employed or utilized in the production process?

2. *What* is to be produced? What collection of goods and services will best satisfy society's material wants?

3. *How* is that output to be produced? How should production be organized? What firms should do the producing and what productive techniques should they use?

4. *Who* is to receive the output? How should the output of the economy be shared by consumers?

5. Can the system *adapt* to change? Can it appropriately adjust to changes in consumer wants, resource supplies, and technology?

Two points are relevant. First, we will defer the "how much" question for the moment. Macroeconomics deals in detail with the complex question of the level of resource employment.

Second, the Five Fundamental Questions are merely an elaboration of the choices underlying Chapter 2's production possibilities curve. These questions would be irrelevant were it not for the economizing problem.

THE MARKET SYSTEM AT WORK

Chapter 2's circular flow diagram (Figure 2-6) provides the setting for our discussion.

DETERMINING WHAT IS TO BE PRODUCED

Given the product and resource prices established by competing buyers and sellers in both the product and resource markets, how would a market economy decide the types and quantities of goods to be produced? Since businesses seek profits and want to avoid losses, we can generalize that those goods and services that can be produced at a profit will be produced and those whose production entails a loss will not. Those industries that are profitable usually expand, those that incur losses usually contract.

ORGANIZING PRODUCTION

How is production to be organized in a market economy? This Fundamental Question is composed of three subquestions:

1. How should resources be allocated among specific industries?
2. What specific firms should do the producing in each industry?
3. What combinations of resources — what technology — should each firm employ?

The market system steers resources to those industries whose products consumers want badly enough to make their production profitable. It simultaneously deprives unprofitable industries of scarce resources. If all firms had sufficient time to enter prosperous industries and to leave unprosperous industries, the output of each industry would be large enough for the firms to make normal profits (Chapter 8).

The second and third subquestions are closely intertwined. In a competitive market economy, the firms that do the producing are those that are willing and able to employ the economically most efficient technique of production. And what determines the most efficient technique? Economic efficiency depends on:

1. Available technology, that is, the alternative combinations of resources or inputs that will produce the desired output.
2. The prices of needed resources.

DISTRIBUTING TOTAL OUTPUT

The market system enters the picture in two ways in solving the problem of distributing total output. Generally speaking, any given product will be distributed to consumers on the basis of their ability and willingness to pay the existing market price for it. This is the rationing function of equilibrium prices.

The size of one's money income determines a consumer's ability to pay the equilibrium price for X and other available products. And money income depends on the quantities of the various resources that the income receiver supplies and the prices that they command in the resource market. Thus, resource prices play a key role in determining the size of each household's income claim against the total output of society. Within the limits of a consumer's money income, his or her willingness to pay the equilibrium price for X determines whether some of this product is distributed to that person. And this willingness to buy X will depend on one's preference for X in comparison with available close substitutes for X and their relative prices. Thus, product prices play a key role in determining the expenditure patterns of consumers.

There is nothing particularly ethical about the market system as a mechanism for distributing output. Households that accumulate large amounts of property by inheritance, through hard work and frugality, through business acumen, or by crook will receive large incomes and thus command large shares of the economy's total output. Others, offering unskilled and relatively unproductive labour resources that elicit low wages, will receive meagre money incomes and small portions of total output.

ACCOMMODATING CHANGE

Industrial societies are dynamic: Consumer preferences, technology, and resource supplies all change. This means that the particular allocation of resources that is *now* the most efficient for a *given* pattern of consumer tastes, for a *given* range of technological alternatives, and for *given* supplies of resources can be expected to become obsolete and inefficient as consumer preferences change, new techniques of production are discovered, and resource supplies change over time. The market economy adjusts to these changes so that resources are still used efficiently.

COMPETITION AND CONTROL

The market mechanism of supply and demand communicates the wants of consumers (society) to businesses and through businesses to resource suppliers. It is competition, however, that forces businesses and resource suppliers to make appropriate responses. But competition does more than guarantee responses appropriate to the wishes of society. It also forces firms to adopt the most efficient productive techniques. In a competitive market, the failure of some firms to use the least costly production technique leads to their eventual elimination by more efficient firms. Finally, competition provides an environment conducive to technological advance.

THE "INVISIBLE HAND"

The operation and the adjustments of a competitive market system create a curious and important identity — the identity of private and social interests. Firms and resource suppliers, seeking to further their own self-interest and operating within the framework of a highly competitive market system, will simultaneously, as though guided by an **"invisible hand,"** promote the public or social interest. For example, in a competitive environment, business firms use the least costly combination of resources in producing a given output because it is in their private self-interest to do so. To act otherwise would be to forgo profits or even to risk bankruptcy. But, at the same time, it is clearly also in the social interest to use scarce resources in the least costly, that is, most efficient, manner. Not to do so would be to produce a given output at a greater cost or sacrifice of alternative goods than is necessary. It is self-interest, awakened and guided by the competitive market system, that induces responses appropriate to the assumed change in society's wants. Businesses seeking to make higher profits and to avoid losses, on the one hand, and resource suppliers pursuing greater monetary rewards, on the other, negotiate the changes in the allocation of resources and therefore the composition of output society demands. The force of competition controls or guides the self-interest motive in such a way that it automatically, and quite unintentionally, furthers the best interests of society. The "invisible hand" tells us that when firms maximize their profits, society's domestic output is also maximized.

THE CASE FOR THE MARKET SYSTEM

The virtues of the market system are implicit in our discussion of its operation. Three merit emphasis.

EFFICIENCY   The basic economic argument for the market system is that it promotes the efficient use of scarce resources. The competitive market system guides scarce resources into production of those goods and services most wanted by society. It forces use of the most efficient techniques in organizing scarce resources for production and is conducive to the development and adoption of new and more efficient production techniques so that the economizing problem — scarce resources and unlimited human wants — can be alleviated.

INCENTIVES   The market system effectively harnesses incentives to alleviate the economizing prob-

lem. Greater work effort is rewarded by higher money incomes that translate into a higher standard of living. Similarly, the assuming of risks by entrepreneurs to provide what consumers want can result in substantial profit incomes. Successful innovations that produce more of what society wants may also generate ample economic rewards.

FREEDOM   The major noneconomic argument for the market system is its great emphasis on personal freedom. In contrast to central planning, the market system can co-ordinate economic activity without coercion. The market system permits — indeed, it thrives on — freedom of enterprise and choice. Entrepreneurs and workers are not herded from industry to industry by government directives to meet production targets established by some omnipotent governmental agency. On the contrary, they are free to further their own self-interests, subject to the rewards and penalties imposed by the market system itself.

QUICK REVIEW 3-3

1. The output mix of the competitive market system is determined by profits. Profits cause industries to expand; losses cause them to contract.

2. Competition forces firms to use the least costly (most efficient) production methods.

3. The distribution of output in a market economy is determined by consumer incomes and product prices.

4. Competitive markets reallocate resources in response to changes in consumer tastes, technological progress, and changes in resource supplies.

CHAPTER SUMMARY

1. The capitalist, or market, system is characterized by private ownership of resources and the freedom of individuals to engage in the economic activities of their choice as a means for advancing their material well-being. Self-interest is the driving force of such an economy, and competition functions as a regulatory or control mechanism.

2. Capitalist production is not organized by a central government, but rather features the market system as a means of organizing and making effective the many individual decisions that determine what is produced, the methods of production, and the sharing of output. A pure capitalist system envisions government playing a minor and relatively passive economic role.

3. Specialization and an advanced technology based on the extensive use of capital goods are common to all modern economies.

4. Functioning as a medium of exchange, money circumvents problems of bartering and thereby permits greater specialization both domestically and internationally.

5. Every economy faces Five Fundamental Questions: **a** At what level should available resources be employed? **b** What goods and services are to be produced? **c** How is that output to be produced? **d** To whom should the output be distributed? **e** Can the system adapt to changes in consumer tastes, resource supplies, and technology?

6. Consumer sovereignty means that both businesses and resource suppliers channel their efforts in accordance with the wants of consumers.

7. The competitive market system can communicate changes in consumer tastes to resource suppliers and entrepreneurs, thereby prompting appropriate adjustments in the allocation of the economy's resources. The competitive market system also provides an environment conducive to technological advance and capital accumulation.

8. Competition, the primary mechanism of control in the market economy, will foster an identity of private and social interests; as though directed by an "invisible hand," competition harnesses the self-interest motives of businesses and resource suppliers so as to simultaneously further the social interest in using scarce resources efficiently.

TERMS AND CONCEPTS

bartering (p. 50)

coincidence of wants (p. 50)

competition (p. 47)

firms (p. 52)

Five Fundamental Questions (p. 52)

freedom of choice (p. 47)

freedom of enterprise (p. 47)

households (p. 52)

"invisible hand" (p. 53)

market economy (p. 48)

medium of exchange (p. 50)

money (p. 50)

private property (p. 46)

roundabout production (p. 49)

self-interest (p. 47)

specialization and division of labour (p. 49)

QUESTIONS AND STUDY SUGGESTIONS

1. "Capitalism may be characterized as an automatic self-regulating system motivated by the self-interest of individuals and regulated by competition." Explain and evaluate.

2. *Key Question* *What advantages result from "roundabout" production? What problem is involved in increasing a full-employment, full-production economy's stock of capital goods? Illustrate this problem in terms of the production possibilities curve. Does an economy with unemployed resources face the same problem?*

3. What are the advantages of specialization in the use of resources? Explain: "Exchange is the necessary consequence of specialization."

4. What problems does barter entail? Indicate the economic significance of money as a medium of exchange. "Money is the only commodity that is good for nothing but to be gotten rid of. It will not feed you, clothe you, shelter you, or amuse you unless you spend or invest it. It imparts value only in parting." Explain this statement.

5. Describe in detail how the market system answers the Fundamental Questions. Why must economic choices be made? Explain: "The capitalist system is a profit and loss economy."

6. Evaluate and explain the following statements:

   a. "The most important feature of capitalism is the absence of a central economic plan."
   b. "Competition is the indispensable disciplinarian of the market economy."
   c. "Production methods that are inferior in the engineering sense may be the most efficient methods in the economic sense."

7. Explain fully the meaning and implications of the following quotation.

   The beautiful consequence of the market is that it is its own guardian. If output prices or certain kinds of remuneration stray away from their socially ordained levels, forces are set into motion to bring them back to the fold. It is a curious paradox which thus ensues: the market, which is the acme of individual economic freedom, is the strictest taskmaster of all. One may appeal the ruling of a planning board or win the dispensation of a minister, but there is no appeal, no dispensation, from the anonymous pressures of the market mechanism. Economic freedom is thus more illusory than at first appears. One can do as one pleases in the market. But if one pleases to do what the market disapproves, the price of individual freedom is economic ruination.[1]

8. (Applying the Theory) What considerations have increased the popularity of barter in recent years?

---

[1] Robert L. Heilbroner, *The Worldly Philosophers*, 3d ed. (New York: Simon & Schuster, Inc., 1967), p. 42.

CHAPTER 4

UNDERSTANDING INDIVIDUAL MARKETS: DEMAND AND SUPPLY

"Teach a parrot to say, 'Demand and supply,' and you have an economist!" There is a strong element of truth in this quip. The tools of demand and supply can take one far in understanding not only specific economic issues, but also how the entire economy works.

The goal of this chapter is to understand the nature of markets and how prices and outputs are determined. Our circular flow model of Chapter 2 identified the participants in both product and resource markets. But we assumed product and resource prices were "given"; here we will explain how prices are determined by discussing more fully the concept of a market.

BOX 4-1 THE BIG PICTURE

In a world of scarcity in relation to unlimited wants, there is constant competition for the available goods and services. The supply and demand curves represent the self-interest of the producers and consumers respectively. Firms are willing to supply *more* of a specific product at successively higher prices, but consumers actually want less at successively higher prices. What quantities of a particular good or service and at what price it is exchanged are determined by the interaction of these two opposing forces. The price mechanism is at the heart of the market system because prices adjust in response to choices made by consumers, suppliers, and other actors in the economy. Price changes mediate the effects of these various choices, leading to a more or less coherent allocation of resources in our society.

As you read this chapter, keep the following points in mind:

- Think of the supply and demand curves as independent of each other. Each of these curves shifts for different reasons. Remember that suppliers of goods and services and the consumers have diverging interests.
- Make sure you understand the distinction between movement along the curves and shifts of the curves.
- The supply and demand curves shift only when certain conditions change. It is imperative that you learn the causes of the demand and supply curve shifts, reproduced in Tables 4-3 and 4-7.
- Supply and demand analysis can appear deceptively easy at first glance. Whenever applying supply and demand analysis, be sure to use graphs; trying to figure out a problem in your head can quickly lead to errors. Supply and demand analysis is mastered by getting "your hands dirty"; you need lots of practice applying it, and graphing is an important part.

MARKETS DEFINED

A **market** *is an institution that brings together buyers and sellers of particular goods and services*. Markets exist in many forms. The corner gas station, the fast-food outlet, the local record shop, a farmer's roadside stand, are all familiar markets. The Toronto Stock Exchange and the Chicago Board of Trade are highly organized markets where buyers and sellers of stocks and bonds and farm commodities, respectively, may communicate with one another. Auctioneers bring together potential buyers and sellers of art, livestock, used farm equipment, and sometimes real estate. The professional hockey player and his agent bargain with the owner of an NHL team. A graduating engineer interviews with Canadian Pacific and Petro-Canada at the university placement office.

All of these situations that link potential buyers with potential sellers constitute markets. Some markets are local while others are national or international in scope. Some are highly personal, involving face-to-face contact between demander and supplier; others are impersonal and buyer and seller never see or know one another.

This chapter looks at *purely competitive markets*. Such markets have large numbers of independently acting buyers and sellers exchanging a standardized product. The kind of market we have in mind is not the record shop or corner gas station, where products have price tags on them, but such competitive markets as a central grain exchange, a stock market, or a market for foreign currencies, where the equilibrium price is "discovered" by the interacting decisions of many buyers and sellers.

DEMAND

Demand *refers to the various amounts of a product consumers are willing and able to purchase at each specific price during a specified period of time, all other things being equal.*[1]

A **demand schedule** shows the amounts consumers will buy at various possible prices. Table 4-1 is a hypothetical demand schedule for a single consumer purchasing bushels of oats.

---

[1] In adjusting this definition to the resource market, substitute the word "resource" for "product" and "businesses" for "consumers."

TABLE 4-1 **An individual buyer's demand for oats**

Price per bushel	Quantity demanded per week
$5	10
4	20
3	35
2	55
1	80

This demand curve reflects the relationship between the price of oats and the quantity that our hypothetical consumer would be willing and able to purchase at each of these prices. We say willing and *able*, because willingness alone will not suffice. I may be willing to buy a Porsche, but if this willingness is not backed by the ability to buy, it will not be effective and therefore not be reflected in the market. In Table 4-1, if the price of oats in the market were $5 per bushel, our consumer would buy 10 bushels per week; if it were $4, the consumer would buy 20 bushels per week, and so forth.

The demand schedule does not tell us which of the five possible prices will actually exist in the oats market. This depends on demand *and supply*. Demand is simply a statement of a buyer's plans or intentions to purchase a product.

To be meaningful the quantities demanded at each price must relate to some specific time period — a day, a week, a month, and so forth. To say "a consumer will buy 10 bushels of oats at $5 per bushel" is vague and meaningless. In the absence of a specific time period we would be unable to tell whether the demand for a product was large or small.

LAW OF DEMAND: A FIRST LOOK

A fundamental characteristic of demand is this: *All else being constant, as price falls, the quantity demanded rises. Or, other things being equal, as price increases, the quantity demanded falls.* There is an inverse relationship between price and quantity demanded. We call this inverse relationship the **law of demand.**

The "other things being constant" assumption is critical. Many factors other than the price of the product under consideration can affect the amount purchased. The quantity of Nikes purchased will depend not only on the price of Nikes, but also on the prices of such substitutes as Reeboks, Adidas, and L.A. Gear. The law of demand in this case says that fewer Nikes will be purchased if the price of Nikes rises *and the prices of Reeboks, Adidas and L.A. Gear all remain constant.* Thus, if the relative price of Nikes increases, fewer Nikes will be bought.

What is the foundation for the law of demand? Why is it that as price falls, the quantity demanded of a good rises, and vice versa?

1. In any time period, each buyer of a product will derive less satisfaction or utility from each successive unit consumed. The second Big Mac will yield less satisfaction than the first; the third still less than the second, and so forth. Because consumption is subject to **diminishing marginal utility** — successive units of a particular product yield less and less extra satisfaction — consumers will buy additional units only if price is reduced.

2. The law of demand can also be explained in terms of substitution effects and income effects. The **substitution effect** tells us that at a lower price, you have the incentive to substitute the cheaper good for similar goods that are now relatively more expensive.

The **income effect** indicates that at a lower price, you can afford more of the good without giving up other goods. A decline in the price of a product will increase the purchasing power of your money income, allowing you to buy more of the product than before.

For example, at a lower price, beef is relatively more attractive and it is substituted for pork, lamb, chicken, and fish (the substitution effect). A decline in the price of beef will increase the purchasing power of consumer incomes, enabling them to buy more beef (the income effect). The substitution and income effects combine to make consumers able and willing to buy more of a product at a low price than at a high price.

THE DEMAND CURVE

This inverse relationship between product price and quantity demanded can be represented on a simple two-dimensional graph, measuring quantity demanded on the horizontal axis and price on the vertical axis. The process involves locating on the graph those five price-quantity possibilities in Table 4-1.

Assuming the same inverse relationship between price and quantity demanded at all points between the ones graphed, we can generalize on the inverse relationship between price and quantity demanded by drawing a curve to represent *all* price–quantity-demanded possibilities within the limits shown on the graph. The resulting curve is called a **demand curve** and is labelled *D* in Figure 4-1. It slopes downward and to the right because the relationship it portrays between price and quantity demanded is negative or inverse. The law of demand is reflected in the downward slope of the demand curve.

FIGURE 4-1   An individual buyer's demand curve for oats

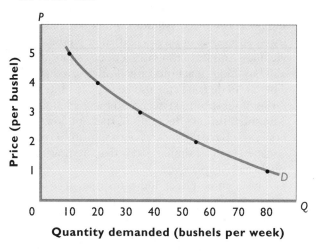

An individual's demand schedule graphs as a downsloping curve such as **D**, because price and quantity demanded are inversely related. Specifically, the law of demand generalizes that consumers will buy more of a product as its price declines.

The advantage of graphing is that it permits us to represent clearly a given relationship — in this case, the law of demand — in a much simpler way. A single curve on a graph, if understood, is simpler to state *and to manipulate* than tables and lengthy verbal presentations. Graphs are invaluable tools in economic analysis. They permit clear expression and handling of sometimes complex relationships.

INDIVIDUAL AND MARKET DEMAND

Until now we have been dealing with one consumer. We can get from an *individual* to a *market* demand schedule easily by summing the quantities demanded by each consumer at the various possible prices. If there were just three buyers in the market, as in Table 4-2, it would be easy to determine the total quantities demanded at each price. Figure 4-2 shows the same summing procedure graphically, using only the $3 price to illustrate the adding-up process. Note that we are simply summing the three individual demand curves *horizontally* to derive the total demand curve.

Competition requires many more than three buyers of a product. For simplicity, let's suppose there are 200 buyers of oats in the market, each choosing to buy the same amount at each of the various prices as our original consumer. We can determine total or market demand multiplying the quantity demanded data of Table 4-1 by 200, as in Table 4-3. Curve D_0 in Figure 4-3 indicates this market demand curve for the 200 buyers.

DETERMINANTS OF DEMAND

Constructing a demand curve such as D_0 in Figure 4-3 assumes that price is the most important determinant of the amount of any product purchased. But factors other

FIGURE 4-2   The market demand curve is the sum of the individual demand curves

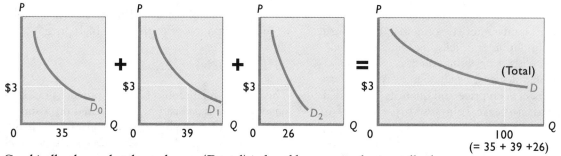

Graphically, the market demand curve (*D* total) is found by summing horizontally the individual demand curves (D_0, D_1, and D_2) of all consumers in the market.

FIGURE 4-3 **Change in the demand for oats**

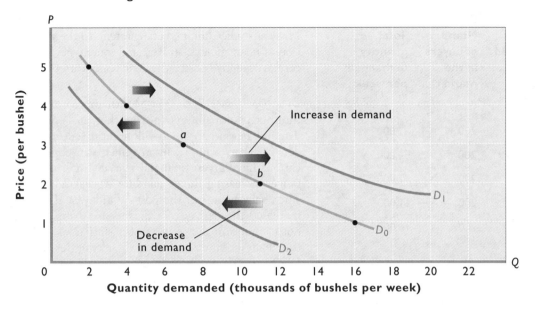

Quantity demanded (thousands of bushels per week)

A change in one or more of the determinants of demand — consumer tastes, the number of buyers in the market, money incomes, the prices of other goods, or consumer expectations — will cause a change in demand. An increase in demand shifts the demand curve to the right, as from D_0 to D_1. A decrease in demand shifts the demand curve to the left, as from D_0 to D_2. A change in the quantity demanded involves a movement, caused by a change in the price of the product under consideration, from one point to another — as from a to b — on a fixed demand curve.

than price can and do affect purchases. In locating a specific demand curve such as D_0, it must be assumed that other *determinants* of the amount demanded are constant. When these determinants of demand do change, the location of the demand curve will shift to some new position to the right or left of D_0. For this reason these determinants are also referred to as "demand shifters."

The determinants of market demand are: (1) the tastes or preferences of consumers, (2) the number of consumers in the market, (3) the money incomes of consumers, (4) the prices of related goods, and (5) consumer expectations with respect to future prices and incomes.

TABLE 4-2 **Market demand for oats, three buyers**

Price per bushel	Quantity demanded, first buyer		Quantity demanded, second buyer		Quantity demanded, third buyer		Total quantity demanded per week
$5	10	+	12	+	8	=	30
4	20	+	23	+	17	=	60
3	35	+	39	+	26	=	100
2	55	+	60	+	39	=	154
1	80	+	87	+	54	=	221

TABLE 4-3   **Market demand for oats, 200 buyers**

(1) Price per bushel	(2) Quantity demanded per week, single buyer		(3) Number of buyers in the market		(4) Total quantity demanded per week
$5	10	x	200	=	2,000
4	20	x	200	=	4,000
3	35	x	200	=	7,000
2	55	x	200	=	11,000
1	80	x	200	=	16,000

CHANGES IN DEMAND

A change in one or more of the determinants will change the demand schedule data in Table 4-3, and therefore the location of the demand curve in Figure 4-3. A change in the demand schedule data or, graphically, a shift in the location of the demand curve, is called a **change in demand.**

If consumers buy more oats at each possible price than is reflected in column 4 of Table 4-3, the result will be an *increase in demand*. In Figure 4-3, this increase in demand is reflected in a shift of the demand curve to the right from D_0 to D_1. Conversely, a *decrease in demand* occurs when, because of a change in one or more of the determinants, consumers buy less oats at each possible price than is indicated in column 4 of Table 4-3. Graphically, a decrease in demand is shown as a shift of the demand curve to the left, from D_0 to D_2, in Figure 4-3.

Let's now examine how changes in each of the determinants affects demand.

1. **TASTES**   A change in consumer tastes or preferences favourable to a product — possibly prompted by advertising or fashion changes — will result in more being demanded at each price; that is, demand will increase. An unfavourable change in consumer preferences will decrease demand, shifting the curve to the left. Technological change in the form of new products may affect consumer tastes. The introduction of compact discs has greatly decreased the demand for long-playing records. Consumer concerns over the health hazards posed by cholesterol and obe-

sity have increased the demands for broccoli, low-calorie sweeteners, and fresh fruits, while decreasing the demands for beef, veal, eggs, and whole milk. Medical studies linking beta carotene to the prevention of heart attacks, strokes, and some types of cancer have greatly boosted the demand for carrots.

2. **NUMBER OF BUYERS**   An increase in the number of consumers in a market will increase demand. Fewer consumers will result in a decrease in demand. For example, improvements in communications have given financial markets international range, increasing the demand for stocks and bonds. The "baby boom" of the post–World War II period increased the demand for diapers and baby lotion, not to mention the services of obstetricians. When the "baby boomers" reached their twenties in the 1970s, the demand for housing greatly increased. Conversely, the aging of the baby boomers in the late 1980s and 1990s has been a factor in the recent "slump" in housing demand. Increasing life expectancy has increased the demands for medical care, retirement communities, and nursing homes. Note, too, that recent international trade agreements such as the North American Free Trade Agreement (NAFTA) and the General Agreement on Tariffs and Trade (GATT) have reduced foreign trade barriers to Canadian products, increasing the demand for them.

3. **INCOME**   For most commodities, a rise in income will cause an increase in demand. Consumers typically buy more shoes, steaks, sunscreen, and stereos as their incomes increase. Conversely, the demand for such products will decline as incomes fall. Commodities whose demand varies *directly* with money income are called **superior** or **normal goods**.

Although most products are normal goods, there are a few exceptions. As incomes increase beyond some point, the amounts of bread or potatoes or cabbages purchased at each price may diminish because higher incomes now allow consumers to buy more high-protein foods, such as dairy products and meat. Rising incomes may also decrease the demands for used clothing and third-hand automobiles. Rising incomes may cause the demands for hamburger to decline, as wealthier consumers switch to T-bone steak. Goods whose demand varies *inversely* with a change in money income are called **inferior goods**.

4. PRICES OF RELATED GOODS Whether a particular change in the price of a related good will increase or decrease the demand for the product under consideration will depend on whether the related good is a substitute for, or a complement to, the product. A substitute good is one that can be used in place of another good. A complementary good is one that is used in conjunction with another good.

SUBSTITUTES Butter and margarine are examples of **substitute goods**. When the price of butter rises, consumers buy less butter, increasing the demand for margarine.[2] Conversely, as the price of butter falls, consumers buy more butter, decreasing the demand for margarine. *When two products are substitutes, the price of one good and the demand for the other are directly related.* So it is with sugar and NutraSweet, Toyotas and Hondas, Coke and Pepsi, and tea and coffee.

COMPLEMENTS Other products are **complementary goods**; they "go together" in that they are used in tandem and jointly demanded. If the price of gasoline falls, you drive your car more, and this extra driving will increase your demand for motor oil. Conversely, an increase in the price of gasoline will diminish the demand for motor oil.[3] Thus gas and oil are jointly demanded; they are complements. And so it is with ham and eggs, university courses and textbooks, movies and popcorn, VCRs and video cassettes, golf clubs and golf balls, cameras and film. *When two commodities are complements, the price of one good and the demand for the other are inversely related.*

Many goods are not related to one another — they are *independent* goods. For example, butter and golf balls, potatoes and automobiles, bananas and wristwatches. A change in the price of one would have little or no impact on the demand for the other.

---

[2] Note that the consumer is moving up a stable demand curve for butter. But the demand curve for margarine shifts to the right. Given the supply of margarine, this rightward shift in demand means that more margarine will be purchased and that its price will also rise.

[3] While the buyer is moving up a stable demand curve for gasoline, the demand for motor oil shifts to the left (decreases). Given the supply of motor oil, this decline in demand for motor oil will decrease both the amount purchased and its price.

5. EXPECTATIONS Consumer expectations about future products prices, product availability, and future income can shift demand. Consumer expectations of higher future prices may prompt them to buy now to "beat" the anticipated price rises. The expectation of rising incomes may induce consumers to be less tight-fisted in their current spending. Conversely, expectations of falling prices and income will decrease current demand for products.

For example, if freezing weather destroys a substantial portion of Florida's citrus crop, consumers may reason that forthcoming shortages of frozen orange juice will escalate its price. They may stock up on orange juice by purchasing large quantities now.

A first-round NHL draft choice might splurge on a new Rolls-Royce in anticipation of a lucrative professional hockey contract.

Table 4-4 provides a convenient listing of the determinants of demand along with additional illustrations. **(Key Question 2)**

TABLE 4-4 Determinants of demand: factors that shift the demand curve

1. ***Change in buyer tastes*** Example: Physical fitness increases in popularity, increasing the demands for jogging shoes and bicycles.

2. ***Change in number of buyers*** Examples: Japanese reduce import restrictions on Canadian telecommunications equipment, increasing the demand for it; a birthrate decline reduces the demand for education.

3. ***Change in income*** Examples: An increase in incomes increases the demand for such normal goods as butter, lobster, and filet mignon, while reducing the demand for such inferior goods as cabbage, turnips, retreaded tires, and used clothing.

4. ***Change in the prices of related goods*** Examples: An increase in air fares because of increased concentration of ownership (mergers) increases the demand for bus transportation (substitute goods); a decline in the price of compact disc players increases the demand for compact discs (complementary goods).

5. ***Change in expectations*** Example: Inclement weather in South America causes the expectation of higher future coffee prices, thereby increasing the current demand for coffee.

CHANGES IN QUANTITY DEMANDED

A "change in demand" must not be confused with a "change in the quantity demanded." A **change in demand** refers to a shift in the entire demand curve either to the right (an increase in demand) or to the left (a decrease in demand). The term "demand" refers to a schedule or curve; therefore, a "change in demand" must mean that the entire schedule has changed, and that graphically, the curve has shifted its position.

In contrast, a **change in the quantity demanded** designates the movement from one point to another point — from one price combination to another — on a fixed demand curve. The cause of a change in the quantity demanded is a change in the price of the product under consideration. In Table 4-3, a decline in the price asked by suppliers of oats from $5 to $4 will increase the quantity of oats demanded from 2,000 to 4,000 bushels.

In Figure 4-3 the shifts of the demand curve D_0 to either D_1 or D_2 are each a "change in demand." But the movement from point a to point b on curve D_0 is a "change in the quantity demanded."

Is a change in demand or a change in the quantity demanded illustrated in each of the following?

1. Consumer incomes rise, with the result that more jewellery is purchased.
2. A barber raises the price of haircuts and experiences a decline in volume of business.
3. The price of Toyotas goes up and, as a consequence, the sales of Chevrolets increase.

QUICK REVIEW 4-1

1. A market is any arrangement that facilitates the purchase and sale of goods, services, or resources.

2. The law of demand indicates that, other things being constant, the quantity of a good purchased will vary inversely with its price.

3. The demand curve will shift as a consequence of changes in (a) consumer tastes, (b) the number of buyers in the market, (c) incomes, (d) the prices of substitute or complementary goods, and (e) expectations.

4. A "change in the quantity demanded" refers to a movement from one point to another on a stable demand curve; a "change in demand" designates a shift in the entire demand curve.

SUPPLY

The term supply *refers to the various amounts of a product that a producer is willing and able to produce and make available for sale at each specific price in a series of possible prices during some specified time period.*[4] The **supply schedule** portrays a series of alternative possibilities, such as those shown in Table 4-5 for a single producer.

Suppose in this case that our producer is a farmer producing oats, the demand for which we have just considered. Our definition of supply indicates that supply is viewed from the vantage point of price. That is, we read supply as showing the amounts producers will offer at various prices.

LAW OF SUPPLY

Table 4-5 shows a positive or *direct* relationship between price and quantity supplied. As price rises, the corresponding quantity supplied rises; as price falls, the quantity supplied also falls. This relationship is called the **law of supply**. It tells us that producers are willing to produce and offer for sale more of their product at a high price than they are at a low price.

Price is a deterrent from the consumer's standpoint. The higher the price, the less the consumer buys. To a supplier, price is revenue per unit and therefore an incentive to produce and sell a product. Given production costs, a higher product price will result in larger profits and thus an incentive to increase the quantity supplied.

Consider a farmer who can shift resources among alternative products. As price moves up in Table 4-5, the farmer will find it profitable to take land out of wheat, rye, and barley production and put it into oats. Higher oat prices will make it possible for the farmer to cover the costs associated with more intensive cultivation and the use of larger quantities of fertilizers and pesticides. The result is more output of oats.

Now consider a manufacturer. As output increases manufacturers generally find that costs rise after some point. They rise because certain productive resources — in particular, the firm's plant and machinery — cannot

---

[4] In discussing the resource market, our definition of supply reads: The various amounts of a resource that its owners are willing to supply in the market at each possible price during some specified time, all other things being equal.

be expanded in a short period of time. As the firm increases the amounts of more readily variable resources such as labour, materials, and component parts, the fixed plant will at some point become crowded or congested. Productive efficiency will decline and the cost of successive units of output will increase. Producers must receive a higher price to produce costly units.

TABLE 4-5 An individual producer's supply of oats

Price per bushel	Quantity demanded per week
$5	60
4	50
3	35
2	20
1	5

THE SUPPLY CURVE

As with demand, it is convenient to present graphically the concept of supply. Our axes in Figure 4-4 are the same as in Figure 4-3, except for the change of "quantity demanded" to "quantity supplied" on the horizontal axis. The graphing procedure is the same as that previously explained, but the quantity

TABLE 4-6 Market supply of oats, 200 producers

(1) Price per bushel	(2) Quantity supplied per week, single producer		(3) Number of sellers in the market		(4) Total quantity supplied per week
$5	60	×	200	=	12,000
4	50	×	200	=	10,000
3	35	×	200	=	7,000
2	20	×	200	=	4,000
1	5	×	200	=	1,000

data and relationship are different. The market supply data graphed in Figure 4-4 as S_0 are shown in Table 4-6, which assumes there are 200 suppliers in the market having the same supply schedules as the producer previously portrayed in Table 4-5.

DETERMINANTS OF SUPPLY

In constructing a supply curve, we assume that price is the most significant determinant of the quantity supplied of any product. But, as with the demand curve, the supply curve is anchored on the "other

FIGURE 4-4 Changes in the supply of oats

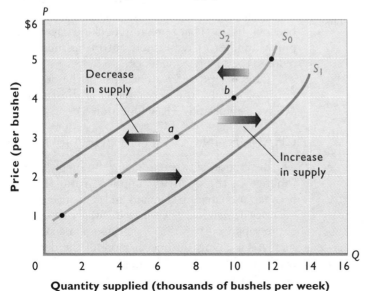

A change in one or more of the determinants of supply — productive techniques, resource prices, taxes and subsidies, the prices of other goods, price expectations, or the number of sellers in the market — will cause a change in supply. An increase in supply shifts the supply curve to the right, as from S_0 to S_1. A decrease in the supply is shown graphically as a movement of the curve to the left, as from S_0 to S_2. A change in the quantity supplied involves a movement, caused by a change in the price of the product under consideration, from one point to another — as from a to b — on a fixed supply curve.

things are equal" assumption. The supply curve is drawn assuming that certain determinants of the amount supplied are given and do not change. If any of these determinants of supply do in fact change, the location of the supply curve will shift.

The basic determinants of supply are (1) the technique of production, (2) resource prices, (3) taxes and subsidies, (4) prices of other goods, (5) price expectations, and (6) the number of sellers in the market.

A change in any one or more of these determinants or "supply shifters" will cause the supply curve for a product to move to either the right or the left. A shift to the *right*, from S_0 to S_1 in Figure 4-4, designates *an increase in supply*: producers will supply larger quantities of the product at each possible price. A shift to the left, S_0 to S_2 in Figure 4-4, indicates a *decrease in supply*: suppliers offer less at each price.

CHANGES IN SUPPLY

Let's consider how changes in each of these determinants affect supply.

1. RESOURCE PRICES The relationship between production costs and supply is a close one. A firm must receive higher prices for additional units of output because those extra units are more costly to produce. It follows that a decrease in resource prices will lower production costs and increase supply (shift the supply curve to the right). If the prices of oat seed and fertilizer decrease, we can expect the supply of oats to increase. Conversely, an increase in input prices will raise production costs and reduce supply (shift the supply curve to the left). Increases in the prices of iron ore and coke will increase the cost of producing steel and reduce its supply.

2. TECHNOLOGY A technological improvement means producing a unit of output with fewer resources. Given the prices of resources, this will lower production costs and increase supply. Example: Currently about 30% of electric power is lost when transmitted by copper cable. Recent breakthroughs in the area of superconductivity point to the possibility of transporting electrical power with little or no loss. The consequence is significant cost reductions and supply increases may occur in a wide range of products where electricity is an important input.

3. TAXES AND SUBSIDIES An increase in taxes on business will increase costs and reduce supply. Conversely, subsidies are "taxes in reverse." If government subsidizes the production of some good, it in effect lowers costs and increases supply.

4. PRICES OF OTHER GOODS Changes in the prices of other goods can also shift the supply curve of a product. A decline in the price of wheat may cause a farmer to produce and offer more oats at each possible price. A firm making sports equipment might reduce its supply of basketballs in response to a rise in the price of soccer balls.

5. EXPECTATIONS Expectations concerning the future price of a product can affect a producer's current willingness to supply that product. It is difficult, however, to generalize about how the expected higher price will affect the present supply. Farmers might withhold some their current harvest of oats from the market, anticipating a higher future price for oats. This will decrease the current supply of oats. On the other hand, in many types of manufacturing, expected price increases may induce firms to expand production facilities, causing supply to increase.

6. NUMBER OF SELLERS Generally, the larger the number of suppliers, the greater will be market supply. As more firms enter an industry, the supply curve will shift to the right. As firms leave an industry, the supply curve shifts to the left. For example, Canada and the United States recently imposed restrictions on haddock fishing to replenish dwindling stocks. The requirement that every haddock fishing boat remain in dock 80 days a year put a number of fishermen out of business and reduced the supply of haddock.

Table 4-7 provides a checklist of the determinants of supply; the accompanying illustrations deserve careful study. **(Key Question 5)**

CHANGES IN QUANTITY SUPPLIED

The distinction between a "change in supply" and a "change in the quantity supplied" parallels that between a change in demand and a change in the quantity demanded. A **change in supply** means the entire supply curve shifts. The cause of a change in supply is a change in one or more of the determinants of supply. The term "supply" refers to a schedule or curve.

A **change in the quantity supplied**, on the other hand, refers to the movement from one point to another point on a supply curve. The cause of such a movement is a change in the price of the product under consideration. In Table 4-6, a decline in the price of oats from $5 to $4 decreases the quantity of oats supplied from 12,000 to 10,000 bushels.

TABLE 4-7 Determinants of supply: factors that shift the supply curve

1. ***Change in technology*** Example: The development of a more effective insecticide for corn rootworm increases the supply of corn.

2. ***Change in resource prices*** Examples: A decline in the price of bauxite increases the supply of aluminum; an increase in the price of irrigation equipment reduces the supply of corn.

3. ***Changes in taxes and subsidies*** Examples: An increase in the excise tax on cigarettes reduces the supply of cigarettes; a decline in provincial grants to universities reduces the supply of higher education.

4. ***Changes in prices of other goods*** Example: Declines in the prices of mutton and pork increase the supply of beef cattle.

5. ***Change in expectations*** Example: Expectations of substantial declines in future oil prices cause oil companies to increase current supply.

6. ***Change in number of suppliers*** Example: An increase in the number of firms producing personal computers increases the supply of personal computers; a new professional football league increases the supply of professional football games on Canadian TV.

Shifting the supply curve from S_0 to S_1 or S_2 in Figure 4-4 each entails a "change in supply." The movement from point *a* to point *b* on S_0, however, is a "change in the quantity supplied."

You should determine which of the following involves a change in supply and which a change in the quantity supplied.

1. Because production costs decline, producers sell more automobiles.
2. The price of wheat declines, causing the number of oats sold per month to increase.
3. Fewer apples are offered for sale because their price has decreased in retail markets.

4. The federal government doubles its excise tax on the production of liquor.

QUICK REVIEW 4-2

1. The law of supply states that, other things being unchanged, the quantity of a good supplied varies directly with its price.

2. The supply curve will shift because of changes in (a) resource prices, (b) technology, (c) taxes or subsidies, (d) expectations regarding future product prices, and (e) the number of suppliers.

3. A "change in supply" means a shift in the supply curve; a "change in the quantity supplied" designates the movement from one point to another point on a given supply curve.

SUPPLY AND DEMAND: MARKET EQUILIBRIUM

Let's now bring supply and demand together to see how the interaction of the buying decisions of households and the selling decisions of producers determines the price of a product and the quantity that is actually bought and sold. In Table 4-8, columns 1 and 2 reproduce the market supply schedule for oats (from Table 4-6), and columns 2 and 3 show the market demand schedule for oats (from Table 4-3). Note in column 2 we are using a common set of prices. We assume competition — a large number of buyers and sellers.

TABLE 4-8 Market supply and demand for oats

(1) Total quantity supplied per week	(2) Price per bushel	(3) Total quantity demanded per week	(4) Surplus (+) or shortage (-) (arrows indicate effect on price)
12,000	$5	2,000	+10,000↓
10,000	4	4,000	+6,000↓
7,000	3	7,000	0
4,000	2	11,000	−7,000↑
1,000	1	16,000	−15,000↑

SURPLUSES

Of the five possible prices at which oats might sell in this market, which will actually prevail as the market price? Could $5 be the prevailing market price for oats? No, because producers are willing to produce and offer in the market some 12,000 bushels of oats, while buyers are willing to take only 2000 bushels at this price. The $5 price encourages farmers to produce lots of oats, but discourages most consumers from buying it. Other products appear as better buys when oats are high-priced. The result, in this case, is a 10,000-bushel **surplus** or *excess quantity supply* of oats. This surplus, shown in column 4, is the excess of quantity supplied over quantity demanded at $5. Oat farmers find themselves with unwanted inventories of output. Thus, the price of $5 could not persist over a period of time.

SHORTAGES

Let's jump to $1 as the possible market price for oats. Observe in column 4 that at this price quantity demanded exceeds quantity supplied by 15,000 units. This price discourages farmers from devoting resources to oats production and encourages consumers to attempt to buy more oats than are available. The result is a 15,000-bushel **shortage** of, or *excess quantity demand* for, oats. This $1 price cannot persist as the market price. Competition among buyers will bid up the price to something greater than $1.

EQUILIBRIUM

At $3, *and only at this price*, the quantity of oats farmers are willing to produce and supply in the market is identical with the amount consumers are willing and able to buy. There is neither a shortage nor a surplus. A surplus causes price to decline and a shortage causes price to rise.

With neither a shortage nor a surplus at $3, there is no reason for the price of oats to change. This price is the *market clearing* or **equilibrium price**, equilibrium meaning "in balance" or "at rest." At $3, quantity supplied and quantity demanded are in balance, and thus **equilibrium quantity** is 7000 bushels. Thus, $3 is the only stable price of oats under the supply and demand conditions shown in Table 4-8.

Figure 4-5 (Key Graph) puts the market supply and market demand curves for oats on the same graph. At any price above the equilibrium price of $3, quantity supplied will exceed quantity demanded. This surplus will bid down the price by sellers eager to rid themselves of their surplus. The falling

KEY GRAPH

FIGURE 4-5 **The equilibrium price and quantity for oats as determined by market demand and supply**

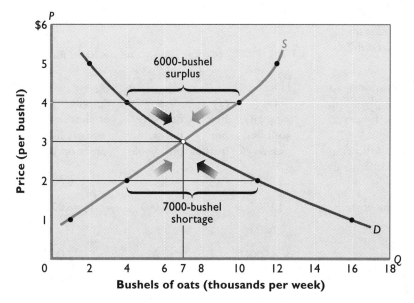

The intersection of the downsloping demand curve D and the upsloping curve S indicates the equilibrium price and quantity, $3 and 7000 bushels in this instance. The shortages of oats that would exist at below-equilibrium prices, for example, 7000 bushels at $2, drive price up and in so doing increase the quantity supplied and reduce the quantity demanded until equilibrium is achieved. The surpluses that above-equilibrium prices would entail, for example 6000 bushels at $4, push price down and thereby increase the quantity demanded and reduce the quantity supplied until equilibrium is achieved.

BOX 4-2 APPLYING THE THEORY

TICKET SCALPING: A BUM RAP?

Some market transactions get a bad name that is unwarranted.

Tickets to athletic and artistic events are sometimes resold at higher-than-original prices — a market transaction known by the unsavoury term "scalping." For example, a $40 ticket to an NHL hockey game may be resold by the original buyer for $200, $250, or more. The media often denounce scalpers for "ripping off" buyers by charging "exorbitant" prices. Scalping and extortion are synonymous in some people's minds.

But is scalping really sinful? We must first recognize that such ticket resales are voluntary, not coerced, transactions. This correctly implies that both buyer and seller gain from the exchange or it would not occur. The seller must value the $200 more than seeing the game and the buyer must value seeing the game more than the $200. There are no losers or victims here; both buyer and seller benefit from the transaction. The "scalping" market simply redistributes assets (game tickets) from those who value them less to those who value them more.

Does scalping impose losses or injury on other parties — in particular, the sponsors of the event? If the sponsors are injured, it is because they initially priced tickets below the equilibrium level. In so doing they suffer an economic loss in the form of less revenue and profit than they might have otherwise received. But the loss is self-inflicted because of their pricing error. That mistake is quite separate and distinct from the fact that some tickets were later resold at a higher price.

What about spectators? Does scalping somehow impose losses by deteriorating the quality of the game's audience? No! People who most want to see the game — generally those with the greatest interest in and understanding of the game — will pay the scalper's high prices. Ticket scalping will benefit athletic teams and performing artists — they will appear before more understanding and appreciative audiences.

So, is ticket scalping undesirable? Not on economic grounds. Both buyer and seller of a "scalped" ticket benefit and a more interested and appreciative audience results. Game sponsors may sacrifice revenue and profits, but that derives from their own misjudgement of equilibrium price.

price will mean less oats offered and will simultaneously encourage consumers to buy more. These adjustments are shown in Figure 4-5 by the arrows pointing down the supply and demand curves.

Any price below the equilibrium price will produce a shortage; quantity demanded will exceed quantity supplied. Competitive bidding by buyers will push the price up towards equilibrium. This rising price will simultaneously cause producers to increase the quantity supplied and buyers to want less, eliminating the shortage. These adjustments are shown in Figure 4-5 by the arrows pointing up the supply and demand curves. *The intersection of the supply curve and the demand curve for the product indicates the equilibrium point.* In this case, equilibrium price and quantity are $3 and 7000 bushels.

RATIONING FUNCTION OF PRICES

The ability of the competitive forces of supply and demand to establish a price where selling and buying decisions are synchronized is called the **rationing function of prices**. In this case, the equilibrium price of $3 "clears the market," leaving no burdensome surplus for the sellers and no inconvenient shortage for buyers. Freely made individual buying and selling decisions set this price that clears the market. The market mechanism of supply and demand dictates that any buyer who is willing and able to pay $3 for a bushel of oats will be able to acquire one. Similarly, any seller who is willing and able to produce bushels of oats and offer them for sale at a price of $3 will be able to do so. **(Key Question 7)**

CHANGES IN SUPPLY AND DEMAND

We know demand might change because of fluctuations in consumer tastes or incomes, changes in consumer expectations, or variations in the prices of related goods. Supply might vary in response to changes in technology, resource prices, or taxes. Now we are ready to consider the effect of changes in supply and demand on equilibrium price and quantity.

CHANGING DEMAND   First we analyze the effects of a change in demand, assuming supply is constant. Suppose that demand *increases*, as shown in Figure 4-6(a). What is the effect on price? The new intersection of the supply and demand curves is at a higher point on both the price and quantity axes, and an increase in demand, other things (supply) being equal, will have a *price-increasing effect* and a *quantity-increasing effect*. A decrease in demand, as illustrated in Figure 4-6(b), reveals a *price-decreasing effect* and a *quantity-decreasing effect*. Price falls and so does quantity. *Thus we find a direct relationship between a change in demand and the resulting changes in both equilibrium price and quantity.*

FIGURE 4-6   **Changes in demand and supply and the effects on price and quantity**

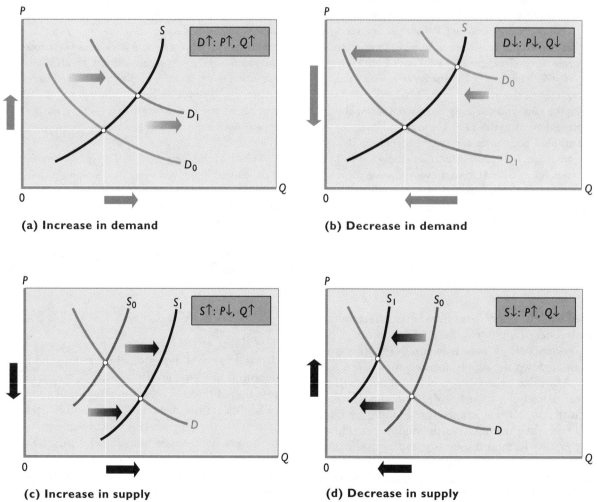

(a) Increase in demand

(b) Decrease in demand

(c) Increase in supply

(d) Decrease in supply

The increase in demand of (a) and the decrease in demand of (b) indicate a direct relationship between a change in demand and the resulting changes in equilibrium price and quantity. The increase in supply of (c) and the decrease in supply of (d) show an inverse relationship between a change in supply and the resulting change in equilibrium price, but a direct relationship between a change in supply and the accompanying change in equilibrium quantity.

CHANGING SUPPLY   Let's analyze the effect of a change in supply on price, assuming that demand is constant. If supply increases, as in Figure 4-6(c), the new intersection of supply and demand is at a lower equilibrium price. Equilibrium quantity, however, increases. If supply decreases, product price will rise. Figure 4-6(d) illustrates this situation. Here, price increases but quantity declines. In short, an increase in supply has a *price-decreasing* and a *quantity-increasing effect*. A decrease in supply has a *price-increasing* and a *quantity-decreasing effect. There is an inverse relationship between a change in supply and the resulting change in equilibrium price, but the relationship between a change in supply and the resulting change in equilibrium quantity is direct.*

SIMULTANEOUS CHANGES IN SUPPLY AND DEMAND

There may be situations in which both supply and demand change at the same time. There are four possibilities: (1) supply increases and demand decreases; (2) supply decreases and demand increases; (3) supply increases and demand increases; and (4) supply decreases and demand decreases. Table 4-9 summarizes these four cases. Draw a supply and demand diagram for each case to determine the effects on equilibrium price and quantity indicated in the table. **(Key Question 8)**

THE RESOURCE MARKET

As in the product market, resource supply curves are typically upsloping and resource demand curves are downsloping because they reflect a *direct* relationship between resource price and quantity supplied. It is in the interests of resource owners to supply more of a resource at a high price than at a low price. High-income payments in a particular occupation or industry encourage households to supply more of their resources. Low-income payments do the opposite.

On the demand side, businesses buy less of a given resource as its price rises and they substitute other, relatively low-priced, resources for it. More of a particular resource will be demanded at a low price than at a high price as entrepreneurs try to minimize costs. The result is a downsloping demand curve for the various resources.

"OTHER THINGS EQUAL" REVISITED

In Chapter 1 we explained that because of the difficulty of conducting controlled experiments, economists assume "other things are equal" in their analyses. We have seen in this chapter that a number of forces bear on both demand and supply. Therefore, in locating specific supply and demand curves such as D_0 and S in Figure 4-6(a), economists are isolating the impact of what they judge to be the most important determinant of the amounts supplied and demanded — that is, the price of the specific product under consideration. In thus representing the laws of demand and supply by downsloping and upsloping curves respectively, we assume that all determinants of demand (incomes, tastes, and so forth) and supply (resource prices, technology, and other factors) are constant. That is, price and quantity demanded are inversely related, *other things being equal*. And price and quantity supplied are directly related, *other things being equal*.

If you forget the "other things equal" assumption you can encounter confusing situations that *seem* to be in conflict with these laws. For example:

TABLE 4-9   **Effects of changes in both supply and demand**

	Change in supply	Change in demand	Effect on equilibrium price	Effect on equilibrium quantity
(1)	increase	decrease	decrease	indeterminate
(2)	decrease	increase	increase	indeterminate
(3)	increase	increase	indeterminate	increase
(4)	decrease	decrease	indeterminate	decrease

BOX 4-3   IN THE MEDIA

STEEL MAKERS FACE SOFTENING PRICES AND GROWING GLUT

HAMILTON (CP) — Another stormy year awaits steel makers as their market is flooded by production capacity and their profits are eroded by low prices.

Stelco Inc. chairman Fred Telmer offers a blunt forecast.

"I'm looking forward to a very gloomy winter," said Telmer in an interview from his company's downtown Stelco Tower headquarters.

"There's a lot of nervousness in the marketplace and prices are being held down. We're expecting a continuation of difficult conditions in 1992."

Dofasco chairman Paul Phoenix offers a similar assessment from his headquarters in Hamilton's industrialized northeast end.

"There's no pricing relief that we can see," Phoenix said. "And we're looking at ongoing poor market conditions."

Phoenix said a worldwide oversupply of steel and shrinking demand continue to drive down steel prices despite rising production costs.

The Toronto Star, January 2, 1992. By permission of The Canadian Press.

The Story in Brief

Executives at Stelco Inc. and Dofasco Inc. — Canada's two largest steel producers — complain of "ongoing poor market conditions" driving down steel prices.

The Economics Behind the Story

• Demand and supply determine both the market price and quantity transacted in a market.

• The world supply of steel is increasing, while the demand for steel is falling.

• We know that the supply and demand curves shift when certain factors change (see Tables 4-4 and 4-7). There is no indication in the story of why the world supply of steel is increasing while the demand for it is falling.

• We expect the price of steel to drop and the quantity exchanged to fall when the supply of steel shifts right and the demand for steel shifts left.

• Draw a graph that represents the economic analysis behind this story. What are some of the likely factors that caused the demand and supply curves for steel to shift?

Suppose General Motors of Canada sells 100,000 Cutlasses in 1994 at $21,000; 150,000 at $22,000 in 1995; and 200,000 in 1996 at $23,000. Price and the number purchased vary *directly,* and these real-world data seem to be at odds with the law of demand.

These data do *not* refute the law of demand. The catch is that the law of demand's "other things equal" assumption has been violated over the three years in the example. Because of, for example,

growing incomes, population growth, and relatively high gasoline prices, all increasing the attractiveness of intermediate and compact cars, the demand curve for Cutlasses has increased over the years — shifted to the right as from D_0 to D_1 in Figure 4-6(a) — causing price to rise and, simultaneously, a larger quantity to be purchased.

Conversely, consider Figure 4-6(d). Comparing the original S_0D and the new S_1D equilibrium positions, we note that *less* of the product is being sold or supplied at a higher price. Price and quantity supplied seem to be *inversely* related, rather than *directly* related as the law of supply indicates. The catch, again, is that the "other things equal" assumption underlying the upsloping supply curve has been violated. Perhaps production costs have gone up or a specific tax has been levied on this product, shifting the supply curve from S_0 to S_1. These examples also emphasize the importance of our earlier distinction between a "change in the quantity demanded (or supplied)" and a "change in demand (supply)."

QUICK REVIEW 4-3

1. In competitive markets, price adjusts to the equilibrium level at which quantity demanded equals quantity supplied.

2. A change in demand changes both equilibrium price and equilibrium quantity in the same direction as the change in demand.

3. A change in supply causes equilibrium price to change in the opposite direction, but equilibrium quantity to change in the same direction, as the change in supply.

4. Over time, equilibrium price and quantity may change in directions that seem at odds with the laws of demand and supply because the "other things equal" assumption is violated.

CHAPTER SUMMARY

1. A market is any institution or arrangement that brings together buyers and sellers of some product or service.

2. Demand refers to the willingness of buyers to purchase a given product during a specific time period at each of the various prices at which it might be sold. According to the law of demand, consumers will ordinarily buy more of a product at a low price than they will at a high price. Other things being equal, the relationship between price and quantity demanded is negative or inverse and demand graphs as a downsloping curve.

3. Changes in one or more of the basic determinants of demand — consumer tastes, the number of buyers in the market, the money incomes of consumers, the prices of related goods, and consumer expectations — will cause the market demand curve to shift. A shift to the right is an increase in demand; a shift to the left, a decrease in demand. A "change in demand" is distinguished from a "change in the quantity demanded," the latter involving the movement from one point to another point on a fixed demand curve because of a change in the price of the product under consideration.

4. Supply is the amounts of a product producers would be willing to offer in the market during a given time period at each possible price. The law of supply says that producers, other things being equal, will offer more of a product at a higher price than they will at a low price. The relationship between price and quantity supplied is a positive or direct one, and the supply curve is upsloping.

5. A change in resource prices, production techniques, taxes or subsidies, the prices of other goods, price expectations, or the number of sellers in the market will cause the supply curve of a product to shift. A shift to the right is an increase in supply; a shift to the left, a decrease in supply. In contrast, a change in the price of the product under consideration will result in a change in the quantity supplied, a movement from one point to another on a given supply curve.

6. Under competition, the interaction of market demand and market supply will adjust price until the quantity demanded and the quantity supplied are equal. This is the equilibrium price. The corresponding quantity is the equilibrium quantity.

7. The ability of market forces to synchronize selling and buying decisions to eliminate potential surpluses or shortages is termed the "rationing function" of prices.

8. A change in either demand or supply will cause equilibrium price and quantity to change. There is a direct relationship between a change in demand and the resulting changes in equilibrium price and quantity. Though the relationship between a change in supply and the resulting change in equilibrium price is inverse, the relationship between a change in supply and equilibrium quantity is direct.

9. The concepts of supply and demand are also applicable to the resource market.

TERMS AND CONCEPTS

change in demand (supply) versus change in the
    quantity demanded (supplied) (pp. 62, 64, 66, 67)
complementary goods (p. 63)
demand (p. 58)
demand curve (p. 60)
demand schedule (p. 58)
diminishing marginal utility (p. 59)
equilibrium price and quantity (p. 68)
income and substitution effects (p. 59)
inferior goods (p. 62)

law of demand (p. 59)
law of supply (p. 64)
market (p. 58)
normal (superior) goods (p. 62)
rationing function of prices (p. 69)
shortage (p. 68)
substitute goods (p. 63)
supply (p. 64)
supply schedule (curve) (p. 64)
surplus (p. 68)

QUESTIONS AND STUDY SUGGESTIONS

1. Explain the law of demand. Why does a demand curve slope downward? What are the determinants of demand? What happens to the demand curve when each of these determinants changes? Distinguish between a change in demand and a change in the quantity demanded, noting the cause(s) of each.

2. *Key Question* *What effect will each of the following have on the demand for product B?*

    a. *Product B becomes more fashionable.*
    b. *The price of substitute product C falls.*
    c. *Incomes decline if B is an inferior good.*
    d. *Consumers anticipate the price of B will be lower in the near future.*
    e. *The price of complementary product D falls.*
    f. *Foreign tariff barriers on B are eliminated.*

3. Explain the following news dispatch from Hull, England: "The fish market here slumped today to what local commentators called 'a disastrous level' — all because of a shortage of potatoes. The potatoes are one of the main ingredients in a dish that figures on almost every café menu — fish and chips."

4. Explain the law of supply. Why does the supply curve slope upward? What are the determinants of supply? What happens to the supply curve when each of these determinants changes? Distinguish between a change in supply and a change in the quantity supplied, noting the cause(s) of each.

5. *Key Question*   What effect will each of the following have on the supply of product B?

a. A technological advance in the methods of producing B.

b. A decline in the number of firms in industry B.

c. An increase in the prices of resources required in the production of B.

d. The expectation that the equilibrium price of B will be lower in the future than it is currently.

e. A decline in the price of product A, a good whose production requires substantially the same techniques and resources as does the production of B.

f. The levying of a specific sale tax on B.

g. The granting of a 50-cent-per-unit subsidy for each unit of B produced.

6. "In the oats market, demand often exceeds supply and supply sometimes exceeds demand." "The price of oats rises and falls in response to changes in supply and demand." In which of these two statements are the terms "supply" and "demand" used correctly? Explain.

7. *Key Question*   Suppose the total demand for eggs (Grade A large) and the total supply of eggs (Grade A large) per month in the Halifax market are as follows:

Thousands of dozens demanded	Price per dozen	Thousands of dozens supplied	Surplus (+) or shortage (-)
85	$1.25	72	_____
80	1.30	73	_____
75	1.35	75	_____
70	1.40	77	_____
65	1.45	79	_____
60	1.50	81	_____

a. What will be the market or equilibrium price? What is the equilibrium quantity? Using the surplus-shortage column, explain why your answers are correct.

b. Using the above data, graph the demand for eggs and the supply of eggs. Be sure to label the axes of your graph correctly. Label equilibrium price "P" and equilibrium quantity "Q".

c. Why will $1.25 not be the equilibrium price in this market? Why not $1.50? "Surpluses drive prices up; shortages drive them down." Do you agree?

d. Now suppose that the government establishes a ceiling price of, say, $1.30 for these eggs. Explain carefully the effects of this ceiling price. Demonstrate your answers graphically. What might prompt government to establish a ceiling price?

e. "Government-fixed prices strip the price mechanism of its rationing function." Explain this statement relating your explanation to your answers to 7d.

8. *Key Question*   How will each of the following changes in demand and/or supply affect equilibrium price and equilibrium quantity in a competitive market; that is, do price and quantity rise, fall, remain unchanged, or are the answers indeterminate, depending on the magnitudes of the shifts in supply and demand? You should rely on a supply and demand diagram to verify answers.

a. Supply decreases and demand remains constant.

b. Demand decreases and supply remains constant.

c. Supply increases and demand is constant.

d. Demand increases and supply increases.

e. *Demand increases and supply is constant.*

f. *Supply increases and demand decreases.*

g. *Demand increases and supply decreases.*

h. *Demand decreases and supply decreases.*

9. "Prices are the automatic regulator that tends to keep production and consumption in line with each other." Explain.

10. Explain: "Even though parking meters may yield little or no net revenue, they should nevertheless be retained because of the rationing function they perform."

11. Critically evaluate: "In comparing the two equilibrium positions in Figure 4-6a, I note that a larger amount is actually purchased at a higher price. This refutes the law of demand."

12. Suppose you go to a recycling centre and are paid 25¢ per kilogram for your aluminum cans. However, the recycler charges you 20¢ per bundle to accept your old newspapers. Use demand and supply diagrams to portray both markets. Can you explain how different government policies with respect to the recycling of aluminum and paper might account for these different market outcomes?

13. **Advanced Analysis**   Assume that the demand for a commodity is represented by the equation $P = 10 - 0.2Q_d$ and supply by the equation $P = 2 + 0.2Q_s$, where Q_d and Q_s are quantity demanded and quantity supplied respectively and P is price. Using the equilibrium condition $Q_s = Q_d$ solve the equations to determine equilibrium price. Then determine equilibrium quantity. Graph the two equations to equations to substantiate your answers.

14. (Applying the Theory) Discuss the economic aspects of ticket scalping, specifying gainers and losers.

CHAPTER 5

THE PUBLIC SECTOR

We noted in Chapter 2 that a society can choose various ways to deal with the economizing problem. A pure market system is one possibility; at the other extreme is a command economy, in which a central government makes the decisions as to what to produce, how much to produce, by what method to produce it, and how that production is distributed.

In fact, all economies are "mixed" to some extent; government and the market system share the responsibility of responding to the Five Fundamental Questions. In Canada, we have an economy dominated by markets, but government has played a significant role in the economic system of this country from the time of Confederation.

In this chapter we investigate the possible economic functions of the public sector in a market economy. Much emphasis is put on the crucial role of government when markets fail to fulfil their function of co-ordinating economic activity. The chapter ends with a discussion of the growth of government in recent decades and the ongoing debate on the extent of government involvement in self-regulating markets.

BOX 5-1   THE BIG PICTURE

Private markets are very good at getting the most out of available resources. Markets also produce those goods and services that people with income to spend want most. But the market system does not arise instantaneously on its own. It requires certain institutions to function well. Among the most important of these is a central government that provides an environment conducive to a market economy.

Sometimes the market system fails to do its job of co-ordinating production and consumption decisions, or does it badly. We call these instances "market failures," and they require government intervention.

As you read this chapter, keep the following points in mind:

- At times market participants have an effect on individuals not involved in market transactions. These effects can be negative, as in the case of a firm polluting the water supply of a village, or positive, as when a neighbour undertakes to beautify her house.
- Sometimes the market system does not produce enough of a specific good that is economically or socially justified. In such instances the government either produces the good itself or gives subsidies to private firms to supply it.

THE ECONOMIC FUNCTIONS OF GOVERNMENT

There is a mistaken view held by some that in an economy dominated by markets, less government is better since government action distorts the efficient function of markets. These critics point out that private markets are regulated by an "invisible hand" that co-ordinates economic activities for the good of both individuals and society.

While economists generally agree that self-regulating markets are efficient at allocating scarce resources, they also hold that governments have crucial roles in a market economy. The following outlines what a government must provide to strengthen and facilitate the operation of the market system.

LEGAL AND SOCIAL FRAMEWORK

Government provides the legal framework and the basic services needed for a market economy to operate effectively. The legal framework provides the legal status of business enterprises, defines the rights of private ownership, and makes it possible to provide for the enforcement of contracts. Government also establishes legal "rules of the game" governing the relationships of businesses, resource suppliers, and consumers with one another. Through legislation, government can referee economic relationships, detect foul play, and impose appropriate penalties.

Services provided by government include police powers to maintain internal order, a system of standards for measuring the weight and quality of products, and a monetary system to facilitate exchange of goods and services.

The Food and Drug Act and Regulations of 1920 is an example of how government has strengthened the market system. This act sets rules of conduct governing producers in their relationships with consumers. It prohibits the sale of adulterated and misbranded foods and drugs, requires net weights and ingredients of products to be specified on their containers, establishes quality standards that must be stated on labels of canned foods, and prohibits deceptive claims on patent-medicine labels. These measures help prevent fraudulent activities by producers and increase the public's confidence in the integrity of the market system. Similar legislation pertains to labour-management relations and relations of business firms to one another.

This type of government activity is presumed to improve resource allocation. Supplying a medium of exchange, ensuring product quality, defining ownership rights, and enforcing contracts all increase the volume of exchange. This widens markets and permits greater specialization in the use of property and human resources. Such specialization means a more efficient allocation of resources. However, some argue that government overregulates interactions of businesses, consumers, and workers, stifling economic incentives and impairing productive efficiency.

MAINTAINING COMPETITION

Competition is the basic regulatory mechanism in a market economy. It is the force that subjects producers and resource suppliers to the dictates of consumer sovereignty. With competition, buyers are the boss, the market is their agent, and businesses are their servants.

It's completely different with **monopoly**. *Monopoly exists if the number of sellers becomes small enough for each seller to influence total supply and therefore the price of the commodity being sold.*

In a monopoly, sellers can influence, or "rig," the market in their own interests, to the detriment of society as a whole. Through their ability to influence total supply, monopolists can restrict the output of products and charge higher prices and, frequently, have substantial economic profits. These above-competitive prices and profits directly conflict with the interests of consumers. Monopolists are not regulated by the will of society as are competitive sellers. Producer sovereignty replaces consumer sovereignty. In a monopoly resources are allocated according to the profit-seeking interests of sellers rather than the wants of society as a whole. Monopoly causes a misallocation of economic resources.

In Canada government has attempted to control monopoly in two ways.

1. REGULATION AND OWNERSHIP In the case of "natural monopolies" — industries in which technological and economic realities rule out competitive markets — government has created public commissions regulating prices and service standards. Transportation, communications, and electric and other utilities are industries that are regulated in varying degrees. At municipal levels of government, public ownership of electric and water utilities is common.

2. ANTI-COMBINES LAWS In nearly all markets, efficient production can be attained with a high degree of competition. The federal government has therefore enacted a series of anti-combines laws, to maintain and strengthen competition as a regulator of business behaviour.

Even if the legal foundation of market institutions is assured and competition is maintained, there is still a need for certain additional economic functions by government. *The market economy has certain biases and shortcomings that make it necessary for government to supplement and modify its operation in certain instances.*

REDISTRIBUTION OF INCOME

The market system is impersonal. It may distribute income with more inequality than society desires. The market system yields very large incomes to those whose labour, by virtue of inherent ability and acquired education and skills, commands high wages. Similarly, those who possess — through hard work or easy inheritance — valuable capital and land receive large incomes.

But others in our society have less ability; have received modest amounts of education and training; and have not accumulated or inherited property resources. Thus, their incomes are very low. Furthermore, many of the aged, the physically and mentally handicapped, and female-headed families earn only very small incomes or, like the unemployed, no incomes at all through the market system. In the market system, there is considerable inequality in the distribution of money income and therefore in the distribution of total output among individual households. Poverty in the midst of overall plenty in our economy persists and is a major economic and political issue.

Government's role in attempting to reduce income inequality is reflected in a variety of policies and programs.

1. TRANSFERS *Transfer payments* provide relief to the destitute, aid to the dependent and handicapped, and unemployment insurance to the unemployed. Social insurance programs provide financial support for the retired and aged sick. These programs transfer income from government to households that would otherwise have little or none.

2. MARKET INTERVENTION Government also alters the distribution of income by *market intervention*, that is, by modifying the prices established by market forces. Price supports for farmers and minimum-wage legislation are examples of government price fixing designed to raise incomes of specific groups.

3. TAXATION   The personal income tax is used to take a larger proportion of the incomes of the rich than the poor.

REALLOCATION OF RESOURCES

Economists recognize *market failure* occurs when the competitive market system either (1) produces the "wrong" amounts of certain goods and services, or (2) fails to allocate any resources whatsoever to the production of certain goods and services whose output is economically justified. The first case involves "spillovers" or "externalities," and the second "public" or "social" goods.

SPILLOVERS OR EXTERNALITIES

The idea that competitive markets automatically bring about efficient resources rests on the assumption that *all* the benefits and costs of production and consumption of each product are fully reflected in the market demand and supply curves. It is assumed that there are no *spillovers* or *externalities* associated with the production or consumption of any good or service.

A *spillover* occurs when benefits or costs of production or consumption of a good "spill over" onto parties other than the immediate buyer or seller. Spillovers are also called *externalities* because they are benefits and costs to a third party external to the market transaction.

SPILLOVER COSTS   When production or consumption of a commodity inflicts costs on a third party without compensation, these costs are **spillover costs**. Examples of spillover costs include environmental pollution. When a chemical manufacturer or meat-packing plant dumps its wastes into a lake or river, swimmers, fishing enthusiasts, and boaters — not to mention communities' water supplies — suffer spillover costs. Human health hazards may arise and wildlife may be damaged or destroyed. When a petroleum refinery pollutes the air with smoke or a paint factory creates distressing odours, the community bears spillover costs for which it is not compensated. Acid rain and global warming are spillover costs that receive almost daily media attention.

What are the economic effects? Recall that costs underlie the firm's supply curve. When a firm avoids some costs by polluting, its supply curve will

lie further to the right than when it bears the full costs of production. This results in a larger output and causes an *overallocation* of resources to the production of this good.

CORRECTING FOR SPILLOVER COSTS   Government can do two things to correct this overallocation of resources. Both are designed to *internalize* the external costs, that is, to make the offending firm pay these costs rather than shift them to society.

1. LEGISLATION   In our examples of air and water pollution, the most direct action is *legislation* prohibiting or limiting pollution. Such legislation forces potential polluters to bear costs of properly disposing of industrial wastes. Firms must buy and install smoke-abatement equipment or facilities to purify water contaminated by manufacturing processes. The idea is to force potential offenders, under the threat of legal action, to bear *all* costs associated with their production.

2. SPECIFIC TAXES   A less direct action is based on the fact that taxes are a cost and therefore a determinant of a firm's supply curve (Chapter 4). Government might levy a *specific tax* that equals or approximates the spillover costs per unit of output. Through this tax, government attempts to shove back onto the offending firm those spillover costs that private industry would otherwise avoid and thus eliminate the overallocation of resources.

SPILLOVER BENEFITS   But spillovers may also appear as benefits. Production or consumption of certain goods and services may bring spillover or external benefits on third parties or the community at large for which payment or compensation is not required. Measles and polio immunization shots result in direct benefits to the immediate consumer. But immunization against these contagious diseases brings widespread and substantial spillover benefits to the entire community. Discovery of an AIDS vaccine would benefit society far beyond those vaccinated. Unvaccinated individuals would benefit by the slowing of the spread of the disease.

Education is another example of **spillover benefits**. Education benefits individual consumers: "More educated" people generally earn higher incomes than "less educated" people. But education also provides benefits to society. The economy as a whole benefits

BOX 5-2   IN THE MEDIA

SCALING BACK TO SAVE SALMON

BY MIRO CERNETIG

KINCOLITH, B.C. — Just as they have done for millenniums, salmon are swimming back to the Nass River, triggering familiar sights around this often-forgotten Indian fishing village on the edge of the Alaskan Panhandle.

Bald eagles skim the bay, diving to snag a fish with their talons. Indians fish along the tidal flats for dinner. And 70-year-old Sydney Alexander is out in his yard, tending nets and warning passers-by that the West Coast's greatest fishery is on the edge of ruin.

"There's far too many people fishing," he complains, looking out toward the ice-blue bay that is filled each summer with an armada of Canadian fishing boats. "They're spreading the fish too thin."

That, in a dozen words, is as good as you will get of what ails the West Coast salmon fishery, now into another hot summer, complete with the threat of a fish war with the United States, racial tension between Indians and non-natives, and charges of rampant overfishing.

Standing on a tidal flat, upon which his nine-tonne skiff sits in clumps of windswept elephant grass, Mr. Alexander points out why most Pacific salmon never make it back up into the Nass River's spawning grounds.

To the east, beyond the mouth of the rushing river, Nisga'a Indians are fishing, one of many aboriginal-only fisheries proliferating along the British Columbia coast.

To the west, where the Queen Charlotte Islands are a purple blur on the horizon, sit fishing lodges where thousands of trophy hunters catch the endangered chinook, the largest of the salmon.

To the north, across the U.S. border, floats the Alaskan fishing fleet, a 2,500-vessel flotilla that is accused by Canada of overfishing. And just over the southern horizon is Canada's own commercial fleet, now universally viewed as a killing machine that could obliterate, in a few hours, salmon runs that have taken generations to build.

"If they're not careful," Mr. Alexander laments, "there won't be enough salmon left."

The complexities of managing the province's salmon stocks could — and do — fill volumes. But the major threat to the salmon is that the West Coast fishing fleet has grown in size and efficiency, thanks to new boats and better technology.

The best measure of this is the drastically reduced time it takes to fish, even though the amount of salmon the fleet has been allowed to catch actually has gone up. In 1972, the salmon season in Johnstone Strait, a rich fishing ground, was 51 days for seine boats, the most potent fish-harvesting machines on the ocean. By 1982, that had shrunk to 24 days. Last year, it was 3.25 days.

For fishermen who use gill nets, the season shrank from 125 days in 1972 to 32 days in 1982 and to only 19 days in 1994.

That has caused headaches for Fisheries Department officers charged with regulating the amount of fish taken.

"Such a large number of vessels can put fisheries managers in difficult-if-not-impossible situations, as slight miscalculations of the catch can have severely detrimental effects on salmon stocks," says a new DFO report that looks into the department's attempts to gauge the amount of fish the powerful fleet is harvesting. "There is growing concern that the present management system used to manage the commercial Salmon [fleet] is not sustainable."

None of this is good news. But it finally is forcing fishing companies, fishermen and the Fisheries Department to agree that Canada's salmon fleet must be trimmed, and the system of UI, which keeps marginal players in the industry, overhauled. This fall, industry and the federal government will begin to develop a strategy to reduce the fleet by from 10 to 50 per cent. If no consensus is reached, Ottawa warns, it will cut the fleet unilaterally.

SOURCE: *Globe and Mail*, July 8, 1995 pp. A1 and A6. Reprinted with permission.

The Story in Brief

The West Coast salmon stocks are dwindling because of overfishing by Canadian and American fishing fleets, as well as thousands of recreational fishing enthusiasts.

The Economics Behind the Story

• Too many people fishing with modern boats and technology are able to wipe out the West Coast salmon stocks. This is an example of market failure; it is the result of the absence of private property rights. A market failure requires government intervention.

• Since fish do not stay in one place, it is impossible to establish private property rights. Thus, the only solution is for the federal government to reduce the salmon taken in each season — to the point where the existing fish stocks will be maintained. The easiest way to cut down on the number of salmon taken each year is to reduce the fishing fleet. Since a licence is already required, the federal government would reduce the number of fishing licences issued.

• In recent years salmon "fish farms" have appeared in Canada. Fish are raised in an enclosed area. Why do you not expect overfishing under such circumstances? Use marginal benefit-cost analysis to help you answer the question.

from a more versatile and more productive labour force, on the one hand, and smaller outlays in crime prevention, law enforcement, and welfare programs, on the other. There is evidence indicating that any worker with a *given* educational or skill level will be more productive if associated workers have more education. In other words, worker X becomes more productive because fellow-workers Y and Z are more educated. Also significant is the fact that political participation increases with the level of education; the percentage of persons who vote increases with the educational level of the population.

Spillover benefits mean the market demand curve, which reflects only private benefits, understates total benefits. The demand curve for the product lies further to the left than if all benefits were taken into account by the market. This means that a smaller amount is produced or, alternatively stated, there is an *underallocation* of resources to the product.

CORRECTING FOR SPILLOVER BENEFITS   How might the underallocation of resources associated with spillover benefits be corrected? The answer is to either subsidize consumers (increase demand) or subsidize producers (increase supply), or, in the extreme, have government produce the product.

1. INCREASE DEMAND   In the care of higher education, government provides low-interest student loans and grants to provide student employment.

2. INCREASE SUPPLY   In some cases, government might find it administratively simpler to subsidize producers. This is also true with higher education where provincial governments provide substantial portions of the budgets of colleges and universities. These subsidies lower costs to students and increase educational supply. Public subsidizing of immunization programs, hospitals, and medical research are additional examples.

3. GOVERNMENT PROVISION   A third policy option arises if spillover benefits are extremely large: Government may choose to finance or, in the extreme, to own and operate such industries. This option leads us into a discussion of public goods and services.

PUBLIC GOODS AND SERVICES

Private goods, which are produced through the market system, are *divisible* in that they come in units small enough to be afforded by individual buyers. Also, private goods are subject to the **exclusion**

principle: those willing and able to pay the equilibrium price get the product but those unable or unwilling to pay are excluded from the benefits provided by that product.

Certain goods and services — **public goods** — would not be produced by the market system because their characteristics are opposite those of private goods. Public goods are *indivisible*, involving such large units that they cannot ordinarily be sold to individual buyers. Individuals can buy hamburgers, computers, and automobiles through the market, but not missiles, highways, space telescopes, and air-traffic control.

More importantly, the exclusion principle does *not* apply to public goods; there is no effective way of excluding individuals from their benefits. Benefits from private goods come from their *purchase*; benefits from public goods accrue to society from their *production*.

ILLUSTRATIONS   The classic public goods example is a lighthouse on a treacherous coast. The construction of a lighthouse would be economically justified if benefits (fewer shipwrecks) exceeded production costs. But the benefit accruing to each individual user would not justify the purchase of such a large and indivisible product. But once in operation, its warning light is a guide to *all* ships. There is no practical way to exclude certain ships from its benefits. Therefore, why should any ship owner voluntarily pay for the benefits received from the light? The light is there for all to see, and a ship captain cannot be excluded from seeing it if the ship owner chooses not to pay. This is called the **free-rider problem**; *people can receive benefits from a good without contributing to its costs.*

Because the exclusion principle does not apply, there is no economic incentive for private enterprises to supply lighthouses. If the services of the lighthouse cannot be priced and sold, it will be unprofitable for private firms to devote resources to lighthouses. Here is a service that brings substantial benefits but for which the market would allocate no resources. National defence, flood control, public health, satellite navigation systems, and insect-abatement programs are other public goods. If society is to enjoy such goods and services, they must be provided by the public sector and financed by compulsory charges in the form of taxes.

LARGE SPILLOVER BENEFITS   While the exclusion principle distinguishes public from private goods, many other goods and services are provided by government even though the exclusion principle *could* be applied. Such goods and services as education, streets and highways, police and fire protection, libraries and museums, preventive medicine, and sewage disposal could be subject to the exclusion principle. All could be priced and provided by private producers through the market system. But, as noted earlier, these are all services with substantial spillover benefits and would be underproduced by the market system. Therefore, government provides them to avoid the underallocation of resources that would otherwise occur. Such goods and services are called *quasi-public goods*.

ALLOCATING RESOURCES TO PUBLIC GOODS

The price system will fail to allocate resources for public goods and will underallocate resources for quasi-public goods. What is the mechanism by which such goods get produced?

Public goods are purchased through the government on the basis of group, or collective, choices, in contrast to private goods, which are purchased from private enterprises on the basis of individual choices. The types and quantities of public goods produced are determined in a democracy by voting. The quantities of the various public goods consumed are a matter of public policy.[1] These group decisions supplement the choices of households and businesses in answering the Five Fundamental Questions.

How are resources reallocated from production of private goods to production of public goods? In a full-employment economy, government must free resources from private employment to make them available for production of public goods. The means of releasing resources from private uses is to reduce private demand

---

[1] There are differences between *dollar voting*, which dictates output in the private sector of the economy, and *political voting*, which determines output in the public sector. The rich person has many more votes to cast in the private sector than does the poor person. In the public sector, each — at least in theory — has an equal say. Furthermore, the children who cast their votes for bubble gum and comic books in the private sector are banned by virtue of their age from the registering of social choices.

for them. This is accomplished by levying taxes on businesses and households, diverting some of their incomes — some of their potential purchasing power — out of the income-expenditure streams. With lower incomes, businesses and households must cut back their investment and consumption spending. *Taxes diminish private demand for goods and services, which in turn prompts a drop in the private demand for resources.* By diverting purchasing power from private spenders to government, taxes free resources from private uses.

Government expenditure of the tax revenues can then reabsorb these resources in the provision of public goods and services. Corporation and personal income taxes release resources from production of investment goods — printing presses, boxcars, warehouses — and consumer goods — food, clothing, and television sets. Government expenditures can reabsorb these resources in production of post offices, military aircraft, and new schools and highways. Government purposely reallocates resources to bring about significant changes in the composition of the economy's total output. **(Key Questions 3 and 4)**

STABILIZATION

Historically, the most recent function of government is that of stabilizing the economy — assisting the private economy to achieve full employment and a stable price level. Here we will only outline (rather than fully explain) how government tries to do this.

The level of output depends directly on total or aggregate expenditures. A high level of total spending will be profitable for industries to produce large outputs. This means that resources be employed at high levels. But aggregate spending may either fall short of, or exceed, that particular level that will provide for full employment and price stability. Two possibilities, unemployment or inflation, may then occur.

1. UNEMPLOYMENT The level of total spending in the private sector may be too low for full employment. Thus, the government may choose to increase private spending so that total spending — private and public — will be sufficient to generate full employment. Government can do this by using the same techniques — government spending and taxes — as

---

[2] In macroeconomics we learn that government can also use monetary policy — changes in the nation's money supply and interest rates — to help achieve economic stability.

it uses to reallocate resources to production of public goods. Specifically, government might increase its own spending on public goods and services on the one hand, and reduce taxes to stimulate private spending on the other.[2]

2. INFLATION If total expenditures are greater than the economy's capacity to produce, the price level will rise. Excessive aggregate spending is inflationary. Government's obligation here is to eliminate the excess spending. It can do this by cutting its own expenditures and by raising taxes to curtail private spending.

QUICK REVIEW 5-1

1. Government enhances the operation of the market system by providing an appropriate legal foundation and promoting competition.

2. Transfer payments, direct market intervention, and the tax system are ways government can lessen income inequality.

3. Government can correct the overallocation of resources associated with spillover costs through legislation or specific taxes; the underallocation of resources associated with spillover benefits can be offset by government subsidies.

4. Government must provide public goods because they are indivisible and the exclusion principle does not apply to them.

5. Government spending and tax revenues can be manipulated to stabilize the economy.

THE CIRCULAR FLOW REVISITED

Government is thoroughly integrated into the real and monetary flows that make up our economy. Let's re-examine the redistributional, allocative, and stabilization functions of government in terms of Chapter 2's circular flow model. In Figure 5-1 flows (1) through (4) restate Figure 2-6. Flows (1) and (2) show business expenditures for the resources provided by households. These expenditures are costs to businesses, but represent wage, rent, interest, and profit income to households. Flows (3) and (4) portray households making consumer expenditures for the goods and services produced by businesses.

FIGURE 5-1   The circular flow and the public sector

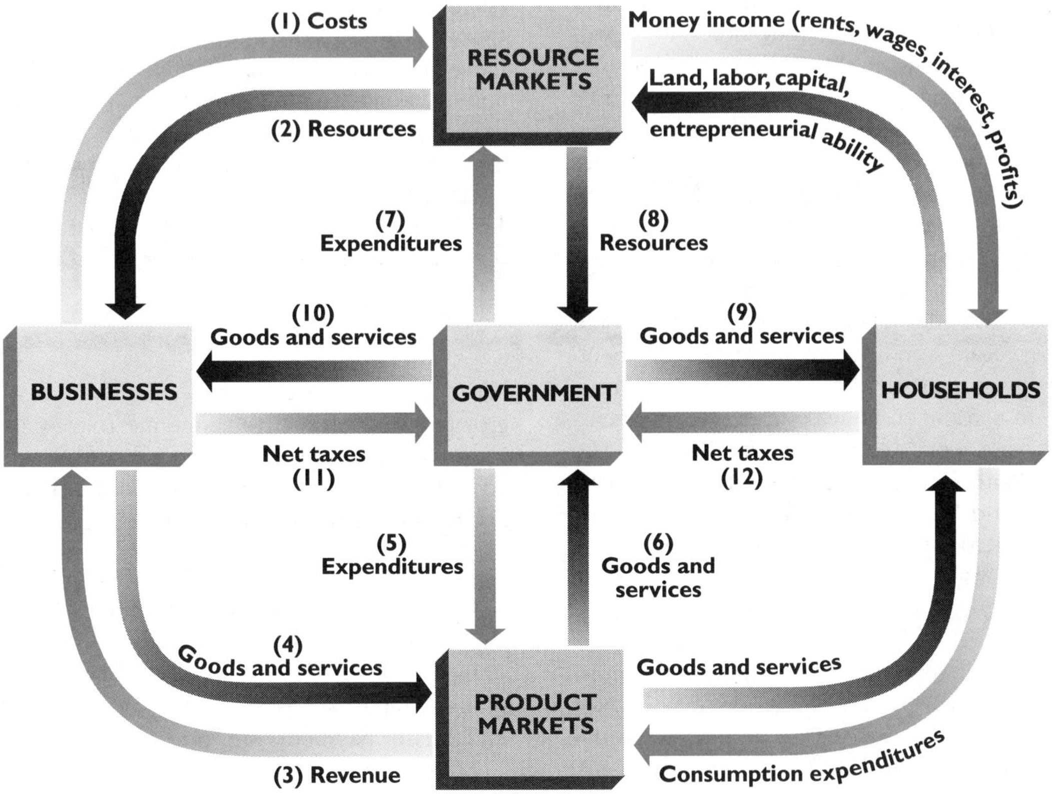

Government expenditures, taxes, and transfer payments affect the distribution of income, the allocation of resources, and the levels of economic activity.

Now consider the numerous modifications that stem from the addition of government. Flows (5) through (8) tell us that government makes purchases in both product and resource markets. Specifically, flows (5) and (6) represent government purchasing such things as paper, computers, and military hardware from private businesses. Flows (7) and (8) reflect government purchases of resources. The federal government employs and pays salaries to members of Parliament, the armed forces, and various other bureaucrats. Provincial and municipal governments hire teachers, bus drivers, police, and firefighters. The federal government might lease or purchase land to expand a military base; a city may buy land to build a new elementary school.

Government then provides public goods and services to both households and businesses as shown by flows (9) and (10). Financing public goods and services requires tax payments by businesses and house-

holds as reflected in flows (11) and (12). We have labelled these flows as *net* taxes to acknowledge that they also include "taxes in reverse" in the form of transfer payments to households and subsidies to businesses. Thus, flow (11) reflects not merely corporate income, sales, and excise taxes flowing from businesses to government but also various subsidies to farmers and some private sector firms. Most business subsidies are "concealed" in the form of low-interest loans, loan guarantees, tax concessions, or the public provision of facilities at prices less than costs. Similarly, government collects taxes (personal income taxes, payroll taxes) directly from households and makes available transfer payments, for example, welfare payments and social insurance benefits as shown by flow (12).

Our circular flow model shows us how government can alter the distribution of income, reallocate resources, and change the level of economic activity. The structure of taxes and transfer payments can have a significant impact on income distribution. In flow (12) a tax structure that draws tax revenues primarily from well-to-do households combined with a system of transfer payments to low-income households will result in greater equality in the distribution of income.

Flows (6) and (8) reflect an allocation of resources different from that of a purely private economy. Government buys goods and labour services that differ from those purchased by households.

Finally, all governmental flows suggest ways government might try to stabilize the economy. If there is unemployment, an increase in government spending, while taxes and transfers are held constant, would increase aggregate spending, output, and employment. Similarly, given the level of government expenditures, a decline in taxes or an increase in transfer payments would increase spendable incomes and boost private spending. With inflation, the opposite government policies would be in order: reduced government spending, increased taxes, and reduced transfers.

THE SIZE OF GOVERNMENT

The size of governments has increased significantly since the end of World War II. Not only have the number of employees of the federal, provincial, and municipal governments

increased, but the shares of the total output of goods and services governments take in taxes and spend have also risen significantly. In 1994 the expenditures of all three levels of governments in Canada collectively represented about 45% of the annual production of the country; this is more than double what it was in 1945. Figure 5-2 shows the growth of government expenditures and revenues of all three levels of governments in Canada since 1970. Expenditures have risen more rapidly than revenues, giving rise to persistent deficits.

GROWTH OF GOVERNMENT OUTLAYS

We can get a general impression of the size and growth of government's economic role by examining government purchases of goods and services and government transfer payments. The distinction between these two types of outlays is significant.

1. **Government purchases** are "exhaustive"; they directly absorb or employ resources. For example, the purchase of a car absorbs the labour of engineers along with steel, plastic, and a host of other inputs.

2. **Transfer payments** are "nonexhaustive"; they do not directly absorb resources or account for pro-

---

FIGURE 5-2   The growth of government

Government* Balance

An indication of the increasing growth of government is the expanding combined expenditures and revenues of the federal, provincial, and municipal governments. Both government revenues and expenditures have increased rapidly since 1970.

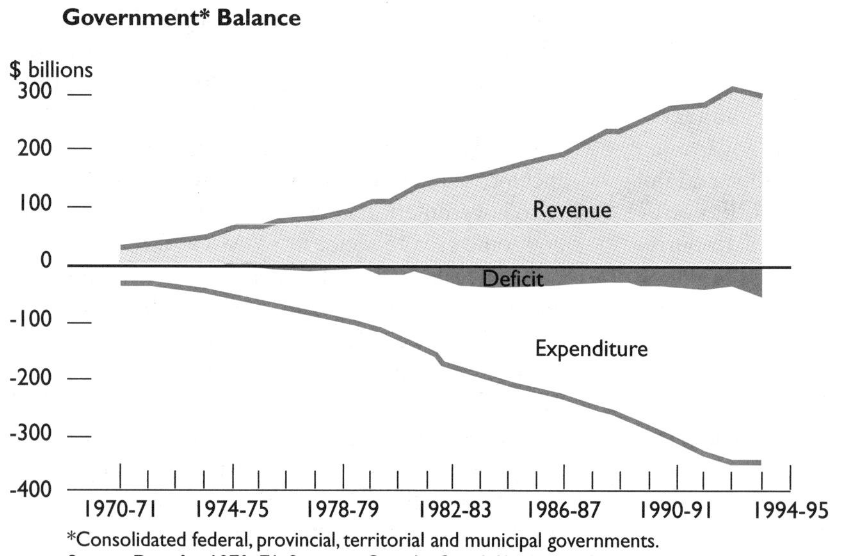

*Consolidated federal, provincial, territorial and municipal governments.
Source: Data for 1970–71, Statistics Canada, *Canada Yearbook, 1994*; for the remaining years computed from data in Statistic Canada, *Canadian Economic Observer, Statistical Summary*.

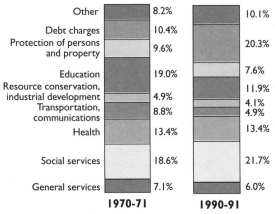

FIGURE 5-3 The trend in government expenditures

Government* Expenditures

Category	1970-71	1990-91
Other	8.2%	10.1%
Debt charges	10.4%	20.3%
Protection of persons and property	9.6%	
Education	19.0%	7.6%
Resource conservation, industrial development	4.9%	11.9%
Transportation, communications	8.8%	4.1% / 4.9%
Health	13.4%	13.4%
Social services	18.6%	21.7%
General services	7.1%	6.0%

*Consolidated federal, provincial, territorial and municipal governments.
Source: Statistics Canada, *Canada Yearbook, 1994.*

The two main changes in the pattern of government expenditures have been the increase in debt payment and the significant reduction in education spending.

duction. Social and health benefits, welfare payments, veterans' benefits, and unemployment insurance payments are examples of transfer payments. Their key characteristic is that those who receive them make no current contribution to output in return for these payments.

Figure 5-3 shows the changing pattern of government expenditures in the last quarter of a century. The two areas in which there have been significant changes are debt charges and education. Debt charges have doubled, while expenditure on education has dropped from 19% in 1970–71 to less than 12% in 1990–91.

SOURCES OF GOVERNMENT EXPENDITURES AND REVENUES

Now let's disaggregate the public sector into federal, provincial, and municipal units of government to compare their expenditures. Figure 5-4(a) tells the story for the federal government.

FEDERAL EXPENDITURES AND REVENUES

Figure 5-4 (a) shows that three important areas of federal spending stand out: (1) social services, (2) protection of persons and property, and (3) interest on the public debt. The social services category, representing

a third of total expenditures, reflects the myriad income-maintenance programs for the aged, the disabled, the unemployed, the handicapped, and families with no breadwinner. *Transfers to other governments* constitute about 18% of the federal budget and underscore the fact that provinces and municipalities have constitutional responsibilities but inadequate sources of revenues. *Interest on the public debt* has grown dramatically in recent years because the public debt itself has grown.

On the revenue side, **personal income taxes** continue to contribute the largest share of federal government revenues at about 47%; **corporate income taxes** represent almost 7%, while unemployment insurance contributions account for 13%. The remaining 24% is raised by a variety of taxes, including the Goods and Services Tax (GST), which contributes about 12%.

GLOBAL PERSPECTIVE 5-1

The tax burden in selected countries, 1993

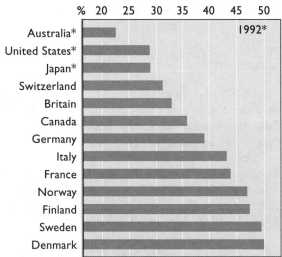

Source: Organization for Economic Cooperation and Development

Tax burdens in Canada are closer to those in Western European countries such as Italy and Germany, than those of our immediate neighbour to the south, the United States.

FIGURE 5-4   **The major components of expenditures and revenues of the three levels of governments in Canada, 1992–93**

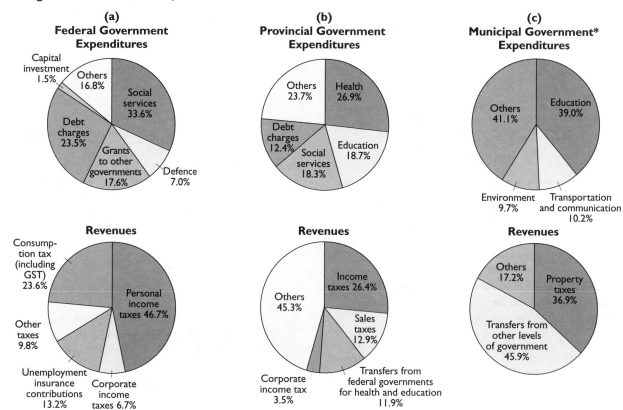

Source: Statistics Canada, *Canada Yearbook, 1994.*
* Municipal government data are for 1991.

PROVINCIAL EXPENDITURES AND REVENUES

Health is the largest provincial and territorial outlay at an estimated 27% of total expenditures in 1992–93. Education was the second largest outlay at about 19%, and social services, the third largest expenditure, accounted for about the same percentage (18.3%).

Figure 5-4(b) shows that income taxes, general sales taxes, and transfers from other levels of governments represented the main generators of revenues at 26.4%, 12.9%, and 11.9% respectively.

MUNICIPAL GOVERNMENT EXPENDITURES AND REVENUES

Education is the largest component of municipal government spending at almost 40% of total expenditures, as Figure 5-4(c) shows. The other main categories of expenditures are transportation and communications, environmental, person and property protection, and social services outlays.

Municipal government revenues come primarily from **property taxes** (37% of the total); provincial government transfers make up the bulk of the rest.

THE DEBATE OVER THE SIZE OF GOVERNMENT

The debate over the appropriate size of government is a long-standing one, but it has received considerable attention in the last decade as government debt has spiralled upwards.

There are those who argue passionately for reducing government expenditure as a way of bringing down government deficits and reducing the size of government itself. Others maintain the govern-

FIGURE 5-5   Public debt* as a percentage of GDP

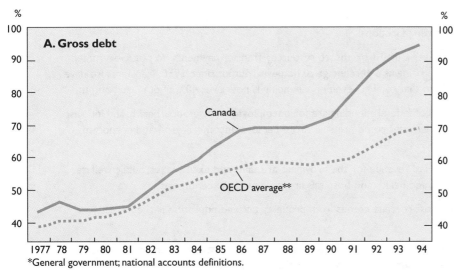

Since 1981, Canada's public debt has grown much more rapidly than the OECD average.

*General government; national accounts definitions.

**Weighted average of 17 countries (1987 GDP weights and exchange rates).

Source: Copyright ©OECD, 1994, *OECD Survey Canada*. Reproduced by permission of the OECD.

ment debt problem has been exaggerated and that if it is, or becomes, a problem the government ought to raise revenues by taxing corporations and well-off Canadians at a higher rate.

These differing views arise because of the different perceptions of the effectiveness of government policies in the past. Those in favour of reducing the size of government argue that instances of government success at alleviating social and economic problems are rare. Those who favour increasing taxes

to deal with the mounting debt point out how much worse the social and economic problems would have been and are likely to become if drastic government expenditure cutbacks were implemented.

Whichever side of the debate you are on, there is no dispute over the fact that in the last 20 years the public debt in Canada has risen steeply, and more so than the OECD average. Figure 5-5 shows the steep rise in the Canadian public net debt compared with the OECD average.

CHAPTER SUMMARY

1. Government enhances the operation of the market system by **a** providing an appropriate legal and social framework, and **b** acting to maintain competition.

2. Government alters the distribution of income by direct market intervention and through the tax-transfer system.

3. Spillovers or externalities cause the equilibrium output of certain goods to vary from the optimal output. Spillover costs result in an overallocation of resources that can be corrected by legislation or specific taxes. Spillover benefits are accompanied by an underallocation of resources that can be corrected by subsidies to either consumers or producers.

4. Government must provide public goods because such goods are indivisible and entail benefits from which nonpaying consumers cannot be excluded.

5. The manipulation of taxes and its expenditures is one way government can reduce unemployment and inflation.

6. The circular flow model helps us envision how government performs its redistributional, allocative, and stabilizing functions.

7. Government purchases exhaust or absorb resources; transfer payments do not. Government purchases have been rising as a percentage of domestic output since 1950. Transfers also have grown significantly, so that total government spending is now over 40% of domestic output.

8. The main categories of federal spending are for unemployment insurance, health, and interest on the public debt; revenues come primarily from personal income, payroll, and corporate income taxes.

9. The primary sources of revenue for the provinces are sales and excise taxes; public welfare, education, highways, and health and hospitals are their major expenditures.

10. At the local level, most revenue comes from property tax, and education is the largest expenditure.

11. Under our system of fiscal federalism, provincial and municipal tax revenues are supplemented by sizable revenue transfers from the federal government.

TERMS AND CONCEPTS

corporate income taxes (p. 87)
exclusion principle (p. 82)
free-rider problem (p. 83)
government purchases (p. 86)
monopoly (p. 79)

personal income taxes (p. 87)
property taxes (p. 88)
public goods (p. 83)
spillover costs and spillover benefits (p. 80)
transfer payments (p. 86)

QUESTIONS AND STUDY SUGGESTIONS

1. List and briefly discuss the main economic functions of government.

2. What divergences arise between equilibrium and an efficient output when a. spillover costs and b. spillover benefits are present? How might government correct for these discrepancies? "The presence of spillover costs suggests underallocation of resources to that product and the need for governmental subsidies." Do you agree? Explain how zoning and seat belt laws might be used to deal with a problem of spillover costs.

3. *Key Question   What are the basic characteristics of public goods? Explain the significance of the exclusion principle. By what means does government provide public goods?*

4. *Key Question   Draw a production possibilities curve with public goods on the vertical axis and private goods on the horizontal axis. Assuming the economy is initially operating on the curve, indicate how the production of public goods might be increased. How might the output of public goods be increased if the economy is initially functioning at a point inside the curve?*

5. Use your understanding of the characteristics of private and public goods to determine whether the following should be produced through the market system or provided by government: a. bread; b. street lighting; c. bridges; d. parks; e. swimming pools; f. medical care; g. mail delivery; h. housing; i. air traffic control; j. libraries.

6. Explain how government might manipulate its expenditures and tax revenues to reduce a. unemployment and b. the rate of inflation.

7. "Most governmental actions affect the distribution of income, the allocation of resources, and the levels of unemployment and prices." Use the circular flow model to confirm this assertion for each of the following: a. the construction of a new high school in Huron County; b. a 2% reduction in the corporate income tax; c. an expansion of preschool programs for disadvantaged children; d. a $50 million increase in spending for space research; e. the levying of a tax on air polluters; and f. a $1 increase in the minimum wage.

8. What is the most important source of revenue and the major type of expenditure for the federal government? For provincial governments? For municipal governments?

CHAPTER 6

CANADA IN THE GLOBAL ECONOMY

Backpackers in the wilderness like to think they are "leaving the world behind." Ironically, like Atlas, they carry the world on their shoulders. Much of their backpacking equipment is imported — knives from Switzerland, rain gear from South Korea, cameras from Japan, aluminum pots made in England, miniature stoves from Sweden, sleeping bags from China, and compasses from Finland. Some backpackers wear hiking boots from Italy, sunglasses made in France, and watches from Japan or Switzerland. Moreover, they may drive to the trailheads in Japanese-made Toyotas or Swedish-made Volvos, sipping coffee from Brazil or snacking on bananas from Honduras.

International trade and the global economy affect all of us daily, whether we are hiking in the wilderness, driving our cars, listening to music, or working at our jobs. We cannot "leave the world behind." We are enmeshed with the rest of the world in a complex web of economic relationships — trade of goods and services, multinational corporations, co-operative ventures among the world's firms, and ties among the world's financial markets. This web is so complex that is difficult to determine just what is — or isn't — a Canadian product! Japanese auto companies have set up factories in Ontario, while many "Canadian" manufacturers have factories or outlets in other countries, particularly in the United States.

The goal of this chapter is to introduce you to the basic principles underlying the global economy. (We defer a more advanced discussion of international economics to Part 5 of this book.)

In this chapter we will first look at the growth of world trade, Canada's role in it, and the factors causing the growth. Next, we will modify Chapter 5's circular flow diagram to account for international trade flows. Third, we will explore the basis for world trade, focusing on the concept of comparative advantage. This discussion is followed by a look at foreign currencies and exchange rates. Then we will examine some restrictive trade practices implemented by nations. That leads us to a discussion of multilateral trade agreements and free-trade regions of the globe. We conclude with some answers to the question: "Can Canadian firms compete?"

BOX 6-1 THE BIG PICTURE

The scarcity problem can be lessened if a society can produce more goods and services from its limited resources. One powerful way for all societies to produce more from the limited resources available to them is to specialize in producing specific goods. If all nations specialized in producing what each was especially good at, each could get its other needs by trading. If all nations specialized, the whole world would be materially better off since we would increase the total goods and services we could produce from available resources. As the twentieth century is coming to a close, this lesson is being followed by more and more nations. Not surprisingly, trade among nations is growing, and Canada is no exception in this trend.

As you read this chapter, keep the following points in mind:

- Opportunity cost plays a central role in specialization, and determines what products a nation

ought to specialize in. Keep asking yourself what a particular good would cost to produce domestically compared to purchasing it from another nation. We could grow bananas in Canada (in greenhouses, of course), but could we purchase bananas at a lower price from a nation better suited to grow bananas?
- Specialization necessarily implies trade. Since nations have different currencies, there is a market for them called the foreign exchange market. As with any market, there are suppliers and those that demand a particular currency. The exchange rate is determined by supply and demand conditions at any given time period.
- Trade is reciprocal in nature: one nation's exports are another's imports, and a nation cannot import unless it also exports.

GROWTH OF WORLD TRADE

The volume of world trade is so large and its characteristics so unique that it requires special consideration.

VOLUME AND PATTERN

Figure 6-1 shows the importance of world trade for several representative countries. Many nations, such as Canada, with limited domestic markets cannot produce with reasonable efficiency the variety of goods they want to consume. For such countries, exports — sales abroad — are the route for obtaining imported goods they desire. In Canada exports make up about 30% of our national output. Other countries, the United States, for example, have rich and diversified resource bases and vast internal markets and are less dependent on world trade.

VOLUME   For Canada and the world, the volume of international trade has been increasing both absolutely and relatively. A comparison of the boxed data within Figure 6-2 reveals the substantial growth in the absolute dollar volume of both Canadian exports and imports over the past several decades. The lines in the figure show the growth of exports and imports as a percent of gross domestic

FIGURE 6-1 Exports of goods and services as a percentage of GDP, selected countries, 1993

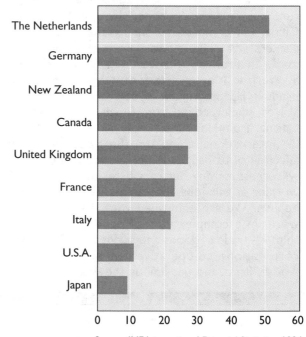

Source: IMF, International Financial Statistics, 1994.

Canada's exports make up almost 30% of domestic output of goods and services.

FIGURE 6-2 **Canada's imports and exports as a percentage of GDP**

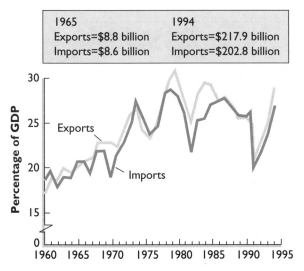

1965	1994
Exports=$8.8 billion	Exports=$217.9 billion
Imports=$8.6 billion	Imports=$202.8 billion

Source: Statistics Canada, *Canadian International Merchandise Trade*.

Canada's imports and exports have expanded since 1960, but have fluctuated over this period.

product (GDP) — the dollar value of all goods and services produced within Canadian borders. Exports and imports currently are 29 and 27% of GDP respectively, up substantially from 1960.

DEPENDENCE   Canada depends heavily on the world economy. We are almost entirely dependent on other countries for bananas, cocoa, coffee, spices, tea, raw silk, and natural rubber. Imported goods compete strongly in many of our domestic markets — for example, French and Italian wines, and Japanese autos. Foreign cars now account for about a third of the total automotive sales in Canada. Even the great Canadian pastime — hockey — relies heavily on imported equipment.

But world trade is a two-way street, and many Canadian industries are highly dependent on foreign markets. Almost all segments of agriculture rely heavily on foreign markets — wheat exports vary from one-fourth to more than one-half of total output. The chemical, aircraft, automobile, machine tool, and forest industries are only a few of many Canadian industries that sell significant portions of their output in

FIGURE 6-3   **Canadian exports and imports, 1994**

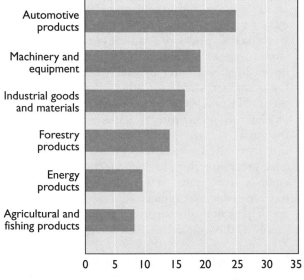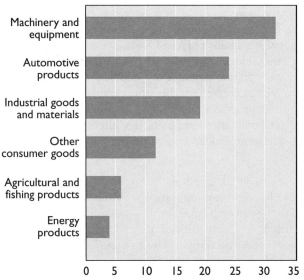

Source: Statistics Canada, *Canadian International Merchandise Trade*, October 1994.

Automotive products (vehicle and parts) are our largest export and second largest import. Machinery and equipment, industrial goods and machinery, and forestry products are Canada's largest export categories.

FIGURE 6-4   Canadian international trade by geographical areas, 1994

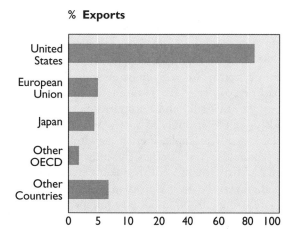

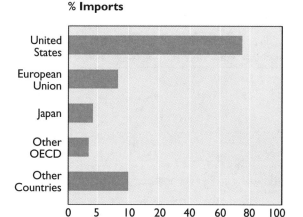

Source: Statistics Canada, *Canadian International Merchandise Trade*, October 1994.

The bulk of our exports and imports are with the United States.

international markets. Figure 6-3 shows some of Canada's major commodity exports and imports.

TRADE PATTERNS   Figure 6-4 provides an overall picture of the pattern of Canada's merchandise trade. Note the following:

1. The bulk of our export and import trade is with other industrially advanced nations, not with the less developed nations or the countries of Eastern Europe.
2. The United States is our most important trading partner quantitatively. Over 80% of our exports are sold to Americans, who in turn provide us with three-quarters of our imports.
3. We import some of the same categories of goods that we export (specifically, automobiles, industrial machinery and materials, chemicals, and telecommunications equipment).

LINKAGES   Figure 6-4 also implies complex financial linkages among nations. A nation can have either an overall trade surplus or deficit. How does a nation — or an individual — obtain more goods from others than it provides to them? The answer is by either borrowing from them or by giving up ownership of some of its assets or wealth.

FACILITATING FACTORS

Several factors have facilitated the rapid growth of international trade since World War II.

TRANSPORTATION TECHNOLOGY   High transportation costs are a barrier to any type of trade, and particularly to trade between distance places. But improvements in transportation have shrunk the globe, fostering world trade. Airplanes now transport low-weight, high-value items such as diamonds and semiconductors quickly from one nation to another. We now routinely transport oil in massive tankers, greatly reducing the cost of transportation per barrel. Grain is loaded onto ocean-going ships at modern, efficient grain silos located at Great Lakes ports and the coastal ports of Vancouver and Halifax. Container ships transport self-contained railroad boxes directly to foreign ports, where cranes place the containers onto railroad cars for internal shipment. Natural gas flows through large diameter pipelines from exporting to importing countries, for instance, from Russia to Germany and from this country to the United States. Workers clean fish on large processing ships located directly on the fishing grounds. Refrigerated vessels then transport the fish to overseas ports. Commercial airplane manufacturers deliver new aircraft in a matter of hours; they simply fly them directly to their foreign customers.

COMMUNICATIONS TECHNOLOGY   Perhaps equally important to the explosion of world trade has been dramatic improvements in communications technology. Telephones, facsimile machines, and computers now directly link traders around the world. These devices have aided exporters in assessing the potential for selling products abroad and in consummating trade deals. The communications revolution has also globalized financial markets and banking industries. People can move money around the world in the blink of an eye. Exchange rates, stock prices, and interest rates flash onto computer screens nearly simultaneously in Vancouver, Toronto, London, and Lisbon.

In short, exporters and importers in today's world can as easily communicate between Sweden and Australia as between Calgary and Winnipeg. A distributor in Montreal can get a price quote on 1000 thatched baskets in Thailand just as quickly as a quotation on 1000 tonnes of steel in Hamilton.

GENERAL DECLINE IN TARIFFS   Tariffs — excise taxes or duties on imported products — have had their ups and downs, but since 1940 have generally fallen worldwide. A glance ahead to Figure 6-8 reveals that Canada's tariff duties as a percent of dutiable imports are now about 5%, down substantially from the highs of 1930. Many nations still have barriers to free trades, but on average, tariffs have fallen greatly, increasing international trade.

PEACE   World War II matched powerful industrial countries against one another and thus disrupted commercial international trade. Not only has trade been restored since World War II, but it has been greatly bolstered by peaceful relations and by trade-conducive institutions linking most industrial nations. In particular, Japan and Germany — two defeated World War II powers — now are major participants in world trade.

PARTICIPANTS

Nearly all nations of the world participate to some extent in international trade.

CANADA, UNITED STATES, JAPAN, AND WESTERN EUROPE   As indicated in Global Perspective 6-1, the top participants in world trade are the United States, Germany, and Japan. In 1993 these three nations had combined exports of U. S. $1.2 trillion. Along with Germany, other Western European nations such as France, Britain, and Italy are major exporters and importers. In fact, Canada, the United States, Japan, and the Western European nations now dominate world trade. These areas also are at the heart of the world's financial system and headquarter most of the world's large **multinational**

GLOBAL PERSPECTIVE 6-1

Comparative exports in billions of dollars

The United States, Germany, and Japan are the world's largest exporters. Canada ranks seventh.

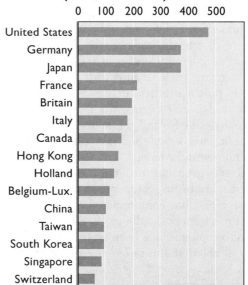

Merchandise exports, 1993 (billions of dollars)

Source: GATT.

corporations, which are firms with sizable foreign production and distribution assets.

NEW PLAYERS   New, important participants have arrived on the world trade scene. One such group of nations is the newly industrializing Asian economies of Hong Kong, Singapore, South Korea, and Taiwan. These "**Asian tigers**" have expanded their share of world exports from about 3% in 1972 to more than 9% today. Their combined exports roughly match that of Japan and greatly exceed those of either France, Britain, or Italy. Other countries in southeast Asia, particularly Malaysia and Indonesia, have also expanded their international trade.

China is another emerging trading power. Since initiating market reforms in 1979, its annual growth of output has averaged nearly 10% (compared to 2 to 3% annually in Canada). At this remarkable rate of growth, China's total output nearly doubles every seven years! An upsurge of exports and imports has accompanied this expansion of output. In 1989 Chinese exports and imports each were about $45 billion. In 1993 they each topped $89 billion, with 30% of the exports going to Canada and the United States. Also, China has been a recent magnet for foreign investment. In 1993 alone, it contracted for about $100 billion of foreign-produced capital to be delivered during the next several years. Experts predict that China eventually will become one of the world's leading trade nations.

The collapse of communism in Eastern Europe and the former Soviet Union has also altered world trade patterns. Before this collapse, the Eastern European nations of Poland, Hungary, Czechoslovakia, and East Germany traded mainly with the Soviet Union and its political allies such as North Korea and Cuba. Today, East Germany is reunited with West Germany, and Poland, Hungary, and the Czech Republic have established new trade relationships with Europe and America.

Russia itself has initiated far-reaching market reforms, including widespread privatization of industry, and has consummated major trade deals with firms from across the globe. Although its transition to capitalism has been far from smooth, there is no doubt that Russia has the potential to be a major trading power. Other former Soviet republics — now independent nations — such as Ukraine and Estonia also are opening their economies to international trade and finance.

BACK TO THE CIRCULAR FLOW MODEL

Now that we have an idea of the size and growth of world trade, we need to incorporate it into Chapter 5's circular flow model. Fortunately, this is a rather straightforward matter. In Figure 6-5 we make two adjustments to Figure 5-1:

1. Our previously labelled "Resource Markets" and "Product Markets" now become "Canadian Resource Markets" and "Canadian Product Markets." Similarly, we add the modifier "Canadian" to the "Businesses," "Government," and "Households" sectors.
2. We place the foreign sector — the "Rest of the World" — at the bottom of the circular flow diagram. This sector designates all foreign nations that we deal with and the individuals, businesses, and governments that make them up.

Flow (13) shows that people, businesses, and governments abroad buy Canadian products — our exports — from our product market. This real flow of Canadian exports to foreign nations is accompanied by an opposite monetary revenue flow (14) from the rest of the world to us. In response to these revenues from abroad, Canadian businesses demand more domestic resources to produce the exported goods; they are on the demand side of the resource market. Thus, the domestic flow (1) of money income (rents, wages, interest, and profits) to Canadian households rises.

But our exports are only half the picture. Flow (15) shows that Canadian households, businesses, and government spend some of their income on foreign products. These products, of course, are our imports (flow 16). These purchases of imports, say, autos and electronic equipment, contribute to foreign output and income, which in turn provides the means for foreign households to buy our exports.

Our circular flow model is a simplification that emphasizes product market effects. But a few other Canada-Rest of the World relationships also merit mention. Specifically, there are linkages between the Canadian resource market and the rest of the world.

Canada imports and exports not only products, but resources as well. For example, we import some crude oil and export raw logs. Moreover, some Canadian firms choose to engage in "offshore" production, which diverts spending on capital from our domestic resource market to resource markets in other nations. For instance, Northern Telecom might build an assembly plant in Germany. Or flowing the other direction, Sony might construct a plant for manufacturing CD players in Canada. There are also international flows of labour. About 250,000 immigrants enter Canada each year. These immigrants expand the availability of labour resources in Canada, raising our total output and income. On the other hand, immigration increases labour supply in specific Canadian labour markets, pulling down wage rates for some types of Canadian labour.

The expanded circular flow model also demonstrates that a nation engaged in world trade faces potential sources of instability that would not affect a "closed" nation. For example, recessions and inflation can be highly contagious among nations. Suppose that the nations of Western Europe experienced a rather severe recession. As their income declined, they would curtail purchases of Canadian exports. As a result flows (13) and (14) in Figure 6-5 would decline and inventories of unsold Canadian goods would rise. Canadian firms would respond by limiting their production and employment, reducing the flow of money income to Canadian households (flow 1). Recession in Europe might contribute to a recession in Canada.

Figure 6-5 also helps us to see that the foreign sector alters resource allocation and incomes in the Canadian economy. In the presence of the foreign sector, we produce more of some goods (our exports) and fewer of others (our imports) than we would otherwise. Thus, Canadian labour and other productive resources are shifted towards export industries and away from import industries. We use more of our resources to manufacture autos and telecommunication equipment. So we ask: "Do these shifts of resources make any economic sense? Do they enhance our total output and thus our standard of living?" We look at some answers next. **(Key Question 3)**

FIGURE 6-5   The circular flow with the foreign sector

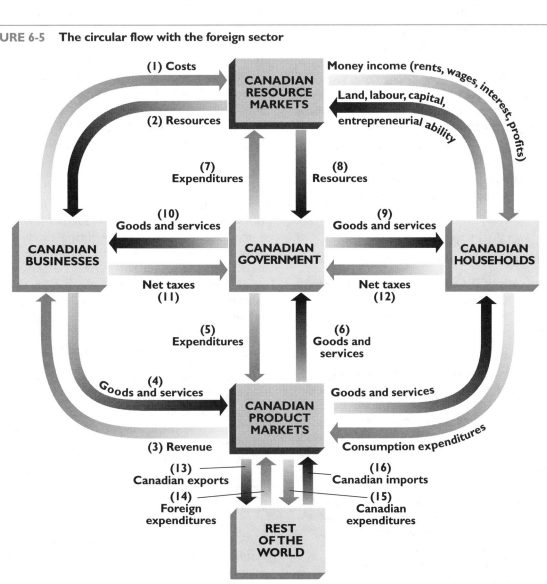

Flows 13-16 in the lower portion of the diagram show how the Canadian economy interacts with "The Rest of the World." People abroad buy Canadian exports, contributing to our business revenue and money income. Canadians, in turn, spend part of their incomes to buy imports from abroad. Income from a nation's exports helps pay for its imports.

QUICK REVIEW 6-1

1. World trade has increased globally and nationally. Canada is a leading international trader, with our exports and imports being about 27 to 29% of our national output.

2. Transportation technology, communications technology, declines in tariffs, and peaceful relations among major industrial countries have all helped to expand world trade.

3. World trade is dominated by Canada, the United States, Japan, and the Western European nations, but has recently been bolstered by new participates such as the "Asian tigers" (Hong Kong, Singapore, South Korea, and Taiwan), China, Eastern European nations, and the newly independent states formerly making up the Soviet Union.

4. The circular flow model now incorporates the foreign sector by adding flows of exports from our domestic product market, imports to our domestic product market, and the corresponding flows of spending.

SPECIALIZATION AND COMPARATIVE ADVANTAGE

Specialization and trade increase the productivity of a nation's resources and allow for larger total output than otherwise. This notion is not new! According to Adam Smith in 1776:

> It is the maxim of every prudent master of a family, never to attempt to make at home what it will cost him more to make than to buy. The taylor does not attempt to make his own shoes, but buys them from the shoemaker. The shoemaker does not attempt to make his own clothes, but employs a taylor. The farmer attempts to make neither the one or the other, but employs those different artificers....
>
> What is prudence in the conduct of every private family, can scarce be folly in that of a great kingdom. If a foreign country can supply us with a commodity cheaper than we can make it, better buy it of them with some part of the produce of our own industry, employed in a way in which we have some advantage.[1]

---

[1] Adam Smith, *The Wealth of Nations* (New York: Modern Library, Inc., 1937), p. 424. [Originally published in 1776.]

Nations specialize and trade for the same reasons as individuals: Specialization and exchange among individuals, regions, and nations results in greater overall output and income.

BASIC PRINCIPLE

In the early 1800s British economist David Ricardo expanded Smith's idea, observing that it pays for a person or a country to specialize and exchange even if that person or nation is more productive than a potential trading partner in *all* economic activities.

Consider an example of a chartered accountant (CA) who is also a skilled house painter. Suppose the CA can paint her house in less time than the professional painter she is thinking of hiring. Also suppose the CA can earn $50 per hour doing her accounting and must pay the painter $15 per hour. Let's say that it will take the accountant 30 hours to paint her house; the painter, 40 hours.

Should the CA take time from her accounting to paint her own house or should she hire the painter? The CA's opportunity cost of painting her house is $1500 (= 30 hours × $50 per hour of sacrificed income). The cost of hiring the painter is only $600 (40 hours × $15 per hour paid to the painter). Although the CA is better at both accounting and painting — she has an **absolute advantage** in both accounting and painting — her relative or comparative advantage lies in accounting. She will *lower the cost of getting her house painted* by specializing in accounting and using some of the earnings from accounting to hire a house painter.

Similarly, the house painter can reduce his cost of obtaining accounting services by specializing in painting and using some of his income to hire the CA to prepare his income tax forms. Suppose that it would take the painter ten hours to prepare his tax return, while the CA could handle this task in two hours. The house painter would sacrifice $150 of income (= 10 hours × $15 per hour of sacrificed time) to accomplish a task that he could hire the CA to do for $100 (= 2 hour × $50 per hour of the CA's time). By using the CA to prepare his tax return, the painter lowers *his cost of getting the tax return completed.*

What is true for our CA and house painter is also true for nations. Countries can reduce their cost of obtaining desirable goods by specializing in production where they have comparative advantages.

COMPARATIVE COSTS

Our simple example clearly shows that specialization is economically desirable because it results in more efficient production. Because it is vital to understanding the global economy, let's tackle an illustration that puts specialization in the context of trading nations. Since you are already familiar with the concept of the production possibilities table, let's use it in our analysis. Suppose production possibilities for Mexico and Canada are as shown in Tables 6-1 and 6-2.

In these production possibilities tables we assume constant costs. Each country must give up a constant amount of one product in securing constant increments of the other product. (This assumption will simplify our discussion without impairing the validity of our conclusions.)

TABLE 6-1   Mexico's production possibilities table (in tonnes)

Product	Production alternatives				
	A	B	C	D	E
Corn	0	20	24	40	60
Soybeans	15	10	9	5	0

Specialization and trade are mutually beneficial or "profitable" to the two nations if the comparative costs of the two products within the two nations differ. What are the domestic comparative costs of corn and soybeans in Mexico? Comparing production alternatives A and B in Table 6-1, we see that 5 tonnes of soybeans (= 15 − 10) must be sacrificed to produce 20 tonnes of corn (= 20 − 0). Or more simply, in Mexico it costs 1 tonne of soybeans to produce 4 tonnes of corn — that is, 1S = 4C. Because we assumed constant costs, this domestic comparative-cost relationship will not change as Mexico expands the output of either product. This is evident from looking at production possibilities B and C, where we see that 4 more tonnes of corn (= 24 − 20) cost 1 unit of soybeans (= 10 − 9).

Similarly, in Table 6-2, a comparison of production alternatives R and S reveals that at a domestic opportunity cost of 10 tonnes of soybeans (= 30 − 20), Canadians can obtain 30 tonnes of corn (= 30 − 0). That is, the domestic comparative-cost ratio for the

TABLE 6-2   Canada's production possibilities table (in tonnes)

Product	Production alternatives				
	R	S	T	U	V
Corn	0	30	33	60	90
Soybeans	30	20	19	10	0

two products in Canada is 1S = 3C. A comparison of production alternative S and T demonstrates this. Note that an extra 3 tonnes of corn (= 33 − 30) comes at the direct sacrifice of 1 tonne of soybeans (= 20 − 19).

The comparative cost of the two products within the two nations is clearly different. Economists say that Canada has a domestic comparative-cost advantage, or simply, a **comparative advantage**, in soybeans. Canada must forgo less corn — 3 tonnes — to get 1 tonne of soybeans than in Mexico where 1 tonne of soybeans costs 4 tonnes of corn. In terms of domestic opportunity costs, soybeans are relatively cheaper in Canada. *A nation has a comparative advantage in some product when it can produce that product at a lower domestic opportunity cost than can a potential trading partner.* Mexico, on the other hand, has a comparative advantage in corn. While it costs $\frac{1}{3}$ tonne of soybeans to get 1 tonne of corn in Canada, by comparison 1 tonne of soybeans costs only $\frac{1}{4}$ tonne of soybeans in Mexico. Comparatively speaking, corn is cheaper in Mexico. In summary:

Mexico's domestic cost conditions 1S = 4C
Canada's domestic cost conditions 1S = 3C

Because of these differences in domestic opportunity costs, we can show that if both nations specialize, each according to its comparative advantage, then each can achieve a larger total output with the same total input of resources. Together, they will be using their scarce resources more efficiently.

TERMS OF TRADE

Since Canada's cost ratio of 1S equals 3C, it makes sense that Canadians would be pleased to specialize in soybeans, if they could obtain *more than* 3 tonnes of corn for a tonne of soybeans through trade with Mexico. Similarly, recalling Mexico's 1S equals 4C cost ratio, it will be advantageous to Mexicans to specialize in corn, provided they can get 1 tonne of soybeans *for less than* 4 tonnes of corn.

Suppose through negotiation the two nations agree on an exchange rate of 1 tonne of soybeans for 3 ½ tonnes of corn. These **terms of trade** will be mutually beneficial to both countries since each can "do better" through trade than via domestic production alone. Canadians get 3 ½ tonnes of corn by sending 1 tonne of soybeans to Mexico, while they can get only 3 tonnes of corn by shifting resources domestically from soybeans to corn. It would cost Mexicans 4 tonnes of corn to obtain 1 tonne of soybeans by shifting their domestic resources. Instead they can obtain 1 tonne of soybeans through trade with Canada at the lower cost of 3 ½ tonnes of corn.

GAINS FROM SPECIALIZATION AND TRADE

Let's pinpoint the size of the gains in total output from specialization and trade. Suppose that before specialization and trade, production alternative C in Table 6-1 and alternative T in 6-2 were the optimal product mixes for each country. These outputs are shown in column 1 of Table 6-3. That is, Mexicans preferred 24 tonnes of corn and 9 tonnes of soybeans (Table 6-1) and Canadians preferred 33 tonnes of corn and 19 tonnes of soybeans (Table 6-2) to all other alternatives available within their respective domestic economies.

Now let's assume both nations specialize according to comparative advantage, Mexico producing 60 tonnes of corn and no soybeans (alternative E) and Canada producing no corn and 30 tonnes of soybeans (alternative R) as reflected in

column 2 of Table 6-3. Using our 1S = 3 ½ terms of trade, assume Mexico exchanges 35 tonnes of corn for 10 tonnes of Canadian soybeans. Column 3 of Table 6-3 shows quantities exchanged in this trade. As observed in Column 4, Mexicans will now have 25 tonnes of corn and 10 tonnes of soybeans, while Canadians will obtain 35 tonnes of corn and 20 tonnes of soybeans. Compared with their optimum product mixes before specialization and trade (column 1), *both* nations now enjoy more corn and more soybeans! Specifically, Mexico will gain 1 tonne of corn and 1 tonne of soybeans. Canada will gain 2 tonnes of corn and 1 tonne of soybeans. These gains are shown in column 5 where we have subtracted the *before*-specialization outputs of column (1) from the outputs realized *after* specialization in column (4).

The point germane to our understanding the world economy is that *specialization according to comparative advantage improves resource allocation. The same total inputs of world resources have resulted in a larger global output.* By having Mexico and Canada allocate all their resources to corn and soybeans respectively, the same total inputs of resources have produced more output between them, indicating that resources are being more efficiently used or allocated.

We saw in Chapter 2 that through specialization and international trade a nation can overcome the production constraints imposed by its domestic production possibilities curve. Although the domestic production possibilities frontiers of the two countries have not been pushed outward, specialization and trade have circumvented the constraints of the production possibilities curve. The economic effects of specialization and trade between two

TABLE 6-3 **Specialization according to comparative advantage and the gains from trade (in tonnes)**

Country	(1) Outputs before specialization	(2) Outputs after specialization	(3) Amounts traded	(4) Outputs available after trade	(5) = (4) – (1) Gains from specialization and trade
Mexico	24 corn	60 corn	-35 corn	25 corn	1 corn
	9 soybeans	0 soybeans	+10 soybeans	10 soybeans	1 soybeans
Canada	33 corn	0 corn	+35 corn	35 corn	2 corn
	19 soybeans	30 soybeans	−10 soybeans	20 soybeans	1 soybeans

nations are tantamount to having more or better resources or to having achieved technological progress. The national self-interests of trading partners is the foundation of the world economy. Such trade provides mutual gains in consumable output and thus higher domestic standards of living. **(Key Question 4)**

FOREIGN EXCHANGE MARKET

People, firms, or nations specializing in the production of specific goods or services exchange those products for money and then use the money to buy other products or to pay for the use of resources. Within an economy — for example, Mexico — prices are stated in pesos and buyers use pesos to purchase domestic products. The buyers possess pesos, exactly the currency sellers want.

International markets are different. How many dollars does it take to buy a truckload of Mexican corn selling for 3000 pesos, a German automobile selling for 90,000 marks, or a Japanese motorcycle priced at 300,000 yen? Producers in Mexico, Germany, and Japan want payment in pesos, marks, and yen, respectively, so they can pay their wages, rent, interest, dividends, and taxes. This need is served by a **foreign exchange market**, *the market where various national currencies are exchanged for one another.* At the outset two points about this market require emphasis.

1. A COMPETITIVE MARKET Real-world foreign exchange markets conform closely to the kinds of markets studied in Chapter 4. These are competitive markets characterized by large numbers of buyers and sellers dealing in a standardized "product" such as the Canadian dollar, the German mark, the British pound, Swedish krona, or the Japanese yen.

2. LINKAGE TO ALL DOMESTIC AND FOREIGN PRICES The price or exchange value of a nation's currency is an unusual price; it links all domestic (say, Canada) prices, with all foreign (say, Japanese or German) prices. Exchange rates enable consumers in one country to translate prices of foreign goods into units of their own currency — just multiply the foreign product price by the exchange rate. If the dollar-yen exchange rate is $.01 (1 cent) per yen, a Sony cassette player priced at 20,000 yen will cost a Canadian $200 (=

20,000 × $.01). If the exchange rate is $.02 per yen, it would cost a Canadian $400 (= 20,000 × $.02). Similarly, all other Japanese products will double in price to Canadian buyers. As we will see, a change in exchange rates has important implications for a nation's levels of domestic production and employment.

DOLLAR-YEN MARKET

Let's look at how the foreign exchange market for dollars and yen works. (We defer technical details until Chapter 21.) When nations trade they need to exchange their currencies. Canadian exporters want to be paid in dollars, not yen; but Japanese importers of Canadian goods possess yen, not dollars. This problem is resolved by Japanese importers who offer to supply their yen in exchange for dollars. Conversely, there are Canadian importers who need to pay Japanese exporters with yen, not dollars. So these Canadians go to the foreign exchange market as demanders of yen.

GLOBAL PERSPECTIVE 6-2

Exchange rates: foreign currency per Canadian dollar

The amount of foreign currency that a dollar will buy varies greatly from nation to nation. These amounts are for February 1995 and fluctuate in response to supply and demand changes in the foreign exchange market.

One Canadian dollar will buy:

1.08 German marks
.45 British pounds
.71 U.S. dollars
3.9 Mexican pesos
.92 Swiss francs
3.8 French francs
71 Japanese yen
562 South Korean won
15,420 Polish zloty

FIGURE 6-6 **The market for foreign exchange**

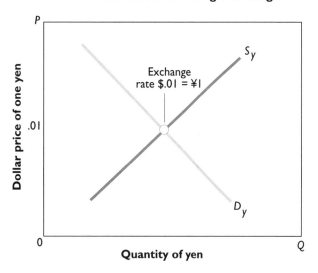

Canadian imports from Japan create a demand for yen, while Canadian exports to Japan create a supply of yen. The dollar price of one yen — the exchange rate — is determined at the intersection of the supply and demand curves. In this case the equilibrium price is $.01, meaning that 1¢ will buy 1 yen (or $1 will buy 100 yen).

Figure 6-6 shows Japanese importers as suppliers of yen and Canadian importers as demanders of yen. The intersection of the demand for yen curve D_y and the supply of yen curve S_y establishes the equilibrium dollar price of yen. Note that the equilibrium dollar price of 1 yen — the dollar-yen exchange rate — is $.01 = 1 yen, or $1 = 100 yen. At this price, the yen market clears; there is neither a shortage nor a surplus of yen. The equilibrium $.01 price of 1 yen means that $1 will buy 100 yen and therefore 100 yen worth of Japanese goods. Conversely, 100 yen will buy $1 worth of Canadian goods.

CHANGING RATES: DEPRECIATION AND APPRECIATION

What might cause the exchange rate to change? The determinants of the demand for and the supply of yen are similar to the determinants of supply and demand discussed in Chapter 4. Looking at it from Canada, several things might take place to increase the demand for — and therefore the dollar price of — yen. Incomes might rise in Canada, enabling Canadians to buy not only more domestic goods, but also more Sony televisions, Nikon cameras, and Nissan automobiles from Japan. So Canadians need more yen and the demand for yen increases. Or, there may be a change in Canadian tastes that enhances our preferences for Japanese goods. For instance, when gas prices soared in the 1970s, many Canadian auto buyers shifted their demands from gas-guzzling domestic cars to gas-efficient Japanese compact cars. The result? An increased demand for yen.

An increase in the Canadian demand for Japanese goods will increase the demand for yen and raise the dollar price of yen. Suppose the dollar price of yen rises from $.01 = ¥1 (or $1 = ¥100) to $.02 = ¥1 (or $2 = ¥100). When the dollar price of yen increases, a **depreciation** of the dollar relative to the yen has occurred. Dollar depreciation means that it takes more dollars (pennies in this case) to buy a single unit of a foreign currency (the yen). A dollar is worth less because it will buy fewer yen and therefore fewer Japanese goods; the yen and therefore all Japanese goods become more expensive to Canadians. Result: Canadian consumers shift their expenditures from Japanese to Canadian goods. The Ford Taurus becomes relatively more attractive than the Honda Accord to Canadian consumers. Conversely, because each yen will buy more dollars, Canadian goods become cheaper to people in Japan and our exports to them rise.

If opposite events occurred — if incomes rise in Japan and Japanese prefer more Canadian goods — then the supply of yen in the foreign exchange market would increase. This increase in the supply of yen relative to demand would decrease the equilibrium dollar price of yen. For example, yen supply might increase, causing the dollar price of yen to decline from $.01 = ¥1 (or $1 = ¥100) to $.005 = ¥1 (or $1 = ¥200). This decrease in the dollar price of yen means there has been an **appreciation** of the dollar relative to the yen. Appreciation of the dollar means that it takes fewer dollars (or pennies) to buy a single yen; the dollar is worth more because it can purchase more yen and therefore more Japanese goods. Each Sony Walkman becomes less expensive in terms of dollars, so Canadians purchase more of them. In general, Canadian imports rise. Meanwhile, because it takes more yen to get a dollar, Canadian exports to Japan fall.

We summarize these currency relationships in Figure 6-7 and you should examine this figure closely. **(Key Question 6)**

FIGURE 6-7 **Currency appreciation and depreciation**

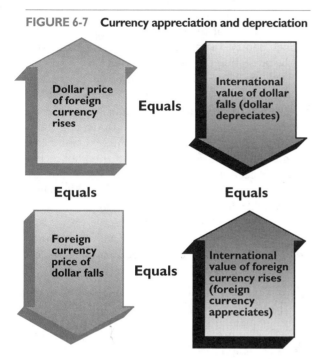

An increase in the dollar price of foreign currency is equivalent to a decline in the international value of the dollar (dollar depreciation). An increase in the dollar price of foreign currency also implies a decline in the foreign currency price of dollars. That is, the international value of foreign currency rises relative to the dollar (foreign currency appreciates).

QUICK REVIEW 6-2

1. A country has a comparative advantage in some product when it can produce it at a lower domestic opportunity cost than can a potential trading partner.

2. Specialization based on comparative advantage increases the total output available for nations that trade with one another.

3. The foreign exchange market is the market where the currency of one nation is exchanged for that of another nation.

4. Appreciation of the dollar is an increase in the international value of the dollar relative to the currency of some other nation; a dollar now buys more units of another currency. Depreciation of the dollar is a decrease in the international value of the dollar relative to other currencies; a dollar now buys fewer units of another currency.

GOVERNMENT AND TRADE

If people and nations benefit from specialization and international exchange, why do governments sometimes try to restrict the free flow of imports or to subsidize exports? What kinds of world trade barriers exist? And what is the rationale for them?

TRADE IMPEDIMENTS AND SUBSIDIES

The major government interferences with free trade are fourfold:

1. *Protective tariffs* are excise taxes or duties placed on imported goods. Most are designed to shield domestic producers from foreign competition. They impede free trade by increasing the prices of imported goods, shifting demand towards domestic products.

2. *Import quotas* are maximum limits on the quantity or total value of specific imported items. Once the quotas are "filled," they choke off imports that domestic consumers might prefer to domestic goods. Import quotas can be more effective in retarding international commerce than tariffs. A particular product might be imported in large quantities despite high tariffs; low import quotas completely prohibit imports once quotas are filled.

3. *Nontariff barriers* include licensing requirements, unreasonable standards pertaining to product quality, or simply unnecessary bureaucratic red tape in customs procedures. Some nations require their domestic importers of foreign goods to obtain licences. By restricting the issuance of licences, imports can be effectively impeded. Great Britain bars coal importation in this way. Also, some nations impede imports of fruit by insisting that each individual crate of fruit be inspected for worms and insects.

4. *Export subsidies* consist of governmental payments to domestic producers to reduce their production costs. With lower production costs, domestic producers can charge lower prices and thus sell more exports in world markets. Two examples: Participating European governments have heavily subsidized Airbus Industries, which produces commercial aircraft. Canada and other nations have subsidized domestic farmers, boosting domestic food supply. This has reduced the market price of food, artificially decreasing export prices on agricultural produce.

WHY GOVERNMENT TRADE INTERVENTIONS?

Why would a nation want to send more of its output for consumption abroad than it gains as imported output in return? Why the impulse to impede imports or boost exports through government policy when free trade is beneficial to a nation? There are several reasons — some legitimate, most not. We will look at two here, and examine others in a later chapter.

1. MISUNDERSTANDING OF THE GAINS FROM TRADE   It is a commonly accepted myth that the fundamental benefit of international trade is larger domestic employment in the export sector. This suggests that exports are "good" because they increase domestic employment, whereas imports are "bad" since they deprive people of jobs at home. In reality, the true benefit from international trade is the *overall* increase in output obtained through specialization and exchange. A nation can fully employ its resources, including labour, with or without international trade. International trade, however, enables society to use its resources in ways that increase its total output and therefore its overall material well-being.

A nation does not need international trade to locate *on* its production possibilities curve. A closed (nontrading) national economy can have full employment without international trade. But through world trade an economy can reach a point *beyond* its domestic production possibilities curve. The gain from trade is the extra output obtained from abroad — the imports got for less cost than if they had to be produced using domestic resources. The only valid reason for exporting part of our domestic output is to obtain imports of greater value to us. Specialization and international exchange make this possible.

2. POLITICAL CONSIDERATIONS   While a nation as a whole gains from trade, trade may harm particular domestic industries and groups of resource suppliers. In our example of comparative advantage, specialization and trade adversely affected the Canadian corn industry and the Mexican soybean industry. These industries may seek to preserve or improve their economic positions by persuading their respective governments to impose tariffs or quotas to protect them from harm. The costs of protectionism are hidden because tariffs and quotas are embedded in the prices of goods. Thus policy makers face fewer political restraints in responding positively to demands for protectionism even if the costs far outweigh the benefits to the country. Inevitably, consumers end up paying for the protection through higher prices.

Indeed, the public may be won over, not only by the vigour of the arguments for trade barriers, but also by the apparent plausibility ("Cut imports and prevent domestic unemployment") and patriotic ring ("Buy Canadian!") of the protectionists. Alleged tariff benefits are immediate and clear-cut to the public. The adverse effects cited by economists are obscure and dispersed over the economy. Then, too, the public is likely to stumble on the fallacy of composition: "If a quota on Japanese automobiles will preserve profits and employment in the Canadian automobile industry, how can it be detrimental to the economy as a whole?"

MULTILATERAL AGREEMENTS AND FREE TRADE ZONES

When one nation enacts barriers against imports, the nations whose exports suffer may retaliate with trade barriers of their own. In a "trade war" tariffs escalate, choking off world trade and reducing everyone's economic well-being. The raising of tariffs by many nations in the early 1930s to fight domestic unemployment is a classic example. Rather than reduce imports and stimulate domestic production, high tariffs prompted affected nations to retaliate with equally high tariffs. International trade across the globe fell, lowering the output, income, and employment levels of all nations. Economic historians generally agree that the tariffs were a contributing cause of the Great Depression. In view of this fact, the world's nations have pursued avenues to lower tariffs worldwide. This pursuit of free trade has been aided by the expansion of powerful domestic interest groups. Specifically, exporters of goods and services, importers of foreign components used in "domestic" products, and domestic sellers of imported products all strongly support lower tariffs worldwide.

Figure 6-8 shows that Canada was a high-tariff nation in the past. But it also demonstrates that, in general, Canadian tariffs have declined during the past half century.[2]

---

[2] Average tariff-rate figures understate the importance of tariffs, however, by not accounting for the fact that some goods are excluded from Canadian markets because of existing tariffs. Then, too, average figures conceal the high tariffs on particular items.

BOX 6-2 APPLYING THE THEORY

PETITION OF THE CANDLEMAKERS, 1845

The French economist Frédéric Bastiat (1801–1850) devastated the proponents of protectionism by satirically extending their reasoning to its logical and absurd conclusions.

Petition of the Manufacturers of Candles, Waxlights, Lamps, Candlesticks, Street Lamps, Snuffers, Extinguishers, and of the Producers of Oil Tallow, Rosin, Alcohol, and, Generally, of Everything Connected with Lighting.

TO MESSIEURS THE MEMBERS OF THE CHAMBER OF DEPUTIES.

Gentlemen — You are on the right road. You reject abstract theories, and have little consideration for cheapness and plenty. Your chief care is the interest of the producer. You desire to emancipate him from external competition, and reserve the *national market* for *national industry*.

We are about to offer you an admirable opportunity of applying your — what shall we call it? your theory? No; nothing is more deceptive than theory; your doctrine? your system? your principle? but you dislike doctrines, you abhor systems, and as for principles, you deny that there are any in social economy: we shall say, then, your practice, your practice without theory and without principle.

We are suffering from the intolerable competition of a foreign rival, placed, it would seem, in a condition so far superior to ours for the production of light, that he absolutely inundates our national market with it at a price fabulously reduced. The moment he shows himself, our trade leaves us — all consumers apply to him; and a branch of native industry, having countless ramifications, is all at once rendered completely stagnant. This rival ... is no other than the Sun.

What we pray for is, that it may please you to pass a law ordering the shutting up of all windows, skylights, dormerwindows, outside and inside shutters, curtains, blinds, bull's-eyes; in a word, of all openings, holes, chinks, clefts, and fissures, by or through which the light of the sun has been in use to enter houses, to the prejudice of the meritorious manufactures with which we flatter ourselves we have accommodated our country, — a country which, in gratitude, ought not to abandon us now to a strife so unequal.

If you shut up as much as possible all access to natural light, and create a demand for artificial light, which of our French manufactures will not be encouraged by it?

If more tallow is consumed, then there must be more oxen and sheep; and, consequently, we shall behold the multiplication of artificial meadows, meat, wool, hides, and, above all, manure, which is the basis and foundation of all agricultural wealth.

The same remark applies to navigation. Thousands of vessels will proceed to the whale fishery; and, in a short time, we shall possess a navy capable of maintaining the honor of France, and gratifying the patriotic aspirations of your petitioners, the undersigned candlemakers and others.

Only have the goodness to reflect, Gentlemen, and you will be convinced that there is, perhaps, no Frenchman, from the wealthy coalmaster to the humblest vender of lucifer matches, whose lot will not be ameliorated by the success of this our petition.

SOURCE: Frédéric Bastiat, *Economic Sophisms* (Edinburgh: Oliver and Boyd, Tweeddale Court, 1873), pp. 49-53, abridged.

FIGURE 6-8 **Candian tariffs: 1930-1994**

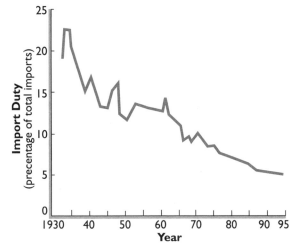

Source: Historical Statistics of Canada and Statistics Canada.

Canadian tariffs have been coming down steadily since 1930.

BILATERAL AGREEMENTS AND GATT

The across-the-board reduction of tariffs has come about because of various bilateral (between two nations) agreements Canada has signed. By incorporating **most-favoured-nation clauses** in these agreements, the reduced tariffs would apply not only to the specific nation negotiating with Canada, but to all nations previously granted most-favoured nation status.

This approach was broadened in 1947 when 23 nations, including Canada, signed a **General Agreement on Tariffs and Trade (GATT)**. GATT is based on three cardinal principles: (1) equal, nondiscriminatory treatment for all member nations; (2) the reduction of tariffs by multilateral negotiations; and (3) the elimination of import quotas.

Basically, GATT is a forum to negotiate reductions in trade barriers on a multilateral basis among nations. More than 100 nations now belong to GATT, and there is little doubt that it has been a positive force in the trend towards liberalized trade. Under its sponsorship, member nations have completed eight "rounds" of negotiations to reduce trade barriers in the post-World War II period.

URUGUAY ROUND The eighth "round" of GATT negotiations began in Uruguay in 1986. After seven years of wrangling, in 1993 the participant nations reached a new agreement. This new agreement took effect on January 1, 1995, and its provisions will be phased in through 2005.

The major provisions of the new GATT agreement are:

1. TARIFF REDUCTION Tariffs will be eliminated or reduced on thousands of products, including construction equipment, medical equipment, paper, steel, chemicals, wood, memory chips, and aluminum. Overall, tariffs will drop by about 33%.
2. INCLUSION OF SERVICES Services are now a $900-billion segment of world trade and GATT will apply to them for the first time. The GATT accord will liberalize governmental rules that in the past have impeded the global market for advertising, insurance, consulting, accounting, legal, tourist, financial, and other services.
3. AGRICULTURAL All member nations together agree to cut agricultural subsidies they pay to farmers, reducing the collective total subsidy by about 21%, or $300 billion annually.
4. INTELLECTUAL PROPERTY International protection against piracy is provided for intellectual property such as patents, trademarks, and copyrights. This protection will greatly benefit Canadian book publishers, music producers, and software firms.
5. PHASED REDUCTION OF QUOTAS ON TEXTILES AND APPAREL Quotas on imported textiles and apparel will be phased out over a ten-year period, to be replaced with tariffs. These quotas have choked off apparel and clothing imports to the industrial nations. Eliminating them will benefit the developing countries having comparative advantages in these areas.
6. WORLD TRADE ORGANIZATION GATT becomes the World Trade Organization with judicial powers to mediate among members disputing the new rules.

When fully implemented, the GATT agreement will boost the world's GDP by $6 trillion, or 8%! Consumers in Canada will save about $3 billion annually.

BOX 6-3 IN THE MEDIA

CHILE VIEWED AS NAFTA TRAIL BLAZER

BY DREW FAGAN

SANTIAGO — Chile is acting as a prototype for other South American countries by entering into free-trade negotiations with North America, the leaders of Chile and Canada said yesterday.

At the end of a two-day official visit by Prime Minister Jean Chrétien, Chilean President Eduardo Frei said free trade will force Chilean companies to become more productive and the government to help prepare sensitive sectors such as agriculture for open trade.

"Chile is actually blazing a trail ... towards integration of the market of the Americas," Mr. Frei said at a press conference.

"Every day, companies need to be more efficient, their costs have to be lower and they have to train their people more."

Mr. Chrétien said he expects that the talks to add Chile to the North American free-trade agreement will make future negotiations to add other countries easier. "After Chile, others will fall in line."

Mr. Chrétien added that the continuing economic crisis in Mexico has not set back talks with Chile.

Canadian Trade Minister Roy MacLaren said in an interview yesterday that his meetings with Eduardo Aninat, the Chilean minister responsible for NAFTA accession, have reaffirmed his view that the negotiations will be relatively simple. "I don't anticipate any problems."

Indeed, an unreleased report commissioned by the Canadian government concludes that existing Chilean laws and policies make the country virtually ready to enter NAFTA. The study was done by a handful of Chilean legal, economic and trade experts and has not been challenged by the U.S. or Mexican governments.

The main changes Chile will have to make to enter NAFTA include, according to the report: extension of patent protection to 17 from 15 years; elimination of a one-year restriction on repatriation of foreign capital; inclusion of improved trade remedy rules; and harmonized procedures for enforcement of environmental standards.

Chile has an 11-per-cent tariff on goods that would be phased out for its NAFTA partners. It has practically no non-tariff barriers to elimi-

nate, has open government procurement procedures, and has services regulations generally in accordance with NAFTA standards.

"This openness would greatly facilitate the negotiation of a trade agreement," the report concludes....

The Chilean government toughened its environmental regulations late last year in an attempt to address criticism, mentioned in the Canadian government study, that the standards were haphazardly applied.

Mr. Aninat has committed the Chilean government to accepting the NAFTA environmental side deal, according to Canadian officials.

But Mr. Frei also implied yesterday that environmental laws must take a back seat in a developing country like Chile. Lax environmental rules are one reason that Canadian mining companies have invested heavily in countries like Chile and Mexico.

"We must use our natural resources ... to develop our industry," Mr. Frei said.

SOURCE: *Globe and Mail*, January 27, 1995, p. B1. Reprinted with permission.

The Story in Brief

In early 1995 Canada, the United States, and Mexico entered into negotiations with Chile in an effort to reach an agreement that would make the South American country a member of the North American Free Trade Agreement (NAFTA).

The Economics Behind the Story

- Negotiations between Chile and NAFTA members to allow the former into NAFTA stem from the desire of both parties to gain from increased trade. Chile had an 11% duty on goods entering its borders. These would be phased out, forcing domestic producers to become more competitive — producing more output with the same, or fewer, inputs. Likewise, Canada, the United States, and Mexico would reduce tariffs on Chilean goods entering their countries — for example, fresh fruits and wine. Consumers of all four countries would benefit from lower prices.

- Do you agree with the Chilean minister responsible for NAFTA accession that "environmental laws must take a back seat in a developing country like Chile"? Would your answer be different if you lived in Chile and were very poor? Use marginal benefit-cost analysis to help you answer the question.

EUROPEAN UNION

Countries have also sought to reduce tariffs by creating regional free-trade zones or trade blocs. The most dramatic example is the **European Union (EU)**, formerly called the European Economic Community. Initiated as the "Common Market" in 1958, the EU now comprises 15 Western European nations — France, Germany, Italy, Belgium, the Netherlands, Luxembourg, Denmark, Ireland, United Kingdom, Greece, Spain, Portugal, Austria, Finland, and Sweden.

GOALS   The original "Common Market" called for (1) gradual abolition of tariffs and import quotas on all products traded among the 12 participating nations; (2) establishment of a common system of tariffs applicable to all goods received from nations outside the EU; (3) free movement of capital and labour within the common market; and (4) creation of common policies with respect to other economic matters of joint concern, such as agriculture, transportation, and restrictive business practices. The EU has achieved most of these goals and is now a strong **trade bloc**.

RESULTS   Motives for creating the European Union were both political and economic. The main economic motive was freer trade for members. While it is difficult to determine how much of EU prosperity and growth has resulted from economic integration, integration has created the mass markets essential to EU industries. The economies of large-scale production have enabled European industries to achieve the lower costs denied them by small, localized markets.

Effects on nonmember nations, such as Canada, are less certain. On one hand, a peaceful and increasingly prosperous EU makes its member nations better customers for Canadian exports. On the other hand, Canadian and other nonmember firms encounter tariffs that make it difficult to compete against firms within the EU trade bloc. For example, before the establishment of the EU, North American, German, and French automobile manufacturers all faced the same tariff selling their products in, say, Belgium. However, with the establishment of internal trading among EU members, Belgium tariffs on German Volkswagens and French Renaults fell to zero, but an external tariff still applies to North American Chevrolets and Fords. This puts North American automobile firms at a serious disadvantage. Similarly, EU trade restrictions hamper Eastern European exports of metals, textiles, and farm products, goods that the Eastern Europeans produce in abundance.

By giving preferences to other countries within their free-trade zone, trade blocs such as the EU may reduce their trade with nonbloc members. Thus, the world loses some of the benefits of a completely open global trading system. Eliminating this disadvantage has been one of the motivations for promoting freer global trade through GATT.

NORTH AMERICAN FREE TRADE AGREEMENT

In 1993 Canada, Mexico, and the United States formed a trade bloc. The **North American Free Trade Agreement (NAFTA)** established a free-trade zone having about the same combined output as the EU, but a much larger geographical area. A

1989 free-trade agreement between Canada and the United States — the **Canada-U.S. Free Trade Agreement (FTA)** — preceded NAFTA. Through the FTA Canadian producers have gained increased access to a market ten times the size of Canada; Canadian consumers have gained the advantage of lower-price American goods. But eliminating tariffs has also helped American producers and consumers. Because Canada and the United States are each other's largest trade partners, there have been large gains for both countries from the Canadian-United States accord. When fully implemented in 1999, the agreement is expected to generate $1 billion to $3 billion of annual gains for each nation.

Free trade with Mexico is more controversial in Canada than is free trade with the United States. NAFTA will eliminate tariffs and other trade barriers between Mexico and Canada and the United States over a 15-year period. Critics of the agreement fear a loss of Canadian jobs as firms move to Mexico to take advantage of lower wages and less stringent regulations on pollution and workplace safety. These detractors also are concerned that Japan and South Korea will build plants in Mexico to transport goods duty-free to Canada, further hurting Canadian firms and workers.

Defenders of NAFTA reject these concerns and cite several strong arguments in its favour.

1. Specialization according to comparative advantage will enable Canada to obtain more total output from its scarce resources.
2. The reduction of high Mexican tariffs will increase Canadian exports to Mexico.
3. This free-trade zone will encourage worldwide investment in Mexico, enhancing Mexican productivity and national income. Mexican consumers will use some of that increased income to buy Canadian exports.
4. A higher standard of living in Mexico will enable Mexico to afford more pollution-control equipment and to provide safer workplaces.
5. The loss of specific Canadian jobs to Mexico may have occurred anyway to low-wage countries such as South Korea, Taiwan, and Hong Kong. NAFTA will enable and encourage Canadian firms to be more efficient, enhancing their long-term competitiveness with firms in Japan and the European Union.

It may appear that the world's nations are combining into potentially hostile trade blocs. But NAFTA constitutes a vehicle to negotiate reductions in trade barriers with the EU, Japan, and other trading countries. Access to the vast North American market is as important to the EU and Japan as is access to their markets by Canada, the United States, and Mexico. NAFTA gives Canada a lever in future trade negotiations with the EU and Japan. Conceivably, direct negotiations between NAFTA and the EU could eventually link the two free-trade zones. Japan and other major trading nations, not wishing to be left out of the world's wealthiest trade markets, would be forced to eliminate their high trade barriers — to open their domestic markets to additional imports. Nor do other nations and trade blocs want to be excluded from North America. Example:

1. **APEC** In late 1994 Canada and 17 other members of the Asia-Pacific Economic Cooperation (APEC) nations agreed to establish freer trade and more open investment over the next few decades. APEC nations are Australia, Brunei, Canada, Chile, Hong Kong, Indonesia, Japan, Malaysia, Mexico, New Zealand, the Philippines, Papua New Guinea, Singapore, South Korea, Taiwan, Thailand, and the United States.

2. **ADMISSION OF CHILE INTO NAFTA** At the invitation of Canada, Mexico, and the United States, Chile has agreed to become the fourth partner in NAFTA (see Box 6-3).

3. **MERCOSUR** The free-trade area encompassing Brazil, Argentina, Uruguay, and Paraguay — called *Mercosur* — is interested in linking up with NAFTA. So are other South American countries. In late 1994 the Canadian prime minister and 33 other prime ministers and presidents of Western hemisphere nations agreed to begin negotiations on a free-trade area from "Alaska to Argentina."

Economists agree that the *ideal* free-trade area would be the world. (**Key Question 10**)

QUICK REVIEW 6-3

I. Governments promote exports and reduce imports through tariffs, quotas, nontariff barriers, and export subsidies.

2. The various "rounds" of the General Agreement on Tariffs and Trade (GATT) have established multinational reductions in tariffs and import quotas among the more than 120 member nations.

3. The Uruguay Round of GATT that went into effect in 1995: **a** reduced tariffs worldwide; **b** liberalized rules impeding barriers to trade in services; **c** reduced agricultural subsidies; **d** created new protections for intellectual property; **e** phased out quotas on textiles and apparel, and **f** set up the World Trade Organization.

4. The European Union (EU), the Canada-U.S. Free Trade Agreement (FTA), and the North American Free Trade Agreement (NAFTA) have reduced trade barriers by establishing large free-trade zones.

CAN CANADIAN FIRMS COMPETE?

Freer international trade has brought with it intense competition in a number of product markets in Canada and worldwide. Not many decades ago three large domestic producers dominated our automobile industry. Imported autos were an oddity that accounted for a minuscule portion of the market. But General Motors, Ford, and Chrysler now face intense competition as they struggle for market shares with Nissan, Honda, Toyota, Hyundai, BMW, and others. Similarly, imports have gained major market shares in automobile tires, clothing, sporting goods, electronics, motorcycles, outboard motors, and toys.

Nevertheless, thousands of firms — large and small — have thrived and prospered in the global marketplace. Northern Telecom, Bombardier, and MacMillan-Bloedel are just a few cases in point. These and many other firms have continued to retain high market shares at home and have expanded their sales broad. Of course, not all firms have been so successful. Some corporations simply have not been able to compete; their international competitors make better quality products, have lower production costs, or both. Not surprisingly, the Canadian firms that have been most vulnerable to foreign competition are precisely those that have enjoyed long periods of trade protection via tariffs and quotas. These barriers to imports have artificially limited competition, greatly dampening incentives to innovate, reduce costs, and improve products. Also, trade barriers have shielded some domestic firms from the usual consequences of national shifts in comparative advantages over time. As trade protection declines under GATT and NAFTA, some Canadian firms will surely discover that they are producing goods for which Canada clearly has a comparative *disadvantage* (apparel, for example).

Is the greater competition accompanying the global economy a good thing? Although some domestic producers and their workers do not like it, foreign competition benefits consumers. Imports reduce product prices and provide consumers with a greater variety of goods. Foreign competition also forces domestic producers to become more efficient and to improve product quality — precisely the outcome in several Canadian industries, including autos and steel. Evidence shows that most — clearly not all — Canadian firms *can* and *do* compete successfully in the global economy.

What about Canadian firms that cannot successfully compete in open markets? The harsh reality is that they should go out of business, much like an unsuccessful corner boutique. Persistent economic losses mean valuable scarce resources are not being used efficiently. Shifting these resources to alternative, profitable, uses will increase the total value of Canadian output.

CHAPTER SUMMARY

1. International trade is growing in importance globally and for Canada. World trade is vital to Canada in two respects. **a** Canadian imports and exports as a percentage of national output are significant. **b** Canada is completely dependent on trade for certain commodities and materials that cannot be obtained domestically.

2. Our principal exports include automotive products, machinery and equipment, and grain; our major imports are general machinery and equipment, automobiles, and industrial goods and machinery. Quantitatively, the United States is our most important trading partner.

3. Global trade has been greatly facilitated by **a** improvements in transportation technology; **b** improvements in communications technology; **c** general declines in tariffs; and **d** peaceful relations among major industrial nations. Canada and the United States, Japan, and the Western European nations dominate the global economy. But the total volume of trade has been increased by several new trade participants, including the "Asian tigers" (Hong Kong, Singapore, South Korea, and Taiwan), China, the Eastern European countries, and the newly independent countries of the former Soviet Union.

4. The "open economy" circular flow model connects the domestic Canadian economy to the "Rest of the World." Customers from abroad enter our product market to buy some of our output. These Canadian exports create business revenues and generate income in Canada. Canadian households spend some of their money income on products made abroad and imported to Canada.

5. Specialization according to comparative advantage permits nations to achieve higher standards of living through exchange with other countries. A trading partner should specialize in products and services where its domestic opportunity costs are lowest. The terms of trade must be such that both nations can get more of a particular output via trade than they can at home.

6. The foreign exchange market sets exchange rates between nations' currencies. Foreign importers are suppliers of their currencies and Canadian exporters are demanders of foreign currencies. The resulting equilibrium exchange rates link the price levels of all nations. Depreciation of the dollar reduces our imports and increases our exports, dollar appreciation increases our imports and reduces our exports.

7. Governments shape trade flows through **a** protective tariffs; **b** quotas; **c** nontariff barriers; and **d** export subsidies. These are impediments to free trade; they result from misunderstanding about the gains from trade and from political considerations. By driving up product prices, trade barriers cost Canadian consumers billions of dollars annually.

8. The post-World War period has seen a trend towards lower Canadian tariffs. In 1947 the General Agreement on Tariffs and Trade (GATT) was formed to **a** encourage nondiscriminatory treatment for all trading nations; **b** reduce tariffs; and **c** eliminate import quotas.

9. The Uruguay Round of GATT negotiations, completed in 1993: **a** reduced tariffs; **b** liberalized trade in services; **c** reduced agricultural subsidies; **d** reduced pirating of intellectual property; **e** phased out import quotas on textiles and apparel; and **f** established the World Trade Organization, which replaces GATT.

10. Free-trade zones (trade blocs) may liberalize trade within regions but may also impede trade with nonbloc members. Three examples of free-trade arrangements are **a** the European Union (EU), formerly the European Community or "Common Market"; **b** the Canada-U.S. Free Trade Agreement (FTA); and **c** the North American Free Trade Agreement (NAFTA), comprising Canada, Mexico, and the United States, and later, Chile.

11. The global economy has created intense foreign competition in many Canadian product markets.

TERMS AND CONCEPTS

absolute advantage (p. 100)
appreciation (p. 104)
"Asian tigers" (p. 97)
Canada-U.S. Free Trade Agreement (FTA)
    (p. 111)
comparative advantage (p. 101)
depreciation (p. 104)
European Union (EU) (p. 110)
export subsidies (p. 105)
foreign exchange market (p. 103)

General Agreement on Tariffs and Trade (GATT) (p. 108)
import quotas (p. 105)
most-favoured-nation clauses (p. 108)
multinational corporations (p. 97)
nontariff barriers (p. 105)
North American Free Trade Agreement (NAFTA)
    (p. 110)
protective tariffs (p. 105)
terms of trade (p. 102)
trade bloc (p. 110)

QUESTIONS AND STUDY SUGGESTIONS

1. What is the quantitative importance of world trade to Canada? Who is quantitatively Canada's most important trade partner? How can persistent trade deficits be financed? "Trade deficits mean we get more merchandise from the rest of the world than we provide them in return. Therefore, trade deficits are economically desirable." Do you agree?

2. Account for the rapid growth of world trade since World War II. Who are the major players in international trade? Who are the "Asian tigers" and how important are they in world trade?

3. *Key Question*   *Use the circular flow model (Figure 6-5) to explain how an increase in exports would affect revenues of domestic firms, money income of domestic households, and imports from abroad. Use Figure 6-3 to find the amounts (1994) of Canada's exports (flow 13) and imports (flow 16) in the circular flow model. What do these amounts imply for flows 14 and 15?*

4. *Key Question*   *The following are production possibilities tables for South Korea and Canada. Assume that before specialization and trade the optimal product mix for South Korea is alternative B and for Canada alternative D.*

Product	South Korea's production alternatives					
	A	B	C	D	E	F
Radios (in thousands)	30	24	18	12	6	0
Chemicals (in tonnes)	0	6	12	18	24	30

Product	Canada's production alternatives					
	A	B	C	D	E	F
Radios (in thousands)	10	8	6	4	2	0
Chemicals (in tonnes)	0	4	8	12	16	20

a. *Are comparative-cost conditions such that the two areas should specialize? If so, what product should each produce?*

b. *What is the total gain in radio and chemical output that results from this specialization?*

c. *What are the limits of the terms of trade? Suppose actual terms of trade are 1 unit of radios for 1 1/2 units of chemicals and that 4 units of radios are exchanged for 6 units of chemicals. What are the gains from specialization and trade for each area?*

d. *Can you conclude from this illustration that specialization according to comparative advantage results in more efficient use of world resources? Explain.*

5. Suppose that the comparative-cost ratios of two products — baby formula and tuna fish — are as follows in the hypothetical nations of Canswicki and Tunata.

Canswicki: 1 can baby formula = 2 cans tuna fish

Tunata: 1 can baby formula = 4 cans tuna fish

In what product should each nation specialize? Explain why terms of trade of 1 can baby formula = 2 1/2 cans tuna fish would be acceptable to both nations.

6. *Key Question* *"Our exports create a demand for foreign currencies; foreign imports of our goods generate supplies of foreign currencies." Do you agree? Other things being equal, would a decline in Canadian incomes or a weakening of Canadian preferences for foreign products cause the dollar to depreciate or appreciate? What would be the effects of that depreciation or appreciation on our exports and imports?*

7. If the French franc declines in value (depreciates) in the foreign exchange market, will it be easier or harder for the French to sell their wine in Canada? If you were planning a trip to Paris, how would the depreciation of the franc change the dollar price of this trip?

8. True or false? "An increase in the Canadian dollar price of the German mark implies that the German mark has depreciated in value." Explain.

9. What tools do governments use to promote exports and restrict imports? What are the benefits and the costs of protectionist policies? What is the net outcome for consumers?

10. *Key Question* *What is GATT? How does it affect nearly every person in the world? What were the major outcomes of the Uruguay Round of GATT? How is GATT related to the European Union (EU), the Canada-U.S. Free Trade Agreement (FTA), and the North American Free Trade Agreement (NAFTA)?*

11. Explain: "Free trade zones such as the EU and NAFTA lead a double life: They can promote free trade among members, but pose serious trade obstacles for nonmembers." Do you think the net effects of these trade blocs are good or bad for world trade?

12. Do you think Canadian firms will be able to compete with foreign firms in world trade during the next 20 years? What do you see as the competitive strengths of Canadian firms? Competitive weaknesses? Explain: "Even if Japan captured the entire worldwide auto market, that simply would mean that Japan would have to buy a whole lot of other products from abroad. Thus, Canada and other industrial nations would necessarily experience an increase in exports to Japan."

13. (Applying the Theory) What point is Bastiat trying to make with his petition of the candlemakers?

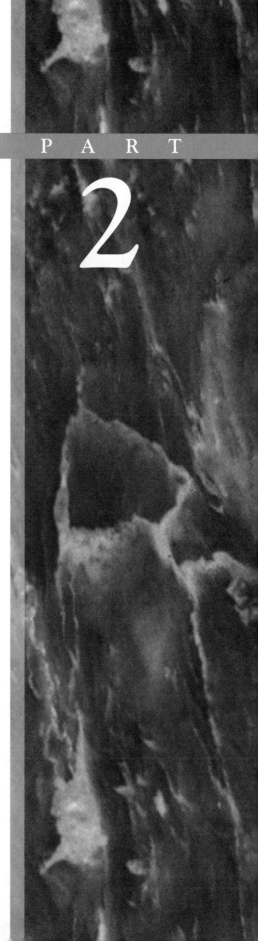

THE ECONOMICS OF CONSUMPTION, PRODUCTION, AND COST

CHAPTER 7

DEMAND AND SUPPLY: ELASTICITIES AND APPLICATIONS

S carce resources. Unlimited wants. That's what economics is all about. It's because of unlimited wants that we must efficiently manage our scarce resources. Our economic system tries to do that in two ways. One is the full employment of all available resources — the subject matter of macroeconomics. The other is to use those employed resources efficiently. This is the focus of microeconomics to which we now turn.

We'll begin by looking at individual prices and the market system. How does the market operate and how efficient is it in utilizing resources? To examine that efficiency, we will analyze individual prices under a variety of contrasting market arrangements.

Demand and supply analysis is a powerful tool with which to explain prices. But is not the demand for insulin by a diabetic very different from the demand for perfume or after-shave lotion? Would a diabetic consumer change the quantity demanded of insulin and perfume by the same amount if their prices both doubled? This question can be answered using the concept of elasticity.

In this chapter we will extend our understanding of demand and supply as follows:

1. Explain the concept of price elasticity as it applies to both demand and supply and present a number of applications;

2. Generalize the elasticity concept by introducing cross and income elasticity of demand.

3. Apply demand and supply analysis to government-imposed price ceilings and floors.

BOX 7-1   THE BIG PICTURE

You should think of elasticity as a refinement of supply and demand analysis. In a world of scarcity, you must choose among alternative needs and wants every day. The choices you make are influenced by prices. As price changes, your choices about how much to purchase of each good or service changes. But your response to price changes for each good or service you want will vary. The quantity demanded of antibiotics prescribed by your doctor is unlikely to change much even if there is a sizable change in price, either up or down! But if the price of chocolate bars were to rise to $10 each, you would undoubtedly consume fewer chocolate bars each year.

As you read this chapter, keep the following points in mind:

- Elasticity has important application to business decisions; it helps predict consumer response to price changes.
- Government policy choices are often made on the basis of elasticity. For example, if a government wants to raise its revenues from taxation, it should choose goods or services whose demand is relatively insensitive to a price change.
- Elasticity can help to explain some social phenomenon — for example, a change in drug-related crime due to a change in the price of drugs.

PRICE ELASTICITY OF DEMAND

The law of demand tells us that consumers will respond to a price decline by buying more of a product. But the degree of consumer responsiveness to a price change may vary considerably from product to product and between different price ranges for the same product.

The responsiveness or sensitivity of consumers to a change in the price of a product is measured by the **price elasticity of demand**. Demand for some products is such that consumers are highly responsive to price changes: modest price changes give rise to very large changes in the quantity purchased. The demand for such products is said to be *relatively elastic* or simply *elastic*. For other products, consumers are quite unresponsive to price changes: substantial price changes result in modest changes in the amount purchased. In such cases demand is *relatively inelastic* or simply *inelastic*.

THE PRICE ELASTICITY FORMULA

We measure the degree of elasticity of demand by the elasticity coefficient E_d, in the price elasticity formula:

$$E_d = \frac{\text{percentage change in quantity demanded of product X}}{\text{percentage change in price of product X}}$$

These *percentage* changes are calculated by dividing the change in price by the original price and the change in quantity demanded by the original quantity demanded. Thus we can restate our formula as:

$$E_d = \frac{\text{change in quantity demanded of product X}}{\text{original quantity demanded of product X}} \div \frac{\text{change in price of product X}}{\text{original price of product X}}$$

USE OF PERCENTAGES   But why use percentages rather than absolute amounts in measuring consumer responsiveness? The answer is two-fold.

1. **CHOICE OF UNITS**   If we use absolute changes, our impression of buyer responsiveness will be arbitrarily affected by the choice of units. If the price of product X falls from $3 to $2 and consumers, as a result, increase their purchases from 60 to 100 kilograms, it may appear that consumers are quite sensitive to price changes and therefore that demand is elastic. After all, a price change of "one" has caused a change in the amount demanded of "forty." But by changing the monetary unit from dollars to cents (why not?), we find that a price change of "one hundred" causes a quantity change of "forty," giving the impression that demand is inelastic. Using percentage changes avoids this problem. This particular price decline is 33% whether measured in dollars ($1/$3) or cents (100 cents/300 cents).

2. **COMPARING PRODUCTS**   By using percentages we can better compare consumer responsiveness to

changes in the prices of different products. It makes little sense to compare the effects on quantity demanded of a $1 increase in the price of a $10,000 auto with a $1 increase in the price of a $1 can of beer. Here the price of the auto is rising by 0.0001% while the beer price is up by 100%! If we increase the price of both products by 1% — $100 for the car and 1¢ for the beer — we obtain a more sensible comparison of consumer sensitivity to the price changes.

IGNORE MINUS SIGN   We know from the downsloping demand curve that price and quantity demanded are inversely related. This means that the price elasticity coefficient of demand will always be a *negative* number. For example, if price declines, then quantity demanded will increase. This means that the numerator in our formula will be negative and the denominator positive, yielding a negative E_d. We therefore ignore the minus sign and simply present the *absolute value* of the elasticity coefficient to avoid an ambiguity that might otherwise arise.

INTERPRETATIONS   Now let's interpret our formula.

1. ELASTIC   Demand is **elastic** if a given percentage change in price results in a *larger* percentage change in quantity demanded. If a 2% decline in price results in a 4% increase in quantity demanded, demand is elastic. Where demand is elastic, E_d will be greater than 1; in this case it is 2.

2. INELASTIC   If a given percentage change in price is accompanied by a relatively *smaller* change in quantity demanded, demand is **inelastic.** If a 3% decline in price leads to only a 1% increase in the amount demanded, demand is inelastic. Specifically, E_d is .33 in this instance. The elasticity coefficient will always be less than 1 when demand is inelastic.

3. OTHER CASES   The borderline case that separates elastic and inelastic demands occurs when a percentage change in price and the accompanying percentage change in quantity demanded are equal. For example, if a 1% drop in price causes a 1% increase in the amount sold. This special case is termed **unit elasticity,** because E_d is exactly 1, or unity.

The term **perfectly inelastic demand** refers to the extreme situation where a change in price results in

no change in the quantity demanded. Approximate examples: An acute diabetic's demand for insulin or an addict's demand for heroin. A demand curve parallel to the vertical axis — such as D_0 in Figure 7-1 — shows this graphically. In the extreme situation where a small price reduction would cause buyers to increase their purchases from zero to all they could obtain, we say that demand is **perfectly elastic**. A perfectly elastic demand curve is a line parallel to the horizontal axis, such as D_1 in Figure 7-1.

REFINEMENT: MIDPOINTS FORMULA

The hypothetical demand data shown in Table 7-1 are useful in explaining an annoying problem that arises in applying the price elasticity formula. In calculating E_d for the $5–$4 price range, should we use the $5–4 units price-quantity combination or the $4–5 units combination as a point of reference in calculating the percentage changes in price and quantity the elasticity formula requires? Our choice will influence the outcome.

Using the $5–4 unit reference point, the percentage decrease in price is 20% and the percentage increase in quantity is 25%. Substituting in the formula, the elasticity coefficient is 25/20 or 1.25, indicating the demand is somewhat elastic. But using the $4–5 unit bushel reference point, the percentage increase in price is 25% and the percentage decline in quantity is 20%. The elasticity coefficient is there-

---

FIGURE 7-1   **Perfectly inelastic and elastic demand**

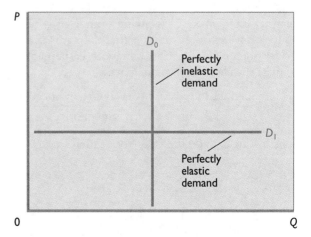

A perfectly inelastic demand curve, D_0, graphs as a line parallel to the vertical axis; a perfectly elastic demand curve, D_1, is drawn parallel to the horizontal axis.

TABLE 7-1 **Price elasticity of demand as measured by the elasticity coefficient and the total revenue test**

(1) Total quantity demanded per week	(2) Price per unit	(3) Elasticity coefficient, E_d	(4) Total revenue (1) x (2)	(5) Total revenue test
1	$8		$ 8	
		5.00		Elastic
2	7		14	
		2.60		Elastic
3	6		18	
		1.57		Elastic
4	5		20	
		1.00		Unit elastic
5	4		20	
		0.64		Inelastic
6	3		18	
		0.38		Inelastic
7	2		14	
		0.20		Inelastic
8	1		8	

fore 20/25, or .80, meaning demand is slightly inelastic. Which is it? Is demand elastic or inelastic?

A solution to this problem is to use the *averages* of two prices and the two quantities under consideration for reference points. In the $5–$4 price range case, the price reference is $4.50 and the quantity reference 4.5 units. The percentage change in price is now about 22% and the percentage change in quantity is also about 22%, giving us an E_d of 1. This solution estimates elasticity at the midpoint of the $5–$4 price range. We can refine our earlier statement of the elasticity formula to read

$$E_d = \frac{\text{change in quantity}}{\text{sum of quantities}/2} \div \frac{\text{change in price}}{\text{sum of prices}/2}$$

Substituting data for the $5–$4 price range, we get

$$E_d = \frac{1}{9/2} \div \frac{1}{9/2} = 1$$

This indicates that at the $4.50–4.5 price-quantity point the price elasticity of demand is unity. A 1% price change would result in a 1% change in quantity demanded.

In column 3 you should verify the elasticity cal-culations for the $1–$2 and $7–$8 price ranges. The interpretation of the E_d for the $1–$2 range is that a 1% change in price will change quantity demanded by 0.2%. For the $7–$8 range a 1% change in price will change quantity demanded by 5%.

GRAPHIC ANALYSIS

In Figure 7-2(a) we have plotted our demand curve from Table 7-1. This portrayal brings two points into focus.

1. **ELASTICITY AND PRICE RANGE** Elasticity varies over the different price ranges of the same demand schedule or curve. For all straight-line and most demand curves, demand is more elastic in the upper-left segment ($5–$8 price range) than in the lower-right segment ($4–$1 price range).

This is a consequence of the arithmetic properties of the elasticity measure.

Specifically, in the upper-left segment the percentage change in quantity is large because the original quantity from which the percentage quantity change is derived is small. In this segment the percentage change in price is small because the original price from which the percentage price

FIGURE 7-2 **Price elasticity of demand and its relation to total revenue**

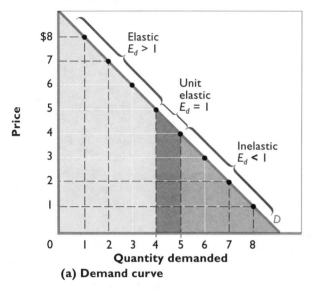

(a) Demand curve

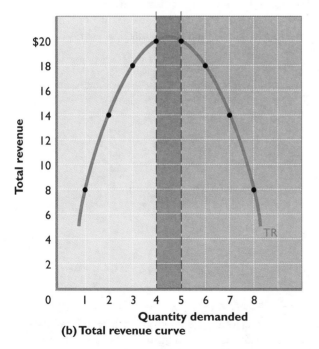

(b) Total revenue curve

As shown in (a), the typical demand curve is elastic in high price ranges and inelastic in lower price ranges. In (b) we observe that total revenue rises in the elastic range as price is reduced. Where demand elasticity is unity, a change in price will not change total revenue. In this range total revenue is maximized. Price reductions in the inelastic range of the demand curve cause total revenue to fall.

change is calculated is large. The relatively large percentage change in quantity divided by the relatively small change in price results in an elastic demand — a large E_d.

The reverse is true for the lower-right segment of the demand curve. Here the percentage change in quantity is small, because the original quantity from which the percentage change is determined is large. Similarly, the percentage change in price is large, because the original price from which the relative price change is calculated is small. The relatively small percentage change in quantity divided by the relatively large change in price results in an inelastic demand — a low E_d.

Assignment: Draw two linear demand curves parallel to one another. Demonstrate that for any specific given price change demand is more elastic on the curve closer to the origin.

2. ELASTICITY VERSUS SLOPE The graphic appearance — the slope — of a demand curve is *not* a sound basis for judging its elasticity. The catch is that the slope — the flatness or steepness — of a demand curve is based on *absolute* changes in price and quantity, while elasticity involves *relative* or *percentage* changes in price and quantity.

Observe in Figure 7-2(a) that our demand curve is linear, which, by definition, means the slope is constant throughout. But we have demonstrated that such a curve is elastic in its high-price ($8–$5) range and inelastic in its low-price ($4–$1) range. **(Key Question 2)**

QUICK REVIEW 7-1

1. Price elasticity of demand measures the extent to which consumers change the quantity of a product they purchase when its price changes.

2. Price elasticity of demand is the ratio of the percentage change in quantity demanded to the percentage change in price. The average of the prices and quantities are used in calculating the percentage changes.

3. When price elasticity is greater than 1, demand is elastic; when less than 1, it is inelastic. When equal to 1, demand is of unit elasticity.

4. Demand is elastic in the high-price (low-quantity) range and inelastic in the low-price (high-quantity) range of the demand curve.

BOX 7-2 IN THE MEDIA

UNIVERSITY APPLICATIONS FALL: FEAR OF TUITION HIKES CITED

BY ANDREW DUFFY
EDUCATION REPORTER

The number of high school students applying to university has declined sharply this year amid fears that tuition fees could double because of government cutbacks.

Five per cent fewer high school students have applied to Ontario universities, compared to last year when 56,314 graduates filled out application forms.

It's the most significant drop in at least a decade, said Greg Marcotte, executive director of the Ontario Universities' Application Centre in Guelph.

University student groups have suggested the federal government's recently announced budget cuts could double university tuition to $6,000 by 1998.

York University has placed ads in Toronto newspapers, informing students about the "facts" of tuition. Applications to York are up by 1 per cent, but university president Susan Mann said she's concerned some students will not apply because of "misinformation."

At York tuition fees — including all of the ancillary fees — will increase by 10 per cent to $3,000 this fall.

University of Toronto applications from high school students are down about 2 per cent.

At Ryerson Polytechnic University, high school applicants are down about 4.5 per cent. The university last year received about 30,000 applications —

a 27 per cent over-all increase — for its 3,800 first-year places.

High school students make up the bulk of university applicants. This year, up to 40,000 mature or out-of-province students are also expected to compete for the 52,000 first year places available.

Applications to most faculties are down: engineering 8.9 per cent, arts 7.9 per cent, science 2.2 per cent, business administration 0.6 per cent, physical education 3.9 per cent, environmental studies 13.5 per cent and journalism 1 per cent.

SOURCE: *Toronto Star*, March 14, 1995, p. A1. Reprinted with permission — The Toronto Star Syndicate.

The Story in Brief

In Ontario the number of students applying to universities in the province fell 5% because of fears of hefty tuition fee increases.

The Economics Behind the Story

• There are many forces that affect the demand for university education. To distinguish these forces, it is essential to invoke the *ceteris paribus* provision you have learned in an earlier chapter.

• We are not told by how much tuition will increase on average across the university system. We know that at one university, tuition increased 10%. If tuition fees increased 10% at all Ontario universities, a 5% drop in application implies a price elasticity of demand of .5, *ceteris paribus*. Note that we have assumed that a drop in the number of applications will automatically lead to a drop in the number of students actually attending university, which is not necessarily the case.

• But the price elasticity coefficient seems to vary among universities. At one university the 10% tuition fee hike resulted in only a 2% drop in applications, while at another university applications actually increased by 1%.

• If indeed the price elasticity of demand for university education were less than one, speculate on applications to universities in the future should tuition fees rise significantly.

THE TOTAL-REVENUE TEST

Total revenue is determined by multiplying price by quantity demanded. Price elasticity of demand compares the relative size of changes in price and quantity demanded. Therefore, it must tell us what happens to total revenue. Indeed, perhaps the easiest way to tell whether demand is elastic or inelastic is to employ the **total-revenue test**, that is, to observe what happens to total revenue when product price changes.

1. ELASTIC DEMAND If demand is *elastic*, a *decrease* in price will *increase* total revenue. Even though a lower price is received per unit, enough additional units are sold to more than make up for the lower price. This is shown in Figure 7-2(a) for the $8–$7 price range of our demand curve from Table 7-1. (Ignore Figure 7-2[b] for the moment.) Total revenue is price times quantity. Total revenue is $8 when price is $8 and quantity demanded is 1 unit. When price declines to $7, increasing the quantity demanded to 2 units, total revenue changes to $14, which is clearly larger than $8. It is larger because the *loss* in revenue due to the lower price per unit is *less* than the *gain* in revenue due to the larger sales that accompany the lower price.

This reasoning is reversible: If demand is elastic, a price *increase* will *reduce* total revenue. The *gain* in total revenue caused by the higher unit price is *less* than the *loss* in revenue associated with the accompanying fall in sales. **If demand is elastic, a price change will change total revenue in the opposite direction.**

2. INELASTIC DEMAND If demand is *inelastic*, a price *decrease* will *reduce* total revenue. The modest increase in sales will not offset the decline in revenue per unit, and the net result is that total revenue declines. This situation exists for the $2–$1 price range of our demand curve, as shown in Figure 7-2(a). Initially total revenue is $14 when price is $2 and quantity demanded is 7 units.

If we reduce price to $1, quantity demanded will increase to 8 units. Total revenue will change to $8, which is clearly less than $14. It is smaller because the loss in revenue due to the lower unit price is larger than the *gain* in revenue due to the accompanying increase in sales.

Again, our analysis is reversible: if demand is inelastic, a price increase will increase total rev-

enue. **If demand is inelastic, a price change will change total revenue in the same direction.**

3. UNIT ELASTICITY In the special case of unit elasticity, an increase or decrease in price will leave total revenue unchanged. Loss in revenue due to a lower unit price will be exactly offset by the gain in revenue from the accompanying increase in sales.

In Figure 7-2(a) we find that at the $5 price 4 units will be sold to yield total revenue of $20. At $4 a total of 5 units will be sold, again resulting in $20 of total revenue. The $1 price reduction causes the loss of $4 in revenue on the 4 units that could have been sold for $5 each. This is exactly offset by a $4 revenue gain that results from the sale of 1 more unit at the lower $4 price.

GRAPHIC PORTRAYAL The relationship between price elasticity of demand and total revenue can be demonstrated graphically by comparing Figures 7-2(a) and 7-2(b). In Figure 7-2(b) we have graphed the eight total revenue-quantity demanded points from columns 1 and 4 of Table 7-1.

Lowering price over the $8–$5 price range increases total revenue. We know from the elasticity coefficient calculations in Table 7-1 that demand is *elastic* in this range so any given percentage decline in price results in a larger percentage increase in quantity demanded. The lower price per unit is more than offset by the increase in sales and, consequently, total revenue rises.

The $5–$4 price range is characterized by *unit* elasticity. Here the percentage decline in price produces an equal percentage increase in quantity demanded. The price cut is exactly offset by increased purchases so total revenue is unchanged.

Finally, our calculations of E_d tell us that in the $4–$1 price range demand is *inelastic*, meaning that any given percentage decline in price will be accompanied by a smaller percentage increase in sales, causing total revenue to diminish.

Our logic is reversible. A price *increase* in the elastic $8–$5 price range will reduce total revenue. Similarly, a price *increase* in the inelastic $4–$1 range raises total revenue. **(Key Questions 4 and 5)**

REPRISE Table 7-2 provides a convenient summary of the characteristics of price elasticity of demand and merits careful study.

TABLE 7-2 **Price elasticity of demand: a summary**

Absolute value of elasticity coefficient	Terminology	Description	Impact on total revenue (expenditures) of a price:	
			Increase	Decrease
Greater than 1 $(E_d > 1)$	Elastic or relatively elastic	Quantity demanded changes by a larger percentage than does price	Total revenue decreases	Total revenue increases
Equal to 1 $(E_d = 1)$	Unit or unitary elastic	Quantity demanded changes by the same percentage as does price	Total revenue is unchanged	Total revenue is unchanged
Less than 1 $(E_d < 1)$	Inelastic or relatively inelastic	Quantity demanded changes by a smaller percentage than does price	Total revenue increases	Total revenue decreases

DETERMINANTS OF PRICE ELASTICITY OF DEMAND

There are no iron-clad generalizations about the determinants of the elasticity of demand. The following points, however, are helpful.

1. SUBSTITUTABILITY Generally, the larger the number of good substitute products available, the greater the elasticity of demand. Also, the elasticity of demand for a product depends on how narrowly the product is defined. The demand for Petro-Canada motor oil is more elastic than is the overall demand for motor oil. A number of other brands are readily substitutable for Petro-Canada's oil, but there is no good substitute for motor oil per se. Similarly, we would expect the lowering of world trade barriers to increase the elasticity of demand for most products by making more substitutes available. With unimpeded trade Hondas, Toyotas, Nissans, Mazdas, Volkswagens, and other foreign cars become effective substitutes for domestic autos.

2. PROPORTION OF INCOME Other things equal, the higher the price of a service or product relative to your budget, the greater will be the elasticity of demand for it. A 10% increase in the price of pencils or chewing gum will amount to a few pennies and elicit little response in the amount you demand. A 10% increase in the price of automobiles or housing means price increases of perhaps $1,500 and $15,000, respectively. These latter increases are significant fractions of the annual incomes of many families, and quantities purchased could be expected to diminish significantly.

3. LUXURIES VERSUS NECESSITIES The demand for necessities tends to be inelastic; for luxuries, it is elastic. Bread and electricity are generally regarded as necessities. A price increase will not significantly reduce the amount of bread consumed or the amount of lighting and power used in a household. Note the low price elasticity of the latter in Table 7-3. An extreme case: You will not decline an operation for acute appendicitis on being told the physician has found a way to extra-bill!

Caribbean cruises and emeralds, on the other hand, are luxuries that can be forgone without undue inconvenience. If the price of cruises or emeralds rises, one need not purchase them.

The demand for salt is highly inelastic for several reasons. It is a necessity, and there are no good substitutes available. Moreover, salt is a negligible item in the family budget.

TABLE 7-3   Selected price elasticities of demand

Product or service	Price elasticity of demand	
Housing	.01	
Electricity (household)	.13	
Bread	.15	
Telephone service	.26	
Medical care	.31	
Eggs	.32	
Legal services	.37	inelastic
Automobile repair	.40	
Clothing	.49	
Milk	.63	
Household appliances	.63	
Movies	.87	
Beer	.90	
Shoes	.91	
Motor vehicles	1.14	
China, glassware, tableware	1.54	elastic
Restaurant meals	2.27	
Lamb and mutton	2.65	

Main sources: H.S. Houthakker and Lester D. Taylor, *Consumer Demand in the United States : Analyses and Projections*, 2d ed. (Cambridge, Mass.: Harvard University Press, 1970); P.S. George and G.A. King, *Consumer Demand for Food Commodities in the United States with Projections for 1980* (Berkeley: University of California, 1971); and Ahsan Mansur and John Whalley, "Numerical Specification of Applied General Equilibrium Models: Estimation, Calibration, and Data," in Herbert E. Scarf and John B. Shoven, *Applied General Equilibrium Analysis* (New York: Cambridge University Press, 1984).

4. TIME   Usually, the demand for a product is more elastic the longer the time period under consideration. When the price of a product rises, it takes time to find and experiment with other products to see if they are acceptable. Consumers may not immediately reduce purchases very much when the price of beef rises by 10%. But in time they might switch to chicken or fish. Another consideration is product durability. Studies show that "short-run demand" for gasoline is more inelastic at 0.2 than is "long-run demand" at 0.7. In the long run, large gas-guzzling automobiles wear out and, with rising gasoline prices, are replaced by smaller, more fuel-efficient, cars.

An empirical study of commuter rail transportation in the Philadelphia area estimates that the long-run elasticity of demand is almost three times as great as the short-run elasticity. Short-run commuter responses (defined as occurring immediately at the time of a fare change) are inelastic at 0.68. In contrast, the long-run response (defined as occurring over a four-year period) is elastic at 1.84. The greater long-run elasticity occurs over time because potential rail commuters can make choices concerning automobile purchases, car pooling, and the locations of residences and employment. These different elasticities led to the prediction that the commuter system, with about 100,000 riders, could immediately *increase* daily revenues by $8000 by raising the price of a one-way ticket by 25¢ or about 9%, since short-run demand is inelastic. But, in the long run, the same 9% fare increase is estimated to *reduce* total revenue per day by over $19,000 because demand is elastic. This implies that a fare increase that is profitable in the short run may lead to financial difficulties in the long run.[1]

Table 7-3 shows price elasticities of demand for a variety of products. Use the elasticity determinants just discussed to explain each of these elasticity coefficients. (**Key Question 9**)

QUICK REVIEW 7-2

1. A price change will cause total revenue to vary in the opposite direction when demand is elastic and in the same direction when demand is inelastic.

2. Price elasticity of demand is greater **a** the larger the number of substitutes available; **b** the larger the product is in one's budget; **c** the greater the extent to which the product is a luxury; and **d** the longer the time period involved.

SOME PRACTICAL APPLICATIONS

The concept of price elasticity of demand is of great practical significance, as the following examples make evident.

[1] Richard Voith, "Commuter Rail Ridership: The Long and the Short Haul," *Business Review* (Federal Reserve Bank of Philadelphia), November-December 1987, pp. 13-23.

1. BUMPER CROPS The demand for most farm products is highly inelastic, perhaps 0.20 or 0.25. As a result, increases in the output of farm products, arising from a good growing season or productivity increases, depress both the price of farm products and total revenues (incomes) of farmers. For farmers as a group, the inelastic nature of demand for their products means a bumper crop may be undesirable. For policy makers it means higher total farm income depends on the restriction of farm output.

2. AUTOMATION The impact of rapid technological advance on the level of employment depends in part on the elasticity of demand for the product being manufactured. Suppose a firm installs new labour-saving machinery, resulting in the technological unemployment of 500 workers. Assume also that part of the cost reduction resulting from this technological advance is passed on to consumers as reduced product prices. The effect of this price reduction on the firm's sales, and therefore the quantity of labour it needs, will depend on the elasticity of product demand. An elastic demand might increase sales to the extent that some of, all, or even more than, the 500 displaced workers are reabsorbed by the firm. An inelastic demand will mean that few, if any, of the displaced workers will be re-employed, because the increase in the volume of the firm's sales and output will be small.

3. EXCISE TAXES Government pays attention to the elasticity of demand when selecting goods and services upon which to levy excise taxes. If a $1 tax is levied on some product, and $10,000 units are sold, tax revenue will be $10,000. If the tax will be raised to $1.50 and the consequent higher price causes sales to decline to 5000 because of an elastic demand, tax revenue will *decline* to $7500. A higher tax on a product with an elastic demand will bring in less tax revenue. Therefore, legislatures will seek out products with inelastic demand — for example, liquor, gasoline, and cigarettes — when levying excises.

4. DRUGS AND STREET CRIME The fact that the demand for heroin by addicts is highly inelastic poses some awkward trade-offs in law enforcement. The approach used to reduce heroin addiction is to restrict supply by cracking down on its shipment into Canada.

But if this policy is successful, given the highly inelastic demand, the street price to addicts will rise sharply while the amount purchased will decrease only slightly. For the drug dealers this means increased revenues and profits. For the addicts it means greater total expenditures on heroin. Because much of the income that addicts spend on heroin comes from crime — shoplifting, burglary, prostitution, and muggings — these kinds of crimes will increase as addicts increase their total expenditures for heroin. Thus, the effort of law-enforcement authorities to control the spread of drug addiction may increase the amount of crime committed by addicts.

In recent years proposals to legalize drugs has been widely debated. Proponents contend drugs should be treated like alcohol, should be made legal for adults, and regulated for purity and potency. The current war on drugs, it is argued, has been unsuccessful and the associated costs — including enlarged police forces, an overburdened court system, and untold human costs — have increased markedly. Legalization would allegedly reduce drug trafficking greatly by taking the profit out of it. Heroin, for example, is cheap to produce and could be sold at a low price in a legal market. Because the demand of addicts is highly inelastic, the amount consumed at the lower price will only increase modestly. Total expenditures for heroin by addicts will decline and so will the street crime that finances these expenditures.

Opponents of legalization say that, in addition to the addict's inelastic demand, there is another segment of the market where demand may be more elastic. These are the occasional users or "dabblers." Dabblers will use heroin when its price is low, but abstain or substitute, say, alcohol when heroin's price is high. For this group the lower price of heroin associated with legalization will increase consumption by dabblers and in time turn many of them into addicts. This will increase street crime and enlarge all of the social costs associated with drug use.

5. MINIMUM WAGE The federal minimum wage prohibits employers from paying covered workers less than $4 per hour, although provincial minimum wages are higher. Critics contend that an above-equilibrium minimum wage moves employers back up their downsloping labour demand curves and causes unemployment, particularly among teenage workers. On the other hand, workers who remain employed at the minimum wage will receive higher incomes than otherwise. The amount of income lost by the unemployed and the income gained by those who keep their jobs will depend on the elasticity of demand for teenage labour. Research suggests demand for teenage labour is quite inelastic, possibly as low as 0.15 or 0.25. If correct, it means income gains associated with the minimum wage exceed income losses. The case made by critics of the minimum wage would be stronger if the demand for teenage workers were elastic.

PRICE ELASTICITY OF SUPPLY

Price elasticity also applies to supply. If producers are responsive to price changes, supply is elastic. If they are relatively unresponsive to price changes, supply is inelastic.

We calculate the degree of elasticity of supply in the same way as for demand, except we substitute "percentage change in quantity *supplied*" for "percentage change in quantity *demanded*."

$$E_S = \frac{\text{percentage change in quantity supplied of product X}}{\text{percentage change in price of product X}}$$

For reasons explained earlier, the midpoints of the changes in quantity supplied and price are used in calculations. Suppose price were to increase from $4 to $6, causing quantity supplied to rise from 10 to 14. The percentage change in quantity supplied would be 4/12 or 33% and the percentage change in price would be 2/5 or 40%. Substituting in our formula, we determine elasticity of supply to be 40 ÷ 33 or 1.21. Note that, because price and quantity supplied are directly related, E_S will always be positive.

The main determinant of the **elasticity of supply** is the amount of *time* a producer has to respond to a specific change in product price. We can expect a greater output response — and therefore greater elasticity of supply — the longer the amount of time a firm has to adjust to a given price change. A firm's response to an increase in the price of product X depends on the ability to shift resources from the production of other products (whose prices we assume remain constant) to the production of X. The shifting of resources takes time.

In analyzing the impact of time on the elasticity of supply, economists distinguish between the immediate market period, the short run, and the long run.

1. THE MARKET PERIOD The immediate **market period** is so short a time that producers cannot respond to a change in demand and price. Suppose a small farmer brings an entire season's output of tomatoes — one truckload — to market. The supply curve will be perfectly inelastic (vertical). The farmer will sell the truckload whether the price is high or low because he/she cannot offer more tomatoes than the one truckload if the price of tomatoes should be higher than anticipated. It will take another full growing season to respond to a higher-than-expected price by producing more than one truckload. Similarly, because the product is perishable, the farmer cannot withhold it from the market. If the price is lower than anticipated, the farmer will still sell the entire truckload. Even though the price of tomatoes may fall far short of production costs, the farmer will sell out to avoid a total loss through spoilage.

Figure 7-3(a) illustrates the farmer's perfectly inelastic supply curve in the market period. Note that truck farmers cannot respond to an assumed increase in demand since they do not have time to increase the amount supplied. The price increase from P_o to P_m rations a fixed supply to buyers, but elicits no increase in output.[2]

2. THE SHORT RUN In the **short run**, the plant capacity of individual producers and the industry is fixed. But firms *do* have time to use their fixed plants more or less intensively. Thus in the short run, our truck farmer's plant, comprising land and farm machinery, is fixed, but the farmer does have time to cultivate tomatoes more intensively by applying more labour and more fertilizer and pesticides to the crop. The result is a greater output response to the presumed increase in demand. This greater output response is reflected in a more elastic supply of tomatoes as shown by S_s in Figure 7-3(b). Note that the increase in demand is met by a larger quantity adjustment (Q_o to Q_s) and a smaller price adjustment (P_o to P_s) than in the market period: price is therefore lower than in the market period.

---

[2] The supply curve need not be perfectly inelastic (vertical) in the market period. If the product is not perishable, producers may choose, at low current prices, to store some of their product for future sale. This will cause the market period supply curve to have some positive slope.

FIGURE 7-3 **Time and the elasticity of supply**

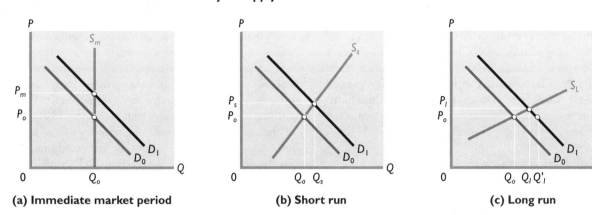

(a) Immediate market period   **(b) Short run**   **(c) Long run**

The greater the amount of time producers have to adjust to a change in demand, the greater will be their output response. In the immediate market period (a) there is insufficient time to change output, and so supply is perfectly inelastic. In the short run (b) plant capacity is fixed, but output can be altered by changing the intensity of its use; supply is therefore more elastic. In the long run (c) all desired adjustments — including changes in plant capacity — can be made, and supply becomes still more elastic.

3. THE LONG RUN The **long run** is a time period long enough that firms can make all desired resource adjustments. Individual firms can expand (or contract) their plant capacities, and new firms can enter (or existing firms can leave) the industry. In the "tomato industry," the farmer can acquire additional land and buy more machinery and equipment. More farmers may be attracted to tomato production by the increased demand and higher price. These adjustments mean an even greater supply response, that is, an even more elastic supply curve S_L. The result, shown in Figure 7-3(c), is a small price effect (P_o to P_l) and a large output effect (Q_o to Q_l) in response to the assumed increase in demand. **(Key Question 14)**

There is no total-revenue test for elasticity of supply. Supply shows a positive or direct relationship between price and amount supplied — the supply curve is upsloping. Regardless of the degree of elasticity, price and total revenue will always move together.

CROSS AND INCOME ELASTICITY OF DEMAND

While price elasticities measure the responsiveness of the quantity of a product demanded or supplied to a change in its price, it is also useful to know how the consump-

tion of a good is affected by a change in the price of a related product or by a change in income.

CROSS ELASTICITY OF DEMAND

Suppose Coca-Cola is considering a reduction in the price of its Sprite brand. Not only will it want to know something about the price elasticity of demand for Sprite (will the price cut increase or decrease total revenue?), but it will also be interested in knowing if the increased sales of Sprite will come at the expense of Coke itself. How sensitive is the quantity demanded of one product (Coke) to a change in the price of a second product (Sprite)? To what extent will the lower price and increased sales of Sprite reduce the sales of Coke?

The concept of **cross elasticity of demand** sheds light on such questions by measuring how sensitive consumer purchases of *one* product (X) are to a change in the price of some *other* product (Y). We calculate cross elasticity of demand like simple price elasticity except we relate the percentage change in the consumption of X to a percentage change in the price of Y:

$$E_{xy} = \frac{\text{percentage change in quantity demanded of X}}{\text{percentage change in price of Y}}$$

This elasticity concept allows us to quantify and more fully understand substitute and complementary goods introduced in Chapter 4.

SUBSTITUTE GOODS   If cross elasticity of demand is *positive* — the quantity demanded of X varies directly with a change in the price of Y — then X and Y are *substitute goods*. For example, an increase in the price of butter (Y) will cause consumers to buy more margarine (X). The larger the positive coefficient, the greater the substitutability between the two products.

COMPLEMENTARY GOODS   When cross elasticity is *negative*, then we know that X and Y "go together" and are *complementary goods*. Thus an increase in the price of cameras will decrease the amount of film purchased. The larger the negative coefficient, the greater the complementarity between the two goods.

INDEPENDENT GOODS   A zero or near-zero coefficient suggests that the two products are unrelated or *independent goods*. For example, we would not expect a change in the price of butter to have any impact on the purchases of film.

INCOME ELASTICITY OF DEMAND

Income elasticity of demand measures the percentage change in the quantity of a product demanded that results from some percentage change in consumer incomes:

$$E_i = \frac{\text{percentage change in quantity demanded}}{\text{percentage change in income}}$$

NORMAL GOODS   For most goods the income elasticity coefficient will be *positive*. Those products of which more is purchased as incomes increase are called *normal goods*. But the positive elasticity coefficient varies greatly among products. For example, the income elasticity of demand for automobiles has been estimated to be about +3.00, while for most farm products it is only about +0.20.

INFERIOR GOODS   A *negative* income elasticity coefficient designates an *inferior good*. Retreaded tires, potatoes, cabbage, and used clothing are likely candidates. Consumers *decrease* their purchases of such products as incomes *increase*.

APPLICATIONS   Estimates of income elasticity can be useful for individuals and policy makers. If you are investing in the stock market, you may be seeking out "growth industries" whose stock values are forecast to rise substantially over time Other things equal, a high income elasticity for industry X's product provides a clue that it will be such an industry, while a low income elasticity for Y suggests it will not. For example, the indicated high positive income

TABLE 7-4   Cross and income elasticity of demand: a summary

Value of coefficient	Description	Type of good(s)
Cross elasticity:		
Positive ($E_{wz} > 0$)	Quantity demanded of W changes in same direction as change in price of Z	Substitutes
Negative ($E_{xy} < 0$)	Quantity demanded of X changes in opposite direction as change in price of Y	Complements
Income elasticity:		
Positive ($E_i > 0$)	Quantity demanded of the product changes in same direction as change in income	Normal or superior
Negative ($E_i < 0$)	Quantity demanded of the product changes in opposite direction as change in income	Inferior

elasticity of demand for automobiles suggests a greater likelihood of long-run prosperity in comparison to agriculture, which has a low income elasticity.

A municipal government would find the income elasticity of demand for new real estate invaluable in estimating future receipts from property taxes. If local incomes are rising by, say, 3% per year, will that result in a proportionately larger or smaller increase in the purchases of new housings and therefore in the property tax base? **(Key Questions 16 and 17)**

Table 7-4 provides a convenient synopsis of the cross and income elasticity concepts.

APPLICATIONS

Supply and demand analysis and the elasticity concept will be applied repeatedly in the remainder of this book. Let's strengthen our understanding of these analytical tools and their significance by examining (a) elasticity and tax incidence, and (b) some of the implications of prices fixed by law.

ELASTICITY AND TAX INCIDENCE

It may be a surprise for you to learn that taxes do not always fall on whom they were levied. The tools of elasticity of supply and demand can help us determine the *tax incidence* — whether producers or consumers bear the tax. Let's focus on a hypothetical excise tax levied on wine producers. Do producers pay this tax, or do they shift it to wine consumers?

Figure 7-4 shows the market for a certain domestic wine and the no-tax equilibrium price and quantity of $4 per bottle and 15 million bottles. Assume that government levies a specific sales or excise tax of $1 per bottle on this wine. What is the incidence of this tax?

DIVISION OF BURDEN   Assuming that government places the tax on sellers (suppliers), the tax can be viewed as an addition to the supply price of the product. While sellers were willing to offer, for example, 5 million bottles of untaxed wine at $2 per bottle, they must now receive $3 per bottle — $2 plus the $1 tax — to offer the same 5 million bottles. Sellers must get $1 more for each quantity supplied to receive the same per unit price they were getting before the tax. The tax shifts the supply curve upward as shown in Figure 7-4, where S is the "no-tax" supply curve and S_t is the "after-tax" supply curve.

Careful comparison of after-tax supply and demand with the pretax equilibrium reveals that with the new tax the new equilibrium price is $4.50 per bottle, compared with the before-tax price of $4. In this case, one-half of the tax is paid by consumers as a higher price and the other half by producers as a lower after-tax price. Consumers pay 50¢ more per bottle and, after remitting the $1 tax per unit to government, producers receive $3.50, or 50¢ less than the $4 before-tax price. In this instance, consumers and producers share the burden of the tax equally; producers shift half the tax forward to consumers in the form of a higher price and bear the other half themselves. .

ELASTICITIES   If the elasticities of demand and supply were different from those shown in Figure 7-4 the incidence of tax would also be different. Two generalizations are relevant.

1. *With a specific supply, the more inelastic the demand for the product, the larger the portion of the tax shifted to consumers.* To verify this, sketch graphically the

---

FIGURE 7-4   The incidence of an excise tax

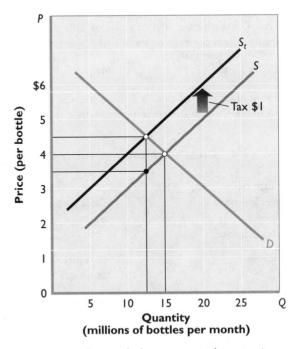

An excise tax of a specified amount, say, $1 per unit, shifts the supply curve upward by the amount of the tax. This results in a higher price ($4.50) to the consumer and a lower after-tax price ($3.50) to the producer. In this particular case, consumers and producers equally share the burden of the tax.

FIGURE 7-5   Demand elasticity and the incidence of an excise tax

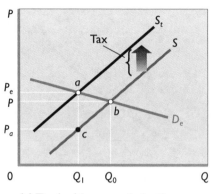

(a) Tax incidence and elastic demand

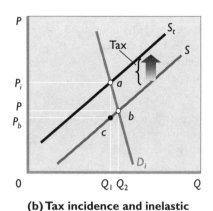

(b) Tax incidence and inelastic demand

In (a) we find that, if demand is elastic in the relevant price range, price will rise modestly (P to P_e) when an excise tax is levied. Hence, the producer bears most of the tax burden. But if demand is inelastic as in (b), the price to the buyer will increase substantially (P to P_i) and most of the tax is shifted to consumers.

extreme cases where demand is perfectly elastic and perfectly inelastic. In the first case the incidence of the tax is entirely on sellers; in the second, the tax is shifted entirely to consumers.

Figure 7-5 contrasts the more likely cases where demand might be relatively elastic (D_e) or relatively inelastic (D_i) in the relevant price range. In the elastic demand case of Figure 7-5(a), a small portion of the tax (PP_e) is shifted to consumers and most of the tax (PP_a) is borne by producers. In the inelastic demand case of Figure 7-5(b), most of the tax (PP_i) is shifted to consumers and only a small amount (PP_b) is paid by producers.

The decline in equilibrium quantity is smaller, the more inelastic the demand. This recalls one of our previous applications of the elasticity concept:

Revenue-seeking legislatures place heavy sales taxes on liquor, cigarettes, automobile tires, and other products whose demand is thought to be inelastic.

2. *With a specific demand, the more inelastic the supply, the larger the portion of the tax borne by producers.* While the demand curves are identical, the supply curve is elastic in Figure 7-6(a) and inelastic in Figure 7-6(b). For the elastic supply curve most of the tax (PP_e) is shifted to consumers and only a small portion (PP_a) is borne by producers or sellers. But where supply is inelastic, the reverse is true. The major portion of the tax (PP_b) falls on sellers and a relatively small amount (PP_i) is shifted to buyers. Quantity also declines less with an inelastic supply than it does with an elastic supply.

FIGURE 7-6   Supply elasticity and the incidence of an excise tax

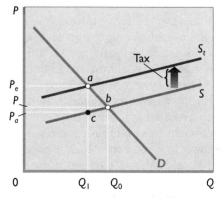

(a) Tax incidence and elastic supply

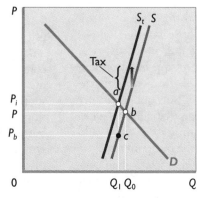

(b) Tax incidence and inelastic supply

Part (a) indicates that with an elastic supply an excise tax results in a large price increase (P to P_e) and the tax is therefore paid largely by consumers. But if supply is inelastic as in (b), the price rise will be small (P to P_i) and sellers will have to bear most of the tax.

Gold is an example of a product with an inelastic supply and therefore one where the burden of an excise tax would fall mainly on producers. On the other hand, because the supply of baseballs is elastic, much of an excise tax on baseballs would get passed to consumers. **(Key Question 18)**

PRICE CEILINGS AND FLOORS

On occasion the general public and government feel that supply and demand result in prices either unfairly high to buyers or unfairly low to sellers. In such instances government may intervene by limiting by law how high or low the price may go. Let's examine what happens to the functioning of the market when government price-fixing occurs.

PRICE CEILINGS AND SHORTAGES

A **price ceiling** *is the maximum legal price that a seller may charge for a product or service.* The rationale for price ceilings on specific products is that they purportedly enable consumers to obtain some "essential" good or service they could not afford at the equilibrium price. Rent controls and usury laws (which specify maximum interest rates that may be charged to borrowers) are examples. Price ceilings or general price controls have been used in attempting to restrain the overall rate of inflation in the economy. Wage and price controls were invoked during World War II, as well as from 1975 to 1979.

WORLD WAR II PRICE CONTROLS Let's turn back the clock to World War II and analyze the effects of a price ceiling on butter. The booming wartime prosperity of the early 1940s was shifting demand for butter to the right so that, as in Figure 7-7 the equilibrium or market price P_0 was, say, $1.20 per pound. The rapidly rising price of butter made it difficult to get for those families whose money incomes were not keeping pace with the increasing cost of living. To help stop inflation and to keep butter on the tables of the poor, government imposed a price ceiling P_c, of, say, $0.90 per pound. To be effective a ceiling price must be *below* equilibrium price. A price ceiling of $1.50 would have no immediate impact on the butter market.

What will be the effects of this $0.90 price ceiling? The rationing ability of the competitive market will be ineffective. At the price ceiling, there will be a persistent shortage of butter. The quantity of butter

FIGURE 7-7   Price ceilings result in persistent shortages

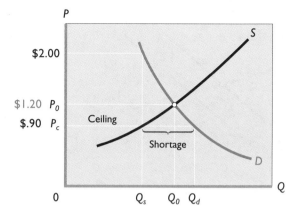

Because the imposition of a price ceiling, such as P_c, results in a persistent product shortage (as indicated by the distance Q_sQ_d), government must undertake the job of rationing the product in order to achieve an equitable distribution.

demanded at P_c is Q_d and the quantity supply is only Q_s; a persistent excess demand or shortage in the amount Q_sQ_d occurs. The size of this shortage varies directly with the price elasticities of supply and demand. The greater the elasticities, the greater the shortage. The important point is that the fixed price P_c prevents the usual market adjustment, where competition among buyers would bid up price, inducing more production and rationing some buyers out of the market until the shortage disappears at the equilibrium price and quantity, P_0 and Q_0.

By preventing market-clearing adjustments from occurring, the price ceiling poses problems born of the market disequilibrium.

1. RATIONING PROBLEM How is the available supply, Q_s, to be apportioned among buyers who want amount Q_d? Should supply be distributed on a first-come, first-served basis? Or should the grocer distribute butter on the basis of favouritism? An unregulated shortage is hardly conducive to the equitable distribution of butter. To avoid a haphazard distribution of butter, the government must establish some formal system of rationing it to consumers. This was accomplished during World War II by issuing ration coupons to individuals on an equitable basis. An effective rationing system requires the printing of ration coupons equal to Q_s pounds of butter and their equitable distribution among consumers so that the rich family of four and the poor family of four will both get the same number of coupons.

2. BLACK MARKETS But ration coupons do not prevent a second problem from arising. The demand curve in Figure 7-7 tells us there are many buyers willing to pay more than the ceiling price. And of course it is more profitable for grocers to sell above the ceiling price. Thus, despite the sizable enforcement bureaucracy that accompanied World War II price controls, illegal *black markets* — markets where products were bought and sold at prices above the legal limits — flourished for many goods. Counterfeiting of ration coupons was also a problem. As Figure 7-7 indicates, there is an excess demand of butter at the ceiling price of $0.90. Since only quantity Q_s is available, a black market price of P_1 ($2) would result. The black market would be given impetus by coupon holders willing to forgo part of their ration to get $2 cash for each pound of butter they would be willing to part with.

RENT CONTROLS Rent controls are another example of attempts to intervene in the functioning of the market to achieve a well-intentioned social goal. Rent control legislation has been fairly common in Canada in the past few decades as provincial governments have attempted to maintain existing stocks of "affordable" rental housing. In several provinces these laws have since been phased out, although as of mid-1995 rent controls were still in force in Ontario.

When controls are first imposed they usually restrict increases in rents above current levels. The short-run supply curve for rental accommodation is inelastic because it takes landlords some time to react to price changes and bring new units on the market. Most tenants benefit, since the quantity of rental accommodation currently on the market or under construction is not significantly affected. Thus the program appears to be successful even if shortages begin to appear. Figure 7-8 portrays a market for rental accommodation with rents fixed at R_c and a short-run supply curve, S_s. A shortage Q_1Q_2 exists in the short run.

In the long run the shortage of rental accommodation will become worse since the supply of rental accommodation is more elastic in the long run. Construction of new units decreases and landlords try to convert existing units to other uses or allow them to deteriorate. The supply curve becomes more elastic in the long run as shown by S_L in Figure 7-8(b), making the shortage worse, and increasing it to Q_3Q_1.

The gradually worsening shortage in the long run leads to several related problems. As in the case of controls on food prices, a black market will emerge. The black market in rental accommodation is characterized by the charging of "key money." Prospective tenants will often be forced to bribe a landlord or a subletting tenant to acquire a particular rental unit. The acceptance of key money is illegal in most jurisdictions with rent controls, but the practice is difficult to stamp out because it is to the advantage of both parties. Those desperate for rental accommodation will have to pay the black market rate of as much as R_1, shown in Figure 7-8(b).

FIGURE 7-8   Rent controls

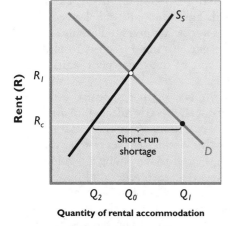

(a) Short run

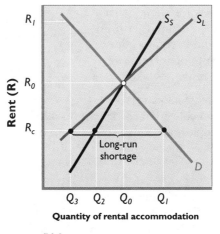

(b) Long run

In the short run the supply for rental accommodation is inelastic. If rent controls are set at R_c a shortage of Q_1Q_2 will occur in the short run. In the long run, supply becomes more elastic as landlords are able to add or withdraw rental units from the market. In the long run the shortage will worsen to Q_3Q_1. On the black market, rents of as much as R_1 will be charged.

Another problem that results from controls is the emergence of a dual rental market if new buildings are exempt from controls. Apartment units whose rents are below market levels are almost always rented informally or with some form of key money attached. The units that have recently come on the market will be offered at rents above the levels that would exist without controls as landlords attempt to compensate for future restrictions on rent increases. Because of discrimination by landlords and the ability to pay key money, middle-class tenants will find it easier to secure units in the controlled market, while the poor will be forced to seek units in the uncontrolled market. Perversely, tenants with higher incomes can be the major beneficiaries of the program.

Rent controls distort market signals and misallocate resources: too few resources are allocated to rental housing, too many to alternative uses. Ironically, although rent controls are often legislated to mitigate the effects of housing shortages, in fact controls contribute to such shortages.

CREDIT CARD INTEREST CEILINGS   In 1988, attempts were made in Parliament by private members to have a nationwide interest-rate ceiling imposed on credit card accounts. In the United States several states now have such laws and others have legislation under consideration. The rationale for interest-rate ceilings is that the banks and retail stores issuing such cards are presumably "gouging" users, particularly lower-income users.

What are the likely responses to the imposition by law of below-equilibrium interest rates on credit cards? According to a study by the U.S. central bank, the Federal Reserve,[3] profits on bank-issued credit cards have been low, while retail store cards have generally generated losses for their issuers. Thus, lower interest income associated with an interest ceiling set by law would require adjustments by issuers to reduce costs or increase revenues. What forms might these responses take?

1. Card issuers might tighten credit standards to reduce nonpayment losses and collection costs. In particular, low-income people and young people who have not yet established their credit-

worthiness would find it more difficult to get credit cards.
2. The annual fee charge to card holders might be increased, as might the fee charged to merchants for processing credit card sales. Card users might also be charged a fee for every transaction.
3. Card users now have a "grace period" when credit provided is interest-free. This period could be shortened or eliminated.
4. Certain "enhancements" that accompany some cards — for example, extended warranties on products bought with a card — might be eliminated.
5. Retail stores that issue cards might increase their merchandise prices to help offset the decline of interest income. This would mean that customers who pay cash would in effect be subsidizing customers who use credit cards.

ROCK CONCERTS   Below-equilibrium pricing should not be associated solely with government policies. Rock superstars frequently price their concert tickets below the market-clearing price. Tickets are usually rationed on a first-come, first-served basis, and ticket "scalping" is common. Why should rock stars want to subsidize their fans — at least those who are fortunate enough to obtain tickets — with below-equilibrium prices? Why not set ticket prices at a higher, market-clearing level and realize more income from a tour?

The answer is that long lines of fans waiting hours or days for bargain-priced tickets catch the attention of the press, as does an occasional attempt by those who do not get tickets to crash a sold-out concert. The millions of dollars worth of free publicity undoubtedly stimulates cassette and CD sales, from which a major portion of any rock star's income is derived. Thus, the "gift" of below-equilibrium ticket prices a rock star gives to fans also benefits the star. The gift also imposes costs to fans — the opportunity cost of the time spent waiting in line to buy tickets.

Incidentally, many people regard the ticket scalping often associated with musical or athletic events as a form of extortion, where the extortionist's (seller's) gain is the victim's (buyer's) loss. But to most economists, the fact that scalping is a voluntary transaction suggests that both seller and buyer gain or the exchange would not occur. Such exchanges redistribute assets (tickets) from those who value them less to those who value them more. The con-

---

[3] See Glenn B. Canner and James T. Fergus, "The Economic Effects of Proposed Ceilings on Credit Card Interest Rates," *Federal Reserve Bulletin*, January 1987, pp. 1-13.

cert or game also benefits from having an audience that most wants to be there (see Applying the Theory box in Chapter 4).

PRICE FLOORS AND SURPLUSES

Price floors *are minimum prices fixed by government that are above equilibrium prices.* Price floors have been implemented when society has believed the free functioning of the market system was not providing a sufficient income for certain groups of resource suppliers or producers. Minimum-wage legislation and the support of agricultural prices are the two most widely discussed examples of government price floors. Let's examine price floors as applied to a specific farm commodity.

Suppose the going market price for oats is $2 per bushel, and as a result of this price, many farmers realize low incomes. Government decides to help out by establishing a price fixed by law or "price support" of $3 per bushel.

What will be the effects? At any price above the equilibrium price, quantity supplied will exceed quantity demanded. There will be a persistent excess

supply or surplus of the product. Farmers will be willing to produce and offer for sale more than private buyers are willing to purchase at the price floor. The size of this surplus will vary directly with the elasticity of demand and supply. The greater the elasticity of demand and supply, the greater the surplus. As with a ceiling price, the rationing ability of the free market is disrupted by imposing a legal price.

Figure 7-9 illustrates the effect of a price floor. Let S and D be the supply and demand curves for corn. Equilibrium price and quantity are P_0 and Q_0, respectively. If government imposes a price floor of P_f, farmers will produce Q_s, but private buyers will only take Q_d off the market at that price. The surplus is the excess of Q_s over Q_d.

Government may cope with the surplus in two basic ways.

1. It might restrict supply (for example, allotments by which farmers agree to take a certain amount of land out of production) or increase demand (for example, researching new uses for agricultural products). In these ways the difference between the equilibrium price and the price floor and the size of the surplus might be reduced.
2. If these efforts are not successful, then government must purchase the surplus output (thereby subsidizing farmers) and store or otherwise dispose of it.

Price ceilings and price floors rob the free-market forces of supply and demand of their ability to bring the supply decisions of producers and the demand decisions of buyers into accord with one another. Freely determined prices automatically ration products to buyers, prices fixed by law do not. Therefore, government must accept the administrative problem of rationing that stems from price ceilings and the problem of eliminating surpluses brought about by price floors. Prices fixed by law bring about controversial trade-offs. Alleged benefits of price ceilings and floors to consumers and producers respectively must be set against costs associated with consequent shortages and surpluses.

Our discussions of World War II price controls, rent controls, and interest-rate ceilings on credit cards indicate that governmental interference with the market can have unintended side effects. Rent controls are likely to discourage housing construction and repair. Instead of protecting low-income families from high interest charges, interest-rate ceilings may simply make credit unavailable to them.

FIGURE 7-9 **Price floors result in persistent surpluses**

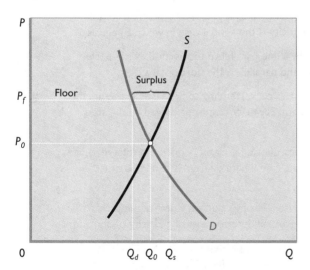

A price floor such as P_f gives rise to a persistent product surplus as indicated by the distance Q_dQ_s. Government must either purchase these surpluses or take measures to eliminate them by restricting product supply or increasing product demand.

QUICK REVIEW 7-3

1. Price elasticity of supply is the ratio of the percentage change in quantity supplied to the percentage change in price. The elasticity of supply varies directly with the amount of time producers have to respond to the price change.

2. Cross elasticity of demand is the percentage change in the quantity demanded of one product divided by the percentage change in the price of another product. If the cross elasticity coefficient is positive, the two products are substitutes; if negative, they are complements.

3. Income elasticity is the percentage change in quantity demanded divided by the percentage change in income. A positive coefficient indicates a normal or superior good. The coefficient is negative for an inferior good.

4. For a product having an excise tax, the more inelastic the demand the more the tax is borne by consumers; the more inelastic the supply, the larger the portion borne by producers.

5. Price ceilings and floors negate the rationing function of prices and have unintended side effects.

CHAPTER SUMMARY

1. Price elasticity of demand measures the responsiveness of consumers to price changes. If consumers are relatively sensitive to price changes, demand is elastic. If consumers are relatively unresponsive to price changes, demand is inelastic.

2. The price elasticity formula measures the degree of elasticity or inelasticity of demand. The formula is

$$E_d = \frac{\text{percentage change in quantity demanded of X}}{\text{percentage change in price of X}}$$

The averages of the prices and quantities under consideration are used as reference points in determining the percentage changes in price and quantity. If E_d is greater than 1, demand is elastic. If E_d is less than 1, demand is inelastic. Unit elasticity is the special case in which E_d equals 1.

3. A perfectly inelastic demand curve is portrayed by a line parallel to the vertical axis. A perfectly elastic demand curve is shown by a line above and parallel to the horizontal axis.

4. Elasticity varies at different price ranges on a demand curve, tending to be elastic in the northwest segment and inelastic in the southeast segment. Elasticity cannot be judged by the steepness or flatness of a demand curve on a graph.

5. If price and total revenue move in opposite directions, demand is elastic. If price and total revenue move in the same direction, demand is inelastic. In the case where demand is of unit elasticity, a change in price will leave total revenue unchanged.

6. The number of available substitutes, the size of an item in one's budget, whether the product is a luxury or necessity, and the time period involved are all determinants of elasticity of demand.

7. The elasticity concept also applies to supply. Elasticity of supply depends on the shiftability of resources between alternative employments. This shiftability varies with the time producers have to adjust to a given price change.

8. Cross elasticity gauges how sensitive the purchases of one product are to changes in the price of another product. It is measured by the percentage change in the quantity demanded of product X divided by the percentage change in the price of product Y. A positive coefficient identifies substitute goods; a negative coefficient indicates complementary goods.

9. Income elasticity indicates the responsiveness of consumer purchases to a change in income. It is measured by the percentage change in the quantity demanded of the product divided by the percentage change in income. The coefficient is positive for normal goods and negative for inferior goods.

10. Excise taxes affect demand or supply and therefore equilibrium price and quantity. The more inelastic the demand for a product the greater the portion of the tax shifted to consumers. The greater the inelasticity of supply, the larger portion of the tax borne by the seller.

11. Prices fixed by law upset the rationing function of equilibrium prices. Effective price ceilings result in persistent product shortages and, if an equitable distribution of the product is sought, government will have to ration the product to consumers. Price floors lead to product surpluses; government must purchase these surpluses or eliminate them by imposing restrictions on production or by increasing private demand.

TERMS AND CONCEPTS

cross elasticity of demand (p. 130)
elastic versus inelastic demand (p. 121)
income elasticity of demand (p. 131)
market period (p. 129)
perfectly elastic demand (p. 121)
perfectly inelastic demand (p. 121)
price ceiling (p. 134)

price elasticity of demand (p. 120)
price elasticity of supply (p. 129)
price floor (p. 137)
short run and long run (pp. 129, 130)
total-revenue test (p. 125)
unit elasticity (p. 121)

QUESTIONS AND STUDY SUGGESTIONS

1. Review questions 1, 4, and 8 at end of Chapter 4.

2. *Key Question*   *Graph the accompanying demand data and then use the midpoints to determine price elasticity of demand for each of the four price changes. What can you conclude about the relationship between the slope of a curve and its elasticity? Explain in a nontechnical way why demand is elastic in the northwest segment of the demand curve and inelastic in the southeast segment.*

Product price	Quantity demanded
$5	1
4	2
3	3
2	4
1	5

3. In 1987 the average price of a home rose from $97,000 in April to $106,800 in May. During the same period home sales fell from 724,000 to 616,000 units. If we assume that mortgage interest rates and all other factors affecting home sales are constant, what do these figures suggest about the elasticity of demand for housing?

4. *Key Question*   *Calculate total revenue data from the demand schedule in question 2. Graph total revenue below your demand curve. Generalize in the relationship between price elasticity and total revenue.*

5. *Key Question*   *How will the following changes in price affect total revenue (expenditures) — that is, will total revenue increase, decline, or remain unchanged?*

   a. *Price falls and demand is inelastic.*

   b. *Price rises and demand is elastic.*

   c. *Price rises and supply is elastic.*

   d. *Price rises and supply is inelastic.*

   e. *Price rises and demand is inelastic.*

   f. *Price falls and demand is elastic.*

   g. *Price falls and demand is of unit elasticity.*

6. In some industries — for example, the petroleum industry — producers justify their reluctance to lower prices by arguing that demand for their products is inelastic. Explain.

7. You are sponsoring an outdoor rock concert. Your major costs — for the band, land rent, and security — are largely independent of attendance. Use the concept of price elasticity of demand to explain how you might establish ticket prices to maximize profits.

8. In the 1970s the Organization of Petroleum Exporting Countries (OPEC) became operational as a cartel that reduced the world supply of oil, greatly increasing OPEC's revenues and profits. What can you infer regarding the elasticity of demand for oil? Would you expect countries exporting bananas or pineapples to be able to emulate OPEC? Explain.

9. *Key Question*   *What are the major determinants of price elasticity of demand? Use these determinants in judging whether demand for each of the following products is elastic or inelastic: a. oranges; b. cigarettes; c. Export cigarettes; d. gasoline; e. butter; f. salt; g. automobiles; h. football games; i. diamond bracelets; and j. this textbook.*

10. Empirical estimates suggest the following demand elasticities: 0.6 for physicians' services; 4.0 for foreign travel; and 1.2 for radio and television receivers. Use the generalizations for the determinants of elasticity developed in this chapter to explain each of these figures.

11. What effect would a rule stating that university students must live in university dormitories have on the price elasticity of demand for dormitory space? What impact might this in turn have on room rates?

12. "If the demand for farm products is highly price inelastic, a bumper crop may reduce farm incomes." Evaluate and illustrate graphically.

13. You are chairperson of a provincial tax commission responsible for establishing a program to raise new revenue through sales taxes. Would elasticity of demand be important to you in determining those products on which sales taxes should be levied? Explain.

14. *Key Question*   *In May 1990 Vincent van Gogh's painting "Portrait of Dr. Gachet" sold at auction for $82.5 million. Portray this sale in a demand and supply diagram and comment on the elasticity of supply.*

15. In the 1950s the local Boy Scout troop in Kamloops, British Columbia, decided to gather and sell at auction elk antlers shed by thousands of elk wintering in the area. Buyers were mainly local artisans who used the antlers to make belt buckles, buttons, and tie clasps. Price per kilogram was 6¢ and the troop took in $500 annually. In the 1970s a fad developed in Asia that involved grinding antlers into powder to sprinkle on food for purported aphrodisiac benefits.

In 1979 the price per kilogram of elk antlers in the Kamloops auction was $6 per kilogram and the Boy Scouts earned $51,000! Show graphically and explain these dramatic increases in price and total revenue. Assuming no shift in the supply curve of elk antlers, use the midpoints formula to calculate the coefficient for the elasticity of supply.

16. *Key Question*   *Suppose the cross elasticity of demand for products A and B is +3.6 and for products C and D it is -5.4. What can you conclude about how products A and B and products C and D are related?*

17. *Key Question*   *The income elasticities of demand for movies, dental services, and clothing have been estimated to be +3.4, +1.0, and +0.5, respectively. Interpret these coefficients. What does it mean if the income elasticity coefficient is negative?*

18. *Key Question*   *What is the incidence of an excise tax when demand is highly inelastic? Elastic? What effect does the elasticity of supply have on the incidence of an excise tax?*

19. Why is it desirable for ceiling prices to be accompanied by government rationing? And for price floors to be accompanied by surplus-purchasing or output-restricting or demand-increasing programs? Show graphically why price ceilings entail shortages and price floors result in surpluses. What effect, if any, does elasticity of demand and supply have on the size of these shortages and surpluses? Explain.

20. "Rent controls are a kind of self-fulfilling prophecy. They are designed to cope with housing shortages, but instead create such shortages." Do you agree?

21. To contain rising health care costs, some reformers have proposed a maximum salary (salary ceiling) for all doctors in Canada. What would be the likely consequences?

CHAPTER 8

CONSUMER BEHAVIOUR AND UTILITY MAXIMIZATION[1]

Because resources are scarce in relation to our wants, all of us have to choose among the vast array of available goods and services. This chapter investigates how consumers decide which goods and services to purchase.

If you were to compare the shopping carts of two consumers, you would observe striking differences. Why does Paula have potatoes, parsnips, pomegranates, and Pepsi in her cart, while Sam has sugar, saltines, soap, and 7-Up in his? Why didn't Paula also buy pork and pimentos? Why didn't Sam have soup and spaghetti on his grocery list? Why does a consumer buy some specific bundle of goods rather than any one of a number of other collections of goods available? As we examine these issues we will learn about the forces that underlie consumer decisions, and also strengthen our understanding of the law of demand.

---

[1] Some instructors may choose to omit this chapter. This can be done without impairing the continuity and meaning of ensuing chapters.

BOX 8-1   THE BIG PICTURE

We now leave general supply-demand analysis behind to focus exclusively on the details of the demand curve. What motivates consumer behaviour; why do consumers buy more of a specific good or service when its price falls and buy less of it when its price rises (*ceteris paribus*)? Recall that the economizing problem has two components: limited resources and unlimited wants. Faced with this, consumers try to do the best they can — buy those goods and services that will yield the greatest satisfaction — with the money income at their disposal. This is what is meant by "utility maximization" in the title of this chapter.

As you read this chapter, keep the following points in mind:

- We assume individuals maximize utility automatically; they don't have to be told how to do it.
- Consumers could always do with a few more goods and services to make life a little easier. Because of unlimited wants, money income is never quite enough, and consumers try to stretch that money income as far as it can go. Thus, consumers prefer lower prices to higher prices for a specific good or service. (When was the last time you heard someone say they were disgusted at how *low* prices were for a specific good or service?)

TWO EXPLANATIONS OF THE LAW OF DEMAND

It is common knowledge that there is an inverse relationship between price and quantity demanded; if the price of a good rises, the quantity demanded of it falls, and vice versa. What is the basis for the inverse relationship between price and quantity demanded?

We now explore two complementary explanations of the downsloping demand curve. (A third explanation, based on indifference curves, is summarized in the appendix of this chapter.)

INCOME AND SUBSTITUTION EFFECTS

In Chapter 4, we saw the downsloping demand curve explained in terms of the income and substitution effects. Whenever a product's price decreases, two things happen to cause the amount demanded to increase.

1. INCOME EFFECT   The **income effect** is the impact of a change in the price of a product on the real income of a consumer and, thus, on the quantity demanded. If the price of a product — say, steak — declines, the real income or purchasing power of anyone buying that product will increase. This increase in real income will result in increased purchases of many products, including steak. With

a constant money income of $40 per week you can purchase 5 kg of steak at a price of $8 per kilogram. But if the price of steak falls to $4 per kilogram and you buy 5 kg, $20 per week is freed to buy more of both steak and other commodities. A decline in the price of steak increases the real income of the consumer, enabling him or her to purchase more steak.[2]

2. SUBSTITUTION EFFECT   The **substitution effect** is the impact of a change in the price of a product on the relative cost of that product, thus on the quantity demanded. When the price of a product falls, it becomes cheaper relative to all other products. Consumers will substitute the less expensive product for other products that are now relatively more expensive. In our example, as the price of steak falls — the prices of other products remaining unchanged — steak will become more attractive to the buyer. At $4 per kilogram it is a better buy than at $8 per kilogram. Steak may be substituted for pork, chicken, veal, fish, and a variety of other foods.

The substitution and income effects combine to make a consumer able and willing to buy more of a specific good at a low price than at a high price.

---

[2] We assume here that steak is a *normal* or *superior* good.

LAW OF DIMINISHING MARGINAL UTILITY

A second explanation of the downsloping demand curve is that the more of a specific product consumers obtain, the less willing they are to get additional units of the same product. This can be most readily seen for durable goods. A consumer's want for an automobile, when he or she has none, may be very strong; the desire for a second car is much less intense; for a third or fourth, very weak. Even the wealthiest families rarely have more than a half-dozen cars, although their incomes would allow them to purchase a whole fleet of them.

TERMINOLOGY   The falling satisfaction derived from one more unit of a product is referred to as the law of diminishing marginal utility. Recall that **utility** is the benefit or satisfaction one gets from consuming a good or service. Three characteristics of this concept must be emphasized.

1. "Utility" and "usefulness" are not synonymous. Paintings by Picasso may be useless in the functional sense and yet offer great utility to art connoisseurs.
2. Utility is a subjective notion. The utility of a specific product will vary widely from person to person. A bottle of cheap wine may yield substantial utility to the alcoholic, but zero or negative utility to a nondrinker. Eyeglasses have great utility to someone who is extremely far- or near-sighted, but no utility to a person with 20-20 vision.
3. Because utility is subjective, it is difficult to quantify. But for purposes of illustration, assume we can measure satisfaction with units we will call "utils." This hypothetical unit of satisfaction is a convenient device that will allow us to quantify consumer behaviour.

TOTAL UTILITY AND MARGINAL UTILITY

We must carefully distinguish between total utility and marginal utility. **Total utility** is the total amount of satisfaction or pleasure a person derives from the consumption of some specific quantity — say, 10 units — of a good or service. **Marginal utility** is the *extra* satisfaction a consumer realizes from an additional unit of that product, in this case the eleventh unit. Alternatively, we can say that marginal utility is the *change* in total utility resulting from the consumption of one or more unit of a product.

Figure 8-1(a) and (b) and the accompanying table reveal the total utility—marginal utility relationship for fast-food hamburgers. Starting at the origin in Figure 8-1(a), we observe that through the first five units total utility increases but at a diminishing rate. Total utility reaches a maximum at the sixth unit and then declines (column 2 of the table). The change in total utility accompanying each additional hamburger, by definition, measures marginal utility (column 3 of the table). Thus in Figure 8-1(b) we find marginal utility is positive but diminishing through the fifth unit (because total utility increases at a declining rate). Marginal utility is zero for the sixth unit (because total utility is at a maximum). Marginal utility then becomes negative with the seventh unit and beyond (because total utility is falling). Figure 8-1(b) and the table tell us that each successive hamburger yields less and less extra utility than the previous one as the consumer's want for hamburgers comes closer and closer to fulfilment.[3] The notion that marginal utility will decline as the consumer acquires additional units of a product is known as the **law of diminishing marginal utility. (Key Question 2)**

RELATION TO DEMAND AND ELASTICITY

How does the law of diminishing marginal utility explain why the demand curve for a specific product is downsloping? If successive units of a good yield smaller and smaller amounts of marginal, or extra, utility, then the consumer will buy additional units of a product only if its price falls. The consumer for whom these utility data are relevant may buy two hamburgers at a price of $1. But owing to diminishing marginal utility from additional hamburgers, a consumer will choose *not* to buy more at this price. After all, giving up money really means giving up other

---

[3] For a time the marginal utility of successive units of a product may increase. A second glass of lemonade on a hot day may yield more extra satisfaction than the first. But beyond some point we can expect the marginal utility of additional glasses to decline. Also note in Figure 8-1(b) that marginal utility is graphed at the halfway points. For example, we graph marginal utility of 4 utils at 3 1/2 units because the 4 utils refers neither to the third nor the fourth unit per se, but to the *addition* of the fourth unit.

FIGURE 8-1   Total and marginal utility

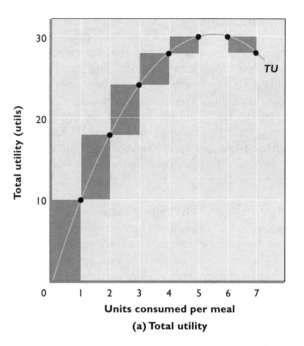

(1) Hamburgers consumed per meal	(2) Total utility	(3) Marginal utility, Δ (2)
0	0	
		10
1	10	
		8
2	18	
		6
3	24	
		4
4	28	
		2
5	30	
		0
6	30	
		-2
7	28	

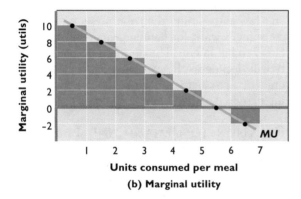

(a) Total utility

(b) Marginal utility

In (a) we observe that, as more of a product is consumed, total utility increases at a diminishing rate, reaches a maximum, and then declines. Marginal utility, by definition, reflects the changes in total utility. Thus, in (b) we find marginal utility diminishes with increased consumption; becomes zero where total utility is at a maximum; and is negative when total utility declines.

goods, that is, alternative ways of getting utility. Therefore, additional hamburgers are not worth it unless the price (sacrifice of other goods) declines. (When marginal utility becomes negative, McDonalds or Burger King would have to pay *you* to eat another hamburger!)

The amount by which marginal utility declines as more units of a product are consumed will determine its price elasticity of demand. Other things being equal, if marginal utility falls sharply as successive units are consumed, we would expect demand to be inelastic. Conversely, modest declines in marginal utility as consumption increases imply an elastic demand.

QUICK REVIEW 8-1

1. The law of demand can be explained in terms of the income effect (a decline in price increases the consumer's purchasing power) and the substitution effect (a product whose price falls is substituted for other products).

2. Utility is the benefit or satisfaction one gets from consuming a good or service.

3. The law of diminishing marginal utility indicates that the gains in satisfaction will decline as successive units of a given product are consumed.

4. Diminishing marginal utility provides a rationale for (a) the law of demand and (b) differing price elasticities.

THEORY OF CONSUMER BEHAVIOUR

In addition to providing a basis for explaining the law of demand, diminishing marginal utility also explains how consumers allocate their money income among the many goods and services available to them.

CONSUMER CHOICE AND BUDGET CONSTRAINT

The typical consumer has the following attributes and constraints:

1. RATIONAL BEHAVIOUR The average consumer is a rational person attempting to dispose of money income so as to derive the greatest amount of satisfaction, or utility, from it. Consumers want to get the most for their money or, more technically, to maximize total utility.

2. PREFERENCES The consumer has clear-cut preferences for various goods and services available in the market. We assume buyers have a good idea of how much marginal utility they will get from successive units of the various products they might choose to purchase.

3. BUDGET CONSTRAINT At any point in time, the consumer's money income is limited. Because the consumer supplies limited amounts of resources to businesses, the income payments to him or her are also limited. Thought of this way, all consumers face a **budget constraint**, even those who earn millions of dollars annually. Of course, this income limitation is more severe for typical consumers with average incomes than for those with extraordinarily high incomes.

4. PRICES If a consumer has a limited income, he or she will be able to purchase only a limited amount of goods. The consumer cannot buy everything wanted when each purchase exhausts a portion of a limited money income. The consumer must choose among alternative goods to obtain with limited money resources the most satisfying collection of goods and services. Individuals will choose different mixes of goods. As Global Perspective 8-1 shows, mixes of goods will vary among nations.

UTILITY-MAXIMIZING RULE

To maximize satisfaction, *the consumer's money income should be allocated so that the last dollar spent on each product purchased yields the same amount of extra (marginal) utility.* We call this the **utility maximizing rule**. When the consumer is "balancing margins" in accordance with this rule, the consumer will be in *equilibrium* and, barring a change in tastes, income, or the prices of the various goods, will be worse off — total utility will decline — by any alteration in the collection of goods purchased.

NUMERICAL EXAMPLE An illustration will help explain this rule. For simplicity's sake, we limit our discussion to just two products. Keep in mind that the analysis can readily be extended to any number of goods. Suppose that consumer Holly is trying to decide which combination of two products — A and B — she should purchase with her limited daily income of $10. Holly's preferences for these two products and their prices will be basic data determining the combination of A and B that will maximize her satisfactions.

GLOBAL PERSPECTIVE 8-1

Shares of household budgets spent on food, selected nations

Consumer spending patterns differ not only among individuals, but among nations. One striking feature is that, although households in rich countries spend larger absolute amounts on food than do poor countries, households in poor nations spend a much larger proportion of their budgets on food.

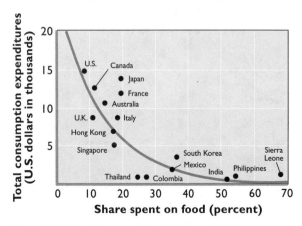

Source: Judith Jones Putnam and Jane E. Allhouse, *Food Consumption, Prices, and Expenditures, 1970-92* (U.S. Department of Agriculture, 1993, Economic Research Service Statistical Bulletin 867).

Table 8-1 summarizes Holly's preferences for products A and B. Column 2(a) shows the amount of marginal utility she will get from each successive unit of A. Column 3(a) reflects her preferences for product B. In each case, the relationship between the number of units of the product consumed and the corresponding marginal utility reflects the law of diminishing marginal utility. Diminishing marginal utility is assumed to begin with the first unit of each product purchased.

MARGINAL UTILITY PER DOLLAR Before we can apply the utility-maximizing rule to these data, we must put the marginal-utility information of columns 2(a) and 3(a) on a per-dollar-spent basis. A consumer's choices will be influenced not only by the extra utility successive units of product A will yield, but also by how many dollars (and therefore how many units of alternative good B) she must give up to obtain those added units of A. The rational consumer will compare the extra utility from each product with its added cost (that is, its price).

Suppose you prefer a pizza whose marginal utility is 36 utils to a movie whose marginal utility is 24 utils. But if the pizza's price is $12 and to go to a movie only

$6, the choice would be for the movie rather than the pizza. Why? Because the *marginal utility per dollar spent* would be 4 utils for the movie (4 = 24 ÷ $6) compared with only 3 utils for the pizza (3 = 36 ÷ 12). You could go to two movies for $12 and, assuming the marginal utility of the second movie is 16 utils, your total utility would be 40 utils. Forty units of satisfaction from two movies is clearly superior to 36 utils from the same $12 expenditure on one pizza.

To make the amounts of extra utility derived from differently priced goods comparable, marginal utility must be put on a per-dollar-spent basis. This is done in columns 2(b) and 3(b). These figures are obtained by dividing the marginal-utility data of columns 2(a) and 3(a) by the assumed prices of A and B — $1 and $2, respectively.

DECISION-MAKING PROCESS Now we have Holly's preferences — on unit and per dollar basis — and the price tags of A and B before us. With $10 to spend, in what order should Holly allocate her dollars on units of A and B to achieve the highest degree of utility within the $10 limits imposed by her money income? What specific combination of A and B will she have obtained at the time that she exhausts her $10?

TABLE 8-1 **The utility-maximizing combination of products A and B obtainable with an income of $10***

(1) Unit of product	(2) Product A: price $1		(3) Product B: price = $2	
	(a) Marginal utility, utils	(b) Marginal utility per dollar (MU/price)	(a) Marginal utility, utils	(b) Marginal utility per dollar (MU/price)
First	10	10	24	12
Second	8	8	20	10
Third	7	7	18	9
Fourth	6	6	16	8
Fifth	5	5	12	6
Sixth	4	4	6	3
Seventh	3	3	4	2

* It is assumed in this table that the amount of marginal utility received from additional units of each of the two products is independent of the quantity of the other product. For example, the marginal-utility schedule for product A is independent of the amount of B obtained by the consumer.

Concentrating on columns 2(b) and 3(b) of Table 8-2, we find that Holly should first spend $2 on the first unit of B because its marginal utility per dollar of 12 utils is higher than A's. But now Holly finds herself indifferent about whether she should buy a second unit of B or the first unit of A, because the marginal utility per dollar of both is 10, so she buys both of them. Holly now has 1 unit of A and 2 of B.

With this combination of goods, the last dollar spent on each yields the same amount of extra utility. Does this combination of A and B therefore represent the maximum amount of utility Holly can obtain? The answer is no. This collection of goods only costs $5 [= (1 × $1) + (2 × $2)]; Holly has $5 remaining, which she can spend to achieve a still higher level of total utility.

Examining columns 2(b) and 3(b) again, we find Holly should spend the next $2 on a third unit of B because marginal utility per dollar for the third unit of B is 9, compared with 8 for the second unit of A. But now with 1 unit of A and 3 of B, we find she is again indifferent to a second unit of A and a fourth unit of B. So Holly purchases one more unit of each. Marginal utility per dollar is now the same at 8 utils for the last dollar spent on each product, *and* Holly's money income of $10 is exhausted [(2 × $1) + (4 × $2)]. *The utility-maximizing combination of goods attainable by Holly is 2 units of A and 4 of B.*[4]

---

[4] To simplify, we assume in this example that Holly spends her entire income; she neither borrows nor saves. Saving can be regarded as a utility-yielding commodity and incorporated in our analysis. We treat it as such in question 4 at the end of the chapter.

By summing the marginal utility information of columns 2(a) and 3(a) we find that Brooks is realizing 18 (= 10 + 8) utils of satisfaction from the 2 units of A and 78 (= 24 + 20 + 18 + 16) utils of satisfaction from the 4 units of B. Her $10, optimally spent, yields 96 (= 18 + 78) utils of satisfaction. Table 8-2 summarizes this step-by-step process for maximizing consumer utility and merits careful study.

INFERIOR OPTIONS   There are other combinations of A and B obtainable with $10. But none will yield a level of total utility as high as 2 units of A and 4 of B. For example, 4 units of A and 3 of B can be obtained for $10. However, this combination violates the utility-maximizing rule; total utility here is only 93 utils, clearly inferior to the 96 utils yielded by 2 of A and 4 of B. Furthermore, there are other combinations of A and B (such as 4 of A and 5 of B *or* 1 of A and 2 of B) wherein the marginal utility of the last dollar spent is the same for both A and B. But all such combinations are either unobtainable with Holly's limited money income (as 4 of A and 5 of B) or fail to exhaust her money income (as 1 of A and 2 of B) and therefore do not yield her the maximum utility attainable.

Problem: Suppose that Holly's money income was $14 rather than $10. What now would be the utility-maximizing combination of A and B? Are A and B normal or inferior goods? **(Key Question 4)**

ALGEBRAIC RESTATEMENT

Our rule says that a consumer will maximize satisfaction when he or she allocates money income so that the last dollar spent on product A, the last on product B, and so forth, yield equal amounts of marginal utility.

TABLE 8-2   **Sequence of purchases in achieving consumer equilibrium**

Potential choice	Marginal utility per dollar	Purchase decision	Income remaining
1. First unit of A First unit of B	10 12	First unit of B for $2	$8 = $10 − $2
2. First unit of A Second unit of B	10 10	First unit of A for $1 and second unit of B for $2	$5 = $8 − $3
3. Second unit of A Third unit of B	8 9	Third unit of B for $2	$3 = $5 − $2
4. Second unit of A Fourth unit of B	8 8	Second unit of A for $1 and fourth unit of B for $2	$0 = $3 − $3

The marginal utility per dollar spent on A is indicated by MU of product A divided by the price of A [column 2(b) of Table 8-2] and the marginal utility per dollar spent on B by MU of product B divided by the price of B [column 3(b) of Table 8-2]. Our utility-maximizing rule merely requires that these ratios be equal. That is,

$$\frac{\text{MU of product A}}{\text{price of A}} = \frac{\text{MU of product B}}{\text{price of B}}$$

The consumer must exhaust her available income. Our illustration in Table 8-1 shows us that the combination of 2 units of A and 4 of B fulfils these conditions in that

$$\frac{8}{1} = \frac{16}{2}$$

and the consumer's $10 income is spent.

If the equation is not fulfilled, there will be some reallocation of the consumer's expenditures between A and B, from the low to the high marginal-utility-per-dollar product, that will increase the consumer's total utility. For example, if the consumer spent $10 on 4 of A and 3 of B, we would find that

$$\frac{\text{MU of A: 6 utils}}{\text{price of A: \$1}} < \frac{\text{MU of B: 18 utils}}{\text{price of B: \$2}}$$

The last dollar spent on A provides only 6 utils of satisfaction, and the last dollar spent on B provides 9 (= 18 ÷ $2). On a per dollar basis, units of B provide more extra satisfaction than units of A. The consumer will increase total satisfaction by purchasing more of B and less of A. As dollars are reallocated from A to B, the marginal utility from additional units of B will decline as the result of moving *down* the diminishing marginal-utility schedule for B, and the marginal utility of A will rise as the consumer moves *up* the diminishing marginal-utility schedule for A. At some new combination of A and B — specifically, 2 of A and 4 of B — the equality of the two ratios, and therefore consumer equilibrium, will be achieved. As we already know, the net gain in utility is 3 utils (= 96 – 93).

MARGINAL UTILITY AND THE DEMAND CURVE

It is a simple step from the utility-maximizing rule to the construction of an individual's downsloping demand curve. Recall that the basic determinants of an individual's demand curve for a specific product are (1) preferences or tastes, (2) money income, and (3) the prices of other goods. The utility data of Table 8-1 reflect our consumer's preferences. We continue to suppose that money income is given at $10. And, concentrating on the construction of a simple demand curve for product B, we assume that the price of A — representing "other goods" — is at $1.

DERIVING THE DEMAND CURVE We can now derive a simple demand schedule for B by considering alternative prices at which B might be sold and by determining the quantity our consumer will purchase. We have already determined one such price-quantity combination in explaining the utility-maximizing rule: given tastes, income, and prices of other goods, our rational consumer will purchase 4 units of B at $2. Now assume the price of B falls to $1. The marginal-utility-per-dollar data of column 3(b) will double, because the price of B has been halved; the new data for column 3(b) in Table 8-1 are in fact identical to those in column 3(a). The purchase of 2 units of A and 4 of B is no longer an equilibrium combination. By applying the same reasoning used to develop the utility-maximizing rule, we now find Holly's utility-maximizing position is 4 units of A and 6 of B. We can sketch Holly's demand curve for B as in Table 8-3, confirming the downsloping demand curve.

TABLE 8-3   **The demand schedule for product B**

Price per unit of B	Quantity demanded
$2	4
1	6

INCOME AND SUBSTITUTION EFFECTS REVISITED At the beginning of this chapter we indicated that increased purchases of a good whose price had fallen could be understood in terms of the substitution and income effects. Although our analysis does not permit us to sort out these two effects, quantitatively, we can see intuitively how each is involved in the increased purchase of product B.

The *substitution effect* can be understood by referring back to our utility-maximizing rule. Before the price of B declined, Holly was in equilibrium in that $MU_A(8)/P_A(\$1) = MU_B(16)/P_B(\$2)$ when purchasing 2 units of A and 4 units of B. But after B's price falls from $2 to $1, $MU_A(8)/P_A(\$1) < MU_B(16)/P_B(\$1)$ or, simply stated, the last dollar spent on B now yields more utility (16 utils) than does the last dollar spent on A (8 utils). This indicates that a switching of expenditures from A to B is needed to restore equilibrium. A *substitution* of now cheaper B for A will occur in the bundle of goods that Holly purchases.

What about the *income effect*? The assumed decline in the price of B from $2 to $1 increases Holly's real income. Before the price decline, Holly was in equilibrium when buying 2 of A and 4 of B. But at the lower $1 price for B, Holly would have to spend only $6 rather than $10 on this combination of goods. She has $4 left over to spend on more of A, more of B, or more of both products. The decline in the price of B has caused Holly's *real* income to increase so that she can now obtain larger amounts of A and B with the same $10 nominal or *money* income. The portion of the 2 unit increase in her purchase of B that is due to this increase in real income is the income effect. (**Key Question 5**)

QUICK REVIEW 8-2

1. The theory of consumer behaviour assumes that, with limited money incomes and given product prices, consumers make rational choices on the basis of well-defined preferences.

2. A consumer maximizes utility by allocating money income so that the marginal utility per dollar spent is the same for every good purchased.

3. A downsloping demand curve can be derived by changing the price of one product in the consumer-behaviour model.

APPLICATIONS AND EXTENSIONS

Many real-world phenomena can be explained by applying the theory of consumer behaviour.

THE COMPACT DISC TAKEOVER

It is difficult to realize that compact discs made their debut as recently as 1983. The CD revolutionized the retail music industry, pushing the vinyl long-playing record to virtual extinction. In 1983 fewer than 1 mil-

FIGURE 8-2   Explaining the success of compact discs

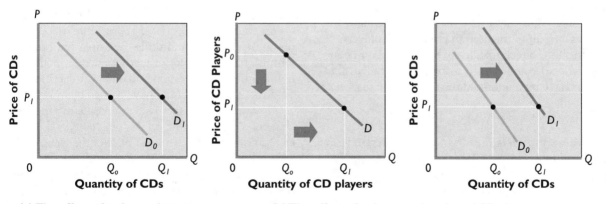

(a) The effect of a change in taste   (b) The effect of a decrease in price of CD players

The demand for CDs has increased because of a change in taste and a decline in the price of CD players. The better sound quality of CDs has translated into a shift from LPs to CDs. The change in taste is reflected in (a) by the rightward shift of the demand for CDs. The decline in the price of CD players has led to an increase in the quantity demanded of them. This is portrayed in (b) in the diagram on the left. CD players and CDs are complementary goods. The lower price for CD players has led to an increase in demand for CDs, shown in the diagram on the right in (b).

lion CDs were sold in North America as compared to almost 210 million LPs. But by 1992 over 440 million CDs were sold, while the sales of LPs plummeted to some 3 million. What caused this dramatic turnabout?

1. PREFERENCE CHANGES CDs have quality characteristics that prompted a massive shift of consumer preferences from LPs to CDs. CDs are played with a laser beam, not a phonograph needle and therefore are virtually impervious to the scratches and wear that plague LPs. CDs provide a wider range of sound and greater brilliance of tone. They can also hold more than 70 minutes of music. All these features make CDs preferable to LPs for most consumers. This change in taste is portrayed in Figure 8-2(a), by a rightward shift of the demand curve. (Recall from Chapter 4 that a change in taste is one of the factors that shifts the demand curve.)

2. CD PLAYER PRICES While the prices of CDs themselves have not fallen significantly, declines in the prices of CD players have been dramatic. Costing $1000 or more a scant decade ago, most players currently sell for under $200. While CDs and LPs are substitute goods, CD players and CDs are clearly complementary goods. Thus, the lower prices for players have increased the demand for CDs. This is shown in Figure 8-2(b): on the left side we see that a fall in the price of CD players increases the quantity demanded for them; on the right side is portrayed the increase in demand for CDs as a result of the drop in price of CD players.

In short, a technologically based change in consumer tastes coupled with a sharp price fall in CD players have revolutionized the retail music market.

THE DIAMOND-WATER PARADOX

Before economists understood the distinction between total and marginal utility, they were puzzled by the fact that some "essential" goods had much lower prices than other "unimportant" goods. Why would water, which is essential to life, be priced far below diamonds, whose usefulness is much less?

The paradox is resolved when we first acknowledge that in most places water is in great supply relative to demand. Thus, it carries a low price. Diamonds, in contrast, are rare and costly to mine, cut, and polish. Their supply is small relative to demand and their price is high.

Second, our utility-maximizing rule tells us that consumers should purchase any good until the ratio of its marginal utility to price is the same as that for all other goods. Although the *marginal* utility of water may be low because it is plentiful and its price is low, the *total* utility derived from its consumption is exceedingly large because of the great quantity consumed. Conversely, the total utility derived from diamonds is low because the very high price, which reflects the scarcity of diamonds, causes consumers to purchase relatively few of them. The total utility derived from water is relatively great and the total utility derived from diamonds is relatively small, but it is *marginal* utility that is relevant to the price people are willing to pay for a good. Water yields much more total utility to us than do diamonds, even though the utility of an additional litre of water is much less than the utility of an additional diamond. Society would gladly give up *all* of the diamonds in the world if that were necessary to obtain *all* of the water in the world. But society would rather have an *additional* diamond than an *additional* litre of water, given the abundant stock of water available.

THE VALUE OF TIME

The theory of consumer behaviour has been generalized to take the economic value of time into account. Both consumption and production activities have a common characteristic — they take time. Time is a valuable economic resource; by working — by using an hour in productive activity — one may earn $6, $10, $50, or more, depending on one's education and skills. By using that hour for leisure or in consumption activities, one incurs the opportunity cost of forgone income; you sacrifice the $6, $10, or $50 you could have earned by working.

Imagine a consumer who is considering the purchase of a round of golf, on the one hand, and a concert, on the other. The market price of the golf game is $15 and the concert is $20. But the golf game is more time-intensive than the concert. Suppose you will spend four hours on the golf course, but only two hours at the concert. If your time is worth $7 per hour — as evidenced by the $7 wage rate you can obtain by working — then the "full price" of the golf game is $43 (the $15 market price *plus* $28 worth of time). Similarly, the "full price" of the concert is $34 (the $20 market price *plus* $14 worth of time). We find that, contrary to what market prices alone indicate, the "full price" of the concert is really *less* than the "full price" of the golf game.

If we now assume that the marginal utilities derived from successive golf games and concerts are identical, traditional theory would indicate that one should consume more golf games than concerts because the market price of the former is lower ($15) than the latter ($20). But when time is taken into account, the situation is reversed and golf games are more expensive ($43) than concerts ($34). Hence, it is rational in this case to consume more concerts than golf games.

By taking time into account, we can explain certain observable phenomena that traditional theory does not. It may be rational for the unskilled worker or retiree whose time has little or no market value to ride a bus from Winnipeg to Vancouver. But the corporate executive, whose time is very valuable, will find it cheaper to fly, even though bus fare is only a fraction of plane fare. It is sensible for the retiree, living on a modest pension cheque and having ample time, to spend many hours shopping for bargains. It is equally intelligent for the highly paid physician, working 55 hours per week, to patronize the hospital cafeteria and to buy a new television set over the phone.

People in other nations feel affluent Canadians are "wasteful" of food and other material goods, but "overly economical" in the use of time. Canadians who visit less developed countries find that time is

---

BOX 8-2   APPLYING THE THEORY

THE INEFFICIENCY OF CHRISTMAS GIFT-GIVING

The theory of consumer behaviour assumes that individual consumers know their preferences better than anyone else. I know what goods and services satisfy my wants better than you do and vice versa. This raises the question of whether gift-giving — consumer choices rendered by someone other than the ultimate consumer — is inefficient.

A recent study by Yale University's Joel Waldfogel* suggests that Christmas gift-giving is inefficient to the extent that between a tenth and one-third of the value of those gifts is lost because they do not match their recipients' tastes. Professor Waldfogel surveyed two groups of his students, asking them to compare the estimated price of each Christmas gift with what they would be willing to pay for it. For example, Aunt Flo may have paid $13 for the Barry Manilow CD she gave you, but you would pay only $6.50 for it. Hence, a $6.50 or 50% loss of value.

In one of the surveys students estimated that, while family and friends paid an average of $438 for the recipient's total gifts, the recipient students would be willing to pay only $313 for the same gifts, reflecting a value loss of $125. Conclusion: Christmas gift-giving destroyed about one-third of the gift value.

Two other questions were explored. First, does the value loss vary with the social distance between giver and receiver? Second, which givers are most likely to give cash?

On the first question it was found that noncash gifts from more distant relatives such as grandparents, aunts, and uncles resulted in greater value loss than gifts received from friends, siblings, parents, and "significant others." Furthermore, gifts from grandparents, aunts, and uncles were much more likely to be exchanged. The point is that more distant relatives are less likely to be aware of the recipient's consumption preferences.

The answer to the second question entails an offsetting consideration. Many grandparents, aunts, and uncles apparently realize they are uninformed about the receiver's tastes and therefore are more likely to give cash. For example, about 42% of grandparents gave cash, while only about 10% of parents and no "significant others" did so. Cash gifts, of course, can be spent by the recipient precisely in accord with his or her preferences and therefore do not result in an efficiency loss.

Conclusions: There is a value loss or inefficiency in noncash gift-giving. Noncash gifts from more distant relatives result in greater value losses than do gifts from those "close" to the recipient. Those more socially distant are more likely to give cash, which avoids any value loss.

* Joel Waldfogel, "The Deadweight Loss of Christmas," *American Economic Review*, December, 1993, pp. 1328-1336.

used casually or "squandered," while material goods are very highly prized and carefully used. These differences are not a paradox or a case of radically different temperaments. The differences are primarily a rational reflection that the high labour productivity characteristic of an advanced society gives time a high market value, whereas the opposite is true in a less developed country.

TRANSFERS AND GIFTS

Government provides eligible households with both *cash transfers* (such as welfare payments and unemployment insurance benefits) and in-kind or *noncash transfers* that specify particular purchases (for examples, subsidies for housing). Most economists contend that noncash transfers are less efficient than cash transfers because the specified uses may not match the recipient's preferences. Stated differently, consumers know their own preferences better than does the government.

Look back to Table 8-2. Suppose Holly has zero earned income, but is given the choice of a $2 cash transfer or a noncash transfer of 2 units of A. Because 2 units of A can be bought with $2, these two transfers are of equal monetary value. But by spending the $2 *cash* transfer on the first unit of B, Holly could obtain 24 utils. The *noncash* transfer of the first 2 units of A would yield only 18 (= 10 + 8) units of utility. Conclusion: The noncash transfer is less efficient (it yields less utility) than the cash transfer.

CHAPTER SUMMARY

1. The law of demand can be explained in terms of the substitution and income effects or the law of diminishing marginal utility.

2. The income effect says that a decline in the price of a product will enable the consumer to buy more of it with a fixed money income. The substitution effect points out that a lower price will make a product relatively more attractive and therefore increase the consumer's willingness to substitute it for other products.

3. The law of diminishing marginal utility states that beyond some point, additional units of a specific good will yield ever-declining amounts of extra satisfaction to a consumer.

4. We may assume that the typical consumer is rational and acts on the basis of rather well-defined preferences. Because income is limited and goods have prices on them, consumers cannot purchase all the goods and services they might like to have. They therefore select that attainable combination of goods that will maximize their utility or satisfaction.

5. The consumer's utility will be maximized when income is allocated so that the last dollar spent on each product purchased yields the same amount of extra satisfaction. Algebraically, the utility-maximizing rule is fulfilled when

$$\frac{\text{MU of product A}}{\text{price of A}} = \frac{\text{MU of product B}}{\text{price of B}}$$

and the consumer's total income is spent.

6. The utility-maximizing rule and the downsloping demand curve are logically consistent. Since marginal utility declines, a lower price is needed to induce consumers to buy more.

TERMS AND CONCEPTS

budget constraint (p. 147)
income effect (p. 144)
law of diminishing marginal utility (p. 145)
substitution effect (p. 144)

utility (p.145)
total utility (p. 145)
marginal utility (p. 145)
utility-maximizing rule (p. 147)

QUESTIONS AND STUDY SUGGESTIONS

1. Explain the law of demand through the substitution and income effects, using a price increase as a point of departure for your discussion. Explain the law of demand in terms of diminishing marginal utility.

2. *Key Question*   *Complete the following table.*

Units consumed	Total utility	Marginal utility
0	0	—
1	8	8
2		10
3	25	
4	30	
5		3
6	34	

3. Mr. Peterson buys loaves of bread and litres of milk each week at prices of $1.20 and $1 respectively. At present, he is buying these two products in amounts such that the marginal utilities from the last units purchased of the two products are 120 and 110 units, respectively. Is Peterson currently buying the utility-maximizing combination of bread and milk? If not, in what manner should he reallocate his expenditures between the two goods?

4. *Key Question*   *Columns 1 to 4 of the following table show the marginal utility, measured in terms of utils, that Ricardo would get by purchasing various amounts of products A, B, C, and D. Column 5 shows the marginal utility Ricardo gets from saving. Assume that the prices of A, B, C, and D are $18, $6, $4 and $24, respectively, and that Ricardo has a money income of $106.*

Column 1 Units of A	MU	Column 2 Units of B	MU	Column 3 Units of C	MU	Column 4 Units of D	MU	Column 5 No. of dollars saved	MU
1	72	1	24	1	15	1	36	1	5
2	54	2	15	2	12	2	30	2	4
3	45	3	12	3	8	3	24	3	3
4	36	4	9	4	7	4	18	4	2
5	27	5	7	5	5	5	13	5	1
6	18	6	5	6	4	6	7	6	$1/2$
7	15	7	2	7	$3 1/2$	7	4	7	$1/4$
8	12	8	1	8	3	8	2	8	$1/8$

a. What quantities of A, B, C, and D will Ricardo purchase to maximize satisfactions?

b. How many dollars will Ricardo choose to save?

c. Check your answers by substituting in the algebraic statement of the utility-maximizing rule.

5. *Key Question* You are choosing between two goods, X and Y, and your marginal utility from each is as shown below. If your income is $9 and the prices of X and Y are $2 and $1 respectively, what quantities of each will you purchase in maximizing utility? Specify the amount of total utility you will realize. Assume that, other things remaining unchanged, the price of X falls to $1. What quantities of X and Y will you now purchase? Using the two prices and quantities for X, derive a demand schedule for X.

Units of X	MU_x	Units of Y	MU_y
1	10	1	8
2	8	2	7
3	6	3	6
4	4	4	5
5	3	5	4
6	2	6	3

6. How can time be incorporated into the theory of consumer behaviour? Foreigners frequently point out that Canadians are very wasteful of food and other material goods and very conscious of, and overly economical in, their use of time. Can you explain this observation?

7. Explain:

a. "Before economic growth, there were too few goods; after growth, there is too little time."

b. "It is irrational for an individual to take the time to be completely rational in economic decision-making."

8. In the last decade or so there has been a dramatic expansion of small retail convenience stores — such as Mac's Milk and Beckers — although their prices are generally much higher than those in the large supermarkets. Can you explain the success of the convenience stores?

9. "Nothing is more useful than water: but it will purchase scarce any thing; scarce any thing can be had in exchange for it. A diamond, on the contrary, has scarce any value in use; but a very great quantity of other goods may frequently be had in exchange for it." Explain.

10. Use the theory of consumer behaviour to explain how the purchase of health care insurance can lead to its overconsumption.

11. Advanced Analysis Let $MU_a = z = 10 - x$ and $MU_b = z = 21 - 2y$, where z is marginal utility measured in utils, x is the amount spent on product A, and y is the amount spent on product B. Assume the consumer has $10 to spend on A and B; that is, $x + y = 10$. How is this $10 best allocated between A and B? How much utility will the marginal dollar yield?

12. (Applying the Theory) Explain why private and public gift-giving might entail economic inefficiency. Distinguish between cash and noncash gifts in your answer.

APPENDIX TO CHAPTER 8

INDIFFERENCE CURVE ANALYSIS

Another explanation of consumer behaviour and consumer equilibrium is based upon (1) budget lines and (2) indifference curves.

THE BUDGET LINE: WHAT IS ATTAINABLE

A budget line *shows various combinations of two products that can be purchased with a given money income.* If the price of product A is $1.50 and the price of B $1, the consumer could purchase all of the combinations of A and B shown in Table A8-1 with $12 of money income. At one extreme the consumer might spend all of his or her income on 8 units of A and have nothing left to spend on B. Or, by giving up 2 units of A, the consumer could have 6 units of A and 3 of B. And so on to the other extreme, at which the consumer could buy 12 units of B at $1 each.

Figure A8-1 shows the budget line graphically. The slope of the budget line measures the ratio of the price of B to the price of A. The absolute value of the slope is $P_B/P_A = \$1/\$1.50 = 2/3$. This is the mathematical way of saying that the consumer must forgo 2 units of A (measured on the vertical axis) at $1.50 each to have $3 to spend on 3 units of B (measured on the horizontal axis). In moving down the budget line, 2 of A (at $1.50 each) must be given up to obtain 3 of B (at $1 each). This yields a slope of 2/3.

TABLE A8-1 **The budget line: combinations of A and B obtainable with income of $12**

Units of A (Price = $1.50)	Units of B (Price = $1)	Total expenditures
8	0	$12 (= $12 + $0)
6	3	$12 (= $9 + $3)
4	6	$12 (= $6 + $6)
2	9	$12 (= $3 + $9)
0	12	$12 (= $0 + $12)

Two other characteristics of the budget line merit comment.

1. **INCOME CHANGES** The location of the budget line varies with money income. An *increase* in money income will shift the budget line to the *right*, a *decrease* in money income will move it to the *left*. To verify, simply recalculate Table A8-1 on the assumption that money income is (a) $24 and (b) $6, and plot the new budget lines in Figure A8-1.

2. **PRICE CHANGES** A change in product prices will also shift the budget line. A decline in the prices of both products — the equivalent of a real income increase — will shift the curve to the right. You can verify this by recalculating Table A8-1 and replotting Figure A8-1 assuming that $P_A = \$0.75$ and $P_B = \$0.50$. Conversely, an increase in the prices of A and B will shift the curve to the left.

FIGURE A8-1 **A consumer's budget line**

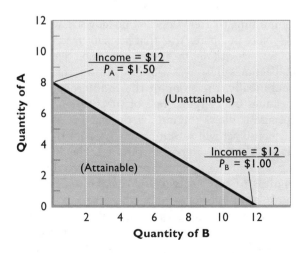

The budget line shows all of the various combinations of any two products that can be purchased, given the prices of the products and the consumer's money income.

Assume P_A = $3 and P_B = $2 and rework Table A8-1 and Figure A8-1 to substantiate this statement.

Note also what happens if we change P_B while holding P_A (and money income) constant. If we lower P_B from $1 to $0.50, the budget line will fan outward to the right. Conversely, by increasing P_B from $1 to $1.50, the line will fan inward to the left. In both instances, the line remains "anchored" at 8 units on the vertical axis because P_A has not changed.

INDIFFERENCE CURVES: WHAT IS PREFERRED

Budget lines reflect "objective" market data involving income and prices. The budget line reveals the combinations of A and B that are obtainable, given money income and prices. Indifference curves, on the other hand, embody "subjective" information about consumer preferences for A and B. **An indifference curve *shows all combinations of products A and B that will yield the same total level of satisfaction or utility to the consumer.***

Table A8-2 and Figure A8-2 present a hypothetical indifference curve involving products A and B. The consumer's preferences are such that he or she will realize the same total utility from each combination of A and B shown in the table or curve. Thus, the consumer will be indifferent as to which combination is obtained.

It is essential to understand several characteristics of indifference curves.

1. DOWNSLOPING Indifference curves are downsloping because both product A and product B yield utility to the consumer. Moving from combination *j* to combination *k*, the consumer is obtaining more of B and less of A but total utility remains the same. More of A necessitates less of B, so that the quantities of A and B are inversely related. Any curve that reflects inversely related variables is downsloping.

TABLE A8-2 **An indifference schedule**

Combination	Units of A	Units of B
j	12	2
k	6	4
l	4	6
m	3	8

2. CONVEX TO ORIGIN Viewed from the origin, a downsloping curve can be concave (bowed outward) or convex (bowed inward). A concave curve has an increasing (steeper) slope as one moves down the curve, while a convex curve has a diminishing (flatter) slope as one moves down it.

Note in Figure A8-2 that *the indifference curve is convex viewed from the origin.* The slope diminishes or becomes flatter as we move down the curve. Technically, the slope of the indifference curve measures the **marginal rate of substitution (MRS)** because it shows the rate, at the margin, at which the consumer will substitute one good for the other (B for A) to remain equally satisfied. The diminishing slope of the indifference curve means the willingness to substitute B for A *diminishes* as one moves down the curve.

The rationale for this convexity, that is, for a diminishing MRS, is that a consumer's willingness to substitute B for A (or vice versa) will depend on the amounts of B and A he or she has to begin with. Consider Table A8-2 and Figure A8-2 once again, beginning at point *j*. Here, in relative terms, the con-

FIGURE A8-2 **A consumer's indifference curve**

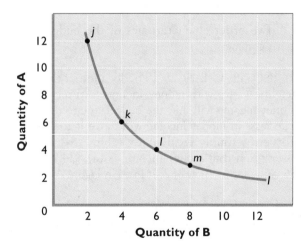

Every point on an indifference curve represents some combination of products A and B that is equally satisfactory to the consumer; that is, each combination of A and B embodies the same level of total utility.

sumer has a substantial amount of A and very little of B. This means that, "at the margin," B is very valuable (its marginal utility is high), while A is less valuable at the margin (its marginal utility is low). The consumer will be willing to give up a substantial amount of A to get a few more units of B. In this particular case the consumer is willing to forgo 6 units of A to get 2 more units of B. Thus the MRS is 6/2 or 3.

In general, as the amount of B *increases*, the marginal utility of additional units of B *decreases*. Similarly, as the quantity of A *decreases*, its marginal utility *increases*. In Figure A8-2 we see that in moving down the curve the consumer will be willing to give up smaller and smaller amounts of A to offset acquiring each additional unit of B. The result is a curve with a diminishing slope, one that is convex when viewed from the origin. The MRS declines as one moves southeast along the indifference curve.

3. INDIFFERENCE MAP   The single indifference curve of Figure A8-2 reflects some constant (but unspecified) level of total utility or satisfaction. It is possible — and useful for our analysis — to sketch a whole series of indifference curves, an **indifference map** as shown in Figure A8-3. Each curve reflects a different level of total utility. Each curve to the right of our original curve (labelled I_2 in Figure A8-3) reflects combinations of A and B that yield *more* utility than I_2. Each curve to the *left* of I_2 reflects *less* total utility than I_2. As *we move out from the origin each successive indifference curve represents a higher level of utility.* This can be demonstrated by drawing a line in a northeasterly direction from the origin. Note that its points of intersection with each successive curve entail larger amounts of *both* A and B, and therefore a higher level of total utility.

EQUILIBRIUM AT TANGENCY

We can now determine the consumer's **equilibrium position** by combining the budget line and the indifference map, as shown in Figure A8-4. By definition, the budget line indicates all combinations of A and B that the consumer can attain, given his or her money income and the prices of A and B. Of these attainable combinations, the consumer will most prefer the combination that yields the greatest satisfaction or utility. *The utility-maximizing combination will be the one lying on the highest attainable indifference curve.* In terms of Figure A8-4, the consumer's utility-maximizing or equilibrium combination of A and B is at point X, where the budget line is *tangent* to I_2.

But why not point Y? Because Y is on a lower indifference curve, I_1. By trading "down" the budget line — by shifting dollars from purchases of A to purchases of B — the consumer can get on an indifference curve further from the origin and thereby increase total utility from the same income.

How about point W on indifference curve I_3? While it is true that W would yield a higher level of total utility than does X, point W is beyond (outside of) the budget line and hence not attainable to the consumer.

Point X is the best or optimum *attainable* combination of products A and B. At this point, by definition of tangency, we note that the slope of the highest obtainable indifference curve equals the slope of the budget line. Because the slope of the indifference curve reflects the MRS and the slope of the budget line is P_B/P_A, the optimum or equilibrium position is where

$$MRS = P_B/P_A$$

Appendix Key Question 3 is recommended at this point.

FIGURE A8-3   An indifference map

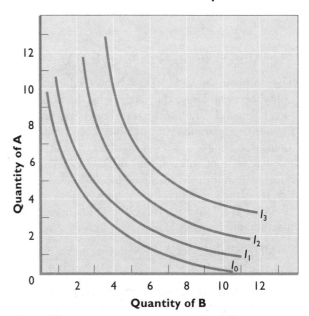

An indifference map comprises a set of indifference curves. Each successive curve further from the origin indicates a higher level of total utility. That is, any combination of products A and B shown by a point on I_3 is superior to any combination of A and B shown by a point on I_2, I_1, or I_0.

FIGURE A8-4 **The consumer's equilibrium position**

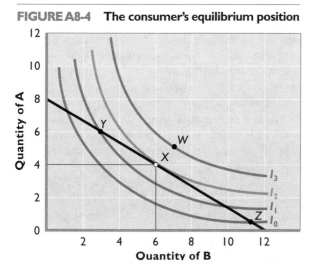

The consumer's equilibrium position is at point *x*, where the budget line is tangent to the highest attainable indifference curve, I_2. In this case, the consumer will buy 4 units of A at $1.50 per unit and 6 of B at $1 per unit with a $12 money income. Points Z and Y also represent attainable combinations of A and B, but yield less total utility, as is evidenced by the fact that they are on lower indifference curves. While W would entail more utility than X, it is outside of the budget line and therefore unattainable.

THE MEASUREMENT OF UTILITY

There is an important difference between the marginal utility theory and the indifference curve theory of consumer demand. The marginal utility theory assumes the utility is *numerically* measurable. The consumer is assumed to be able to say *how much* extra utility he or she derives from an extra unit of A or B. Given the prices of A and B, the consumer must be able to measure the marginal utility derived from successive units of A and B in order to realize the utility-maximizing (equilibrium) position, as previously indicated by

$$\frac{\text{Marginal utility of A}}{\text{Price of A}} = \frac{\text{Marginal utility of B}}{\text{Price of B}}$$

The indifference curve approach poses a less stringent requirement for the consumer: he or she need only be able to specify whether a given combination of A and B yields more, less, or the same amount of utility than some other combinations of A and B. The consumer need only say, for example, that 6 of A and 7 of B yield more (or less) satisfaction than 4 of A and 9 of B. Indifference curve

analysis does *not* require the consumer to specify *how much* more (or less) satisfaction will be realized.

When the equilibrium situations in the two approaches are compared we find that (1) in the indifference curve analysis the MRS equals P_B/P_A; (2) in the marginal utility approach the ratio of marginal utilities also equals P_B/P_A. We therefore deduce that the MRS is equivalent in the marginal utility approach to the ratio of marginal utilities of the two goods.[5]

DERIVING THE DEMAND CURVE

We earlier noted that given the price of A, an increase in the price of B will cause the budget line to fan inward to the left. This can now be used to derive a demand curve for product B. In Figure A8-5(a) we have simply reproduced Figure A8-4, showing our initial consumer equilibrium at point X. The budget line involved in determining this equilibrium position assumes that the money income is $12 and that P_A = $1.50 and P_B = $1. Let's examine what happens to the equilibrium position if we increase P_B to $1.50, holding money income and the price of A constant.

The result is shown in Figure A8-5(a). The budget line fans to the left, yielding a new equilibrium point of tangency with indifference curve I_1 at point X'. At X', the consumer is buying 3 units of B and 5 of A (compared to 4 of A and 6 of B at X). We now have sufficient information to locate the demand curve for product B. We know that, at equilibrium point X, the price of B is $1 and 6 units are purchased; at equilibrium point X', the price of B is $1.50 and 3 units are purchased.

These data are shown graphically as a demand curve for B in Figure A8-5(b). Note that the horizontal axes of Figures 8-5(a) and A8-5(b) are identical; both measure the quantity demanded of B. We can therefore drop dashed perpendiculars from Figure A8-5(a) down to the horizontal axis of Figure A8-5(b). On the vertical axis of Figure A8-5(b), we locate the two chosen prices of B. Connecting these prices with the relevant quantities demanded, we locate two points on the demand curve for B.

---

[5] If we begin with the utility-maximizing rule, $MU_A/P_A = MU_B/P_B$, then multiply through by P_B and divide through by MU_A, we obtain $P_B/P_A = MU_B/MU_A$. In indifference curve analysis we know that the optimum or equilibrium position is where MRS = P_B/P_A. Hence, MRS also equals MU_B/MU_A.

FIGURE A8-5 **Deriving the demand curve**

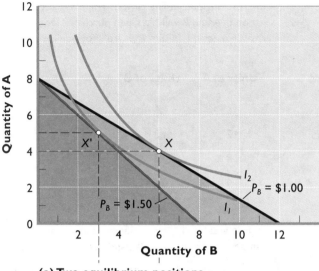

(a) Two equilibrium positions

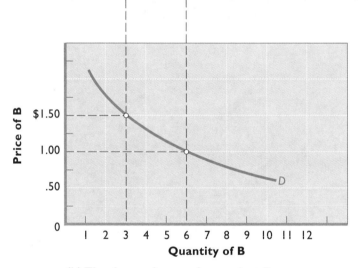

(b) The demand curve for product B

When the price of B is increased from $1 to $1.50 in (a), the equilibrium position moves from X to X′, decreasing the quantity demanded from 6 to 3 units. The demand curve for B is determined in (b) by plotting the $1.00–6 units and the $1.50–3 units price-quantity combinations for B.

By simple manipulation of the price of B in an indifference curve-budget line context, a downsloping demand curve for B can be derived. We have derived the law of demand under the correct assumption of "other things equal" since *only* the price of B has been changed. The price of A as well as the consumer's income and tastes have remained constant when deriving the consumer's demand curve for product B.

APPENDIX SUMMARY

1. The indifference curve approach to consumer behaviour is based upon the consumer's budget line and indifference curves.

2. The budget line shows all combinations of two products the consumer can purchase, given money income and product prices.

3. A change in product prices or money income will shift the budget line.

4. An indifference curve shows all combinations of two products that will yield the same level of total utility to the consumer. Indifference curves are downsloping and convex to the origin.

5. An indifference map consists of a number of indifference curves; the further from the origin, the higher the level of utility associated with each curve.

6. The consumer will select that point on the budget line that puts him or her on the highest attainable indifference curve.

7. Changing the price of one product shifts the budget line and determines a new equilibrium position. A downsloping demand curve can be determined by plotting the price-quantity combinations associated with the old and new equilibrium positions.

TERMS AND CONCEPTS

budget line (p. 157)
equilibrium position (p. 159)
indifference curve (p. 158)
indifference map (p. 159)
marginal rate of substitution (p. 158)

APPENDIX QUESTIONS AND STUDY SUGGESTIONS

1. What information is embodied in a budget line? What shifts will occur in the budget line as money income a. increases and b. decreases? What shifts will occur in the budget line as the product price shown on the horizontal axis a. increases and b. decreases?

2. What information is contained in an indifference curve? Why are such curves a. downsloping and b. convex to the origin? Why does total utility increase as the consumer moves to indifference curves further from the origin? Why can't indifference curves intersect?

3. *Appendix Key Quesion*   *Using Figure A8-4, explain why the point of tangency of the budget line with an indifference curve is the consumer's equilibrium position. Explain why any point where the budget line intersects an indifference curve will not be equilibrium. Explain: "The consumer is in equilibrium where MRS = P_B/P_A."*

4. Assume that the data in the accompanying table is an indifference curve for Ms. Chen. Graph this curve,

putting A on the vertical and B on the horizontal axis. Assuming the prices of A and B are $1.50 and $1.00 respectively and that Ms. Chen has $24 to spend, add the resulting budget line to your graph. What combination of A and B will Ms. Chen purchase? Does your answer meet the MRS = P_B/P_A rule for equilibrium?

Units of A	Units of B
16	6
12	8
8	12
4	24

5. Explain graphically how indifference curve analysis can be used to derive a demand curve.

6. *Advanced analysis.* Demonstrate that the equilibrium condition MRS = P_B/P_A is the equivalent of the utility-maximizing rule $MU_A/P_A = MU_B/P_B$.

CHAPTER 9

THE ORGANIZATION AND COSTS OF PRODUCTION

Product prices are determined by the interaction of demand and supply. In preceding chapters we focused our attention on factors underlying demand. As observed in Chapter 4, the basic factor underlying the ability and willingness of firms to supply a product or service is the cost of production. Production of a good requires economic resources that, because of their relative scarcity, have a price. The amount of any product a firm is willing to supply depends on the prices (costs), the productivity of the resources needed to produce it, and the price the product will bring on the market.

This chapter considers the organization of firms and the general nature of production costs. Product prices are introduced in the following chapters, and supply decisions of producers are then explained.

BOX 9-1 THE BIG PICTURE

Let's put the demand curve on the back burner for the moment and concentrate on the supply curve. What is behind the supply curve? Why is it upward sloping?

Firms are organizations that bring together the factors of production (land, labour, capital, and entrepreneurial talent) to produce goods and services consumers want. Firms function in a world of scarcity, thus competing for available resources. In the last chapter, we noted that the goal of the consumer is to get as much satisfaction as possible from the income he or she has. The aim of the firm is to make as much profit as possible.

In trying to maximize their profits in a world of scarcity, business owners must make a number of choices. These include: (a) what form of organizational structure to adopt (proprietorship, partnership, or corporation); (b) what combination of resources to use; and (c) whether to continue operating in their current line of production. Over the next number of chapters, we will delve deeper into various constraints or limitations the firm must operate under. These range from the time frame within which the firm is making choices, to policy and legal constraints, to the extent and type of competition that the firm faces from other businesses trying to maximize their profits in the same market.

As you read this chapter, keep the following points in mind:

- A firm will choose the form of organization most conducive to its goal of maximizing profit.
- Whatever your normative stance (opinion) on profit, it is the prime motivating drive of firms. It is imperative you accept this fact.
- A firm will stay in a specific line of production or service as long as it cannot make more profits elsewhere.
- In the short run, there are fixed plant and equipment that can't be altered. In the long run, all input variables can be changed.
- The bulk of this chapter is concerned with often tedious details about production and costs. It is crucial you take the time to master the concepts. Unless you do so, the following chapters will be much more difficult for you to comprehend.

THE NEED FOR FIRMS

Businesses, or firms, constitute one of the two major aggregates of the private sector, the other being the household — or consumption — sector.

As will be discussed shortly, there are many ways to organize a firm. But why is there a need for the firm in a market economy? Could we not have people working in their own homes? While this could be possible, it would greatly decrease the efficiency of an economy. Production and distribution could be much more efficiently carried out at a centralized location. The task of organizing production and distribution at a centralized location would be easier and less costly.

THE MAIN GOAL OF THE FIRM

It cannot be emphasized enough that the main goal of a firm is to maximize profits. The firm may have many objectives — behaving in a socially responsible manner, giving to charities, offering scholarships, etc. — but the overriding goal is to maximize profit.

THE BUSINESS SECTOR

PLANTS, FIRMS, AND INDUSTRIES

To avoid any possible confusion, we preface our discussion of sector with some comments concerning terminology: we must distinguish between a plant, a firm, and an industry.

1. A **plant** is a physical establishment — a factory, farm, mine, retail or wholesale store, or warehouse that performs one or more functions in the making and distribution of goods and services.
2. A business **firm** is the business organization that owns and operates these plants. Most firms operate on only one plant, but many own and operate a number of plants. Multiplant firms may be

"horizontal," "vertical," or "conglomerate" combinations. For example, every large steel firm — Dofasco, Stelco — are **vertical combinations** of plants. Both firms own plants at various stages of the production process. Each steelmaker owns ore and coal mines, limestone quarries, coke ovens, blast furnaces, rolling mills, forge shops, foundries, and, in some cases, manufacturing shops.

The large chain stores in the retail field — Zellers, Safeway, The Bay — are **horizontal combinations** in that each plant is at the same stage of production.

Other firms are **conglomerates**; they are made up of plants operating across many different markets and industries. For example, Canadian Pacific is involved through affiliated plants on a large-scale basis in such diverse fields as hotels, baking products, educational materials, and insurance.

3. An **industry** is a group of firms producing the same or similar products. Industries are usually difficult to actually identify in practice. For example, how do we identify the automobile industry? The simplest answer is, "All firms producing automobiles." But automobiles are heterogeneous products. While Cadillacs and Buicks are similar products, Geos and Cadillacs are not. At least most buyers think so. And what about trucks? Small pickup trucks are similar in some respects to station wagons. Is it better to speak of the "motor vehicle industry" rather than of the "automobile industry"?

Delineating an industry becomes even more complex because most firms are multiproduct firms. Automobile manufacturers also make such diverse products as diesel locomotives, buses, refrigerators, guided missiles, and air conditioners. For these reasons, industry classifications are usually somewhat arbitrary.

LEGAL FORMS OF BUSINESS ORGANIZATION

Business firms are diverse, ranging from giant corporations like Bell Canada Enterprises, Inc. to neighbourhood specialty shops and "mom and pop" groceries with one or two employees. This diversity makes it necessary to classify business firms by some criterion such as legal structure, industry or product, or size. Business firms are distributed among the three major legal forms: (1) the sole proprietorship, (2) the partnership, and (3) the corporation.

SOLE PROPRIETORSHIP

A **sole proprietorship** is an individual in business for himself or herself. The proprietor owns or obtains the materials and equipment needed by the business and personally runs it.

ADVANTAGES This simple type of business organization has the following advantages:

1. A sole proprietorship is easy to organize.
2. The proprietor is his or her own boss and has substantial freedom of action. Since the proprietor's profit income depends on the enterprise's success, there is a strong incentive to manage the business efficiently.

DISADVANTAGES But the disadvantages of this form of business organization are great.

1. With rare exceptions, the financial resources of a sole proprietorship are insufficient to allow the firm to grow into a large enterprise. Finances are usually limited to what the proprietor has in the bank and what can be borrowed. Since proprietorships often fail, banks are not eager to extend much — or often, any — credit to them.
2. Complete control of a firm forces the proprietor to carry out all management functions. A proprietor must make decisions concerning buying, selling, and the hiring and training of personnel, not to mention the technical aspects of producing, advertising, and distributing the product. Thus, the potential benefits of specialization in business management are usually not available to the typical small-scale proprietorship.
3. Most important, the proprietor is subject to **unlimited liability**. Individuals in business for themselves risk not only the assets of the firm but also their personal assets. If assets of an unsuccessful proprietorship are insufficient to satisfy the claims of creditors, creditors can file claims against the proprietor's personal property.

PARTNERSHIP

The **partnership** is a natural outgrowth of the sole proprietorship. A partnership is a form of business organization in which two or more individuals agree to own and operate a business. Usually they pool their financial resources and business skills. They share the risks and the profits or losses.

ADVANTAGES   The advantages of a partnership are:

1. It is easy to organize. Although a written agreement is almost invariably involved, legal red tape is not great.
2. Greater specification in management is possible because there are more participants.
3. Financial resources of a partnership are usually greater than those of a sole proprietorship. Partners can pool their money capital and are often somewhat better risks in the eyes of lending institutions.

DISADVANTAGES   The partnership raises some potential problems the sole proprietorship does not.

1. When several people participate in management, this division of authority can lead to inconsistent policies or to inaction when action is required. Worse, partners may disagree on basic policy.
2. The finances of partnerships are limited, although generally better than a sole proprietorship. But the financial resources of partners may not be enough for the growth of a successful enterprise.
3. The continuity of a partnership is precarious. The withdrawal or death of a partner generally means dissolution and complete reorganization of the firm, disrupting its operations.
4. Unlimited liability plagues a partnership, just as it does a proprietorship. In fact each partner is liable for all business debts incurred, not only as a result of each partner's own management decisions, but also as a consequence of the actions of any other partner. A wealthy partner risks money on the prudence of less affluent partners.

CORPORATION

Corporations are legal entities, distinct and separate from the individuals who own them. These governmentally designated "legal persons" can acquire resources, own assets, produce and sell products, incur debts, extend credit, sue and be sued, and carry on all the functions any other type of enterprise performs.

ADVANTAGES   The advantages of the corporate form of business enterprise have catapulted it into a dominant position in the modern market economy. Although corporations are relatively small in num-

ber, they are frequently large in size and scale of operations. In fact, they account for roughly 70% of all private business.

1. The corporation is by far the most effective form of business organization for raising money capital. The corporation features unique methods of finance — the selling of stocks and bonds — which allow the firm to tap the savings of untold thousands of households. Through the securities market (stock and bond market) corporations can pool the financial resources of large numbers of people. Financing by the sale of securities also has advantages from the viewpoint of the purchasers of these securities.

   First, households can now participate in enterprise and share the expected monetary reward without assuming an active part in management. In addition, an individual can spread any risks by buying the securities of several corporations. Finally, it is usually easy for the holder of corporate securities to sell them. Organized stock exchanges make it easy to buy and sell securities, increasing the willingness of savers to buy them.

   Corporations have easier access to bank credit than other types of business organizations. Corporations are better risks and are more likely to provide banks with profitable accounts.
2. Corporations have the distinct advantage of **limited liability**. The owners (stockholders) of a corporation risk *only* what they paid for the stock purchased. Their personal assets are not at stake if the corporation becomes bankrupt. Creditors can sue the corporation as a legal person, but can't sue the owners of the corporation as individuals. Limited liability eases the corporation's task in getting money capital.
3. Because of their advantage in attracting money capital, successful corporations find it easier to expand the size and scope of their operations and to realize the benefit of expansion. They can take advantage of mass-production technologies and greater specialization in the use of resources. While a sole proprietor may be forced to share time among production, accounting, and marketing functions, a corporation can hire specialized personnel in these areas and achieve greater efficiency.
4. As a legal entity, the corporation has a life independent of its owners and its officers. Proprietorships are subject to sudden and unpredictable demise, but legally at least corporations are immortal. The transfer of corporate ownership through the sale of

stock will not disrupt the continuity of the corporation. Corporations have a permanence, lacking in other forms of business organization, which is conducive to long-range planning and growth.

DISADVANTAGES The corporation's advantages are of tremendous significance and typically override any accompanying disadvantages, yet there are drawbacks to the corporate form.

1. Red tape and legal expense are involved in obtaining a corporate charter.
2. From the social point of view, the corporate form of enterprise lends itself to certain abuses. Because the corporation is a legal entity, unscrupulous business owners sometimes can avoid personal responsibility for questionable business activities by adopting the corporate form of enterprise.
3. A further disadvantage of corporations has to do with the **double taxation** of corporate income. That part of corporate income paid out as dividends to stockholders is taxed twice — once as part of corporate profits and again as part of stockholders' personal incomes.
4. In sole proprietorships and partnerships the owners of the real and financial assets of the firm also directly manage or control those assets. In large corporations where ownership is widely diffused over tens or hundreds of thousands of stockholders, there is **separation of ownership and control**.

Most stockholders vote, or, if they do not, merely delegate their votes to the corporation's present officers. Not voting, or the automatic signing over of one's proxy votes to current corporate officials, makes those officials self-perpetuating.

The separation of ownership and control is of no consequence so long as the actions of the control (management) group and the wishes of the ownership (stockholder) group are in accord. But the interests of the two groups are not always identical. Management, seeking the power and prestige that accompany control over a *large* enterprise, may favour unprofitable expansion of the firm's operations. Or a conflict of interest can develop over dividend policies. What portion of corporate earnings after taxes should be paid out as dividends, and what amount should be retained by the firm as undistributed profits? And corporation officials may vote themselves large salaries, pensions, bonuses, and so forth, out of corporate

earnings that might otherwise be used for increased dividend payments. **(Key Question 2)**

INCORPORATE OR NOT?

The need for money capital is critical to whether a firm incorporates. The money capital required to establish and operate a barbershop, a shoeshine stand, or a small gift shop is modest, making incorporation unnecessary. In contrast, modern technology makes incorporation imperative in many lines of production. In most branches of manufacturing — automobiles, steel, fabricated metal products, electrical equipment and household appliances — substantial amounts of money are needed for investment in fixed assets and working capital. Here there is no choice but to incorporate.

QUICK REVIEW 9-1

1. Business firms are either sole proprietorships, partnerships, or corporations.

2. Although relatively small in number, corporations dominate our economy because of their superior ability to raise money capital.

THE STRUCTURE OF THE CANADIAN ECONOMY AND ITS EVOLUTION OVER TIME

Table 9-1 sets out the contribution to domestic output (GDP) by each sector and industry. The major sectors of any economy are: **primary**, **secondary**, and **tertiary** (which is more commonly referred to as the service sector). Table 9-1 also breaks each sector into sub-sectors or industries.

The service sector has come to dominate in terms of its contributing share to domestic output, followed by the secondary sector in which manufacturing dominates. The primary sector has experienced an almost continuous decline in GDP share over the last century.

Table 9-2, which shows employment shares by each sector and industry, reflects contribution to domestic output. For example, agriculture's employment share fell from about a quarter of the workforce in 1947 to a mere 4% in 1987. Manufacturing has also experienced a decline in employment share, but a much less steep decline. The service sector, on the other hand, has almost doubled its employment share of the economy.

BOX 9-2 APPLYING THE THEORY

THE FINANCING OF CORPORATE ACTIVITY

One of the main advantages of corporations is their ability to finance their operations through the sale of stocks and bonds. It is informative to examine the nature of corporate finance in more detail.

Corporations finance their activities in three different ways. First, a large portion of a corporation's activity is financed internally out of undistributed corporate profits. Second, like individuals or unincorporated businesses, corporations may borrow from financial institutions. For example, a small corporation that wants to build a new plant or warehouse may obtain the funds from a chartered bank, a trust company, or an insurance company. Also, unique to corporations, common stocks and bonds can be issued.

Stocks versus Bonds A common stock is an ownership share. The purchaser of a stock certificate has the right to vote in the selection of corporate officers and to share in any declared dividends. If you own 1000 of the 100,000 shares issued by Specific Motors, Inc. (hereafter SM), then you own 1% of the company, are entitled to 1% of any dividends declared by the board of directors, and control 1% of the votes in the annual election of corporate officials. In contrast, a bond is not an ownership share. A bond purchaser is simply lending money to a corporation. A bond is merely an IOU, in acknowledgement of a loan, whereby the corporation promises to pay the holder a fixed amount at some specified future date and other fixed amounts (interest payments) every year up to the bond's maturity date. For example, one might purchase a ten-year SM bond with a face value of $1000 with a 10% stated rate of interest. This means that in exchange for your $1000 SM guarantees you a $100 interest payment for each of the next ten years and then to repay your $1000 principal at the end of that period.

Differences There are important differences between stocks and bonds. First, as noted, the bondholder is not an owner of the company, but is only a lender. Second, bonds are considered to be less risky than stocks for two reasons. On the one hand, bondholders have a "legally prior claim" on a corporation's earnings. Dividends cannot be paid to stockholders until all interest payments due to bondholders have been paid. On the other hand, holders

of SM stock do not know how much their dividends will be or how much they might obtain for their stock if they decide to sell. If Specific Motors falls on hard times, stockholders may receive no dividends at all and the value of their stock may plummet. Provided the corporation does not go bankrupt, the holder of an SM bond is guaranteed a $100 interest payment each year and the return of his or her $1000 at the end of ten years.

Bond Risks But this is not to imply that the purchase of corporate bonds is riskless. The market value of your SM bond may vary over time in accordance with the financial health of the corporation. If SM encounters economic misfortunes that raise questions about its financial integrity, the market value of your bond may fall. Should you sell the bond prior to maturity you may receive only $600 or $700 for it (rather than $1000) and thereby incur a capital loss.

Changes in interest rates also affect the market prices of bonds. Increases in interest rates cause bond prices to fall and vice versa. Assume you purchase a $1000 ten-year SM bond this year (1996) when the going interest rate is 10%. This obviously means that your bond provides a $100 fixed interest payment each year. But now suppose that by next year the interest rate has jumped to 15% and SM must now guarantee a $150 fixed annual payment on its new 1997 $1000 ten-year bonds. No sensible person will pay you $1000 for your bond that pays only $100 of interest income per year when new bonds can be purchased for $1000 that pay the holder $150 per year. Thus if you sell your 1996 bond before maturity, you will suffer a capital loss.

Bondholders face another element of risk due to inflation. If substantial inflation occurs over the ten-year period you hold an SM bond, the $1000 principal repaid to you at the end of that period will represent substantially less purchasing power than the $1000 you loaned to SM ten years earlier. You will have lent "dear" dollars, but will be repaid in "cheap" dollars.

We noted in Chapter 3 that industries expand and contract on their profitability. The inter-sectoral shifts are due to a number of factors, of which technological improvements and accompanying productivity increases are dominant. For example, while there has been a continuous decline in agriculture's employment share, it has come about because of large labour (and land) productivity improvements. While this may at first seem odd, a large labour productivity improvement means you need fewer people in that sector, unless there is an accompanying increase in the demand for foodstuffs. Since there is a limit to our capacity to increase our food intake, the excess labour had to find work elsewhere. Throughout the nineteenth and early twentieth centuries, excess agricultural workers found jobs in the secondary sector, primarily in manufacturing.

Since about the time of World War II, the secondary sector has been losing employment share as productivity in that sector rose. Manufacturing in particular has seen a significant drop in its employment share. Table 9-1 shows manufacturing's GDP share has dropped somewhat from a high of 26% in 1960, dropping to just over 18% by 1994.

While it is true that natural resources are important to Canada's economy, the output and employment share of the primary sector continues to fall. Only the mining, quarrying, and oil wells category has maintained a relatively steady employment share, but a decreasing GDP share.

TABLE 9-1   Production shares by sector, selected years 1870-1994

	% of Gross Domestic Product at Factor Cost							
	1870	**1911**	**1926**	**1960**	**1970**	**1980**	**1986**	**1994**
PRIMARY	46.2	39.4	23.4	10.4	8.3	11.2	10.0	7.3
Agriculture	34.3	30.8	18.1	4.9	3.3	3.3	3.3	2.0
Forestry	9.9	4.6	1.3	1.3	0.8	0.9	0.7	0.9
Fishing and trapping	1.1	1.5	0.8	0.2	0.2	0.2	0.2	0.1
Mining, quarrying, oil wells	0.9	2.5	3.2	4.0	4.0	6.8	5.8	4.3
SECONDARY	22.6	29.7	38.7	44.8	41.4	38.3	36.7	35.4
Manufacturing	na	18.8	21.7	26.4	23.3	20.6	19.5	18.3
Construction	na	10.3	4.1	6.0	6.3	5.9	7.0	5.2
Transportation and communication	na	na	12.9	9.6	8.9	8.3	7.3	8.6
Electric power, gas, and water utilities	na	0.6		2.8	2.9	3.5	2.9	3.3
TERTIARY	31.2[a]	30.8[a]	37.9	44.8	50.2	50.5	53.3	57.3
Trade (wholesale, retail)	na	na	11.6	12.8	12.4	11.0	11.7	12.6
Finance, insurance, real estate	na	na	10.0	11.6	11.3	11.3	14.1	16.3
Public administration, defence	na	na	3.4	6.9	7.3	7.4	7.2	6.3
Service	na	na	12.9	13.5	19.2	20.8	20.3	22.1
Total	100.0	100.0	100.0	100.0	100.0	100.0	100.0	100.0

[a] Includes income generated by the railway and telephone industries.

* Figure for Forestry calculated as a residual.

Source: Data for 1870 to 1986 from C. Green, *Canadian Industrial Organization and Policy* (Toronto: McGraw-Hill Ryerson Ltd., 1990), p. 4. Data for 1994 calculated from Statistics Canada, *Canadian Economic Observer*, Statistical Summary, June 1995.

TABLE 9-2 Employment shares (%) by economic sector and industry

	1891[a]	1921[a]	1947	1960	1970	1980	1987	1994
PRIMARY	49	36	27.5	14.3	9.3	7.3	6.4	5.3
Agriculture			24.1	11.3	6.5	4.5	4.0	3.2
Forestry			1.2	1.1	0.9	0.7	0.6	0.5
Fishing and trapping			0.7	0.4	0.3	0.3	0.3	0.6
Mining, quarrying, oil wells			1.5	1.5	1.6	1.8	1.5	1.0
SECONDARY	31	34	40.3	40.7	37.5	34.0	30.4	27.7
Manufacturing			26.7	24.9	22.7	19.7	17.1	14.7
Construction			5.2	7.2	6.0	5.8	5.7	5.6
Transportation and communication			7.7	7.5	7.7	7.3	6.6 ⎫	7.4
Public utilities			0.7	1.1	1.1	1.2	1.0 ⎭	
TERTIARY	20	30	32.1	45.0	53.2	58.7	63.2	67.0
Trade (wholesale, retail)			12.3	16.2	16.7	17.2	17.7	17.4
Finance, insurance, real estate			2.7	3.8	4.6	5.7	5.8	5.9
Community, business, personal services (including health, education)		⎫ 17.1 ⎬ ⎭		⎫ 25.0 ⎬ ⎭	25.7	28.9	32.9	37.1
Public administration					6.2	6.9	6.8	6.6
Total	100.0	100.0	100.0	100.0	100.0	100.0	100.0	100.0

[a] Based on occupational data in which all clerical workers are allocated to the tertiary sector and all nonprimary sector labourers are allocated to the secondary sector.

Source: Data for 1891 to 1987 from C. Green, *op. cit.*, (Toronto: McGraw-Hill Ryerson Ltd., 1990), p. 6. Data for 1994 calculated from Statistics Canada, *Canadian Economic Observer*, Statistical Summary, June 1995.

There is good evidence to suggest that some Canadian industries are highly concentrated in their market power. More will be said about this topic in Chapter 14. For now it will suffice to say that compared with the U.S. economy, many of our industries are dominated by a few firms that control a significant percentage of the market.

FOREIGN OWNERSHIP

Another distinguishing characteristic of our economy is that a high percentage is **foreign owned**, particularly by Americans. Table 9-3 shows the extent of foreign ownership in a number of industries. The term "foreign owned" generally connotes outright ownership of a firm or at least owning 51% of the stocks, which means control of a firm.

Foreign ownership has costs and benefits. These have been extensively debated. Given the difficulties of measuring costs and benefits, it is not surprising that the issue of foreign ownership often arouses strong emotions. Perhaps the most serious accusation against foreign ownership is that it jeopardizes Canada's political autonomy. However, such an accusation is difficult to prove or disprove.

There are various explanations of the high incidence of foreign direct investment in Canada. Some attribute it to the relatively high Canadian tariffs instituted in 1879 with the formation of the National Policy. Since foreign firms, particularly American firms, couldn't compete by exporting here, they established production facilities. Our patent laws in the past, which allowed no protec-

TABLE 9-3   Foreign ownership and control of Canadian industry

Industrial division	Percentage of capital employed	
	Foreign-owned in 1987	Foreign-controlled in 1991
Manufacturing	48%	56%
Petroleum and natural gas	35	41
Mining and smelting	40	36
Railways	40	0
Other utilities	27	2
Total of above specified industries, merchandising and construction	31%	26%

Source: Statistics Canada, Canada's International Investment Position, 1991 (Ottawa, March 1992).

tion to their foreign owner, also helped to stimulate foreign ownership as firms not wishing to have their technologies imitated quickly established themselves in Canada. The fact that our country shares a border with the United States also has stimulated foreign ownership, as firms often viewed Canada as an extension of their American domestic market.

All these explanations have some merit. However, all that can be said with certainty is that if firms decided to establish productive capacities in Canada, it must have been because it was the most profitable alternative.

ECONOMIC COSTS

Costs exist because resources are scarce and have alternative uses. To use a bundle of resources in producing a particular good means that other production opportunities have been forgone. *Costs are forgoing opportunities to produce alternative goods and services.* The economic cost, or opportunity cost, of a resource in producing a good is its value in its best alternative use.

This concept of costs can be seen in the production possibilities curve of Chapter 2. At point C in Table 2-1 the opportunity cost in real terms of producing 100,000 *more* pizzas is the 3000 industrial robots that must be forgone. If an assembly-line worker can produce automobiles or washing machines, then the cost to society in employing that worker in an automobile plant is the contribution the worker could have made in producing washing machines. The cost to you in reading this chapter is the alternative uses of your time —

studying for a biology exam or going to a movie — that you must forgo.

EXPLICIT AND IMPLICIT COSTS

Consider costs from the viewpoint of an individual firm. Keeping in mind the notion of opportunity costs, we can say *that economic costs are payments a firm must make to resource suppliers to attract these resources away from alternative production opportunities.* These payments may be either explicit or implicit.

The monetary payments — the out-of-pocket or cash expenditures a firm makes to those "outsiders" who supply labour services, materials, fuel, transportation services, and power — are called **explicit costs.**

But, in addition, a firm may use certain resources the firm itself owns. Our concept of opportunity costs tells us that regardless of whether a resource is owned or hired by an enterprise, there is a cost involved in using that resource in a specific employment. The costs of such self-owned, self-employed resources are **implicit costs** — the money payments the self-employed resources could have earned in their best alternative uses. The best alternative uses refer to those that have the highest money payments.

Example: Suppose you are earning $20,000 a year as a sales representative for a compact disc manufacturer. But now you decide to open a store to sell CDs at the retail level. In doing so you invest $20,000 in savings, which has been earning you $1000 per year in interest. You decide your new firm will occupy a small store you own and have been renting for $5000 per year. One clerk is hired to help you in the store.

After a year's operations, you total up your accounts and find the following:

Total sales revenue		$120,000
Cost of CDs	$40,000	
Clerk's salary	20,000	
Utilities	5,000	
Total (explicit) costs		$65,000
Accounting profit		$55,000

But this accounting profit does not accurately reflect the economic status of your venture because it ignores implicit costs. What is economically significant is the total amount of resources used (as opposed to dollars expended) in your enterprise. By providing your own financial capital, building, and labour, you are forging incomes of $1000 in interest, $5000 in rent, and $20,000 in wages. Also, suppose that your entrepreneurial talent is worth $5000 annually in other business endeavours of similar scope. Thus:

Accounting profit		$55,000
Forgone interest	$1,000	
Forgone rent	5,000	
Forgone wages	20,000	
Forgone entrepreneurial income	5,000	
Total implicit costs		$31,000
Economic profit		$24,000

NORMAL PROFITS AS A COST

The $5000 minimum payment required to keep your entrepreneurial talents engaged in this enterprise is called a **normal profit**. As is true of implicit rent or implicit wages, the normal return for performing entrepreneurial functions is an implicit cost. If this minimum, or normal, return is not realized, you will withdraw your efforts from this line of production and reallocate them to a more profitable line of production. Or you may cease being an entrepreneur, collect your $1000 interest per year, rent your store for $5000, and become a $20,000 wage or salary earner.

The economist includes as costs all payments — explicit and implicit, the latter including a normal profit — required to attract and retain resources in a specific line of production.

ECONOMIC, OR PURE, PROFITS

Economists and accountants use the term "profits" differently. *Accounting profits are the firm's total revenue less its explicit costs*. But to economists, **economic profits are total revenue less all costs (explicit and implicit, the latter including a normal profit to the entrepreneur)**. Therefore, when an economist says that a firm is just covering its costs, it means all explicit and implicit costs are being met and the entrepreneur is receiving a return just large enough to retain his or her talents in the present line of production.

If a firm's total revenue exceeds all its economic costs, any residual goes to the entrepreneur. This residual is called an **economic profit**:

$$\frac{\text{Economic}}{\text{profit}} = \frac{\text{total}}{\text{revenue}} - \frac{\text{opportunity cost}}{\text{of all inputs}}$$

In our example, this economic profit is $24,000 (= $120,000 − $96,000). An economic profit is not a cost, because by definition it is a return in excess of the normal profit required to retain the entrepreneur in this particular line of production. Even if the economic profit is zero, the entrepreneur is still covering all explicit and implicit costs, including a normal profit. In our example, so long as accounting profits are $31,000 or more (economic profits zero or more), you will be earning the $5000 normal profit and will continue to operate your CD store.

Figure 9-1 shows the relationship among various cost and profits concepts. From our example, pencil in the various cost data in the appropriate blocks. **(Key Question 5)**

SHORT RUN AND LONG RUN

The costs a firm incurs in producing any specific output will depend on the adjustments it can make in the amounts of the various resources it employs. The quantities employed of many resources — most labour, raw materials, fuel, and power — can be varied easily and quickly. Other resources require more time for adjustment. The capacity of a manufacturing plant — the size of the factory building and the amount of machinery and equipment in it — can be varied only over a considerable period of time. In some heavy industries, it may take several years to alter plant capacity.

SHORT RUN: FIXED PLANT Because of these differences in the time necessary to vary quantities of various resources used in production, we need to

FIGURE 9-1   Economic and accounting profits

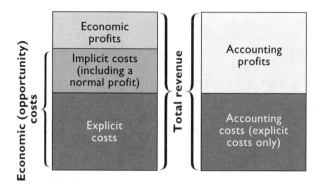

Economic profits are equal to total revenue less opportunity costs. Economic or opportunity costs are the sum of explicit and implicit costs, the latter including a normal profit to the entrepreneur. Accounting profits are equal to total revenue less accounting (explicit) costs.

distinguish between the short run and the long run. The **short run** is a period of time too brief for a firm to change its plant capacity. The firm's plant capacity is fixed in the short run, but output can be varied by applying larger or smaller amounts of labour, materials, and other resources to that plant. Existing plant capacity can be used more or less intensively in the short run.

LONG RUN: VARIABLE PLANT   The **long run** refers to a period extensive enough to allow firms to change the quantities of *all* resources employed, including plant capacity. The long run also leaves enough time for existing firms to dissolve and leave the industry and for new firms to be created and to enter the industry. *While the short run is a "fixed-plant" period, the long run is a "variable-plant" period.*

ILLUSTRATIONS   If a Northern Telecom plant hired 100 extra workers or added an entire shift of workers, these would be short-run adjustments. If the same Northern Telecom plant added a new wing to its building and installed more equipment, this would be a long-run adjustment.

Note that the short run and long run are *conceptual* rather than specific calendar time periods. In light manufacturing industries, changes in plant capacity may be negotiated almost overnight. A

small T-shirt firm can increase its plant capacity in a few days or less by ordering and installing new cutting tables and several extra sewing machines. But heavy industry is a different story. It may take Petro-Canada several years to construct a new oil refinery.

QUICK REVIEW 9-2

1. Explicit costs are money payments a firm makes to outside suppliers of resources; implicit costs are the opportunity costs associated with a firm's use of resources it owns.

2. Economic profits are total revenue less all explicit and implicit costs, including a normal profit.

3. In the short run a firm's plant capacity is fixed; in the long run a firm can vary its plant size.

SHORT-RUN PRODUCTION COSTS

In the short run, a firm can change its output by adding variable resources to a fixed plant. But how does output change as more and more variable resources are added to the firm's fixed resources?

LAW OF DIMINISHING RETURNS

The answer is provided in general terms by the **law of diminishing returns,** also called the "law of diminishing marginal product" and the "law of variable proportions." This law states that *as more units of a variable resource are added to a fixed resource, beyond some point the extra, or marginal, output from each additional unit of the variable resource will decline.* For example, if additional workers are hired to operate a constant amount of capital equipment, output will eventually rise by smaller and smaller amounts as more workers are employed.

RATIONALE   Consider a small manufacturer of wood furniture frames. The firm has a given amount of equipment in the form of lathes, planers, saws, sanders, and so forth. If this firm hired just one or two workers, total output and productivity (output per worker) would be very low. These workers would have a number of different jobs to perform, and the advantages of specialization would be lost. Time would also be lost in switching from one job operation to another, and the machines would stand idle much of the time. Production would be inefficient because there is too much capital relative to labour.

These difficulties would disappear as more workers were added. Equipment would be more fully utilized, and workers could now specialize on a single job. Time would no longer be lost as a result of job-switching. Thus as more workers are hired by the initially understaffed plant, the extra or marginal product of each will rise as a result of more efficient production.

But this cannot go on indefinitely. As still more workers are added, problems of overcrowding arise. Workers must wait in line to use the machinery, so now *workers* will be underutilized. Total output increases at a diminishing rate because, with the fixed plant size, each worker will have less capital equipment to work with as more and more labour is hired. The marginal product of additional workers declines because the plant is overstaffed. There will be more labour in proportion to the fixed amount of capital equipment. In the extreme case, the continuous addition of labour to the plant would use up all standing room, and production would be brought to a standstill.

It is to be emphasized that the law of diminishing returns assumes all units of variable inputs are of equal quality. In the case of labour, for example, each successive worker is presumed to have the same innate ability, motor co-ordination, education, training, and work experience. Marginal product ultimately diminishes, not because successive workers are qualitatively inferior, but because too many workers are being used relative to the amount of plant and equipment available.

NUMERICAL EXAMPLE   Table 9-4 presents a numerical illustration of the law of diminishing returns. Column 2 indicates the **total product** resulting from combining each level of labour input in column 1 with a fixed amount of capital equipment.

Marginal product in column 3 shows the *change* in total output associated with each additional input of labour. Note that with no labour inputs, total product is zero; a plant with no workers will not produce any output. The first two workers reflect increasing returns, their marginal products being 10 and 15 units respectively. But then, beginning with the third worker, marginal product diminishes continuously, and actually becomes zero with the eighth worker and negative with the ninth.

Average product or output per worker (also called "labour productivity") is shown in column 4. It is calculated by dividing total product (column 2) by the corresponding number of workers that produced it (column 1).

GRAPHIC PORTRAYAL   **Figures 9-2(a) and (b) (Key Graphs)** on page 175 show the law of dimin-

TABLE 9-4   The law of diminishing returns

(1) Inputs of the variable resource (labour)	(2) Total product	(3) Marginal product $\left(\dfrac{\Delta 2}{\Delta 1}\right)$		(4) Average product (2 ÷ 1)
0	0			—
1	10	10		10
2	25	15	Increasing marginal returns	12 $^1/_2$
3	37	12		12 $^1/_3$
4	47	10		11 $^3/_4$
5	55	8	Diminishing marginal returns	11
6	60	5		10
7	63	3		9
8	63	0	Negative marginal returns	7 $^7/_8$
9	62	-1		6 $^8/_9$

KEY GRAPH

FIGURE 9-2   The law of diminishing returns

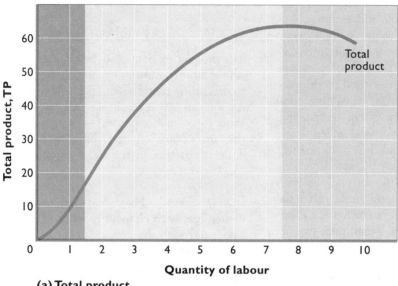

(a) Total product

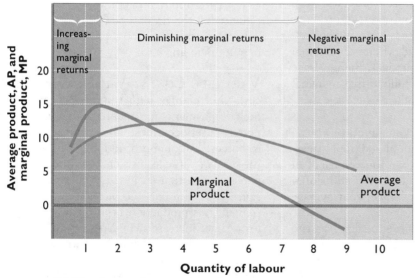

(b) Marginal and average product

As a variable resource (labour) is added to fixed amounts of other resources (land, capital), the resulting total product will eventually increase by diminishing amounts, reach a maximum, and then decline as in (a). Marginal product in (b) reflects the changes in total product associated with each input of labour. Average product is simply output per worker. Note that marginal product intersects average product at the maximum average product.

ishing returns graphically and will help to explain more fully the relationships between total, marginal, and average product. Note that total product goes through three phases; it rises initially at an increasing rate; then it increases, but at a decreasing rate; and finally it reaches a maximum and declines.

Geometrically, marginal product is the slope of the total product curve. Marginal product measures the changes in total product with each successive worker. Thus, the three phases of total product are also reflected in marginal product. Where total product is increasing at an increasing rate, marginal product is rising. As extra workers are added, larger and larger amounts are also added to total product. Where total product is increasing but at a decreasing rate, marginal product is positive but falling. Each additional worker adds less to total product than did preceding workers. When total product is at a maximum, marginal product is zero. When total product declines, marginal product becomes negative.

Average product also reflects the same general "increasing-maximum-diminishing" relationship between variable inputs of labour and output as does marginal product. But note the relationship between marginal product and average product: where marginal product exceeds average product, average product will rise. And wherever marginal product is less than average product, then average product must be declining. It follows that marginal product intersects average product where the average product is at a maximum.

For example, you raise your average course grade only when your score on an additional (marginal) examination is greater than the average of all your past scores. If your grade on an additional exam is below your current average, your average will be pulled down.

In our production example, so long as the amount an additional worker adds to total product exceeds the average product of all workers already employed, average product will rise. Conversely, when an extra worker adds an amount to total product that is less than the present average product, then that worker will lower average product.

The law of diminishing returns is reflected in the shapes of all three curves. But, as our earlier definition of the law of diminishing returns indicates, we are most concerned with marginal product. The stages of increasing, diminishing, and negative marginal product (returns) are shown in Figure 9-2.

Glancing back at columns 1 and 3 of Table 9-4, we observe increasing returns for the first two workers, decreasing returns for workers 3 to 7, zero returns for the eighth worker, and negative returns for the ninth. **(Key Question 7)**

FIXED, VARIABLE, AND TOTAL COSTS

The production data described by the law of diminishing returns must be coupled with resource prices to determine the total and per unit costs of producing various levels of output. We know that in the short run, some resources — those associated with the firm's plant — are fixed. Others are variable. This means that in the short run, costs are either fixed or variable.

FIXED COSTS   **Fixed costs** *are those costs that do not vary with changes in output.* Fixed costs are associated with the very existence of a firm's plant and must be paid even if the firm's output is zero. Such costs as interest on a firm's debt, rental payments, insurance premiums, and the salaries of top management and key personnel are generally fixed costs. In column 2 of Table 9-5 (page 177) we assume that the firm's total fixed costs are $100. By definition, this fixed cost prevails at all levels of output, including zero.

VARIABLE COSTS   **Variable costs** *are those costs that change with the level of output.* They include payments for materials, fuel, power, transportation services, most labour, and similar variable resources. In column 3 of Table 9-5, we find that the total of variable costs changes directly with output. But note that *the increases in variable costs associated with each one-unit increase in output are not constant.* As production begins, variable costs will, for a time, increase by a *decreasing* amount; this is true up to the fourth unit of output. Beyond the fourth unit, however, variable costs rise by *increasing* amounts for each successive unit of output.

Variable costs act in this way because of the law of diminishing returns. At first, because of *increasing* marginal product, smaller and smaller increases in the amounts of variable resources will be needed to get each successive unit of output produced. Because all units of the variable resources have the same price, total variable costs will increase by decreasing amounts. But when marginal product begins to decline as diminishing returns set in, larger and larger additional amounts of variable resources are needed to produce each successive unit of output. Total variable costs will therefore increase by increasing amounts.

TOTAL COST   **Total cost** *is the sum of fixed and variable costs at each level of output.* It is shown in column 4 of Table 9-5. At zero units of output, total cost is equal to the firm's fixed costs. Then for each unit of production — 1 to 10 — total cost increases by the same amounts as variable cost.

Figure 9-3 shows graphically the fixed-cost, variable-cost, and total-cost data of Table 9-5.

The distinction between fixed and variable costs is significant to the business manager. Variable costs can be controlled or altered in the short run by changing production levels. Fixed costs are beyond the business executive's control; they are incurred in the short run and must be paid regardless of output level.

PER UNIT, OR AVERAGE, COSTS

Producers are certainly interested in their total costs, but they are equally concerned with *per unit*, or *average*, costs. Average-cost data are better for making comparisons with product price, which is always stated on a per-unit basis. Average fixed cost, average variable cost, and average total cost are shown in columns 5 to 7 of Table 9-5. Let's see how these unit-cost figures are calculated and how they vary as output changes.

1. AFC   Average fixed cost (AFC) for any output is found by dividing total fixed cost (TFC) by that output (Q):

$$\text{AFC} = \frac{\text{TFC}}{Q}$$

While total fixed costs are, by definition, independent of output, AFC will decline as output increases. As output increases, a given total fixed cost of $100 is being spread over a larger and larger output. When output is just 1 unit, total fixed costs and AFC are equal at $100. But at 2 units of output, total fixed costs of $100 become $50 worth of fixed costs per unit; then $33.33, as $100 is spread over 3 units; and $25, when spread over 4 units. This is referred to as "spreading the overhead." We find, in Figure 9-4, that AFC continually declines as total output rises.

2. AVC   Average variable cost (AVC) for any output is calculated by dividing total variable cost (TVC) by that output (Q):

TABLE 9-5   **Total- and average-cost schedules for an individual firm in the short run**

TOTAL-COST DATA, PER WEEK				AVERAGE-COST DATA, PER WEEK			
(1) Total product (Q)	(2) Total fixed cost (TFC)	(3) Total variable cost (TVC)	(4) Total cost (TC) TC=TFC +TVC	(5) Average fixed cost (AFC) $AFC = \frac{TFC}{Q}$	(6) Average variable cost (AVC) $AVC = \frac{TVC}{Q}$	(7) Average total cost (ATC) $ATC = \frac{TC}{Q}$	(8) Marginal cost (MC) $MC = \frac{\text{change in TC}}{\text{change in Q}}$
0	$100	$ 0	$ 100				
1	100	90	190	$100.00	$90.00	$190.00	$ 90
2	100	170	270	50.00	85.00	135.00	80
3	100	240	340	33.33	80.00	113.33	70
4	100	300	400	25.00	75.00	100.00	60
5	100	370	470	20.00	74.00	94.00	70
6	100	450	550	16.67	75.00	91.67	80
7	100	540	640	14.29	77.14	91.43	90
8	100	650	750	12.50	81.25	93.75	110
9	100	780	880	11.11	86.67	97.78	130
10	100	930	1030	10.00	93.00	103.00	150

FIGURE 9-3   **Total cost is the sum of fixed and variable costs**

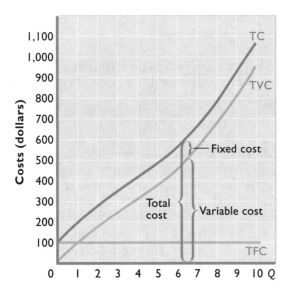

Total variable costs (TVC) change with output. Fixed costs are independent of the level of output. The total cost (TC) of any output is the vertical sum of the fixed and variable costs of that output.

$$AVC = \frac{TVC}{Q}$$

AVC declines initially, reaches a minimum, and then increases again. Graphically, this is reflected by a U-shaped AVC curve, as shown in Figure 9-4.

Because total variable cost reflects the law of diminishing returns, so must the AVC figures, which are derived from total variable cost. Due to increasing returns, it takes fewer and fewer additional variable resources to produce each of the first 4 units of output. As a result, variable cost per unit will decline. AVC hits a minimum with the fifth unit of output, and, beyond this point, AVC rises as diminishing returns require more and more variable resources to produce each additional unit of output.

You can verify the U shape of the AVC curve by returning to Table 9-4. Assume the price of labour is $10 per unit. By dividing average product (output per worker) into $10 (price per worker), labour cost per unit of output can be determined. Because we have assumed labour to be the only variable input, labour cost per unit of output is variable cost per unit of output, or AVC. When average product is initially low,

AVC will be high. As workers are added, average product rises and AVC falls. When average product is at its maximum, AVC will be at its minimum. As still more workers are added and average product declines, AVC will rise. The "hump" of the average product curve is reflected in the U-shaped AVC curve. A glance ahead at Figure 9-7 will confirm this graphically.

3. ATC   **Average total cost** (ATC) for any output is found by dividing total cost (TC) by that output (Q) or by adding AFC and AVC at that level of output.

$$ATC = \frac{TC}{Q} = AFC + AVC$$

These data are shown in column 7 of Table 9-5.

MARGINAL COST

One final and very crucial cost concept remains — marginal cost. **Marginal cost (MC)** *is the additional cost of producing one more unit of output.* MC can be determined for each additional unit of output by noting the *change* in total cost that each unit brings about and is calculated as follows:

$$MC = \frac{\text{change in TC}}{\text{change in } Q}$$

FIGURE 9-4   **The average-cost curves**

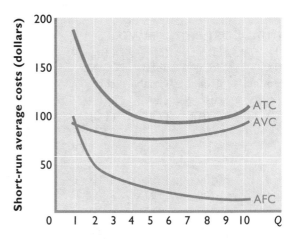

AFC necessarily falls as a given amount of fixed costs is apportioned over a larger and larger ouput. AVC initially falls because of increasing returns but then rises because of diminishing returns. Average total cost (ATC) is the vertical sum of average variable cost (AVC) and average fixed cost (AFC).

Our data are structured so that the "change in Q" is always "1," so we have defined MC as the cost of *one* more unit of output.

CALCULATIONS   In column 4 of Table 9-5, production of the first unit of output increases total cost from $100 to $190. Therefore, the additional, or marginal, cost of that first unit is $90 (column 8). The marginal cost of the second unit is $80 ($270 – $190); the MC of the third is $70 ($340 – $270); and so forth. MC for each of the 10 units of output is shown in column 8.

MC can also be calculated from the total-variable-cost column because the only difference between total cost and total variable cost is the constant amount of fixed costs ($100). Thus, the *change* in total cost and the *change* in total variable cost associated with each additional unit of output are always the same.

MARGINAL DECISIONS   Marginal cost designates those costs that the firm can directly and immediately control. Specifically, MC indicates those costs incurred in the production of the last unit of output and, simultaneously, the cost that can be "saved" by reducing total output by the last unit. A firm's decisions as to what output level to produce are marginal decisions, that is, decisions to produce a few more or a few less units.

GRAPHIC PORTRAYAL   Marginal cost is shown graphically in **Figure 9-5 (Key Graph)**. Marginal cost declines sharply, reaches a minimum, and then rises rather abruptly. This mirrors the fact that variable cost, and therefore total cost, increases first by decreasing amounts and then by increasing amounts (see Figure 9-3 and columns 3 and 4 of Table 9-5).

MC AND MARGINAL PRODUCT   The shape of the marginal-cost curve reflects the law of diminishing returns. The relationship between marginal product and marginal cost can be seen in Table 9-4. If each successive unit of a variable resource (labour) is hired at a constant price, the marginal cost of each extra unit of output will *fall* so long as the marginal product of each additional worker is *rising*. This is so because marginal cost is the (constant) price or cost of an extra worker divided by his or her marginal product. In Table 9-4, suppose each worker can be hired for $10. Because the first worker's marginal product is 10 and the hire of this worker increases

FIGURE 9-5   The relationship of marginal cost to average total cost and average variable cost

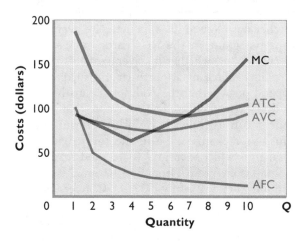

Marginal cost (MC) cuts both ATC and AVC at their minimum points. This is so because whenever the extra or marginal amount added to total cost (or variable cost) is less than the average of that cost, the average will necessarily fall. Conversely, whenever the marginal amount added to total (or variable) cost is greater than the average of that cost, the average must rise.

the firm's costs by $10, the marginal cost of each of these 10 extra units of output will be $1 (= $10 ÷ 10). The second worker also increases costs by $10, but the marginal product is 15, so that the marginal cost of each of these 15 extra units of output is $0.67 (= $10 ÷ 15). In general, so long as marginal product is rising, marginal cost will be falling.

But as diminishing returns set in — in this case, with the third worker — marginal cost will begin to rise. Thus for the third worker, marginal cost is $0.83 (= $10 ÷ 12); $1.00 for the fourth worker; $1.25 for the fifth; and so on. ***Assuming a constant price (cost) of the variable resource, increasing returns will be reflected in a declining marginal cost and diminishing returns in a rising marginal cost.*** The MC curve is a mirror reflection of the marginal product curve.

As Figure 9-6 shows, when marginal product is rising, marginal cost is necessarily falling. When marginal product is at its maximum, marginal cost is at its minimum. And when marginal product is falling, marginal cost is rising.

RELATION OF MC TO AVC AND ATC   The marginal cost curve intersects both the AVC and ATC curves at their minimum points. As noted earlier, this marginal-average relationship is a mathematical necessity, which a simple illustration will reveal. Suppose a professional baseball pitcher has allowed his opponents an average of 3 runs per game in the first three games he has pitched. Now, whether his average falls or rises as a result of pitching a fourth (marginal) game will depend on whether the additional runs he allows in that extra game are fewer or more than his current 3-run average. If he allows fewer than 3 runs— for example, 1—in the fourth game, his total runs will rise from 9 to 10, and his average will fall from 3 to $2\frac{1}{2}$ from 9 to 10, and his average will fall from 3 to $2\frac{1}{2}$ (= 10 ÷ 4). Conversely, if he allows more than 3 runs— say, 7— in the fourth game, his total will increase from 9 to 16 and his average will rise from 3 to 4 (=16 ÷ 4)

So it is with costs. When the amount added to total cost (marginal cost) is less than the average of total cost, ATC will fall. Conversely, when marginal cost exceeds ATC, ATC will rise. This means, in Figure 9-5, that so long as MC lies below ATC, the ATC will fall, and where MC is above ATC, ATC will rise. Therefore at the point of intersection where MC equals ATC, ATC has just ceased to fall but has not yet begun to rise. This, by definition, is the minimum point on the ATC curve. *The marginal cost curve intersects the average total cost curve at the ATC curve's minimum point.*

Because MC can be defined as the addition either to total cost or to total variable cost resulting from one more unit of output, this same rationale explains why the MC curve also crosses the AVC curve at its minimum point. **(Key Question 10)**

SHIFTING THE COST CURVES

Changes in either resource prices or technology will shift the cost curves. If fixed costs had been higher — say, $200 rather than the $100 we assumed in Table 9-5 — then the AFC curve in Figure 9-5 would shift upward. The ATC curve would also be at a higher position because AFC is a component of ATC. But the positions of the AVC and MC curves would be unaltered because their locations are based on the prices of variable rather than fixed resources. Thus, if the price (wage) of labour or some other variable input rose, the AVC, ATC, and

FIGURE 9-6   The relationship between productivity curves and cost curves

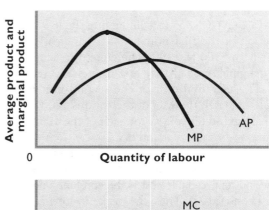

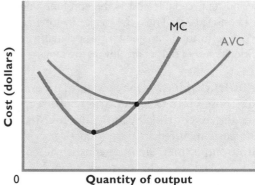

The marginal cost (MC) and average variable cost (AVC) curves are mirror images of the marginal product (MP) and average product (AP) curves respectively. Assuming labour is the only variable input and that its price (the wage rate) is constant, MC is found by dividing the wage rate by MP. Hence when MP is rising, MC is falling; when MP reaches its maximum, MC is at its minimum; and when MP is diminishing, MC is rising. A similar relationship holds between AP and AVC.

MC curves would all shift upward but the position of AFC would remain unchanged. Reductions in the prices of fixed or variable resources will shift the cost curves exactly opposite to those just described.

A more efficient technology increases the productivity of all inputs and the cost figures in Table 9-4 would all be lower. To illustrate, if labour is the only variable input and wages are $10 per hour and average product is 10 units, then AVC would be $1. But if a technological improvement increases the average product of labour to 20 units, then AVC will decline to $0.50. More generally, an upshift in the productivity curves shown in the top portion of

Figure 9-6 will mean a downshift in the cost curves portrayed in the bottom portion of that diagram. (See Global Perspective 9-1.)

GLOBAL PERSPECTIVE 9-1

Unit labour costs in manufacturing, selected nations

Labour costs — wages to workers — are a large percentage of ATC for most firms. Average labour costs in manufacturing have risen in Canada, shifting many ATC curves upward. But labour costs have risen even faster in many other countries.

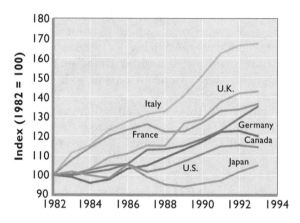

Source: Federal Reserve Bank of Cleveland, *Economic Trends,* November 1994, p. 19.

PRODUCTION COSTS IN THE LONG RUN

In the long run firms can make all desired resource adjustments. The firm can alter its plant capacity; it can build a larger plant or revert to a smaller plant than assumed in Table 9-5. The long run is also sufficient time for new firms to enter or existing firms to leave an industry. The impact of the entry and exodus of firms from an industry will be discussed in the next chapter; here we are concerned only with changes

FIGURE 9-7   **The long-run average-total-cost curve: five possible plant sizes**

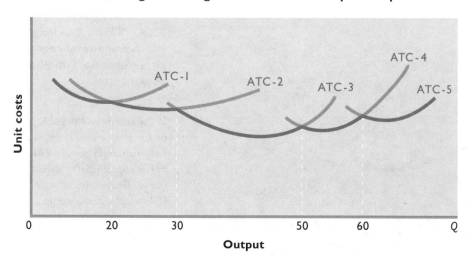

The long-run average-total-cost curve is made up of segments of the short-run cost curves (ATC-1, ATC-2, etc.) of the various-sized plants from which the firm might choose. Each point on the bumpy planning curve shows the least unit cost attainable for any output when the firm has had time to make all desired changes in its plant size.

in plant capacity made by a single firm. Our analysis will be in terms of ATC, making no distinction between fixed and variable costs because all resources, and therefore all costs, are variable in the long run.

FIRM SIZE AND COSTS

Suppose a single-plant manufacturer starts out on a small scale and, as the result of successful operations, expands to successively larger plant sizes. For a time, larger plants will lower average total costs. However, eventually the building of a still larger plant may cause ATC to rise.

Figure 9-7 illustrates this situation for five possible plant sizes. ATC-1 is the average-total-cost curve for the smallest of the five plants, and ATC-5 for the largest. Constructing larger plants will mean lower minimum per unit costs to plant size 3. But beyond this point, a larger plant will mean a higher level of minimum average total costs.

THE LONG-RUN COST CURVE

The dotted lines indicate those outputs at which the firm should change plant size in order to realize the lowest attainable per-unit costs of production. For all outputs up to 20 units, the lowest per unit costs are attainable with plant size 1. However, if the firm expands to some level greater than 20 but less than 30 units, it can achieve lower per unit costs by constructing a larger plant — plant size 2. Although *total* cost will be higher at the greater levels of pro-

duction, the cost *per unit* of output will be less. For any output between 30 and 50 units, plant size 3 will yield the lowest per-unit cost. For the 50- to 60-unit range of output, plant size 4 must be built to achieve the lowest unit costs. Lowest per unit costs for any output over 60 units demand the construction of the still larger plant size 5.

Tracing these adjustments, we can conclude that the long-run ATC curve for the enterprise will comprise segments of the short-run ATC curves for the various plant sizes that can be constructed. *The long-run ATC curve shows the least per-unit cost at which any output can be produced after the firm has had time to make all appropriate adjustments in its plant size.* In Figure 9-7, the heavy curve is the firm's long-run ATC curve or, as it is often called, the firm's planning curve.

In most lines of production, the choice of plant sizes is much wider than assumed in our illustration. In many industries the number of possible plant sizes is virtually unlimited and, in time, quite small changes in the volume of output will lead to changes in plant size.

Graphically, this implies an unlimited number of short-run ATC curves, as suggested by **Figure 9-8 (Key Graph)**. The minimum ATC of producing each possible level of output is shown by the long-run ATC curve. Rather than being made up of *segments* of short-run ATC curves, as in Figure 9-7, the long-run ATC curve is made up of all the *points of tangency* of the short-run ATC curves from which the long-run ATC curve is derived.

KEY GRAPH

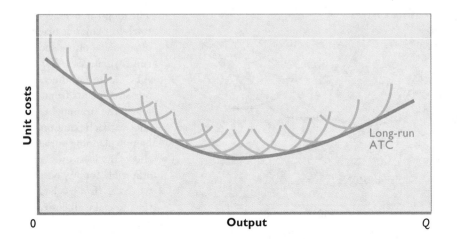

FIGURE 9-8 **The long-run average-total-cost curve: unlimited number of plant sizes**

If the number of possible plant sizes is very large, the long-run average-total-cost curve approximates a smooth curve. Economies of scale, followed by diseconomies of scale, cause the curve to be U-shaped.

ECONOMIES AND DISECONOMIES OF SCALE

We have accepted the contention that for a time, a larger and larger plant size will translate into lower unit costs but that beyond some point, successively larger plants will mean higher average total costs. Exactly why is the long-run ATC curve U-shaped? Note, first, that *the law of diminishing returns does not apply in the long run.* That's because diminishing returns presumes one resource is fixed in supply while the long run assumes resource prices

are constant. Also, our discussion assumes resource prices are constant. We can explain the U-shaped long-run average-cost curve in terms of *economies* and *diseconomies* of large-scale production.

ECONOMIES OF SCALE **Economies of scale** or, more commonly, economies of mass production, explain the downsloping part of the long-run ATC curve, as indicated in Figure 9-9(a). As plant size increases, a number of factors will lead to lower average costs of production.

FIGURE 9-9 Various possible long-run average-total-cost curves

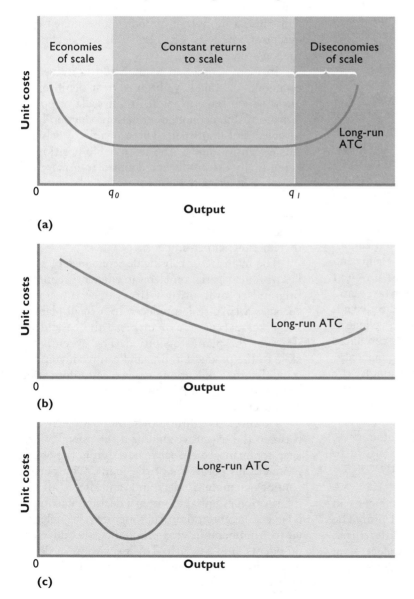

(a) Where economies of scale are rather rapidly exhausted and diseconomies not encountered until a considerably larger scale of output has been achieved, long-run average total costs will be constant over a wide range of output. (b) When economies of scale are extensive and diseconomies remote, the ATC will fall over a wide range of production. (c) If economies of scale are exhausted quickly, followed immediately by diseconomies, minimum unit costs will be encountered at a relatively low output.

1. LABOUR SPECIALIZATION Increased labour specialization is feasible as a plant increases in size. Hiring more workers means that jobs can be divided and subdivided. Each worker may now have just one task to perform instead of five or six. Workers can be used full-time on those particular operations at which they have special skills, thereby becoming highly efficient. Greater specialization also eliminates the loss of time that accompanies the shifting of workers from one job to another. Thus, specialization reduces labour costs.

2. MANAGERIAL SPECIALIZATION Large-scale production means better utilization of, and greater specialization in, management. A supervisor who can handle twenty workers will be underutilized in a small plant with only ten people. The production staff can be doubled with no increase in administrative costs. Nor will small firms be able to use management specialists to best advantage. In a small plant, a sales specialist may have to divide his or her time between several executive functions — for example, marketing, personnel, and finance. A larger scale of operations will mean that the marketing expert can supervise sales and product distribution full time, while appropriate specialists perform other managerial functions. Greater efficiency and lower unit costs are the net result.

3. EFFICIENT CAPITAL Small firms often cannot employ the most technologically efficient equipment. In many lines of production, the most efficient machinery is available only in very large and extremely expensive units. Furthermore, effective utilization of this equipment demands a high volume of production, so only large-scale producers can afford and efficiently operate the best available equipment.

In the automobile industry, for example, the most efficient fabrication method employs robotics and elaborate assembly-line equipment. The efficient use of this equipment demands an annual output of an estimated 200,000 to 400,000 automobiles. Only very large-scale producers can afford to purchase and use this equipment efficiently.

4. BY-PRODUCTS The large-scale producer can better use by-products than can a small firm. The large meat-packing plant makes glue, fertilizer, pharmaceuticals, and a host of other products from animal remnants that would be discarded by smaller producers.

5. OTHER FACTORS Many products require design, development, and certain other "start-up" costs that must be incurred irrespective of sales. These costs decline per unit as output is increased. Similarly, advertising costs decline per auto, per computer, and per case of beer as more units are produced.

All these technological considerations — greater specialization in labour and management, the ability to use the most efficient equipment, and effective use of by-products — will contribute to lower unit costs for the firm able to expand its scale of operation.

Another way of thinking about economies of scale is that an increase in *all* resources of, say, 10% will cause a more-than-proportionate increase in output of, say, 20%. The result will be a decline in the long-run ATC.

In many Canadian manufacturing industries economies of scale have been of great significance. Firms which have expanded their scale of operations to realize economies of mass production have survived and flourished. Those unable to achieve this expansion are in the unenviable position of being high-cost producers, doomed to a marginal existence or ultimate insolvency.

DISECONOMIES OF SCALE But in time, the expansion of a firm *may* lead to diseconomies and therefore higher per-unit costs.

The main factor causing **diseconomies of scale** lies with managerial problems in efficiently controlling and co-ordinating a firm's operations as it becomes a large-scale producer. In a small plant, a single key executive may make all the basic decisions for the plant's operation. The executive is close to the production line and can readily understand the firm's operations, easily digest information gained from subordinates, and make clear and efficient decisions.

However, as a firm grows, the many echelons between the executive suite and the assembly line keep top management far removed from the actual production operations of the plant. One person cannot assemble, understand, and digest all the information essential to rational decision making in a large-scale enterprise. Authority must be delegated to innumerable vice-presidents, second vice-presidents, and so forth. This expansion in depth and width of the management hierarchy leads to problems of communication, co-ordination, and bureaucratic red tape, and the possibility that the decisions of various subordinates will fail to mesh. Similarly, decisions may be sluggish in that they fail to quickly incorporate important changes in consumer tastes or technology. The result is impaired efficiency and rising average total costs.

Another way of thinking about diseconomies of scale is that an increase in *all* resources of, say, 10% will cause a less-than-proportionate increase in output of, say, 5%. As a consequence, ATC will increase. Diseconomies of scale are illustrated by the rising portion of the long-run ATC in Figure 9-9(a).

CONSTANT RETURNS TO SCALE   In some instances there may exist a rather wide range of output between the output level at which economies of scale are exhausted and the point at which diseconomies of scale are encountered. That is, there will exist a range of **constant returns to scale** over which long-run average cost is constant. The q_0q_1 output range of Figure 9-9(a) is relevant. Here a given percentage increase in *all* inputs of, say, 10% will cause a proportionate 10% increase in output. Thus the long-run ATC does not change.

APPLICATIONS AND ILLUSTRATIONS   There are many examples and applications of economies and diseconomies of scale.

TEXTBOOKS   Next semester when you buy texts at your bookstore, compare the prices of introductory or basic texts with prices of more specialized, advanced books. You may be surprised that the price of a two-semester principles of economics text is not much more — and sometimes less — than that of a one-semester advanced text. This is true even though the principles text may be 200 pages longer and has a multi-colour format, while the advanced book is in black and white. Economies of scale are at work here. Both introductory and advanced texts require design, editing, and typesetting costs that are more or less the same per page whether 1000 copies (of the advanced text) or 50,000 copies (of the basic text) are printed. With basic books these costs are spread over many more units of output, meaning lower unit costs and a comparatively low price per book.

GENERAL MOTORS   In recent years GM (the world's largest corporation) has found itself with both a declining market share and a substantial cost disadvantage. GM's labour costs per car are nearly $800 more than Ford's and $500 more than Chrysler's. To offset scale diseconomies, GM has given each of its five automotive divisions (Chevrolet, Buick, Pontiac, Oldsmobile, and Cadillac) greater autonomy with respect to styling, engineering, and marketing decisions. The goal is to reduce the layers of managerial approval required in decision making so each division can respond more rapidly and with greater precision to changes in technology and consumer tastes. For its Saturn automobile GM created a separate company. In late 1994 GM announced it will reorganize into a Small Car Group and a Midsize and Luxury Group in an attempt to cut costs and bring new car models to the market faster.

MES AND INDUSTRY STRUCTURE

Economies and diseconomies of scale are an important determinant of an industry's structure. To understand this, it is helpful to introduce the concept of **minimum efficient scale (MES)**, which is the smallest level of output at which a firm can minimize long-run average costs. In Figure 9-9(a) this occurs at $0q_0$ units of output. Because of the extended range of constant returns to scale, firms producing substantially larger outputs could also realize the minimum attainable average costs. Specifically, firms would be equally efficient within the q_0q_1 range. An industry with such costs conditions is populated by firms of quite different sizes. The apparel, food processing, furniture, wood products, and small-appliance industries provide approximate examples. With an extended range of constant returns to scale, relatively large and relatively small firms could coexist in an industry and be equally viable.

Compare this with Figure 9-9(b), where economies of scale are extensive and diseconomies are remote. Here the long-run average-cost curve will decline over an extended range of output, as is the case in the automobile, aluminum, steel, and other heavy industries. Given consumer demand, efficient production will be achieved only with a small number of industrial giants. Small firms cannot realize the minimum efficient scale and will not be viable. In the extreme, economies of scale might extend beyond the market's size, resulting in what is termed a natural monopoly. A **natural monopoly** is a market situation where unit costs are minimized by having a single firm produce the particular good or service. A natural monopoly has a continuously falling ATC curve; as scale increases, the per-unit cost falls.

Where economies of scale are few and diseconomies quickly encountered, minimum efficient size occurs at a small level of output as shown in Figure 9-9(c). In such industries, a particular level of consumer demand will support a large number of relatively small producers. Many retail trades, some types of farming, and certain types of light manufacturing, such as the baking, clothing, and shoe industries, fall into this category. Fairly small firms are as efficient as, or more efficient than, large-scale producers in such industries.

The point is that the shape of the long-run average-cost curve, as determined by economies and diseconomies of scale, can be significant in determining the structure and competitiveness of an industry. Whether an industry is "competitive" — populated by a relatively large number of small firms — or "concentrated" — dominated by a few large producers — is sometimes a reflection of an industry's technology and the resulting shape of its long-run average-total-cost curve.

But we must be cautious because industry structure does not depend on cost conditions alone. Government policies, the geographic size of a market, managerial ability, and a variety of other factors must be considered in explaining the structure of a given industry. **(Key Question 13)**

QUICK REVIEW 9-4

1. Most firms have U-shaped long-run average-cost curves, reflecting economies and then diseconomies of scale.

2. Economies of scale are the consequence of greater specialization of labour and management, more efficient capital equipment, and the use of by-products.

3. Diseconomies of scale are caused by problems of coordination and communication that arise in large firms.

4. Minimum efficient scale is the lowest level of output at which a firm's long-run average total costs are at a minimum.

CHAPTER SUMMARY

1. The firm is the most efficient form of organizing production and distribution. The main goal of a firm is to maximize profit.

2. Sole proprietorships, partnerships, and corporations are the major legal forms that business enterprises may assume. Though proprietorships dominate numerically, the bulk of total output is produced by corporations. Corporations have grown to their position of dominance in the business sector primarily because they are **a** characterized by limited liability and **b** can acquire money capital for expansion more easily than other firms.

3. In terms of both employment share and contribution to domestic production, the service sector dominates in the Canadian economy.

4. Compared to the U.S. economy, many of our industries are highly concentrated; a relatively few firms represent a high percentage of output and sales. A high proportion of our industries are foreign owned.

5. Economic costs include all payments that must be received by resource owners to assure continued supply of these resources in a particular line of production. This definition includes explicit costs, which flow to resource suppliers separate from a given enterprise, and also implicit costs, the remuneration of self-owned and self-employed resources. One of the implicit cost payments is a normal profit to the entrepreneur.

6. In the short run, a firm's plant capacity is fixed. The firm can use its plant more or less intensively by adding or subtracting units of variable resources, but the firm does not have sufficient time to alter plant size.

7. The law of diminishing returns describes what happens to output as a fixed plant is used more intensively. As successive units of a variable resource such as labour are added to a fixed plant, beyond some point the resulting marginal product associated with each additional worker declines.

8. Because some resources are variable and others fixed, costs can be classified as variable or fixed in the short run. Fixed costs are independent of the level of output. Variable costs vary with output. The total cost of any output is the sum of fixed and variable costs at that output.

9. Average fixed, average variable, and average total costs are fixed, variable, and total costs per unit of output. Average fixed costs decline continuously as output increases, because a fixed sum is being spread over a larger and larger number of units of production. Average variable costs are U-shaped, reflecting the law of diminishing returns. Average total cost is the sum of average fixed and average variable cost; it, too, is U-shaped.

10. Marginal cost is the extra, or additional, cost of producing one more unit of output. Graphically, the marginal cost curve intersects the ATC and AVC curves at their minimum points.

11. Lower resource prices shift cost curves downward, as does technological progress. Higher input prices shift cost curves upward.

12. The long run is a period of time sufficiently long for a firm to vary the amounts of all resources used, including plant size. In the long run all costs are variable. The long-run ATC, or planning, curve is composed of segments of the short-run ATC curves, representing the various plant sizes a firm can construct in the long run.

13. The long-run ATC curve is generally U-shaped. Economies of scale are first encountered as a small firm expands. Greater specialization in the use of labour and management, ability to use the most efficient equipment, and more complete utilization of by-products — all contribute to economies of scale. Diseconomies of scale stem from the managerial complexities that accompany large-scale production. The relative importance of economies and diseconomies of scale in an industry is often an important determinant of the structure of that industry.

TERMS AND CONCEPTS

average fixed cost (p. 177)
average total cost (p. 178)
average variable cost (p. 177)
conglomerates (p. 165)
constant returns to scale (p. 185)
corporation (p. 166)
double taxation (p. 167)
economic (opportunity) cost (p. 171)
economies and diseconomies of scale (pp. 183, 184)
explicit and implicit costs (p. 171)
firm (p. 164)
fixed costs (p. 176)
foreign ownership (p. 170)
horizontal and vertical combinations (p.165)
industry (p. 165)
law of diminishing returns (p. 173)

limited liability (p. 166)
marginal cost (p. 178)
minimum efficient scale (p. 185)
natural monopoly (p. 185)
normal and economic profits (p. 172)
partnership (p. 165)
plant (p.164)
primary, secondary, and tertiary sectors (p. 167)
separation of ownership and control (p. 167)
short run and long run (p. 173)
sole proprietorship (p.165)
total cost (p. 177)
total, marginal, and average product (p. 174)
variable costs (p. 176)
unlimited liability (p. 165)

QUESTIONS AND STUDY SUGGESTIONS

1. Distinguish between a plant, a firm, and an industry. Why is an "industry" often difficult to define in practice?

2. *Key Question* *What are the major legal forms of business organization? Briefly state the advantages and disadvantages of each. How do you account for the dominant role of corporations in our economy?*

3. "The legal form of an enterprise is dictated primarily by the financial requirements of its particular line of production." Do you agree?

4. Distinguish between explicit and implicit costs, giving examples of each. What are the explicit and implicit costs of attending college or university? Why does the economist classify normal profits as a cost? Are economic profits a cost of production?

5. *Key Question* *Bozzelli runs a small pottery firm. He hires one helper at $12,000 a year, pays annual rent of $5000 for his shop, and materials cost $20, 000 per year. Bozzelli has $40,000 of his own funds invested in equipment (pottery wheels, kilns, and so forth) that could earn him $4000 a year if alternatively invested. Bozzelli has been offered $15,000 a year to work as a potter for a competitor. He estimates his entrepreneurial talents are worth $3000 a year. Total annual revenue from pottery sales is $72,000. Calculate accounting profits and economic profits for Bozzelli's pottery.*

6. Which of the following are short-run and which are long-run adjustments? a. Petro-Canada builds a new oil refinery; b. Dofasco hires 200 more workers; c. a farmer increases the amount of fertilizer used on the corn crop; d. an Alcan plant adds a third shift of workers.

7. *Key Question* *Use the following data to calculate marginal product and average product.*

Inputs of labour %	Total product %	Marginal product	Average product
1	15		
2	34		
3	51		
4	65		
5	74		
6	80		
7	83		
8	82		

Plot total, marginal, and average product and explain in detail the relationship between each pair of curves. Explain why marginal product first rises, then declines, and ultimately becomes negative. What bearing does the law of diminishing returns have on short-run costs? Be specific. "When marginal product is rising, marginal cost is falling. And when marginal product is diminishing, marginal cost is rising." Illustrate and explain graphically and through a numerical example.

8. Why can the distinction between fixed and variable costs be made in the short run? Classify the following as fixed or variable costs: advertising expenditures, fuel, interest on company-issued bonds, shipping charges, payments for raw materials, real estate taxes, executive salaries, insurance premiums, wage payments, depreciation and obsolescence charges, sales taxes, and rental payments on leased office machinery. "There are no fixed costs in the long run; all costs are variable." Explain.

9. List the fixed and variable costs associated with owning and operating an automobile. Suppose you are considering whether to drive your car or fly 1000 km to a ski resort for spring break. Which costs — fixed, variable, or both — would you take into account in making your decision? Would any implicit costs be relevant? Explain.

10. *Key Question* *A firm has fixed costs of $60 and variable costs as indicated in the table below. Complete the table. When finished, check your calculations by referring to question 6 at the end of Chapter 10.*

Total product	Total fixed cost	Total variable cost	Total cost	Average fixed cost	Average variable cost	Average total cost	Marginal cost
0	$____	$ 0					$____
1	____	45	$____	$____	$____	$____	____
2	____	85	____	____	____	____	____
3	____	120	____	____	____	____	____
4	____	150	____	____	____	____	____
5	____	185	____	____	____	____	____
6	____	225	____	____	____	____	____
7	____	270	____	____	____	____	____
8	____	325	____	____	____	____	____
9	____	390	____	____	____	____	____
10	____	465	____	____	____	____	____

a. Graph fixed cost, variable cost, and total cost. Explain how the law of diminishing returns influences the shapes of the variable-cost and total-cost curves.

b. Graph AFC, AVC, ATC, and MC. Explain the derivation and shape of each of these four curves and their relationships to one another. Specifically, explain in nontechnical terms why the MC curve intersects both the AVC and ATC curves at their minimum points.

c. Explain how the locations of each curve graphed in question 10b would be altered if (1) total fixed cost had been $100 rather than $60 and (2) total variable cost had been $10 less at each level of output.

11. Indicate how each of the following would shift the (a) marginal cost curve, (b) average variable cost curve, (c) average fixed cost curve, and (d) average total cost curve of a manufacturing firm. In each case specify the direction of the shift.

a. A reduction in business property taxes.
b. An increase in the nominal wages of production workers.
c. A decrease in the price of electricity.
d. An increase in insurance rates on plant and equipment.
e. An increase in transportation costs.

12. Suppose a firm has only three possible firm size options as shown in the accompanying figure. What plant size will the firm choose in producing a. 50, b. 130, c. 160, and d. 250 units of out-

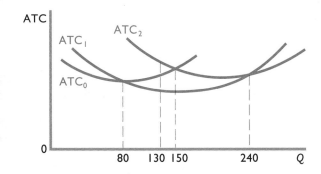

put? Draw the firm's long-run average-cost curve on the diagram and define this curve.

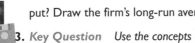 **3.** *Key Question*   *Use the concepts of economies and diseconomies of scale to explain the shape of a firm's long-run ATC curve. What is the concept of minimum efficient scale? What bearing may the exact shape of the long-run ATC curve have on the structure of an industry?*

14. Use the concept of minimum efficient scale to explain the number of efficient firms an industry can support. Is market concentration — the presence of only a few firms in an industry — explainable in terms of economies of scale?

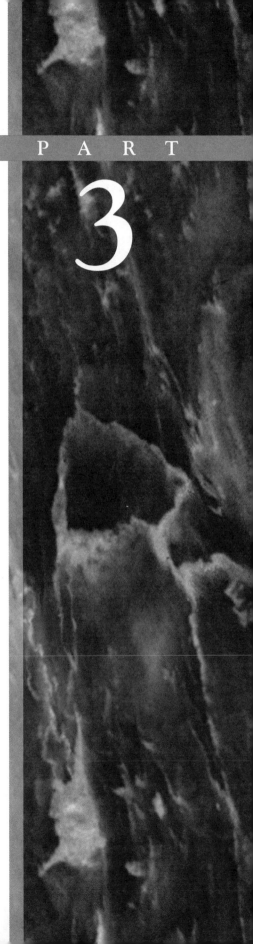

MARKETS, PRICES, AND RESOURCE ALLOCATION

CHAPTER 10

PRICE AND OUTPUT DETERMINATION: PURE COMPETITION

We now have the basic tools of analysis for understanding how product price and output are determined. But a firm's decisions concerning price and production will vary depending on the character of the industry in which it is operating. There is no "average" or "typical" industry. The business sector of our economy has a number of different market structures. At one extreme we find a single producer dominating a market; at the other we discover thousands of firms, each supplying a minute fraction of market output. In this chapter we first introduce the four basic market structures, and then focus in on the first of these — pure competition.

BOX 10-1   THE BIG PICTURE

The goal of the firm is to make as much profit as possible. Scarcity *automatically* brings about competition among firms as each tries to do the best it can for itself.

But competing for scarce resources in the input (or factor) market and customers in the product market is hard work; the more firms compete, the harder each firm has to work, in some cases just to survive. For a firm, an ideal world is one in which it would have no competition and lots of profits. Alas, the probability that such an ideal situation could persist in a world pervaded by scarcity is small. There will always be competitors — or at least potential competitors — unless a firm is protected from competition, a topic we will take up in the next chapter.

With this chapter we begin to examine firm behaviour under different market structures. Note that we are now focusing on the product market — the market for goods and services; the factor market is analyzed in later chapters. The main goal of the firm never changes, but its behaviour will be influenced by the amount of competition (or lack of it) it has, and this is dictated by the market structure. There are almost limitless shades of competition possible. To get an idea of the amount of competition between firms, we study four models: the two extremes, pure competition and monopoly, and the much more prevalent forms found in the real world, monopolistic competition and oligopoly.

As you read this chapter, keep the following points in mind:

- Pure competition is the ideal system against which to compare the other market structures. In this market structure, firms produce the most out of the available resources, and produce the goods and services most wanted by society.
- The pure competitive model stresses the underlying force in a market economy: competition. Never lose sight of the fact that in a market economy there are inconstant competitive, or potentially competitive, forces at work no matter what the market structure.
- Be sure to clearly distinguish between the firm and the industry.
- The dynamics of the pure competitive model will be easier to understand if you distinguish between the short and long run. Short-run losses mean firms leave the industry; short-run economic profits attract firms to the industry; in the long run, only normal profits are possible.

FOUR BASIC MARKET STRUCTURES

Any attempt to examine each specific industry is an impossible task. We seek a more realistic objective — to define and discuss several basic market structures, or models. We will acquaint ourselves with the *general* way in which price and output are determined in most of the market types that characterize our economy.

There are four distinct market structures. These are (1) pure competition, (2) pure monopoly, (3) monopolistic competition, and (4) oligopoly. These four market models differ in the number of firms in the industry, whether the product is standardized or differentiated, and how easy or difficult it is for new firms to enter the industry.

Table 10-1 indicates the main characteristics of these four models. A more detailed analysis of each will follow in the next three chapters.

1. In **pure competition** there are a very large number of firms producing a standardized product (for example, wheat or corn). New firms can enter the industry very easily.

2. At the other extreme **pure monopoly** (Chapter 11) is a market in which one firm is the sole seller of a product or service (a local electric company). Entry of additional firms is blocked so that the firm is the industry. Because there is only one product, there is no product differentiation.

3. **Monopolistic competition** (Chapter 12) is characterized by a relatively large number of sellers producing differentiated products (women's clothing, furniture, books). Differentiation is the basis for product promotion and development. Entry to a monopolistically competitive industry is quite easy.

4. In **oligopoly** (Chapter 13) there are a few sellers, and this "fewness" means that pricing and output decisions are interdependent. Each firm is affected by the decisions of rivals and must take these decisions into account in determining its own price–output behaviour. Products may be stan-

TABLE 10-1 **Characteristics of the four basic market models**

Characteristic	MARKET MODEL			
	Pure competition	Monopolistic competition	Oligopoly	Pure monopoly
Number of firms	A very large number	Many	Few	One
Type of product	Standardized	Differentiated	Standardized or differentiated	Unique; no close substitutes
Control over price	None, price taker	Some, but within rather narrow limits	Circumscribed by mutual interdependence; considerable with collusion	Considerable, price maker
Conditions of entry	Very easy, no obstacles	Relatively easy	Significant obstacles present	Blocked
Nonprice competition	None	Considerable emphasis on advertising, brand names, trademarks, and so on	Typically a great deal, particularly with product differentiation	Mostly public relations advertising ("goodwill")
Examples	Agriculture	Retail trade, dresses, shoes	Steel, automobiles, farm implements, many household appliances	Bell Canada, local utilities

dardized (such as steel or aluminum) or differentiated (automobiles). Generally, entry into oligopolistic industries is very difficult.

These definitions and the characteristics outlined in Table 10-1 will come into sharper focus as we examine each market structure in detail.

We will find it convenient to occasionally distinguish between the characteristics of a purely competitive market and those of all other basic market structures — pure monopoly, monopolistic competition, and oligopoly. To facilitate such comparisons, we will employ **imperfect competition** as a generic term to designate all those market structures deviating from the purely competitive market model.

THE IMPORTANCE OF MARKET STRUCTURE

The market structure in which a firm exists will be an important determinant of what price it can charge for its output and the quantity it will produce. The overriding goal of a firm is to maximize profits. But how a firm pursues that goal, and whether it can make normal or economic profit, is determined by the market structure it is in. A monopolist's output and price behaviour is significantly different from a firm in pure competition, where there are many firms selling a homogeneous product. In a pure competitive industry a firm has to be on the alert to *adapt* to constantly changing market conditions, whereas a monopolist can *influence* market conditions.

But no matter what market structure prevails, as the firm attempts to maximize its profits it must continuously look over its shoulder since other and potentially new firms are trying to do the same. Even a monopolist, unless protected by entry barriers, is under a constant threat as potential competitors enviously eye its healthy (economic) profits. On the other hand, firms will naturally attempt to outdo their competitors with lower prices, unique products and services, or erection of entry barriers of different types. This is the dynamics of the supply side in a market economy.

PURE COMPETITION: CONCEPT AND OCCURRENCE

A purely competitive market has several distinct characteristics that distinguish it from other market structures.

1. VERY LARGE NUMBERS   A basic feature of a purely competitive market is the presence of a large number of independently acting sellers, offering their products in an organized market. Markets for farm commodities (in the absence of marketing boards), stock markets, and the foreign-exchange market are close approximations.

2. STANDARDIZED PRODUCT   Competitive firms produce a standardized, or homogeneous, product. Given price, the consumer is indifferent as to the firm from which a purchase is made. Because of product standardization, there is no reason for *nonprice competition* — competition based on differences in product quality, advertising, or sales promotion.

3. "PRICE TAKER"   In a purely competitive market, *individual firms* exert no significant control over product price. This characteristic follows from the preceding two. Under pure competition, each firm produces such a small fraction of total output that increasing or decreasing its output will not perceptibly influence total supply or product price.

Assume there are 10,000 competing firms, each currently producing 100 units of output. Total supply is 1,000,000. Now suppose one of these firms cuts its output to 50 units. This will not affect price because this restriction of output by a single firm has almost no impact on total supply. The total quantity supplied declines from 1,000,000 to 999,950 — not enough of a change in total supply to noticeably affect product price.

Thus, the individual competitive firm is a **price taker**; it cannot adjust market price, but can only adjust to it.

4. EASY ENTRY AND EXIT   New firms can easily enter and existing firms can easily leave purely competitive industries. No significant obstacles — legal, technical, financial, or other — prohibit new firms from coming into being and selling their outputs in competitive markets.

RELEVANCE   Pure competition is rare in practice. But this does not mean that an analysis of how competitive markets work is irrelevant.

1. A few industries more closely approximate the competitive model than they do any other market structure. For example, much can be learned about Canadian agriculture by understanding competitive markets.
2. Pure competition provides the simplest context in which to apply the revenue and cost concepts developed in the previous chapter. Pure competition is a clear and meaningful starting point for any discussion of price and output determination.
3. The operation of a purely competitive economy provides us with a standard against which the efficiency of the real-world economy can be compared and evaluated.

Our analysis of pure competition has four objectives: First, we will examine demand from the competitive seller's viewpoint. Second, we consider how a competitive producer adjusts to market price in the short run. Third, the nature of long-run adjustments in a competitive industry is explored. Finally, we evaluate the efficiency of competitive industries from the standpoint of society.

DEMAND TO A COMPETITIVE SELLER

Because each competitive firm offers a negligible fraction of total supply, the individual firm cannot perceptibly influence the market price. Rather, the firm can merely *adjust* to the market price, which it must regard as determined by the market. The competitive seller is a *price taker*, not a *price maker*.

PERFECTLY ELASTIC DEMAND

Thus, *the demand curve facing the individual competitive firm is perfectly elastic*. Columns 1 and 2 of Table 10-2 show a perfectly elastic demand curve, where market price is assumed to be $131. The firm cannot obtain a higher price by restricting output; nor need it lower price to increase its sales volume.

We are *not* saying that the *market* demand curve is perfectly elastic in a competitive market. Instead, it is a downsloping curve, as a glance ahead at Figure 10-7(b) indicates. However, the demand schedule faced by the *individual firm* in a purely competitive industry is perfectly elastic.

The distinction comes about in this way. For the industry a larger sales volume can be realized only by accepting a lower product price. All firms, acting independently but simultaneously, can and do affect total supply and therefore market price. But not so for the individual firm. If a *single* producer increases or decreases output, the outputs of all other competing firms being constant, the effect on total supply and market price is negligible. The single firm's demand or sales schedule is therefore perfectly elastic, as shown in Figures 10-1 and 10-7(a). This is the fallacy of composition at work. What is true for the group of firms (a downsloping, less than perfectly elastic demand curve), is *not* true for the individual firm (a perfectly elastic demand curve).

AVERAGE, TOTAL, AND MARGINAL REVENUE

The firm's demand schedule is simultaneously a revenue schedule. What appears in column 1 of Table 10-2 as price per unit to the purchaser is revenue per unit, or **average revenue**, to the seller. To say that a buyer must pay $131 per unit is to say that the revenue per unit, or average revenue, received by the seller is $131. Price and average revenue are the same thing seen from different viewpoints.

Total revenue for each sales level can be determined by multiplying price by the corresponding quantity the firm can sell. Multiply column 1 by column 2, and the result is column 3. In this case, total receipts increase by a constant amount, $131, for each additional unit of sales. Each unit sold adds exactly its constant price to total revenue.

When a firm is pondering a change in its output, it will consider how its revenue will *change* as a result of that shift in output. What will be the additional revenue from selling another unit of output? **Marginal revenue** is the change in total revenue, that is, the extra revenue that results from selling one more unit of output. In column 3 of Table 10-2 total revenue is zero

FIGURE 10-1 **Demand, marginal revenue, and total revenue of a purely competitive firm**

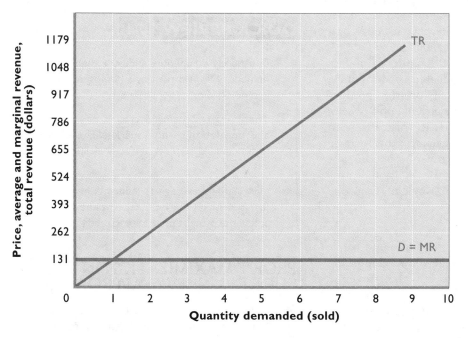

Because it can sell additional units of output at a constant price, the marginal-revenue curve (MR) of a purely competitive firm coincides with its perfectly elastic demand curve (D). The firm's total-revenue curve (TR) is a straight upsloping line.

TABLE 10-2 The demand and revenue schedules for an individual purely competitive firm

FIRM'S DEMAND OR AVERAGE-REVENUE SCHEDULE		REVENUE DATA	
(1) Product price (average revenue)	(2) Quantity demanded (sold)	(3) Total revenue	(4) Marginal revenue
$131	0	$ 0	$131
131	1	131	131
131	2	262	131
131	3	393	131
131	4	524	131
131	5	655	131
131	6	786	131
131	7	917	131
131	8	1048	131
131	9	1179	131
131	10	1310	131

when zero units are sold. The first unit of output sold increases total revenue from zero to $131; marginal revenue is therefore $131. The second unit sold increases total revenue from $131 to $262, so marginal revenue is again $131, Note in column 4 that marginal revenue is a constant $131, because total revenue increases by a constant amount with every extra unit sold.

Under purely competitive conditions, product price is constant to the individual firm; added units, therefore, can be sold without lowering product price. This means that each additional unit of sales adds exactly its price — $131, in this case — to total revenue. And marginal revenue *is* this increase in total revenue. Marginal revenue is constant under pure competition, because additional units can be sold at a constant price. **(Key Question 3)**

GRAPHIC PORTRAYAL

The competitive firm's demand curve and total- and marginal-revenue curves are shown graphically in Figure 10-1. The demand or average-revenue curve is perfectly elastic. The marginal-revenue curve coincides with the demand curve because product price is constant to the competitive firm. Each extra unit of sales increases total revenue by

$131. Total revenue is a straight line up to the right. Its slope is constant — it is a straight line — because marginal revenue is constant.

QUICK REVIEW 10-1

1. In a purely competitive industry there are a large number of firms producing a homogeneous product and no significant entry barriers.

2. There are two demand curves, one for the firm and one for the whole market. The competitive firm's demand curve is perfectly elastic at the market price.

3. Marginal and average revenues coincide with the firm's demand curve; total revenue rises by the amount of product price for each additional unit sold.

PROFIT MAXIMIZATION IN THE SHORT RUN: TWO APPROACHES

In the short run, the competitive firm has a fixed plant and maximizes its profits or minimizes its losses by adjusting its output through changes in the amounts of variable resources (materials, labour, and so forth) it employs. The economic profits it seeks are the difference between total revenue and total costs. Indeed, this is the direction of our analysis. The revenue data of the previous section and the cost data of Chapter 9 must be brought together so that the profit-maximizing output for the firm can be determined.

There are two ways of calculating the level of output at which a competitive firm will realize maximum profits or minimum losses. One compares total revenue and total costs; the other compares marginal revenue and marginal cost. Both approaches apply not only to a purely competitive firm but also to firms operating in any of the other three basic market structures. To understand output determination under pure competition, we will use both approaches, emphasizing the marginal approach. Also, hypothetical data will be employed to clarify the two approaches.

TOTAL-REVENUE–TOTAL-COST APPROACH

Confronted with the market price of its product, the competitive producer is faced with three related questions: (1) Should we produce? (2) If so, what amount? (3) What profit (or loss) will be realized?

At first, the answer to question one seems obvious: "You should produce if it is profitable to do so." But the situation is more complex than this. In the short run, part of the firm's total costs is variable costs, and the remainder is fixed costs. Fixed costs have to be paid "out of pocket" even when the firm is closed down. In the short run, a firm takes a loss equal to its fixed costs when it produces zero units of output. This means that although there may be no level of output at which the firm can realize a profit, the firm might still produce if it can realize a loss less than the fixed-cost loss it will face in closing down. Thus, the correct answer to "Should we produce?" is: *The firm should produce in the short run if it can realize either (1) a profit or (2) a loss that is less than its fixed costs.*

Assuming the firm *will* produce, the second question is: "How much should be produced?" The answer: *In the short run, the firm should produce that output at which it maximizes profits or minimizes losses.*

We now examine three cases to demonstrate the validity of these two generalizations and answer our third query by indicating how profits and losses can be calculated. In the first case, the firm will maximize its profits by producing. In the second case, it will minimize its losses by producing. In the third case, the firm will

minimize its losses by closing down. We will assume the same short-run cost data for all three cases and explore the firm's production decisions when faced with three different product prices.

PROFIT-MAXIMIZING CASE Columns 2 through 4 of Table 10-3 repeat the fixed-cost, variable-cost, and total-cost data developed in Table 9-2. Assuming that market price is $131, we derive total revenue for each output level by multiplying output by price, as we did in Table 10-2. These data are presented in column 5. Then in column 6, the profit or loss at each output level is found by subtracting total cost from total revenue. Now we have all the data needed to answer the three questions.

Should the firm produce? Yes, because it can realize a profit by doing so. How much? Nine units, because column 6 tells us this is the output at which total economic profits will be at a maximum. The size of that profit is $299.

Figure 10-2(a) graphically compares total revenue and total cost. Total revenue is a straight line because under pure competition each additional unit adds the same amount to total revenue (Table 10-2).

Total costs increase with output; more production requires more resources. But the rate of increase in total costs varies with the relative efficiency of the firm. The cost data reflect Chapter 9's law of diminishing returns. For a time the rate of increase in total cost diminishes as the firm uses its fixed resources more efficiently. Then after a time, total cost begins to rise by ever-increasing amounts because of the inefficiencies accompanying more intensive use of the firm's plant.

Comparing total cost with total revenue in Figure 10-2(a), note that a **break-even point** (normal profit position) occurs at 2 units of output. If our data were extended beyond 10 units of output, another such point would occur where total cost would catch up with total revenue, as is shown in Figure 10-2(a). Any output outside of these break-even points will entail losses. Any output within these points will produce an economic profit. Maximum profit is achieved where the vertical difference between total revenue and total cost is greatest. For our data, this is at 9 units of output where maximum profit is $299.

LOSS-MINIMIZING CASE Assuming no change in costs, the firm may not realize economic profits if

FIGURE 10-2 **The (a) profit-maximizing (b) loss-minimizing, and close-down cases as shown by the total-revenue-total-cost approach**

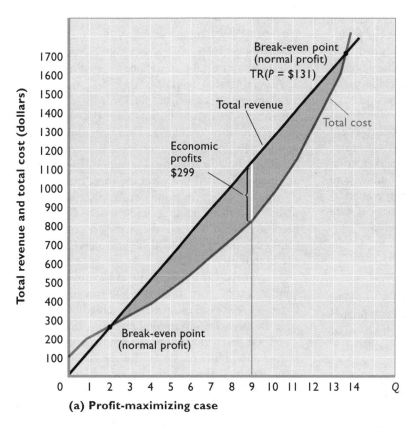

(a) Profit-maximizing case

In (a), a firm's profits are maximized at that output where total revenue exceeds total cost by the maximum amount. In (b), a firm will minimize its losses by producing at that output at which total cost exceeds total revenue by the smallest amount. However, if there is no output where total revenue exceeds total variable costs, the firm will minimize losses in the short run by closing down.

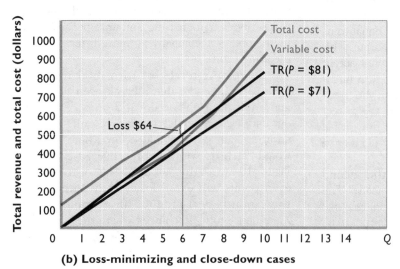

(b) Loss-minimizing and close-down cases

the market yields a price considerably below $131. Suppose the market price is $81. As column 8 of Table 10-3 indicates, at this price all levels of output will lead to losses. But the firm will *not* close down because, by producing, it realizes a loss considerably less than the $100 fixed-cost loss it would incur by closing down. The firm will minimize its losses by producing 6 units of output. The resulting $64 loss is clearly preferable to the $100 loss from producing no units — closing down. By producing 6 units the firm earns a total revenue of $486, sufficient to pay all the firm's variable cost ($450) and also a substantial portion — $36 worth — of the firm's $100 of fixed costs.

In general, whenever total revenue exceeds total *variable* costs, the firm will produce because all variable costs as well as some portion of total fixed costs can be paid out of revenue. If the firm closed down, all of its total fixed costs would have to be paid out of the entrepreneur's pocket. By producing some output, the firm's loss will be less than total fixed costs.

Note that there are several other outputs that entail a loss less than the firm's $100 fixed costs, but at 6 units of output the loss is minimized.

CLOSE-DOWN CASE Assume that the market price is $71. Given short-run costs, column 10 of Table 10-3 indicates that at all levels of output, losses will exceed the $100 fixed-cost loss the firm will incur by closing down. It follows that the firm will minimize its losses by closing down.

Figure 10-2(b) demonstrates the loss-minimizing and close-down cases graphically. In the loss-minimizing case, the total-revenue line TR (P = $81) exceeds total variable cost by the maximum amount at 6 units of output. Here total revenue is $486, and the firm recovers all its $450 of variable costs and also $36 worth of fixed costs. The firm's minimum loss is $64, better than the $100 fixed-cost loss involved in closing down.

In the close-down case, the total-revenue line TR (P = $71) lies below the total-variable-cost curve at all points; there is no output at which variable costs can be recovered. By producing, the firm would incur losses exceeding its fixed costs. The firm's best choice is to close down and pay its $100 fixed-cost loss out of pocket.

TABLE 10-3 **The profit-maximizing output for a purely competitive firm: total-revenue–total-cost approach (prices: $131, $81, $71)**

(1) Total product	(2) Total fixed cost	(3) Total variable cost	(4) Total cost	PRICE: $131		PRICE: $81		PRICE: $71	
				(5) Total revenue	(6) Profit	(7) Total revenue	(8) Profit	(9) Total revenue	(10) Profit
0	$100	$ 0	$100	0	$−100	$ 0	$−100	$ 0	$−100
1	100	90	190	131	−59	81	−109	71	−119
2	100	170	270	262	−8	162	−108	142	−128
3	100	240	340	393	+53	243	−97	213	−127
4	100	300	400	524	+124	324	−76	284	−116
5	100	370	470	655	+185	405	−65	355	−115
6	100	450	550	786	+236	486	−64	426	−124
7	100	540	640	917	+277	567	−73	497	−143
8	100	650	750	1048	+298	648	−102	568	−182
9	100	780	880	1179	+299	729	−151	639	−241
10	100	930	1030	1310	+280	810	−220	710	−320

1. In the short run a firm should produce if it can realize a profit or a loss that is smaller than its total fixed costs.

2. Profits are maximized where the excess of total revenue over total cost is greatest.

3. Losses are minimized where the excess of total cost over total revenue is smallest and is some amount less than total fixed costs.

4. If losses at all levels of output exceed total fixed costs, the firm should close down in the short run.

MARGINAL-REVENUE–MARGINAL-COST APPROACH

Another way a competitive firm decides the amounts it would produce at each possible price is to determine and compare the amounts that each *additional* unit of output will add to total revenue and to total cost. The firm should compare the *marginal revenue* (MR) and the *marginal cost* (MC) of each successive unit of output. Any unit whose marginal revenue exceeds its marginal cost should be produced because, on each such unit, the firm gains more in revenue from its sale than it adds to costs producing the unit.

MR = MC RULE At relatively low levels of output, marginal revenue will usually (but not always) exceed marginal cost. It is therefore profitable to produce through this range of output. But as output increases, marginal cost will exceed marginal revenue. To maximize profits, the firm must not produce in this range.

Separating these two production ranges will be a unique point at which marginal revenue equals marginal cost. This point is the key to the output-determining rule: *The firm will maximize profits or minimize losses by producing at the point where marginal revenue equals marginal cost.* We call this profit-maximizing guide the **MR = MC** rule. For most sets of MR and MC data, there will not be a nonfractional level of output at which MR and MC are precisely equal. In such instances, the firm should produce the last complete unit of output whose MR *exceeds* its MC.

THREE CHARACTERISTICS There are three features of this MR = MC rule you should know.

1. The rule presumes the firm will choose to produce rather than close down. Shortly, we will note that marginal revenue must be equal to, or must exceed, average variable cost, or the firm will prefer to close down rather than produce the MR = MC output.
2. The MR = MC rule is an accurate guide to profit maximization for all firms, be they purely competitive, monopolistic, monopolistically competitive, or oligopolistic.
3. The MR = MC rule can be restated in a slightly different form when applied to a purely competitive firm. Product price is determined by the market forces of supply and demand and, although the competitive firm can sell as much or as little as it chooses at that price, the firm cannot manipulate the price itself. The demand schedule faced by a competitive seller is perfectly elastic at the going market price. The result is that product price and marginal revenue are equal; each extra unit sold adds precisely its price to total revenue, as shown in Figure 10-1.

Thus under pure competition — and *only* under pure competition — we may substitute price for marginal revenue in the rule, so that it reads as follows: *To maximize profits or minimize losses, the competitive firms should produce at that point where price equals marginal cost (P = MC).* This **P = MC** rule is simply a special case of the MR = MC rule.

PROFIT-MAXIMIZING CASE Table 10-4 reproduces the unit- and marginal-cost data derived in Table 9-2. It is, of course, the marginal-cost data of column 5 in Table 10-4 that we wish to compare with price (equal to marginal revenue) for each unit of output. Suppose first that market price, and therefore marginal revenue, is $131, as shown in column 6.

What is the profit-maximizing output? We see that each and every unit of output up to and including the ninth adds more to total revenue than to total cost, thus marginal revenue exceeds marginal cost on all of the first 9 units of output. Each unit therefore adds to the firm's profits and should be produced. The tenth unit, however, will not be produced, because it would add more to costs ($150) than to revenue ($131).

PROFIT CALCULATIONS The economic profits realized by the firm can be calculated from the unit-cost data. Multiplying price ($131) by output (9), we find total revenue is $1179. Total cost of $880 is found by

TABLE 10-4 The profit-maximizing output for a purely competitive firm: marginal-revenue-equals-marginal-cost approach (price = $131)

(1) Total product	(2) Average fixed cost	(3) Average variable cost	(4) Average total cost	(5) Marginal cost	(6) Price = marginal revenue	(7) Total economic profit (+) or loss −
0						$ −100
1	$100.00	$90.00	$190.00	$90	$131	− 59
2	50.00	85.00	135.00	80	131	− 8
3	33.33	80.00	113.33	70	131	− 53
4	25.00	75.00	100.00	60	131	+124
5	20.00	74.00	94.00	70	131	+185
6	16.67	75.00	91.67	80	131	+236
7	14.29	77.14	91.43	90	131	+277
8	12.50	81.25	93.75	110	131	+298
9	11.11	86.67	97.78	130	131	+299
10	10.00	93.00	103.00	150	131	+280

multiplying average total cost ($97.78) by output (9).[1] The difference of $299 (= $1179 −$880) is economic profits.

Another means of calculating economic profits is to determine profit *per unit* by subtracting average total cost ($97.78) from product price ($131) and multiplying the difference (per unit profits of $33.22) by the level of output (9).

GRAPHIC PORTRAYAL Figure 10-3 (Key Graph) compares price and marginal cost graphically. Here per unit economic profit is indicated by the distance AP. When multiplied by 9 units, the profit-maximizing output, the total economic profit is shown by the shaded rectangular area, labelled "economic profit."

Note that the firm is seeking to maximize its *total* profits, not its *per unit* profits. Per unit profits are largest at 7 units of output, where price exceeds average total cost by $39.57 ($131 minus $91.43).

---

[1] In most instances, the unit-cost data are rounded figures. Therefore, economic profits calculated from them will typically vary by a few cents from the profits determined in the total-revenue–total-cost approach. We here ignore the few cents differentials and make our answers consistent with the results of the total-revenue–total-cost approach.

But by producing only 7 units, the firm would be forgoing the production of two additional units of output that would clearly contribute to total profits. The firm is happy to accept lower per-unit profits if the resulting extra units of sales more than compensate for the lower per-unit profits.

LOSS-MINIMIZING CASE Now, let's assume that market price is $81 rather than $131. Should the firm produce? If so, how much? And what will the resulting profits or losses be? The answers are, respectively, "Yes," "6 units," and "A loss of $64."

Column 6 of Table 10-5 shows the new price (equal to marginal revenue) alongside the same unit- and marginal-cost data presented in Table 10-4. Comparing columns 5 and 6, we find that the first unit of output adds $90 to total cost but only $81 to total revenue. One might conclude, "Don't produce — close down!" But this would be hasty. Remember that at very low levels of production, marginal product is low, making marginal cost unusually high. The price–marginal-cost relationships improve with increased production.

On the next 5 units — 2 through 6 — price exceeds marginal cost. Each of these 5 units adds more to revenue than to cost, more than compensating for the "loss" taken on the first unit. Beyond 6 units, however, MC exceeds MR (= P). The firm

KEY GRAPH

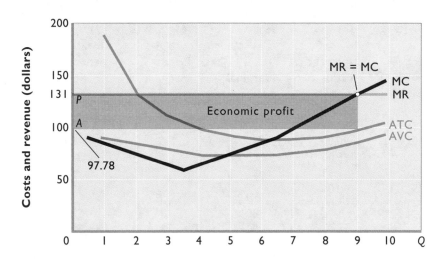

FIGURE 10-3 The short-run profit-maximizing position of a purely competitive firm

The P = MC output allows the competitive producer to maximize profits or minimize losses. In this case, price exceeds average total cost at the P = MC output of 9 units. Economic profits per unit of AP are realized; total economic profits are indicated by the shaded rectangle.

should therefore produce at 6 units. In general, the profit-seeking firm should always compare marginal revenue (or price under pure competition) with the *rising* portion of its marginal-cost schedule or curve.

LOSS DETERMINATION Will production be profitable? No, because at 6 units of output, average total costs of $91.67 exceed price of $81 by $10.67 per unit. Multiply by the 6 units of output, and we

find the firm's total loss is $64. Alternatively, comparing total revenue of $486 (= 6 × $81) with total cost of $550 (= 6 × $91.67), the firm's loss is $64.

Then why produce? Because this loss is less than the firm's $100 worth of fixed costs — the $100 loss the firm would incur in the short run by closing down. The firm receives enough revenue per unit ($81) to cover its variable cost of $75 and also provide $6 per unit, or a total of $36, to apply

TABLE 10-5 The loss-minimizing outputs for a purely competitive firm: marginal-revenue-equals-marginal-cost approach (prices = $81 and $71)

(1) Total product	(2) Average fixed cost	(3) Average variable cost	(4) Average total cost	(5) Marginal cost	(6) $81 price = marginal revenue	(7) Profit (+) or loss (−), $81 price	(8) $71 price = marginal revenue	(9) Profit (+) or loss (−), $71 price
0						$ −100		$ −100
				$ 90	$81		$71	
1	$100.00	$90.00	$190.00			−109		−119
				80	81		71	
2	50.00	85.00	135.00			−108		−128
				70	81		71	
3	33.33	80.00	113.33			− 97		−127
				60	81		71	
4	25.00	75.00	100.00			− 76		−116
				70	81		71	
5	20.00	74.00	94.00			− 65		−115
				80	81		71	
6	16.67	75.00	91.67			− 64		−124
				90	81		71	
7	14.29	77.14	91.43			− 73		−143
				110	81		71	
8	12.50	81.25	93.75			−102		−182
				130	81		71	
9	11.11	86.67	97.78			−151		−241
				150	81		71	
10	10.00	93.00	103.00			−220		−320

FIGURE 10-4 **The short-run loss-minimizing position of a purely competitive firm**

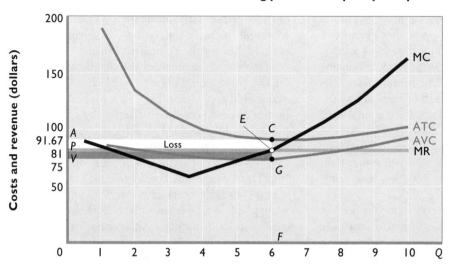

If price exceeds the minimum AVC but is less than ATC, the P = MC output of 6 units will permit the firm to minimize its losses. In this instance, losses are AP per unit; total losses are shown by the area PACE.

FIGURE 10-5 **The short-run close-down position of a purely competitve firm**

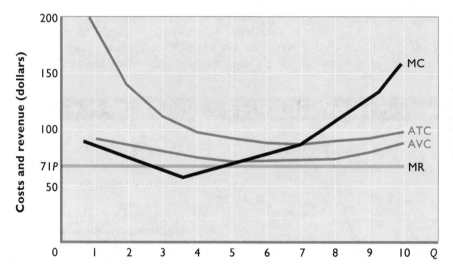

If price falls short of minimum AVC, the competitive firm will minimize its losses in the short run by closing down. There is no level of output at which the firm can produce and realize a loss smaller than its total fixed cost.

against fixed costs. Therefore, the firm's loss is only $64 ($100 – $36), rather than $100.

GRAPHIC PORTRAYAL This case is shown in Figure 10-4. Whenever price exceeds the minimum average variable cost but falls short of average total cost, the firm can pay part of, but not all, its fixed costs by producing. In this instance, total variable costs are shown by the area 0VGF. Total revenue, however, is 0PEF, greater than total variable costs by VPEG. This excess of revenue over variable costs can be applied against total fixed costs, repre-

sented by area VACG. By producing 6 units, the firm's loss is only area PACE; by closing down, its loss would be its fixed costs shown by the larger area VACG.

CLOSE-DOWN CASE Suppose now that the market yields a price of only $71. It will now pay the firm to close down because there is no output at which the firm can cover its average variable costs, much less its average total cost. In other words, the smallest loss it can realize by producing is greater than the $100 worth of fixed costs it will lose by closing down.

This can be verified by comparing columns 3 and 8 of Table 10-5 and can be seen in Figure 10-5. Price comes closest to covering average variable costs at the MR (= P) = MC output of 5 units. But even here, price or revenue per unit would fall short of average variable cost by $3 (= $74 minus $71). By producing at the MR (= P) = MC output, the firm would lose its $100 worth of fixed costs, *plus* $15 ($3 on each of the five units) worth of variable costs, for a total loss of $115. This clearly compares unfavourably with the $100 fixed-cost loss the firm would incur by closing down. It will pay the firm to close down rather than operate at a $71 price or at any price less than minimum average variable cost of $74.

The close-down case obligates us to modify our MR (= P) = MC rule. **A competitive firm will maximize profits or minimize losses in the short run by producing that output at which MR (= P) = MC, provided that price exceeds minimum average-variable-cost.**

MARGINAL COST AND THE SHORT-RUN SUPPLY CURVE

You will recognize that we have simply selected three different prices and asked how much the prof-it-seeking competitive firm, faced with certain costs, would choose to supply in the market at each of these prices. This information — price and corresponding quantity supplied — constitutes the supply schedule for the competitive firm.

Table 10-6 summarizes the supply-schedule data for the three prices chosen — $131, $81, and $71. You should apply the MR (= P) = MC rule (modified by the close-down case) to verify the quantity-supplied data for the $151, $111, $91, and $61 prices and calculate the corresponding profits or losses.

We confirm that the supply schedule is upsloping. Here price must be $74 (equal to minimum average variable cost) or greater before any output is supplied. And because the marginal cost of successive units of output is increasing, the firm must get successively higher prices for it to be profitable to produce these additional units of output.

GENERALIZED DEPICTION   **Figure 10-6 (Key Graph)** generalizes on our application of the MR (= P) = MC rule. We have drawn the relevant cost curves and from the vertical axis have extended a series of marginal-revenue lines from some possible prices the market might set for the firm. The crucial prices are P_1 and P_3.

KEY GRAPH

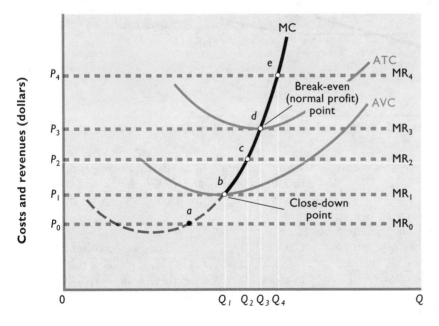

FIGURE 10-6   The P = MC rule and the competitive firm's short-run supply curve

Application of the P = MC rule, as modified by the close-down case, reveals that the (solid) segment of the firm's MC curve that lies above AVC is the firm's short-run supply curve. More specifically, at price P_0, P = MC at point *a*, but the firm will produce no output because P_0 is less than minimum AVC. At price P_1 the firm is in equilibrium at point *b*, where it produces Q_1 units and incurs a loss equal to its fixed costs. At P_2 equilibrium is at point *d* if price is P_3. In this case the firm earns a normal profit because at output Q_3 price equals ATC. At price P_4 the firm reaches an equilibrium at point *e* and maximizes its economic profit by producing Q_4 units.

Our close-down case reminds us that at any price *below* P_1 — the price that is equal to the minimum average variable cost — the firm should close down and supply nothing.

P_3 is strategic because it is the price at which the firm will just break even — earn a normal profit — by producing Q_3 units of output, as indicated by the MR (= P) = MC rule. Here, total revenue will just cover total costs (including a normal profit).

At P_2 the firm supplies Q_2 units of output and minimizes its losses. At any other price between P_1 and P_3, the firm will minimize its losses by producing to the point where MR (– P) = MC.

TABLE 10-6 **The supply schedule of a competitive firm confronted with the cost data of Table 10-4**

Price	Quantity supplied	Maximum profit (+) or minimum loss (-)
$151	10	$ _____
131	9	+299
111	8	_____
91	7	_____
81	6	– 64
71	0	–100
61	0	_____

At any price above P_3, the firm will maximize its economic profits by producing to the point where MR (= P) = MC. Thus at P_4 the firm will realize the greatest profits by supplying Q_4 units of output.

The basic point is that each of the various MR (= P) = MC intersection points shown as b, c, d, and e in Figure 10-6 indicates a possible product price (on the vertical axis) and the corresponding quantity the profit-seeking firm would supply at that price (on the horizontal axis). These points locate the supply curve of the competitive firm. We can conclude that *the portion of the firm's marginal-cost curve lying above its average-variable-cost curve is its short-run supply curve*. The heavy segment of the marginal-cost curve is the short-run supply curve in Figure 10-6.

SUPPLY CURVE SHIFTS In Chapter 9 we saw that changes in such factors as the prices of variable inputs or in technology will shift the marginal-cost or short-run supply curve to a new location. For example, a wage increase would shift the supply curve in Figure 10-6 upward, constituting a decrease in supply. Technological progress that increases the productivity of labour would shift the marginal cost or supply curve downward, representing an increase in supply. You should determine how (1) a specific tax on the product and (2) a per unit subsidy on this product would shift the supply curve.

TABLE 10-7 **Summary of competitive output determination in the short run**

Question	Total-revenue–total-cost approach	Marginal-revenue–marginal-cost approach
Should the firm produce?	Yes, if TR exceeds TC or if TC exceeds TR by some amount less than total fixed costs.	Yes, if price is equal to, or greater than, minimum average variable cost.
What quantity should be produced to maximize profits?	Produce where the excess of TR over TC is a maximum or where the excess of TC over TR is a minimum (and less than total fixed costs).	Produce where MR or price equals MC.
Will production result in an economic profit?	Yes, if TR exceeds TC. No, if TC exceeds TR.	Yes, if price exceeds average total cost. No, if average total cost exceeds price.

FIRM AND INDUSTRY: EQUILIBRIUM PRICE

We must now determine which of the various price possibilities will actually be the equilibrium price. From Chapter 4, we know that in a purely competitive market, equilibrium price is determined by *total* supply and total demand. To derive total supply, the sales schedules or curves of the individual competitive firms must be summed. Thus in Table 10-8, columns 1 and 3 repeat the individual competitive firm's supply schedule just derived in Table 10-6. We now assume that there are a total of 1000 competitive firms in this industry, each having the same total and unit costs as the single firm we have discussed. This lets us calculate the total- or market-supply schedule (columns 2 and 3) by multiplying the quantity-supplied figures of the single firm (column 1) by 1000.

MARKET PRICE AND PROFITS To determine equilibrium price and output, this total-supply data must be compared with total-demand data. For purposes of illustration, let's assume total-demand data are as shown in columns 3 and 4 of Table 10-8. Comparing the total quantity supplied and total quantity demanded at the seven possible prices, we determine that equilibrium price is $111 and equilibrium quantity 8000 units for the industry, and 8 units for each of the 1000 identical firms.

Will these conditions of market supply and demand make this a prosperous industry? Multiplying product price ($111) by output (8 units), we find the total revenue of each firm is $888. Total cost is $750,

found by multiplying average total cost of $93.75 by 8, or simply by looking at column 4 of Table 10-3. The $138 difference is the economic profit of each firm. For the industry, total economic profit is $138,000. This is a prosperous industry.

GRAPHIC PORTRAYAL Figures 10-7(a) and (b) show this analysis graphically. The individual supply curves of each of the 1000 identical firms — one of which is shown as *s* in Figure 10-7(a) — are summed horizontally to get the total-supply curve *S* of Figure 10-7(b). Given total demand *D*, equilibrium price is $111, and equilibrium quantity for the industry is 8000 units. This equilibrium price is given and unalterable to the individual firm; that is, each firm's demand curve is perfectly elastic at the equilibrium price, indicated by *d*. Because price is given and constant to the individual firm, the marginal-revenue curve coincides with the demand curve. This $111 price exceeds average total cost at the firm's equilibrium MR (= *P*) = MC output, resulting in a situation of economic profits similar to that already portrayed in Figure 10-3.

Assuming no changes in costs or market demand occur, these diagrams reveal a *short-run* equilibrium situation. There are no shortages or surpluses in the market to cause price or total quantity to change. Nor can any of the firms in the industry improve its profits by altering output. Note, too, that higher unit and marginal costs or a weaker market demand situation could have created a loss situation similar to Figure 10-4. You are urged to sketch, in Figures 10-7(a) and (b), how higher costs and a less favourable demand could cause short-run losses.

FIRM VERSUS INDUSTRY Figures 10-7(a) and (b) underscore a point made earlier: Product price is a given to the *individual* competitive firm, but, at the same time, the supply plans of all competitive producers *as a group* are a basic determinant of product price. If we recall the fallacy of composition, we find there is no inconsistency here. Though each firm, supplying a negligible fraction of total supply, cannot affect price, the sum of the supply curves of all the many firms in the industry constitutes the industry supply curve, and this curve does have an important bearing on price. *Under competition, equilibrium price is a given to the individual firm and simultaneously is the result of the production (supply) decisions of all firms taken as a group.* **(Key Question 4)**

FIGURE 10-7   Short-run competitive equilibrium for (a) a representative firm and (b) the industy

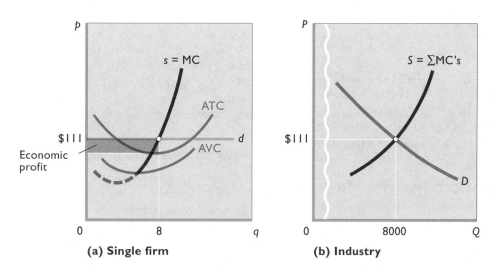

(a) Single firm   **(b) Industry**

The horizontal sum of the 1000 firms' supply curves (S) determines the industry supply curve (S). Given industry demand (D), the short-run equilibrium price and output for the industry are $111 and 8000 units. Taking the equilibrium price as given datum, the representative firm establishes its profit-maximizing output at 8 units and, in this case, realizes the economic profit shown by the shaded area.

TABLE 10-8   Firm and market supply and market demand

(1) Quantity supplied, single firm	(2) Total quantity supplied, 1000 firms	(3) Product price	(4) Total quantity demanded
10	10,000	$151	4,000
9	9,000	131	6,000
8	8,000	111	8,000
7	7,000	91	9,000
6	6,000	81	11,000
0	0	71	13,000
0	0	61	16,000

PROFIT MAXIMIZATION IN THE LONG RUN

In the short run there is a specific number of firms in an industry, each with a fixed plant. In the long run firms already in an industry have sufficient time either to expand or to contract their plant capacities. More importantly, the number of firms in the industry may either increase or decrease

as new firms enter or existing firms leave. We now examine how these long-run adjustments modify our conclusions about short-run output and price determination.

ASSUMPTIONS

We will make three simplifying assumptions, none of which will impair the validity of our conclusions.

1. ENTRY AND EXIT The only long-run adjustment is the entry and exit of firms. Furthermore, we ignore the short-run adjustments already analyzed, to grasp more clearly the nature of long-run competitive adjustments.

2. IDENTICAL COSTS All firms in the industry have identical cost curves. This assumption lets us discuss an "average," or "representative," firm knowing that all other firms in the industry are similarly affected by any long-run adjustments that occur.

3. CONSTANT-COST INDUSTRY The industry under discussion is a constant-cost industry. This means the entry and exit of firms will *not* affect resource prices or, therefore, the locations of the unit-cost schedules of individual firms.

GOAL

We will describe long-run competitive adjustments both verbally and graphically. The basic conclusion we seek to explain is as follows: ***After all long-run adjustments are completed, product price will be exactly equal to, and production will occur at, each firm's point of minimum average total cost.***

This conclusion follows from two basic facts: (1) firms seek profits and shun losses, and (2) under competition, firms are free to enter and leave industries. If price initially exceeds average total costs, the resulting economic profits will attract new firms to the industry. But this expansion of the industry will increase product supply until price is brought back down into equality with minimum average total cost. Conversely, if price is initially less than average total cost, resulting losses will cause firms to leave the industry. As they leave, total product supply will decline, bringing price back up into equality with minimum average total cost.

ZERO ECONOMIC PROFIT MODEL

Suppose that a representative firm in a purely competitive industry is initially in long-run equilibrium. This is shown in Figure 10-8(a), where price and minimum average total cost are equal at $50. Economic profits here are zero; the industry is in equilibrium, or "at rest," because there is no tendency for firms to enter or leave the industry. The existing firms are earning normal profits, which are incorporated in their cost curves. The market price in Figure 10-8(b) is determined by total, or industry, demand and supply, as shown by D_0 and S_0. (The market supply schedule is a *short-run* schedule; the industry's long-run supply schedule will be developed below.) By examining the quantity axes of the two graphs, we note that if all firms are identical, there must be 1000 firms in the industry, each producing 100 units, to achieve the industry's equilibrium output of 100,000 units.

FIGURE 10.8 **Temporary profits and the re-establishment of long-run equilibrium in (a) a representative firm and (b) the industry**

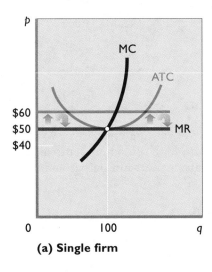

(a) Single firm

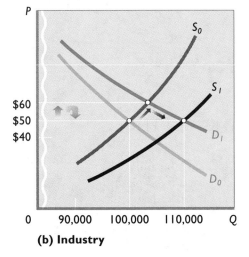

(b) Industry

A favourable shift in demand (D_0 to D_1) will upset the original equilibrium and cause economic profits. But profits will cause new firms to enter the industry, increasing supply (S_0 to S_1) and lowering product price until economic profits are once again zero.

ENTRY ELIMINATES ECONOMIC PROFITS

Let's upset the long-run equilibrium in Figure 10-8 and trace the subsequent adjustments. Suppose a change in consumer tastes increases product demand from D_0 to D_1. This favourable shift in demand will create economic profit; the new price of $60 exceeds average total cost of $50, creating an economic profit of $10 per unit. *These economic profits will lure new firms into the industry.* Some of the entrants will be newly created firms; others will shift from less prosperous industries.

As the firms enter, the market supply of the product will increase, pushing product price below $60. Economic profits will persist and entry will continue until short-run market supply has increased to S_1. At this point, price (= $50) is again equal to minimum average total cost at $50. The economic profits caused by the boost in demand have been competed away to zero and as a result, the previous incentive for more firms to enter the industry has disappeared. Long-run equilibrium is restored.

Figure 10-8 tells us that on the re-establishment of long-run equilibrium, industry output is 110,000 units, and that each firm in the now expanded industry is producing 100 units. We can conclude that the industry is now composed of 1100 firms; that is, 100 new firms have entered the industry.

EXIT ELIMINATES LOSSES

Now let's suppose the consumer demand falls from D_0 to D_2 in Figures 10-9(a) and (b). This forces price down to $40, making production unprofitable. *In the long run, resulting losses will induce firms to leave the industry.* Owners can realize a better return elsewhere. As capital equipment wears out and contractual obligations expire, some firms will simply fold.

As this exit of firms proceeds, industry supply will decrease, moving from S_0 towards S_2. Price will begin to rise from $40 back towards $50. Losses will force firms to leave the industry until supply has declined to S_2, at which point price is again exactly $50, barely consistent with minimum average total cost. The exodus of firms has continued until losses have been eliminated and long-run equilibrium has once again been restored.

Observe in Figures 10-9(a) and (b) that total quantity supplied is now 90,000 units and each firm is producing 100 units. This means that the industry is now populated by only 900 firms, rather than the original 1000.

LONG-RUN SUPPLY FOR A CONSTANT-COST INDUSTRY

What is the character of the **long-run supply curve** that evolves from this analysis of the expansion or contraction of a competitive industry? Although

---

FIGURE 10.9 **Temporary losses and the re-establishment of long-run equilibrium in (a) a representative firm and (b) the industry**

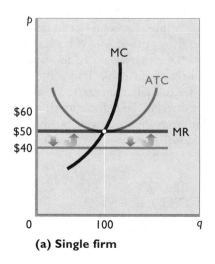

(a) Single firm

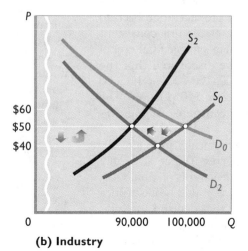

(b) Industry

An unfavourable shift in demand (D_0 to D_1) will upset the original equilibrium and cause losses. But losses will cause firms to leave the industry, decreasing supply (S_0 to S_2) and increasing product price until all losses have disappeared.

our discussion is concerned with the long run, we have noted that the market supply curves of Figures 10-8(b) and 10-9(b) are short-run industry supply curves. However, the analysis permits us to sketch the nature of the long-run supply curve for this competitive industry. The crucial factor in determining the shape of the industry's long-run supply curve is the effect, if any, that changes in the number of firms in the industry will have on the costs of the individual firms in the industry.

CONSTANT-COST INDUSTRY   In the foregoing analysis of long-run competitive equilibrium, we assumed the industry under discussion was a **constant-cost industry**. This means that industry expansion or contraction through the entry or exodus of firms will not affect resource prices or, therefore, production costs. Graphically, the entry or exodus of firms does *not* change the position of the long-run average-total-cost curves of the individual firms in the industry.

When will this be the case? For the most part, when the industry's demand for resources is small in relation to the total demand for those resources. This is most likely to occur when the industry employs unspecialized resources that are being demanded by many other industries.

PERFECTLY ELASTIC SUPPLY   What will the long-run supply curve for a constant-cost industry look like? The answer is contained in our previous discussion of the long-run adjustments towards equilibrium. Here we assumed that entrance or departure of firms would not affect costs. The result was that entry or exodus of firms would alter industry output but always bring product price back to the original $50 level, where it is just consistent with the unchanging minimum average total cost of production. Specifically, we discovered that the industry would supply 90,000, 100,000, or 110,000 units of output, all at a price of $50 per unit. *The long-run supply curve of a constant-cost industry is perfectly elastic.*

This is demonstrated graphically in Figure 10-10, where the data from Figures 10-8 and 10-9 are retained. Suppose industry demand is originally D_0, industry output is Q_0 (100,000), and product price is $Q_0 P_0$ ($50). Now assume that demand increases to D_1, upsetting this equilibrium. The resulting economic profits will attract new firms. Because this is

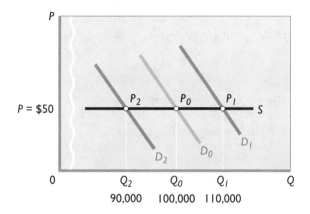

Because the entry or exodus of firms does not affect resource prices or therefore unit costs, an increase in demand (D_0 to D_1) will cause an expansion in industry output (Q_0 to Q_1) but no alteration in price ($Q_0 P_0 = Q_1 P_1$). Similarly, a decrease in demand (D_0 to D_2) will cause a contraction of output (Q_0 to Q_2) but no change in price ($Q_0 P_0 = Q_2 P_2$). This means that the long-run industry supply curve (S) will be perfectly elastic.

a constant-cost industry, entry will continue and industry output will expand until price is driven back down to the unchanged minimum average-total-cost level. This will be at price $Q_1 P_1$ ($50) and output Q_1 (110,000).

This analysis is reversible. A decline in short-run industry demand from D_0 to D_2 in Figure 10-9 will cause an exodus of firms and, ultimately, a restoration of equilibrium at price $Q_2 P_2$ ($50) and output Q_2 (90,000). A line that connects all points, such as these three, shows the various price-quantity supplied combinations that would be most profitable for the industry when it has had sufficient time to make *all* desired adjustments to assumed changes in industry demand. By definition, this line is the industry's long-run supply curve. In the case of a constant-cost industry, we note that this line — S in Figure 10-10 — is perfectly elastic.

LONG-RUN SUPPLY FOR AN INCREASING-COST INDUSTRY

But constant-cost industries are a special case. Usually, the entry of firms will bid up resource prices and therefore unit costs for individual firms in the industry. Such industries are **increasing-cost industries**. When an industry is using a significant portion of some resource whose total supply is not readily increased, the entry of new firms will increase resource demand in relation to supply and increase resource prices. This is particularly so in industries using specialized resources whose initial supply is not readily increased. Higher resource prices will result in higher long-run average total costs for firms in the industry. The higher costs take the form of an upward shift in the firm's long-run average total cost.

The net result is that when an increase in product demand causes economic profits and attracts new firms to the industry, a two-way squeeze on profits will eliminate those profits. The entry of new firms will increase market supply and lower product price, and the entire average-total-cost curve will shift upward. The equilibrium price will now be higher than it was originally. The industry will produce a larger output at a higher price only because industry expansion has increased average total costs and, in the long run, product price must cover these costs. A greater

industry output will be forthcoming at a higher price, thus the industry supply curve for an increasing-cost industry will be upsloping. Instead of getting either 90,000, 100,000, or 110,000 units at the same price of $50, in an increasing-cost industry 90,000 units might be forthcoming at $45; 100,000 at $50; and 110,000 at $55. The higher price is required to induce more production because costs per unit of output increase as the industry expands.

We show this in Figure 10-11. Original market demand, industry output, and price are D_0, Q_0 (100,000), and Q_0P_0 (50) respectively. An increase in demand to D_1 will upset this equilibrium and lead to economic profits. As firms enter, (1) industry supply will increase, tending to drive product price down to minimum average total cost, and (2) resource prices will rise, causing the average total costs of production to rise. Because of these average-total-cost increases, the new long-run equilibrium price will be established at some level *above* the original price, such as Q_1P_1 (55).

Conversely, a decline in demand from D_0 to D_2 will make production unprofitable and cause firms to leave the industry. The new equilibrium price will be established at some level *below* the original price, such as Q_2P_2 (45). Connecting these three equilibrium positions, we derive an upsloping long-run supply curve shown by S in Figure 10-11.

LONG-RUN SUPPLY FOR A DECREASING-COST INDUSTRY

In industries known as **decreasing-cost industries**, firms may experience lower costs as the industry expands. Classic example: As more mines are established in a given locality, each firm's costs in pumping out water seepage may decline. With more mines pumping, seepage into each is less, and pumping costs are therefore reduced. Furthermore, with only a few mines in an area, industry output might be so small that only relatively primitive and therefore costly transportation facilities are available. But as the number of firms and industry output expand, a railroad might build a spur into the area and thereby significantly reduce transportation costs.

You are urged to replicate the analysis underlying Figure 10-11 to show that the long-run supply curve of a decreasing-cost industry will be *downsloping*. **(Key Question 8)**

FIGURE 10-11 The long-run supply curve for an increasing-cost industry is upsloping

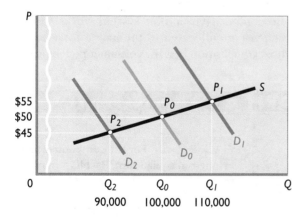

In an increasing-cost industry, the entry of firms in response to increases in demand (D_2 to D_0 to D_1) will bid up resource prices and thereby increase unit costs. As a result, an increased industry output (Q_2 to Q_0 to Q_1) will be forthcoming only at higher prices ($Q_1P_1 > Q_0P_0 > Q_2P_2$). The long-run industry supply curve (S) is therefore upsloping.

PURE COMPETITION AND EFFICIENCY

Whether a purely competitive industry is one of constant or increasing costs, the final long-run equilibrium position for each firm will have the same basic characteristics. As shown in **Figure 10-12 (Key Graph)**, price (and marginal revenue) will settle where they are equal to minimum average total cost. However, we discovered in Chapter 9 that the marginal-cost curve intersects, and is therefore equal to, average total cost at the point of minimum average total cost. In the long-run equilibrium position, "everything is equal." MR (= P) = MC = minimum ATC.

This triple equality tells us that although a competitive firm may realize economic profits or losses in the short run, it will earn only a normal profit by producing in accordance with the MR (= P) = MC rule in the long run. Also, this triple equality suggests certain conclusions of great social significance concerning the efficiency of a purely competitive economy. Subject to certain limitations and exceptions, a purely competitive economy will lead to the most efficient use of society's scarce resources. *A competitive economy will use the limited amounts of resources available to society in a way that maximizes the satisfactions of consumers.* Efficient use of limited resources requires that two conditions — allocative efficiency and productive efficiency — be fulfilled.

First, to achieve **allocative efficiency** resources must be apportioned among firms and industries to obtain the particular mix of products that is most desired by society (consumers). Allocative efficiency is realized when it is impossible to change the composition of total output to achieve a net gain for society.

Second, **productive efficiency** requires that each good in this optimum product mix be produced in the least costly way. To facilitate our discussion of how these conditions would be achieved under purely competitive conditions, let's examine the second point first.

1. PRODUCTIVE EFFICIENCY: *P* = MINIMUM ATC

In the long run, competition forces firms to produce at the point of minimum average total cost of production and to charge that price that is just consistent with these costs. This is a most desirable situation from the consumer's point of view. It means that firms must use the best available (least-cost) technology or they will not survive.

For example, glance back at the final equilibrium position shown in Figure 10-9(a). Each firm in the industry is producing 100 units of output by using $5000 (equal to average cost of $50 *times* 100 units) worth of resources. If that same output had been produced at a total cost of $7000, resources would be used inefficiently. Society would be faced with the net loss of $2000 worth of alternative products. Note too that consumers benefit from the lowest product price possible under the cost conditions currently prevailing.

2. ALLOCATIVE EFFICIENCY: *P* = MC

Production must not only be technologically efficient, but must also be goods consumers want most. The competitive market system works so that resources are allocated to produce a total output whose composition best fits consumer preferences.

KEY GRAPH

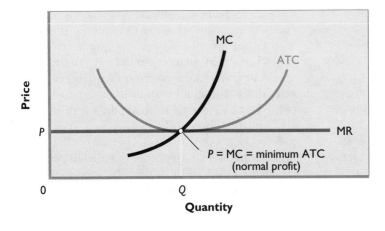

FIGURE 10-12 **For the competitive firm in long-run equilibrium, *P* = MC = minimum ATC**

The equality of price and minimum average total cost indicates that the firm is using the most efficient known technology and is charging the lowest price, P, and producing the greatest output, Q, consistent with its costs. The equality of price and marginal cost indicates that resources are being allocated in accordance with consumer preferences.

BOX 10-2 APPLYING THE THEORY

"CREATIVE DESTRUCTION" AS A COMPETITIVE FORCE

The famous Austrian — later American — economist, Joseph Schumpeter (1883–1950) believed that models such as that of pure competition are inadequate because they view markets in a static or point-in-time framework. Schumpeter argued that technological progress is a much more important dynamic form of competition that occurs over extended periods of time.

Schumpeter viewed competition as a dynamic process involving the development of new products and markets, new production and transportation techniques, and even new forms of business organization. Such innovations were viewed by Schumpeter as a process of "creative destruction" because the creation of new products and production methods simultaneously destroyed the market (often monopoly) positions of firms committed to existing products and old ways of doing business. In Schumpeter's words:

> In capitalist reality ... it is ... competition from the new commodity, the new technology, the new source of supply, the new type of organization (the largest-scale unit of control for instance) — competition which commands a decisive cost or quality advantage and which strikes not at the margins of the profits and the outputs of the existing firms but at their foundations and their very lives. This kind of competition is ... so ... important that it becomes a matter of comparative indifference whether competition in the ordinary sense functions more or less promptly; the powerful lever that in the long run expands output and brings down prices is in any case made of other stuff.[*]

Historical examples of creative destruction as a competitive force are abundant. In the 1800s railroads began to compete with wagons, ships, and barges in transporting freight, only to have their dominant market position undermined by trucks and, still later, by airplanes. Similarly,

the rapid development of the dehydrated and quick-frozen food industries during World War II intensified competition that paper and plastic containers provide for the tin-can industry. Movies competed with the live theatre, only to be challenged in turn by television. Typewriter manufacturers face severe competition because of the development of word processors and personal computers. Cable television assaults the networks; fax machines replace mail; mass discounters such as Wal-Mart attack Eaton's and The Bay; personal computers challenge mainframe computers, to the dismay of IBM.

Acetate 78-rpm phonograph records were supplanted by vinyl long-playing records after World War II. Cassettes then challenged LP records. More recently, the development of compact discs has doomed the LP record. In 1983, when CDs were introduced, record companies shipped over 295 million LPs and only 800,000 CDs. In 1991 less than 5 million LPs were produced, compared to 333 million CDs. CDs have also put a competitive squeeze on cassettes, whose shipments fell from 450 million in 1988 to 360 million in 1991.

The point is that competition must be defined more broadly than simply entry of firms to existing profitable industries. Technological progress leads to a competitive force that over time can undermine existing industries — even monopolies — and eliminate economic profits.

[*] Joseph A. Schumpeter, *Capitalism, Socialism, and Democracy*, 3d ed. (New York: Harper & Row, Publishers, Incorporated, 1950), pp. 84-85.

We must first grasp the social meaning of competitive product and resource prices. *The price of any product — product X — is society's measure of the relative worth of that product at the margin.* Price reflects the marginal benefit derived from that good. Similarly, recalling the notion of opportunity costs, *the marginal cost of producing X measures the value of*

the other goods that the resources used in the production of an extra unit of X could otherwise have produced. In short, product price measures the marginal benefit, or satisfaction, that society gets from additional units of X, and the marginal cost of an additional unit of X measures the sacrifice, or cost to society, of other goods in using resources to produce more of X.

UNDER-ALLOCATION: P > MC Under competition, the production of each product will occur up to that precise point at which price is equal to marginal cost (Figure 10-12). The profit-seeking competitor will realize the maximum possible profit only by equating price and marginal cost. To produce short of the MR (= P) = MC point will mean less than maximum profits to the individual firm and an *under*-allocation of resources to this product from society's standpoint. The fact that price exceeds marginal cost indicates that society values additional units of X more highly than the alternative products the appropriate resources could otherwise produce.

OVER-ALLOCATION: P < MC For similar reasons, the production of X should not go beyond the output at which price equals marginal cost. To do so means less than maximum profits for producers and an *over*-allocation of resources to X from the standpoint of society. To produce X at some point at which marginal cost exceeds price means that resources are being used in the production of X at the sacrifice of alternative goods that society values more highly than the added units of X.

EFFICIENT ALLOCATION Our conclusion is that **under pure competition, producers will produce each commodity up to that precise point where price (marginal benefit) and marginal cost are equal. This means that resources are efficiently allocated under competition**. Each good is produced to the point at which the value of the last unit is equal to the value of the alternative goods sacrificed by its production.

DYNAMIC ADJUSTMENTS A further attribute of purely competitive markets is their ability to restore efficiency in the use of resources when disrupted by dynamic changes in the economy. In a competitive economy, any changes in consumer tastes, resource supplies, or technology will automatically set in motion appropriate realignments of resources.

As we have already explained, an increase in consumer demand for product X will increase its price. Disequilibrium will occur in that at its present output, the price of X will now exceed its marginal cost. This will create economic profits in industry X and stimulate its expansion. Its profitability will permit the industry to bid resources

away from now less pressing uses. Expansion in this industry will end only when the price of X again equals its marginal cost, that is, when the value of the last unit produced once again equals the value of the alternative goods society forgoes in producing the last unit of X.

"INVISIBLE HAND" REVISITED A final point: The highly efficient allocation of resources that a purely competitive economy fosters comes about because businesses and resource suppliers seek to further their own self-interests. The "invisible hand" (Chapter 3) is at work in a competitive market system. In a competitive economy, businesses employ resources until the extra, or marginal, costs of production equal the product price. This not only maximizes profits for individual producers but simultaneously results in a pattern of resource allocation that maximizes consumer satisfaction. The competitive market system organizes the private interests of producers along lines that are fully in accord with society's interest in using scarce resources efficiently. **(Key Question 10)**

QUICK REVIEW 10-4

1. In the long run the entry of firms will compete away profits and the exodus of firms will eliminate losses so that price equals minimum average total cost.

2. The long-run supply curves of constant-, increasing-, and decreasing-cost industries are perfectly elastic, upsloping, and downsloping, respectively.

3. In purely competitive markets both productive efficiency (price equals minimum average total cost) and allocative efficiency (price equals marginal cost) are achieved in the long run.

QUALIFICATIONS

Our conclusion that a purely competitive market system results in both productive and allocative efficiency must be qualified in several respects.

THE INCOME DISTRIBUTION PROBLEM The contention that pure competition will allocate resources efficiently is predicated on some particular distribution of money income resulting in a certain structure of demand. The competitive market system then brings about an efficient allocation of resources or, stated differently, an output of goods and services whose composition maximizes fulfilment of these particular consumer demands.

But if the distribution of money income is altered so that the structure of demand changes, would the competitive market system negotiate a new allocation of resources? Yes, the market system would reallocate resources and therefore change the composition of output to maximize the fulfilment of this new pattern of consumer wants. The question, then, is which of these two "efficient" allocations of resources is the "most efficient"? Which allocation of resources yields the greatest level of satisfaction to society?

There is no *scientific* answer to this question. If all people were alike in their capacities to get satisfaction from income and their contribution to output, economists could recommend that income be distributed equally and that the allocation of resources appropriate to *that* distribution would be the "best" or "most efficient" of all. But people differ in their education, productivity, experiences, and environment, as well as their mental and physical characteristics. Such differences can be used to argue for an unequal distribution of income.

The distribution of income associated with the working of the competitive market system is quite unequal and therefore may lead to the production of luxury items for the rich while denying the basic needs of the poor. Many economists believe that the distribution of income that pure competition provides should be modified by public action. They maintain that allocative efficiency is hardly a virtue if it is a response to an income distribution that offends prevailing standards of equity.

MARKET FAILURE: SPILLOVERS AND PUBLIC GOODS

Under competition each producer will assume only those costs which it *must* pay. This correctly implies that in some lines of production there are significant costs producers can and do avoid, usually by polluting the environment. Recall from Chapter 5 that these avoided costs accrue to society and are aptly called **spillover** or **external costs**. On the other hand, consumption of certain goods and services, such as education and measles vaccinations, yields widespread satisfactions, or benefits, to society as a whole. These satisfactions are called **external** or **spillover benefits**.

The profit-seeking activities of producers will bring about an allocation of resources that is efficient from society's point of view only if marginal cost embodies *all* the costs that production entails and product price accurately reflects *all* the benefits that society gets from a good's production. Only in this case will competitive production at the MR (= P) = MC point balance the *total* sacrifices and satisfactions of society and result in an efficient allocation of resources. If price and marginal cost are not accurate indexes of sacrifices and satisfactions — if sizable spillover costs and benefits exist — production at the MR (= P) = MC point will *not* signify an efficient allocation of resources.

Remember, too, the point of the lighthouse example in Chapter 5: The market system does not provide for social or public goods, that is, for goods to which the exclusion principle does *not* apply. Despite its other virtues, the competitive price system ignores an important class of goods and services — national defence, flood-control programs, and so forth — which can and do yield satisfaction to consumers but which cannot be priced and sold through the market system.

PRODUCTION TECHNIQUES

Purely competitive markets may not always entail the use of the most efficient productive techniques or encourage development of improved techniques. There are both a static (or "right now") aspect and a dynamic (or "over time") aspect of this criticism.

NATURAL MONOPOLIES

The static aspect involves the *natural monopoly* problem introduced in Chapter 9. In certain lines of production, existing technology may be such that a firm must be a large-scale producer to realize the lowest unit costs of production. Given consumer demand, this suggests that a relatively small number of large-scale producers is needed if production is to be carried on efficiently. Existing mass-production economies might be lost if such an industry were populated by the large number of small-scale producers that pure competition requires.

TECHNOLOGICAL PROGRESS

The dynamic aspect of this criticism concerns the willingness and ability of purely competitive firms to undertake technological advance. The progressiveness of pure competition is debated by economists. Some authorities believe that a purely competitive economy would *not* foster a very rapid rate of technological progress. They argue, first, that the incentive for technological advance may be weak under pure competition because the profit rewards accruing to an innovating firm from a cost-reducing technological improvement will be quickly competed away by rival firms adopting the new technique. Second, the small size of the typical competitive firm and the fact that it tends to "break even" in the long run raise serious questions whether such producers could finance substantial programs of organized research.

RANGE OF CONSUMER CHOICE   A purely competitive economy might not provide sufficient range of consumer choice or foster development of new products. This criticism, like the previous one, has both a static and a dynamic aspect. Pure competition means product standardization, whereas other market structures — for example, monopolistic competition and, frequently, oligopoly — encom-

pass a wide range of types, styles, and quality gradations of any product. This product differentiation widens the consumer's range of free choice and simultaneously allows buyers to more completely fulfil their preferences. Similarly, critics of pure competition point out that, just as pure competition is not likely to be progressive in developing new productive techniques, neither is this market structure conducive to improving existing products or creating completely new ones.

The question of the progressiveness of various market structures in terms of both productive techniques and product development will recur in the following three chapters.[2]

---

[2] Instructors who want to consider agriculture as a case study in pure competition should insert Chapter 21 at this point.

CHAPTER SUMMARY

1. The market structures of **a** pure competition, **b** pure monopoly, **c** monopolistic competition, and **d** oligopoly are classifications into which most industries can be fitted with reasonable accuracy.

2. A purely competitive industry comprises a large number of independent firms producing a standardized product. Pure competition assumes that firms and resources are mobile among different industries.

3. No single firm can influence market price in a competitive industry; the firm's demand curve is perfectly elastic and price therefore equals marginal revenue.

4. Short-run profit maximization by a competitive firm can be analyzed by a comparison of total revenue and total cost or through marginal analysis. A firm will maximize profits by producing that output at which total revenue exceeds total cost by the greatest amount. Losses will be minimized by producing where the excess of total cost over total revenue is at a minimum and less than total fixed costs.

5. Provided price exceeds minimum average variable cost, a competitive firm will maximize profits or minimize losses in the short run by producing at that output at which price or marginal revenue equals marginal cost. If price is less than average variable cost, the firm will minimize its losses by closing down. If price is greater than average variable cost but less than average total cost, the firm will minimize its losses by producing the $P = MC$ output. If price exceeds average total cost, the $P = MC$ output will provide maximum economic profits for the firm.

6. Applying the MR $(= P) = MC$ rule at various possible market prices leads to the conclusion that the segment of the firm's short-run marginal-cost curve lying above average variable cost is its short-run supply curve.

7. In the long run, competitive price will equal the minimum average total cost of production because economic profits will cause firms to enter a competitive industry until those profits

have been competed away. Conversely, losses will force the exodus of firms from the industry until product price once again barely covers unit costs.

8. The long-run supply curve is perfectly elastic for a constant-cost industry, upsloping for an increasing-cost industry, and downsloping for a decreasing cost industry.

9. The long-run equality of price and minimum average total cost means that competitive firms will use the most efficient known (least-cost) technology and charge the lowest price consistent with their production costs. The equality of price and marginal cost implies that resources will be allocated in accordance with consumer tastes. The competitive price system will reallocate resources in response to a change in consumer tastes, technology, or resource supplies to maintain allocative efficiency over time.

10. The equality of price and marginal cost implies that resources will be allocated in accordance with consumer tastes. The competitive price system will reallocate resources in response to a change in consumer tastes, technology, or resource supplies to maintain allocative efficiency over time.

11. There are four possible deterrents to allocative efficiency in a competitive economy. **a** There is no reason why the competitive market system will result in an optimal distribution of income. **b** In allocating resources, the competitive model does not allow for spillover costs and benefits or for the production of public goods. **c** A purely competitive industry may preclude the use of the best-known productive techniques and foster a slow rate of technological advance. **d** A competitive system provides neither a wide range of product choice nor an environment conducive to the development of new products.

TERMS AND CONCEPTS

allocative efficiency (p. 214)
average, total, and marginal revenue (p. 197)
break-even point (p. 199)
close-down case (p. 201)
constant-cost industry (p. 212)
decreasing-cost industries (p. 213)
external costs and benefits (p. 217)
imperfect competition (p. 194)
increasing-cost industries (p. 213)
long-run supply curve (p. 211)
loss-minimizing case (p. 203)
market failure (p. 217)

monopolistic competition (p. 194)
MR (= P) = MC rule (p. 202)
oligopoly (p. 194)
P = MC rule (p. 202)
price taker (p. 196)
productive efficiency (p. 214)
profit-maximizing case (p. 202)
pure competition (p. 194)
pure monopoly (p. 194)
short-run supply curve (p. 206)
spillover costs and benefits (p. 217)

QUESTIONS AND STUDY SUGGESTIONS

1. Briefly indicate the basic characteristics of pure competition, pure monopoly, monopolistic competition, and oligopoly. Under which of these market structures does each of the following most accurately fit: a. a supermarket in your home town; b. the steel industry; c. Manitoba wheat farm; d. the chartered bank in which you or your family has an account; e. the automobile industry. In each case justify your classification.

2. Strictly speaking, pure competition never has existed and probably never will. Then why study it?

3. *Key Question* Use following demand schedule to determine total and marginal revenues for each possible level of sales.

Product price	Quantity demanded	Total revenue	Marginal revenue
$2	0	$ _____	
2	1	_____	$ _____
2	2	_____	_____
2	3	_____	_____
2	4	_____	_____
2	5	_____	_____

a. What can you conclude about the structure of the industry in which this firm is operating? Explain.

b. Graph the demand, total-revenue, and marginal-revenue curves for this firm.

c. Why do the demand and marginal-revenue curves coincide?

d. "Marginal revenue is the change in total revenue." Do you agree? Explain verbally and graphically, using the above data.

4. *Key Question* Assume the following unit-cost data for a purely competitive producer:

Total product	Average fixed cost	Average variable cost	Average total cost	Marginal cost
0				
1	$60.00	$45.00	$105.00	
2	30.00	42.50	72.50	40
3	20.00	40.00	60.00	35
4	15.00	37.50	52.50	30
5	12.00	37.00	49.00	35
6	10.00	37.50	47.50	40
7	8.57	38.57	47.14	45
8	7.50	40.63	48.13	55
9	6.67	43.33	50.00	65
10	6.00	46.50	52.50	75

a. At a product price of $32, will this firm produce in the short run? Why or why not? If it does produce, what will be the profit-maximizing or loss-minimizing output? Explain. Specify the amount of economic profit or loss per unit of output.

b. Answer the questions of 4(a) assuming product price is $41.

c. Answer the questions of 4(a) assuming product price is $56.

d. Complete the short-run supply schedule shown below for the firm, and indicate the profit or loss incurred at each output (columns 1 to 3).

(1) Price	(2) Quantity supplied, single firm	(3) Profit (+) or loss (-)	(4) Quantity supplied, 1500 firms
$26	_____	$ _____	_____
32	_____	_____	_____
38	_____	_____	_____
41	_____	_____	_____
46	_____	_____	_____
56	_____	_____	_____
66	_____	_____	_____

e. *Explain:"That segment of a competitive firm's marginal-cost curve that lies above its average-variable-cost curve constitutes the short-run supply curve for the firm." Illustrate graphically.*

f. *Now assume there are 1500 identical firms in this competitive industry; that is, there are 1500 firms, each of which has the same cost data as shown here. Calculate the industry supply schedule (column 4).*

g. *Suppose the market demand for the product is as follows:*

Price	Total quantity demanded
$26	17,000
32	15,000
38	13,500
41	12,000
46	10,500
56	9,500
66	8,000

What will equilibrium price be? What will equilibrium output be for the industry? For each firm? What will profit or loss be per unit? Per firm? Will this industry expand or contract in the long run?

5. Why is the equality of marginal revenue and marginal cost essential for profit maximization in all market structures? Explain why price can be substituted for marginal revenue in the MR = MC rule when an industry is purely competitive.

6. Explain:"A competitive producer must look to average variable cost in determining whether to produce in the short run, to marginal cost in deciding upon the best volume of production, and to average total cost to calculate profits or losses." Why might a firm produce at a loss in the short run rather than close down?

7. Many grocery stores in urban areas now stay open 24 hours a day even though they have rela- tively few customers at night. Distinguishing between fixed and marginal costs, explain how this strategy might maximize a firm's profits.

8. *Key Question* *Using diagrams for both the industry and a representative firm, illustrate competitive long- run equilibrium. Employing these diagrams, show how a. an increase, and b. a decrease in market demand will upset this long-run equilibrium. Trace graphically and describe verbally the adjustment processes by which the long-run equilibrium is restored. Assume the industry is one of constant costs. Now rework your analysis for increasing and decreasing cost industries and compare the three long-run supply curves.*

9. Suppose a decrease in demand occurs in a competitive increasing-cost industry. Contrast the product price and industry output existing after all long-run adjustments are completed with those that originally prevailed.

10. *Key Question* *In long-run equilibrium, P = minimum ATC = MC. Of what significance for the alloca- tion of resources is the equality of P and minimum ATC? The equality of P and MC? Distinguish between productive and allocative efficiency in your answer.*

11. Explain why some economists believe that an unequal distribution of income might impair the efficiency with which a competitive market system allocates resources. What other criticisms can be made of a purely competitive economy?

12. (Applying the Theory) What is Schumpeter's process of "creative destruction"? How does it function as a competitive force?

PRICE AND OUTPUT DETERMINATION: PURE MONOPOLY

We deal with monopolies — sole sellers of various products and services — daily. When we mail a letter, we are using the services of Canada Post, a government-sponsored monopoly. Similarly, when we use the telephone, turn on the lights, or subscribe to cable TV, we are patronizing monopolies.

We now jump to the opposite end of the industry spectrum and examine the characteristics, price-output behaviour, and social desirability of pure monopoly. How is a pure monopoly defined? What conditions underlie its existence? How does a monopolist's price-output behaviour compare with that of a purely competitive industry? Do monopolists achieve the allocative and productive efficiency associated with pure competition? If not, can government policies improve the price-output behaviour of a pure monopolist?

BOX 11-1 THE BIG PICTURE

If you owned a firm producing a product or providing a service, you would prefer it to be the only firm of its type, and the demand for its product to be strong and price inelastic. Under these conditions, your firm would probably make economic profits. You would undoubtedly attract envy from competitors and potential competitors; in a world pervaded by scarcities, others would want a piece of the (your) action.

But consumers would not be happy; they would have to pay a higher price for your firm's product compared to a situation where your firm had many competitors. Thus, there is a serious conflict between what is good for your firm and what is good for society (consumers). Monopoly — what you wish for your firm — stands much in contrast to pure competition, where the conflict between the firm and consumers is mitigated. Recall that the pure competitive model ensures firms produce at the lowest possible price (productive efficiency) and also produce those goods and services consumers want most (allocative efficiency). To this end, the pure competitive model ensures a society is getting the most out of its limited resources. The monopoly model serves to demonstrate two important points: (a) the inefficiencies of a one-firm

industry — neither productive nor allocative efficiencies are achieved — and (b) the difficulty of maintaining a monopoly. A monopoly is difficult to maintain because economic profits attract other firms to the industry. Only if it is impossible for others to enter the industry will a monopoly persist.

As you read this chapter, keep the following points in mind:
- Despite what you may believe, a monopolist cannot charge any price it wants; a monopolist is constrained by the demand curve.
- There is no industry supply curve. Whatever is supplied by the monopolist is also the industry supply curve.
- A natural monopoly is one in which the average total cost falls continuously over a significant range as the size of the firm increases. Examples of natural monopolies are utility companies — water, gas, hydro. Since natural monopolies can produce at the lowest possible unit cost, they are beneficial. But in the absence of competition, a natural monopoly could make economic profits, thus to protect consumers' interests, natural monopolies are regulated by governments.

PURE MONOPOLY: AN INTRODUCTION

Absolute or pure monopoly *exists when a single firm is the sole producer of a product or provider of a service for which there are no close substitutes.* Let's first examine the characteristics of pure monopoly and then discuss a few examples.

CHARACTERISTICS

1. SINGLE SELLER   A pure monopolist is a one-firm industry. A single firm is the only producer of a given product or the sole supplier of a service; the firm and the industry are synonymous.

2. NO CLOSE SUBSTITUTES   The monopolist's product is unique in that there are no close substitutes available. From the buyer's viewpoint, there are no reasonable alternatives. The buyer who does

not buy the product or service from the monopolist has no alternative but to do without.

3. "PRICE MAKER"   The individual firm operating under pure competition exercises no influence over product price; it is a "price taker." This is so because it contributes only a negligible portion of total supply. In contrast, the pure monopolist is a **price maker**; the firm exercises considerable control over price because it controls the total quantity supplied. Confronted with a downsloping demand curve for its product, the monopolist can change product price by manipulating the quantity of the product supplied. If it is advantageous, the monopolist will use this power.

4. BLOCKED ENTRY   A pure monopolist has no immediate competitors because there are **barriers to entry**. Economic, technological, legal, or other obstacles must exist to keep new competitors from coming into the industry if monopoly is to

persist. Entry under conditions of pure monopoly is totally blocked.

EXAMPLES

In most cities government-owned or -regulated public utilities — gas and electric companies, the water company, the telephone company, the cable TV company, and the public transit system — are all monopolies or virtually so. There are no close substitutes for goods and services provided by these public utilities. Candles or kerosene lights are very imperfect substitutes for electricity; telegrams, letters, and courier services can be substituted for the telephone. But such substitutes are either costly, less convenient, or unappealing.

The classic example of a private, unregulated monopoly is the De Beers diamond syndicate, which effectively controls 80% to 90% of the world's supply of diamonds. But in Canada major manufacturing monopolies are rare and frequently transient because in time new competitors emerge to erode their single-producer status.

Professional sports leagues create monopoly power by granting member clubs franchises to be the sole suppliers of their services in designated geographic areas. The larger Canadian cities are served by a single professional baseball, football, or hockey team. If you want to see a live major-league professional hockey game in Calgary or Montreal, you have no choice but to patronize the Flames and the Canadiens, respectively.

Monopoly may also be geographic. A small town may be served by only one airline or railway. The local bank branch, movie theatre, or bookstore may approximate a monopoly in a small and isolated community.

IMPORTANCE

We should understand the workings of pure monopoly for two reasons.

1. A not insignificant amount of economic activity — perhaps 5 or 6% of the GDP — is carried out under conditions approaching pure monopoly.
2. A study of pure monopoly yields valuable insights into monopolistic competition and oligopoly, which will be discussed in Chapters 12 and 13. These two market structures combine in differing degrees characteristics of pure competition and pure monopoly.

BARRIERS TO ENTRY

The absence of competitors in pure monopoly is explainable by factors that prohibit firms from entering an industry. These barriers to entry also explain the existence of oligopoly and monopolistic competition between the market extremes of pure competition and pure monopoly. In pure monopoly, entry barriers effectively block all potential competition.

What forms do these entry barriers assume?

ECONOMIES OF SCALE

Modern technology in some industries is such that efficient, low-cost production can be achieved only if producers are extremely large both absolutely and in relation to the market. Where economies of scale are very significant, a firm's long-run average-cost schedule will decline over a wide range of output [Figure 9-9(b)]. Given market demand, achieving low unit costs depends on the existence of a small number of firms or, in the extreme case, only one firm.

Figure 11-1 is helpful. Here we observe economies of scale — that is, declining average total costs — throughout the relevant range of production. As a result, any particular level of output can be produced at the least cost when there is a single producer — a monopoly. Note that the monopoly could produce 200 units at a per-unit cost of $10 for a total cost of $2000. If two firms

FIGURE II-I Economies of scale: the natural monopoly case

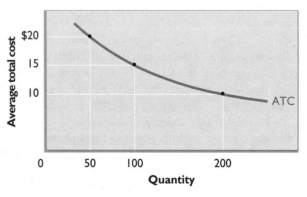

If average total costs decline over an extended range of output, least cost production may be realized only if there is a single producer. This is what defines a natural monopoly.

made up the industry and each produced 100 units, unit cost would be $15 and total cost would rise to $3000 (200 × $15). A still more competitive situation with four firms each producing 50 units would boost unit and total costs to $20 and $4000 (200 × $20) respectively. Conclusion: To produce any output with minimum total cost — with the fewest resources — the industry must be a pure monopoly.

If a pure monopoly initially exists, it is easy to see why economies of scale will function as an entry barrier to protect that firm from competition. New firms attempting to enter the industry as small-scale producers will have little or no chance to survive and expand. Small-scale entrants cannot realize the cost economies of the monopolist and therefore cannot realize the profits necessary for survival and growth.

The other option is to start out big — to enter the industry as a large-scale producer. But it is extremely difficult for a new and untried firm to secure the money capital needed to obtain the massive capital facilities required to realize all economies of scale. The financial obstacles to "starting big" are so great in most cases as to be prohibitive. Economies of scale explain why efforts to enter such industries as automobiles, aluminum, and basic steel are rare.

The circumstances we have just described define a natural monopoly. A **natural monopoly** exists when economies of scale are so great that a good or service con be produced by one firm at an average total cost lower than if produced by more than one firm. The monopoly's lower unit costs allow it to charge a lower price than if the industry were more competitive. But this may not happen. As we will see, a pure monopolist may set its price far above unit costs and realize substantial economic profits. The cost advantage of a natural monopoly may accrue to the monopolist as profits and not to consumers in the form of lower prices. It is for this reason that governments regulate natural monopolies, specifying the price they may charge.

Most of the so-called public utilities — electric and gas companies, local water and telephone companies — are regulated natural monopolies. It would be wasteful if a community had several firms supplying water or electricity. Technology is such in these industries that large-scale and extensive capital expenditures on generators, pumping and purification equipment, water mains, and transmission lines are required. This problem is aggravated because

capital equipment must be sufficient to meet peak demands on hot summer days when lawns are being watered and air conditioners operated.

So single producers are given exclusive franchises by government. But in return for this sole right to supply electricity, water, or telephone services to a particular geographic area, government reserves the right to regulate their prices and services to prevent abuses of the monopoly power it has granted. Some of the problems associated with regulation are considered later in this chapter and in Chapter 14.

LEGAL BARRIERS: PATENTS AND LICENCES

We have just noted that government frequently gives exclusive franchises to natural monopolies. Government also creates legal entry barriers in awarding patents and licences.

PATENTS By granting an inventor the exclusive right to produce or license a product for 17 years, Canadian patent laws are aimed at protecting the inventor from having the product or process usurped by rivals who have not shared in the time, effort, and money outlays that have gone into its development. At the same time patents may provide the inventor with a monopoly position for the life of the patent.

Patent control was important in the growth of modern-day industrial giants — National Cash Register, General Motors, Xerox, Polaroid, General Electric, and Du Pont. The United Shoe Machinery Company in the United States is a notable example of how patent control can be abused to achieve monopoly power. United Shoe became the exclusive supplier of certain essential shoemaking machinery by requiring all lessees of its patented machine to sign a "tying agreement" in which shoe manufacturers agreed also to lease all other shoemaking machinery from United Shoe. This allowed United Shoe to monopolize the market until partially effective anti-trust action was taken by the United States government in 1955.

Research is usually required for the development of patentable products. Firms that gain monopoly power by their own research or by purchasing the patents of others can consolidate and strengthen their market position. The profits from one patent can finance the research required to develop new patentable products. In the pharmaceutical industry patents on prescription drugs have produced large monopoly profits that have helped finance the discovery of new patentable medicines. Monopoly power achieved through patents may well be self-sustaining.

LICENCES   Entry into an industry or occupation may be limited by government licensing. At the national level the Canadian Radio-television and Telecommunications Commission licenses radio and television stations. In many large cities you need a municipal licence to drive a taxicab. The restriction of the supply of cabs creates monopoly earnings for cab owners and drivers. In a few instances government might license itself to provide some product and thereby create a public monopoly. For example, the sale of liquor in each province is exclusively through provincially owned retail outlets. Many provinces have "licensed" themselves to run lotteries.

OWNERSHIP OF ESSENTIAL INPUTS

A firm owning or controlling a resource that is essential in production can prohibit the creation of rival firms. The Aluminum Company of America retained its monopoly position in the aluminum industry for many years through its control of all basic sources of bauxite, the major ore used in producing aluminum ingots. The International Nickel Company of Canada (Inco) used to control approximately 90% of the world's known nickel reserves. Most of the world's diamond mines are owned or effectively controlled by the De Beers Company of South Africa. Similarly, it is very difficult for new professional sports leagues to evolve when existing leagues have contracts with the best players and leases on the major stadiums and arenas.

TWO IMPLICATIONS

Our discussion of barriers to entry suggests two important points about monopoly.

1. RELATIVELY RARE   Barriers to entry are rarely complete — meaning pure monopoly is relatively rare. Although research and technological advances may strengthen the market position of a firm, technology may also undermine existing monopoly power.

Over time the creation of new technologies can destroy existing monopoly positions. The development of courier delivery systems, fax machines, and electronic mail has eroded the monopoly power of the postal service. Cable television monopolies are challenged by new technologies that enable telephone companies to transmit audio and visual signals and thereby provide TV programs to consumers at any time they choose to view them.

Similarly, existing patent advantages may be circumvented by the development of new and distinct, yet substitutable, products. New sources of strategic resources may be found. It is probably only a modest overstatement to say that monopoly in the sense of a one-firm industry persists over time only with the sanction or aid of government, as with the postal service's monopoly on the delivery of first-class mail.

2. DESIRABILITY   We have implied that monopolies may be desirable or undesirable from the standpoint of economic efficiency. The public-utilities and economics-of-scale arguments suggest that market demand and technology may be such that efficient, low-cost production presupposes the existence of monopoly. On the other hand, our comments on inputs ownership, patents, and licensing as sources of monopoly imply undesirable connotations of monopoly.

MONOPOLY DEMAND

Let's begin our analysis of the price-output behaviour of a pure monopolist by making three assumptions.

1. Our monopolist's status is secured by patents, economies of scale, or resource ownership.
2. The firm is *not* regulated by government.
3. The firm is a single-price monopolist; it charges the same price for all units of output.

The crucial difference between a pure monopolist and a purely competitive seller is on the demand side of the market. Recall from Chapter 10 that the purely competitive seller faces a perfectly elastic demand schedule at the market price determined by industry supply and demand. The competitive firm is a "price taker" that can sell as much or as little as it wants at the going market price.

The monopolist's demand curve — indeed, the demand curve of *any* imperfectly competitive seller — is much different. Because the pure monopolist is the industry, its demand curve is the industry demand curve.[1] And the industry demand curve is not perfectly elastic; it is downsloping. This is illustrated by columns 1 and 2 of Table 11-1.

There are three implications of a downsloping demand curve you must understand.

1. PRICE EXCEEDS MARGINAL REVENUE A downsloping demand curve means that a pure monopoly can increase its sales only by charging a lower unit price for its product. *Since the monopolist must lower price to boost sales, marginal revenue is less than price (average revenue) for every level of output except the first.* The reason? Price cuts will apply not only to the extra output sold but also to *all* other units of output.

In Figure 11-2 we have extracted two price-quantity combinations — $142-3 units and $132-4 units — from the monopolist's demand curve. By lowering price from $142 to $132, the monopolist can sell one

_____
[1] Recall in Chapter 10 that we presented separate diagrams for the purely competitive industry *and* for a single firm in that industry. Because with pure monopoly the firm and the industry are one and the same, we need only a single diagram.

FIGURE 11-2   Price and marginal revenue under pure monopoly

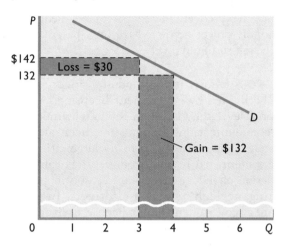

A pure monopolist — or any imperfect competitor with a downsloping demand curve — must reduce price to sell more output. As a consequence, marginal revenue will be less than price. In our example, by reducing price from $142 to $132 the monopolist gains $132 from the sale of the fourth unit. But from this gain must be subtracted $30, which reflects the $10 price cut that has been made on each of the first three units. Hence, the fourth unit's marginal revenue is $102 (= $132 − $30), considerably less than its $132 price.

TABLE 11-1   Revenue and cost data of a pure monopolist

Revenue data				Cost data			
(1) Quantity of output	(2) Price (average revenue)	(3) Total revenue	(4) Marginal revenue	(5) Average total cost	(6) Total cost	(7) Marginal cost	(8) Profit (+) or loss (−)
0	$172	$ 0			$ 100		$ −100
1	162	162	$162	$190.00	190	$ 90	− 28
2	152	304	142	135.00	270	80	+ 34
3	142	426	122	113.33	340	70	+ 86
4	132	528	102	100.00	400	60	+128
5	122	610	82	94.00	470	70	+140
6	112	672	62	91.67	550	80	+122
7	102	714	42	91.43	640	90	+ 74
8	92	736	22	93.73	750	110	− 14
9	82	738	2	97.78	880	130	−142
10	72	720	− 18	103.00	1030	150	−310

more unit and gain as revenue the fourth unit's price of $132 as indicated. This gain is designated as the shaded rectangle in Figure 11-2. But to sell this fourth unit for $132, the monopolist must lower price on the first three units from $142 to $132. This $10 price reduction on 3 units results in a $30 revenue loss. The *net* change in total revenue or, in other words, marginal revenue, from selling the fourth unit is $102 — the $132 gain minus the $30 loss.

This same idea is evident in Table 11-1 where we observe that marginal revenue of the second unit of output is $142 rather than its $152 price because a $10 price cut must be taken on the first unit to increase sales from 1 to 2 units. Similarly, to sell 3 units, the firm must lower price from $152 to $142.

The resulting marginal revenue will be $122 — the $142 addition to total revenue the third unit of sales provides less $10 price cuts on the first 2 units of output. This rationale explains why the marginal-revenue data of column 4 of Table 11-1 fall short of product price in column 2 for all levels of output except the first. Because marginal revenue is by definition the increase in total revenue associated with each additional unit of output, the declining marginal revenue figures mean total revenue will increase at a diminishing rate, as shown in column 3 of Table 11-1.

The relationships between the demand, marginal revenue, and total revenue curves are shown in Figure 11-3(a) and (b). In this diagram we have extended the demand and revenue data of columns 1 to 4 of Table

---

FIGURE 11-3   Demand, marginal revenue, and total revenue of an imperfectly competitive firm

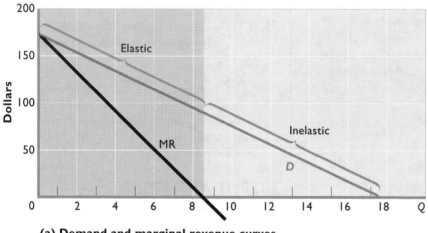

(a) Demand and marginal revenue curves

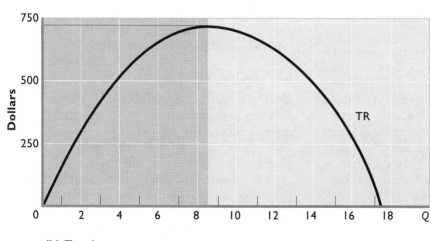

(b) Total revenue curve

Because it must lower price to increase its sales, an imperfectly competitive firm's marginal-revenue curve (MR) lies below its downsloping demand curve (D). Total revenue (TR) increases at a decreasing rate, reaches a maximum, and then declines. Note that because MR is the change in TR, a unique relationship exists between MR and TR. In moving down the elastic segment of the demand curve, TR is increasing and hence MR is positive. When TR reaches its maximum, MR is zero. In moving down the inelastic segment of the demand curve, TR is declining, so MR is negative. A monopolist or other imperfectly competitive seller will never choose to lower price into the inelastic segment of its demand curve because by doing so, it will simultaneously reduce total revenue and increase production costs, thereby lowering profits.

11-1 by continuing to assume that successive $10 price cuts will each elicit one additional unit of sales. That is, 11 units can be sold at $62, 12 at $52, and so forth.

In addition to the fact that the marginal revenue curve lies *below* the demand curve, note the special relationship between total revenue and marginal revenue. Because marginal revenue is by definition the change in total revenue, we observe that so long as total revenue is increasing, marginal revenue is positive. When total revenue reaches its maximum, marginal revenue is zero. When total revenue is diminishing marginal revenue is negative.

2. PRICE MAKER

In all imperfectly competitive markets in which downsloping demand curves are relevant — purely monopolistic, oligopolistic, and monopolistically competitive markets — firms have a price policy. By virtue of their ability to influence total supply, the output decisions of these firms necessarily affect product price. This is most evident in pure monopoly, where one firm controls total output. Faced with a downsloping demand curve in which each output is associated with some unique price, the monopolist automatically determines price in deciding what volume of output to produce.

The monopolist simultaneously chooses both price and output. In columns 1 and 2 of Table 11-1, we find that the monopolist can sell only an output of 1 unit at a price of $162, only an output of 2 units at a price of $152, and so forth.

This does not mean that the monopolist is "free" of market forces in establishing price and output, or that the consumer is completely at the monopolist's mercy. The monopolist's downsloping demand curve means that it cannot raise price without losing sales or gain sales without charging a lower price.

3. PRICE ELASTICITY

The total-revenue test for price elasticity of demand is the basis for our third conclusion. Recall from Chapter 7 that the total-revenue test tells us that when demand is elastic, a decline in price will increase total revenue. Beginning at the top of the demand curve in Figure 11-3(a), observe that for all price reductions from $172 down to approximately $82, total revenue increases (and marginal revenue therefore is positive). This means that demand is elastic in this price range. Conversely, for price reductions below $82, total revenue decreases (marginal revenue is negative), which indicates the demand is inelastic.

Our generalization is that a monopolist will never choose a price-quantity combination where total revenue is decreasing (marginal revenue is negative). *The profit-maximizing monopolist will always want to avoid the inelastic segment of its demand curve in favour of some price-quantity combination in the elastic segment.* By lowering price into the inelastic range, total revenue will decline. But the lower price is associated with a larger output and therefore increased total costs. Lower revenue and higher costs mean diminished profits. **(Key Question 4)**

QUICK REVIEW 11-1

1. A pure monopolist is the sole supplier of a product or service for which there are no close substitutes.

2. Monopolies exist because of entry barriers such as economies of scale, patents and licences, and the ownership of essential resources.

3. The monopolist's demand curve is downsloping, causing the marginal revenue curve to lie below it.

4. The downsloping demand curve means that the monopolist is a "price maker."

5. As long as a firm is on the inelastic segment of its demand curve, it can increase total revenue and reduce total costs — thereby increasing profits — by raising price.

OUTPUT AND PRICE DETERMINATION

What specific price-quantity combination on its demand curve will a profit-maximizing monopolist choose? To answer this question we need to add production costs to our understanding of monopoly demand.

COST DATA

On the cost side, we will assume that although the firm is a monopolist in the product market, it hires resources competitively and employs the same technology as our competitive firm in the preceding chapter. This allows us to use the cost data developed in Chapter 9 and applied in Chapter 10 so we can compare the price-output decisions of a pure monopoly with those of a pure competitor. Columns 5 to 7 of Table 11-1 reproduce the pertinent cost concepts of Table 9-2.

MR = MC RULE

A profit-seeking monopolist will employ the same rationale as a profit-seeking firm in a competitive industry. A monopolist will produce each successive unit of output so long as it adds more to total revenue than it does to total costs. The firm will produce up to that output at which marginal revenue equals marginal cost (MR = MC).

A comparison of columns 4 and 7 in Table 11-1 indicates that the profit-maximizing output is 5 units; the fifth unit is the last unit of output whose marginal revenue exceeds its marginal cost. What price will the monopolist charge? The downsloping demand curve of columns 1 and 2 of the table indicates that there is only one price at which 5 units can be sold: $122.

This analysis is presented graphically in **Figure 11-4 (Key Graph)**, where the demand, marginal-revenue, average-total-cost, and marginal-cost data of Table 11-1 have been drawn. Comparing marginal revenue and marginal cost confirms that the profit-maximizing output is 5 units or, more generally, Q_m. The indicated price is $122, or more generally P_m. To charge a price higher than P_m, the monopolist must move up the demand curve, meaning that sales will fall short of the profit-maximizing level Q_m. If the monopolist charges less, it would involve a sales volume in excess of the profit-maximizing output.

Columns 2 and 5 of Table 11-1 indicate that at 5 units of output, product price of $122 exceeds average total cost of $94. Economic profits are therefore $28 per unit; total economic profits are then $140 (= 5 × $28). In Figure 11-4, per-unit profit is indicated by the distance AP_m, and total economic profits — the shaded area — are found by multiplying this unit profit by the profit-maximizing output, Q_m. **(Key Question 5)**

NO MONOPOLY SUPPLY CURVE

Recall that the supply curve of a purely competitive firm is that portion of its marginal cost curve lying above average variable costs (Figure 10-6). At first glance we would suspect that the pure monopolist's marginal cost curve would also be its supply curve. But this is *not* the case. ***The pure monopolist has no supply curve.*** The reason is that there is no unique relationship between price and quantity supplied. The price and amount supplied depend on the location of the demand (and therefore marginal revenue) curves. Like the competitive firm, the monopolist equates marginal revenue and marginal cost, but for the monopolist marginal revenue is less than price. Because the monopolist does *not* equate marginal cost to price, it is possible for different demand conditions to bring about different profit-

KEY GRAPH

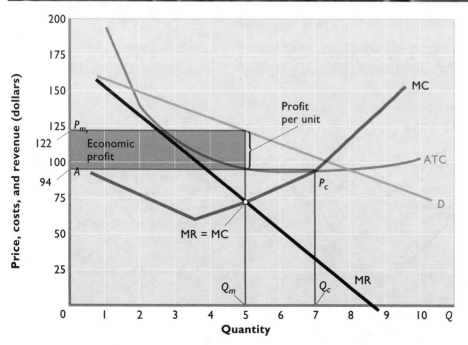

FIGURE 11-4 **The profit-maximizing position of a pure monopolist**

The pure monopolist maximizes profits by producing the MR = MC output. In this instance, profit is AP_m per unit; total profits are measured by the shaded rectangle.

maximizing prices for the same output. To convince yourself of this, go back to Figure 11-4 and pencil in a steeper (less elastic) demand curve, drawing its corresponding marginal revenue curve so that it intersects marginal cost at the same point as does the present marginal revenue curve. With the steeper demand curve this new MR = MC output will yield a higher price. Thus, our conclusion is that no single, unique price is associated with output level Q_m, and therefore there is no supply curve for the pure monopolist.

MISCONCEPTIONS ABOUT MONOPOLY PRICING

Our analysis explodes some popular fallacies about monopoly behaviour.

1. NOT HIGHEST PRICE Because a monopolist can manipulate output and price, people often believe it "will charge the highest price it can get." This is wrong. There are many prices above P_m in Figure 11-4, but the monopolist shuns them because they will result in a smaller-than-maximum profit. These higher prices move the monopolist back into output ranges where MR exceeds MC, indicating that larger outputs are profitable. *Total* profits are the difference between *total* revenue and *total* costs, and each of these two determinants of profits depends on quantity sold as much as on price and unit cost.

2. TOTAL, NOT UNIT, PROFITS The monopolist seeks maximum *total* profits, not maximum *unit* profits. In Figure 11-4, a careful comparison of the vertical distance between average total cost and price at various possible outputs indicates that per-unit profits are greater at a point slightly to the left of the profit-maximizing output, Q_m. This is seen in Table 11-1, where unit profits at 4 units of output are $32 (= $132 – $100) as compared with $28 (= $122– $94) at the profit-maximizing output of 5 units. Here the monopolist is accepting a lower-than-maximum per-unit profit because the additional sales more than compensate for the lower unit profits. A profit-seeking monopolist would rather sell 5 units at a profit of $28 per unit (for a total profit of $140) than 4 units at a profit of $32 per unit (for a total profit of only $128).

3. LOSSES Pure monopoly does *not* guarantee economic profits. True, the likelihood of economic profits is greater for a pure monopolist than for a purely competitive producer. In the long run, a competitive firm can only make a normal profit; barriers to entry permit the monopolist to perpetuate economic profits in the long run. Unlike the competitive situation, entry barriers keep out potential entrants who would increase supply, drive down price, and eliminate economic profits.

Like the pure competitor, the monopolist will not persistently operate at a loss. Thus we can

---

FIGURE 11-5 **The loss-minimizing position of a pure monopolist**

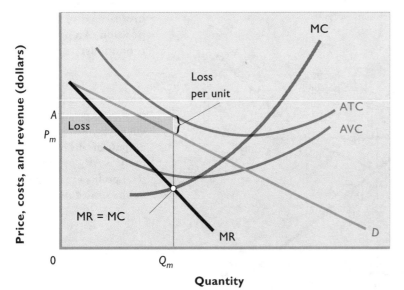

If demand, **D,** is weak and costs are high, the pure monopolist may be unable to make a profit. Because P_m exceeds AVC at Q_m, it will minimize losses in the short run by producing at that output where MR = MC. Loss per unit is AP_m, and total losses are indicated by the shaded rectangle.

expect the monopolist to realize a normal profit or better in the long run. However, if the demand-and-cost situation faced by the monopolist is sufficiently less favourable than the one shown in Figure 11-4, short-run losses will be realized. Despite its dominance in the market, the monopolist shown in Figure 11-5 suffers a loss because of weak demand and relatively high costs.

ECONOMIC EFFECTS OF MONOPOLY

Let's now evaluate pure monopoly from the standpoint of society as a whole. We will examine (1) price, output, and efficiency; (2) income distribution; (3) some uncertainties caused by difficulties in making cost comparisons between competitive firms and a monopolist; and (4) technological progress.

BOX 11-2   APPLYING THE THEORY

DE BEERS' DIAMONDS: ARE MONOPOLIES FOREVER?

De Beers Consolidated Mines of South Africa is one of the world's strongest and most enduring monopolies, having dominated the diamond market for over 60 years.

De Beers produces about 50% of all rough-cut diamonds in the world and buys for resale a large portion of the diamonds produced by other mines worldwide. As a result, it markets over 80% of the world's diamonds to a select group of diamond manufacturers and dealers.

Monopoly Behaviour   De Beers' behaviour and results are closely portrayed by the unregulated monopoly model of Figure 11-4. It sells only that quantity of diamonds that will yield an "appropriate" (monopoly) price. This price bears little relationship to production costs, and profits have been enormous. In "good" years profits are 60% of total revenues and rates of return on equity capital are 30% or more.

When demand falls, De Beers will restrict sales to maintain price. The excess of production over sales is reflected in growing diamond stockpiles held by De Beers. It also attempts to bolster demand through advertising ("diamonds are forever"). When demand is strong, it increases sales by reducing its diamond inventories.

De Beers controls the production of mines it does not own in several ways. First, it tries to convince independent producers that "single-channel" or monopoly marketing through De Beers is in their best interests in that it maximizes profits. Second, mines that circumvent De Beers are likely to find that the market is suddenly flooded from De Beers' stockpiles with the particular kind of diamonds that the "rogue" mine produces. The resulting price decline and loss of

profits are likely to bring the mine into the De Beers fold. Finally, De Beers will simply purchase and stockpile diamonds produced by independent mines so their added supply will not "spoil" the market.

Threats and Problems   But even such an enduring monopoly as De Beers faces threats and problems. First, new diamond discoveries have resulted in a growing leakage of diamonds into world markets outside De Beers' control. For example, wildcat prospecting and trading in Angola have forced De Beers to spend $300 million or more per year to keep such diamonds off the market. The recent discovery of potentially great diamond supplies in our Northwest Territories poses a future threat. Similarly, although Russia has been a part of the De Beers monopoly, this cash-strapped country has been selling as much as $500 million in diamonds per year (about one-fourth of its annual output) directly onto world markets. When new Siberian mines are brought into production, the additional output will pose a further threat to De Beers. Russia's estimated $4 to $8 billion stockpile of diamonds constitutes another potential future source of uncontrolled supply.

De Beers' diamond inventories are now an estimated $5 billion, an amount exceeding its annual sales. Observers wonder whether De Beers' capacity to absorb future unregulated production will reach a breaking point, at which time the monopoly will unravel. Although diamonds may be forever, De Beers may not.

PRICE, OUTPUT, AND EFFICIENCY

In Chapter 10, we concluded that pure competition would result in both "productive efficiency" and "allocative efficiency." Productive efficiency is realized because in the long run, the free entry and exodus of firms would force firms to operate at the optimum rate of output where unit costs of production would be at a minimum. Product price would be at the lowest level consistent with average total costs. In Figure 11-4, in long-run equilibrium, the competitive firm would sell Q_c units of output at a price of P_c.

Allocative efficiency is reflected in the fact that production under competition would occur up to the point at which price (the measure of a product's value or marginal benefit to society) would equal marginal cost (the measure of the alternative products forgone by society in producing any given commodity).

Figure 11-4 indicates that, *given the same costs,* a pure monopoly will produce much less desirable results. As we have already discovered, the pure monopolist will maximize profits by producing an output of Q_m and charging a price of P_m. ***The monopolist will find it profitable to sell a smaller output and to charge a higher price than would a competitive producer.***[2] Output Q_m is short of the

Q_c point where average total costs are minimized (the intersection of MC and ATC). Looking back at column 5 of Table 11-1, ATC at the monopolist's 5 units of output is $94.00, compared to the $91.43 that would result under pure competition. Also, at Q_m units of output, product price is considerably greater than marginal cost. This means that society values additional units of this monopolized product more highly than it does the alternative products that resources could otherwise produce. The monopolist's profit-maximizing output results in an underallocation of resources; the monopolist finds it profitable to restrict output and therefore employ fewer resources than are justified from society's standpoint. Neither productive nor allocative efficiency is achieved in monopolized markets.

INCOME DISTRIBUTION

In general, monopoly contributes to inequality in income distribution. By virtue of their market power, monopolists charge a higher price than would a purely competitive firm with the same costs; monopolists in effect can levy a "private tax" on consumers and obtain substantial economic profits. These monopoly profits are not widely distributed

---

[2] In Figure 11-4 the price-quantity comparison of monopoly and pure competition is from the vantage point of the single purely competitive *firm* of Figure 10-7(a). An equally illuminating approach is to start with the purely competitive *industry* of Figure 10-7(b), reproduced opposite. Recall that the competitive industry's supply curve, *S,* is the horizontal sum of the marginal-cost curves of all the firms in the industry. Comparing this with industry demand, *D,* we get the purely competitive price and output of P_c and Q_c. Now suppose that this industry becomes a pure monopoly as a result of a wholesale merger or one firm's somehow buying out all its competitors. Assume, too, that no changes in costs or market demand result from this dramatic change in the industry's structure. What were formerly, say, 100 competing firms are now a pure monopolist, consisting of 100 branch plants.

The industry supply curve is now the marginal-cost curve of the monopolist, the sum of the MC curves of its many branch plants. The important change, however, is on the market-demand side. From the viewpoint of each individual competitive firm, demand was perfectly elastic, and marginal revenue was therefore equal to price. Each firm equated MC to MR (and therefore to P) in maximizing profits (Chapter

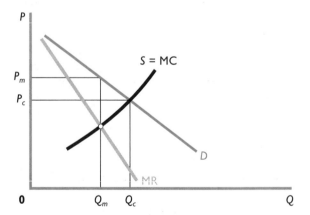

10). But industry demand and individual demand are the same to the pure monopolist; the firm is the industry, and thus the monopolist correctly envisions a downsloping demand curve, D. This means that marginal revenue, MR, will be less than price; graphically, the MR curve lies below the demand curve. In choosing the profit-maximizing MC = MR position, the monopolist selects an output Q_m that is smaller, and a price P_m that is greater, than if the industry were organized competitively.

because corporate stock ownership is largely concentrated in the hands of upper income groups. The owners of a monopoly firm tend to be enriched at the expense of the rest of society.

Exception: If the buyers of a monopoly product are wealthier than the owners, suppliers, and workers of the monopoly, the monopoly may *reduce* income inequality. Undoubtedly, some international commodity monopolies such as those involving metals, bananas, and coffee redistribute the world's income from wealthy consuming nations to poorer developing nations. But, in general, monopoly contributes to income inequality.

COST COMPLICATIONS

Our evaluation of pure monopoly has led us to conclude that, *given identical costs*, a purely monopolistic firm will find it profitable to charge a higher price, produce a smaller output, and lead to an allocation of economic resources inferior to that of a purely competitive industry. These results are rooted in the entry barriers characterizing monopoly.

Now we must recognize that costs may *not* be the same for purely competitive and monopolistic producers. Unit costs incurred by a monopolist may be either larger or smaller than those facing a purely competitive firm. There are four reasons why costs may differ: (1) economies of scale, (2) the notion of "X-inefficiency," (3) monopoly-preserving expenditures, and (4) the "very long run" perspective that allows for technological progress. We examine the first three issues in this section, and technological progress in the ensuing section.

ECONOMIES OF SCALE REVISITED The assumption that unit costs available to the competitive firm and a monopoly are the same may not hold in practice. Given production techniques and therefore production costs, consumer demand may not be sufficient to support a large number of competing firms producing at an output that permits each to realize all *existing* economies of scale. In such instances, a firm must be large in relation to the market — it must be a monopoly — to produce efficiently (at low unit cost). This is the natural monopoly case discussed earlier.

Most economists conclude that the natural monopoly or public utilities case is not significant enough to undermine our general conclusions about the restrictive nature of monopoly. Evidence suggests

that the large corporations in many manufacturing industries now have more monopoly power than can be justified on the grounds that these firms are merely availing themselves of existing economies of scale.

X-INEFFICIENCY While economies of scale *might* argue for monopoly in a few cases, the notion of X-inefficiency tends to suggest that monopoly costs might be *higher* than costs associated with more competitive industries. What is X-inefficiency? Why might it plague monopolists more than competitive firms?

All the average-total-cost curves used in this and other chapters are based on the assumption that the firm chooses from *existing* technologies the most efficient one or, in other words, that technology permitting the firm to achieve the minimum average total cost for each level of output. **X-inefficiency** occurs when a firm's actual costs of producing any output are greater than the minimum possible costs. In Figure 11-6, X-inefficiency is represented by unit costs of ATC_x (as opposed to ATC_c) for output Q_c and average costs of ATC'_x (rather than ATC_m) for output Q_m. Any point above the average cost curve in Figure 11-6 is attainable but reflects internal inefficiency or "bad management."

Why does X-inefficiency occur if it reduces profits? Managers may often have goals — for example, firm growth, an easier work life, the avoidance of business risk, providing jobs for incompetent friends and relatives — that conflict with cost minimization. Or X-inefficiency may arise because a firm's workers are poorly motivated or ineffectively supervised.

RENT-SEEKING EXPENDITURES The term **rent-seeking behaviour** refers to activities designed to transfer income or wealth to a particular firm or resource supplier at someone else's or society's expense. We have seen that a monopolist can earn economic profits even in the long run. Therefore, it is no surprise a firm may go to considerable expense to acquire or maintain monopoly privileges granted by government. A monopolist's barrier to entry may depend on legislation or an exclusive licence provided by government, as in radio and television broadcasting. To sustain or enhance the consequent economic profits, the monopolist may spend large amounts on legal fees, lobbying, and public relations advertising to persuade government to grant or sustain its privileged position.

FIGURE 11-6   Economies of scale and X-inefficiency

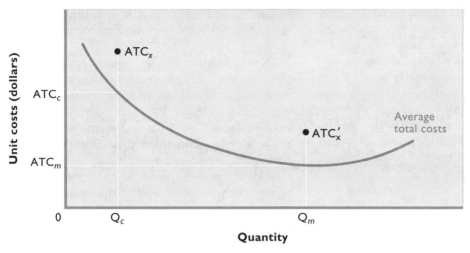

This diagram serves to demonstrate two unrelated points. First, given the existence of extensive economies of scale, we note that a monopolist can achieve low unit costs of ATC_m at Q_m units of output. In contrast, if the market were divided among a number of competing firms so that each produced only Q_c, then scale economies would be unrealized and unit costs of ATC_c would be high. The second point is that X-inefficiency — the inefficient internal operation of a firm — results in higher-than-necessary costs. For example, unit costs might be ATC_x, rather than ATC_c for Q_c units of output and ATC'_x rather than ATC_m for the Q_m level of output.

These expenditures add nothing to the firm's output, but increase its costs. Rent-seeking expenditures mean that monopoly might entail higher costs and a greater efficiency loss than suggested by Figure 11-4.

TECHNOLOGICAL PROGRESS: DYNAMIC EFFICIENCY

We have noted that our condemnation of monopoly must be qualified where *existing* mass-production economies might be lost if an industry comprises a large number of small, competing firms. Now we must consider the issue of **dynamic efficiency**, or whether monopolists are more likely to develop more efficient production techniques over time than competitive firms. Are monopolists more likely to improve productive technology, thereby lowering (shifting downward) their average-total-cost curves, than are competitive producers? Although we will concentrate on changes in productive techniques, the same question applies to product improvement. Do monopolists have greater means and incentives to improve their products and thus enhance consumer satisfaction? This is fertile ground for honest differences of opinion.

THE COMPETITIVE MODEL   Competitive firms certainly have the incentive to employ the most efficient *known* productive techniques. Their survival depends on being efficient. But competition deprives firms of economic profit — an important means and a major incentive to develop *new* improved productive techniques or *new* products. The profits from technological innovation may be short-lived to the innovating competitor. An innovating firm in a competitive industry will find that its many rivals will soon duplicate or imitate any technological advance it may achieve; rivals will share the rewards but not the costs of successful technological research.

THE MONOPOLY MODEL   In contrast — thanks to entry barriers — a monopolist may persistently realize substantial economic profits. Hence the pure monopolist will have greater financial resources for technological innovation than will competitive firms. But what about the monopolist's incentives for technological advance? Here the picture is clouded.

There is one imposing argument suggesting that the monopolist's incentives to develop new techniques or products will be weak: the absence of

BOX 11-3   IN THE MEDIA

OTTAWA REJECTS RAIL MERGER: DEAL WOULD HAVE LEFT EASTERN CANADA WITH ONE OPERATOR

BY BARRIE McKENNA, Ottawa
OLIVER BERTIN, Toronto

The federal government rejected **Canadian Pacific Ltd.'s** $1.4-billion bid for **Canadian National Railways** operations east of Winnipeg yesterday, a decision that shelves the idea of privatizing the Crown corporation.

Transport Minister Douglas Young said the biggest problem with CP's offer is that it would have left much of the country with a single railway operator.

"The government was not prepared to have a total loss ... of competition in the rail sector east of Winnipeg and to privatize all the rail operations east of Winnipeg based on an unsolicited bid," Mr. Young told reporters outside the House of Commons.

He said the government, which owns CN, won't "entertain further proposals at this time."

Mr. Young said the government also did not like the financial terms of the proposed deal and feared job losses at both railways after a merger.

"This bid has been set aside and we felt we should close the door very firmly," he said.

In a statement issued after Mr. Young's announcement, CP spokesman B. C. Scott said the Montreal-based energy and transportation giant "believes it made a realistic offer that was in line with the federal government's objectives of commercializing Crown corporations and reducing public debt. The offer was a sound one for the government, for taxpayers and for the future viability of the railway industry."

CP said it was also disappointed because the rejection does nothing to solve a persistent industry problem — too many railways in Eastern Canada....

Source: *The Globe and Mail*, December 14, 1994, p. B1. Reproduced with permission.

The Story in Brief

The federal government rejects a bid by Canadian Pacific Ltd., a private company, to purchase Canadian National Railways. The reason given was that "it would have left much of the country with a single railway operator."

The Economics Behind the Story

• From Chapter 11 we learned the favourable outcome of a pure competitive market structure: production at lowest cost (productive efficiency, P = min ATC), production of those goods and services society most wants (allocative efficiency, P = MC), and a quick response to changes in consumer wants. From Chapter 12 we have learned that a monopoly achieves none of these desirable results — thus, the reason for public policy facilitating competition and making it unlawful for producers to collude or impede competition.

• If Canadian Pacific Ltd. had purchased Canadian National Railways there would have been only one railway company east of Winnipeg, with the expected negative consequences for consumers and producers relying on that mode of transportation.

• Once you have read the section in this chapter on regulated monopoly, consider whether railways are natural monopolies and should be subjected to government regualation. If Canadian Pacific had purchased Canadian National Railways, would it have had a "monopoly" on transportation east of Winnipeg? Explain.

competitors. Because of its sheltered market position, the pure monopolist can afford to be inefficient and lethargic. The monopolist has every reason to be satisfied with the status quo, to become complacent. It might well pay the monopolist to withhold or "file" technological improvements in both productive techniques and products to exploit existing capital equipment fully.

And even when improved techniques are belatedly introduced by monopolists, the accompanying cost reductions will accrue to the monopolist as increases in profits and only partially, if at all, to consumers in the form of lower prices and an increased output. Proponents of this view point out that in a number of industries that approximate monopoly the interest in research has been minimal. Such advances as have been realized have come largely from outside the industry or from the smaller firms making up the competitive fringe of the industry.

There are at least two counter-arguments:

1. Technological advance lowers unit costs and expands profits. As our analysis of Figure 11-4 implies, lower costs will give rise to a profit-maximizing position that involves a larger output and a lower price. Any expansion of profits will not be transitory; barriers to entry protect the monopolist from profit encroachment by rivals. Thus, technological progress is profitable to the monopolist, and therefore will be undertaken.
2. Research and technological advance may be one of the monopolist's barriers to entry; hence the monopolist must persist and succeed in these areas or eventually fall prey to new competitors, including those located abroad. Technological progress, it is argued, is essential to the maintenance of monopoly.

A MIXED PICTURE What can be said as a summarizing generalization on the economic efficiency of pure monopoly? In a static economy where economies of scale are equally accessible to a monopolist and purely competitive firms, pure competition will be superior because it forces use of the best-known technology and allocates resources according to the wants of society. However, when economies of scale available to the monopolist are not attainable by small competitive producers, the inefficiencies of pure monopoly are less evident.

TWO POLICY OPTIONS There are two policy options when pure monopoly creates substantial economic inefficiency and appears to be long-lasting.

1. ANTI-COMBINES As we will detail in Chapter 14, government can file charges against monopoly under the anti-combines laws, seeking to break up the monopoly into competing firms.

2. PUBLIC UTILITY REGULATION Society can allow the monopoly to continue, but directly regulate its prices and operations. We will explore this option — public utility regulation — later in this chapter.

QUICK REVIEW 11-2

1. The monopolist maximizes profits (or minimizes losses) at the MR = MC output and charges the price on its demand curve that corresponds to this output.

2. Assuming identical costs, a monopolist will be less efficient than a purely competitive firm because it produces less output and charges a higher price.

3. The inefficiencies of monopoly may be offset by economies of scale and technological progress, but intensified by the presence of X-inefficiency and rent-seeking expenditures.

PRICE DISCRIMINATION

We have assumed the monopolist charges a uniform price to all buyers. But under certain conditions, the monopolist can exploit its market position more fully and increase profits by charging different prices to different buyers. In so doing, the seller is engaging in price discrimination. **Price discrimination** *occurs when a given product is sold at more than one price and these price differences are not justified by cost differences.*

CONDITIONS

The opportunity to engage in price discrimination is not readily available to all sellers. Price discrimination can occur when three conditions are realized.

1. MONOPOLY POWER The seller must be a monopolist, or at least possess some degree of monopoly power — some ability to control output and price.

2. MARKET SEGREGATION The seller must be able to segregate buyers into separate classes, where each group has a different willingness or ability to pay for the product. This separation of buyers is usually based on different elasticities of demand, as later illustrations will make clear.

3. NO RESALE The original purchaser cannot resell the product or service. If buyers in the low-price segment of the market can easily resell in the high-price segment, the resulting decline in supply would increase price in the low-price segment and the increase in supply would lower price in the high-price segment. The price discrimination policy would thereby be undermined. This suggests that service industries, such as the transportation industry or legal and medical services, are especially susceptible to price discrimination.

ILLUSTRATIONS

Price discrimination is widely practised in our economy. The sales representative who must communicate important information to corporate headquarters has a highly inelastic demand for long-distance telephone service and pays the high daytime rate. The college or university student "reporting in" to the folks at home has an elastic demand and defers the call to take advantage of lower evening or weekend rates. Electric utilities frequently segment their markets by end uses, such as lighting and heating. The absence of reasonable substitutes means the demand for electricity for illumination is inelastic and the price per kilowatt hour for this use is high. But the availability of natural gas and petroleum as alternatives to electrical heating makes the demand for electricity elastic for this purpose, and the price charged is therefore lower. Similarly, industrial users of electricity are typically charged lower rates than residential users because the former can construct their own generating equipment while the individual household cannot.

Movie theatres and golf courses vary their charges on the basis of time (higher rates in the evening and on weekends when demand is strong) and age (ability to pay). Railways vary the freight rate charged according to the market value of the product being shipped; the shipper of 10 tonnes of television sets or costume jewellery will be charged more than the shipper of 10 tonnes of gravel or coal. Airlines charge high fares to travelling executives, whose demand for travel is inelastic, and offer lower fares in the guise of "family rates" and "standby fares" to attract vacationers and others whose demands are more elastic.

CONSEQUENCES

There are two economic consequences of price discrimination.

1. A monopolist will be able to increase its profits by practising price discrimination.
2. Other things being equal, a discriminating monopolist will produce a larger output than a nondiscriminating monopolist.

1. MORE PROFITS The simplest way to understand why price discrimination can yield additional profits is to look again at our monopolist's downsloping demand curve, in Figure 11-4. We note that, although the profit-maximizing uniform price is $122, the segment of the demand curve lying above the profit area in Figure 11-4 tells us there are buyers who would be willing to pay *more than* P_m ($122) rather than forgo the product.

If the monopolist can identify and segregate each of these buyers and charge the maximum price each would pay, the sale of any given level of output will be more profitable. In columns 1 and 2 of Table 11-1, we note that the buyers of the first 4 units of output would be willing to pay more than the equilibrium price of $122. If the seller could practise perfect price discrimination by extracting the maximum price each buyer would pay, total revenue would increase from $610 (= $122 × 5) to $710 (= $122 + $132 + $142 + $152 + $162) and profits would increase from $140 (= $610 − $470) to $240 (= $710 − $470).

2. MORE PRODUCTION Other things being the same, the discriminating monopolist will in fact choose to produce a larger output than the nondiscriminating monopolist. Recall that when the nondiscriminating monopolist lowers price to sell additional output, the lower price will apply not only to the additional sales but also to *all* prior units of output. But when a perfectly discriminating monopolist lowers price, the reduced price applies *only* to the additional unit sold and *not* to prior units. Thus, price and marginal revenue are equal for any unit of output.

As indicated in Table 11-1, because marginal revenue now equals price, the discriminating monopolist will find that it is profitable to produce

7, rather than 5, units of output. The additional revenue beyond the 5 units level is $214 (= $112 + $102). Thus total revenue for 7 units is $924 (= $710 + $214). Total cost for 7 units is $640 (= 7 × $91.43), so profits are $284.

Ironically, although price discrimination increases the monopolist's profit compared to a nondiscriminating monopolist, it also results in greater output and thus less allocative inefficiency. In our example, the output level of 7 units matches the output that would occur in pure competition. That is, allocative efficiency ($P = MC$) is achieved.

GRAPHIC SUMMARY Figure 11-7 summarizes the effects of price discrimination. Figure 11-7(a) merely restates Figure 11-4 in a generalized form to show the position of a nondiscriminating monopolist as a benchmark. The nondiscriminating monopolist produces output Q_0 where $MR = MC$ and charges a price of Q_0c (= $0b$). Total revenue is area $0bcQ_0$ and economic profit is area $abcd$.

In Figure 11-7(b) the monopolist engages in perfect price discrimination, charging each buyer the highest price he or she is willing to pay. Starting at zero, each successive unit is sold for the price indicated by the corresponding point on the demand curve. This means that the demand and marginal revenue curves coincide because the monopolist need *not* cut

price on preceding units to sell more output. Thus, the most profitable output is Q_1 (where $MC = MR$), which is greater than Q_0. Total revenue is area $0fgQ_1$ and total cost is area $0hjQ_1$. The discriminating monopolist's economic profit of $hfgj$ is clearly larger than the single-price monopolist's profit of $abcd$.

The impact of discrimination on consumers is mixed. Those buying each unit out to Q_0 will pay more than the nondiscriminatory price of Q_0c. But those additional consumers brought into the market by discrimination will pay less than Q_0c. Specifically, they will pay the various prices shown on the cg segment of the D = MR curve.

To summarize: As compared to a one-price monopoly, price discrimination results in more profits; a greater output; and higher prices for many consumers but lower prices for those purchasing the extra output. **(Key Question 6)**

REGULATED MONOPOLY

Most purely monopolistic industries are "natural monopolies" and subject to regulation. The prices or rates public utilities — railways, airlines, telephone companies, natural gas and electricity suppliers — charge are determined by a federal, provincial, or local regulatory commission or board.

FIGURE 11-7 **A single-price versus a perfectly discriminating monopolist**

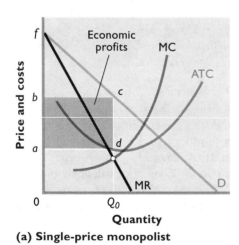

(a) Single-price monopolist

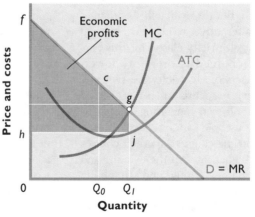

(b) Perfectly discriminating monopolist

The perfectly discriminating monopolist realizes a larger profit (*hfgj* as compared to *abcd*) and produces a larger output (Q_1 rather than Q_0) than would a single-price monopolist. Consumers on the *fc* range of the demand curve will pay higher prices with discrimination, while those on the *cg* segment will pay less.

FIGURE 11-8   **Regulated monopoly**

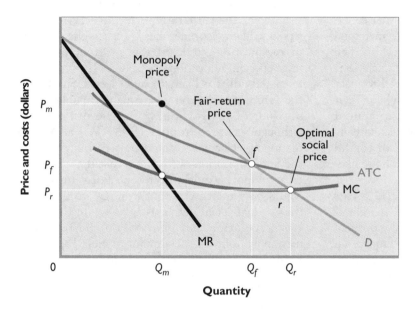

Price regulation can improve the social consequences of a natural monopoly. The socially optimum price, P_r, will result in an efficient allocation of resources, but is likely to entail losses and therefore call for permanent public subsidies. The "fair-return" price, P_f, will allow the monopolist to break even, but will not fully correct the underallocation of resources.

Figure 11-8 shows the demand and cost conditions of a natural monopoly; the ATC comes down as the scale of the firm increases. Because of the advantages of larger firm size, demand cuts the long-run average-total-cost curve where it is still falling. It would be inefficient to have many firms in such an industry because, by dividing the market, each firm would move further to the left on its average-total-cost curve so unit costs would be substantially higher. The relationship between market demand and costs is such that the attainment of low unit costs presumes only one producer.

We know by application of the MR = MC rule that P_m and Q_m are the profit-maximizing price and output that the unregulated monopolist would choose. Because price exceeds average total cost at Q_m, the monopolist enjoys a substantial economic profit. Furthermore, price exceeds marginal cost, which indicates an underallocation of resources to this product or service. Can government regulation bring about better results for society?

OPTIMAL SOCIAL PRICE: P = MC

If the objective of our regulatory commission is to achieve allocative efficiency, it should attempt to establish a ceiling price for the monopolist that is

equal to *marginal cost*. Since each point on the market demand curve designates a price-quantity combination, and noting that marginal cost cuts the demand curve only at point *r*, it is clear the P_r is the only price equal to marginal cost. The imposition of this maximum or ceiling price causes the monopolist's effective demand curve to become P_rrD; the demand curve becomes perfectly elastic, and therefore P_r = MR, out to point *r*, where the regulated price ceases to be effective.

By imposing the fixed price P_r and letting the monopolist choose its profit-maximizing or loss-minimizing output, the allocative results of pure competition can be simulated. Production takes place where P_r = MC, and this equality indicates an efficient allocation of resources to this product or service.[3] This price, which achieves allocative efficiency, is called the **optimal social price**.

---

[3] While "allocative efficiency" is achieved, "productive efficiency" would be achieved only by chance. In Figure 11-8 we note that production takes place at Q_r, which is less than the output at which average total costs are minimized. Can you redraw Figure 11-8 to show those special conditions where both allocative and productive efficiency are realized?

"FAIR-RETURN" PRICE: $P = ATC$

But the optimal social price, P_r, may pose a problem of losses for the regulated firm. The price that equals marginal cost is likely to be so low that average total costs are not covered, as is shown in Figure 11-8. The result is losses. The reason lies in the basic character of public utilities. Because they are required to meet peak demands (both daily and seasonally) for their product or service, they tend to have substantial excess productive capacity when demand is relatively normal. This high level of investment in capital facilities means that unit costs of production are likely to decline over a wide range of output.

The market demand curve in Figure 11-8 cuts marginal cost at a point to the left of the marginal-cost–average-total-cost intersection, so the optimal social price is below ATC. Therefore, to enforce an optimal social price on the regulated monopolist means short-run losses and, in the long run, bankruptcy for the utility.

What to do? One option is a public subsidy sufficient to cover the loss marginal-cost pricing would entail. Another possibility is to condone price discrimination, in the hope that the additional revenue gained will permit the firm to cover costs.

In practice, regulatory commissions have pursued a third option: they have tended to back away from the objective of allocative efficiency and marginal-cost pricing. Most regulatory agencies in Canada are concerned with establishing a **"fair-return" price**. This is because an optimal social price leads to losses and eventual bankruptcy.

We see that the fair or fair-return price in Figure 11-8 is P_f, where price equals *average* cost. Because the demand curve cuts average total cost only at point f, P_f is the only price that permits a fair return. The corresponding output at regulated price P_f will be Q_f.

DILEMMA OF REGULATION

Comparing the results of the optimal social price ($P = MC$) and the fair-return price ($P = ATC$) suggests a policy dilemma, sometimes known as the **dilemma of regulation**. When price is set to achieve the most efficient allocation of resources ($P = MC$), the regulated utility is likely to suffer losses. Survival of the firm would depend on permanent public subsidies out of tax revenues. On the other hand, although a fair-return price ($P = ATC$) allows the monopolist to cover costs, it only partially resolves the underallocation of resources that the unregulated monopoly would foster. The fair-return price would only increase output from Q_m to Q_f, while the optimal social output is Q_r. Despite this problem, regulation can improve on the results of monopoly from the social point of view. Price regulation can simultaneously reduce price, increase output, and reduce the economic profits of monopolies. **(Key Question 14)**

QUICK REVIEW 11-3

1. Price discrimination occurs when a seller charges different prices that are not based on cost differentials.

2. The conditions necessary for price discrimination are: **a** monopoly power; **b** the segregation of buyers on the basis of different demand elasticities; and **c** the inability of buyers to resell the product.

3. Monopoly price can be reduced and output increased through government regulation.

4. The optimal social price ($P = MC$) achieves allocative efficiency but may result in losses; the fair-return price ($P = ATC$) yields a normal profit but falls short of allocative efficiency.

CHAPTER SUMMARY

1. A pure monopolist is the sole producer of a commodity for which there are no close substitutes.

2. Barriers to entry, in the form of **a**. economies of scale, **b** patent ownership and research, and **c** ownership or control of essential inputs, help explain the existence of pure monopoly and other imperfectly competitive market structures.

3. The pure monopolist's market situation differs from a competitive firm in that the monopolist's demand curve is downsloping, causing the marginal-revenue curve to lie below the demand

curve. Like the competitive seller, the pure monopolist will maximize profits by equating marginal revenue and marginal cost. Barriers to entry may permit a monopolist to acquire economic profits even in the long run. Note, however, that **a** the monopolist does not charge "the highest price it can get"; **b** the maximum total profit sought by the monopolist rarely coincides with maximum unit profits; **c** high costs and a weak demand may prevent the monopolist from realizing any profit at all; **d** the monopolist will want to avoid the inelastic range of its demand curve.

4. With the same costs, the pure monopolist will find it more profitable to restrict output and charge a higher price than would a competitive seller. This restriction of output causes resources to be misallocated, as is evidenced by the fact that price exceeds marginal costs in monopolized markets.

5. In general, monopoly increases income inequality.

6. The costs of monopolists and competitive producers may not be the same. On the one hand, economies of scale may make lower unit costs accessible to monopolists but not to competitors. On the other hand, there is evidence that X-inefficiency — the failure to produce with the least-costly combination of inputs — is more common to monopolists than it is to competitive firms and that monopolists may make sizable expenditures to maintain monopoly privileges conferred by government.

7. Economists disagree as to how conducive pure monopoly is to technological advance. Some believe pure monopoly is more progressive than pure competition, because its ability to realize economic profits helps finance technological research. Others, however, argue that the absence of rival firms and the monopolist's desire to exploit fully its existing capital facilities weaken the monopolist's incentive to innovate.

8. A monopolist can increase its profits by practising price discrimination, provided it can segregate buyers on the basis of different elasticities of demand and the product or service cannot be readily transferred between the segmented markets. Other things being equal, the discriminating monopolist will produce a larger output than will the nondiscriminating monopolist.

9. Price regulation can be invoked to eliminate wholly or partially the tendency of monopolists to underallocate resources and to earn economic profits. The "optimal social" price is determined where the demand and marginal cost curves intersect; the "fair-return" price is determined where the demand and average-total-cost curves intersect.

TERMS AND CONCEPTS

barriers to entry (p. 224)
dilemma of regulation (p. 242)
dynamic efficiency (p. 236)
"fair-return" price (p. 242)
natural monopoly (p. 226)
optimal social price (p. 241)

price discrimination (p. 238)
price maker (p. 224)
pure monopoly (p. 224)
rent-seeking behaviour (p. 235)
X-inefficiency (p. 235)

QUESTIONS AND STUDY SUGGESTIONS

1. "No firm is completely sheltered from rivals; all firms compete for consumers' dollars. Pure monopoly, therefore, does not exist." Do you agree? Explain. How might you use Chapter 7's concept of cross-elasticity of demand to judge whether monopoly exists?

2. Discuss the major barriers to entry. Explain how each barrier can foster monopoly or oligopoly. Which barriers, if any, do you think give rise to monopoly that is socially justifiable?

3. How does the demand curve faced by a purely monopolistic seller differ from that confronting a purely competitive firm? Why does it differ? Of what significance is the difference? Why is the pure monopolist's demand curve not perfectly inelastic?

4. *Key Question   Use the demand schedule below to calculate total revenue and marginal revenue. Plot the demand, total revenue, and marginal revenue curves and carefully explain the relationships between them. Explain why the marginal revenue of the fourth unit of output is $3.50, even though its price is $5. Use Chapter 5's total-revenue test for price elasticity to designate the elastic and inelastic segments of your graphed demand curve. What generalization can you make regarding the relationship between marginal revenue and elasticity of demand? Suppose that somehow the marginal cost of successive units of output was zero. What output would the profit-seeking firm produce? Finally, use your analysis to explain why a monopolist would never produce in the inelastic range of its demand curve.*

Price	Quantity demanded	Price	Quantity demanded
$7.00	0	$4.50	5
6.50	1	4.00	6
6.00	2	3.50	7
5.50	3	3.00	8
5.00	4	2.50	9

5. *Key Question   Suppose a pure monopolist is faced with the demand schedule shown below and the same cost data as the competitive producer discussed in question 4 at the end of Chapter 10. Calculate total and marginal revenue and determine the profit-maximizing price and output for this monopolist. What is the level of profits? Verify your answer graphically and by comparing total revenue and total cost.*

Price	Quantity demanded	Total revenue	Marginal revenue
$115	0	$_____	$_____
100	1	_____	_____
83	2	_____	_____
71	3	_____	_____
63	4	_____	_____
55	5	_____	_____
48	6	_____	_____
42	7	_____	_____
37	8	_____	_____
33	9	_____	_____
29	10	_____	

6. *Key Question*   If the firm described in question 5 could engage in perfect price discrimination, what would be the level of output? Of profits? Draw a diagram showing the relevant-demand, marginal-revenue, average-total-cost, and marginal-cost curves and the equilibrium price and output for a nondiscriminating monopolist. Use the same diagram to show the equilibrium position of a monopolist able to practise perfect price discrimination. Compare equilibrium outputs, total revenues, economic profits, and consumer prices in the two cases. Comment on the economic desirability of price discrimination.

7. Assume a pure monopolist and a purely competitive firm have the same unit costs. Contrast the two with respect to a. price, b. output, c. profits, d. allocation of resources, and e. impact upon the distribution of income. Since both monopolists and competitive firms follow the MC = MR rule in maximizing profits, how do you account for the different results? Why might the costs of a purely competitive firm and monopolist *not* be the same? What are the implications of such cost differences?

8. Critically evaluate and explain:

    a. "Because they can control product price, monopolists are always assured of profitable production by simply charging the highest price consumers will pay."

    b. "The pure monopolist seeks that output that will yield the greatest per-unit profit."

    c. "An excess of price over marginal cost is the market's way of signalling the need for more production of a good."

    d. "The more profitable a firm, the greater its monopoly power."

    e. "The monopolist has a price policy; the competitive producer does not."

    f. "With respect to resource allocation, the interests of the seller and of society coincide in a purely competitive market but conflict in a monopolized market."

    g. "In a sense, the monopolist makes a profit for not producing: the monopolist produces profits more than it does goods."

9. Carefully evaluate the following widely held viewpoint. Can you offer any arguments to the contrary?

    A monopoly is usually not under pressure to *invent* new products or methods. Nor does it have strong incentives to *innovate*: to apply those new inventions in practice and bring new products to the market. *The monopoly may choose to invent and innovate, but it will do so only at its own pace.* Because the new product cuts the value of the existing products, the monopoly will tend to hold back on innovation. Typically it innovates only when a smaller competitor forces its hand. Even if its capital is outdated or its products mediocre, a monopolist may prefer to protect and continue them rather than to replace them with better ones.[4]

10. Assume a monopolistic publisher has agreed to pay an author 15% of the total revenue from the sales of a text. Will the author and the publisher want to charge the same price for the text? Explain.

11. Suppose a firm's demand curve lies below its average-total-cost curve at all levels of output. Can you conceive of any circumstances by which production might be profitable?

12. Are community colleges and universities engaging in price discrimination when they charge full tuition to some students and provide financial aid to others? What are the advantages and disadvantages of this practice?

---

[4] William G. Shepherd, *Public Policies Toward Business*, 8th ed. (Homewood, Ill.: Richard D. Irwin, Inc., 1991), p. 36.

13. Explain verbally and graphically how price (rate) regulation may improve the performance of monopolies. In your answer distinguish between a. optimal social (marginal cost) pricing and b. fair-return (average cost) pricing. What is the "dilemma of regulation"?

14. *Key Question* *It has been proposed that natural monopolists should be allowed to determine their profit-maximizing outputs and prices and then government should tax their profits away and distribute them to consumers in proportion to their purchases from the monopoly. Is this proposal as socially desirable as requiring monopolists to equate price with marginal cost or average total cost?*

15. (Applying the Theory) Explain how De Beers has an almost complete monopoly of the world diamond market, although it produces only one-half of world output. What are the threats to its market power?

CHAPTER 12

PRICE AND OUTPUT DETERMINATION: MONOPOLISTIC COMPETITION

A consumer living in a sizable town or city will have an array of choices when buying many products. Take the purchase of a sweater. You could go to a discount store and buy an imported acrylic sweater for about $15; or purchase a fleece pullover with your school's logo and colours for $35. You might buy a cotton knit from a mail-order catalogue for $45, or go to an upscale clothier to purchase a top-of-the-line wool sweater for over $100. The product choices reflect monopolistic competition: a market structure in which competition occurs not only on the basis of price, but also product quality, service, and advertising.

Pure competition and pure monopoly are the exceptions, not the rule, in our economy. Most market structures fall somewhere between these two extremes. In the present chapter, we examine monopolistic competition. This market structure is a blending of a considerable amount of competition with a small dose of monopoly power.

Our objectives in this chapter are to:

1. Examine the nature and prevalence of monopolistic competition.

2. Analyze and evaluate the price-output behaviour of monopolistically competitive firms.

3. Explain and assess the role of nonprice competition, based on product quality, service, and advertising, in monopolistically competitive industries.

BOX 12-1   THE BIG PICTURE

The pure competitive market structure is the ideal against which we measure other market structures. The monopoly model demonstrates the other extreme, the inefficiencies of a one-firm industry. But most industries do not approach either extreme. We now use what you learned in the last two chapters to investigate market structures prevalent in the real world.

Monopolistic competition: the term tells us a great deal about this market structure. There are elements of monopoly and elements of competition. The monopoly part applies because each firm produces a unique product. There may be close substitutes — for example, Coke and Pepsi — but each product has a quality (or qualities) that make its producer the "only" supplier. The competition part comes in because there are close substitutes and many firms in the industry.

Monopolistic competition is the most prevalent market structure found in most economies, including Canada. And we should be thankful! Can you imagine the appearance of the world if it were dominated by pure competition? All goods and services produced would be homogeneous — there would be no quality or aesthetic differences among them! While a monopolistic competition does not lead to either productive or allocative efficiency, it is a market structure that provides consumers a greater variety of products at any point in time, and improved products over time.

As you read this chapter, keep the following points in mind:

- A pivotal distinguishing feature of monopolistic competition is product differentiation — each firm produces a variation of a particular good or service. There are also a relatively large number of firms in any industry competing with each other.
- Since each firm produces a unique product, it faces a downward-sloping demand curve and, thus, a revenue curve below the demand curve, just as in the case of a monopoly.
- There is no industry supply curve; each firm produces a slightly different version of a product compared to its competitors.
- As with the pure competitive model, losses in the short run will lead to firms leaving the industry and economic profits will attract firms to the industry. In the long run, firms generally earn normal profits.

MONOPOLISTIC COMPETITION: CONCEPT AND OCCURRENCE

The defining characteristics of **monopolistic competition** are: (1) a relatively large number of sellers; (2) product differentiation; and (3) easy entry to, and exit from, the industry. The first and third characteristics provide the "competitive" aspect of monopolistic competition; the second characteristic contributes the "monopolistic" aspect.

RELATIVELY LARGE NUMBERS

Monopolistic competition does not require hundreds of thousands of firms as in pure competition, but only a fairly large number — say, 25, 35, 60, or 70.

Several characteristics of monopolistic competition follow from the relatively large numbers of firms.

1. SMALL MARKET SHARE   Each firm has a comparatively small percentage of the total market, so each has a limited control over market price.

2. NO COLLUSION   A relatively large number of firms also ensures that collusion — concerted action by firms to restrict output and rig price — is all but impossible.

3. INDEPENDENT ACTION   With numerous firms in the industry, there is no mutual interdependence among them. Each firm determines its policies without considering the possible reactions of rival firms. The 15% increase in sales that firm X may realize by cutting price will be spread so thinly over its 20, 40, or 60 rivals that for all practical purposes, the impact on their sales will be imperceptible.

PRODUCT DIFFERENTIATION

In contrast to pure competition, monopolistic competition has the fundamental feature of **product differentiation**. Purely competitive firms produce a standardized or homogeneous product such as wheat or corn; monopolistically competitive producers turn out variations of a particular product.

Because of product differentiation, economic rivalry typically takes the form of **nonprice competition**, that is, competition in terms of product quality, services to consumers, location and accessibility, and advertising.

Let's examine these aspects of nonprice competition.

1. PRODUCT QUALITY   Product differentiation may take the form of physical or qualitative differences in products themselves. "Real" differences in functional features, materials, design, and workmanship are vital aspects of product differentiation. Personal computers, for example, differ in hardware capacity, software, graphics, and how user-friendly they are. There are scores of competing principles of economics texts that differ in content, organization, presentation and readability, pedagogical aids, graphics and design. Most cities will have a variety of retail stores selling men's and women's clothing that vary greatly in styling, materials, and quality of workmanship. Similarly, one fast-food hamburger chain may feature lean beef while a competitor stresses the juiciness of its hamburgers.

Credit cards may seem like homogeneous "products," differing only in annual fees and interest rate charges. Not so. Some provide rebates on purchases; others offer free airline travel miles, and still others offer extended warranties on products purchased on credit.

2. SERVICES   Services and conditions surrounding the sale of a product are forms of product differentiation. One grocery store may stress the helpfulness of its clerks who bag your groceries and carry them to your car. A "warehouse" competitor may leave bagging and carrying to its customers but feature lower prices. One-day clothes cleaning may be preferred to cleaning of equal quality that takes three days. The snob appeal of a store, the courteousness and helpfulness of clerks, the firm's reputation for service or exchanging its products, and credit availability are all service aspects of product differentiation. Pizza restaurants compete on the basis of whether they offer delivery services.

3. LOCATION   Products may also be differentiated by location and accessibility. Small mini-groceries or convenience stores successfully compete with large supermarkets, even though they have a much more limited range of products and charge significantly higher prices. They compete on the basis of being close to customers and situated on much-travelled streets — and by staying open 24 hours a day. A gas station's close proximity to the Trans-Canada highway gives it a locational advantage that allows it to sell gasoline at a higher price than the same brand sells for in a town located two or three kilometres from the highway.

4. ADVERTISING AND PACKAGING   Product differentiation may also arise from perceived differences created through advertising, the use of brand

GLOBAL PERSPECTIVE 12-1

Some of the world's most valuable brand names

Using such factors as sales, profitability, and growth potential, *Financial World* magazine estimates the value of product brands. The graph shows that the brands of selected international firms, some of which have subsidiaries in Canada, were valuable assets in 1993.

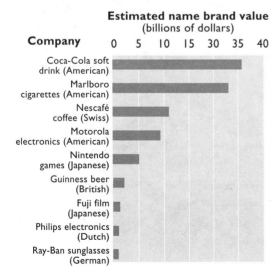

Estimated name brand value
(billions of dollars)

Source: *Financial World*, August 2, 1994, pp. 40-56.

BOX 12-2   IN THE MEDIA

AULT LAUNCHES "FILTERED" MILK: RIVAL FIRM FAILS TO STOP CAMPAIGN

CANADIAN PRESS AND STAFF

TORONTO — **Ault Foods Ltd.** today begins the launch of what it calls longer-lasting, fresher-tasting "filtered" milk, after rival **Beatrice Foods Inc.** failed in its attempt to keep the new milk off the market.

Lawyers for Beatrice appealed for an injunction in an Ontario court Friday, saying people would be "scared" to drink regular milk if Ault was permitted to go ahead with an advertising campaign claiming microfiltered milk contains less bacteria than ordinary pasteurized milk.

"Trying to get in the way of an innovation like this was a little hard to take," Graham Freeman, president of Toronto-based Ault, said after learning the injunction was denied.

Beatrice, also of Toronto, said in a statement that it remains concerned "that Ault's misleading and meaningless claims about bacteria will cause significant loss of consumer confidence in the safety and value of Beatrice and other milk brands."

In court, Beatrice lawyer Alan Aucoin argued: "We're not saying don't market the new milk. We're saying don't market it in such a way that it casts aspersions on everyone else's milk."

Mr. Aucoin told the court that all milk is 99.4-per-cent pure after being pasteurized. The new milk could be 99.9-per-cent bacteria free but that's not the impression people will get when they hear claims of "92 times fewer bacteria," he said.

Ault lawyer Clifford Lax told the judge Beatrice was "trying to get the court's help to avoid competition."

He pointed out none of the other major dairies, including giant Sealtest, was backing Beatrice's complaint.

Outside the courtroom, Mr. Freeman accused rival Beatrice of trying to thwart the launch of the premium milk, set to hit Ontario stores today, because of the 15- to 20-per-cent market share it is expected to grab.

He pointed out that the lower bacteria level does not just improve the taste.

"The difference is the difference between an 18-day shelf life and a 30-day shelf life. We have to be able to explain why this process works," he said.

Ault is planning to sell the new milk in Quebec by spring and throughout Canada within six months. It will be sold in the United States as soon as it receives approval, Mr. Freeman said.

In a bid to fatten its profit margins, Ault plans to sell its PurFiltre at 10 cents a litre more than regular milk. For example, a four-litre bag of PurFiltre will cost $3.89 compared with $3.49 for a four-litre bag of regular milk.

Ault has already poured $8-million into developing the filtered milk, which some analysts have dubbed "cold-filtered milk," borrowing a page from trendy beers. The company has slated another $7-million for advertising this year, Ault spokeswoman Pamela Kempthorne said.

SOURCE: *The Globe and Mail,* January 9, 1995. Reproduced with permission of the Canadian Press.

The Story in Brief

Ault Foods Ltd. launches what it claims is a fresher-tasting, longer-lasting "filtered" milk. The company claims it is 99.9% bacteria-free.

Beatrice Food Inc. has taken exception to the advertisement campaign of its rival, claiming it leaves the public with the mistaken impression that "regular" milk may not be safe to drink.

The Economics Behind the Story

- Prior to Ault Foods' introduction of its new product, consumers perceived milk to be essentially a homogeneous product — there was no difference in taste or quality according to producers.

- The aim of Ault Foods Ltd. is to increase its market share for milk by introducing a differentiated brand of milk. All milk is at least 99.4% bacteria-free, but Ault Foods is playing up the added purity and that it is "better" tasting, and has a longer shelf life. Moreover, it is betting consumer are willing to pay 10¢ per litre more than "regular" milk.

- What economic reason might there be for Beatrice Foods to go to the expense of taking Ault Foods to court? Use marginal cost-benefit analysis to help you answer the question.

names and trademarks, and packaging. While there are many aspirin-type products, promotion and advertising may convince headache sufferers that Bayer or Anacin is superior and worth a higher price than a generic substitute. A celebrity's name associated with jeans or perfume may enhance those products in the minds of buyers. Many consumers regard toothpaste in a "pump" container to be preferable to the same toothpaste in a conventional tube. Environment-friendly "green" packaging or "clear" beverages and liquid soaps are used to attract additional customers.

One implication of product differentiation is that, despite the relatively large number of firms, monopolistically competitive producers do have limited control over the prices of their products. Consumers prefer the products of specific sellers and *within limits* will pay more to satisfy those preferences. Sellers and buyers are not linked at random, as in a purely competitive market.

EASY ENTRY

Entry into monopolistically competitive industries is relatively easy. The fact that monopolistically competitive producers are typically small-sized firms, both absolutely and relatively, suggests that economies of scale and capital requirements are few. Compared with pure competition, however, added financial barriers may result from the need to develop a product different from that of one's rivals and to advertise it. Some existing firms may hold patents on their products and copyrights on their brand names and trademarks, making it more difficult and costly to successfully imitate them.

ILLUSTRATIONS

Table 12-1 lists industries approximating monopolistic competition. Also, grocery stores, gasoline stations, barber shops, dry cleaners, clothing stores, and restaurants operate under conditions similar to those just described.

PRICE AND OUTPUT DETERMINATION

Let's analyze the price-output behaviour of a monopolistically competitive firm. Assume initially that the firms in the industry are producing *specific* products and engaging in a *specific* amount of promotional activity. Later we'll see how product variation and advertising modify our discussion.

THE FIRM'S DEMAND CURVE

Our explanation can be followed in **Figure 12-1 (Key Graph)**. The basic feature of this diagram, which distinguishes it from our analyses of pure competition and pure monopoly, is the elasticity of the firm's individual demand curve. *The demand curve faced by a monopolistically competitive seller is highly, but not perfectly, elastic.* It is much more elastic than the demand curve of the pure monopolist, because the monopolistically competitive seller faces many rivals producing close-substitute goods. Yet for two reasons, the monopolistically competitive seller's sales curve is not perfectly elastic. First, the monopolistically competitive firm has fewer rivals; second, the products of these rivals are close but not perfect substitutes.

TABLE 12-1 **Percentage of output* produced by firms in selected low-concentration manufacturing industries**

Industry	Four largest firms	Eight largest firms	Twenty largest firms
Hosiery	34.4	51.6	79.6
Knitted fabric manufacturers	25.3	42.9	73.6
Footwear	24.9**	40.7	61.7
Feed industry	23.1	32.5	48.3
Boatbuilding and repair	22.8	35.3	52.0
Concrete products	22.7	35.2	51.1
Miscellaneous furniture and fixtures	18.1	32.4	57.0
Children's clothing industry	16.2	27.4	51.1
Kitchen cabinets	15.2**	24.3	37.6
Wooden household furniture	12.5	20.7	37.3
Miscellaneous metal fabricating	12.2	21.9	42.5
Men's and boys' clothing contractors	11.8	20.4	41.0
Platemaking, typesetting, etc.	11.8	18.7	31.4
Metal dies, moulds, patterns	8.5	15.5	31.9
Women's clothing contractors	7.3	11.8	21.1

* As measured by value of shipments. Data for 1985.

** Data for 1984.

Source: Statistics Canada, *Industrial Organization and Concentration in the Manufacturing, Mining and Logging Industries,* 1985 (Ottawa, June 1989).

The precise degree of elasticity of the monopolistically competitive firm's demand curve will depend on the number of rivals and the degree of product differentiation. The larger the number of rivals and the weaker the product differentiation, the greater will be the elasticity of each seller's demand curve; that is, the closer monopolistic competition will be to pure competition.

THE SHORT RUN: PROFITS OR LOSSES

The firm will maximize its profits or minimize its losses in the short run by producing that output designated by the intersection of marginal cost and marginal revenue, for reasons with which we are now familiar. The representative firm of Figure 12-1(a) produces output Q, charges price P, and realizes an economic profit. But a less favourable cost-and-demand situation may exist, putting the monopolistically competitive firm in the position of incurring losses in the short run. This is illustrated

in Figure 12-1(b). In the short run, the monopolistically competitive firm may either realize an economic profit or face losses.

THE LONG RUN: NORMAL PROFITS

In the long run, a monopolistically competitive firm will earn only a normal profit.

PROFITS: FIRMS ENTER In the short-run profits case, in Figure 12-1(a), economic profits will attract new rivals because it's easy to enter the industry. As new firms enter, the demand curve faced by the typical firm will fall (shift to the left) and become more elastic. Why? Because each firm has a smaller share of the total demand and now faces a larger number of close-substitute products. This in turn causes economic profits to disappear. When the demand curve is tangent to the average total-cost curve at the profit-maximizing output, as shown in Figure 12-1(c), the firm is just making normal profits. Output Q is

KEY GRAPH

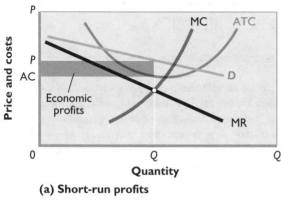

(a) Short-run profits

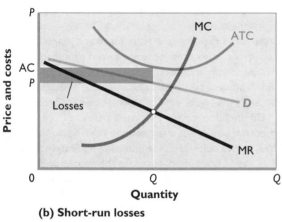

(b) Short-run losses

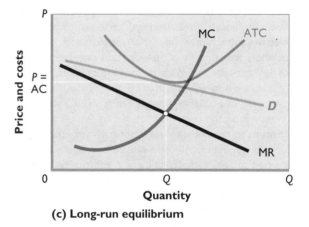

(c) Long-run equilibrium

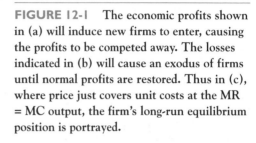

FIGURE 12-1 The economic profits shown in (a) will induce new firms to enter, causing the profits to be competed away. The losses indicated in (b) will cause an exodus of firms until normal profits are restored. Thus in (c), where price just covers unit costs at the MR = MC output, the firm's long-run equilibrium position is portrayed.

the equilibrium output for the firm. As Figure 12-1(c) indicates, any deviation from that output will entail average total costs that exceed product price and, therefore, losses for the firm. Furthermore, economic profits have been competed away and there is no incentive for additional firms to enter.

LOSSES: FIRMS LEAVE   When the industry suffers short-run losses — as shown in Figure 12-1(b) — some firms will exit in the long run. Faced with fewer substitute products and an expanded share of total demand, surviving firms will see their losses disappear and gradually give way to approximately normal profits. (For simplicity we have assumed constant costs; shifts in the cost curve as firms enter or leave would complicate our discussion slightly, but would not alter the conclusions.)

COMPLICATIONS   The representative firm in the monopolistic competition model earns only a nor-

mal profit in the long run. This outcome may not always occur, however, in a world of small firms that have some monopoly power but also face competition. Three possible complications may arise.

1. Some firms may achieve product differentiation to an extent that cannot be duplicated by rivals even over a long time. A particular gasoline station may have the only available location at the busiest intersection in town. Or a firm may hold a patent giving it a slight and more-or-less permanent advantage over imitators. Such firms are, in effect, monopolists and may realize economic profits even in the long run.

2. Remember that entry is not completely unrestricted. Because of product differentiation, there are likely to be greater financial barriers to entry than otherwise. This again suggests monopoly power, with some economic profits persisting even in the long run.

BOX 12-3   APPLYING THE THEORY

THE MARKET FOR PRINCIPLES OF ECONOMICS TEXTBOOKS[*]

The market for principles texts embraces a number of the characteristics of monopolistic competition.

There are many more economics texts that could be used in the principles course. If you compared a number of them, you would find considerable differences. While there is some variation in subject matter, most cover the same core topics. Book do vary considerably as to the rigour and detail with which material is presented. They also vary as to reading level. Some books have a one-colour format, others multicolour diagrams and tables. Books vary greatly in the use of such pedagogical devices as photos, "boxed features," cartoons, learning objectives, intrachapter summaries, and glossaries. Publishers seek the mix of these features that they hope will be most appealing to instructors and students.

Texts are also differentiated by their accompanying "packages" of ancillary materials. These include study guides, videos, and computer tutorial and simulation programs to aid student understanding. Instructor manuals, test banks, and overhead transparencies are designed to save instructor time and enhance teacher productivity. Were you to trace the introduction and development of these various pedagogical aids and instructional materials, you would find that when any one of them was introduced and proved attractive to adopters, that feature would be quickly incorporated into future editions of most other old and new books.

Product differentiation is accompanied by considerable nonprice competition. Texts are advertised by direct mail and in widely read economics journals. Publishers provide potential adopters with free copies and use "trade fair" booths at economics conventions to publicize their wares. Sales representatives of the various publishers — who receive bonuses for exceeding sales quotas — prowl the halls of academia to make professors aware of the distinguishing features and alleged advantages of their particular text. Over 1 million students take principles course each year so the battle for market shares is vigorous.[**]

[*] Based on Timothy Tregarthen, "The Market for Principles of Economics Texts," *The Margin*, March 1987, pp. 14–15; and Joseph E. Stiglitz, "On the Market for Principles of Economics Textbooks: Innovation and Product Differentiation," *Journal of Economic Education*, Spring 1988, pp. 171–177.

[**] In Canada over 65,000 students take principles courses each year, less than 10% of the U.S. market. However, the price of entry for Canadian publishers into this market runs between

Price competition plays a secondary role in the textbook market. First, unlike most markets, the product is chosen for the consumer by a second party. Your instructor — who gets a free text (and teachers' aids) from the publisher and may not even be aware of its retail price — decides the text you must read for the course. Second, instructors usually put textbook quality above price. It would prove very costly to students to use an inaccurate, poorly written text that might impair the teaching-learning process. The significant exception is that over the years more and more instructors have opted for lower-priced paperbacks that split micro and macro components of the course. Thus, a student taking only one semester of economics can avoid the higher cost of a two-semester hardback.

Competition for any given text arises not only from rival books, but also from the used-book market. While new copies of a text dominate its first-year sales, used books often dominate the second and third years of its revision cycle. That means publishers and authors (who receive no income from used-book sales) "compete with themselves" shortly after a revision is published. Many students prefer a used book selling at $25 to a new copy at $35. Furthermore, bookstores typically make a larger profit on used textbooks and therefore "push" them over new ones. Used copies of a given text are very good substitutes for new copies and they undoubtedly increase the price elasticity of demand for new copies.

While there are no artificial barriers to entering the market, the widespread use of multicolour formats and the obligation to provide an array of student-instructor ancillary items poses a significant financial barrier. It may take an investment of $1 million or more for a publisher to enter the market with a text and ancillaries comparable to those already on the market. Even so, it is not uncommon to find two or three new entries in the market every year.

In summary, the economics textbook market is characterized by product differentiation and nonprice competition. Price competition is muted and the only entry barrier is financial.

$100,000 and $300,000, considerably higher than 10% of the average U.S. investment per text.

3. A final consideration may work in the opposite direction, causing losses — below-normal profits — to remain in the long run. The proprietors of a corner delicatessen persistently accept a return less than they could earn elsewhere because their business is a way of life to them. The suburban barber ekes out a meagre existence, because cutting hair is all the barber wants to do. All things considered, however, the long-run normal profit equilibrium of Figure 12-1(c) is a reasonable portrayal of reality.

MONOPOLISTIC COMPETITION AND ECONOMIC INEFFICIENCY

We know that economic efficiency requires the triple equality of price, marginal cost, and average cost. When price and marginal cost are equal, there will be *allocative efficiency*: the allocation of the right amount of resources to the product. When price equals minimum average total cost *productive effi-*ciency, or the use of the most efficient (least-cost) technology, will result. Productive efficiency means consumers will enjoy the largest volume of the product and the lowest price which least-cost conditions allow.

EXCESS CAPACITY

In monopolistically competitive markets excess capacity occurs, and neither allocative nor productive efficiency is realized. An examination of Figure 12-2, which enlarges the relevant portion of Figure 12-1(c) and adds detail, shows that the monopolistic element in monopolistic competition causes a modest underallocation of resources to goods produced. Price (*p*) exceeds marginal cost (*m*) in long-run equilibrium, indicating that society values additional units of this commodity more than the alternative products the needed resource could otherwise produce.

We also observe in Figure 12-1(c) that the monopolistically competitive firms are characterized by **excess capacity**, meaning they produce short of

FIGURE 12-2 **The efficiency aspects of monopolistic competition**

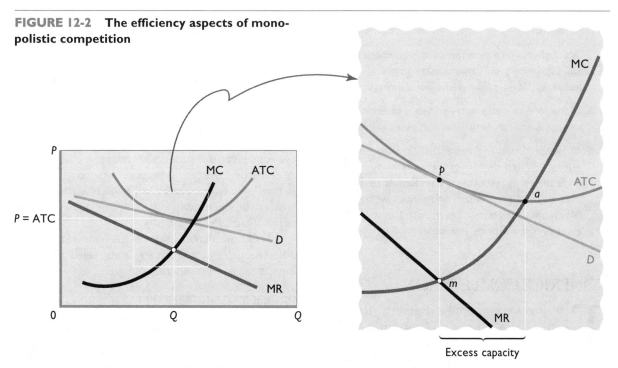

In long-run equilibrium a monopolistically competitive firm achieves neither allocative nor productive efficiency. An underallocation of resources occurs because the product price of *p* exceeds the marginal cost of *m*. Productive efficiency is not realized because production occurs where unit costs of *a* exceed the minimum attainable cost of *a*.

the most efficient (least unit cost) output. There is a higher unit cost than the minimum attainable. This means a higher price (*p*) than would result under competition (*a*). Consumers do *not* benefit from the largest output and lowest price that cost conditions permit. Indeed, the monopolistically competitive firms must charge a higher than competitive price in the long run in order to achieve a normal profit.

Monopolistically competitive industries are overcrowded with firms, each of which is underutilized, or operating short of optimum capacity. That is typified by many kinds of retail establishments; for example, the 30 or 40 gasoline stations, all operating with excess capacity, that populate a medium-sized city. Monopolistic competition results in underutilized plants, and consumers who are penalized through higher than competitive prices for this underutilization. (**Key Question 2**)

QUICK REVIEW 12-1

1. Monopolistic competition refers to industries comprising a relatively large number of firms, operating noncollusively, in the production of differentiated products.

2. In the short run a monopolistically competitive firm will maximize profits or minimize losses at an output at which marginal revenue equals marginal cost.

3. In the long run easy entry and exit of firms causes monopolistically competitive firms to earn a normal profit.

4. A monopolistically competitive firm's equilibrium output is such that price exceeds marginal cost (indicating that resources are underallocated to the product) and price exceeds minimum average total cost (consumers do not get the product at the lowest unit cost and price attainable).

NONPRICE COMPETITION

The situation portrayed in Figure 12-1(c) and Figure 12-2 is not very satisfying to the monopolistically competitive producer that captures only a normal profit. Therefore, monopolistically competitive producers will try to improve on the long-run equilibrium position.

How do they do this? Through nonprice competition in the form of product differentiation and adver-

tising. Each firm has a product distinguishable in some more-or-less tangible way from those of its rivals. The product is presumably subject to further variation, that is, to product development. The emphasis on real product differences and the creation of perceived differences may be achieved through advertising and related sales promotion. The profit-realizing firm of Figure 12-1(a) will not stand by and watch new competitors encroach on its profits by duplicating or imitating its product, copying its advertising, and matching its services to consumers. Rather, the firm will attempt to sustain its profits and stay ahead of competitors through further product development and by enhancing the quantity and quality of its advertising. In this way it might prevent the long-run outcome of Figure 12-1(c) from becoming a reality. True, product development and advertising will add to the firm's costs, but they can also increase the demand for its product. If demand increases by more than enough to compensate for development and promotional costs, the firm will have improved its profit position. As Figure 12-1(c) suggests, the firm may have little or no prospect of increasing profits by price cutting. So why not practice nonprice competition?

The likelihood that easy entry will promote product variety and product improvement is possibly a redeeming feature of monopolistic competition that may offset, wholly or in part, its inefficiencies. In fact, there is a trade-off between product differentiation and the production of a given product at the minimum average total cost. The stronger the product differentiation (the less elastic the demand curve), the further to the left of the minimum average total costs will production take place (Figure 12-2). But the greater the product differentiation, the more likely diverse tastes will be fully satisfied. The greater the excess capacity problem, the wider the range of consumer choice.

There are two considerations here: (1) product differentiation at a point in time, and (2) product improvement over a period of time.

PRODUCT DIFFERENTIATION

Product differentiation means that at any point in time the consumer will be offered a wide range of types, styles, brands, and quality gradations of any given product. Compared with pure competition, this suggests possible advantages to the consumer. The range of choice is widened, and variations and shadings of consumer tastes are more fully met by producers.

But sceptics warn that product differentiation may reach the point where the consumer becomes confused and rational choice becomes time-consuming and difficult. Variety may add spice to the consumer's life, but only up to a point. A woman shopping for lipstick may be bewildered by the vast array of products available. Revlon alone offers more than 150 shades of lipstick, of which over 40 are "pink"! Worse, some observers fear that the consumer, faced with a myriad of similar products, may judge product quality by price; the consumer may irrationally assume that price is an index of product quality.

PRODUCT DEVELOPMENT

Product competition is vital to technological innovation and product betterment over a period of time. Such product development may be cumulative in two different ways. First, a successful product improvement by one firm obligates rivals to imitate or, if they can, improve on this firm's temporary market advantage or suffer losses. Second, profits realized from a successful product improvement can finance further improvements.

Again, there are critics. They say many product alterations are more apparent than real, consisting of frivolous and superficial changes which do *not* improve the product's durability, efficiency, or usefulness. A more exotic container or bright packaging is frequently the extent of product development. It is argued, too, that particularly with durable and semi-durable consumer goods, development may follow a pattern of "planned obsolescence," where firms improve a product only by that amount necessary to make the average consumer dissatisfied with last year's model.

Do the advantages of product differentiation, properly discounted, outweigh the inefficiencies of monopolistic competition? It is difficult to say, short of examining specific cases; and even then, concrete conclusions are hard to come by.

THE ECONOMICS OF ADVERTISING

A monopolistically competitive firm may gain at least a temporary edge on rivals by altering its product. It may also seek the same result by attempting to influence consumer preferences through advertising and sales promotion. Advertising *may* be a mechanism through which a firm can increase its share of the market and enhance consumer loyalty to its particular product.

CONTROVERSY AND SCOPE

There is considerable disagreement as to the economic and social desirability of advertising. Advertising and promotional expenditures in Canada are estimated to be $10 billion. Thus, if advertising is wasteful, any potential virtues of monopolistically competitive markets are thereby dimmed, and the need for corrective public policies is indicated.

TWO VIEWS

The controversy has generated two opposite views.[1] In outlining these two views, bear in mind that advertising is not confined to monopolistic competition. Product differentiation and heavy advertising are also characteristic of many oligopolistic industries (Chapter 13). Thus, our comments are equally germane to these industries.

The **traditional view** sees advertising as a redundant and economically wasteful expenditure that generates economic concentration and monopoly power. The **new perspective** on advertising sees it as an efficient means for both providing information to consumers and enhancing competition. Let's contrast these two views in three critical areas.

1. **PERSUASION OR INFORMATION?** The traditional view holds that the main purpose of advertising is to manipulate or persuade consumers to alter their preferences in favour of the advertiser's product. A television beer commercial conveys little or no useful information to consumers. Advertising is often based on misleading and extravagant claims that confuse and frequently insult the intelligence of consumers, not enlighten them. Indeed, advertising may well persuade consumers in some cases to pay high prices for much-acclaimed but inferior products, forgoing better but unadvertised products selling at lower prices.

The new perspective contends that consumers need information about product characteristics and

---

[1] The following discussion draws on Robert B. Eklund, Jr. and David S. Saurman, *Advertising and the Market Process* (San Francisco: Pacific Research Institute for Public Policy, 1988).

prices in order to make rational decisions. Advertising is alleged to be a low-cost means of providing that information. Suppose you are in the market for a CD player and there was no newspaper or magazine advertising of this product. To make a rational choice you might have to spend several days visiting electronics stores to determine the prices and features of various brands. This entails both direct costs (gasoline, parking fees) and indirect costs (the value of your time). Advertising, it is argued, reduces your "search time" and minimizes these costs.

2. CONCENTRATION OR COMPETITION?

Does advertising generate monopoly or stimulate competition? The traditional view says some firms are more successful than others in establishing "brand loyalty" through advertising. As a consequence, such firms are able to increase their sales, expand their market share, and enjoy enlarged profits. Larger profits permit still more advertising and further enlargement of the firm's market share and profits. Successful advertising can lead to the expansion of some firms at the expense of others and therefore to increased industrial concentration. Consumers eventually lose all the advantages of

competitive markets. Furthermore, potential new entrants to the industry need to incur large advertising costs to establish their product in the marketplace; thus, advertising costs may be a barrier to entry.

The traditional view is portrayed graphically in Figure 12-3(a). By successfully generating brand loyalty through advertising, the firm's demand curve shifts rightward from D_0 to D_1, implying a larger market share. The fact that curve D_1 is less elastic than D_0 indicates a lessening of competition; successful advertising has convinced consumers that there exist fewer good substitutes for this firm's product. The less elastic demand curve also means that the producer can charge higher prices with less loss of sales.

The new perspective says advertising enhances competition. By providing information about the wide variety of substitute products available, advertising diminishes monopoly power. In fact, advertising is frequently associated with the introduction of new products designed to compete with existing brands. Could the Hyundai and Isuzu automobiles have gained a foothold in the North American market without advertising?

In terms of Figure 12-3(b) advertising, in a world of costly and imperfect knowledge, makes

FIGURE 12-3   Advertising and a firm's demand curve: traditional and new perspective views

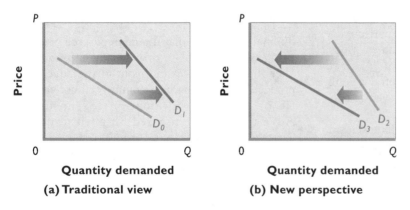

(a) Traditional view   **(b) New perspective**

The traditional view of advertising sees advertising as a device that increases the successful advertiser's market share and enhances brand loyalty. The result is greater market concentration as the demand curve of the successful advertiser shifts rightward and becomes more inelastic as shown by the D_0 to D_1 movement in panel (a). The new perspective regards advertising as a means of increasing consumer awareness of substitute products, thereby enhancing competition. Consequently, advertising in an industry will cause a firm's demand curve to shift leftward and become more elastic as portrayed by the movement from D_2 to D_3 in panel (b).

consumers more aware of the range of substitutable products available to them and provides them with valuable information on the prices and characteristics of these goods. With no advertising, consumers may be aware only that products B and C were good substitutes for A. But advertising provides them with the knowledge that D, E, and F are also substitutable for A. As a consequence of the advertising of all firms in the industry, the demand curve of each firm shifts leftward as from D_2 to D_3 in Figure 12-3(b) and becomes more elastic. Both of these changes reflect enhanced competition.

3. WASTEFUL OR EFFICIENT? The traditional view says that advertising is wasteful. First, it makes markets less competitive and therefore obstructs the realization of either allocative or productive efficiency. Second, advertising allegedly diverts resources from higher-valued uses. For example, timber, which is needed in the production of housing, is squandered on unsightly billboards and on producing the paper used for the ubiquitous advertising supplements in local newspapers. Advertising allegedly constitutes an inefficient use of scarce resources. Finally, advertising expenditures contribute to higher costs, ultimately reflected in higher prices to consumers.

The new perspective views advertising as an efficiency-enhancing activity. It is an inexpensive means of providing useful information to consumers and thus lowers search costs. By enhancing competition, advertising is conducive to both greater allocative and productive efficiency. Finally, by facilitating the successful introduction of new products, advertising is conducive to technological progress.

A narrower perspective on the efficiency aspects of advertising is shown in Figure 12-4. It focuses on the notion that advertising has two effects: (1) it is designed to increase demand and (2) it increases costs.

Scenario one: Through successful advertising a firm increases its demand, permitting it to expand production and sales from, say, Q_0 to Q_1. Despite the fact that advertising outlays will shift the firm's average-total-cost curve upward, unit costs will nevertheless decline from ATC_0 to ATC_1 as the firm moves from point a to b. Greater productive efficiency resulting from economies of scale more than offsets the increase in unit costs due to advertising. Consumers will therefore get the product at a lower price with advertising than they would without.

Scenario two: What if the advertising efforts of firms are essentially self-cancelling? The advertising campaign of one clothing manufacturer is offset by equally costly campaigns waged by rivals so that each firm's demand curve is unchanged. Little or no additional clothing is actually purchased and each firm's market share stays the same. But, because of the advertising, the cost and therefore the price of clothing is higher. Instead of moving from a to b, self-cancelling advertising moves the firm from a to c. The consumer faces a higher product price because of advertising.

These conflicting scenarios suggest that the impact of advertising on output, unit costs, and prices is unclear and ambiguous. **(Key Questions 6 and 9)**

EMPIRICAL EVIDENCE

Evidence on the economic effects of advertising is mixed because studies are usually plagued by data problems and difficulties in determining cause and effect. For example, suppose it is found that firms

FIGURE 12-4 The possible effects of advertising upon a firm's output and average costs

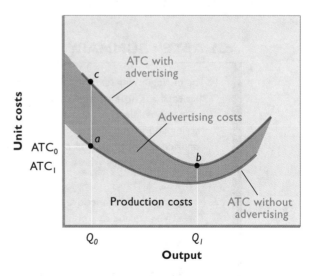

Proponents of advertising contend that advertising will expand the firm's production from, say, a to b and lower unit costs as economies of scale are realized. Some critics argue that advertising is more likely to increase costs and leave output largely unchanged, as is suggested by the movement from a to c.

that do a great deal of advertising seem to have considerable monopoly power and large profits. Does this mean advertising creates barriers to entry that generate monopoly power and profits? Or do entry barriers associated with factors remote from advertising cause monopoly profits that allow firms to spend lavishly in advertising their products? In any event, at this time there is no consensus on the economic implications of advertising.

QUICK REVIEW 12-2

1. Monopolistically competitive firms may seek economic profits through product differentiation, product development, and advertising.

2. The traditional view of advertising alleges that it is a persuasive rather than informative activity; it promotes economic concentration and monopoly power; and it is a source of economic waste and inefficiency.

3. According to the new perspective, advertising is a low-cost source of information for consumers; a means of increasing competition by making consumers aware of substitutable products; and a source of greater efficiency in the use of resources.

MONOPOLISTIC COMPETITION AND ECONOMIC ANALYSIS

Our discussion of nonprice competition implies that the equilibrium situation of a monopolistically competitive firm is more complex than the previous graphic analysis indicates. Figure 12-1 *assumes* a given product and a given level of advertising expenditures. The monopolistically competitive firm, however, must juggle three factors — price, product, and promotion — in seeking maximum profits. What specific variety of product, selling at what price and supplemented by what level of promotional activity, will result in the greatest level of profits? There is no simple answer.

At best, we can note that each possible combination of price, product, and promotion poses a different demand and cost (production plus promotion) structure for the firm, some of which will allow it maximum profits. This optimum combination cannot be readily forecast but must be sought by trial and error. Even here, certain limitations may be imposed by the actions of rivals. A firm may not eliminate advertising expenditures for fear its share of the market will decline sharply, benefiting rivals who do advertise. Similarly, patents held by rivals will rule out certain desirable production variations.

CHAPTER SUMMARY

1. The distinguishing features of monopolistic competition are: **a** there are enough firms so that each has little control over price, mutual interdependence is absent, and collusion is virtually impossible; **b** products are characterized by real and perceived differences and by varying conditions surrounding their sale so that economic rivalry entails both price and nonprice competition; and **c** entry to the industry is relatively easy. Many aspects of retailing, and some industries where economies of scale are few, approximate monopolistic competition.

2. Monopolistically competitive firms may earn economic profits or incur losses in the short run. The easy entry and exit of firms results in a normal profit in the long run.

3. The long-run equilibrium position of the monopolistically competitive producer is less socially desirable than that of a purely competitive firm. Under monopolistic competition, price exceeds marginal cost, resulting in an underallocation of resources to the product, and price exceeds minimum average total cost, indicating that consumers do not get the product at the lowest price cost conditions would allow.

4. Product differentiation provides a means by which monopolistically competitive firms can offset the long-run tendency for economic profits to approximate zero. Through product development and advertising outlays, a firm may strive to increase the demand for its product more than nonprice competition increases its costs.

5. Product differentiation affords the consumer a greater variety of products at any point in time, and improved, products over time. Whether these features fully compensate for the inefficiencies of monopolistic competition is an unresolved question.

6. The traditional and new perspective views of advertising differ as to whether advertising **a** is persuasive or informative, **b** promotes monopoly or competition, and **c** impairs or improves efficiency in resource use. Empirical evidence reveals no consensus about whether advertising is an anti- or pro-competitive force.

7. In practice, the monopolistic competitor seeks that specific combination of price, product, and promotion that will maximize its profits.

TERMS AND CONCEPTS

excess capacity (p. 255)
monopolistic competition (p. 248)
nonprice competition (p. 249)

product differentiation (p. 249)
traditional and new perspective on advertising (p. 257)

QUESTIONS AND STUDY SUGGESTIONS

1. How does monopolistic competition differ from pure competition? From pure monopoly? Explain fully what product differentiation entails.

2. *Key Question   Compare the elasticity of the monopolistically competitive producer's demand curve with that of a. a pure competitor, and b. a pure monopolist. Assuming identical long-run costs, compare graphically the prices and output that would result under pure competition and monopolistic competition. Contrast the two market structures in terms of allocative and productive efficiency. Explain: "Monopolistically competitive industries are characterized by too many firms, each of which produces too little."*

3. "Monopolistic competition is monopoly up to the point at which consumers become willing to buy close substitute products and competitive beyond that point." Explain.

4. "Competition in quality and in service may be quite as effective in giving buyers more for their money as is price competition." Do you agree? Explain why monopolistically competitive firms frequently prefer nonprice to price competition.

5. Critically evaluate and explain:

   a. "In monopolistically competitive industries, economic profits are competed away in the long run; hence there is no valid reason to criticize the performance and efficiency of such industries."

   b. "In the long run, monopolistic competition leads to a monopolistic price but not to monopolistic profits."

6. *Key Question   Compare the traditional and new perspective views of advertising. Which do you think is more accurate?*

7. Do you agree or disagree with the following statements?

   a. "The amount of advertising a firm does is likely to vary inversely with the real differences in its product."

   b. "If each firm's advertising expenditures merely tend to cancel the effects of its rivals' advertising, it is clearly irrational for these firms to maintain large advertising budgets."

8. Carefully evaluate the two views expressed in the following statements:

   a. "It happens every day. Advertising builds mass demand. Production goes up — costs come down. More people can buy — more jobs are created. These are the ingredients of economic growth. Each stimulates the next in a cycle of productivity and plenty that constantly creates a better life for you."

   b. "Advertising constitutes 'inverted education' — a costly effort to induce people to buy without sufficient thought and deliberation and therefore to buy things they don't need. Furthermore, advertising intensifies economic instability because advertising outlays vary directly with the level of consumer spending."

   Which view do you think is more accurate? justify your position.

9. *Key Question* *Advertising can have two effects: It increases a firm's output and it increases unit costs. Explain how the relative size of these two effects may affect consumers.*

10. (Applying the Theory) Describe the price and nonprice competition that is present in the market for economics textbooks. What is the effect of the used book market?

CHAPTER 13

PRICE AND OUTPUT DETERMINATION: OLIGOPOLY

I n many of our manufacturing, mining, and wholesaling industries, a few firms are dominant. Such industries are called oligopolies, the subject of this chapter. We have five objectives. (1) We first define oligopoly, assess its occurrence, and note the reasons for its existence. (2) Our major goal is to survey the possible courses of price-output behaviour that oligopolistic industries might follow. (3) The role of nonprice competition, based on product development and advertising, in oligopolistic industries is briefly discussed. (4) Next, we comment on the economic efficiency and social desirability of oligopoly. (5) Finally, many of the salient aspects of oligopoly are underscored in a brief case study of the automobile industry.

BOX 13-1   THE BIG PICTURE

Monopolistic competition is the most prevalent form of market structure found in the real world. But there is yet another market structure that is not uncommon: oligopoly. Oligopoly refers to a market structure in which there are a few large firms that dominate the market. The fact that there are a few firms makes it difficult to come up with one model that adequately explains an oligopolist's price and output behaviour. We lack one good model of oligopoly because each firm's price and output behaviour depends on what its rivals do, or expect to do. If all firms think in this way, it is far from certain what price or quantity will materialize in an oligopolistic market structure. Because we do not have one good model, we have to look at more than one.

Whether an oligopolistic market structure persists will depend on entry conditions. If it is easy to enter the industry, an oligopoly is unlikely to continue, perhaps transforming into a monopolistically competitive market structure. If entry conditions are next to impossible, an oligopoly could lead to a monopoly.

As you read this chapter, keep the following points in mind:

- Because one firm's move depends on what others do, there is a tendency for firms to agree, overtly or covertly, to co-ordinate output and price.

- Even if firms do not overtly or covertly agree to set price and output, there is a tendency not to rock the boat for fear of market share losses and price wars. This leads to infrequent price changes.

- If firms do co-operate to set price and output, the result will be the same as that of a pure monopolist.

- There are anti-combines laws against collusion. But even in the absence of such laws, collusive agreements are unstable in the long run. In a world of scarce resources in relation to wants, participants in the collusion game will be tempted to cheat.

OLIGOPOLY: CONCEPT AND OCCURRENCE

What are the characteristics of oligopoly? How frequently is it encountered in our economy?

OLIGOPOLY DEFINED

Oligopoly exists when a few large firms, producing a homogeneous or differentiated product, dominate a market. "Fewness" means that the firms are mutually interdependent in that each must consider the possible reactions of its rivals to its price, advertising, and product development decisions.

But what is meant by "a few" firms? This is necessarily vague, because the market model of oligopoly covers much ground. Thus oligopoly encompasses the tin can industry, in which two firms dominate an entire national market, and the situation in which 10 or 15 gasoline stations may enjoy roughly equal shares of the petroleum products market in a medium-sized town. Generally, when we hear of the "Big Three," "Big Four" or "Big Six," we can be sure they refer to an oligopoly market structure.

HOMOGENEOUS OR DIFFERENTIATED PRODUCTS Firms in an oligopoly may produce **homogeneous** (standardized) or **differentiated** products. Many industrial products — steel, zinc, copper, aluminum, lead, cement, and industrial alcohol — are virtually standardized products in the physical sense and are produced under oligopolistic conditions. On the other hand, many consumer goods — automobiles, tires, detergents, greeting cards, breakfast cereals, cigarettes, and many household appliances — are differentiated but also produced by oligopolies.

CONCENTRATION RATIOS Economists use **concentration ratios** as an approximate measure of the structure of an industry. Table 13-1 shows the four-firm concentration ratios — the percentage of total industry sales accounted for by the four largest firms — for a number of industries. For example, almost 100% of tobacco products and about 70% of the batteries produced in Canada are manufactured by the four largest firms in each industry.

When the largest four firms control 40% or more of the total market, that industry is considered oligopolistic. Using this benchmark, more than one-half of Canada's manufacturing industries are oligopolies.

While concentration ratios provide useful insights on the competitiveness or monopolization of various industries, they have several shortcomings.

1. LOCALIZED MARKETS Concentration ratios pertain to the nation as a whole, while markets for some products are actually highly localized because of high transportation costs. For example, the four-firm concentration ratio for concrete products (Table 12-1) suggests a competitive industry. But the sheer bulk of this product limits the market to a given town or metropolitan area and in such localized markets we typically find oligopolistic suppliers. At the local level, some aspects of the retail trade — particularly in small- and medium-sized towns — are characterized by oligopoly.

2. INTERINDUSTRY COMPETITION Definitions of industries are somewhat arbitrary and we must be aware of **interindustry competition**, that is, competition between two products associated with different industries. Table 13-1's high concentration ratios for the aluminum and copper industries understate the degree of competition because aluminum and copper compete in many applications — for example, in the market for electrical transmission lines.

3. WORLD TRADE The data are for Canadian products and therefore often overstate monopoly power because they do not take into account the **import competition** of foreign suppliers. The automobile industry is a highly relevant illustration. While Table 13-1 tells us that four firms account for 95% of the domestic production of motor vehicles, it ignores the fact that about 30% of the automobiles purchased in Canada are imports.

4. HERFINDAHL INDEX Another problem with concentration ratios is that they fail to measure accurately the distribution of market power among the several dominant firms. Suppose in the long-distance telephone industry one firm controlled all service. In a second industry — say, the automobile industry — assume four firms exist and each has 25% of the market. For both industries the four-firm concentration ratio would be 100%. But the telecommunications industry would be a pure monopoly, while the auto

TABLE 13-1 **Percentage of output* produced by firms in selected high-concentration manufacturing industries**

Industry	Percent of industry output produced by first four firms
Glass**	100.0
Cane and beet sugar processors**	100.0
Tobacco products	99.4
Breweries	97.7
Motor vehicles	95.1
Abrasives**	91.0
Aluminum rolling and casting	88.8
Asphalt roofing	86.1
Major appliances	85.0
Copper rolling	82.4
Cement	81.7
Fibre and filament yarn	79.4
Railroad rolling stock	78.8
Leather tanneries	77.4
Distilleries	77.0
Lubricating oils and greases	76.4
Shipbuilding and repair	71.4
Batteries	69.4
Wood preservation industry	68.9
Wire and wire rope industry	68.2
Petroleum products	64.0
Steel pipe and tubes	63.7

* As measured by value of shipments. Data for 1985.

** First eight firms.

Source: Statistics Canada, *Industrial Organization and Concentration in the Manufacturing, Mining and Logging Industries*, 1985 (Ottawa, June 1989).

industry would be an oligopoly characterized perhaps by significant rivalry. The market power would be substantially greater in the telecommunications than in the auto industry, a fact not reflected in the identical 100% concentration ratios.

The **Herfindahl Index** deals with this problem. This index is *the sum of the squared market shares of all firms in the industry*. By squaring the market shares, much greater weight is given to larger firms than smaller ones. In the hypothetical case of the single-firm telecommunications industry the index would be 100^2 or 10,000. For the four-firm auto industry the index would be $25^2 + 25^2 + 25^2 + 25^2$ or 2,500. To generalize, the larger the Herfindahl Index, the greater the degree of market power within an industry. (**Key Questions 3 and 4**)

5. PERFORMANCE   Concentration ratios tell us nothing about the actual market performance of various industries. Industries X and Y may have identical four-firm concentration ratios of 85%. Industry X may be characterized by vigorous price competition and technological progress, evidenced by improved product and production techniques. In contrast, firms of industry Y may price their products collusively and be technologically stagnant. From society's viewpoint the "competitive" performance of industry X is clearly superior to the "monopolistic" performance of Y, a fact concealed by the identical concentration ratios.

CAUSES OF OLIGOPOLY: ENTRY BARRIERS

The same barriers to entry that give rise to pure monopoly are relevant in explaining the existence of oligopoly. Historically, in many industries technological progress has made more and more economies of scale attainable over time. Many industries started out with a primitive technology, few economies of scale, and many competitors. But as technology improved and economies of scale became increasingly pronounced, the less alert or less aggressive firms fell by the wayside and a few producers emerged.

Economies of scale are important in a number of industries such as the aircraft, rubber, and cement industries. While three or four firms can achieve minimum efficient scale (MES), new firms would have such a small market share as to not realize MES. Therefore, they could not survive as high-cost producers.

A closely related barrier is that the capital investment required to enter certain industries — the cost of obtaining necessary plant and equipment — is so great as to discourage entry. The cigarette, automobile, steel, and petroleum-refining industries, for example, are all characterized by very high capital requirements. Prodigious advertising outlays may provide a financial barrier to entry, as some economists have argued is the case in the cigarette industry.

The ownership or control of basic raw materials explains the historical dominance of Inco in the production of nickel. In the electronics, chemicals, photographic equipment, office machine, and pharmaceutical industries, patents have served as entry barriers.

Firm mergers may also give rise to oligopoly. Combining two or more formerly competing firms by merger may increase their market share substantially, enabling the new and larger production unit to achieve greater economies of scale.

Another motive underlying the "urge to merge" is market power. A firm that is larger both absolutely and relative to the market may have greater ability to control the market for and the price of its product than does a smaller, more competitive producer. Also, the large size that merger entails may give the firm the advantage of being a "big buyer" and permit it to demand and obtain lower prices (costs) from input suppliers.

OLIGOPOLY BEHAVIOUR: A GAME THEORY OVERVIEW

Oligopoly pricing behaviour has the characteristics of a game of strategy such as poker, chess, or bridge. The best way to play your hand in a poker game depends on the way rivals play theirs. Players must pattern their actions according to the actions and expected reactions of rivals. Let's use a simple **game theory model** to grasp the basics of oligopolistic pricing behaviour. Specifically, let's assume a **duopoly** — a two-firm oligopoly — exists.

Consider Figure 13-1, which shows the price-profit or profits-payoff matrix for two firms producing athletic shows. Pricing strategies for the firms — say, Leapers and Jumpers — are shown along the left and top margins respectively. Entries in the matrix show the profit payoffs to the two firms associated with any given combination of pricing strate-

BOX 13-2 APPLYING THE THEORY

THE THEORY OF CONTESTABLE MARKETS

The concept of contestable markets suggests that the market power of imperfectly competitive producers may be severely constrained by potential industry entrants.

The outcomes of purely competitive markets set standards of efficiency by which imperfectly competitive markets are judged. Both allocative and productive efficiency are realized when an industry is purely competitive. Princeton's William Baumol argues that the *potential* entry of firms to industries that are *not* purely competitive may also bring about the efficient results associated with pure competition.

Baumol has developed the notion of a *contestable market*, which means a market in which firm entry and exit are costless or virtually so. Envision a contestable market that is oligopolistic, that is, comprised of three or four large firms. The contestability of the market means that it is subject to "hit and run" entry by other firms because they can enter and leave virtually without cost. It follows that any economic profits or production inefficiencies on the part of the several firms in the industry will attract new entrants. (Productive inefficiencies imply that profits are being forgone by existing producers and new entrants can realize such profits by producing efficiently.) Thus, in contestable markets the mere presence of potential competition will force existing firms to produce efficiently and to charge prices that yield only a normal profit. Stated differently, incumbent firms are forced to behave as would purely competitive firms in order to forestall entry of other firms. We thus realize the socially desirable outcomes of purely competitive markets in contestable markets even though the latter are populated by only a few firms. The important factor that promotes these outcomes is not the number of firms in the industry, but costless entry and exit.

The most cited example of a contestable market is the airline industry. Assume there are just two airlines flying the Toronto-Vancouver route. If entry and exit were costly, the market would *not* be contestable and the two incumbent airlines might realize substantial economic profits from their protected market position. But in fact additional airlines can enter and leave this particular segment of the air transportation market with minimal cost. The reason is that the relevant capital equipment — the airplanes themselves — are highly mobile. Thus, if an additional airline were to enter and find the Toronto-Vancouver route to be unprofitable, it could simply pull out by flying its equipment to some other route. The important point is that the awareness of the possibility of costless entry will compel the two airlines currently flying the Toronto-Vancouver route to provide their transportation services efficiently and at prices that yield only a normal profit.

The main policy implication of contestable markets is that the focus of anti-monopoly policy should shift from the current structure or competitive conditions within an industry to the conditions of entry. The criticism of contestable market theory is that its applicability is limited. Critics contend that there are few, if any, industries — including the aforementioned airline industry — in which entry and exit are costless.

gies. Leapers' profit (in millions) is shown in the northeast portion of each cell and Jumpers' profit is in the southwest portion. For example, if both firms adopt a high-price strategy (cell A), each will realize a $12 million profit. Alternatively, if Jumpers follows a high-price policy and Leapers a low-price policy (cell B), Jumpers' profit will be only $6 million and Leapers' will be $15 million.

Although the data of Figure 13-1 are hypothetical, the profit figures are not arbitrarily chosen. In reality, if Jumpers committed itself to a high price and did not vary from it, Leapers could increase its profits by choosing a low price and gaining market share at Jumpers' expense. The same rationale applies if Leapers commits to a high price and Jumpers opts for a low price.

FIGURE 13-1

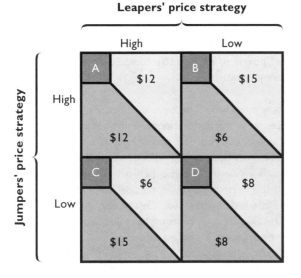

Both firms would realize the largest profit of $12 million if each followed a high-price policy (cell A). But if they are acting independently or competitively, each might achieve a higher profit of $15 million by adopting a low-price policy against its rival's high-price policy (cells B and C). Such independent pricing causes the outcome to gravitate to cell D where profits are only $8 million. Collusion can be used to establish mutual high prices and increase each firm's profits from $8 million (cell D) to $12 million (cell A). But cells B and C remind us of the temptation to cheat on a collusive agreement.

MUTUAL INTERDEPENDENCE

The most evident point demonstrated by Figure 13-1 is the **mutual interdependence** of oligopolists. Each firm's profits will depend not only on its own pricing strategy, but also on that of its rivals. As we have just observed, if Jumpers adopts a high-price policy, its profit will be $12 million *provided* Leapers also employs a high-price strategy (cell A). But if Leapers uses a low-price strategy against Jumpers' high-price strategy (cell B), Leapers will increase its market share and thereby its profits from $12 to $15 million. Leapers' higher profits come at the expense of Jumpers' whose profits fall from $12 to $6 million. Jumpers' high-price strategy is only a "good" strategy *if* Leapers employs the same strategy. Indeed, a good, workable definition of oligopoly is that **oligopoly exists when the number of firms in an industry is** so small that each must consider the reactions of rivals in formulating its price policy.

COLLUSIVE TENDENCIES

A second point is that oligopoly often leads to **collusion,** meaning some sort of formal or informal arrangement to co-ordinate pricing strategies or fix prices. To illustrate in terms of Figure 13-1, suppose that initially both firms are *independently* following high-price strategies. Each realizes a $12 million profit (cell A).

Observe that *either* Leapers or Jumpers could increase its profits by switching to a low-price strategy (cell B or C). If Leapers uses a low-price strategy against Jumpers' high-price strategy, its profits will increase to $15 million and Jumpers' will fall to $6 million. But by comparing cells B and D, we note that when Leapers shifts to a low-price policy, Jumpers would be better off if it also adopted a low-price policy. By doing so its profit would increase from $6 million (cell B) to $8 million (cell D).

Similarly, starting again at cell A, if Jumpers switched to a low-price policy against Leapers' high-price strategy, Jumpers' profit would increase to $15 million and Leapers' would fall to $6 million (cell C). And, again, Leapers could increase its profit from $6 million (cell C) to $8 million (cell D) by also switching to a low-price policy.

What we find is that independent action by oligopolists will likely lead to mutual "competitive" low-price strategies. Independent oligopolists compete with respect to price and this leads to lower prices and lower profits. This is clearly beneficial to consumers, but not to the oligopolists who experience lower profits than if both had used high-price strategies (cell A).

How can oligopolists avoid the low-profit outcome of cell D? The answer is *not* to establish prices competitively or independently, but rather to collude. The two firms must agree to establish and maintain a high-price policy. Each firm will thus increase its profits from $8 million (cell D) to $12 million (cell A). We will discuss a variety of specific collusive practices later in this chapter.

INCENTIVE TO CHEAT

The payoff matrix also explains why an oligopolist might be strongly tempted to cheat on a collusive agreement. Suppose as a result of collusion Jumpers and Leapers both agree to high-price policies with each earning $12 million in profits (cell A). The temptation to cheat on this pricing agreement arises because either firm can increase its profits to $15 million by lowering its price (cell B or C). If Jumpers agrees to a high-price policy but secretly "cheats" on that agreement by actually charging low prices, the outcome moves from cell A to cell C. Result? Jumpers' profit rises to $15 million and Leapers' falls to $6 million. **(Key Question 5)**

QUICK REVIEW 13-1

1. Oligopolistic industries are made up of a "few" firms producing either homogeneous or differentiated products.

2. The four-firm concentration ratio shows the percentage of an industry's sales accounted for by the four largest firms; the Herfindahl Index measures the degree of market power in an industry by summing the squares of the market shares held by each firm.

3. Oligopolies result from scale economies, the control of patents or strategic resources, or mergers.

4. Game theory reveals that **a** oligopolists are mutually interdependent in their pricing policies; **b** collusion will enhance oligopoly profits; and **c** there is a temptation for oligopolists to cheat on a collusive agreement.

FOUR OLIGOPOLY MODELS

To gain further insights on oligopolistic price-output behaviour, we will examine four models: (1) the kinked demand curve, (2) collusive pricing, (3) price leadership, and (4) cost-plus pricing.

Why not a single model as in our discussions of the other market structures? There is no standard portrait of oligopoly for two reasons. -

1. DIVERSITY Oligopoly has a greater range and diversity than other market structures. It includes "tight oligopoly" in which two or three firms dominate an entire market, as well as "loose oligopoly" in which six or seven firms share, say, 70 or 80% of a market while a "competitive fringe" of firms shares the remainder. It includes both product differentiation and standardization. It encompasses cases where firms act in collusion and those where they act independently. It includes situations in which barriers to entry are very strong and those in which they are less so. The diversity of oligopoly precludes development of a simple market model that provides a general explanation of oligopolistic behaviour.

2. INTERDEPENDENCE The fact of mutual interdependence is a significant complication. The inability of a firm to predict with certainty the reactions of its rivals makes it difficult to estimate the demand and marginal-revenue data faced by an oligopolist. Without such data, firms cannot determine their profit-maximizing price and output.

Despite these analytical difficulties, two interrelated characteristics of oligopolistic pricing have been observed. First, if the macroeconomy is generally stable, oligopolistic prices are typically inflexible or "sticky." Prices change less frequently in oligopoly than under pure competition, monopolistic competition, and, in some instances, pure monopoly. Second, when oligopolistic prices do change, firms are likely to change their prices together; oligopolistic price behaviour suggests there are incentives to act collusively in setting and changing prices.

KINKED DEMAND: NONCOLLUSIVE OLIGOPOLY

Imagine an oligopolistic industry comprising just three firms, A, B, and C, each having about one-third of the total market for a differentiated product. Assume the firms are "independent," meaning they do not engage in collusive practices in setting prices. Suppose, too, that the going price for firm A's product is PQ and its current sales are Q, as shown in Figure 13-2(a).

Now the question is, "What does the firm's demand, or sales, curve look like?" Mutual interdependence, and the uncertainty of rivals' reactions make this question difficult to answer. The location and shape of an oligopolist's demand curve depend on how the firm's rivals will react to a price change introduced by A. There are two plausible assumptions about the reactions of A's rivals.

MATCH PRICE CHANGES One possibility is that firms B and C will match any price change initiated by A. In this case, A's demand and marginal-revenue curves will look like D_1D_1 and MR_1 in Figure 13-2(a). If A cuts price, its sales will increase very modestly, because its two rivals will do likewise

FIGURE 13-2

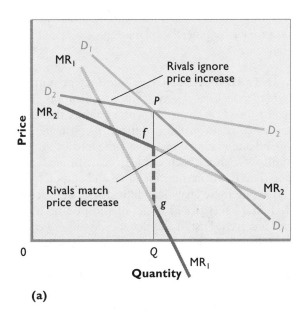

(a)

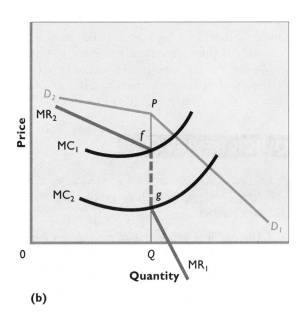

(b)

A noncollusive oligopolist's demand and marginal-revenue curves as shown in (a) will depend upon whether its rivals will match (D_1D_1 and MR_1MR_1) or ignore (D_2D_2 and MR_2MR_2) any price changes that it may initiate from the current price, PQ. In all likelihood, an oligopolist's rivals will ignore a price increase but follow a price cut. This causes the oligopolist's demand curve to be kinked (D_2PD_1) and its marginal-revenue curve to have a vertical break, or gap (MR_2MR_1) as shown in (b). Furthermore, because any shift in marginal costs between MC_1 and MC_2 will cut the vertical (dashed) segment of the marginal-revenue curve, no change in either price, PQ, or output, Q, will occur.

to prevent A from gaining any price advantage over them. The small increase in sales that A (and its two rivals) will realize is at the expense of other industries; A will gain no sales from B and C. If A raises the going price, its sales will fall only modestly, because B and C match its price increase. The industry loses some sales to other industries, but A loses no customers to B and C.

Ignore Price Changes The other possibility is that firms B and C will ignore any price change by A. In this case, the demand and marginal-revenue curves faced by A will resemble D_2D_2 and MR_2MR_2 in Figure 13-2(a). The demand curve in this case is more elastic than under the assumption that B and C will match A's price changes. The reasons are that if A lowers its price and its rivals do not, A will gain sales significantly at the expense of its two rivals because it will be underselling them. If A raises its price and its rivals do not, A will lose many customers to B and C.

Because of product differentiation, however, A's sales do not fall to zero when it raises its price; some of A's customers will pay the higher price because they have strong preferences for A's product.

A Mixed Strategy The most logical assumption for A to make on how its rivals will react to any price change it might initiate is that price declines will be matched as a firm's competitors try to prevent the price cutter from taking their customers; price increases will be ignored because A's rivals stand to gain the business lost by the price booster. The coloured D_2P segment of the "rivals ignore" demand curve seems relevant for price increases, and the coloured PD_1 segment of the "rivals match" demand curve is more realistic for price cuts. It is logical, or at least a good guess, that a noncollusive oligopolist faces a **"kinked" demand curve** on the order of D_2PD_1 as shown in Figure 13-2(b). (Ignore the MC_1 and MC_2 curves for now.) The curve is highly elastic above the going price, but much less elastic below that price.

If it is correct to suppose that rivals will follow a price cut but ignore an increase, the marginal-revenue curve of the oligopolist will also have an odd shape. It, too, will be made up of two segments — the MR_2f part of the marginal-revenue curve appropriate to D_2D_2 and the gMR_1 part appropriate to D_1D_1 in Figure 13-2(a). Because of the sharp differences in elasticity of demand above and below the going price, there is a gap, or what we can treat as a vertical segment, in the marginal-revenue curve. In Figure 13-2(b), the marginal-revenue curve is shown by the two coloured lines connected by the dashed vertical segment, or gap.

PRICE INFLEXIBILITY   This analysis goes far to explain why price changes may be infrequent in noncollusive oligopolistic industries.

1. The kinked demand schedule gives each oligopolist reason to believe that any change in price will be for the worse. Many customers will desert the firm if it raises price. If it lowers price, its sales at best will increase modestly. Even if a price cut increases its total revenue somewhat, the oligopolist's costs may well increase by a more-than-offsetting amount. If the coloured PD_1 segment of its sales schedule be *inelastic*, in that E_d is less than 1, the firm's profit will fall.

   A price decrease will lower the firm's total receipts, and the production of a somewhat larger output will increase total costs. Worse yet, a price cut by A may be *more* than met by B and C, leading to a **price war**; so A's sales may actually decline as its rival firms charge still lower prices. These are all good reasons, on the demand side of the picture, that noncollusive oligopolies might seek the quiet life and follow live-and-let-live price policies.

2. The other reason for price inflexibility under noncollusive oligopoly comes from the cost side of the picture. The broken marginal-revenue curve that accompanies the kinked demand curve suggests that within limits, substantial cost changes will have no effect on output and price. Any shift in marginal cost between MC_1 and MC_2 in Figure 13-2(b) will result in no change in price or output; MR will continue to equal MC at output Q at which price PQ will be charged.

CRITICISM   The kinked demand analysis has two shortcomings. First, *it does not explain how the going price gets to be at PQ (Figure 13-2) in the first place*. Rather, it helps to explain only why oligopolists may be reluctant to deviate from an existing price that yields them a "satisfactory" or "reasonable" profit. The kinked demand curve explains price inflexibility but not price itself.

Second, when the macro environment is unstable, oligopoly prices may not be as rigid — particularly in an upward direction — as the kinked demand theory implies. During inflationary periods such as the 1970s and early 1980s, producers in oligopolistic industries raised their prices substantially. Such price increases might be better explained in terms of collusive oligopoly. (**Key Question 6**)

COLLUSION AND CARTELS

Our game theory model predicts oligopoly is conducive to collusion. Collusion occurs when firms in an industry reach an "observable" or "concealed" agreement to fix prices, divide or share the market, and otherwise restrict competition among themselves. The disadvantages and uncertainties of the noncollusive, kinked-demand model to producers are obvious. There is always the danger of a price war. In a general recession each firm will find itself with excess capacity, and it can reduce per-unit costs by increasing its market share. A new firm may surmount entry barriers and initiate aggressive price cutting to gain a foothold in the market. In addition, the rigid prices suggested by the kinked demand curve may adversely affect profits if general inflationary pressures increase costs. Thus, collusive control over price may permit oligopolists to reduce uncertainty, increase profits, and perhaps even prohibit the entry of new rivals.

PRICE AND OUTPUT   Where will price and output be established under **collusive oligopoly**? Assume once again there are three firms — A, B, and C — producing, in this instance, homogeneous products. Each firm has identical cost curves. Each firm's demand curve is indeterminate unless we know how its rivals will react to any price change. Therefore, suppose each firm assumes its two rivals will match either a price cut or a price increase. In other words, each firm's demand curve is of the D_1D_1 type in Figure 13-2(a). Assume further that the demand curve for each firm is identical. Given

FIGURE 13-3

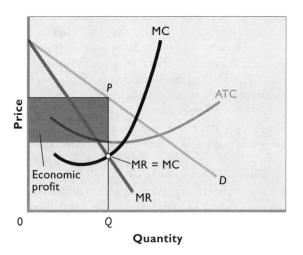

If oligopolistic firms are faced with identical or highly similar demand and cost conditions, they will tend to behave collusively and maximize joint profits. The price and output results are essentially the same as those of pure (unregulated) monopoly; each oligopolist charges price PQ and produces output Q.

identical cost, demand, and marginal-revenue data, we can say that Figure 13-3 represents the position of each of our three oligopolistic firms.

What price-output combination should each firm choose? If firm A were a pure monopolist, the answer would be clear: Establish output at Q, where marginal revenue equals marginal cost, charge the corresponding price, PQ, and enjoy the maximum profit attainable. However, firm A *does* have two rivals selling identical products, and if A's assumption that its rivals will match its price proves to be incorrect, the consequences could be disastrous for A. If B and C actually charge prices below PQ, then firm A's demand curve will shift sharply to the left as its potential customers turn to its rivals, who are now selling the same product at a lower price. Of course, A can retaliate by cutting its price too, but this will move all three firms down their demand curves, lowering their profits, and perhaps even driving them to some point where average cost exceeds price and losses are incurred.

So the question becomes, "Will B and C want to charge a price below PQ?" Under our assumptions, and recognizing that A will have little choice

except to match any price they may set below PQ, the answer is no. Faced with the same demand and cost circumstances, B and C will find it in their interest to produce Q and charge PQ. This is a curious situation; each firm finds it most profitable to charge the same price, PQ, but only if its rivals will actually do so!

How can the three firms realize the PQ-price and Q-quantity solution in which each is keenly interested? The answer is evident: The firms will all be motivated to collude — to get together and talk it over — and agree to charge the same price, PQ. In addition to reducing the possibility of a price war, each firm will realize the maximum profit. And for society, the result is likely to be about the same as if the industry were a pure monopoly composed of three identical plants (Chapter 11).

OVERT COLLUSION: THE OPEC CARTEL
Collusion may assume a variety of forms. The most comprehensive form of collusion is the **cartel**, which typically involves a formal written agreement with respect to both price and production. Output must be controlled — the market must be shared — to maintain the agreed-upon price.

The most spectacularly successful international cartel of recent years has been OPEC (the Organization of Petroleum Exporting Countries). Comprising 13 nations, OPEC was very effective in the 1970s in restricting oil supply and raising prices. The cartel was able to raise world oil prices from U.S. $2.50 to $11 per barrel within a six-month period in 1973–74. By early 1980, price hikes had brought the per barrel price into the U.S. $32 to $34 range. The result was enormous profits for cartel members, greater worldwide inflation, and serious international trade deficits for oil importers.

OPEC was highly effective in the 1970s for several reasons. First, it dominated the world market for oil. If a nation imported oil, it was almost obligated to do business with OPEC. Second, the world demand for oil was strong and expanding in the 1970s. Finally, the short-run demand for oil was highly inelastic, which meant that a small restriction of output by OPEC would result in a relatively large price increase. As shown in Figure 13-4, in 1973–74 and again in 1979–80 OPEC was able to achieve enormous oil price increases and incur only a very modest decline in sales. With this inelastic demand, higher prices translated into greatly

FIGURE 13-4

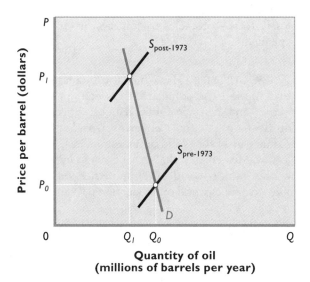

Quantity of oil
(millions of barrels per year)

Because of the inelasticity of the demand for oil, in 1973–74 and again in 1979–80 the OPEC cartel was able to obtain a dramatic increase in the price of oil (P_0 to P_1) accompanied by only a very modest decline in production and sales (Q_0 to Q_1).

increased total revenues for OPEC members. The accompanying smaller output meant lower total costs. The combination of more total revenue and lower total costs resulted in greatly expanded profits.

COVERT COLLUSION: THE ELECTRICAL EQUIPMENT CONSPIRACY   Cartels are illegal in both Canada and the United States; collusion has been covert or secret. For example, in 1960 an extensive price-fixing and market-sharing scheme involving heavy electrical equipment, such as transformers, turbines, circuit breakers, and switchgear, was uncovered in the United States. Elaborate secret schemes were developed by such participants as General Electric, Westinghouse, and Allis-Chalmers to rig prices and divide the market. Twenty-nine manufacturers and forty-six company officials were indicted in this "great electrical conspiracy," which violated United States antitrust laws. Substantial fines, jail penalties, and lawsuits by victimized buyers were the final outcome. In 1933 Borden, Pet, and Dean food companies, among a number of others, either pleaded guilty or

were convicted of rigging bids on the prices of milk products sold to American schools and military bases. By phone or at luncheons, company executives agreed in advance who would submit the low bid for each school district or military base. In 1992 the U.S. government accused eight major airlines of fixing fares during the 1988–92 period. Agreements to increase fares or eliminate discounts were accomplished by communicating fare proposals through their computerized ticket information system. The makers of SOS and Brillo steel wool scouring pads were recently indicted for co-ordinating by telephone their price increases and discounts. In contrast, no one has ever gone to jail for breaches of Canada's Combines Investigation Act (renamed the Competition Act in mid-1986).

In innumerable other instances, collusion is even more subtle. **Gentlemen's agreements** frequently are struck at cocktail parties, on the golf course, by phone calls, or at trade association meetings. Competing firms reach a verbal agreement on product price, leaving market shares to the ingenuity of each seller as reflected in nonprice competition. Although they collide with the Competition Act, the elusive character of gentlemen's agreements makes them more difficult to detect and prosecute successfully.

OBSTACLES TO COLLUSION   Cartels and similar collusive arrangements are often difficult to establish and maintain. Let's briefly consider several important barriers to collusion.

1. DEMAND AND COST DIFFERENCES   When oligopolists' costs and product demands differ, it is more difficult to agree on price, especially where products are differentiated and changing frequently over time. Indeed, even with highly standardized products, we would expect that firms might have somewhat different market shares and would operate with differing degrees of productive efficiency, thus they would have different demand and cost curves.

In either event, unlike the cartel of Figure 13-3, differences in costs and demand will mean that the profit-maximizing price for each firm will differ; there will be no single price that is readily acceptable to all. Price collusion therefore depends on compromises and concessions — to arrive at a degree of "understanding" that in practice is often difficult to attain.

For example, the MR = MC positions of firms A, B, and C may call for them to charge $12, $11, and

$10 respectively, but this price cluster or range may be unsatisfactory to one or more of the firms.

2. NUMBER OF FIRMS Other things equal, the larger the number of firms, the more difficult it is to achieve a cartel or other form of price collusion. Agreement on price by three or four producers that control an entire market is much more readily accomplished than it is when ten firms each have roughly 10% of the market.

3. CHEATING As our game theory made clear, there is also a temptation for collusive oligopolists to make secret price concessions in order to get additional business. The difficulty with cheating is that buyers who are paying a high price may become aware of the lower-priced sales and demand similar treatment. Or buyers receiving price concessions from one oligopolist may use this concession as a wedge to get even larger price concessions from the firm's rivals. The attempt of buyers to play sellers against one another may precipitate a price war among the firms. Although it is potentially profitable, secret price concessions threaten the maintenance of collusive oligopoly over time. Collusion is more likely to persist when cheating is easy to detect and punish.

4. RECESSION Recession is usually an enemy of collusion because slumping markets cause the oligopolists' demand and marginal-revenue curves to shift to the left (Figure 13-3), and each firm moves back to a higher point on its average-total-cost curve. Firms find they have substantial excess productive capacity, sales are down, unit costs are up, and profits are being squeezed. Under these conditions, businesses may feel they can better avoid serious profit reductions by price cutting in the hope of gaining sales at the expense of rivals.

5. POTENTIAL ENTRY The enhanced prices and profits that result from collusion may attract new entrants, including foreign firms. Such entry would increase market supply and reduce prices and profits. Therefore, successful collusion requires that the colluding oligopolists can block entry of new producers.

6. LEGAL OBSTACLES: ANTI-COMBINES Our Competition Act prohibits cartels and the kind of price-fixing collusion we have been discussing. Thus, less obvious means of price rigging — such as price leadership — have evolved in Canada.

OPEC IN DISARRAY The highly successful OPEC oil cartel of the 1970s fell into disarray in the 1980s. The reasons for OPEC's decline relate closely to the obstacles to collusion we have just explained.

1. NEW SUPPLIES The dramatic increase in oil prices in the 1970s stimulated the search for new oil reserves, and soon non-OPEC nations, which OPEC could not block from entering world markets, became part of the world oil industry. Great Britain, Norway, Mexico, and the former Soviet Union have become major world oil suppliers. As a result, OPEC's share of world oil production fell sharply.

2. CONSERVATION On the demand side, oil conservation, a worldwide recession in the early 1980s, and the expanded use of alternative energy sources (such as coal, natural gas, and nuclear power) reduced the demand for oil. The combination of greater production by non-OPEC nations and a decline in world demand generated an oil glut that seriously impaired OPEC's ability to control world oil prices.

3. CHEATING OPEC has had a serious cheating problem stemming from the relatively large number of members (13) and the diversity of their economic circumstances. Saudi Arabia is the dominant cartel member; it has the largest oil reserves and is probably the lowest-cost producer. It has favoured a "moderate" pricing policy because it has feared that very high oil prices would hasten the development of alternative energy sources (such as solar power and synthetic fuels) and increase the attractiveness of existing substitutes such as coal and natural gas. These developments would greatly reduce the value of its vast oil reserves. Saudi Arabia also has a small population and a very high per capita GDP. But other members — for example, Nigeria and Venezuela — are very poor, have large populations, and are burdened with large external debts. Others — Iran, Iraq, and Libya — have had large military commitments. All of these members have had immediate needs for cash. Thus, there has been substantial cheating. Some members have exceeded assigned production quotas and have sold oil at prices below those agreed to by the cartel. As a consequence, although OPEC's official oil price reached U.S. $34 per barrel in 1979, it is currently about U.S. $17 per barrel.

BOX 13-3 IN THE MEDIA

DIAMOND CARTEL MAY NOT BE FOREVER

PETER COOK

JOHANNESBURG — A diamond may be forever. But the world's diamond cartel run by **De Beers** of South Africa is in trouble at the age of 60.

The trouble comes from a not unusual source in the mining industry. The Russians, desperate for foreign exchange, have upset world markets for aluminum and nickel, and are doing the same to diamonds, disrupting the way the Central Selling Organisation, De Beers' price-setting subsidiary, has done business since 1934.

The Russians have signed a deal that commits them to selling their 25 per cent of world production to the CSO. So De Beers has reacted angrily to the quota being exceeded with large sales of rough uncut diamonds that circumvent the cartel and threaten to pull down prices.

Talks on a new five-year quota arrangement with the Russians must be concluded this year. But, according to the chairman of De Beers Centenary AG, Julian Ogilvie Thompson, the Russians are not ready to negotiate.

"They haven't got their brief from whomever decides these things in Russia nowadays," he said last week. "Meanwhile, they are getting away with murder. Retail sales of diamonds are up but our sales are down."

At stake is not just the profitability of De Beers, which is closely linked to the world's largest natural resources group, Anglo American Corp., but the immutable idea — on which the company has spent a fortune in advertising — that diamonds are forever and do not lose their value.

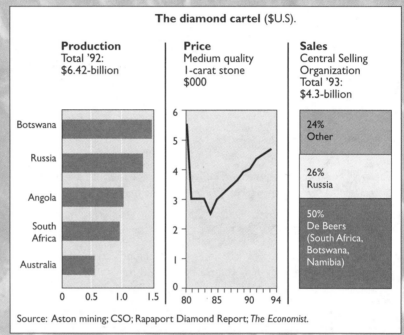

The diamond cartel ($U.S).

Production
Total '92:
$6.42-billion

Botswana
Russia
Angola
South Africa
Australia

0   0.5   1.0   1.5

Price
Medium quality
1-carat stone
$000

6
5
4
3
2
1
0

80   85   90   94

Sales
Central Selling
Organization
Total '93:
$4.3-billion

24% Other

26% Russia

50% De Beers (South Africa, Botswana, Namibia)

Source: Aston mining; CSO; Rapaport Diamond Report; *The Economist.*

Traditionally, cartels work when a single producer has the lion's share of the market and fail when too many new producers arrive on the scene.

Some observers say, in breaking their agreement, the Russians are merely bringing forward the day when De Beers loses control of the price of diamonds. New discoveries are being made. By the turn of the century, Canada, not now a diamond producer, will become one if a consortium led by Broken Hill Pty. Co. Ltd. of Australia is able to exploit its Lac de Gras discovery in the Northwest Territories. And that new mine could account for 3 per cent of world output.

Over the past 30 years, De Beers has maintained prices while three large fields, in Russia, Botswana and Australia, have come into production. Some observers say this cannot

last. As diamonds are discovered outside De Beers' sphere of influence, its ability to organize and finance a cartel and act as the swing producer will become a thing of the past.

Mr. Ogilvie Thompson sees things differently. He says a higher proportion of world diamonds are passing through the hands of the CSO, and its position is under no threat.

"If new people come into the market and they are large producers then it is wise for them to have a contract with De Beers. If they're small, then they can take advantage of us," he says. "But we are used to this."

The Russians are flexing their muscles because they hope to get a better quota in a new agreement. If De Beers gives in, others like Botswana and Australia will demand similar concessions. One estimate puts

Russia's unofficial sales at $500-million (U.S.) above a quota that is worth $1.2-billion. Russia's precious metals and gems committee, which will do the negotiating, says it could join with new producers such as Canada and market diamonds outside the cartel.

De Beers' CSO was established by Ernest Oppenheimer in the 1930s to keep prices high during the Depression (De Beers and Anglo American are still controlled by the Oppenheimer family). The stones are sold to dealers in Antwerp, Tel Aviv, Bombay and New York. Every year, De Beers spends $170-million on advertising, a cost that all producers benefit from.

Since the early 1980s, world output of diamonds has more than doubled, forcing De Beers to stockpile supplies and hold them off the market — another cost that helps cartel and non-cartel producers alike.

By raising their sales, the Russians risk pushing down prices, which would undermine the industry's image. However, sources say the Russians are knowledgeable traders and know that this would be against their own interest. All they want is to expand their share of the business at De Beers' expense.

Source: *The Globe and Mail*, February 20, 1995. Reproduced with permission.

The Story in Brief

The world diamond cartel, run by De Beers for more than half a century, may not be able to keep the cartel intact as new producers come on to the market.

The Economics Behind the Story

- De Beers, the leader that has kept the world diamond cartel intact, has been successful in keeping the price of diamonds high by controlling supply through the Central Selling Organization (CSO), a subsidiary of De Beers.

- Russia, which produces a quarter of the world's diamond production, is selling more than the quota assigned to it by the CSO. If Russia continues to exceed its quota, the rightward shift in the world's supply of diamonds will reduce their price. Such an outcome can be avoided only if all diamond producers co-operate to regulate supply.

- What economic arguments will De Beer's use to persuade Russia to continue selling through the CSO?

PRICE LEADERSHIP

Price leadership is a type of gentlemen's agreement by which oligopolists can co-ordinate their price behaviour without engaging in outright collusion. Formal agreements and clandestine meetings are not involved. Rather, a practice evolves whereby the "dominant" firm — usually the largest or the most efficient in the industry — initiates price changes, and all other firms more or less automatically follow. Such industries as farm machinery, anthracite coal, cement, copper, gasoline, newsprint, tin cans, lead, sulphur, rayon, fertilizer, glass containers, steel, automobiles, and nonferrous metals are practising, or have in the recent past practised, price leadership.

CIGARETTE PRICING   The case of the cigarette industry is a classic example of tight price leadership. In this instance, the American Big Three, producing from 68% to 90% of total output, evolved a highly profitable practice of price leadership, which resulted in virtually identical prices over the entire 1923–41 period.

Since 1946, cigarette pricing has been less rigid, reflecting both successful anti-combines action and the development of increasingly heterogeneous product lines.

LEADERSHIP TACTICS   The examination of price leadership in a variety of industries suggests that the price leader is likely to observe the following tactics.

1. INFREQUENT CHANGES   Because price changes always entail some risk that rivals will not follow, price adjustments will be made infrequently. The price leader will *not* change prices in response to tiny day-to-day changes in cost and demand conditions. Price will be changed only when cost and demand conditions have been altered significantly and on an industry-wide basis. For example, in response to industry-wide wage increases, an increase in taxes, or an increase in the price of some basic input such as energy. In the automobile industry, price adjustments have traditionally been made when new models are introduced each fall.

2. COMMUNICATION   Impending price adjustments are often communicated by the price leader to the industry through speeches by major executives, trade publication interviews, and so forth. By publicizing "the need to raise prices," the price leader can elicit a consensus among its competitors for the actual increase.

3. LIMIT PRICING   The price leader does not necessarily choose the price that maximizes short-run profits for the industry. The industry may want to discourage new firms from entering. If barriers to entry are based on cost advantages (economies of scale) or existing firms, these cost barriers may be surmounted by new entrants *if* product price is set high enough. New firms that are relatively inefficient because of their small size may survive and grow if the industry's price is very high. To discourage new competitors and thereby maintain the current oligopolistic structure of the industry, price may be established below the profit-maximizing level. This strategy of establishing a price that prevents the entry of new firms is called *limit pricing*.

COST-PLUS PRICING

Another model of oligopolistic price behaviour centres on what is variously known as *markup, rule-of-thumb,* or **cost-plus pricing**. The oligopolist estimates cost per unit of output and a markup is applied to cost to determine price. Unit costs, however, vary with output and therefore the firm must assume some typical or target level of output. For example, the firm's average-total-cost figure may be that which is realized when the firm is operating at, say, 75% or 80% of capacity. A markup, usually in the form of a percentage, is applied to average total cost in determining price. For example, an appliance manufacturer may estimate unit costs of dish-

washers to be $250, to which a 50% markup is applied. This yields a $375 price to retailers.

The markup is 50%, rather than 25% or 100% because the firm is seeking some target profit or rate of return on its investment. Consider the pricing techniques used by General Motors for over four decades prior to the advent of aggressive foreign competition in the mid-1970s:

> GM started with the goal of earning, on the average over the years, a return of approximately 15 percent after taxes on total invested capital. Not knowing how many autos would be sold and hence unit costs (including prorated fixed costs), it calculated costs on the assumption of operation at 80 percent of conservatively rated capacity. A standard price was calculated by adding to unit cost a sufficient profit margin to yield the desired 15 percent after-tax return. The rule would be adjusted across the product line to take account of actual and potential competition, business conditions, long-run strategic goals, and other factors. Actual profit then depended on the number of vehicles sold. Between 1960 and 1979, GM's actual return on stockholders' equity fell below 15 percent in only four years, all marked by recession and/or OPEC-induced gasoline price shocks. The average return was 17.6 percent. After 1979, recession and intensifying import competition caused GM frequently to fall short of its target.[1]

Two final points: First, this cost-plus method of pricing is *not* inconsistent with outright collusion or price leadership. If the several producers in an industry have roughly similar costs, adherence to a common pricing formula will result in highly similar prices and price changes. As we will find in a case study later in this chapter, General Motors uses cost-plus pricing *and* is the price leader in the automobile industry.

Second, cost-plus pricing has obvious advantages for multi-product firms, which would otherwise be faced with the difficult and costly process of estimating demand and cost conditions for perhaps hundreds of different products. In practice, it is virtually impossible to allocate correctly certain common overhead costs such as power, lighting, insurance, and taxes to specific products.

[1] F.M. Scherer and David Rose, *Industrial Market Structure and Economic Performance*, 3rd ed. (Boston: Houghton Mifflin Company, 1990), p. 262.

NONPRICE COMPETITION

We explained why oligopolists are averse to price competition. This aversion may lead to informal collusion on price. In North America, however, price collusion is usually accompanied by nonprice competition. It is typically through nonprice competition that each firm's share of total market is determined. This emphasis on nonprice competition has its roots in two facts.

1. LESS EASILY DUPLICATED Price cuts can be quickly and easily met by a firm's rivals. Thus, the possibility of a firm's significantly increasing its share of the market through price competition is small. And of course the risk is always present that price competition will precipitate a disastrous price war. Nonprice competition is less likely to get out of hand. Oligopolists seem to feel that more permanent advantages can be gained over rivals through nonprice competition because product variations, improvements in productive techniques, and successful advertising gimmicks cannot be duplicated as easily as price reductions.

2. GREATER FINANCIAL RESOURCES There is a more evident reason for the tremendous emphasis on nonprice competition: Manufacturing oligopolists typically have substantial financial resources with which to support advertising and product development. Although nonprice competition is a basic characteristic of both monopolistically competitive and oligopolistic industries, oligopolists are typically in a financial position to indulge more fully in nonprice competition.

OLIGOPOLY AND ECONOMIC EFFICIENCY

Is oligopoly an "efficient" market structure from society's standpoint? How does the price-output behaviour of the oligopolist compare with that of a purely competitive firm?

ALLOCATIVE AND PRODUCTIVE EFFICIENCY

Many economists believe that the outcome of oligopolistic markets is approximately that shown in Figure 13-3. As compared to the benchmark of pure competition (Figure 10-12), the oligopolist's production occurs where price exceeds marginal cost and short of that output where average total cost is minimized. In the terminology of Chapters 10 and 11, neither allocative efficiency ($P = MC$) nor productive efficiency (P = minimum ATC) is likely to occur under oligopoly.

One may even argue that oligopoly is actually less desirable than pure monopoly because pure monopoly in Canada is frequently subject to government regulation to mitigate abuses of market power. Informal collusion among oligopolists may yield price and output results similar to pure monopoly, yet at the same time maintain the outward appearance of several independent and "competing" firms.

Two qualifications are relevant. First, in recent years foreign competition has generated more rivalry in a number of oligopolistic markets — autos and steel, for example — and has undermined such cozy arrangements as price leadership and cost-plus pricing and stimulated more competitive pricing. Second, recall that oligopolistic firms may purposely keep prices below the short-run profit-maximizing level to deter entry where entry barriers are less formidable.

DYNAMIC EFFICIENCY

What about the "very long-run" perspective where we allow for innovation in improvements in product quality and more efficient production methods?

COMPETITIVE VIEW One view is that competition provides a compelling incentive to be technologically progressive. If a competitive firm does not seize the initiative, one or more rivals will introduce an improved product or a cost-reducing production technique that may drive it from the market. Both the desire of short-term profits and long-term survival provide competitive firms with the persistent pressure to improve products and lower costs through innovation.

Some adherents to this **competitive view** allege that oligopolists may have an incentive to impede innovation and restrain technological progress. The larger corporation wants to maximize profits by exploiting fully all its capital assets. Why rush to develop and introduce a new product (for example, fluorescent lights) when that product's success will render obsolete all equipment designed to produce an existing product (incandescent bulbs)? It is not difficult to cite oligopolistic industries in which interest in research and development has been modest at best. Examples: the steel, cigarette, and aluminum industries.

SCHUMPETER-GALBRAITH VIEW   In contrast the Schumpeter-Galbraith view holds that technological advance is a competitive force (see Chapter 10's Applying the Theory box) and large oligopolistic firms with market power are necessary for rapid technological progress.

HIGH R&D COSTS   It is argued, first, that modern research to develop new products and new productive techniques is very expensive. Therefore, only large oligopolistic firms can finance extensive research and development (R & D) activities.

BARRIERS AND PROFIT   Second, the existence of barriers to entry gives the oligopolist some assurance that it will realize any profit rewards from successful R & D endeavours. Small competitive firms have neither the *means* nor the *incentives* to be technologically progressive; large oligopolists do.[2]

If the Schumpeter-Galbraith view is correct, it suggests that over time oligopolistic industries will foster rapid product improvement, lower unit production costs, lower prices, and perhaps a greater output and more employment than would the same industry organized competitively. There is anecdotal and case-study evidence suggesting that many oligopolistic manufacturing industries — television and other electronics products, home appliances, automobile tires — have been characterized by substantial improvements in product quality, falling relative prices, and expanding levels of output and employment.

TECHNOLOGICAL PROGRESS: THE EVIDENCE

Which view is correct? Empirical studies have yielded ambiguous results. The consensus, however, seems to be that giant oligopolies are probably *not* a fountainhead of technological progress. A pioneering study[3] of 61 important inventions made from 1880 to 1965 indicates that over half were the work of independent inventors disassociated from corporate industrial research laboratories. Such substantial advances as air conditioning, power

steering, the ballpoint pen, cellophane, the jet engine, insulin, xerography, the helicopter, and the catalytic cracking of petroleum have this individualistic heritage. Other equally important advances have come from small- and medium-sized firms.

According to this study, about two-thirds — 40 out of 61 — of the basic inventions of this century have been fathered by independent inventors or the research activities of relatively small firms. This is not to deny that in a number of oligopolistic industries — for example, the steel, aluminum, and nickel industries — research activity has been pursued vigorously and fruitfully. The Big Two in Canadian steel — Dofasco and Stelco — decided a long time ago that research and development were essential to their survival in the face of competition from U.S. Steel. Since then, the research activity of U.S. Steel (now named USX) has declined markedly, while it has remained at a substantial level in the Canadian industry.

Some leading researchers in this field have tentatively concluded that technological progress in an industry may be determined more by the industry's scientific character and "technological opportunities" than by its market structure. There may simply be more opportunities for progress in the computer and electronics industries than in the brickmaking and cigarette industries, regardless of market structure.

[2] John Kenneth Galbraith, *American Capitalism*, rev. ed. (Boston: Houghton Mifflin Company, 1956), pp. 86–88. Also see Joseph Schumpeter, *Capitalism, Socialism and Democracy* (New York: Harper & Row Publishers, Inc., 1942).

[3] John Jewkes, David Sawers, and Richard Stillerman, *The Sources of Invention*, rev. ed. (New York: St. Martin's Press, Inc., 1968).

QUICK REVIEW 13-2

1. The kinked-demand curve model is based on the assumption that an oligopolist's rivals will match a price cut but ignore a price increase. This model is consistent with observed price rigidity found in some oligopolistic industries.

2. A cartel is a collusive association of firms that establishes a formal agreement to determine price and to divide the market among participants.

3. Price leadership occurs when one firm — usually the largest or most efficient — determines price, and rival firms establish identical or similar prices.

4. Cost-plus pricing means that a firm establishes price by adding a percentage markup to the average cost of its product.

5. Oligopoly is conducive to neither allocative nor productive efficiency. There is disagreement as to whether oligopoly fosters technological progress.

AUTOMOBILES: A CASE STUDY[4]

The North American automobile industry provides an informative case study of oligopoly, illustrating many of the points made in this chapter. It also indicates that market structure is not permanent and, in particular, that foreign competition can upset the oligopolists' "quiet life."

MARKET STRUCTURE

Although there were more than 80 auto manufacturers in the early 1920s in the United States and almost as many in Canada, a number of mergers (most notably the combining of Chevrolet, Pontiac, Oldsmobile, Buick, and Cadillac into General Motors), many failures during the Great Depression of the 1930s, and the increasing role of entry barriers all reduced numbers in the industry. Currently, three large firms — General Motors (GM), Ford, and Chrysler — dominate the North American market for domestically produced automobiles.

These firms are gigantic in size: according to *The Report on Business Magazine*, in 1995, GM was second, Ford third and Chrysler the fourth largest in Canada, ranked by sale. Furthermore, all three firms are leading truck manufacturers, produce a variety of household appliances, are involved in U.S. defence contracting, and have extensive overseas interests.

ENTRY BARRIERS Entry barriers are substantial, as is evidenced by the fact that it has been about six decades since a North American firm successfully entered the automobile industry. The primary barrier is economies of scale. It is estimated that the minimum efficient scale for a producer is about 300,000 autos per year. However, given the uncertainties of consumer tastes, experts believe a truly viable firm must produce at least two different models. Hence to have a reasonable prospect of success, a new firm would have to produce about 600,000 autos per year.

---

[4] This section draws heavily on Walter Adams and James W. Brock, "The Automobile Industry," in Walter Adams (ed.), *The Structure of American Industry*, 7th ed. (New York: Macmillan Publishing Co., Inc., 1986), pp. 126–171 and John E. Kwoka, Jr., "Automobiles: Overtaking an Oligopoly," in Larry Deutsch (ed.), *Industry Studies* (Englewood Cliffs, N.J.: Prentice Hall, Inc., 1993).

The estimated cost of an integrated plant (involving the production of engines, transmissions, other components, and product assembly) might be as much as $1.2 to $1.4 billion. Other entry barriers include the need for extensive advertising and a far-flung dealer network (GM has over 16,000 dealers; Chrysler has over 11,000) that provide spare parts and repair service. A newcomer would also face the expensive task of overcoming existing brand loyalties. Because the North American automobile industry spent over $3 billion per year on advertising in each of the past five years, this is no small matter.

PRICE LEADERSHIP AND PROFITS The indicated industry structure — a few firms with high entry barriers — has been fertile ground for collusive or co-ordinated pricing. GM has traditionally been the price leader. Each fall, with the introduction of new models, GM would establish prices for its basic models, and Ford and Chrysler would set the prices of their comparable models accordingly. (Details of how GM established its prices were outlined in the earlier section on cost-plus pricing.)

In the past several decades automobile prices have moved up steadily and often at a rate exceeding the overall rate of inflation. And despite large periodic declines in demand and sales, automobile prices have displayed considerable downward rigidity, although import competition and recession have caused rebates and financing subsidies to become common in recent years.

Over the years, price leadership has proven to be very profitable. In the 1947–77 period the Big Three earned an average profit rate significantly greater than that of all manufacturing corporations taken as a whole.

STYLING AND TECHNOLOGY In addition to advertising, nonprice competition has centred historically on styling changes and the introduction of new models. In practice styling changes have been stressed over technological advance. As early as the 1920s GM recognized that the replacement market was becoming increasingly important compared to the market for first-time purchasers. Therefore, its strategy — later adopted by other manufacturers — became one of annual styling changes accompanied by model proliferation. The purpose is to achieve higher sales and profits by encouraging consumers to replace their autos with greater frequency and to encourage buyers to shift their purchase from basic to "upscale" models.

But competition did *not* focus on product quality.

Autos were being built in ways that had changed very little in decades. Each company had large and expensive engine, transmission, stamping, and other production plants located all around the country, each of which shipped components to assembly facilities. The latter still resembled Henry Ford's original assembly line, with paramount importance given to maintaining continuous operation of the line. To ensure that the line never stopped, large numbers of all necessary components were held in inventory, extra workers were available to replace those absent or on break at any time, and repair stations were located at the end of each line to fix defective vehicles that came off the line.

This approach provided very little incentive for quality production, since ill-fitting parts could still be installed and poorly assembled vehicles would be attended to elsewhere. The results were both poor quality and high cost.[5]

WAGES AND WORK RULES High costs were also due to high wages and restrictive work rules. The high profits of the Big Three were shared with their union. Wage increases were persistently greater than productivity increases, so that labour costs per auto rose. By 1980 wages in the auto industry were 50% greater than wages for manufacturing as a whole. The companies also accepted union-imposed work rules that restricted management's flexibility in assigning tasks to workers. The effect of such rules was to diminish worker productivity.

To summarize: The post-World War II auto industry was a "complacent oligopoly," characterized by (1) little price competition; (2) substantial profits; (3) emphasis on styling changes, model proliferation, and advertising; (4) neglect of product quality; and (5) high labour costs.

FOREIGN COMPETITION This state of affairs changed abruptly in the early 1970s with the advent of more vigorous competition by foreign — particularly Japanese — producers. There were several reasons for the growth of foreign competition.

First, OPEC-inspired increases in gasoline prices in the early 1970s prompted a shift in consumer demand towards smaller, fuel-efficient imports from Japan and Germany. Second, many consumers perceived the imports as having quality advantages. A 1990 consumer survey found seven Japanese, two German, and only one North American car ranked in the top ten. Third, lower overseas wages and higher labour productivity gave the Japanese and South Koreans a substantial cost advantage in producing compact cars.

RESPONSES North American producers initially responded to this new competition in two ways. First, the industry — with the support of organized labour — successfully lobbied government for protection. The result, beginning in 1981, was "voluntary" import quotas on Japanese cars that effectively restrained competition. But, rather than take their advantage in the form of increased sales and market share, North American producers boosted auto prices. One study suggests that the import quotas increased the profits of the Big Three by over $3 billion in 1983 alone.

The second response of domestic producers was to co-opt and mitigate foreign competition by initiating an elaborate network of joint ownership arrangements and joint ventures with foreign producers. Chrysler owns about one-fourth of Mitsubishi and imports both compact cars and parts from the latter. Mitsubishi in turn is a part owner of Korea's Hyundai Motor Company. General Motors has a joint production arrangement with Toyota in California and Ontario and has significant ownership shares in other lesser-known Japanese auto manufacturers. Ford owns about one-fourth of Mazda. These arrangements cast a cloud of doubt on the contention that foreign competition has had an important "disciplining" effect on North American auto manufacturers. Indeed, this interlocking system of joint ventures may be establishing "the groundwork for cartelizing the world automobile industry."[6]

But the Japanese have responded to import quotas and the uncertainties inherent in the changing dollar-yen exchange rate by building automobile plants in North America. These "trans-plants" produce about 10% of the cars sold in North America. The success of Japanese production in North America is reflected in

---

[5] Kwoka, *op. cit.*, p. 68.

[6] Walter Adams and James W. Brock, "Joint Ventures, Antitrust, and Transnational Cartelization," *Northwestern Journal of International Law & Business*, Winter 1991, p. 465.

the fact that they built ten new factories in Canada and the United States in the 1980s, precisely the number closed by the Big Three in the 1987-89 period.

RESTRUCTURING AND RESURGENCE? Despite record losses in the early 1990s, there are signs in the mid-1990s that the North American Big Three have gone through a difficult period of restructuring and may be meeting the import challenge.

There are several reasons for this revival. First, North American producers have upgraded product quality. While the perceived quality gap between Japanese and North American cars remains, it has narrowed substantially. Second, the Big Three — especially Chrysler and Ford — have increased productivity and reduced costs by imitating Japanese "lean" production methods. These methods entail the use of fewer parts suppliers, carrying smaller inventories, a more flexible work force, and greater attention to quality. Third, the yen has appreciated substantially compared to the dollar, meaning each dollar spent on a Japanese car generates a smaller yen profit for Japanese producers. This has necessitated increases in the dollar prices of Japanese autos to preserve profitability. Thus Japanese cars may now cost $2000 to $3000 more than their North American counterparts, shifting demand to the Big Three.

While the future of the automobile industry is uncertain, it is clear that the competition from abroad has greatly altered the Big Three's "complacent oligopoly" of the 1950s and 1960s. GM's price leadership is a thing of the past. Current pricing is more competitive with ten companies producing and about thirty selling in the North American market. And rising incomes are expected to stimulate auto sales in many of the less developed areas of the world, presenting new competitive challenges (Global Perspective 13-1).

GLOBAL PERSPECTIVE 13-1

North American producers and the global auto market

Big Three automobile sales are heavily concentrated in the North American and western European markets, where currently some 63% of global vehicle sales occur. However, sales growth is accelerating in Asia, Latin American, and central and eastern Europe, where North America's Big Three are generally much less active than European and Japanese producers. In comparison, sales growth is declining in North American and western Europe where the Big Three's presence is strongest. Will North American firms again have to play "catch-up" with their global rivals?

Percent (sales in region/total sales)

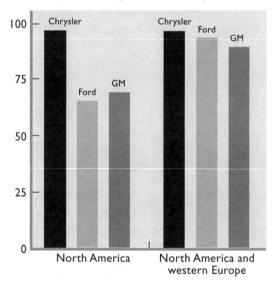

Source: U.S. Department of Commerce and the Federal Reserve Bank of Chicago.

CHAPTER SUMMARY

1. Oligopolistic industries are characterized by the presence of a few firms, each having a significant fraction of the market. Firms thus situated are mutually interdependent; the behaviour of any one firm directly affects, and is affected by, the actions of rivals. Products may be virtually uniform or significantly differentiated. Various barriers to entry underlie and maintain oligopoly.

2. Concentration ratios can be used as a measure of oligopoly and market power. The Herfindahl Index, which gives more weight to larger firms, is designed to measure market dominance in an industry.

3. Game theory shows **a** the mutual interdependence of oligopolists' price policies; **b** reveals the tendency to act collusively; and **c** explains the temptation to cheat on collusive agreements.

4. Important models of oligopoly include: **a** the kinked-demand model, **b** collusive oligopoly, **c** price leadership, and **d** cost-plus pricing.

5. Noncollusive oligopolists may face a kinked demand curve. This curve and the accompanying marginal-revenue curve help explain the price rigidity that often characterizes such markets; they do not, however, explain the level of price.

6. The uncertainties inherent in noncollusive pricing promote collusion. Collusive oligopolists maximize joint profits — that is, they behave like pure monopolists. Demand and cost differences, a "large" number of firms, "cheating" through secret price concessions, recessions, and the Competition Act are all obstacles to collusive oligopoly.

7. Price leadership is an informal means of collusion where the largest or most efficient firm in the industry initiates price changes and the other firms follow.

8. With cost-plus or markup pricing, oligopolists estimate their unit costs at some target level of output and add a percentage "markup" to determine price.

9. Market shares in oligopolistic industries are usually determined on the basis of nonprice competition. Oligopolists emphasize nonprice competition because *a.* advertising and product variations are less easy for rivals to match, and *b.* oligopolists frequently have ample resources to finance nonprice competition.

10. Neither allocative nor productive efficiency is achieved in oligopolistic markets. The competitive view envisions oligopoly as being inferior to more competitive market structures in promoting product improvement and cost-decreasing innovations. The Schumpeter-Galbraith view is that oligopolists have both the incentive and financial resources to be technologically progressive.

TERMS AND CONCEPTS

cartel (p. 272)
collusion (p. 268)
collusive oligopoly (p. 271)
competitive view (p. 278)
concentration ratio (p. 264)
cost-plus pricing (p. 277)
duopoly (p. 266)
game theory model (p. 266)
gentlemen's agreement (p. 273)
Herfindahl Index (p. 266)

homogeneous and differentiated oligopoly (p. 264)
import competition (p. 265)
interindustry competition (p. 265)
kinked demand curve (p. 270)
mutual interdependence (p. 268)
oligopoly (p. 264)
price leadership (p. 276)
price war (p. 271)
traditional and Schumpeter-Galbraith views (p. 279)

QUESTIONS AND STUDY SUGGESTIONS

1. Why do oligopolies exist? List five or six oligopolists whose products you own or regularly purchase. What distinguishes oligopoly from monopolistic competition?

2. "Fewness of rivals means mutual interdependence, and mutual interdependence means uncertainty as to how those few rivals will react to a price change by any one firm." Explain. Of what significance is this for determining demand and marginal revenue? Other things equal, would you expect mutual interdependence to vary directly or inversely with the degree of product differentiation? With the number of firms? Explain.

3. **Key Question**   *What is the meaning of a four-firm concentration ratio of 60%? 90%? What are the shortcomings of concentration ratios as measures of market power?*

4. **Key Question**   *Suppose that in industry A five firms have annual sales of 30, 30, 20, 10, and 10% of total industry sales. For the five firms in industry B the figures are 60, 25, 5, 5, and 5%. Calculate the Herfindahl Index for each industry and compare their likely competitiveness.*

5. **Key Question**   *Explain the general character of the data in the following profits-payoff matrix for oligopolists C and D. All profit figures are in thousands.*

	C's price →	
D's price ↓	$40	$35
$40	$57 / $60	$59 / $55
$35	$50 / $69	$55 / $58

   a. *Use the table to explain the mutual interdependence that characterizes oligopolistic industries.*

   b. *Assuming no collusion, what is the likely outcome?*

   c. *Given your answer to question b., explain why price collusion is mutually profitable. Why might there be a temptation to cheat on the collusive agreement?*

6. **Key Question**   *What assumptions about a rival's responses to price changes underlie the kinked demand curve? Why is there a gap in the marginal-revenue curve? How does the kinked demand curve explain oligopolistic price rigidity? What are the shortcomings of the kinked-demand model?*

7. Why might price collusion occur in oligopolistic industries? Assess the economic desirability of collusive pricing. Explain: "If each firm knows that the price of each of its few rivals depends on its own price, how can the prices be determined?" What are the main obstacles to collusion? Apply these obstacles to the weakening of OPEC in the 1980s.

8. Assume the demand curve shown in question 4 in Chapter 11 applies to a pure monopolist that has a constant marginal cost of $4. What price and output will be most profitable for the monopolist? Now assume the demand curve applies to a two-firm industry (a "duopoly") and that each firm has a constant marginal cost of $4. If the firms collude, what price and quantity

will maximize their joint profits? Demonstrate why it might be profitable for one of the firms to cheat. if the other firm becomes aware of this cheating, what will happen?

9. Explain how price leadership might evolve and function in an oligopolistic industry. Is cost-plus pricing compatible with collusion?

10. "Oligopolistic industries have both the means and the inclination for technological progress." Do you agree? Explain.

11. "If oligopolists really want to compete, they should do so by cutting their prices rather than by squandering millions of dollars on advertising and other forms of sales promotion." Do you agree? Why don't oligopolists usually compete by cutting prices?

12. Using Figure 13-3, explain how a collusive oligopolist might increase its profits by offering secret price concessions to buyers. On the diagram, indicate the amount of additional profits that the firm may realize. What are the risks involved in such a policy?

13. Identify aspects of the structure and behaviour of the automobile industry that are oligopolistic. Why did the Big Three lose domestic market share to foreign producers in the 1970s and 1980s? What have been the responses of domestic producers to increased foreign competition?

14. (Applying the Theory) What is the main criticism of the theory of contestable markets? Would the existence of potential foreign entrants into a specific oligopolistic market structure weaken the criticism of the theory of contestable markets?

GOVERNMENT COMPETITION POLICY AND REGULATION OF MONOPOLIES

H ow are electricity, natural gas, local phone calls, and railroad service related? All are "utilities" and subject to **industrial regulation** — government regulation of prices (rates) within selected industries. Governments also encourage competition by enforcing **anti-combines** laws that make it illegal for firms to collude to affect the market price of their output.

What do workplace safety standards, infant seats, acid rain, affirmative action, and auto fuel economy have in common? All are the objects or results of **social regulation** — government regulation of the conditions under which goods are produced, their physical characteristics, and the impact of their production on society.

What do government subsidies to the auto industry to promote fuel-efficient automobiles, to the computer industry to develop "flat glass" monitor screens, and to manufacturers who export goods have in common? All are components of *industrial policy* — government policies to promote selected industries or products.

Anti-combines, industrial, and social regulation and industrial policy — each is a government intervention in the marketplace. To explain why and how, we first clarify some terms and summarize the debate over the desirability of industrial concentration. Next, we examine government policy towards monopoly and anti-competitive business practices. We then consider both anti-combines legislation and the regulation of industries that are natural monopolies. Finally, we look at examples of industrial policy and issues relating to it.

BOX 14-1 THE BIG PICTURE

When we studied market structures we concluded that in a world of scarce resources, pure competition is the market structure that produces the most out of limited resources, and produces those good and services society wants most. While pure competition itself is rare in the real world, the model tells us that more competition is better than less.

Because competition is desirable, governments encourage it — and discourage the opposite: restriction of competition. That's also the aim of anti-combines laws. But make no mistake; there are trade-offs between regulated versus unregulated markets. The desire for more competition is a societal goal; a firm with a monopoly will not lobby a government for more competition — that would not be in its interest. On the other hand, recall that there are instances when a natural monopoly may deliver the lowest costs for consumers. Thus, it is not easy to find the right balance between regulated and unregulated markets. It is no surprise that governments continually revisit their policy in this regard.

As you read this chapter, keep the following points in mind:

- Some industrial concentration may be beneficial to consumers because of the lower unit costs it can bring about.
- Natural monopolies are desirable because they can produce goods at the lowest possible unit cost. But in the absence of competition the benefits of the scale economies achieved are unlikely to be passed on to consumers. Thus, governments regulate them to ensure the benefits of scale economies are passed on to consumers.
- The aim of deregulation is to promote competition. Deregulation is desirable if it brings about more competition, thus lower prices for consumers. But deregulation can bring about the opposite result: a few firms can come to dominate the industry.
- Government often imposes regulations on firms for perceived beneficial social ends. The regulations sometimes lessen competition.
- Social regulations attempt to lessen undesirable social side effects of a competitive market economy. There are pros and cons to social regulations.
- Industrial policy seeks to intervene in the market system to improve the social and economic outcome in particular sectors of the economy. Industrial policy has its supporters and detractors.

INDUSTRIAL CONCENTRATION: DEFINITIONS

In Chapter 11 we developed and applied a strict definition of monopoly. A *pure*, or *absolute*, monopoly, we said, is a one-firm industry — a situation where a unique product is being produced entirely by a single firm, entry to the industry being blocked by insurmountable barriers.

In this chapter we will use *industrial concentration* to include pure monopoly and markets in which there is much potential monopoly power. **Industrial concentration** *exists whenever a single firm or a small number of firms control the major portion of the output of an industry.* One, two, or three firms dominate the industry, potentially resulting in higher than competitive prices and economic profits. This definition, which is closer to how most people

understand the "monopoly problem," includes many industries we previously designated as oligopolies.

"Industrial concentration" refers to those industries where firms are large in absolute terms *and* in relation to the total market. Examples are the electric equipment industry, in which Northern Telecom, Canadian General Electric, and Westinghouse Canada, large by any absolute standard, dominate the market; the automobile industry, where General Motors of Canada, Ford of Canada, and Chrysler Canada are dominant; the petroleum industry, dominated by Petro-Canada, Imperial Oil (Exxon), and Shell Canada; the aluminum industry, where industrial giant Alcan Aluminum reigns supreme; and the steel industry, where the two large producers, Dominion Foundries & Steel (Dofasco) and Steel Company of Canada (Stelco), command the lion's share of this large market.

INDUSTRIAL CONCENTRATION: BENEFICIAL OR HARMFUL?

I t is unclear whether industrial concentration is, on balance, advantageous or disadvantageous to the working of our economy.

THE CASE AGAINST INDUSTRIAL CONCENTRATION

We stated the case against monopoly and oligopoly in previous chapters. Let's review and extend those arguments.

1. INEFFICIENT RESOURCE ALLOCATION Monopolists and oligopolists find it possible and profitable to restrict output and charge higher prices than if their industry were organized competitively. With pure competition, production occurs where P = MC. This equality specifies an efficient allocation of resources because price measures the marginal value to society of an extra unit of output, while marginal cost reflects the sacrifice of alternative goods. In maximizing profits a monopolist equates not price, but marginal revenue with marginal cost. At this MR = MC point, price will exceed marginal cost, designating an underallocation of resources to the monopolized product. As a result, the economic well-being of society is less than it would be with pure competition.

2. UNPROGRESSIVE Critics say industrial concentration is neither essential for achieving mass-production economies nor conducive to technological progress.

Empirical studies suggest that "fewness" is not essential for achieving economies of scale in most manufacturing industries. In these industries, firms need only realize a small percentage — in many cases less than 3 or 5% — of the total market to achieve low-cost production; industrial concentration is *not* a prerequisite of productive efficiency.

Furthermore, the basic unit for technological efficiency is not the firm, but the individual plant. You can correctly argue that productive efficiency calls for, say, a large-scale, integrated auto-manufacturing plant. But it is perfectly consistent to argue that there is no technological justification for General Motors, which is a giant business corporation composed of a number of geographically distinct plants.

Nor does technological progress depend on huge corporations with substantial monopoly power. Large size and market power do *not* correlate closely with technological progress. Instead, the sheltered position of firms in highly concentrated industries may promote inefficiency and lethargy; there is no competition to spur productive efficiency. Furthermore, monopolists and oligopolists often resist or suppress technological advances that may cause sudden obsolescence of their existing machinery and equipment.

3. INCOME INEQUALITY Industrial concentration is criticized as a contributor to income inequality. Because of entry barriers, monopolists and oligopolists can charge a price above average total cost and consistently realize economic profits. These profits go to corporate stockholders and executives who are generally among the upper income groups.

4. POLITICAL CLOUT Because economic power and political clout go hand in hand, it is argued that giant corporations exert undue influence over government. This is reflected in legislation and government policies that are congenial, not to the public interest, but to the preservation and growth of these large firms. Big businesses allegedly have exerted political power to become primary beneficiaries of tax loopholes, patent policy, tariff and quota protection, and other subsidies and privileges.

DEFENCE OF INDUSTRIAL CONCENTRATION

Industrial concentration *does* have supporters, who make the following points:

1. SUPERIOR PRODUCTS One defence is that monopolists and oligopolists have gained their market dominance by offering superior products. Business monopolists do not coerce consumers to buy, say, Colgate or Crest toothpaste, soft drinks from Coca-Cola and Pepsi, software from Microsoft, ketchup from Heinz, or soup from Campbell. Consumers have collectively decided these products are more desirable than those offered by other producers. Monopoly profits and large market shares have been "earned."

2. UNDERESTIMATING COMPETITION Another defence of industrial concentration is that economists may view competition too narrowly.

While there may be only a few firms producing a specific product, those firms may face **interindustry competition** — competition from other firms producing distinct but highly substitutable products. There may be only a handful of firms responsible for the nation's output of steel. But steel faces competition in specific markets from aluminum, copper, wood, plastics, and a host of other products.

Foreign competition must also be taken into account. While General Motors and Ford dominate domestic automobile production, strong import competition constrains their pricing and output decisions.

Furthermore, the large profits resulting from a monopolist's market power induce potential competitors to enter the industry. **Potential competition** restrains the price and output decisions of firms now possessing market power. These firms wish to deter entry, and one way to do that is to keep prices low.

3. ECONOMIES OF SCALE Where existing technology is highly advanced, only large producers — firms that are large both absolutely and in relation to the market — can obtain low unit costs and therefore sell to consumers at low prices. The traditional antimonopoly contention that industrial concentration means less output, higher prices, and an inefficient allocation of resources assumes that cost economies would be equally available to firms whether the industry's structure was highly competitive or quite monopolistic. This is frequently not so; economies of scale may be accessible only if competition — in the sense of a large number of firms — is absent.

4. TECHNOLOGICAL PROGRESS Recall the *Schumpeter-Galbraith view* that monopolistic industries — in particular, three- and four-firm oligopolies — generate a high rate of technological progress. Oligopolistic firms have both the financial resources *and* the incentives to undertake technological research.

QUICK REVIEW 14-1

1. Industrial concentration exists whenever a single firm or a small number of firms controls the major portion of output of an industry.

2. The case against industrial concentration is that it fosters allocative inefficiency, impedes technological progress, promotes income inequality, and can give some interest groups more political power.

3. Those who defend industrial concentration contend it arises from superior performance and economies of scale; is countered by interindustry, foreign, and potential competition; and generates both the resources and incentives for technological research.

ANTI-COMBINES LEGISLATION

The sharp conflict of opinion over the merits of industrial concentration is likely why government policy towards concentration has not been clear-cut and consistent. Although the thrust of federal legislation and policy has been to maintain and promote competition, we will examine policies and acts that have furthered the development of monopoly and oligopoly.

HISTORICAL BACKGROUND

Our economy has been a fertile ground for development of a suspicious, fearful public attitude towards industrial concentration. Dormant in the nation's early years, this distrust of big business bloomed in the decades following Confederation. The widening of local markets into national markets as transportation facilities improved, the ever-increasing mechanization of production, and the increasingly widespread adoption of the corporate form of business enterprise contributed to the development of industrial concentration between the 1880s and World War I.

Not only were questionable tactics used in the concentration of these industries, the resulting market power was exerted to the detriment of all who did business with them. Farmers and small businesses, being particularly vulnerable to the growth of monopoly power, were among the first to criticize its development. Consumers and labour unions were not far behind in their opposition.

Because of development of industries in which market forces no longer provided adequate control to ensure socially tolerable behaviour, two techniques of control have been adopted as substitutes for, or supplements to, the market.

1. REGULATORY AGENCIES In those few markets where economic realities preclude the effective working of the market — where there is "natural monopoly" — we have established public **regulatory agencies** to control economic behaviour.

FIGURE 14-1

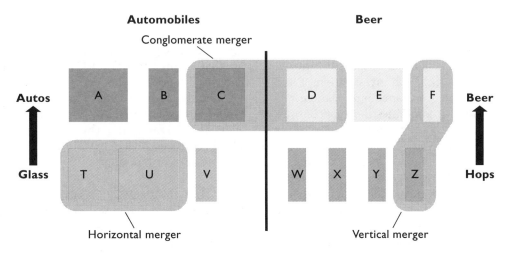

Horizontal mergers (T + U) bring together firms selling similar products; vertical mergers (F + Z) connect firms having a buyer-seller relationship; and conglomerate mergers (C + D) join unrelated firms.

2. ANTI-COMBINES LAWS In most other markets where economic and technological conditions have not made monopoly essential, social control has taken the form of **anti-combines legislation** designed to inhibit or prevent the growth of monopoly.

First, let's consider the anti-combines legislation that, as refined and extended by various amendments, constitutes the basic law of the land with respect to corporate size and concentration. Before we do, let's examine merger types.

MERGER TYPES There are three basic types of mergers, as shown in Figure 14-1. This diagram shows two stages of production, one the input stage, the other the final-good stage of two distinct final-good industries: autos and beer. Each rectangle (A, B, C ... X, Y, Z) represents a particular firm.

A horizontal merger *is a merger between two competitors selling similar products in the same market.* In Figure 14-1 this type of merger is shown as a combination of glass producers T and U. Other hypothetical examples of horizontal mergers would be Ford Motor Company merging with General Motors or Molson merging with Labatts.

A vertical merger — *the merging of firms at different stages of the production process in the same industry* — is shown in Figure 14-1 as a merger between firm Z, a hops producer, and firm F, a

brewery. Vertical mergers involve firms having buyer-seller relationships. Examples of mergers of this type are Pepsico's mergers with Pizza Hut, Taco Bell, and Kentucky Fried Chicken. Pepsico supplies soft drinks to each of these fast-food outlets.

A conglomerate merger *is the merger of a firm in one industry with a firm in another unrelated industry.* In Figure 14-1 a merger between firm C, an auto manufacturer, and firm D, a brewery, fits this description and is a conglomerate merger.

THE ACT OF 1889

Canadian anti-combines legislation began in 1889 with the passage of an Act that made it a misdemeanour to conspire to either restrict trade or output, or competition. Three years later, the Act of 1889 became a section of the Criminal Code and the offence became an indictable one. In the first ten years of this century there were *six* prosecutions under the section, resulting in four convictions. Apparently, securing evidence was particularly difficult, and further changes became necessary.

COMBINES INVESTIGATION ACT, 1910

The result was the passing of the **Combines Investigation Act** in 1910, an Act whose name was with us in successive Acts until June 1986, when it became the Competition Act. The 1910

Act authorized a judge, on receiving an application by six persons, to order an investigation into an alleged combine.

The 1910 Act was hardly a success, for two reasons: (1) Rarely could six private citizens be found willing to bear the publicity and expense of initiating an investigation. (2) Each investigation, if and when ordered by a judge, started afresh; there was no person or body to administer the Act continuously. Thus, there was only *one* investigation under the Act before World War I.

The next 50 years saw no fundamental change. Of note were the 1952 amendments to the Act, which split the duties of the combines commissioner and assigned them to two separate agencies — one for investigation and research, the other for appraisal and report. Thus were established a director of investigation and research and a Restrictive Trade Practices Commission, the latter being superseded in June 1986 by the Competition Tribunal (see below).

In 1960, the Combines Investigation Act was at last amended to include the provisions relating to combinations that had been laid down in the Criminal Code since 1892. As well, mergers and monopolies now were deemed unlawful only if a "detriment or against the interest of the public."

In 1967, the newly formed Department of Consumer and Corporate Affairs took over responsibility for combines, mergers, monopolies, and restraint of trade. Shortly thereafter, in 1969, the Economic Council of Canada reported that the provisions of the Combines Investigation Act making mergers and monopolies criminal offences were "all but inoperative" because a criminal offence had to be proved "beyond a shadow of a doubt" — a very difficult task. However, the Economic Council did *not* recommend barriers be placed in the way of a company achieving dominance through internal growth or superior efficiency. The Economic Council's whole approach then was based on the goal of economic efficiency. It was this same approach that led the Economic Council to recommend that competition policy be extended to services.

On January 1, 1976, new amendments to the Combines Investigation Act became effective, with the result that it became applicable to services as well.

THE COMPETITION ACT, 1986

Successive governments in Ottawa have attempted to bring about changes to Canada's law governing monopolies. Three attempts, Bills brought before Parliament in 1971, 1977, and 1977–79, met with organized opposition from business. Extensive consultations with the private sector and provincial governments preceded the introduction of yet another Bill in 1984. The 1984 election intervened and this Bill, too, was not enacted.

Finally, in June 1986, Parliament passed the Competition Tribunal Act and the **Competition Act**, the latter being the new name for the Combines Investigation Act. Some of the major changes are worth noting.

CIVIL LAW FRAMEWORK   Mergers and monopolies have been removed from the jurisdiction of the criminal law, making it easier to prosecute those mergers and monopolies not in the public interest. A **Competition Tribunal** adjudicates under a civil law framework that will permit the issuing of remedial orders to restore and maintain competition in the market. The tribunal is made up of judges of the Federal Court and lay persons, with a judge as chairperson. The Restrictive Trade Practices Commission is abolished as a result.

MERGER   Only those mergers resulting in an unacceptable lessening of competition could be prohibited or modified by the Competition Tribunal. Mergers that result in gains in efficiency — through, for example, economies of scale — that more than offset the costs stemming from the lessening of competition are allowed.

ABUSE OF DOMINANT POSITION   The abuse-of-dominance provision is designed to ensure that dominant firms compete with other firms on merit, not through the abuse of their market power.

CONSPIRACY   The conspiracy provision in the old Combines Investigation Act is considerably tightened by adding that the existence of a conspiracy may be proven from circumstantial evidence with or without direct evidence of communication among the parties. The maximum fine has been increased from $1 million to $10 million.

EXPORT AGREEMENTS   Export consortia — combines — are permitted, provided they relate only to the export of products from Canada, even should they have the unintended, ancillary effect of lessening domestic competition.

BOX 14-2 IN THE MEDIA

OIL FIRMS NOT GOUGING DRIVERS, REPORT SAYS: NOT ANY EVIDENCE OF PRICE FIXING, WATCHDOG SAYS

By ROB CARRICK
CANADIAN PRESS

OTTAWA — The federal competition watchdog has let the oil industry off the hook on complaints of high gasoline prices and told consumers it's up to them to police the market.

The Bureau of Competition says in a report released yesterday that it found no evidence of price fixing by gasoline companies.

The report also says current laws are adequate to address concerns about the way gas is priced.

People concerned about high gas costs should patronize stations with the lowest prices, the report says.

A survey by The Star for two weeks in July found prices were lowest on a Monday and were higher during the weekend. The survey also found exceptions did exist for customers who wanted to shop around.

Industry Minister John Manley, who commissioned the report, said yesterday he accepts its findings.

"Consumers are going to have to shop around. They are going to have to be vigilant to go where the prices are lowest," he said.

The report says that despite close monitoring, the bureau has never found evidence of an agreement among oil companies to fix prices.

It says neighborhood gas stations that charge the same amount and then move their prices in unison may be responding to "normal market forces."

And differences in gas prices from region to region can be a result of local supply and demand, the number and type of competitors in a market, and transportation costs.

The report did not satisfy two MPs.

John Solomon, a New Democrat MP from Regina, said the Liberals went easy on the oil industry because they received $76,000 in campaign contributions from Imperial Oil, Husky Oil and Amoco.

Mac Harb, an Ottawa Liberal MP, insisted that gasoline companies are gouging Ottawa motorists.

"I know there's price fixing," he said.

A spokesperson for the Canadian Petroleum Products Institute, an industry lobby group, said gas retailers have to better explain their pricing policies to consumers.

"The reality is that the industry is competitive," Brendan Hawley said.

SOURCE: *Toronto Star*, December 1, 1994. Reproduced with permission of The Canadian Press.

The Story in Brief

Complaints had been received about high gasoline prices; consumers suspected oil companies of price fixing. The Bureau of Competition policy found no evidence of price fixing by oil companies. Moreover, it urged consumers to patronize those gasoline stations with the lowest prices.

The Economics Behind the Story

- The aim of consumers is to maximize satisfaction. *Ceteris paribus*, higher prices mean lower levels of consumer welfare and lower prices lead to higher consumer welfare. Firms try to maximize profits; *ceteris paribus*, higher prices lead to higher profits and vice versa.

- Consumers suspected oil companies of colluding to fix prices at a level higher than brought about by competitive market forces. Price fixing is against the law in Canada. The Bureau of Competition Policy investigated the charges and found them unsubstantiated. The bureau reminded consumers that they must compare the price of gasoline among competitors before deciding from whom to buy; consumers play a vital role in keeping firms actively competing with each other. In a market economy, firms are free to set the price at any level they desire; consumers must therefore shop for the lowest prices.

- How can the government assure consumers the lowest possible price for goods and services? Why are anti-combines laws needed?

SPECIALIZATION AGREEMENTS Many of our industries are composed of firms with short production runs of several different products. Efficiency could be gained through greater specialization and longer production runs. Thus, the Competition Tribunal may approve a specialization agreement if the promised gains in efficiency are likely to more than offset the costs caused by the lessening of competition.

BANKS Banking agreements and bank mergers are subject to the Competition Act.

CROWN CORPORATIONS All Crown corporations, both federal and provincial, in commercial activity and in competition with other firms, are subject to the Act.

The thrust of the latest version of the Competition Act is the surveillance of all firms providing goods and services in our economy, but the Act recognizes that some mergers may be warranted from an efficiency viewpoint. This is important because under the Canadian–U.S. Free Trade Agreement (FTA) and the North American Free Trade Agreement (NAFTA), firms must increasingly compete with Mexican and American competitors. Any advantage that may be gained through mergers that increase efficiency would be beneficial.

EXEMPTIONS TO ANTI-COMBINES LEGISLATION

Over the years, government has enacted certain laws that have either exempted certain specific industries or, alternatively, have excluded certain trade practices from anti-combines prosecution. In doing so, the government has fostered the growth of monopoly power.

Labour unions, co-operatives, **caisses populaires**, and credit unions have been exempt — subject to limitations — from the competition law. We will see in Chapter 21 that legislation and policy have provided some measure of monopolistic power for agriculture and kept agricultural prices above competitive levels. Since 1945, federal and provincial legislation has generally facilitated the growth of labour unions. According to some authorities, the government-sponsored growth has resulted in the formation of union monopolies, whose goal is above-competitive wage rates. At provincial and local levels, a wide variety of occupational groups have succeeded in establishing licensing requirements that arbitrarily restrict entry to certain occupations, keeping wages and earnings above competitive levels (Chapter 16). Finally, as we saw in Chapter 11, **patent laws** may encourage monopolies into research and development.

OTHER DESIRABLE GOALS

Achieving economic efficiency through competition is only one of society's goals. Strict enforcement of anti-combines laws occasionally may conflict with some other worthy goal. Examples:

1. BALANCE OF TRADE Governments seek ways to increase exports to pay for imports. Anti-combines actions to undo a merger of, for example, two chemical suppliers, break up a dominant aircraft manufacturer, or dissolve an emerging software monopolist might weaken the targeted firms, reducing their competitiveness and sales abroad. Our total exports might therefore decline and a trade deficit could result or an existing trade deficit worsen. Should government strictly enforce anti-combines laws, even when significant amounts of exports are potentially at stake? Should the anti-combines goal of efficiency supersede the goal of balancing exports and imports?

2. EMERGING NEW TECHNOLOGIES Occasionally, new technologies combine to create new products and services. A current example is the meshing of computers and communications technologies to create the "information superhighway," a generic name for the eventual hookups of computers, telephones, television sets, and other communications devices. This interactive "highway" will improve communications capabilities of households, businesses, and governments across the globe. It will also allow them to access unprecedented amounts of information via a click of a "mouse" and directly buy and sell goods and services. The emergence of this new technology has set off a spate of mergers involving companies from diverse areas. Should government strictly enforce Canada's anti-combines laws to block some of those mergers that increase industrial concentration and threaten to reduce competition? Or should government temporarily "suspend the anti-combines rules" to encourage the major restructuring of industries and to speed the introduction of this new technology? Hastening the development of the information superhighway may also increase our exports of these services.

These trade-offs have stirred controversy. The issue of anti-combines enforcement is more complex when it conflicts with other desirable social goals. Some argue that the gains from an anti-combines policy must be weighed against the effects of the policy on these conflicting objectives. Others contend that selective enforcement of the anti-combines laws is a facet of government industrial policy (discussed later) that interferes with the efficient market process. Different policy makers may well view these considerations and trade-offs differently. (**Key Question 3**)

QUICK REVIEW 14-2

1. There are three types of mergers: horizontal, vertical, and conglomerate.

2. The first Canadian anti-combines legislation was passed in 1889. Its purpose was to make it unlawful to restrict competition unduly.

3. The original anti-combines legislation subsequently came under the Criminal Code, making successful prosecution difficult.

4. The Competition Act, passed in 1986, removed anti-combines activity from the Criminal Code, making prosecution easier. This Act also stressed that even if some mergers lessened competition, they should be allowed if such mergers bring about significant efficiency gains.

5. Some government legislation lessens competitive forces, for example, patent laws. But patent laws may encourage research and development.

NATURAL MONOPOLIES AND THEIR REGULATION

Anti-combines legislation assumes society will benefit by encouraging competition and preventing monopoly power. We now consider a special case in which there is an economic rationale for an industry to be organized monopolistically.

THEORY OF NATURAL MONOPOLY

A **natural monopoly** exists when economies of scale are so extensive that a single firm can supply the entire market at lower unit cost than could a number of competing firms; it means there is a

falling ATC curve for such a firm over an extended range. Such conditions exist for the **public utilities**, such as electricity, water, gas, telephone service, and so on (Chapter 11). In these cases, the economies of scale in producing and distributing the product are very large, so that large-scale operations are necessary if low unit costs — and a low price — are to be obtained (see Figure 11-1). In this situation, competition is uneconomic. If the market were divided among many producers, economies of scale would not be achieved, unit costs would be high, and high prices would be necessary to cover those costs.

Alternatives that present themselves as possible means of promoting socially acceptable behaviour on the part of a natural monopoly are public ownership and public regulation.

Public ownership has been established in several instances; Canada Post, Canadian National Rail, Air Canada — partially privatized in 1988 — and the St. Lawrence Seaway come to mind at the national level. All the provinces except Alberta and Prince Edward Island have Crown corporations producing their electricity, while mass-transit, the water system, and garbage collection are typically public enterprises at the local level.

Public regulation is also an option extensively used in Canada; the transportation, energy, telecommunications, broadcasting, insurance, securities, financial, and pharmaceuticals industries are all subject to public regulation. Table 14-1 lists the major federal regulatory agencies.

The intent of "natural monopoly" legislation is embodied in the **public interest theory of regulation**. This theory says such industries will be regu-

TABLE 14-1   The main federal regulatory agencies

Atomic Energy Control Board
Canadian Dairy Commission
Canadian Grain Commission
Canadian Radio-television and Telecommunications Commission
Canadian Wheat Board
National Energy Board
National Farm Products Marketing Council
National Harbours Board
National Transport Agency of Canada

lated for the benefit of the public, so that consumers may be ensured good service at reasonable rates. The rationale? If competition is inappropriate, *regulated* monopolies should be established to avoid possible abuses of uncontrolled monopoly power. Regulation should guarantee that consumers benefit from the economies of scale — the lower per-unit costs. In practice, regulators seek to establish rates that will cover production costs and yield a "fair" or "reasonable" return to the enterprise.

The goal is to set price equal to average total cost. (Review the "Regulated Monopoly" section of Chapter 11.)

PROBLEMS

There is disagreement on how effective regulation is in practice. Let's examine three criticisms of regulation.

1. COSTS AND INEFFICIENCY   There are a number of interrelated problems associated with cost containment and efficiency in the use of resources.

A goal of regulation is to establish prices so regulated firms will receive a "normal" or "fair" return above their production costs. But this means that firms are operating on the basis of cost-plus pricing and therefore have no incentive to contain costs. Higher costs will mean larger total profits, so why develop or accept cost-cutting innovations if your "reward" will be a reduction in price? Stated technically, regulation tends to foster considerable *X-inefficiency* (Chapter 11).

A regulated firm may resort to accounting trickery to overstate its costs and obtain a higher unjustified profit. In many instances prices are set by the commission so the firm will receive a stipulated rate of return based on the value of its real capital. This poses a special problem. To increase profits, the regulated firm might make an uneconomic substitution of capital for labour, thereby contributing to an inefficient allocation of resources within the firm (X-inefficiency).

2. COMMISSION DEFICIENCIES   Another criticism is that the regulatory commissions function inadequately because they are "captured" or controlled by the industries they are supposed to regulate. Commission members often were executives in these very industries. Therefore, regulation need *not*

be in the public interest, but rather it may protect and nurture the comfortable position of the natural monopolist. It is alleged that regulation becomes a way to guarantee profits and protect the regulated industry from potential new competition that technological change might create.

3. REGULATING COMPETITIVE INDUSTRIES   Perhaps the most profound criticism of industrial regulation is that it has sometimes been applied to industries that are *not* natural monopolies and that, without regulation, would be quite competitive. Regulation has been used in industries such as trucking and airlines, where economies of scale are not great and entry barriers are relatively weak. In such instances regulation itself, by limiting entry, may create the monopoly rather than the conditions portrayed in Figure 11-1. The result is higher prices and less output than without regulation. Contrary to the public interest theory of regulation, the beneficiaries of regulation are the regulated firms and their employees. The losers are the public and potential competitors barred from entering the industry.

Example: Regulation of the railways may have been justifiable in the late 1800s and the early decades of this century. But by the 1930s the nation had developed a network of highways and the trucking industry had seriously undermined the monopoly power of the railways. At this point it would have been desirable to dismantle the regulatory agency and let the railways and truckers, along with barges and airlines, compete with one another. Instead, the regulatory net of what is now the National Transport Agency of Canada was cast wider in the 1930s to include the airlines, while each province created its own trucking oligopoly. **(Key Question 7)**

LEGAL CARTEL THEORY

The regulation of potentially competitive industries has produced the **legal cartel theory of regulation**. In the place of socially minded officials *forcing* regulation on natural monopolies to protect consumers, this view sees practical politicians as supplying the "service" of regulation to firms that *want* to be regulated. Regulation is desired because it constitutes a legal cartel that can be highly profitable to the regulated firms. The regulatory commission performs such functions as dividing up the market and restricting potential competition by enlarging the cartel. While private cartels are unstable and often break down, the special attraction of the government-sponsored cartel under the guise of regulation is that it endures.

Occupational licensing (Chapter 16) is the labour market manifestation of the legal cartel theory. Certain occupational groups — lawyers, physicians, dentists, engineers, barbers, hairdressers, dietitians, among many others — demand licensing because it protects the public from charlatans and quacks. But at least part of the reason may be to limit occupational entry so that practitioners may receive monopoly incomes.

DEREGULATION

The legal cartel theory, increasing evidence of inefficiency in regulated industries, and the contention that government was regulating potentially competitive industries, all contributed to the deregulation of the 1970s and 1980s. Parliament passed legislation that deregulated in varying degrees the airline, trucking, banking, railroad, natural gas, and television broadcasting industries. Moreover, deregulation occurred in the telecommunications industry where anti-combines authorities took away from the *regulated monopoly* known as Bell Canada, its monopoly in the long-distance market.

CONTROVERSY

Deregulation has been controversial and the nature of the dispute is predictable. Basing their arguments on the legal cartel theory, proponents of deregulation contended it would lower prices, increase output, and eliminate bureaucratic inefficiencies. Some critics of deregulation, embracing the public interest theory, argued deregulation would result in gradual monopolization of some of the deregulated industries by one or two firms. The result would be higher prices, diminished output, and deteriorating service. Other critics were concerned deregulation would lead to excessive competition and industry instability and that vital services (for example, transportation) would be withdrawn from smaller communities. Still others stressed that, as increased competition reduced each firm's revenues, firms would lower their safety standards to reduce costs and remain profitable.

DEREGULATION OUTCOMES

It is perhaps still too soon to declare deregulation either a success or a failure in all specific industries. But studies show the overall effect of deregulation has been positive. Deregulation of industries formerly subjected to industrial regulation is now contributing to society's well-being through lower prices, lower costs, and increased output.

DEREGULATION OF THE AIRLINES

Although the airline industry was deregulated more than a decade ago, it is still adjusting to deregulation. In the near future an "open sky" policy will go into effect in which the Canadian and American market will in effect become integrated. Nevertheless, some of the effects of deregulation have become clear.

FARES Deregulation has exerted downward pressure on fares, with overall fares rising less rapidly than the general price level. Discount air tickets, in particular, have increased in availability and declined in price.

Today, fares generally are about 20% lower in real terms than before deregulation. Of course, fare reductions have not been uniform in all airline markets. Passengers flying from some cities have enjoyed greater decreases in fares than passengers originating their flights elsewhere.

Deregulation has produced lower fares for two reasons. First, competition among air carriers has driven down prices. Before regulation, ticket prices greatly exceeded the average total cost (ATC) of passenger service. Competition has reduced fares and economic profits; prices are closer to ATC. Second, competition has pressured firms to reduce costs. The industry's "hub and spoke" route system — analogous to a bicycle wheel — has reduced costs by allowing airlines to use smaller planes on the spoke routes and wide-bodied craft between the major hub airports. Wide-body aircraft cost less to operate per seat mile than smaller aircraft.

Also, some airlines have established two-tier wage systems paying new workers less than current employees. Union work rules have been made more flexible to increase worker productivity and reduce wage costs. Airlines are increasingly leasing work such as airline maintenance to lower-cost outside companies.

SERVICE AND SAFETY While some major air-lines have withdrawn service from a few smaller cities, commuter airlines usually fill the resulting void. The hub and spoke system has increased flight frequencies at most airports. It has also reduced the amount of airline switching required of passengers.

On the negative side, more frequent stopovers now required in hub cities have increased average travel time between cities. Also, by increasing the volume of traffic, deregulation has contributed to greater airport congestion, resulting in more frequent and longer flight delays.

There is mixed evidence whether deregulation has reduced the safety margin of air transportation. The greater volume of air traffic has resulted in higher reported instances of near collisions in midair. But the accident and fatal accident rates of airlines are much lower today than before deregulation. Furthermore, deregulation has prevented an estimated 80 deaths annually on the nation's highways, because lower fares have enticed people to substitute air travel for more dangerous automobile travel.

INDUSTRY STRUCTURE Airline deregulation initially induced entry of new chartered carriers. But in the past several years the industry has gone through a "shakeout" in which some chartered airlines have failed and others have merged with stronger competitors. Moreover, there still remains excess capacity and severe economic losses in some parts of the industry. Thus far, consolidation of the industry has not brought with it sustained profitability, even for the dominant firms.

Growing concentration in the airlines industry is of much concern. Air Canada and Canadian International Airlines now dominate the industry. Some think consolidation of the industry eventually may be detrimental to the very goals of deregulation itself. Studies in the United States show that fares at airports dominated by one or two airlines are as much as 25% higher than at airports where competition is more brisk. Moreover, entry of new carriers into the industry is more difficult than many economists predicted. The lack of airport capacity — at least in the short term — means that airline markets are far from being perfectly competitive. A firm wishing to enter a particular market because existing carriers are earning economic profits cannot do so if long-term leases allow existing carriers to control the airline gates.

Airline tactics also make successful entry difficult. Airline reservation systems developed by the major carriers often give their own flights priority listings on the computers used by travel agents. Frequent-flyer programs — discounts based on accumulated flight mileage — encourage passengers to use dominant existing carriers rather than new entrants. Also, price matching by existing carriers makes it difficult for new entrants to lure customers through lower ticket prices.

CONCLUSION Although it is too soon for a definitive assessment of airline deregulation, most economists see a positive outcome to date. While airlines lost billions of dollars during and immediately following the recession of 1990–91, the survivors are positioned to regain strong profitability. Also, although lasting entry has proved difficult, there are some success stories. In particular, chartered airlines such as Canada 3000 and Air Transat have been able to successfully compete with the two major Canadian airlines, Air Canada and Canadian Airlines International.

QUICK REVIEW 14-3

1. Natural monopoly occurs where economies of scale are so extensive that only a single firm can produce the product at minimum cost.

2. The public interest theory of regulation holds that government must regulate business to prevent allocative inefficiency arising from monopoly power.

3. The legal cartel theory of regulation suggests that firms seek government regulation to reduce price competition and ensure stable profits.

4. Deregulation initiated in the past two decades is now yielding large annual efficiency gains for society. Airline deregulation has reduced fares.

SOCIAL REGULATION

The "regulation" just discussed is economic or **industrial regulation**. With this regulation the government tries to improve the overall economic performance of a few specific industries, by focusing on pricing and service to the public.

Beginning in the early 1960s, government regulation of a new type evolved and grew rapidly. This relatively new **social regulation** has been called "health, safety, and environmental regulation." It controls the conditions under which goods and services are produced, the impact of production on society, and the physical characteristics of the goods themselves. Thus, for example, the Food and Drugs Act and Regulations list chemical additives that may be used in foods; the Canada Labour (Safety) Code and its provincial counterparts attempt to protect workers against occupational injuries; the Hazardous Products Act specifies minimum standards for potentially unsafe products; regulations promulgated under the Fisheries Act restrict the amount of effluents an industry can discharge into waters inhabited by aquatic life; the Environmental Protection Service of the federal Ministry of the Environment develops and enforces environmental protection regulations.

DISTINGUISHING FEATURES

Social regulation differs from economic regulation in several ways.

1. Social regulation is often applied across the board to all industries, and directly affects far more producers. While the Air Transport Committee of the National Transport Agency of Canada controls only the air transport industry, the rules and regulations of the Canada Labour (Safety) Code and its provincial counterparts apply to every employer.
2. Social regulation involves government in the details of the production process. For example, rather than specify safety standards for vehicles, the 1970 federal Motor Vehicle Safety Act includes, among many others, six standards limiting motor vehicle exhaust, evaporative, and noise emissions.
3. Social regulation has expanded rapidly while industrial regulation has waned. Of the 140 federal statutes enacted since Confederation to regulate business, 25 came into being between 1970 and 1978. In the same nine years, the provinces enacted 262 of the 1,608 statutes passed since Confederation.

The reason for the creation and growth of regulatory statutes and agencies is that much of society achieved a reasonably affluent level of living by the 1960s, and attention shifted to improvements in the quality of life. This improvement called for safer and better products, less pollution, better working conditions, and greater equality of opportunity.

COSTS AND CRITICISMS

The overall objectives of social regulation are laudable. But there is controversy as to whether the benefits of these regulatory efforts justify the costs.

COSTS   The costs of social regulation are *administrative costs*, such as salaries paid to employees of the commissions, office expenses, and the like; and *compliance costs*, the costs incurred by businesses and provincial and local governments in meeting the requirements of regulatory commissions.

CRITICISMS   Critics argue that our economy is now subject to overregulation, that regulatory activities have been carried to the point where the marginal costs of regulation exceed the marginal benefits.

UNECONOMIC GOALS   Those concerned with overregulation contend that many of the social regulation laws are poorly drawn so that regulators are virtually prohibited from making economically rational decisions and rules. Regulatory objectives and standards are often stated in legal, political, or engineering terms that result in the pursuit of goals beyond the point at which marginal benefits equal marginal costs. Businesses complain that regulators press for small increments of improvements, unmindful of costs. A requirement to reduce pollution by an additional 5% may cost as much as required to achieve the first 95% reduction.

INADEQUATE INFORMATION   Decisions must often be made and rules put into place on the basis of inadequate information. The federal Health Protection Branch may make decisions about suspected carcinogens in products based on limited experiments with laboratory animals.

UNINTENDED SIDE EFFECTS   Critics argue that regulations produce many unintended side effects which greatly boost the full cost of regulation. For example, gas mileage standards for automobiles may cause hundreds of traffic deaths. The reason? Manufacturers have reduced the weight of vehicles to meet the increasingly stringent standards. All else equal, drivers of lighter cars have a higher fatality rate than drivers of heavier vehicles.

OVERZEALOUS PERSONNEL   Critics also say that the regulatory agencies may attract overzealous personnel who "believe" in regulation. It is argued that the bureaucrats of the new statutory regulatory agencies may be overly sensitive to criticism by some special interest group — for example, environmentalists. The result is bureaucratic inflexibility and the establishment of extreme or nonsensical regulations so that no watchdog group will question the agency's commitment to its social goal.

ECONOMIC IMPLICATIONS

If overregulation does exist — and that is subject to debate — what are its consequences?

1. HIGHER PRICES   Social regulation increases product prices because compliance costs normally get passed on to consumers. Furthermore, social regulation indirectly contributes to higher product prices by reducing labour productivity. Resources invested in anti-pollution equipment are not available for investment in new machinery to increase output per worker. Where wage rates are inflexible downward, declines in labour productivity increase marginal and average total costs of production. In effect, product-supply curves shift leftward, causing product prices to rise.

2. SLOWER INNOVATION   Social regulation may have a negative impact on the rate of innovation. The fear that a new, technologically superior plant will not meet environmental protection regulations or that a new product may run into difficulties with the Hazardous Products Act may persuade a firm to produce the same old product in the same old way.

3. REDUCED COMPETITION   Social regulation may have an anti-competitive effect, since it usually is a relatively greater economic burden for small firms than for large firms. The costs of complying with the new regulations are, in effect, fixed costs. Smaller firms produce less output over which to distribute their costs, thus their compliance costs per unit of output set them at a competitive disadvantage with their larger rivals. The burden of social regulation is more likely to put small firms out of business, contributing to the increased concentration of industry.

IN SUPPORT OF SOCIAL REGULATION

The problems that social regulation confronts are serious and substantial. Thousands of workers die in job-related accidents in Canada each year. Particulate and ozone pollution still plagues our major cities, imposing large costs in reduced property values and increased health-care expenses. Hundreds of children and adults die each year in accidents involving poorly designed products. Discrimination against visible minorities, females, the disabled, and older workers reduces their earnings and also imposes heavy costs on society.

According to proponents of social regulation, the relevant economic test of whether it is worthwhile is not whether its costs are high or low, but rather whether benefits *exceed* costs. After years of neglect, society cannot expect to cleanse the environment, enhance the safety of the workplace, improve the safety of the automobile, and enhance economic opportunity without incurring substantial costs.

Cost calculations may paint too dim a picture. Benefits are taken for granted, are more difficult to measure than costs, and may accrue to society only after an extended period.

Benefits of social regulation have been substantial. Examples: It is estimated that highway fatalities would be substantially greater without auto safety features mandated through regulation. Compliance with child safety-belt laws has significantly reduced the auto fatality rate for small children. Affirmative action regulations have significantly increased labour demand for visible minorities and females. Childproof lids have resulted in a 90% decline in child deaths caused by accidental swallowing of poisonous substances.

Defenders of social regulation assert these and other benefits are well worth the costs of social regulation. These costs are simply the "price" a society must pay to create a hospitable, sustainable, and just society.

Although we can expect social regulation to continue to be controversial, the policy question has moved away from whether social regulation should occur. Rather the questions now are: How and when should social regulation be used? Can we improve social regulation to make it more efficient? Are the decision makers aware of the marginal costs, as well as the marginal benefits? (**Key Question 9**)

INDUSTRIAL POLICY

In recent years industrial policy has joined anti-combines, industrial regulation, and social regulation as a distinct form of government involvement with business. **Industrial policy consists of governmental actions that promote the economic vitality of specific firms or industries**. It differs from anti-combines, industrial regulation, and social regulation. These government policies alter the structure or restrict the conduct of private firms, either by reducing their revenues or increasing their cost. Industrial policy promotes selected firms and industries by adding to their profitability.

ANTECEDENTS

Governmental promotion of industries has a long, controversial history. In the 1600s and 1700s, European governments subscribed to a set of policies known as mercantilism. At the heart of this now discredited policy was the belief that a nation's wealth consisted of its precious metals. Because merchants received inflows of gold in return for their exports, governments established elaborate policies to promote trade surpluses (exports in excess of imports). Such policies included tariffs on finished goods, free importation of resources, and granting of monopoly trading privileges to selected companies (such as the East India Company and the Hudson Bay Company). Governments also regulated production techniques to ensure the quality of exports and, in general, subsidized production in their exporting industries.

Canada's history is replete with examples of industrial policy. In the 1800s government granted free land to railroads to promote their westward expansion. This expansion hastened economic development, increased productivity, and helped raise national output and employment. Government has heavily subsidized Canadian agriculture over the decades, boosting profits in that industry.

RECENT EMPHASIS

There has recently been a growing concern that Canada's industrial strength has been seriously eroded. Our domestic markets have been flooded with foreign steel, automobiles, motorcycles, cameras, watches, sporting goods, and electronic equipment. Some suggest that the growing imports means we have lost our competitive edge.

Noting apparent Japanese success, many politicians, union, and business leaders — but a far fewer number of economists — feel Canada needs a strong industrial policy to reverse our alleged industrial decline. It is argued that government should take a more active and direct role in determining the structure and composition of Canadian industry. Government, they say, should use low-interest loans, loan guarantees, favourable tax treatment, research and development subsidies, anti-combines immunity, and even foreign-trade protection to accelerate the development of "high-tech" industries and to revitalize certain core manufacturing industries such as steel. Presumably the result will be that the Canadian economy will enjoy a higher average level of productivity and be more competitive in world markets.

Although the federal government has not committed itself to a comprehensive industrial policy, there are many examples of specific programs consistent with this concept.

1. AUTO INDUSTRY The surge of Japanese auto imports during the 1970s and 1980s placed tremendous financial pressure on Canadian auto producers. Governments responded with a series of actions to promote the domestic industry. For example, in 1979 the Ontario provincial government "bailed out" both Massey-Ferguson and Chrysler Corporation by providing loan guarantees to financial institutions lending to the two corporations. Second example: In the mid-1980s the government negotiated "voluntary" export restrictions on automobiles imported from Japan. In these agreements the Japanese government and auto firms agreed to limit auto exports to North America to no more than a set number of cars.

2. ALTERNATIVE FUEL PROGRAM

In response to the "oil crisis" of the mid-1970s, the government established a subsidy program to promote the development of alternative fuels. Also, much money went into the development to recover oil from oil shale and the Alberta tar sands. Overall, this government effort has not worked out as well as hoped.

3. EXPORT DEVELOPMENT CORPORATION

This federal entity subsidizes interest rates on loans taken out by foreign buyers of Canadian exports. These subsidies directly benefit Canadian exporters of goods bought on credit. In effect, the subsidies reduce the total price (product price plus interest on loan) to the foreign buyer.

CONTROVERSY

Opponents of industrial policy raise several issues.

1. DEINDUSTRIALIZATION

Has Canada deindustrialized? Has our manufacturing sector experienced serious decline, justifying subsidies to industries? Statistics suggest not. While the composition of manufacturing output has changed, manufacturing in the aggregate accounts for about the same percentage (20%) of GDP as it did in 1950. Manufacturing's share of the nation's expenditures on new plant and equipment was nearly identical in 1994 to 1950. Employment in manufacturing has declined from 27 to 15% of total employment in the 1947–94 period, but that reflects the growth of labour productivity rather than industrial demise.

2. FOREIGN EXPERIENCE

Advocates of industrial policy cite Japan and its Ministry of International Trade and Industry (MITI) as a model. In the post-World War II era, Japan has achieved rapid economic growth; it has been highly successful in penetrating world markets; and it has had a much publicized industrial policy. Yet the overall role of industrial policy as a causal factor in Japanese industrial success is not clear. Subsidies of some targeted industries have succeeded (semiconductors, machine tools, steel, and

ship building). In other cases, Japan's industrial policy has failed (aluminum smelting, petrochemicals, high-definition television). In still other instances, Japanese industries have been successful without government support (electronics, motorcycles).

Neither has European industrial policy been consistently successful. A notable success has been Europe's subsidized development of Airbus Industries, a manufacturer of commercial aircraft. Europe's subsidization of supersonic transport aircraft was a failure.

3. MARKETS AND POLITICS

While "short-circuiting" the market mechanism through promotion of selected industries sounds appealing, critics question the government's ability to identify future industrial "winners" and "losers." The issue here is whether private investors using capital markets have better foresight than public officials in determining where investment funds ought to be channelled. Critics argue that private investors have greater incentive in investing their *own* funds to obtain accurate information on the future prospects of various industries and technologies than might government bureaucrats in investing *taxpayers'* funds.

Furthermore, might not government use its power to allocate investment funds to buy political support of target industries? Might not the economic goal of enhanced industrial efficiency and encouragement of exports be subverted to the political goal of getting re-elected? It is feared that the expansion of industrial policy might lead to "lemon" socialism — government support or ownership of declining industries, dying companies, and inefficient technologies.

Proponents of industrial policy counter that many leading Canadian products developed with direct government support. The argument is that government industrial policy targeted at key, high-technology applications in the private sector facilitates entrepreneurial forces and enhances the dynamic efficiency associated with the market system. By subsidizing research and development efforts, industrial policy reduces the risk of exploring and applying new technologies. These technologies often spur complementary products and entire new industries, boosting a nation's productivity, standard of living, and international competitiveness. (**Key Question 10**)

CHAPTER SUMMARY

1. The case against industrial concentration contends that it **a** causes a misallocation of resources; **b** retards the rate of technological advance; **c** promotes income inequality; and **d** may result in some interest groups having more political clout.

2. The defence of industrial concentration maintains: **a** firms have obtained their large market shares by offering superior products; **b** interindustry and foreign competition, along with potential competition from new industry entrants, makes Canadian industries more competitive than generally believed; **c** some degree of monopoly may be essential to realize economies of scale; and **d** monopolies and oligopolies may be technologically progressive.

3. Mergers can be of three types: horizontal, vertical, and conglomerate.

4. The cornerstone of anti-combines policy consists of amendments to the Criminal Code in 1892 and the Combines Investigation Acts of 1910 and 1923, as subsequently frequently amended. On the fifth attempt since 1971, the Competition Act was finally passed in mid-1986, supplanting the Combines Investigation Act.

5. Issues in applying anti-combines laws include: **a** the problem of determining whether an industry should be judged by its structure or its behaviour; **b** defining the scope and size of the dominant firm's market; and **c** balancing the gains from anti-combines against other desirable goals such as balancing exports and imports and encouraging new technologies.

6. The objective of industrial regulation is to protect the public from the market power of natural monopolies by regulating prices and quality of service. Critics contend that industrial regulation is conducive to inefficiency and rising costs and that, in many instances, it constitutes a legal cartel for the regulated firms. Legislation passed in the last decade brought about varying degrees of deregulation in the airline, trucking, banking, and railroad industries. Studies indicate that deregulation is producing sizable annual gains to society through lower prices, lower costs, and increased output. Deregulation in the airline industry has resulted in lower fares.

7. Social regulation is concerned with product safety, safer working conditions, less pollution, and greater economic opportunity. Critics contend that businesses are overregulated in that marginal costs exceed marginal benefits, while defenders dispute that contention.

8. Industrial policy consists of government actions promoting the economic vitality of specific industries or firms. Proponents of industrial policy see it as a way to strengthen the industrial sector, speed development of new technologies, increase productivity, and increase international competitiveness. Critics charge that industrial policy substitutes the whims of politicians and bureaucrats for the hard scrutiny of entrepreneurs and business executives in allocating society's resources.

TERMS AND CONCEPTS

anti-combines legislation (pp. 287, 291)

caisses populaires (p. 294)

Combines Investigation Act (p. 291)

Competition Act (p. 292)

Competition Tribunal (p. 292)

conglomerate merger (p. 291)

foreign competition (p. 290)

horizontal merger (p. 291)

industrial concentration (p. 288)

industrial policy (p. 301)

industrial regulation (pp. 287, 298)

interindustry competition (p. 290)

legal cartel theory of regulation (p. 296)

natural monopoly (p. 295)

patent laws (p. 294)

potential competition (p. 290)
public interest theory of regulation (p. 295)
public utilities (p. 295)

regulatory agencies (p. 290)
social regulation (pp. 287, 299)
vertical merger (p. 291)

QUESTIONS AND STUDY SUGGESTIONS

1. You are president of one of the Big Three automobile producers. Discuss critically the case against industrial concentration. Now suppose you are a representative for a consumer organization and are attempting to convince a parliamentary committee that the presence of industrial concentration is a significant factor contributing to high prices. Critically evaluate the case for industrial concentration.

2. Explain how strict enforcement of the anti-combines laws might conflict with a. promoting exports to achieve a balance of trade; and b. encouraging new technologies. Do you see any dangers of using selective anti-combines enforcement as part of an industrial policy?

3. *Key Question   How would you expect anti-combines authorities to react to a. a proposed merger of the Canadian subsidiaries of Ford and Chrysler; b. evidence of secret meetings by contractors to rig bids for highway construction projects; c. a proposed merger of a large shoe manufacturer and a chain of retail shoe stores; and d. a proposed merger of a small life insurance company and a regional candy manufacturer?*

4. Suppose a proposed merger of firms will simultaneously lessen competition and reduce unit costs through economies of scale. Do you think such a merger should be allowed?

5. "The anti-combines laws serve to penalize efficiently managed firms." Do you agree?

6. "The social desirability of any given business enterprise should be judged not on the basis of the structure of the industry in which it finds itself, but rather on the basis of the market performance and behaviour of that firm." Analyze critically.

7. *Key Question   What types of industries should be subjected to industrial regulation? What specific problems does industrial regulation bring about? Why might an inefficient combination of capital and labour be employed by a regulated natural monopoly?*

8. In view of the problems in regulating natural monopolies, compare optimal social (marginal-cost) pricing and fair-return pricing by referring again to Figure 11-8. Assuming a government subsidy might be used to cover any loss brought about by marginal-cost pricing, which pricing policy would you favour? What problems might the subsidy entail?

9. *Key Question   How does social regulation differ from industrial regulation? What types of costs and benefits are associated with social regulation?*

10. *Key Question   What is industrial policy and how does it differ from anti-combines, industrial regulation, and social regulation? Why might businesses look more favourably on industrial policy than these other policies? Cite an example of industrial policy. What are the pros and cons of industrial policy?*

11. What does it mean when we say that the airline industry has been deregulated? What have been the impacts of deregulation on fares, service and safety, and industry structure? Some say the "the jury is still out on airline deregulation." Speculate on what they may mean.

FACTOR MARKETS AND THE DISTRIBUTION OF INCOME

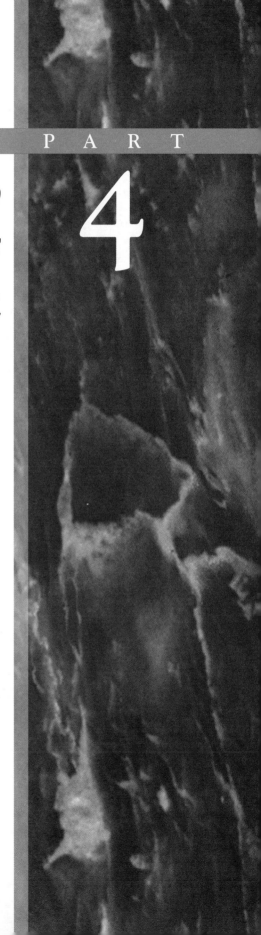

CHAPTER 15

PRODUCTION AND THE DEMAND FOR RESOURCES

In the preceding four chapters we explored the pricing and output of goods and services under a variety of product market structures. The purely competitive cucumber farmer considers the market price and decides how many hectares to plant. The monopolistically competitive local restaurant decides on the best combination of price, quality, and advertising to maximize its profits. The automobile manufacturer pays close attention to the business strategies of rivals and sets its price and production plans accordingly. The provincial natural gas monopoly files requests for rate increases before the provincial utility board, and then provides service to all customers.

Although firms and market structures differ greatly, firms in general have something in common. In producing their product — be it cucumbers, sandwiches, automobiles, or natural gas — they must hire productive resources. Among other resources, the cucumber farmer needs land, tractors, fertilizer, and labourers to harvest the crop. The restaurant buys kitchen equipment and hires cooks and waiters. The auto manufacturer purchases production materials and hires executives, accountants, engineers, and assembly-line workers. The gas company leases land, builds pipeline and storage tanks, and hires billing clerks.

In this chapter we turn from the pricing and production of goods to the pricing and employment of resources needed to produce those goods and services. Land, labour, capital, and entrepreneurial resources directly, or indirectly, are owned and supplied by households. In terms of our circular flow model of the economy (Chapters 2, 5, and 6), we now shift attention from the bottom loop of the diagram, where firms supply and households demand products, to the top loop, where households supply and businesses demand resources.

BOX 15-1   THE BIG PICTURE

Up to this point we have been focusing on the product market — the market for goods and services. But to produce goods and services we require inputs of the factors of production. Recall these are labour, land, capital and entrepreneurial talent. The factors of production are available in limited quantities, thus the economizing problem — scarcity, unlimited wants, and the need for choices — also applies to the factor market. In the product market allocation of goods and services is determined by prices; in the factor market the allocation of land, labour, capital, and entrepreneurial ability is also determined by "price," although "price" for each of the factors goes by a different name. The "price" for labour is wages; the "price" for capital is the interest rate; the "price" for land is rent; and the "price" for entrepreneurial talent is profit. This chapter focuses on the demand for the factors of pro-

duction in general. Chapter 16 looks at the labour markets and the determinants of wages (and salaries). Chapter 17 analyzes the determinants of the "prices" for the other factors: rent, interest, and profits.

As you read this chapter, keep the following points in mind:

- The price of factors is determined by supply and demand conditions.
- The demand for any factor, for example, labour, is determined by the demand for the product the factor is used in making.
- The demand for any factor also depends on its contribution to output.
- As in the product market, the amount of competition in the factor market depends on the relative market power of factor owners and factor sellers.

SIGNIFICANCE OF RESOURCE PRICING

There are several reasons to study resource pricing.

1. MONEY INCOMES   Resource prices constitute a major determinant of money incomes. The expenditures businesses make in acquiring economic resources flow as wage, rent, interest, and profit incomes to those households that supply the resources at their disposal.

2. RESOURCE ALLOCATION   Just as product prices ration finished goods and services to consumers, so resource prices allocate scarce resources among industries and firms. An understanding of how resource prices affect resource allocation is particularly significant since, in a dynamic economy, the efficient allocation of resources over time calls for continuing shifts in resources among alternative uses.

3. COST MINIMIZATION   To the firm, resource prices are costs, and to realize maximum profits, a

firm must produce the profit-maximizing output with the most efficient (least costly) combination of resources. Given technology, resource prices play the major role in determining the quantities of land, labour, capital, and entrepreneurial ability that are to be combined in the productive process.

4. POLICY ISSUES   Finally, there are numerous ethical questions and public policy issues surrounding the resource market. What degree of income inequality is acceptable? Should a special tax be levied on "excess" profits? Is it desirable for government to establish a wage floor in the form of a minimum-wage law? What about ceilings on interest rates? Are current government subsidies to farmers justifiable? Chapter 18 will explore the facts and ethics of income distribution.

COMPLEXITIES OF RESOURCE PRICING

Economists generally agree about the basic principles that determine the price of resources. Yet they disagree as to the variations in these principles that must be made as they are applied to specific resources and particular markets. While economists agree that the pricing and employment of economic resources (factors of production) are a supply and demand phenomenon, they also recognize that in particular markets resource supply and demand may assume unique and often complex dimensions. This is further complicated when supply and demand forces are altered or even supplanted by the policies and practices of government, firms, or labour unions, among other institutional considerations.

Our objective in this chapter is to explain the factors underlying the demand for economic resources. Our discussion is in terms of labour, but the principles outlined also apply to land, capital, and entrepreneurial ability. In Chapter 16, we combine our understanding of resource demand with a discussion of labour supply in analyzing wage rates. Then in Chapter 17, we incorporate the supply side of the markets for resources to analyze the prices of, and returns to, land, capital, and entrepreneurial ability.

MARGINAL PRODUCTIVITY THEORY OF RESOURCE DEMAND

The least complicated approach to resource demand assumes a firm hires a resource in a competitive market and sells its product in a competitive market. The simplicity of this situation lies in the fact that under competition the firm, as a price taker, can dispose of as little or as much output as it chooses at the going market price. The firm is selling such a negligible fraction of total output that it exerts no influence on product price. Similarly, in the resource market, competition means that the firm is hiring such a small fraction of the total supply of the resource that its price is unaffected by the quantity the firm purchases.

RESOURCE DEMAND AS A DERIVED DEMAND

The demand for resources is a **derived demand**; it is derived from the products or services that resources help produce. Resources do not directly satisfy consumer wants, but do so indirectly by producing goods and services. No one wants to consume a hectare of land, a tractor, or the labour services of a farmer, but households do want to consume the food and fibre products these resources help produce. The demand for automobiles generates a demand for automobile workers; the demand for

services such as income tax preparation, hair cuts, and child care creates a derived demand for accountants, barbers, and child-care workers.

MARGINAL REVENUE PRODUCT (MRP)

The derived nature of resource demand implies that the strength of the demand for any resource will depend on (1) the productivity of the resource in helping to create a good, and (2) the market price of the good it is producing. A resource that is highly productive in turning out a commodity highly valued by society will be in great demand. On the other hand, demand will be very weak for a relatively unproductive resource that is capable only of producing some good not in great demand by households.

PRODUCTIVITY The roles of productivity and product price in determining resource demand can be clearly seen in Table 15-1. Here we assume a firm adds one variable resource — labour — to its fixed plant. Columns 1 to 3 remind us that the law of diminishing returns will apply here, causing the **marginal product (MP)** of labour to fall beyond some point. (It might be helpful to review the subsection entitled "Law of Diminishing Returns" in Chapter 9 at this point.) For simplicity, assume diminishing marginal productivity sets in with the first worker hired.

PRODUCT PRICE But the derived demand for a resource also depends on the price of the commodity it produces. Column 4 adds this price information. Note that product price is constant, in this case $2, because we are assuming a competitive product market. The firm is a "price-taker" and can sell as few or as many units of output as it wants at this price.

Multiplying column 2 by column 4, we get the total-revenue data of column 5. From these total-revenue data we can compute **marginal revenue product (MRP)** — *the increase in total revenue resulting from the use of each additional variable input (labour, in this case)*. MRP is indicated in column 6.

RULE FOR EMPLOYING RESOURCES: MRP = MRC

The MRP schedule — columns 1 and 6 — constitutes the firm's demand schedule for labour. To explain why, we must first discuss the rule that guides a profit-seeking firm in hiring any resource. *To maximize profits, a firm should hire additional units of*

GLOBAL PERSPECTIVE 15-1

Labour demand and allocation: less developed countries, industrially advanced countries, and Canada

The notion of derived demand implies that the composition of a country's product market demand will determine the allocation of its labour force among agricultural products, industrial goods, and services. Because poor nations must spend most of their incomes for food and fibre, the bulk of their labour is allocated to agriculture. The much-richer industrially advanced economies allocate most of their labour to industrial products and services.

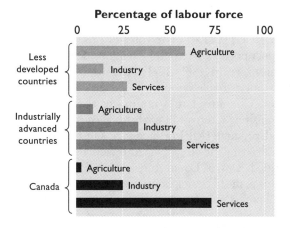

Percentage of labour force

Source: United Nations, *Human Development Report 1994*, p. 194.

any given resource so long as each successive unit adds more to the firm's total revenue than it does to its total costs.

The amount each additional unit of a resource adds to the firm's total (resource) cost is called **marginal resource cost (MRC)**. Thus we can restate our rule for hiring resources as follows: *It will be profitable for a firm to hire additional units of a resource up to the point at which the resource's MRP is equal to its MRC.* If the number of workers a firm is currently hiring is such that the MRP of the last worker exceeds his or her MRC, the firm can clearly profit by hiring more workers. But if the number being hired is such that the MRC of the last worker exceeds the MRP, the firm is hiring workers who are not paying their way, and it can thereby increase its profits by laying off some workers. You may have recognized that this **MRP = MRC rule** is very similar to the MR = MC profit-maximizing rule

employed throughout our discussion of price and output determination. The rationale of the two rules is the same, but the point of reference is now *inputs* of resources rather than *outputs* of product.

MRP IS A DEMAND SCHEDULE

Just as product price and marginal revenue are equal in a purely competitive product market, so *resource price and marginal resource cost are equal when a firm is hiring a resource in a competitive market.* In a purely competitive labour market, the wage rate is set by the total supply and demand for labour. Because it hires such a small fraction of the total supply of labour, a single firm cannot influence this wage rate. This means that total resource cost increases by exactly the amount of the going wage rate for each additional worker hired; the wage rate and MRC are equal. It follows that so long as it is hiring labour in a competitive labour market, *the firm will hire workers to the point at which their wage rate (or MRC) is equal to their MRP.*[1]

The data in column 6 of Table 15-1 show that if the wage rate is $13.95 the firm will hire only one worker. This is because the first worker adds $14 to total revenue and slightly less — $13.95 — to total costs. For each successive worker, however, MRC exceeds MRP, indicating that it will not be profitable to hire another worker. If the wage rate is $11.95, we discover that it will pay the firm to hire both the first and second workers. If the wage rate is $9.95, three will be hired. If $7.95, four. If $5.95, then five. And so forth. It is evident that *the MRP schedule constitutes the firm's demand for labour because each point on this schedule (curve) indicates the number of workers the firm would hire at each possible wage rate that might exist.* This is shown graphically in Figure 15-1.

The rationale employed here is familiar to us. Recall that in Chapter 10 we applied the price-equals-marginal-cost or *P* = MC rule for the profit-maximizing *output* to discover that the portion of the competitive firm's short-run marginal-cost curve lying above average variable cost is the short-run *product* supply curve (Figure 10-6). Now we are applying the MRP = MRC rule for the profit-maximizing *input* to the firm's MRP curve and determining that this curve is the input or *resource demand* curve.

---

[1] The logic here is the same as that which allowed us to change the MR = MC profit-maximization rule to P = MC for the purely competitive seller of Chapter 10.

FIGURE 15-1 **The purely competitive seller's demand for a resource**

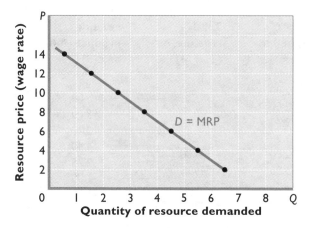

The MRP curve is the resource demand curve. The location of the curve depends on the marginal productivity of the resource and the price of the product. Under pure competition, product price is constant; therefore, it is solely because of diminishing marginal productivity that the resource demand curve is downsloping.

RESOURCE DEMAND UNDER IMPERFECT COMPETITION

Our analysis of labour demand becomes slightly more complex when we assume the firm is selling its product in an imperfectly competitive market. Pure monopoly, oligopoly, and monopolistic competition in the product market all mean that the firm's prod-

uct demand curve is downsloping; the firm must accept a lower price in order to increase its sales.

The productivity data of Table 15-1 are retained in columns 1 to 3, but here we assume in column 4 that product price must be lowered to sell the marginal product of each successive worker. The MRP of the purely competitive seller in Table 15-1 falls for one reason: marginal product diminishes. But the MRP of the imperfectly competitive seller in Table 15-2 falls for two reasons: marginal product diminishes *and* product price falls as output increases.

The result is that the MRP curve — the resource demand curve — of the imperfectly competitive producer is less elastic than that of a purely competitive producer. At a wage rate or MRC of $11.95, both the purely competitive and the imperfectly competitive seller will hire two workers. But at $9.95, the competitive firm will hire three and the imperfectly competitive firm only two. And at $7.95, the purely competitive firm will take on four employees and the imperfect competitor only three. This difference in elasticity can be seen by graphing the MRP data of Table 15-2, as in Figure 15-2, and comparing them with Figure 15-1.[2]

_____

[2] Note that the points in Figures 15-1 and 15-2 are plotted halfway between each number of workers because MRP is associated with the *addition* of one more worker. Thus in Figure 15-2, for example, the MRP of the second worker ($13) is plotted not at 1 or 2, but rather at 1 1/2. This "smoothing" technique also allows us to present a continuously downsloping curve rather than one that moves downward in discrete steps as each worker is hired.

TABLE 15-1 **The demand for a resource: pure competition in the sale of the product**

(1) Units of resource	(2) Total product	(3) Marginal product (MP), or Δ(2)*	(4) Product price	(5) Total revenue, or (2) x (4)	(6) Marginal revenue product (MRP), or Δ(5)
0	0		$2	$ 0	
1	7	7	2	14	$14
2	13	6	2	26	12
3	18	5	2	36	10
4	22	4	2	44	8
5	25	3	2	50	6
6	27	2	2	54	4
7	28	1	2	56	2

* Δ indicates a "change in."

TABLE 15-2   The demand for a resource: imperfect competition in the sale of the product

(1) Units of resource	(2) Total product	(3) Marginal product (MP), or Δ(2)	(4) Product price	(5) Total revenue, or (2) x (4)	(6) Marginal revenue product (MRP), or Δ(5)
0	0		$2.80	$ 0	
		7			$18.20
1	7		2.60	18.20	
		6			13.00
2	13		2.40	31.20	
		5			8.40
3	18		2.20	39.60	
		4			4.40
4	22		2.00	44.00	
		3			2.25
5	25		1.85	46.25	
		2			1.00
6	27		1.75	47.25	
		1			−1.05
7	28		1.65	46.20	

FIGURE 15-2   The imperfectly competitive seller's demand for a resource

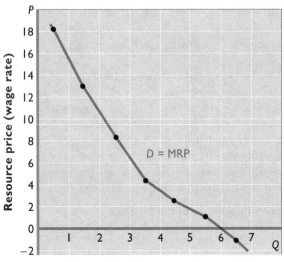

Quantity of resource demanded

An imperfectly competitive seller's resource demand curve slopes downward because marginal product diminishes and product price falls as output increases.

It is not surprising that the imperfectly competitive producer is less responsive to wage cuts in terms of workers employed than is the purely competitive producer. The reluctance of the imperfect competitor to employ more resources and produce more output when resource prices fall reflects the imperfect competitor's tendency to restrict output in the product market. Other things being equal, the imperfectly competitive seller will produce less of a product than would a purely competitive seller. In producing this smaller output, the seller will demand fewer resources. (**Key Question 2**)

MARKET DEMAND FOR A RESOURCE

We can now derive the market demand curve for a resource. You will recall that the total, or market, demand curve for a product is developed by summing up the demand curves of all individual buyers in the market. Similarly, the market demand curve for a particular resource can be derived in essentially the same way: adding up MRP curves for all firms hiring that resource.

QUICK REVIEW 15-1

1. A resource will be employed in the profit-maximizing amount where its marginal revenue product equals its marginal resource cost (MRP = MRC).

2. Application of the MRP = MRC rule to a firm's MRP curve demonstrates that the MRP curve is the firm's resource demand curve.

3. The resource demand curve of a purely competitive seller is downsloping solely because the marginal product of the resource diminishes; the resource demand curve of an imperfectly competitive seller is downsloping because marginal product diminishes and product price falls as output is increased.

DETERMINANTS OF RESOURCE DEMAND

What are the determinants of resource demand? The derivation of resource demand suggests three related factors — the resource's productivity, the market price of the product it is producing, and changes in the prices of other resources.

CHANGES IN PRODUCT DEMAND

Because resource demand is a derived demand, any change in the demand for the product will affect product price and therefore the MRP of the resource. Other things equal, *a change in the demand for the product that a particular type of labour is producing will shift labour demand in the same direction.*

In Table 15-1, assume an increase in product demand that boosts product price from $2 to $3. You should calculate the new labour demand curve and plot it in Figure 15-1 to verify it lies to the right of the old curve. Similarly, a drop in product demand and price will shift the labour demand curve to the left.

PRODUCTIVITY CHANGES

Other things held constant, *a change in the productivity of labour will shift the labour demand curve in the same direction.* If we were to double the MP data of column 3 in Table 15-1 we would find that the MRP data would also double, indicating an increase in labour demand.

The productivity of any resource can be altered in several ways:

1. **NONLABOUR INPUTS** The marginal productivity data for labour will depend on the quantities of other resources with which it is combined. The greater the amount of capital and land resources with which labour is combined, the greater will be the marginal productivity and the demand for labour.

2. **TECHNOLOGICAL PROGRESS** Technological improvements will have the same effect. The better the quality of the capital, the greater the productivity of labour. Steelworkers employed with a given amount of real capital in the form of modern oxygen furnaces are more productive than when employed with the same amount of real capital in the old open-hearth furnaces.

3. **LABOUR QUALITY** Improvements in the quality of the variable resource itself — labour — will increase marginal productivity, and therefore the demand for labour. In effect, we have a new demand curve for a different, more skilled, kind of labour.

All these considerations help explain why the average level of (real) wages is higher in Canada than in most other countries. Canadian workers are usually healthier and better trained than those of other nations, and in most industries they work with a larger and more efficient stock of capital goods and much more abundant natural resources. This translates into a strong demand for labour. On the supply side of the market, labour is *relatively* scarce as compared with most other nations. A strong demand and a relatively scarce supply result in high wage rates. This will be discussed further in Chapter 16.

PRICES OF OTHER RESOURCES

Just as changes in the prices of other products will change the demand for a specific commodity, so changes in the prices of other resources can be expected to alter the demand for a particular resource. And just as the effect of a change in the price of product X on the demand for product Y depends on whether X and Y are substitute or complementary goods (Chapter 4), so the effect of a change in the price of resource A on the demand for resource B will depend on their substitutability or their degree of complementarity.

SUBSTITUTE RESOURCES Suppose that in a certain production process technology is such that labour and capital are substitutable for one another. Now assume the price of machinery falls. The resulting impact on the demand for labour will be the net result of two opposed effects: the substitution effect and the output effect.

1. **SUBSTITUTION EFFECT** The decline in the price of machinery will prompt the firm to substitute machinery for labour. At given wage rates, smaller quantities of labour will now be employed. This **substitution effect** will decrease the demand for labour.

2. **OUTPUT EFFECT** Because the price of machinery has fallen, the costs of producing various outputs will also decline. With lower costs, the firm will find it profitable to produce and sell a larger output. This greater output, which is referred to as the **output effect**, will increase the demand for all resources, including labour.

BOX 15-2 APPLYING THE THEORY

INPUT SUBSTITUTION: THE CASE OF CABOOSES

Substituting among inputs — particularly when jobs are at stake — can be controversial.

A firm will achieve the least-cost combination of inputs when the last dollar spent on each makes the same contribution to total output. This rule also implies that a firm is unimpeded in changing its input mix in response to technological changes or changes in input prices. Unfortunately, in the real world the substitution of new capital for old capital and the substitution of capital for labour may be controversial and difficult to achieve.

Consider railway cabooses. The railways claim that technological advance has made the caboose obsolete. In particular, railways want to substitute a "trainlink" that can be attached to the coupler of the last car of a train. This small black box contains a revolving strobe light and instruments that monitor train speed, air-brake pressure, and other relevant data, which it transmits to the locomotive engineer. The trainlink costs only $4000, compared with $80,000 for a new caboose. And, of course, the trainlink replaces one member of the train crew.

The railways cite substantial cost economies from this rearrangement of capital and labour inputs. But the union that represents railway conductors and brakemen knows that the demise of the caboose

means a decline in the demand for its members. The union therefore made a concerted, but unsuccessful, effort to halt the elimination of cabooses on trains. The union argued that the elimination of cabooses would reduce railway safety.

The union contended that, unlike humans, trainlinks cannot detect broken wheels or axles nor overheated bearings. From the vantage point of the railways this looked like featherbedding — the protection of unnecessary jobs. The railways contended that available data showed no safety differences between trains using and those not using cabooses. Indeed, safety may be enhanced without cabooses because many injuries are incurred by crew who are riding in cabooses.

Cabooses are virtually extinct in Europe, but they were the rule in Canada until 1988. In the United States, the railway unions have lobbied successfully for legislation in several states that makes cabooses mandatory. In all other states, the use of cabooses remains a matter of collective bargaining negotiations. In any event, the case of the cabooses indicates clearly that input substitution is not as simple as economic analysis would suggest.

To repeat: The *substitution effect* indicates a firm will purchase more of an input whose relative price has fallen and, conversely, use less of an input whose relative price has risen. Thus a decline in the price of capital will increase the relative price of labour and decrease the demand for labour. The *output effect* occurs because a change in an input price will alter production costs and the profit-maximizing output in the same direction. A decrease in the price of capital will lower production costs, increase the profit-maximizing output, and increase the demand for labour.

The substitution and output effects work in opposite directions. For a decline in the price of machinery, the substitution effect decreases and the output effect increases the demand for labour. The

net impact on labour demand will depend on the relative sizes of the two opposed effects. *If the substitution effect outweighs the output effect, a change in the price of a substitute resource will change the demand for labour in the same direction. If the output effect exceeds the substitution effect, a change in the price of a substitute resource will change the demand for labour in the opposite direction.*

COMPLEMENTARY RESOURCES Recall from Chapter 4 that certain products, such as cameras and film or computers and software, are complementary goods in that they go together and are jointly demanded. Resources may also be complementary; an increase in the quantity of one of them employed in the production process will require an increase in the amount used of the other as well, and vice versa. Suppose a small manufacturer of metal products uses punch presses as its basic piece of capital equipment. Each press is designed to be operated by one worker, the machine is not automated — it won't run itself — and a second worker would be wholly redundant.

Assume a technological advance in the production of these presses substantially reduces their costs. Now there can be no negative substitution effect because labour and capital must be used in *fixed proportions*, one person for one machine. Capital cannot be substituted for labour. But there is a positive output effect for labour. Other things equal, the reduction in the price of capital goods means lower production costs. It will therefore be profitable to produce a larger output. In doing so the firm will use both more capital and more labour.

When labour and capital are complementary, for example, a decline in the price of machinery will increase the demand for labour through the output effect. Conversely, in the case of an *increase* in the price of capital, the output effect will reduce the demand for labour. **A change in the price of a complementary resource will cause the demand for labour to change in the opposite direction.**

Recap: The demand curve for labour will *increase* (shift rightward) when:

1. the demand for (and therefore the price of) the product produced by that labour increases;
2. the productivity (MP) of labour increases;
3. the price of a substitute input decreases, provided the output effect is greater than the substitution effect;
4. the price of a substitute input increases, provided the substitution effect exceeds the output effect;
5. the price of a complementary input decreases.

Be sure that you can reverse these generalizations to explain a *decrease* in labour demand.

APPLICATIONS

The determinants of labour demand have practical repercussions, as seen in the following examples.

1. NORTH AMERICAN AUTO WORKERS In 1995 there were about 440,000 fewer workers in the North American automobile industry than in 1979. Two factors help explain this dramatic decline in jobs.

First, foreign competition, particularly from Japanese producers, has reduced the demand for North American cars. The share of the North American market accounted for by North American firms has fallen from about 80% in 1979 to about 66% today. This decline in demand for North American cars has sharply reduced the derived demand for auto workers. A second factor has been the spread of robotic technology in auto manufacturing. Industrial robots have been substituted for assembly-line labour, further reducing the demand for auto workers.

2. FAST-FOOD WORKERS In the past several years, McDonald's and other fast-food establishments have advertised to attract housewives and older people to work in their restaurants. A major reason for this is that more and more women are working outside the home, causing families to substitute restaurant meals for home-prepared meals. The increase in the demand for restaurant meals has increased the demand for fast-food workers. But because the labour supply of traditional fast-food workers — teenagers — has not kept pace, many restaurants are now recruiting housewives and retired workers.

3. PERSONAL COMPUTERS During the last decade there has been a remarkable drop in the average price of personal computers and an equally impressive rise in the computing power of the typical machine. The effects of these developments on labour demand have been both positive and negative. Between 1975 and 1990, employment in the computer services industry (programming and software) grew at an annual rate of over 12%. In some offices computers and labour (keyboard personnel) have been complementary inputs. Thus, the decline in computer prices has reduced production costs to the extent that product or service prices have dropped, sales have increased, and the derived demand for computer operators has increased. On the downside, in some offices personal computers have been substituted for labour, reducing the demand for labour and allowing these firms to use fewer workers to produce their goods and services.

4. DEFENCE CUTBACKS The end of the Cold War and the resulting reductions in defence spending have substantially reduced labour demand by the military. An estimated 16,500 Canadian Forces jobs will be lost between 1994 and 1998. Also, the federal spending cuts on defence will significantly reduce the demand for labour in associated industries.

5. PART-TIME WORKERS One of the biggest labour market changes of recent years has been that many employers have reduced the size of their full-time "core" work forces and simultaneously increased their use of part-time workers (temporary and subcontracted workers). Why has the demand for part-time workers increased? First, increasingly expensive fringe benefits such as pension plans, paid vacations, and sick leave are typically not provided for part-time workers, making their employment less costly. Second, part-time workers give firms more flexibility in responding to changing economic conditions. As product demand shifts, firms can readily increase or decrease the sizes of their work forces through altering their employment of part-time workers. This flexibility enhances the competitive positions of firms and often improves their ability to succeed in international markets.

Table 15-3 provides additional illustrations to reinforce your understanding of the determinants of labour demand.

TABLE 15-3 Determinants of labour demand: factors that shift the labour demand curve

1. **Changes in product demand** Examples: Computer software increases in popularity, increasing the demand for workers at software firms; consumers increase their demand for leather coats, increasing the demand for tanners.

2. **Productivity changes** Examples: An increase in the skill levels of glass blowers increases the demand for their services; computer-assisted graphic design increases the productivity of, and demand for, graphic artists.

3. **Changes in the prices of other resources** Examples: An increase in the price of electricity increases the costs of producing aluminum and reduces the demand for aluminum workers; the price of security equipment used by businesses to protect against illegal entry falls, decreasing the demand for security guards; the price of telephone switching equipment decreases, greatly reducing the cost of telephone service, which in turn increases the demand for telemarketers.

ELASTICITY OF RESOURCE DEMAND

What determines the elasticity of resource demand? Several generalizations provide insights in answering this question.

1. RATE OF MP DECLINE A purely technical consideration — the rate at which the marginal product of the variable resource declines — is crucial. *If the marginal product of labour declines slowly as it is added to a fixed amount of capital, the MRP, or demand curve for labour, will decline slowly and tend to be highly elastic.* A small decline in the price of such a resource will yield a relatively large increase in the amount demanded. Conversely, if the marginal productivity of labour declines sharply, the MRP, or labour demand curve, will decline rapidly. This means that a relatively large decline in the wage rate will be accompanied by a modest increase in the amount of labour hired; resource demand will be inelastic.

2. EASE OF RESOURCE SUBSTITUTABILITY The degree to which resources are substitutable is also a determinant of elasticity. *The larger the number of good substitute resources available, the greater will be the elasticity of demand for a particular resource.* If a furniture manufacturer finds that five or six different types of wood are equally satisfactory in making coffee tables, a rise in the price of any one type of wood may cause a sharp drop in the amount demanded, as the producer substitutes other woods. At the other extreme, it may be impossible to substitute: bauxite is absolutely essential in the production of aluminum ingots. Thus, the demand for bauxite by aluminum producers is very inelastic.

Time can play a role in the input substitution process. For example, a firm's truck drivers may obtain a substantial wage increase with little or no immediate decline in employment. But over time, as the firm's trucks wear out and are replaced, the company may purchase larger trucks and thereby be able to deliver the same total output with fewer drivers. Alternatively, as the firm's trucks depreciate, it might turn to entirely different means of transportation.

3. ELASTICITY OF PRODUCT DEMAND The elasticity of demand for any resource will depend on the elasticity of demand for the product it helps to produce. *The greater the elasticity of product demand,* the greater the elasticity of resource demand. The derived nature of resource demand would lead us to expect this relationship. A small rise in the price of a product with great elasticity of demand will sharply reduce output, and therefore bring about a relatively large decline in the amounts of various resources demanded. This implies that the demand for the resource is elastic.

4. LABOUR COST/TOTAL COST RATIO *The larger the proportion of total production costs accounted for by a resource, the greater will be the elasticity of demand for that resource.* For example, if labour costs were the only production cost, then a 20% increase in wage rates would shift the firm's cost curves upward by 20%. Given the elasticity of product demand, this substantial increase in costs would cause a relatively large decline in sales and a sharp decline in the amount of labour demanded. Labour demand would be elastic. But if labour costs were only 50% of production costs, then a 20% increase in wage rates would only increase costs by 10%. Given the same elasticity of product demand, a relatively small decline in sales, and therefore in the amount of labour demanded, would result. The demand for labour would be inelastic. (**Key Question 4**)

QUICK REVIEW 15-2

1. A resource demand curve will shift because of changes in product demand, changes in the productivity of the resource, and changes in the prices of other inputs.

2. If resources A and B are substitutable, a decline in the price of A will decrease the demand for B if the substitution effect exceeds the output effect. But if the output effect exceeds the substitution effect, the demand for B will increase.

3. If resources C and D are complements, a decline in the price of C will increase the demand for D.

4. The elasticity of demand for a resource will be less **a** the more rapid the decline in marginal product; **b** the smaller the number of substitutes; **c** the smaller the elasticity of product demand; and **d** the smaller the proportion of total cost accounted for by the resource.

OPTIMAL COMBINATION OF RESOURCES

So far we have considered one variable input — labour. But in the long run, firms can vary the amounts of *all* the resources they use. That's why we need to consider what combination of resources a firm will choose when all are variable. While our analysis will be based on two resources, it can readily be extended to any number.

We will consider two interrelated questions:

1. What is the least-cost combination of resources producing *any* given level of output?
2. What combination of resources will maximize a firm's profits?

THE LEAST-COST RULE

A firm is producing *any* given output with the **least-cost combination of resources** when the last dollar spent on each resource entails the same marginal product. That is, *the cost of any output is minimized when the marginal product per dollar's worth of each resource used is the same.* With just two resources, labour and capital, total costs are minimized where:

$$\frac{\text{MP of labour}}{\text{price of labour}} = \frac{\text{MP of capital}}{\text{price of capital}} \quad (1)$$

You can see why fulfilling this condition means least-cost production. Suppose the prices of capital and labour are both $1 per unit, but capital and labour are being employed in such amounts that the marginal product of labour is 10 and the marginal product of capital is 5. Our equation tells us that this is clearly *not* the least costly combination of resources: MP_L/P_L is 10/1 and MP_C/P_C is 5/1.

If the firm spends a dollar less on capital and shifts that dollar to labour, it will lose the 5 units of output produced by the marginal dollar's worth of capital, but will gain the 10 units of output from the employment of an extra dollar's worth of labour. *Net* output will increase by 5 (= 10 − 5) units for the same total cost. This shifting of dollars from capital to labour will push the firm down its MP curve for labour and back up its MP curve for capital, moving the firm towards a position of equilibrium wherein equation (1) is fulfilled. At that point, the MP of both labour and capital might be, for example, 7.

BOX 15-3   IN THE MEDIA

DRIVERS WILL PAY TAB FOR NEW TECHNOLOGY

BY TIMOTHY PRITCHARD
Auto Industry Reporter

Today, oil companies are paying a price for the development of increasingly fuel-efficient cars, but more changes lie ahead and drivers will soon begin paying for them.

Refiners will have to invest to keep up with new vehicle and environmental technology — and they will have to be profitable to do it.

So as refinery and service station capacity is cut back, prices at the pump will go up, say investment analysts who follow the industry.

Canada's car population of 13 million is almost 50 per cent higher than it was in the mid-1970s, but gasoline consumption is no greater than it was 15 years ago. Great efficiencies have been achieved by building smaller and lighter cars.

In 1975, the average passenger car in Ontario burned 18.6 litres to travel 100 kilometres in combined city and highway driving, according to calculations by DesRosiers Automotive Consultants of Toronto.

The comparable figure for 1989 was 9.6 litres for 100 kilometres, and a better performance is likely as older cars are replaced.

But flat gasoline sales are only one challenge facing the oil companies.

They soon will have to refit stations to sell a greater variety of fuels, including ethanol, methanol, and natural gas.

SOURCE: *The Globe and Mail*, January 30, 1992. Reprinted by permersion.

The Story in Brief

The efficiency of automobile engines has led to stagnant demand for gasoline, even in the face of an almost 50% increase in the number of automobiles since the 1970s.

New environmentally friendly technology requires refiners to invest to produce a greater variety of fuels, including ethanol, methanol, and natural gas. These costs will likely be passed on to consumers.

The Economics Behind the Story

- The demand for gasoline is a derived demand; as demand for cars increases so does the demand for gasoline.

- Since the 1970s the efficiency of automobile engines has increased enough to completely offset an almost 50% rise in the number of cars. Thus, the demand for gasoline has remained flat, as has price.

- But the demand for environmentally friendly cars necessitates the development of cleaner-burning fuels. The increased cost of these fuels will likely be passed on to consumers.

- How does the price elasticity of demand for automobile fuels affect how much of the increase in new fuel costs will be passed on to consumers?

Whenever the same total cost results in a greater total output, the cost per unit — and therefore the total cost of any given level of output — is being reduced. To be able to produce a *larger* output with a *given* total cost is the same as being able to produce a *given* output with a *smaller* total cost. And as we have seen, the cost of producing any given output can be reduced so long as $MP_L/P_L \neq MP_C/P_C$.

THE PROFIT-MAXIMIZING RULE

Minimizing cost is not sufficient for maximizing profit. There are many different levels of output that a firm can produce in the least costly way. But there is only one unique output that will maximize profits. Recalling our earlier analysis of product markets, this profit-maximizing *output* is where marginal revenue equals marginal cost (MR = MC). Let us now derive a comparable rule from the standpoint of resource *inputs*.

In deriving the demand schedule for labour early in this chapter, we determined that the profit-maximizing quantity of labour to employ is that quantity at which the wage rate, or price of labour (P_L), equals the marginal *revenue* product of labour (MRP_L) or, more simply, $P_L = MRP_L$.

The same rationale applies to any other resource — for example, capital. Capital will also be employed in the profit-maximizing amount when its price equals its marginal revenue product, or $P_C = MRP_C$. Thus in general, we can say that when hiring resources *in competitive markets*, a firm will realize the **profit-maximizing combination of resources** when each input is employed up to the point at which its price equals its marginal revenue product:

$$P_L = MRP_L$$
$$P_C = MRP_C$$

Dividing both sides of the equation by their respective prices, we have:

$$\frac{MRP_L}{P_L} = \frac{MRP_C}{P_C} = 1 \qquad (2)$$

Note in equation (2) that it is not sufficient that the MRPs of the two resources be *proportionate* to their prices: the MRPs must be *equal* to their prices, and the ratios therefore equal to 1. For example, if $MRP_L = \$15$, $P_L = \$5$, $MRP_C = \$9$, and

$P_C = \$3$, the firm would be underemploying both capital and labour, even though the ratios of MRP to resource price were identical for both resources. The firm could expand its profits by hiring additional amounts of both capital and labour until it had moved down their downsloping MRP curves to the points at which MRP_L was equal to \$5 and MRP_C was \$3. The ratios would now be 5/5 and 3/3, and equal to 1.[3]

Although we have separated the two for discussion purposes, the profit-maximizing position of equation (2) subsumes the least-cost position of equation (1). [Note that if we divide the MRP numerators in equation (2) by product price, we would obtain equa-

---

[3] It is not difficult to demonstrate that equation (2) is consistent with (indeed, the equivalent of) the P = MC rule for determining the profit-maximizing output of Chapter 10. We begin by taking the reciprocal of equation (2):

$$\frac{P_L}{MRP_L} = \frac{P_C}{MRP_C} = 1$$

Recall that, assuming pure competition in the product market, marginal revenue product, MRP, is found by multiplying marginal product, MP, by product price, P_x. Thus we can write:

$$\frac{P_L}{MP_L \times P_x} = \frac{P_C}{MP_C \times P_x} = 1$$

Multiplying through by product price, P_x, we get:

$$\frac{P_L}{MP_L} = \frac{P_C}{MP_C} = P_x$$

The two ratios measure marginal cost. That is, if we divide the cost (price) of an additional input of labour or capital by the associated marginal product, we have the addition to total cost, that is, the *marginal* cost, of each additional unit of output. For example, if the price of an extra worker (P_L) is \$10 and that worker's marginal product (MP_L) is, say, 5 units, then the marginal cost of each of those 5 units is \$2. The same reasoning applies to capital. We thus obtain:

$$MC_x = P_x$$

Our conclusion is that equation (2) in the text, showing the profit-maximizing combination of *inputs*, is the equivalent of our earlier P = MC rule, which identified the profit-maximizing *output*.

tion (1).] A firm that is maximizing its profits *must* be producing the profit-maximizing output with the least costly combination of resources. If it is *not* using the least costly combination of labour and capital, then it could produce the same output at a smaller total cost and realize a larger profit. Thus, a necessary condition for profit-maximization is the fulfilment of equation (1). But equation (1) is not a sufficient condition for profit maximization. It is quite possible for a firm to produce the "wrong" output, an output that does not maximize profits, but to produce that output with the least costly combination of resources.

NUMERICAL ILLUSTRATION

A numerical illustration will reinforce your understanding of the least-cost and profit-maximizing rules. In columns 2, 3, 2′, and 3′ of Table 15-4 we show the total products and marginal physical products for various amounts of labour and capital that are assumed to be the only inputs needed in producing product X. Both inputs are subject to the law of diminishing returns.

We also assume that labour and capital are supplied in competitive resource markets at $8 and $12 respectively and that product X is sold competitively at $2 per unit. For both labour and capital we can determine the total revenue associated with each input level by multiplying total product by the $2 product price. These data are shown in columns 4 and 4′. This allows us to calculate the marginal revenue product of each successive input of labour and capital as shown in columns 5 and 5′.

PRODUCING AT LEAST-COST What is the least-cost combination of labour and capital to use in producing, say, 50 units of output? Answer: 3 units of labour and 2 units of capital. Note from columns 3 and 3′ that in hiring 3 units of labour MP_L/P_L = 6/8 = 3/4 and for 2 units of capital MP_C/P_C = 9/12 = 3/4, so equation (1) is fulfilled. And columns 2 and 2′ indicate that this combination of labour and capital does, indeed, result in the specified 50 (= 28 + 22) units of output. How can we verify that costs are actually minimized? First, note that the total cost of employing 3 units of labour and 2 of capital is $48 [= (3 × $8) + (2 × $12)] or, alternatively stated, cost per unit of output is $0.96 (= $48/50).

Observe, too, that there are other combinations of labour and capital that will yield 50 units of output. For example, 5 units of labour and 1 unit of cap-

ital will produce 50 (= 37 + 13) units, but we find that total cost is now higher at $52 [= (5 × $8) + (1 × $12)], meaning average unit cost has risen to $1.04 (= $52/50). By employing 5 units of labour and 1 of capital the least-cost rule would be violated in that MP_L/P_L = 4/8 is less than MP_C/P_C = 13/12, indicating more capital and less labour should be employed to produce this output.

Similarly, 50 units of output also could be produced with 2 units of labour and 3 of capital. The total cost of the 50 units of output would again be $52 [= (2 × $8) + (3 × $12)], or $1.04 per unit. Here equation (1) is not fulfilled in that MP_L/P_L = 10/8, which exceeds MP_C/P_C = 6/12. This inequality suggests that the firm should use more labour and less capital.

MAXIMIZING PROFITS Will 50 units of output maximize the firm's profits? No, because the profit-maximizing rule stated in equation (2) is *not* fulfilled when employing 3 units of labour and 2 of capital. We know that to maximize profits any given input should be employed until its price equals its marginal revenue product (P_L = MRP_L and P_C = MRP_C). But for 3 units of labour we find in column 5 that labour's MRP is $12 while its price is only $8. This means it is profitable to hire more labour. Similarly, for 2 units of capital we observe in column 5′ that MRP is $18 and capital's price is only $12, indicating that more capital should also be employed. When hiring 3 units of labour and 2 of capital to produce 50 units of output, the firm is underemploying both inputs. Labour and capital are both being used in less than profit-maximizing amounts.

The marginal revenue products of labour and capital are equal to their prices and equation (2) is fulfilled when the firm is employing 5 units of labour and 3 units of capital. This is therefore the profit-maximizing combination of outputs.[4] The firm's total cost will be $76, which is made up of $40 (= 5 × $8) worth of labour and $36 (= 3 × $12) worth of capital.

---

[4] Given that we are dealing with discrete (nonfractional) increases in the two outputs, you should also be aware that in fact the employment of 4 units of labour and 2 of capital are equally profitable. The fifth unit of labour's MRP and its price are equal (at $8), so that the fifth unit neither adds to, nor subtracts from, the firm's profits. The same reasoning applies to the third unit of labour.

TABLE 15-4   The least-cost and profit-maximizing combinations of labour and capital*

LABOUR (PRICE = $8)					CAPITAL (PRICE = $12)				
(1)	(2)	(3)	(4)	(5)	(1')	(2')	(3')	(4')	(5')
Quantity	Total product	Marginal product	Total revenue	Marginal revenue product	Quantity	Total product	Marginal product	Total revenue	Marginal revenue product
0	0	0	$ 0	$ 0	0	0	0	$ 0	$ 0
1	12	12	24	24	1	13	13	26	26
2	22	10	44	20	2	22	9	44	18
3	28	6	56	12	3	28	6	56	12
4	33	5	66	10	4	32	4	64	8
5	37	4	74	8	5	35	3	70	6
6	40	3	80	6	6	37	2	74	4
7	42	2	84	4	7	38	1	76	2

*To simplify, it is assumed in this table that the productivity of each resource is independent of the quantity of the other. For example, the total and marginal product of labour is assumed not to vary with the quantity of capital employed.

Total revenue of $130 is determined by multiplying total output of 65 (= 37 + 28) by the $2 product price or, alternatively, by simply summing the total revenue attributable to labour ($74) and to capital ($56). The difference between total revenue and total cost is, of course, the firm's economic profit, which in this instance is $54 (= $130 − $76). Equation (2) is fulfilled when 5 units of labour and 3 of capital are employed: $MRP_L/P_L = 8/8 = MRP_C/P_C = 12/12 = 1$. You should experiment with other combinations of labour and capital to demonstrate that they will yield an economic profit less than $54.

Our example also verifies our earlier assertion that a firm using the profit-maximizing combination of inputs is also necessarily producing the resulting output with the least cost. In fulfilling equation (2) the firm is automatically fulfilling equation (1). In this case, for 5 units of labour and 3 of capital we observe that $MP_L/P_L = 4/8 = MP_C/P_C = 6/12$[5]. (**Key Questions 5 and 7**)

___
[5] Footnote 1 in Chapter 16 modifies our least-cost and profit-maximizing rules for the situation in which a firm is hiring resources under imperfectly competitive conditions. Where there is imperfect competition in the resource market, the marginal resource cost (MRC) — the cost of an extra input — exceeds the resource price (P). Thus, we must substitute MRC for P in the denominators of equations (1) and (2).

MARGINAL PRODUCTIVITY THEORY OF INCOME DISTRIBUTION

Our discussion of resource pricing is the cornerstone of the controversial view that economic justice is one of the outcomes of a competitive market economy. Table 15-1 tells us in effect that labour receives an income payment equal to the marginal contribution it makes to the firm's revenue. Bluntly stated, labour is paid what it is worth. Therefore, if you accept the proposition that we are paid according to what we produce, the marginal productivity theory seems to provide a fair and equitable distribution of income. Because the marginal productivity theory equally applies to capital and land, the distribution of all incomes can be regarded as equitable.

An income distribution whereby workers and owners of property resources are paid in accordance with their contribution to output sounds fair. But there are serious criticisms of the **marginal productivity theory of income distribution**.

1. INEQUALITY Critics argue that the distribution of income resulting from payment according to marginal productivity may be highly unequal because productive resources are very unequally distributed in the first place. Aside from differences in genetic endowments, individ-

uals encounter substantially different opportunities to enhance their productivity through education and training. Some may not be able to participate in production at all, because of mental or physical handicaps, and would obtain no income under a system of distribution based solely on marginal productivity. Ownership of resources is also highly unequal. Many landlords obtain their property by inheritance rather than through their own productive effort. Hence income from inherited property conflicts with the "to each according to what one creates" proposition. This reasoning can lead us to advocate government policies to modify the income distribution resulting from payments made strictly according to marginal productivity.

2. MONOPSONY AND MONOPOLY The marginal productivity theory rests on the assumption of competitive markets. We will find in Chapter 16 that labour markets, for example, are riddled with imperfections. Some employers exert monopsony power in hiring workers. And some workers, through labour unions, professional associations, and occupational licensing laws, wield monopoly power in selling their services. Indeed, the process of collective bargaining over wages suggests a power struggle over the division of income. In this struggle, market forces — and income shares based on marginal productivity — are pushed into the background. In short, we will find that because of market imperfections, wage rates and other resource prices frequently do *not* measure contributions to a nation's domestic output.

CHAPTER SUMMARY

1. Resource prices are a determinant of money incomes and simultaneously ration resources to various industries and firms.

2. The demand for any resource is derived from the product it helps produce. That means the demand for a resource will depend on its productivity and the market value (price) of the good it is producing.

3. The marginal revenue product schedule of any resource is the demand schedule for that resource. This follows from the rule that a firm hiring under competitive conditions will find it most profitable to hire a resource up to the point where the price of the resource equals its marginal revenue product.

4. The demand curve for a resource is downsloping, because the marginal product of additional inputs of any resource declines in accordance with the law of diminishing returns. When a firm is selling in an imperfectly competitive market, the resource demand curve will fall for a second reason: product price must be reduced to permit the firm to sell a larger output. The market demand for a resource can be derived by summing the demand curves of all firms hiring that resource.

5. The demand for a resource will shift as a result of **a** a change in the demand for, and therefore the price of, the product the resource is producing; **b** changes in the productivity of the resource; **c** changes in prices of other resources.

6. If resources A and B are substitutable, a decline in the price of A will decrease the demand for B, provided the substitution effect is greater than the output effect. But if the output effect exceeds the substitution effect, a decline in the price of A will increase the demand for B.

7. If resources C and D are complementary or jointly demanded there is only an output effect, and a change in the price of C will change the demand for D in the opposite direction.

8. The elasticity of resource demand will be greater **a** the slower the rate at which the marginal product of the resource declines, **b** the larger the number of good substitute resources available, **c** the greater the elasticity of demand for the product, and **d** the larger the proportion of total production costs attributable to the resource.

9. Any level of output will be produced with the least costly combination of resources when the marginal product, per dollar's worth of each input, is the same, that is, when

$$\frac{\text{MP of labour}}{\text{price of labour}} = \frac{\text{MP of capital}}{\text{price of capital}}$$

10. A firm will employ the profit-maximizing combination of resources when the price of each resource is equal to its marginal *revenue* product or, algebraically, when

$$\frac{\text{MRP of labour}}{\text{price of labour}} = \frac{\text{MRP of capital}}{\text{price of capital}} = 1$$

TERMS AND CONCEPTS

derived demand (p. 309)
least-cost combination of resources (p. 317)
marginal product (MP) (p. 309)
marginal productivity theory of income
   distribution (p.321)

marginal resource cost (MRC) (p. 310)
marginal revenue product (MRP) (p. 309)
MRP = MRC rule (p. 310)
profit-maximizing combination of resources (p. 319)
substitution and output effects (p. 313)

QUESTIONS AND STUDY SUGGESTIONS

1. What is the significance of resource pricing? Explain in detail how the factors determining resource demand differ from those underlying product demand. Explain the meaning and significance of the notion that the demand for a resource is a *derived* demand. Why do resource demand curves slope downward?

2. *Key Question*   *Complete the following labour demand table for a firm that is hiring labour competitively and selling its product in a competitive market.*

Units of labour	Total product	Marginal product	Product price	Total revenue	Marginal revenue product
1	17	$ _____	$2	$ _____	$ _____
2	31		2	_____	
3	43	_____	2	_____	_____
4	53	_____	2	_____	_____
5	60	_____	2	_____	_____
6	65	_____	2	_____	_____

   a. How many workers will the firm hire if the going rate is $27.95? $19.95? Explain why the firm will not hire a larger or smaller number of workers at each of these wage rates.

   b. Show, in schedule form and graphically, the labour demand curve for this firm.

   c. Redetermine the firm's demand curve for labour on the assumption that it is selling in an imperfectly competitive market and that, although it can sell 17 units at $2.20 per unit, it must lower product price by 5¢ in order to sell the marginal product of each successive worker. Compare this demand curve with that derived in question 2b. Which curve is more elastic? Explain.

3. Distinguish between a change in resource demand and a change in the quantity of a resource demanded. What specific factors might lead to a change in resource demand? A change in the quantity of a resource demanded?

4. *Key Question* *What factors determine the elasticity of resource demand? What effect will each of the following have on the elasticity or the location of the demand for resource C that is being used in the production of commodity X? Where there is any uncertainty as to the outcome, specify the causes of that uncertainty.*

   a. An increase in the demand for product X.

   b. An increase in the price of substitute resource D.

   c. An increase in the number of resources substitutable for C in producing X.

   d. A technological improvement in the capital equipment with which resource C is combined.

   e. A decline in the price of complementary resource E.

   f. A decline in the elasticity of demand for product X, due to a decline in the competitiveness of the product market.

5. *Key Question* *Suppose the productivity of labour and capital are as shown below. The output of these resources sells in a purely competitive market for $1 per unit. Both labour and capital are hired under purely competitive conditions at $1 and $3 respectively.*

Units of capital	MP of capital	Units of labour	MP of labour
1	24	1	11
2	21	2	9
3	18	3	8
4	15	4	7
5	9	5	6
6	6	6	4
7	3	7	1
8	1	8	$1/2$

   a. What is the least-cost combination of labour and capital to employ in producing 80 units of output? Explain.

   b. What is the profit-maximizing combination of labour and capital for the firm to employ? Explain. What is the resulting level of output? What is the economic profit?

   c. When the firm employs the profit-maximizing combination of labour and capital determined in 5b, is this combination also the least costly way of producing the profit-maximizing output? Explain.

6. Using the substitution and output effects, explain how a decline in the price of resource A *might* cause an increase in the demand for substitute resource B. If resources C and D are complementary and used in fixed proportions, what will be the impact of an increase in the price of C upon the demand for D?

7. *Key Question* In each of the following four cases MRP_L and MRP_C refer to the marginal revenue products of labour and capital, respectively, and P_L and P_C refer to their prices. Indicate in each case whether the conditions are consistent with maximum profits for the firm. If not, state which resources should be used in larger amounts and which resources should be used in smaller amounts.

   a. $MRP_L = \$8; P_L = \$4; MRP_C = \$8; P_C = \$4.$

   b. $MRP_L = \$10; P_L = \$12; MRP_C = \$14; P_C = \$9.$

   c. $MRP_L = \$6; P_L = \$6; MRP_C = \$12; P_C = \$12.$

   d. $MRP_L = \$22; P_L = \$26; MRP_C = \$16; P_C = \$19.$

8. **Advanced Analysis** Demonstrate algebraically that the condition for the profit-maximizing level of output is the equivalent of the condition for the profit-maximizing combination of inputs.

9. If each input is paid in accordance with its marginal revenue product, will the resulting distribution of income be ethically just?

10. (Applying the Theory) Use the example of railroad cabooses from Box 15-2 to explain why firms do not always employ the least-cost combination of resources.

CHAPTER 16

THE PRICING AND EMPLOYMENT OF RESOURCES: WAGE DETERMINATION

The most important price you will encounter in your lifetime will be your wage rate. It will be critical in determining the economic well-being of you and your family. Thus, the following facts and questions may be of more than casual interest.

Real wages, and therefore living standards, have increased historically in Canada. What forces account for these increases?

Union workers generally receive higher wages than nonunion workers. How are unions able to accomplish this wage advantage?

The average salary for major league baseball players in 1995 was over $1 million as compared to about $45,000 for schoolteachers. What causes differences in wages and incomes?

Most people are paid an hourly wage rate. But some workers are paid by the number of units produced or receive commissions and royalties. What is the rationale for various compensation schemes?

BOX 16-1 THE BIG PICTURE

Chapter 15 looked at the theory of resource demand; resources include land, labour, capital, and entrepreneurial talent. This chapter focuses specifically on the demand and supply for labour and how wages are determined. If the labour market is competitive, then equilibrium wages in each market are the result of many buyers and sellers of labour services. But if there are impediments to supply and demand forces in the labour market, wages will diverge from their competitive rates.

As you read this chapter, keep the following points in mind:

- In a competitive market the amount of labour employed and the wage rate is determined by supply and demand conditions.
- There are often impediments to competitive market forces in labour markets, among them, unions and market power of buyers of labour services.
- There are also other labour market imperfections that help explain wage differences paid on identical jobs.

Having explored the major factors underlying resource demand, we now introduce supply as it characterizes the markets for labour, land, capital, and entrepreneurial ability to understand how wages, rents, interest, and profits are determined.

We discuss wages prior to other resource prices because to the vast majority of households, the wage rate is the most important price in the economy; it is their sole or basic source of income. About three-quarters of the national income is in the form of wages and salaries.

Our objectives in discussing wage determination are to: (1) understand the forces underlying the general level of wage rates in Canada; (2) see how wage rates are determined in particular labour markets; (3) analyze the impact of unions on the structure and level of wages; (4) discuss the economic effects of the minimum wage; (5) explain wage differentials; and (6) survey a number of compensation schemes that link pay to worker performance.

Throughout this chapter, we rely on the marginal productivity theory of Chapter 15 as an explanation of labour demand.

MEANING OF WAGES

Wages are the price paid for the use of labour. The term "wages" broadly applies to the payments received by (1) blue- and white-collar workers of almost infinite variety; (2) professionals — physicians, lawyers, dentists, teachers; (3) owners of small businesses — barbers, plumbers, and a host of retailers — for the labour services they provide in operating their own businesses.

Wages may take the form of bonuses, royalties, commissions, and monthly salaries, but unless otherwise stated we use the term "wages" to mean wage rates per unit of time — per hour, per day, and so forth. This will remind us that the wage rate is a price paid for units of labour service. It also lets us distinguish between "wages" and "earnings," the latter depending on wage rates *and* the number of hours or weeks of labour service supplied in the market.

We also distinguish between nominal wages and real wages. **Nominal wages** are the amount of money received per hour, per day, per week, and so forth. **Real wages** are the quantity of goods and services you can obtain with nominal wages; real wages are the "purchasing power" of nominal wages.

Your real wages depend on your nominal wages and the prices of the goods and services you buy. The percentage change in real wages can be determined by subtracting the percentage change in the price level from the percentage change in nominal wages. Thus an 8% increase in nominal wages during a year when the price level increases by 5% yields a 3% increase in real wages. Unless otherwise indicated, our discussion will be in terms of real wage rates by assuming the level of product prices is constant.

GENERAL LEVELS OF WAGES

Wages differ among nations, regions, occupations, and individuals. Wage rates are vastly higher in Canada than in China or India; they are generally higher in British Columbia, Ontario, and Alberta than in Quebec and the

Atlantic provinces; plumbers are paid more than general labourers; lawyer A may earn twice as much as lawyer B for the same number of hours of work. Wage rates may also differ according to gender, age, and ethnic background.

The general level of wages, like the general level of prices, encompasses a wide range of different specific wage rates. It includes the wages of bakers, barbers, baseball players, and brain surgeons. Nevertheless, the average wage is a useful point of departure in making and explaining international and interregional wage comparisons.

International wage comparisons are admittedly complex and suspect. But data such as Global Perspective 16-1 suggest that the general level of

real wages in Canada is relatively high — although not the highest — globally.

The simplest explanation for our high real wages is that the demand for labour has been great relative to the supply.

ROLE OF PRODUCTIVITY

We know the demand for labour — or any other resource — depends on its productivity. The greater the productivity of labour, the greater the demand for it. And given the total supply of labour, the stronger the demand, the higher the average level of real wages. The demand for Canadian labour has been strong because Canadian labour is highly productive. But why the high productivity? There are several reasons for this high productivity.

1. CAPITAL Canadian workers are employed in conjunction with large amounts of capital equipment. The average Canadian worker is assisted by more machinery and equipment than any other worker in the world.

2. NATURAL RESOURCES Natural resources are very abundant in relation to the size of the labour force. Canada is richly endowed with arable land, basic mineral resources, and sources of industrial power. The fact that Canadian workers have large amounts of high-quality natural resources to work with is perhaps most evident in agriculture, where historically the growth of productivity has been dramatic.

3. TECHNOLOGY Canadian workers in many industries not only use more capital equipment but technologically superior equipment than do most foreign workers. Similarly, work methods are steadily being improved through detailed scientific study and research.

4. LABOUR QUALITY The health, education, and training of Canadian workers have been generally superior to that of the workers of most other nations. This means that even with the same quantity and quality of natural and capital resources, Canadian workers would be more efficient than many of their foreign counterparts.

5. OTHER FACTORS Less tangible items underlying the high productivity of Canadian labour are (*a*) the efficiency and flexibility of Canadian management; (*b*) a business, social, and political envi-

GLOBAL PERSPECTIVE 16-1

Hourly wages of production workers, selected nations

Wage differentials are pronounced worldwide. The data shown here indicate that hourly compensation in Canada is not as high as in a number of European nations. It is important to note, however, that the prices of goods and services vary greatly among nations, and the process of converting foreign wages into dollars does not fully reflect these differences.

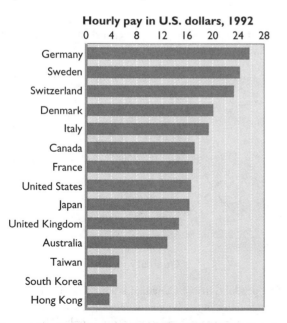

Hourly pay in U.S. dollars, 1992

Source: *International Comparisons of Hourly Compensation Costs for Production Workers, 1992* (U.S. Bureau of Labor Statistics, Report 844).

FIGURE 16-1 Output per hour and real average hourly earnings, all business-sector industries

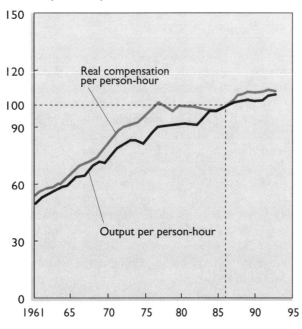

Index (1986=100)

Over a period of years, there has been a close relationship between real hourly wages and output per person-hour. As a result of large nominal wage increases between 1974 and 1977, real wages rose considerably above output per person-hour. Note that real wages have not increased since then, while output per person-hour has caught up.

Source: *Statistics Canada, Aggregate Productivity Measures, 1993* Table 1.

ronment that puts great emphasis on production and productivity; (c) generally, an adequately sized market that provides the opportunity for firms to realize mass-production economies.

REAL WAGES AND PRODUCTIVITY

The dependence of real hourly wages on the productivity level is indicated in Figure 16-1. Note the close long-run relationship between real hourly wages and output per person-hour. Since real income and real output are two ways of viewing the same thing, it is no surprise that *real income (earnings) per worker can increase only at about the same rate as output per worker*. More real output per hour means more real income to distribute for each hour worked. The sim-

plest case is Robinson Crusoe on the desert island. The number of coconuts he can pick or fish he can catch per hour is his real wage per hour.

SECULAR GROWTH

But simple supply and demand analysis suggests that even if the demand for labour is strong in Canada, increases in the supply of labour will reduce the general level of wages over time. It is true that the Canadian population and the labour force have grown significantly over the decades. Historically, increases in the supply of labour have usually been more than offset by increases in the demand for labour, arising from the productivity-increasing factors discussed above. The result has been a long-run, or secular, increase in wage rates and employment, as suggested by Figure 16-2.

But a glance back at Figure 16-1 suggests a more disturbing point. Real hourly wages and weekly earnings have been more or less stagnant since 1979. In 1993 the average real hourly wage (in 1986 dollars) in all private nonmanufacturing industries was $10.67, down from $11.96 in 1979. Average weekly real earnings were $427 in 1993, compared to $478 in 1979. There is no consensus as to the causes of these slowdowns, but the following are frequently cited: diminished rates of capital accumulation and the reallocation of labour from high-productivity manufacturing industries to low-productivity service industries. Also cited are the deterioration of

FIGURE 16-2 The secular trend of real wages in Canada

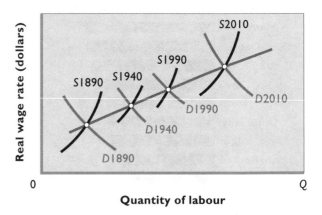

The productivity of Canadian labour has increased substantially in the long run, causing the demand for labour to increase in relation to the supply. The result has been increases in real wages.

labour force skills due to the declining quality of education; the surge of labour force supply associated with large numbers of "baby boomers" and married women entering the labour force; and management strategies that stress short-term profitability at the expense of research and development and innovative labour relations programs that might increase productivity.

The globalization of production may also be a factor. When production can be effectively outsourced to less developed countries, the effective supply of unskilled workers is greatly expanded. This global market for unskilled labour pulls down the real wages of such workers in Canada and other industrialized nations. Stated differently, with the globalization of the market for unskilled labour, unskilled Canadian workers must work for wages roughly equal to those of the unskilled in the less developed nations or lose their jobs because production will be relocated to those less developed countries. In fact, the real wages of less skilled Canadian workers have declined significantly, pulling down the average level of real wages.

WAGES IN PARTICULAR LABOUR MARKETS

We now turn from the general level of wages to specific wage rates. What determines the wage rate received by a specific type of worker? Demand and supply analysis again is revealing. Our analysis covers some half-dozen basic market models.

COMPETITIVE MODEL

In a purely **competitive labour market**:

1. many firms are competing with one another in hiring a specific type of labour;

2. numerous qualified workers with identical skills independently supplying this type of labour service;

3. neither firms nor workers can exert control over market wage rate.

KEY GRAPH

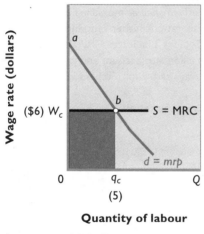

(a) Individual firm

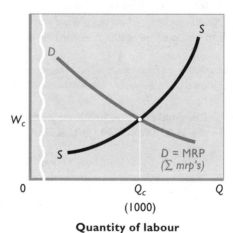

(b) Market

FIGURE 16-3 The supply of, and the demand for, labour in (a) a single competitive firm and (b) a competitive market

In a competitive labour market, the equilibriium wage rate, W_c, and number of workers employed, Q_c, are determined by supply, S, and demand, D, as shown in (b). Because this wage rate is given to the individual firm hiring in the market, its labour supply curve, $S = MRC$, is perfectly elastic as in (a). The firm finds it most profitable to hire workers up to the $MRP = MRC$ point. The area $0abq_c$ represents the firm's total revenue, of which $0W_c bq_c$ is its total wage cost; the remaining area $W_c ab$ is available for paying nonlabour resources.

BOX 16-2   APPLYING THE THEORY

PAY AND PERFORMANCE IN PROFESSIONAL BASEBALL

Professional baseball has provided an interesting "laboratory" in which the predictions of wage theory have been empirically tested.

Until 1976 professional baseball players were bound to a single team through the so-called "reserve clause" that prevented players from selling their talents on the open (competitive) market. Stated differently, the reserve clause conferred monopsony power on the team that originally drafted a player. As we saw in this chapter, labour market theory would lead us to predict that this monopsony power would permit teams to pay wages less than a player's marginal revenue product (MRP). However, since 1976 major league players have been able to become "free agents" at the end of their sixth season of play and at that time can sell their services to any team. Orthodox theory suggests that free agents should be able to increase their salaries and bring them more closely into accord with their MRPs. Research confirms both predictions.

Scully[*] found that before baseball players were legally able to become free agents their salaries were

substantially below their MRPs. Scully estimated a player's MRP as follows. First, he determined the relationship between a team's winning percentage and its revenue. Then he estimated the relationship between various possible measures of player productivity and a team's winning percentage. He found the ratio of strikeouts to walks for pitchers and the slugging averages for hitters (all nonpitchers) to be the best indicators of a player's contribution to the winning percentage. These two estimates were combined to calculate the contribution of a player to a team's total revenue.

Scully calculated that prior to free agency the estimated MRPs of both pitchers and hitters were substantially greater than player salaries. Table 1 shows the relevant data for pitchers. Column 1 indicates pitcher performance as measured by lifetime strike-out-to-walk ratio. A higher ratio indicates a better pitcher. Column 2 indicates MRP after player training costs are taken into account and column 3 shows actual average salary for pitchers in each quality class.

_____

[*] Gerald W. Scully, "Pay and Performance in Major League Baseball," *American Economic Review*, December 1974, pp. 915-930.

TABLE 1   Marginal revenue products and salaries of professional baseball pitchers in the U.S., 1968-1969 (in U.S. dollars)

(1) Performance*	(2) Marginal revenue product	(3) Salary
1.60	$ 57,600	$31,100
1.80	80,900	34,200
2.00	104,100	37,200
2.20	127,400	40,200
2.40	150,600	43,100
2.60	173,900	46,000
2.80	197,100	48,800
3.00	220,300	51,600
3.20	243,600	54,400
3.40	266,800	57,100
3.60	290,100	59,800

*Strikeout-to-walk ratio.

Source: Scully, op. cit., p. 923.

As expected, salaries were far less than MRPs. Even the lowest quality pitchers (those with a 1.60 strike-out-to-walk ratio) received on the average salaries amounting to only about 54% of their MRPs. Observe, too, that the gap between MRP and average salary widens as player quality improves. "Star" players were exploited more than other players. The best pitchers received salaries that were only about 21% of their MRPs. The same general results apply to hitters. For example, the least productive hitters on the average received a salary equal to about 37% of their MRPs.

Sommers and Quinton[**] have assessed the economic fortunes of 14 players who constituted the

between estimated MRPs and salaries. Although MRP and salary differences are larger for hitters, Sommers and Quinton conclude that the overturn of the monopsonistic reserve clause "has forced owners into a situation where there is a greater tendency to pay players in relation to their contribution to team revenues."

How have baseball team owners reacted to the escalating salaries under free agency? In early 1986 the players' union filed a grievance charging that the 26 professional baseball clubs had acted in concert against signing any of the players who became free agents in 1985. In fact, of the 62 players who became

TABLE 2 Estimated marginal revenue products and player costs, 1977 (in U.S. dollars)

(1) Pitcher	(2) Marginal revenue product	(3) Annual contract cost*
Garland	$282,091	$230,000
Gullett	340,846	349,333
Fingers	303,511	332,000
Campbell	205,639	210,000
Alexander	166,203	166,667

*Includes annual salary, bonuses, the value of insurance policies and deferred payments, etc.

Source: Sommers and Quinton, op. cit., p. 432.

"first family" of free agents. In accordance with the predictions of labour market theory, their research indicates that the competitive bidding of free agency brought the salaries of free agents more closely into accord with their estimated MRPs. The data for the five free-agent pitchers are shown in Table 2 where we find a surprisingly close correspondence

free agents in 1985, only two had signed contracts with a different team before the season began. In effect, the players charged that owners had attempted to restore some of the monopsony power they previously possessed. Such collusive action is illegal because it violates the collective bargaining agreement that exists between players and owners. In the fall of 1987 an arbitrator ruled that baseball owners had conspired to "destroy" the free-agent market, and in 1990 the courts in the United States ordered club owners to pay $102.5 million (U.S.) in lost salaries to players.

[**] Paul M. Sommers and Noel Quinton, "Pay and Performance in Major League Baseball: The Case of the First Family of Free Agents," *Journal of Human Resources*, Summer 1982, pp. 426–435.

MARKET DEMAND   Suppose that there are many — say, 200 — firms demanding a particular type of semiskilled or skilled labour. The total, or market, demand for this labour can be determined by adding up the labour demand curves (the MRP curves) of the individual firms, as suggested in **Figure 16-3(a)** and **(b)** (Key Graph).

MARKET SUPPLY   On the supply side, we assume there is no union; workers compete individually for available jobs. The supply curve for a particular type of labour will be upsloping, reflecting that in the absence of unemployment, employers as a group will have to pay higher wage rates to obtain more workers. This is so because the firms must bid these workers away from other industries, occupations, and localities. Within limits, workers have alternative job opportunities; they may work in other industries in the same locality, or they may work in their present occupations in different cities or provinces. In a full-employment economy, the group of firms in this particular labour market must pay higher and higher wage rates to attract this type of labour away from these alternative job opportunities. Similarly, higher wages are necessary to induce individuals not currently in the labour force to seek employment.

More technically, the market supply curve rises because it is an *opportunity cost* curve. To attract workers to this particular employment the wage rate paid must cover the opportunity costs of alternative uses of time spent, either in other labour markets, in household activities, or in leisure. Higher wages attract more people to this employment — people who were not attracted by lower wages because their opportunity costs were too high.

MARKET EQUILIBRIUM   The equilibrium wage rate and the equilibrium level of employment for this type of labour are determined at the intersection of the labour demand and labour supply curves. In Figure 16-3(b), the equilibrium wage rate is W_c ($6), and the number of workers hired is Q_c (1000). To the individual firm, the wage rate W_c is given. Each of the many hiring firms employs such a small fraction of the total available supply of this type of labour that none can influence the wage rate. The supply of labour is perfectly elastic to the individual firm, as shown by S in Figure 16-3(a).

Each individual firm will find it profitable to hire workers up to the point at which the going

TABLE 16-1   The supply of labour: pure competition in the hire of labour

(1) Units of labour	(2) Wage rate	(3) Total labour cost (wage bill)	(4) Marginal resource (labour) cost
0	$6	$ 0	
1	6	6	$6
2	6	12	6
3	6	18	6
4	6	24	6
5	6	30	6
6	6	36	6

wage rate is equal to labour's MRP. This is merely an application of the MRP = MRC rule developed in Chapter 15. [Indeed, the demand curve in Figure 16-3(a) is based upon Table 15-1.]

As Table 16-1 indicates, *because resource price is given to the individual competitive firm, the marginal cost of that resource (MRC) will be constant and equal to resource price (the wage rate).* In this case, the wage rate and hence the marginal cost of labour are constant to the individual firm. Each additional worker hired adds precisely his or her wage rate ($6 in this case) to the firm's total resource cost. The firm, then, will maximize its profits by hiring workers to the point at which their wage rate, and therefore marginal resource cost, equals their marginal revenue product. In Figure 16-3(a), the "typical" firm will hire q_c (5) workers.

Note that the firm's total revenue from hiring q_c workers can be found by summing their MRPs. In this case the total revenue from the five workers is indicated by the area $0abq_c$ in Figure 16-3(a). Of this total revenue, the area $0W_c bq_c$ is the firm's total wage cost and the triangular area $W_c ab$ represents additional revenue available to reward other inputs such as capital, land, and entrepreneurship. (**Key Questions 3 and 4**)

MONOPSONY MODEL

CHARACTERISTICS   Let's now consider the case of a **monopsony**, which describes an employer with monopolistic buying (hiring) power. Monopsony has the following characteristics.

1. The firm's employment is a large portion of the total employment of a particular kind of labour.
2. This type of labour is relatively immobile either geographically or in the sense that, if workers sought alternative employment, they would have to acquire new skills.
3. The firm is a "wage maker" in that the wage rate it must pay varies directly with the number of workers it employs.

In some instances, the monopsonistic power of employers is virtually complete, in the sense that there is only one major employer in a labour market. For example, the economies of some towns and cities depend almost entirely on one major firm. A copper-mining company may be the basic source of employment in a remote British Columbia town. A textile mill in Quebec's Eastern Townships, a Gatineau paper mill, or a Newfoundland fish processor may provide a large proportion of the employment in its locality.

In other cases, *oligopsony* may prevail: three or four firms may each hire a large portion of the supply of labour in a particular market. Our study of oligopoly suggests there is a strong tendency for oligopsonists to act in concert — much like a monopsonist — in hiring labour.

UPSLOPING SUPPLY TO FIRM   When a firm hires a considerable portion of the total available supply of a particular type of labour, its decisions to employ more or fewer workers will affect the wage rate. Specifically, *if a firm is large in relation to the labour market, it will have to pay a higher wage rate to obtain more labour.* For simplicity's sake, suppose there is only one employer of a particular type of labour in a specified geographic area.

In this extreme case, the labour supply curve to that firm and the total supply curve for the labour market are identical. This supply curve, for reasons already made clear, is upsloping, indicating that the firm must pay a higher wage rate to attract more workers. This is shown by S in Figure 16-4. The supply curve is, in effect, the average-cost-of-labour curve from the firm's point of view; each point on it indicates the wage rate (cost) per worker that must be paid to attract the corresponding number of workers.

MRC EXCEEDS WAGE RATE   But the higher wages needed to attract *additional* workers will also have to be paid to *all* workers currently employed at lower wage rates. The payment of a uniform wage to all workers will mean that the cost of an extra worker — the marginal resource (labour) cost (MRC) — will exceed the wage rate by the amount necessary to bring the wage rate of all workers currently employed up to the new wage level.

Table 16-2 illustrates this point. One worker can be hired at a wage rate of $6. But hiring a second worker forces the firm to pay a higher wage rate of $7. Marginal resource (labour) cost is $8 — the

FIGURE 16-4   The wage rate and level of employment in a monopsonistic labour market

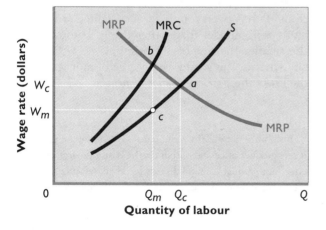

In a monopsonistic labour market, the employer's marginal resource (labour) cost curve (MRC) lies above the labour supply curve (S). Equating MRC with labour demand MRP at point *b*, the monopsonist will hire Q_m workers (as compared with Q_c under competition) and pay the wage rate W_m (as compared with the competitive wage W_c).

TABLE 16-2   The supply of labour: monopsony in the hire of labour

(1)	(2)	(3)	(4)
			Marginal
		Total labour	resource
Units of	Wage	cost	(labour)
labour	rate	(wage bill)	cost
0	$5	$ 0	
1	6	6	$6
2	7	14	8
3	8	24	10
4	9	36	12
5	10	50	14
6	11	66	16

$7 paid the second worker plus a $1 raise for the first worker. That is, total labour cost is $14 (= 2 × $7), rather than the $13 that would be the case if the first worker were paid $6 and the second paid $7. Thus, the MRC of the second worker is $8 (= $14 – $6), not the $7 wage rate paid the second worker. Similarly, the marginal labour cost of the third worker is $10 — the $8 that must be paid to attract this worker from alternative employments plus $1 raises — from $7 to $8 — for the first two workers.

The important point is that *to the monopsonist, marginal resource (labour) cost will exceed the wage rate*. Graphically, the MRC curve (columns 1 and 4 in Table 16-2) will lie above the average cost, or supply, curve of labour (columns 1 and 2). This is shown in Figure 16-4.

EQUILIBRIUM   To maximize profits, the firm will equate marginal resource (labour) cost with the MRP.[1] The number of workers hired by the monopsonist is indicated by Q_m and the wage rate paid, W_m, is indicated by the corresponding point on the resource supply, or average-cost-of-labour, curve.

Contrast these results with those a competitive labour market would yield. With competition in the

hire of labour, the level of employment would have been greater (Q_c) and the wage rate would have been higher (W_c). It simply does not pay the monopsonist to hire workers up to the point at which the wage rate and labour's MRP are equal. *Other things equal, the monopsonist maximizes its profits by hiring a smaller number of workers and thereby paying a less-than-competitive wage rate*. Society gets a smaller output,[2] and workers get a wage rate less by *bc* than their marginal revenue product.

Just as a monopolistic seller finds it profitable to restrict product output to realize an above-competitive price for goods, so the monopsonistic employer of resources finds it profitable to restrict employment to realize below-competitive wage rates.[3]

EXAMPLES   Monopsonistic labour market outcomes are not common in our economy. There are typically many potential employers for most workers, particularly when these workers are occupationally and geographically mobile. Also, unions often counteract monopsony power in labour markets. Nevertheless, there is evidence of monopsony in such diverse labour markets as those for nurses, professional athletes, public school teachers, newspaper employees, and some building trade workers.

In the case of nurses, the major employers in most localities are a relatively small number of hospitals. Furthermore, the highly specialized skills of nurses are not readily transferable to other occupations. It has been found in accordance with the monopsony model that, other things being equal, the smaller the number of hospitals in a town or city (that is, the greater the degree of monopsony), the lower the starting salaries of nurses.

---

[1] The fact that MRC exceeds resource price when resources are hired or purchased under imperfectly competitive (monopsonistic) conditions calls for adjustments in Chapter 15's least-cost and profit-maximizing rules for hiring resources. [See equations (1) and (2) in the "Optimal Combination of Resources" section of Chapter 15.] Specifically, we must substitute MRC for resource price in the denominators of our two equations. That is, with imperfect competition in the hiring of both labour and capital, equation (1) becomes

$$\frac{MP_L}{MRC_L} = \frac{MP_C}{MRC_C} \qquad (1')$$

and equation (2) is restated as

$$\frac{MRP_L}{MRC_L} = \frac{MRP_C}{MRC_C} = 1 \qquad (2')$$

In fact, equations (1) and (2) can be regarded as special cases of (1') and (2'), wherein firms happen to be hiring under purely competitive conditions and resource price is therefore equal to, and can be substituted for, marginal resource cost.

[2] This is analogous to the monopolist's restricting output as it sets product price and output on the basis of marginal revenue, not product demand. In this instance, resource price is set on the basis of marginal labour (resource) cost, not resource supply.

[3] Will a monopsonistic employer also be a monopolistic seller in the product market? Not necessarily. The Eastern Townships textile mill may be a monopsonistic employer, yet face severe domestic and foreign competition in selling its product. In other cases — for example, the automobile and steel industries — firms have both monopsonistic and monopolistic (oligopolistic) power.

Although *potential* employers for professional athletes are quite numerous, the market historically has been characterized by ingenious collusive devices by which employers have attempted, with success, to limit competition. The National Hockey League and the Canadian Football League have established rules that tie a player to one team and prevent him from selling his talents to the highest bidder on the open (competitive) market. In particular, through the new player draft, the team that selects or "drafts" a player has the exclusive right to bargain a contract with that player. Furthermore, the so-called "reserve clause" in each player's contract gives his team the exclusive right to purchase his services for the next season. Though players' associations and collective bargaining agreements that stipulate "free agency" for experienced players have made the labour markets for professional athletes in recent years more competitive, collusive monopsony persists.

Empirical studies have shown that, prior to 1976, baseball players (despite very high salaries) were paid substantially less than their estimated MRPs, which is consistent with Figure 16-4. (See Box 16-2.) However, beginning in 1976, players were allowed to become "free agents" — they became free to sell their services to any interested team — after their sixth season of play. A comparison of the salaries of the first group of free agents with their estimated MRPs indicates that the competitive bidding of teams for free agents brought their salaries and MRPs into close accord, as our competitive model suggests. (**Key Question 6**)

QUICK REVIEW 16-1

1. Real wages have increased historically in Canada because labour demand has increased relative to labour supply.

2. Real wages per worker have increased at approximately the same rate as worker productivity.

3. The competitive employer is a "wage taker" and employs workers at the point where the wage rate or MRC equals MRP.

4. The labour supply curve to a monopsonist is upsloping, causing MRC to exceed the wage rate for each worker. Other things being equal, the monopsonist will hire fewer workers and pay a lower wage rate than would a purely competitive employer.

THREE UNION MODELS

Thus far, we have assumed that workers actively compete in the sale of their labour services. In some markets, workers collectively "sell" their labour services through unions. To see the economic impact of unions in the simplest context, let us first suppose a union is formed in an otherwise competitive labour market. A union is now bargaining with a relatively large number of employers.

Unions seek many goals. The basic one is to raise wage rates. The union can pursue this objective in several ways.

INCREASING THE DEMAND FOR LABOUR

From the unions' viewpoint, the most desirable technique for raising wage rates is to increase the demand for labour. As shown in Figure 16-5, an increase in the demand for labour will result in *both* higher wage rates and more jobs. The relative size of these increases will depend on the elasticity of labour supply.

A union might increase labour demand by altering one or more of the determinants of labour demand (Chapter 15). Specifically, a union can attempt to (1) increase the demand for the product or service it is producing, (2) enhance labour productivity, or (3) alter the prices of other inputs.

FIGURE 16-5 **Unions and the demand for labour**

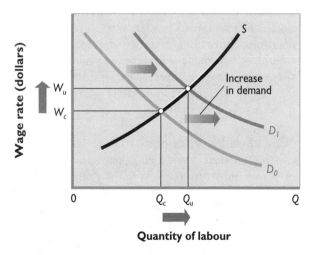

When unions can increase the demand for labour (D_0 to D_1), higher wage rates (W_c to W_u) and a larger number of jobs (Q_c to Q_u) can be realized.

1. INCREASE PRODUCT DEMAND Unions may attempt to increase the demand for the products they help produce — and thus increase the derived demand for their own labour services — by advertising or by political lobbying. Union television ads urging consumers to "buy the union label" are relevant. Historically, the International Ladies Garment Workers Union (ILGWU) has joined with its employers to finance advertising campaigns to bolster the demand for their products.

On the political front we see construction unions lobbying for new highway or urban renewal projects. Teachers' unions and associations push for increased public spending on education. And some unions have vigorously supported their employers in seeking protective tariffs or import quotas designed to exclude competing foreign products. The automobile workers have sought such protection. Thus, a decline in the supply of imported cars through tariffs or negotiated agreements between nations will increase their prices, thereby increasing the demand for North American–made autos and boosting the derived demand for North American auto workers.

Some unions have sought to expand the demand for labour by forcing "make-work," or "featherbedding," rules on employers. It took a Canada-wide strike back in the 1950s before the railways were able to drop firemen from freight-yard diesels – firemen who had no fire to tend since the days of the steam locomotives.

2. INCREASE PRODUCTIVITY While many decisions affecting labour productivity — for example, decisions concerning quantity and quality of real capital — are made unilaterally by management, there is a growing interest in establishing joint labour-management committees designed to increase labour productivity.

3. INCREASE PRICES OF SUBSTITUTES Unions might enhance the demand for their labour by increasing the prices of substitute resources. An example is that unions — whose workers are generally paid significantly more than the minimum wage — strongly support increases in the minimum wage. An alleged reason for this backing is that unions want to increase the price of substitutable low-wage, nonunion labour. A higher minimum wage for nonunion workers will deter employers from substituting them for union workers, thereby bolstering the demand for union workers.

Unions can also increase the demand for their labour by supporting public actions that *reduce* the price of a complementary resource. For example, unions in industries that use large amounts of energy might actively oppose rate increases proposed by electric or natural gas utilities. Where labour and energy are complementary, an energy price increase might reduce the demand for labour through the output effect.

Unions recognize that their capacity to influence the demand for labour is difficult and uncertain. As many of our illustrations imply, unions are frequently trying to forestall *declines* in labour demand rather than actually increase it. In view of these considerations, it is not surprising that union efforts to increase wage rates have concentrated on the supply side of the market.

EXCLUSIVE, OR CRAFT, UNIONISM Unions may boost wage rates by reducing the supply of labour. Historically, organized labour has favoured policies restricting the supply of labour to the economy as a whole to bolster the general level of wages. Labour unions have supported legislation that has (1) reduced child labour, (2) encouraged compulsory retirement, and (3) enforced a shorter work week.

More relevant for present purposes is that specific types of workers have adopted, through unions, techniques designed to restrict their numbers. This is especially true of *craft unions* — unions that comprise workers of a given skill, such as electricians, carpenters, bricklayers, plumbers, and printers. These unions have frequently forced employers to agree to hire only union workers, giving the union virtually complete control of the supply of labour. Then, by following restrictive membership policies — long apprenticeships, exorbitant initiation fees, the limitation or prohibition of new members — the union causes an artificial restriction of the labour supply. As shown in Figure 16-6, this results in higher wage rates. This approach to achieving wage increases is called **exclusive unionism**. Higher wages are the result of excluding workers from the union and therefore from the supply of labour.

Occupational licensing is another means of restricting the supplies of specific kinds of labour. Here a group of workers in an occupation will pressure provincial or municipal governments to pass a law to provide that, say, barbers (or physicians, lawyers, dentists, plumbers, beauticians, opticians,

FIGURE 16-6   Exclusive, or craft, unionism

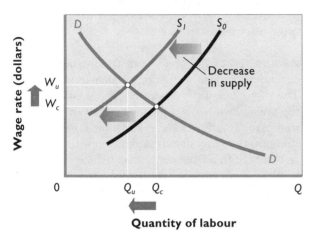

By reducing the supply of labour (S_0 to S_1) through the use of restrictive membership policies, exclusive unions achieve higher wage rates (W_c to W_u). However, the restriction of labour supply also reduces the number of workers employed (Q_c to Q_u).

cinema projectionists) can practise their trade only if they meet certain specified requirements. These requirements might specify the level of education, amount of work experience, passing of an examination, and personal characteristics ("the practitioner must be of good moral character").

The licensing board administering the law is typically dominated by members of the licensed occupation. The result is self-regulation, conducive to policies that reflect self-interest. In short, imposing arbitrary and irrelevant entrance requirements or setting an unnecessarily stringent examination can restrict entrants to the occupation.

Ostensibly, the purpose of licensing is to protect consumers from incompetent practitioners. But licensing laws are frequently abused in that the number of qualified workers is artificially restricted, resulting in above-competitive wages and earnings for those in the occupation (Figure 16-6). Furthermore, licensing requirements often specify a residency requirement that inhibits the interprovincial movement of qualified workers. It is estimated that over 200 occupations are now licensed in Canada.

INCLUSIVE, OR INDUSTRIAL, UNIONISM   Most unions, however, do not attempt to limit their membership. On the contrary, they seek to organize all available or potential workers. This is characteristic of the

so-called *industrial unions* — unions such as the automobile workers and steelworkers that seek as members all unskilled, semiskilled, and skilled workers in a given industry. A union can afford to be exclusive when its members are so highly skilled that substitute workers are not readily available in quantity. But a union that comprises unskilled and semi-skilled workers will undermine its own existence by limiting its membership, causing numerous highly substitutable nonunion workers to be readily available for employment.

If an industrial union includes virtually all workers in its membership, firms will be under great pressure to agree to the wage rate demanded by the union, because by going on strike, the union can deprive the firm of its entire labour supply.

Inclusive unionism is illustrated in Figure 16-7. Initially, the competitive equilibrium wage rate is W_c and the level of employment is Q_c. Now suppose an industrial union is formed, and it imposes a higher, above-equilibrium wage rate of, say, W_u. This wage rate changes the supply curve of labour to the firms from the pre-union S curve to the post-union $W_u aS$ curve.[4] No workers will be forthcoming at a wage rate less than that demanded by the union. If employers decide it is better to pay this higher wage rate than to suffer a strike, they will cut back on employment from Q_c to Q_u.

By agreeing to the union's W_u wage demand, individual employers become "wage takers" at this wage and therefore face a perfectly elastic labour supply curve over the $W_u a$ range. Because labour supply is perfectly elastic, MRC is equal to the W_u wage over this range. The Q_u level of employment results from employers equating MRC (= W_u) with MRP, as embodied in the labour demand curve.

Note that at W_u there is an excess supply or surplus of labour in the amount *ea*. Without the union — in a purely competitive labour market — we expect these unemployed workers to accept

---

[4] Technically, the wage rate W_u makes the labour supply curve perfectly elastic over the $W_u a$ range in Figure 16-7. If employers hire any number of workers in this range, the union-imposed wage rate is effective and must be paid, or the union will supply no labour at all — the employers will be faced with a strike. If employers want a number of workers over $W_u a$, they will have to bid up wages above the union's minimum. This will only occur if the market demand curve for labour shifts rightward so that it intersects the *aS* range of the labour supply curve.

FIGURE 16-7   Inclusive, or industrial, unionism

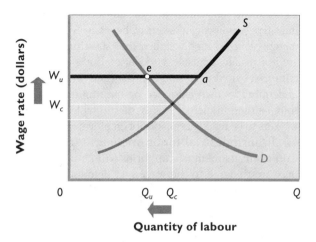

By organizing virtually all available workers and thereby controlling the supply of labour, inclusive industrial unions may impose a wage rate, such as W_u that is above the competitive wage rate, W_c. The effect is to change the labour supply curve from S to $W_u aS$. At the W_u wage rate, employers will cut employment from Q_c to Q_u.

lower wages and the wage rate would as a result fall to the W_c competitive equilibrium level where quantity demanded equals quantity supplied. But this doesn't happen, because workers are acting collectively through their union. Workers cannot individually offer to work for less than W_u; nor can employers contractually pay less.

WAGE INCREASES AND UNEMPLOYMENT

As Figures 16-6 and 16-7 suggest, the wage-raising actions of both exclusive and inclusive unionism reduce employment. A union's success in achieving above-equilibrium wage rates is tempered by the consequent decline in the number of workers employed. This unemployment effect acts as a restraining influence on union wage demands. A union cannot expect to maintain solidarity within its ranks if it seeks a wage rate so high that joblessness will result for, say, 20% or 30% of its members.

The unemployment impact of wage increases might be mitigated in two ways.

1. GROWTH   The normal growth of the economy increases the demand for most kinds of labour through time. Thus a rightward shift of the labour

demand curves in Figures 16-6 and 16-7 could offset, or more than offset, any unemployment effects that would otherwise be associated with the indicated wage increases.

2. ELASTICITY   The size of the unemployment effect depends on the elasticity of demand for labour. The more inelastic the demand, the smaller will be the unemployment accompanying a given wage-rate increase. If unions have sufficient bargaining strength, they *may* obtain provisions in their collective bargaining agreements that reduce the substitutability of other inputs for labour and thereby reduce the elasticity of demand for union labour. For example, a union may force an employer to accept rules blocking the introduction of new machinery and equipment. Or the union may bargain successfully for severance or layoff pay that increases the cost to the firm of substituting capital for labour when wage rates are increased. Similarly, the union might gain a contract provision that prohibits the firm from subcontracting production to nonunion (lower-wage) firms or relocating work to low-wage workers abroad, effectively restricting the substitution of less expensive labour for union workers.

For these and other reasons, the unemployment restraint on union wage demands may be less pressing than our exclusive and inclusive union models suggest.

BILATERAL MONOPOLY MODEL

Suppose a strong industrial union is formed in a labour market that is monopsonistic, rather than competitive. In other words, we combine the monopsony model with the inclusive unionism model. The result is **bilateral monopoly**. The union is a monopolistic "seller" of labour, controls the labour supply, and can exert an influence over wage rates, but it faces a monopsonistic employer (or combination of oligopsonistic employers) of labour, who can also affect wages by altering their employment. This is not an extreme or special case. In such industries as steel, automobiles, meat-packing, and farm machinery, "big labour" — one huge industrial union — bargains with "big business" — a few huge industrial giants.

INDETERMINANT OUTCOME   This situation is shown in Figure 16-8, which merely superimposes Figure 16-7 on 16-4. The monopsonistic employer

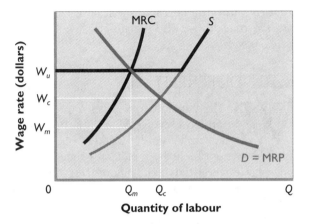

FIGURE 16-8   Bilateral monopoly in the labour market

When a monopsonistic employer seeks the wage rate W_m and the inclusive union it faces seeks an above-equilibrium wage rate such as W_u, the actual outcome is logically indeterminate.

will seek the below-competitive equilibrium wage rate W_m, and the union presumably will press for some above-competitive equilibrium wage rate such as W_u. Which will result? We cannot say with certainty. The outcome is indeterminate, since economic theory does not explain what the resulting wage rate will be. We should expect the wage outcome to lie somewhere between W_m and W_u. Beyond that, all we can say is that the party with the most bargaining power and the most effective bargaining strategy will be able to get its opponent to agree to a wage close to the one it seeks.

DESIRABILITY   It is possible that the wage and employment outcomes might be more socially desirable than the term bilateral monopoly would imply. Monopoly on one side of the market *might* in effect cancel out the monopoly on the other side of the market, yielding competitive or near-competitive results. If either the union or management prevailed in this market — if the actual wage rate were determined at either W_u or W_m — employment would be restricted to Q_m (where MRP = MRC), which is below the competitive level.

But now suppose that the countervailing power of the union roughly offsets the original monopsony power of management, and that a bargained wage

rate of about W_c, which is the competitive wage, is agreed on. Once management agrees to this wage rate, its incentive to restrict employment disappears; no longer can the employer depress wage rates by restricting employment. Thus management equates the bargained wage rate W_c (= MRC) with MRP and finds it most profitable to hire Q_c workers. (**Key Question 8**)

THE MINIMUM-WAGE CONTROVERSY

Both the federal and provincial governments have enacted **minimum wage** legislation. In 1995 the minimum wage was $4 an hour at the federal level. Roughly 80% of all nonsupervisory workers are covered. Our analysis of the effects of union wage-fixing raises the question of how effective minimum-wage legislation is as an anti-poverty device.

CASE AGAINST THE MINIMUM WAGE Critics reasoning in terms of Figure 16-7 contend that the imposition of effective (above-equilibrium) minimum wages will simply push employers back up their MRP or labour demand curves because it is now profitable to hire fewer workers. The higher wage costs may even force some firms out of business. Some of the poor, low-wage workers, whom the minimum wage was designed to help, will now find themselves out of work. Critics say that a worker who is unemployed at a minimum wage of $4.50 per hour is clearly worse off than if he or she were employed at a market wage rate of $4 per hour.

A second criticism is that the minimum wage is poorly targeted as an anti-poverty device. It is designed to provide a "living wage" that will allow less skilled workers to earn enough so that they and their families can escape poverty. However, critics argue that the primary impact of the minimum wage is on teenage workers, many of whom belong to relatively affluent families.

CASE FOR THE MINIMUM WAGE Advocates say critics analyze the impact of the minimum wage in an unrealistic context. Figure 16-7 presumes a competitive and static market. But a minimum wage in a monopsonistic labour market (Figure 16-8) suggests that the minimum wage can increase wage rates without causing unemployment. Indeed, a higher minimum wage may even produce more jobs by eliminating the monopsonistic employer's motive to restrict employment.

Furthermore, an effective minimum wage may increase labour productivity, shifting the labour demand curve to the right and offsetting any unemployment effects the minimum wage might induce.

But how might a minimum wage increase productivity? First, a minimum wage may have a *shock effect* on employers. Firms using low-wage workers may be inefficient in the use of labour; the higher wage rates imposed by the minimum wage will presumably shock these firms into using labour more efficiently, and so the productivity of labour rises. Second, some argue that higher wages will increase the incomes, and therefore the health and motivation of workers, making them more productive.

EVIDENCE   Which view is correct? The consensus from the many research studies of the minimum wage is that it does cause some unemployment, particularly among teenage workers (16–19 years of age). It is estimated that the minimum wage reduced teenage employment opportunities by 15% in Canada. Young adults (age 20–24) are also adversely affected; a 10% increase in the minimum wage increased unemployment by 2.5 to 3.5 percentage points for young men and 1.5 to 3.0 percentage points for young women. Older women, who are disproportionately represented in low-wage occupations, suffer larger declines in employment than men. The other side of the coin is that those who remain employed receive higher incomes and may escape poverty. The overall anti-poverty effect of the minimum wage is thus a mixed, ambivalent one. Those who lose their jobs are forced into the unemployment and social assistance systems; those who remain employed tend to escape poverty.

WAGE DIFFERENTIALS

Why do corporate executives or professional athletes receive $1 million or more a year while laundry workers get a paltry $14,000 a year? Table 16-3 indicates that substantial **wage differentials** exist among certain industries. Our objective now is to gain some insight as to why these differentials exist.

Once again, the forces of supply and demand provide a general answer. If the supply of a particular type of labour is great in relation to the demand for it, the wage rate will be low. But if demand is great and the supply relatively small, wages will be high. But we want to discover *why* supply and demand conditions differ in various labour markets. To do this, we must probe those factors that lie behind the supply and demand of particular types of labour.

If (1) all workers were homogeneous, (2) all jobs were equally attractive to workers, and (3) labour markets were perfectly competitive, all workers would receive precisely the same wage

TABLE 16-3   Average hourly wages in selected industries, 1995

Industry	Average hourly earnings (paid by the hour)
Goods-producing industries	$16.56
Service-producing industries	12.76
Logging and forestry	18.80
Mining, quarrying, and oil wells	21.49
Manufacturing	15.61
Construction	18.67
Transportation, communication, and other utilities	17.75
Trade	11.08
Finance, insurance, and real estate	12.60
Community business and personal service	13.13
Industrial aggregate	14.09

Source: Statistics Canada, *Employment, Earnings, and Hours, March, 1995* (Ottawa, June 1995).

rate. This is not a startling statement. It suggests that in an economy having one type of labour and, in effect, one type of job, competition would result in a single wage rate for all workers. The statement is important only because it suggests reasons wage rates do differ in practice. (1) Workers are not homogeneous. They differ in abilities and in training and, as a result, they fall into noncompeting occupational groups. (2) Jobs vary in attractiveness; the nonmonetary aspects of various jobs are not the same. (3) Labour markets are characterized by imperfections.

NONCOMPETING GROUPS

Workers are not homogeneous; they differ in their mental and physical capacities *and* in their education and training. At any point in time the labour force can be thought of as falling into many **noncompeting groups**, each composed of one or several occupations for which the members of this group qualify.

ABILITY   Few workers have the abilities to be brain surgeons, concert violinists, research chemists, entertainers, or professional athletes. The result is that the supplies of these particular types of labour are very small in relation to the demand for them and consequently wages and salaries are high. These and similar groups do not compete with one another nor with other skilled or semiskilled workers. The violinist does not compete with the surgeon, nor does the laundry worker compete with either the violinist or the surgeon.

The concept of noncompeting groups is a flexible one; it can be applied to various subgroups and even to specific individuals in a given group. Some especially skilled lawyers are able to command fees considerably in excess of their run-of-the-mill colleagues. Wayne Gretzky and a few others demand and get salaries much higher than the average professional hockey player. Their less talented colleagues are only imperfect substitutes.

INVESTING IN HUMAN CAPITAL: EDUCATION
Noncompeting groups — and therefore wage differentials — also exist because of differing amounts of investment in human capital. A **human capital investment** refers to expenditures on education and training that improve the skills and therefore the productivity of workers. Like business purchases of machinery and equipment, expenditures that

increase a worker's productivity can be regarded as investments because *current* expenditures or costs are incurred with the intention that these costs will be more than compensated for by an enhanced *future* flow of earnings.

The statistical evidence is strong that individuals with larger investments in education do achieve on average higher incomes during their careers than those who have made smaller education investments. Moreover, the earnings of more-educated workers rise more rapidly than those of less-educated workers. The primary reason for this is that more-educated workers usually get more on-the-job training.

Although education yields higher incomes, it also has costs. A college or university education has not only direct costs (tuition, fees, books) but also indirect or opportunity costs (forgone earnings). Does the higher pay received by more-educated workers compensate for these costs? The answer is "yes." Rates of return are estimated to be 10 to 13% for investing in a secondary education and 8 to 10% for higher education.

COMPENSATING DIFFERENCES

If a group of workers in a particular noncompeting group is equally capable of performing several different jobs, you might expect the wage rate would be identical for each of these jobs. Not so. A group of high school graduates may be equally capable of becoming bank clerks or unskilled construction workers. But these jobs pay different wages. In virtually all localities, construction labourers receive higher wages than bank clerks.

These differences can be explained on the basis of the *nonmonetary aspects* of the two jobs. The construction job involves dirty hands, a potentially sore back, the hazard of accidents, and irregular employment, both seasonally and cyclically. The banking job usually means physical comfort, pleasant air-conditioned surroundings, and little fear of injury or layoff. Other things equal, it is easy to see why workers would rather pick up a deposit slip than a shovel. That's why contractors must pay higher wages than banks to compensate for the unattractive, nonmonetary aspects of construction jobs. These wage differentials are called **compensating differences**, because they must be paid to compensate for nonmonetary differences in various jobs.

BOX 16-3 IN THE MEDIA

REALITY BITES: NO DIPLOMA, NO JOB OFFERS

BRUCE LITTLE

The economy has been creating jobs for almost three years now, but a very large group of Canadians has been getting almost nothing out of the recovery. They're easy to spot because they lack something employers increasingly demand — solid educational credentials.

A new iron law is taking over in the workplace.

If you have completed some form of postsecondary education — a university degree, a community-college diploma, a training certificate — you're going to get a job. If you have anything less, you won't.

Last year, the economy added 277,000 jobs, its best showing since 1989. Look who got them: For those with a high-school education or less, 145,000 jobs disappeared. For those with a postsecondary education, 422,000 jobs opened up. That means 99.3 per cent of people entering the labour force with a degree or diploma found work.

As the accompanying chart shows, the door has closed on job seekers who have failed to go beyond high school. When you look at the overall job market, the path of recession and recovery is clear. From 1990 to 1992, total employment fell 323,000; from 1992 to 1994, employment climbed by 450,000. Last year, we were 127,000 jobs ahead of 1990.

Now zero in on what happened to people according to their schooling from 1990 to 1994:

• University graduates never missed a beat. For them, employment increased 483,000, a gain of 25 per cent.

• Those with a postsecondary diploma or certificate saw little job growth during the recession, but have cashed in during the recovery. By last year, they were 474,000 jobs ahead of 1990, a 14-per-cent increase.

• Those with some postsecondary schooling, but no certificate, lost 36,000 jobs over the four years, a 3-per-cent drop.

• High-school graduates held their own during the recession and first year of the recovery, but were shut out in 1994. Employment for that group was down 120,000 — 4 per cent — from 1990.

• Canadians with some high school to their credit fared badly throughout, losing 445,000 jobs, more than 17 per cent of the work slots open to them in 1990.

• The hardest hit were people with only an elementary-school education. For them, employment fell 229,000, a decline of 23 per cent.

Regular readers will recognize this chart as one we've run before. Two years ago, it appeared that the recession was having a disproportionate impact on the less educated, but even then, Philip Cross, Statistics Canada's chief of current analysis, was flagging the fact that a historic shift in the labour market was under way.

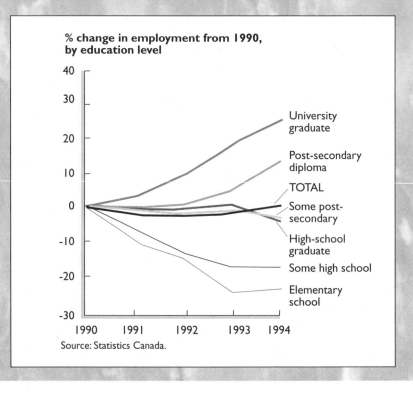

% change in employment from 1990, by education level

Source: Statistics Canada.

It's even clearer now that he was dead on. If the recession was tough on the less educated, the recovery has been even harder; they *know* companies are hiring, but they don't have the certified skills to get any of the jobs.

Look at it this way. From 1990 to 1994, the economy created about 957,000 jobs for people with that essential piece of paper attesting to their postsecondary-school achievements. At the same time, it destroyed 830,000 jobs for people with anything less.

In a 13.3-million-person job market, that's a massive change over such a short period. Last year, people with a postsecondary certificate of some kind held 48 per cent of all jobs, up from 41 per cent in 1990. The share of jobs available to those who didn't finish high school fell to 21 from 27 per cent. Those with a high-school diploma and some post-secondary schooling had the rest.

These rapidly changing shares underline the fundamental transformation of the work world in recent years.

The spread of computers has been wiping out low-skilled clerical and blue-collar jobs. As companies have brought more sophisticated information technology into their offices and factories, they've been able to make do with fewer workers. At the same time, they've had to upgrade the skills of the people they kept; otherwise, their workers wouldn't be able to get the most out of the new equipment.

SOURCE: *The Globe and Mail*, March 13, 1995 p. A9. Reprinted with permission.

The Story in Brief

The author marshals statistical evidence indicating the more education and/or training you have, the more success you will have in the job market, both in pay and stability of employment.

The Economics Behind the Story

• Firms want to maximize profits; they select employees who will help them in this endeavour.

• Technological advances have made it possible to replace employees in jobs with low levels of education and/or training requirements. The new jobs being created in Canada in the last decade of the twentieth century are going overwhelmingly to those with a postsecondary diploma or degree who have either the necessary skills or the educational background to easily acquire those skills. Between 1990 and 1994 almost a million jobs were created, requiring postsecondary-school education; over 800,000 low-skilled jobs were lost.

• How do the education and/or training of a person affect the wage he or she commands on the job market? In your answer be sure to include the impact of supply and demand forces in a given labour market.

MARKET IMPERFECTIONS

Market imperfections, in the form of various immobilities, help explain wage differences paid on identical jobs. These imperfections can be divided into the following categories.

1. GEOGRAPHIC IMMOBILITIES Workers are generally reluctant to leave friends, relatives, and associates, to force their children to change schools, and to incur the costs and inconveniences of adjusting to a new job and a new community. Geographic mobility is likely to be low for older workers with seniority rights and substantial claims to pension payments on retirement. Similarly, an optometrist or dental hygienist who is qualified to practise in one province may not meet the licensing requirements of other provinces, so his or her ability to move geographically is impeded. Language can be a barrier into and out of Quebec. Also, workers who may be willing to move may be ignorant of job opportunities and wage rates in other areas. As Adam Smith noted more than two centuries ago, "A man is of all sorts of luggage the most difficult to be transported." The reluctance or inability of workers to move enables geographic wage differentials for the same occupations to persist.

2. INSTITUTIONAL IMMOBILITIES Geographic immobilities may be reinforced by artificial restrictions on mobility imposed by institutions. We have noted that craft unions find it to their advantage to restrict membership. After all, if carpenters and bricklayers become plentiful, the wages they can command will decline. Thus the low-paid, nonunion carpenter of Epsom, Ontario, may be willing to move to Edmonton in the pursuit of higher wages. But his chances of successfully doing so are slim. He will probably be unable to get a union card — and no card, no job. The professions impose similar artificial restraints. For example, at most universities individuals lacking advanced degrees are simply not considered for employment as professors.

3. SOCIOLOGICAL IMMOBILITIES: DISCRIMINATION We must acknowledge sociological immobilities in the form of discrimination. Despite regulatory legislation to the contrary, women workers frequently receive less pay than men on the same job. The consequence of racial discrimination is that recent immigrants historically have been forced to accept lower wages on given jobs than native-born Canadians. The economic effects of discrimination will be analyzed below in the context of the "crowding hypothesis."

A final point: Usually all three considerations — noncompeting groups, compensating differences, and market imperfections — help explain actual wage differentials. For example, the differential between the wages of a physician and a construction worker is largely explainable on the basis of noncompeting groups. Physicians fall into a noncompeting group where, because of certain abilities and financial requisites to entry, the supply of labour is small in relation to demand, and wages are therefore high. In construction work, where intellectual and financial prerequisites are much less significant, the supply of labour is great in relation to demand, and wages are low compared to those of physicians. However, were it not for certain unattractive features of the construction worker's job and the fact that craft unions pursue restrictive membership policies, the differential would probably be even greater.

PAY AND PERFORMANCE

The models of wage determination presented in this chapter presume that worker compensation is always a standard hourly wage rate. In fact, pay schemes are often more complex in composition and purpose. For example, many workers receive annual salaries rather than hourly pay. Also, pay plans are frequently designed by employers to elicit some desired level of performance by workers.

THE PRINCIPAL–AGENT PROBLEM

Firms hire workers because they help produce goods or services that firms can sell for a profit. Workers may be thought of as the firm's *agents* — hired to advance the interests of the firm. Firms may be regarded as *principals* or parties who hire others (agents) to help them achieve their goals. Principals and their agents have a common interest. The principal's (firm's) objective is profits, and agents (workers) are willing to help firms earn profits in return for payments of wage income.

But the interests of firms and workers are not identical. When these interests diverge, a so-called **principal–agent problem** arises. Agents might increase their utility by **shirking** on the job — providing less than agreed-upon worker effort or by taking unauthorized work breaks. The security guard in a warehouse may leave work early or spend time reading a novel as opposed to making the assigned rounds. A salaried manager may spend much time out of the office, looking after personal interests, rather than attending to company business.

Firms (principals) have a profit incentive to reduce or eliminate shirking. There are essentially two means of accomplishing this. One option is to monitor workers. But monitoring is often difficult and costly. Hiring another worker to supervise or monitor our security guard might double the costs of having a secure warehouse. The other means of resolving a principal–agent problem is through the creation of some sort of **incentive pay plan** that ties worker compensation more closely to worker output or performance. Such incentive pay schemes include piece rates, commissions and royalties, bonuses and profit sharing, seniority pay, and efficiency wages.

PIECE RATES   *Piece rates* are compensation paid in proportion to the number of units of output an individual produces. By paying fruit pickers by the bushel and typists by the page, the principal need not be concerned with shirking or monitoring costs.

COMMISSIONS AND ROYALTIES   Commissions and royalties tie pay to the *value* of sales. Realtors, insurance agents, stockbrokers, and retail salespersons commonly receive *commissions* based on the monetary value of their sales. *Royalties* are paid to recording artists and authors based on a certain percentage of sales revenue.

BONUSES AND PROFIT-SHARING   *Bonuses* are payments beyond one's annual salary based on some factor such as individual or firm performance. A professional baseball player may receive bonuses for a high batting average, the number of home runs, or the number of runs batted in. A manager may receive bonuses based on the profit performance of his or her unit. *Profit-sharing* allocates a specified percentage of a firm's profits to its employees.

SENIORITY PAY   Wages and earnings increase with job tenure. One recent explanation of this is that it is advantageous to both workers and employers to pay junior workers less than their MRPs and senior workers more than their MRPs. Such *seniority pay* may be an inexpensive way of reducing shirking when monitoring costs are high. Workers are discouraged from shirking because detection will mean forgoing the high seniority pay accruing in later years of employment. From the firm's stand-

point, turnover is reduced because workers who quit will forfeit the high seniority pay. The increased productivity of workers is the source of extra sales revenue from which the firm and the workers, respectively, enhance their profits and lifetime pay. Young workers may accept wages that are initially less than their MRPs for the opportunity to participate in a labour market where in time the reverse will be true. The increased work effort and higher average productivity may be appealing to the workers because these factors are the source of higher lifetime earnings.

EFFICIENCY WAGES   The notion of *efficiency wages* suggests that employers might get greater effort from their workers by paying them relatively high, above-equilibrium wage rates. Glance back at Figure 16-3, which shows a competitive labour market where the equilibrium wage rate is $6. What if an employer decided to pay an above-equilibrium wage of $7 per hour? Rather than put the firm at a cost disadvantage in comparison to rival firms that are paying only $6, the higher wage *might* improve worker effort and productivity so that unit labour costs actually fall. For example, if each worker produces 10 units of output per hour at the $7 wage rate as compared to only 6 units at the $6 wage rate, unit labour costs will be only $.70 (= $7 ÷ 10) for the high-wage firm as opposed to $1 (= $6 ÷6) for firms paying the equilibrium wage.

An above-equilibrium wage might enhance worker efficiency in several ways. The higher wage permits the firm to attract higher quality workers. Worker morale should be higher. Turnover will be reduced, resulting in both a more experienced workforce and lower recruitment and training costs. Because the opportunity cost of losing a high-wage job is greater, workers are likely to put forth their best efforts with less supervision and monitoring.

TWO ADDENDA

Our discussion of pay-for-performance schemes requires two additional comments.

SOLUTIONS AS PROBLEMS   "Solutions" to principal–agent problems sometimes yield undesirable results. First example: In the early 1990s Sears, the large department store with outlets all over North America, offered its service advisors at its auto-repair shops sales commissions based on the dollar amounts of parts and services recommended and bought. The goal was to align the interest of these service advisors with the profit interest of the corporation. By aggressively identifying and fixing needed repairs, the service managers could enhance Sears' profit while adding to their own total pay.

But the plan backfired! In 1992 U.S. government officials detected widespread fraud in Sears' auto shops in California. They found that many Sears service representatives were recommending unneeded repairs, such as new springs and shock absorbers, to increase sales and commissions. This fraud pervaded Sears' auto-repair shops throughout California, resulting in negative publicity, government legal action, and a large loss of automotive business at Sears.

EQUILIBRIUM REVISITED Pay-for-performance plans also tell us that labour market equilibrium is often more complex than the simple determination of wage rates and employment (Figures 16-3 through 16-8). When principal–agent problems involving shirking and monitoring costs arise, decisions must also be made with respect to the most effective compensation scheme. When we recognize that work effort and productivity are related to the form of worker compensation, the choice of pay plan is not a matter of indifference to the employer, the employee, or society.

MORE ON THE ECONOMIC EFFECTS OF UNIONS

Are the economic effects of labour unions positive or negative? We will address this issue by examining several questions: Do unions raise wages? Do they increase or diminish economic efficiency? Do they make the distribution of earnings more or less equal? There is considerable uncertainty and debate about the answers to these questions.

THE UNION WAGE ADVANTAGE

Our union models (Figure 16-5, 16-6, and 16-7) all imply that unions have the capacity to raise wage rates. Has unionization brought about higher wage rates?

Empirical research overwhelmingly suggests that *unions do raise the wages of their members relative to comparable nonunion workers*, although the size of the

union wage advantage varies according to occupation, industry, race, and gender. The consensus estimate is that the present union wage advantage is about 15%.

This estimate of the union wage advantage is understated because union workers enjoy substantially larger *fringe benefits* than do nonunion workers. Union workers are more likely to have private pensions, dental insurance, and paid vacations and sick leaves than are nonunion workers. Moreover, unionized workers have the company paying their public health insurance premiums in the provinces that charge them. Where such benefits are available to both union and nonunion workers, their magnitude is greater for the union workers. Thus the total compensation (wage rates plus fringe benefits) advantage of union workers is greater than the previously indicated 15%.

There is also general agreement that **unions have probably had little or no impact on the average level of real wages received by labour — both organized and unorganized — taken as a whole.** At first glance these two conclusions — that unions

GLOBAL PERSPECTIVE 16-2

Union membership as a percentage of employed labour force, selected nations

As compared to most other industrialized nations, union membership in Canada is closer to Western European nations than to our neighbour, the United States.

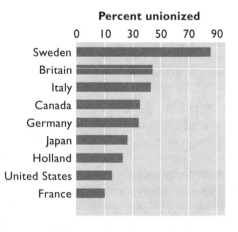

Source: Organization for Economic Cooperation and Development, as reported in *The Economist*, 5 September 1992. Data are for 1988 and 1989.

gain a wage advantage but do not affect the average level of real wages — may seem inconsistent. But they need not be if the wage gains of organized workers are at the expense of unorganized workers. Higher wages in unionized labour markets may cause employers to move back up their labour demand curves and hire fewer workers. These unemployed workers may seek employment in nonunion labour markets. The resulting increase in the supply of labour will depress wage rates in these nonunion markets. The net result may be no change in the average level of wages.

The tight relationship between productivity and the average level of real wages, shown in Figure 16-1, suggests that unions have little power to raise real wage rates for labour as a whole. But Figure 16-1 is an average relationship and is therefore compatible with certain groups of (union) workers getting higher relative wages if other (nonunion) workers are simultaneously getting lower real wages.

EFFICIENCY AND PRODUCTIVITY

Are unions a positive or a negative force insofar as economic efficiency and productivity are concerned? While there is much disagreement about the efficiency aspects of unions, let's consider some of the ways unions might affect efficiency both negatively and positively. We will consider the negative view first.

NEGATIVE VIEW   There are three means by which unions might exert a negative impact on efficiency.

1. FEATHERBEDDING AND WORK RULES   Some unions have undoubtedly diminished productivity growth by engaging in make-work or featherbedding practices and resisting the introduction of output-increasing machinery and equipment. These productivity-reducing practices often come into being against a backdrop of technological change. Labour and management may agree to a team size that is reasonable and appropriate at the time the agreement is concluded, but labour-saving technology may then emerge that renders the team too large. The union is likely to resist the potential loss of jobs. For example, union painters sometimes refused to use spray guns and in some instances limited the width of paint brushes. In more recent years, the typographer unions resisted the introduction of computers in setting type. Historically, the

musicians' union insisted on oversized orchestras for musical shows and required that a union standby orchestra be paid by employers using nonunion orchestras.

More generally, one can argue that unions are responsible for the establishment of work rules and practices that are inimical to efficient production. For example, under seniority rules workers may be promoted in accordance with their employment tenure, rather than based on who can perform the available job with the greatest efficiency. Also, unions may impose jurisdictional restrictions on the kinds of jobs workers may perform. For example, sheet-metal workers or bricklayers may be prohibited from performing the simple carpentry work that is often associated with their jobs. Observance of such rules means, in this instance, that unneeded and underutilized carpenters must be available. Finally, it is often contended that unions constrain managerial prerogatives to establish work schedules, determine production targets, and to make freely the decisions contributing to productive efficiency.

2. STRIKES   A second way unions may adversely affect efficiency is through strikes. If union and management reach an impasse in their negotiations, a strike will result and the firm's production will cease for the strike's duration. The firm will forgo sales and profits and workers will sacrifice income.

Statistics on strike activity suggest strikes are rare and that the associated aggregate economic losses are minimal. While currently an estimated 9000 collective bargaining agreements are in effect, the number of work stoppages in 1994 was 379, involving only 81,245 workers. Furthermore, most of these strikes lasted only a few days. The average amount of work-time lost each year because of strikes is only about one-fifth of 1% of total work-time. This loss is the equivalent of four hours per worker per year, which is less than five minutes per worker per week!

3. LABOUR MISALLOCATION   A more subtle avenue through which unions might adversely affect efficiency is the union wage advantage itself. Figure 16-9 is instructive. Here we have drawn (for simplicity) identical labour demand curves for the unionized and nonunion sectors of the labour market for some particular kind of labour. Our discus-

FIGURE 16-9   **The effect of the union wage advantage on the allocation of labour**

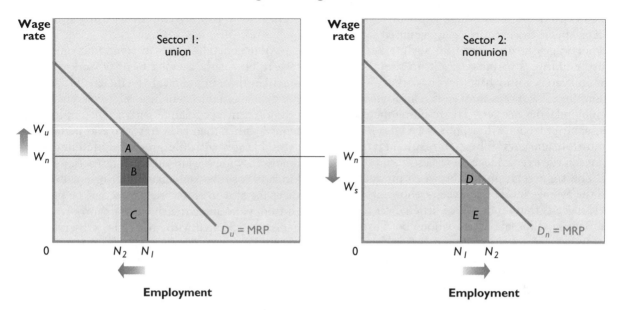

The higher wage W_u that the union achieves in sector 1 causes the displacement of $N_1 N_2$ workers. The re-employment of these workers in nonunion sector 2 reduces the wage rate there from W_n to W_s. The associated loss of output in the union sector is area A + B + C, while the gain in the nonunion sector is only area D + E. The net loss of output is equal to area B. This suggests the union wage advantage has resulted in the misallocation of labour and a decline in economic efficiency.

sion assumes pure competition in both product and resource markets. If there were no union initially, the wage rate that would result from the competitive hire of labour would be, say, W_n. Now assume a union comes into being in sector 1 and succeeds in increasing the wage rate from W_n to W_u. As a consequence, $N_1 N_2$ workers lose their jobs in the union sector. Assume they all move to nonunion sector 2, where they are employed. This increase in labour supply in the nonunion sector depresses the wage rate from W_n to W_s.

Recall that the labour demand curves reflect the marginal revenue products (MRPs) of workers or, in other words, the contributions workers make to domestic output. This means that the shaded area A + B + C in the union sector represents the *decrease* in domestic output caused by the $N_1 N_2$ employment decline in that sector. This A + B + C area is the sum of the MRPs — the total contribution to domestic output — of the workers displaced by the W_n to W_u wage increase achieved by the union. Similarly, the re-employment of these workers in nonunion sector 2 results in an *increase* in

domestic output indicated by the shaded area D + E. Because area A + B + C exceeds area D + E, there is a net loss of domestic output. More precisely, because A = D and C = E, the *net* loss attributable to the union wage advantage is equal to area B. Since the same amount of employed labour is now producing a smaller output, labour is being misallocated and inefficiently used.

Attempts to estimate the output loss due to the allocative inefficiency associated with union wage gains suggest the loss is small. One study assumed a 15% union wage advantage and estimated that approximately 0.14% — only about one-seventh of 1% — of the domestic output was lost! A more recent estimate indicates that union monopoly wage gains cost the U.S. economy 0.2% to 0.4% of gross domestic product. In Canadian terms, in 1994 this amounted to $1.5 billion to $3 billion, or $50 to $100 per person. (**Key Question 17**)

POSITIVE VIEW   Others take the position that, on balance, unions make a positive contribution to productivity and efficiency.

1. MANAGERIAL PERFORMANCE: THE SHOCK EFFECT
The *shock effect* is the idea that a wage increase imposed by a union may induce affected firms to adopt improved production and personnel methods and thereby become more efficient. We may carry Figure 16-9's analysis of labour misallocation one step further and argue that the union wage advantage will prompt union firms to *accelerate* the substitution of capital for labour and *hasten* the search for cost-reducing (productivity-increasing) technologies. When faced with higher production costs due to the union wage advantage, employers will be pushed to reduce costs by using more machinery and by seeking improved production techniques using less of both labour and capital per unit of output. In fact, if the product market is reasonably competitive, a unionized firm with labour costs that are, say, 10% to 15% higher than those of nonunion competitors will not survive unless productivity can be raised. Thus, union wage pressure may inadvertently generate managerial actions that increase national productivity.

2. REDUCED WORKER TURNOVER Unions may also contribute to rising productivity within firms through their effects on worker turnover and worker security. Unions function as a **collective voice** for members in resolving disputes and improving working conditions. If a group of workers is dissatisfied with its conditions of employment, it can respond in two ways: the "exit mechanism" and the "voice mechanism."

The **exit mechanism** refers to the use of the labour market — leave or exit your present job in search of a better one — as a means of reacting to "bad" employers and "bad" working conditions.

The **voice mechanism** involves communication by workers with the employer to improve working conditions and resolve worker grievances. It might be risky for *individual* workers to express their dissatisfaction to employers because employers may retaliate by firing them as "troublemakers." But unions can provide workers with a *collective* voice to communicate problems and grievances to management and to press for their satisfactory resolution.

More specifically, unions may help reduce worker turnover in two ways.

1. Unions provide the voice mechanism as a substitute for the exit mechanism. Unions are effective in correcting job dissatisfactions that would otherwise be "resolved" by workers through the exit mechanism of changing jobs.

2. The union wage advantage is a deterrent to job changes. Higher wages make unionized firms more attractive places to work. Several studies suggest that the decline in quit rates attributable to unionism is substantial, ranging from 31% to 65%.

A lower quit rate increases efficiency in several ways. First, lower turnover means a more experienced and, hence, more productive labour force. Second, fewer quits reduce the firm's recruitment, screening, and hiring costs. Finally, reduced turnover makes employers more willing to invest in the training (and therefore the productivity) of their workers. If a worker quits or "exits" at the end of, say, a year's training, the employer will get no return from the higher worker productivity attributable to that training. Lower turnover increases the likelihood that employers will receive a return on any training they provide, thereby making them more willing to upgrade their labour forces.

3. SENIORITY AND INFORMAL TRAINING Much productivity-increasing training is transmitted informally. More-skilled workers may explain their functions to less-skilled workers on the job, during lunch, or during a coffee break. However, a more-skilled senior worker may want to conceal his or her knowledge from less-skilled junior workers *if* the latter can become competitive for the former's job. Because of union insistence on the primacy of seniority in such matters as promotion and layoff, worker security is enhanced. Given this security, senior workers will be more willing to pass on their job knowledge and skills to new or subordinate workers. This informal training enhances the quality and productivity of the firm's work force.

MIXED RESEARCH FINDINGS Many studies have measured the impact of unionization on productivity. These studies attempt to control for differences in labour quality, the amount of capital equipment used per worker, and other factors aside from unionization that might contribute to productivity differences. Unfortunately, the evidence from the studies is inconclusive. For every study that finds a positive union effect on productivity, another study concludes that there is a negative effect. All we can say is that at present there is no generally accepted conclusion regarding the overall impact of unions on labour productivity.

DISTRIBUTION OF EARNINGS

Labour unions envision themselves as institutions that enhance economic equality. Do unions reduce the inequality with which earnings are distributed? The most convincing evidence suggests they do.

INCREASING INEQUALITY Some economists use Figure 16-9's analysis of labour misallocation to conclude that unions increase earnings inequality. They contend that in the absence of the union, competition would bring wages into equality at W_n in these two sectors or submarkets. But the higher union wage realized in sector 1 displaces workers who seek re-employment in the nonunion sector. In so doing they depress nonunion wages. Instead of wage equality at W_n, we have higher wage rates of W_u for union workers and lower wages of W_s for nonunion workers. The impact of the union is to increase earnings inequality. Furthermore, the fact that unionization is more extensive among the more highly skilled, higher-paid blue-collar workers than among less-skilled, lower-paid blue-collar workers also suggests that the obtaining of a wage advantage by unions increases dispersion of earnings.

PROMOTING EQUALITY There are other aspects of union wage policies that suggest that unionism promotes greater, not less, equality in the distribution of earnings.

1. UNIFORM WAGES WITHIN FIRMS In the absence of unions, employers are apt to pay different wages to individual workers on the same job. These wage differences are based on perceived differences in job performance, length of job tenure, and, perhaps, favouritism. Unions traditionally seek uniform wage rates for all workers performing a particular job. While nonunion firms tend to assign wage rates to *individual workers*, unions — in the interest of worker allegiance and solidarity — seek to assign wage rates to *jobs*. To the extent that unions are successful, wage and earnings differentials based upon supervisory judgements of individual worker performance are eliminated. A side effect of this standard-wage policy is that wage discrimination against minorities and women is likely to be less when a union is present.

2. UNIFORM WAGES AMONG FIRMS In addition to seeking standard wage rates for given occupa-

tional classes *within* firms, unions also seek standard wage rates *among* firms. The rationale is that the existence of substantial wage differences among competing firms may undermine the ability of unions to sustain and enhance wage advantages.

For example, if one firm in a four-firm oligopoly is allowed to pay significantly lower wages to its union workers, the union is likely to find it difficult to maintain the union wage advantage in the other three firms. To avoid this kind of problem, unions seek to "take wages out of competition" by standardizing wage rates among firms, thereby reducing the degree of wage dispersion.

NET EFFECT What is the *net* effect of unions on the distribution of earnings? Although the issue remains controversial, one authoritative study concluded that the wage effects indicated in Figure 16-9 *increase* earnings inequality by about 1%, but the standardization of wage rates within and among firms *decreases* inequality by about 4%. The net result is a 3% decline in earnings inequality due to unions. Because about a third of the labour force is unionized, this 3% reduction in inequality is substantial. **(Key Question 19)**

QUICK REVIEW 16-3

1. Union workers receive average wage rates 15% higher than comparable nonunion workers.

2. Union work rules, strikes, and the misallocation of labour associated with the union wage advantage are means by which unions may reduce efficiency.

3. Unions may enhance productivity through the shock effect, by reducing worker turnover, and by providing the worker security prerequisite to informal on-the-job training.

4. On balance, unions probably reduce wage inequality by achieving wage uniformity within and among firms.

DISCRIMINATION

Discrimination — gender, ethnic, and racial — is a market imperfection that contributes to wage differentials. A society ought to eliminate all types of discrimination not only for reasons of moral justice, but for efficiency as well.

Economic discrimination occurs when female or minority workers, who have the same abilities, education, training, and experience as white male workers, are accorded inferior treatment with respect to hiring, occupational access, promotion, or wage rate. Discrimination also occurs when females or minorities are denied access to education and training.

TYPES OF DISCRIMINATION

Our discussion is in terms of racial and gender discrimination, but these remarks also generally apply to discrimination based on age, religion, or ethnic background.

1. **Wage discrimination** occurs when visible minority workers are paid less than whites for doing the same work. This kind of discrimination is declining because of its explicitness and the fact that it violates federal and provincial laws. But, as Box 16-4 demonstrates, wage discrimination can be very subtle and difficult to detect.
2. **Employment discrimination** means that unemployment is concentrated among minorities. Minorities are frequently the last hired and the first fired.
3. **Human-capital discrimination** occurs when investments in education and training are lower for minority groups compared to whites. The smaller amount and inferior quality of the education cost

minority groups the opportunity to increase their productivity and qualify for better jobs.
4. **Occupational discrimination** means minority workers are arbitrarily restricted or prohibited from entering the more desirable, higher-paying occupations.

OCCUPATIONAL SEGREGATION: THE CROWDING MODEL

This latter form of discrimination — **occupational segregation** — is particularly apparent in our economy. Women are disproportionately concentrated in a limited number of occupations such as nursing, public school teaching, secretarial and clerical jobs, and retail clerks. Minorities are crowded into a limited number of low paying jogs such as laundry workers, cleaners and servants, hospital orderlies, and other manual jobs.

Though racial and ethnic discrimination also exists in Canada, our stress here is on discrimination against women because of their already very great and continuously growing importance in the labour force. As Table 16-4 reveals, women make up 45% of our labour force, the **female participation rate** having doubled to almost 58% since 1961.

ASSUMPTIONS   The character and consequences of occupational discrimination is revealed through a simple supply and demand model. We make three assumptions.

FIGURE 16-10   The economics of occupational discrimination

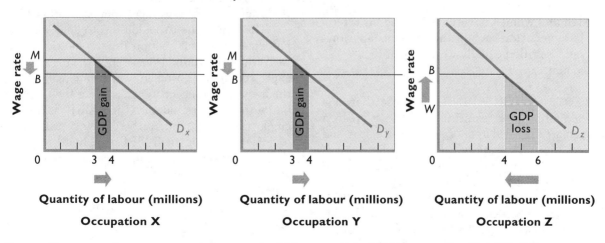

By crowding women into one occupation, men enjoy high wage rates of 0M in occupation X and Y, while women receive low wages of 0W in occupation Z. The abandonment of discrimination will equalize wage rates at 0B and result in a net income increase (real domestic output), or a net gain for society.

TABLE 16-4 Women in the labour force, 1901–1993

Year	Women in labour force (thousands)	Women in labour force as percent of	
		Total labour force	All women aged 15[*] and older
1901	239	13.4%	16%
1911	360	13.2	19
1921	487	15.4	20
1931	706	17.0	22
1941	889	19.9	23
1951	1,149	22.0	24
1961	1,780	27.3	29
1971	2,961	34.3	40
1981	4,812	40.6	52
1991	6,188	44.9	58
1993	6,297	45.1	57.5

[*]For 1901 to 1961, the minimum age was 14.

Source: Gail C.A. Cook (ed.), *Opportunity for Choice* (Ottawa: Information Canada, 1976), p. 97; Statistics Canada, *Labour Force Annual Averages 1993* (Ottawa: February 1994).

1. The labour force is equally divided between male and female workers. Let's say there are 6 million male and 6 million female workers.
2. The economy is made up of three occupations, each with identical labour demand curves, as shown in Figure 16-10.
3. Men and women have identical labour force characteristics; each of the three occupations could be filled equally well by men or women.

EFFECTS OF CROWDING Suppose that as a consequence of discrimination, the 6 million women are excluded from occupations X and Y and crowded into occupation Z. Men distribute themselves equally among occupations X and Y, so there are 3 million male workers in each occupation and the resulting common wage rate for men is 0M. (Assuming no barriers to mobility, any initially different distribution of males between X and Y would result in a wage differential that would prompt labour shifts from low- to high-wage industry until wage equality was realized.)

Women are crowded into occupation Z and because of this occupational segregation, receive a much lower wage rate, 0W. Given the reality of discrimination, this is an "equilibrium" situation. Women *cannot*, because of discrimination, reallocate themselves to occupations X and Y in the pursuit of higher wage rates.

ELIMINATING DISCRIMINATION But now assume that through legislation or sweeping changes in social attitudes, discrimination disappears. Women, attracted by higher wage rates, will shift from Z to X and Y. Specifically, 1 million women will shift into X and another 1 million into Y, leaving 4 million workers in Z. At this point, 4 million workers will be in each occupation and wage rates will be equal to 0B in all three occupations. Wage equality eliminates the incentive for further reallocations of labour.

This new, nondiscriminatory equilibrium is to the obvious advantage of women who now receive higher wages and to the disadvantage of men who now get lower wages. Women were initially exploited through discrimination to the benefit of men; the ending of discrimination corrects that situation.

There is also a net gain to society. Recall that the labour demand curve reflects labour's marginal revenue product (Chapter 15) — labour's contribution to the domestic output.[5] "Society's gain" for occupations X and Y shows the *increases* in domestic output — the market value of the marginal or extra output — realized by adding 1 million women workers in each of those two occupations. Similarly, the "society's loss" for occupation Z shows the *decline* in domestic output caused by the shifting of the 2 million women workers from occupation Z.

The sum of the two additions to domestic output exceeds the subtraction from domestic output in Z when discrimination is ended. This is to be expected. After all, women workers are reallocating themselves from occupation Z, where their contribution to domestic output (their MRP) is low, to employments in X and Y, where their contributions to domestic output (their MRPs) are high.

Conclusion: *Society gains from a more efficient allocation of resources when discrimination is abandoned.* Discrimination places the nation on a point inside its production possibilities curve. (**Key Question 19**)

---

[5] Technical note: This assumes pure competition in product and resource markets.

COSTS OF DISCRIMINATION

Given the diverse types of discrimination, the economic costs of discrimination are difficult to estimate. One estimate for racial discrimination in the United States puts the cost at 4% of the total output of the economy. If ethnic discrimination in Canada were of the same magnitude, in 1995 it would have cost the Canadian economy about $30 billion. A more complex study has concluded that the elimination of gender discrimination would increase domestic output by almost 2.6%.

PUBLIC POLICY CONSEQUENCES

We must consider two more aspects of discrimination.

COMPARABLE WORTH DOCTRINE   The first involves public policy. The reality of pervasive occupational segregation has given rise to the issue of comparable worth. Legislation that forced employers to pay equal wages to men and women performing the same jobs was of no help to many women because occupational segregation limited their access to the jobs held by men. The **comparable worth doctrine — equal pay for work of equal value** — says female secretaries, nurses, and clerks should receive the same salaries as male truck drivers or construction workers if the levels of skill, effort, and responsibility in these disparate jobs are comparable. The basic advantage of comparable worth is that it is a means of quickly correcting perceived pay inequities.

While the concept of comparable worth has considerable appeal, there are objections. For example, any comparison of the relative worth of various jobs is necessarily subjective and therefore arbitrary,

---

BOX 16-4   APPLYING THE THEORY

RACISM IN PROFESSIONAL BASKETBALL?

Although black players earn more than white players in the NBA, researchers have discovered evidence of wage discrimination against blacks.

Casual observation would suggest no racial discrimination in the National Basketball Association (NBA). Almost four-fifths of all NBA players are black. Teams are highly integrated. There are more black coaches in the NBA than in other professional sports. Many of the most highly paid players are black. Raw salary data for 1985–1986 show that black players earned $10,620 (2.7%) more than white players.

Yet research suggests that discrimination *does* exist. Sherer and Kahn* have adjusted 1985–1986 raw salary data for various measures of player performance (productivity) such as number of seasons played, games played per season, career points, field goal percentage, rebounds, assists per game, and so forth. These measures indicate that black players are superior to whites. Adjusting salaries to account for this superiority, Sherer and Kahn have concluded that black players earned about $80,000 or 20% *less* than white players.

What is the source of this discrimination? Sherer and Kahn reject the notion of racist attitudes on the part of owners. By rejecting talented black players, racist owners would find themselves with less successful teams, declining revenues, and franchises of lesser value. Furthermore, the fact that NBA teams are highly integrated suggests that fellow employees (white players) are not the source of discrimination. Sherer and Kahn find that team customers (fans) are the source of NBA discrimination. Their research shows that home game attendance increases with the number of white players on the team. Specifically, they estimate that a team's revenue may increase by about $115,000 to $131,000 per season per additional white player, and suggest that both white players and team owners gain by serving fans' preferences to watch white players. Sherer and Kahn conclude that "as long as fans prefer to see white players, profit-oriented teams will make discriminatory salary offers."**

* Peter D. Sherer and Lawrence M. Kahn, "Racial Differences in Professional Basketball Players' Compensation," *Journal of Labor Economics,* January 1988, pp. 40–61.

** Ibid., p. 60.

opening the door to endless controversies and law-suits. Second, wage-setting by administrative or bureaucratic judgement, rather than supply and demand, does not bode well for long-run efficiency. To the extent that the calculated worth of specific jobs varies from their market or equilibrium values, worker shortages or surpluses will develop. Furthermore, increasing the wages of women could attract even more females to traditionally "women's jobs" and thereby prolong occupational segregation.

NONDISCRIMINATORY FACTORS   Not all of the average income differentials found between males and females are necessarily due to discrimi-nation. Most researchers agree that some part of the male-female earnings differential is attribut-able to factors other than discrimination. For example, the typical work-life cycle of some mar-ried women who have children involves a continu-ous period of work until birth of the first child, then maybe a five- to ten-year period of non-par-ticipation or partial participation in the labour force related to childbearing and child care, fol-lowed by a more continuous period of work experi-ence when the mother is in her late thirties or early forties. The net result is that, on the average, married women with children have accumulated less labour force experience than men in the same age group.

Furthermore, family ties apparently provide mar-ried women with less geographical mobility in job choice than is the case with men. Married women may give up good positions to move with husbands who decide to accept jobs located elsewhere. Some married women may put convenience of job location and flexibility of working hours ahead of occupation-al choice. Women may have purposely crowded into such occupations as nursing and elementary school teaching because such occupations have the greatest carry-over value for productive activity within the home. Finally, in the past decades more women have entered the labour force than men. This large increase in the supply of female workers has acted as a drag on women's wages and earnings.

All this implies that some part of the male-female earnings differential is due to considerations other than sex discrimination. It also suggests that the male-female wage gap will narrow in the future, now that a greater number of women are attending university, maintaining employment through their childbearing years, and pursuing higher-paying pro-fessional jobs. In this regard, a recent StatsCan study reveals that the income of women in the labour force who have never married is at about 90% of the male level.

QUICK REVIEW 16-4

1. Discrimination may mean **a** paying different wages to equally qualified workers, **b** higher unemploy-ment rates for visible minorities, **c** less education and training for women and visible minorities, and **d** the concentration of visible minorities and women in a limited number of occupations.

2. The crowding model demonstrates how **a** men can increase their wages at the expense of women and **b** occupational segregation diminishes the domestic output.

3. Comparable worth is the notion that females in one occupation should receive the same wages as males in another occupation if the levels of skill, effort, responsibility, and working conditions are comparable.

CHAPTER SUMMARY

1. Wages are the price paid per unit of time for the services of labour.

2. The general level of wages is higher in Canada than in most foreign nations because the demand for labour is great in relation to the supply. The strong demand for Canadian labour is based on its high productivity. Over time, various productivity-increasing factors have caused the demand for labour to increase in relation to the supply, accounting for the long-run rise of real wages in Canada.

3. The long-run growth of real wages is closely correlated with labour productivity.

4. Global comparisons show that real wages in Canada are relatively high, but not the highest.

5. Real wages and earnings have been stagnant for the past 15 years.

6. Specific wage rates depend on the structure of the particular labour market. In a competitive market, the equilibrium wage rate and level of employment are determined at the intersection of labour supply and demand.

7. Under monopsony the marginal-resource-cost curve will lie above the resource supply curve, because the monopsonist must bid up wage rates in hiring extra workers and pay that higher wage to *all* workers. The monopsonist will hire fewer workers than under competitive conditions to achieve less-than-competitive wage rates (costs) and thereby greater profits.

8. A union may raise competitive wage rates by **a** increasing the derived demand for labour, **b** restricting the supply of labour through exclusive unionism, and **c** directly enforcing an above-equilibrium wage rate through inclusive unionism.

9. In many industries, the labour market takes the form of bilateral monopoly wherein a strong union "sells" labour to a monopsonistic employer. The wage rate outcome of this labour market model is logically indeterminate.

10. Economists disagree about the desirability of the minimum wage as an antipoverty mechanism. While it causes unemployment for some low-income workers, it raises the incomes of others who retain their jobs.

11. Wage differentials are largely explainable in terms of **a** noncompeting groups arising from differences in the capacities and education of different groups of workers; **b** compensating wage differences, that is, wage differences that must be paid to offset nonmonetary differences in jobs; **c** market imperfections in the form of geographic, artificial, and sociological immobilities.

12. The principal-agent problem arises when workers shirk — provide less-than-expected work effort. Firms may combat this problem by monitoring workers or by creating incentive pay schemes that link worker compensation to work effort.

13. Union workers currently enjoy wages about 15% higher than comparable nonunion workers. There is little evidence that unions have been able to raise the average level of real wages for labour as a whole.

14. There is disagreement as to whether the net effect of unions on allocative efficiency and productivity is positive or negative. The negative view cites **a** inefficiencies associated with featherbedding and union-imposed work rules; **b** loss of output through strikes; and **c** the misallocation of labour to which the union wage advantage gives rise. The positive view holds that **a** through the shock effect, union wage pressure spurs technological advance and mecha-

nization of the production process; **b** as collective voice institutions, unions contribute to rising productivity by reducing labour turnover; and **c** the enhanced security of union workers increases their willingness to teach their skills to less-experienced workers.

15. Those who say unions increase earnings inequality argue that **a** unionization increases the wages of union workers but lowers the wages of nonunion workers and **b** unions are strongest among highly paid skilled blue-collar workers but relatively weak among low-paid unskilled blue-collar workers. But other economists contend that unions contribute to greater earnings equality because unions seek uniform wages both for given jobs within firms and among firms.

16. Historically, an increasing percentage of all working-age women has entered the labour market, and women constitute a rising percentage of the total labour force.

17. The average income of full-time female workers is about 60% that of males. This differential is partially the result of discrimination and, in particular, job segregation.

18. The crowding model of occupational segregation indicates how men may gain higher earnings at the expense of women and visible minorities. The model also shows that discrimination causes a net loss of domestic output.

TERMS AND CONCEPTS

bilateral monopoly (p. 340)

collective voice (p. 351)

comparable worth doctrine — equal pay for
    work of equal value (p. 355)

compensating differences (p. 343)

competitive labour market (p. 331)

crowding model of occupational segregation
    (p. 353)

employment discrimination (p. 353)

exclusive and inclusive unionism
    (pp. 338, 339)

exit and voice mechanisms (p. 351)

female participation rate (p. 353)

human-capital discrimination (p. 353)

human capital investment (p. 343)

incentive pay plan (p. 347)

minimum wage (p. 341)

monopsony (p. 334)

nominal and real wage rates (p. 328)

noncompeting groups (p. 343)

occupational discrimination (p. 353)

occupational licensing (p. 338)

principal–agent problem (p. 346)

shirking (p. 346)

wage differentials (p. 342)

wage discrimination (p. 353)

QUESTIONS AND STUDY SUGGESTIONS

1. Explain why the general level of wages is higher in Canada than in most foreign nations. What is the most important single factor underlying the long-run increase in the average real wage rates in Canada?

2. What factors might explain the stagnation of real wages in the past 15 years?

3. *Key Question*   *Describe wage determination in a labour market in which workers are unorganized and many firms actively compete for the services of labour. Show this situation graphically, using W_1 to indicate the equilibrium wage rate and Q_1 to show the number of workers hired by the firms as a group. Compare the labour supply curve of the individual firm with that of the total market and explain any differences. Identify total revenue, total wage cost, and revenue available for the payment of nonlabour resources.*

4. *Key Question* *Complete the following labour supply table for a firm hiring labour competitively.*

Units of labour	Wage rate	Total labour cost (wage bill)	Marginal resource (labour) cost
1	$ 14	$ _____	$ _____
2	14	_____	_____
3	14	_____	_____
4	14	_____	_____
5	14	_____	_____
6	14	_____	_____

   a. *Show graphically the labour supply and marginal revenue (labour) cost curves for this firm. Explain the relationships of these curves to one another.*

   b. *Compare these data with the labour demand data of question 2 in Chapter 15. What will be the equilibrium wage rate and level of employment be? Explain.*

5. Using the diagram you have drawn in answering question 3, suppose that the formerly competing firms form an employers' association which hires labour as a monopsonist would. Describe verbally the impact upon wage rates and employment. Adjust the graph, showing the monopsonistic wage rate and employment level as W_2 and Q_2, respectively. Using this monopsony model, explain why hospital administrators sometimes complain about a "shortage" of nurses. Do you have suggestions for correcting any such shortage?

6. *Key Question* *Assume a firm is a monopsonist which can hire its first worker for $6, but must increase the wage rate by $3 to attract each successive worker. Show the labour supply and marginal labour cost curves graphically and explain their relationships to one another. Compare these data with the labour demand data of question 2 for Chapter 15. What will be the equilibrium wage rate and the level of employment? Why do these differ from your answer to question 4?*

7. Describe the techniques that unions might employ to raise wages. Evaluate the desirability of each from the viewpoint of a. the union, and b. society as a whole. Explain: "Craft unionism directly restricts the supply of labour; industrial unionism relies upon the market to restrict number of jobs."

8. *Key Question* *Assume a monopsonistic employer is paying a wage rate of W_m and hiring Q_m workers, as indicated in Figure 16-8. Now suppose that an industrial union is formed and that it forces the employer to accept a wage rate of W_c. Explain verbally and graphically why in this instance the higher wage rate will be accompanied by an increase in the number of workers hired.*

9. A critic of the minimum wage has contended, "The effects of minimum wage legislation are precisely the opposite of those predicted by those who support them. Government can legislate a minimum wage, but cannot force employers to hire unprofitable workers. In fact, minimum wages cause unemployment among low-wage workers who can least afford to give up their small incomes." Do you agree? What bearing does the elasticity of labour demand have on this assessment? What factors might possibly offset the potential unemployment effects of a minimum wage?

10. On the average do union workers receive higher wages than comparable nonunion workers?

11. What are the basic considerations which help explain wage differentials? What long-run effect would a substantial increase in safety for underground coal miners have on their wage rates in comparison to other workers?

12. "Many of the lowest-paid people in society — for example, short-order cooks — also have relatively poor working conditions. Thus, the notion of compensating wage differentials is disproved." Do you agree? Explain.

13. What is meant by investment in human capital? Use this concept to explain a. wage differentials, and b. the long-run rise of real wage rates in Canada.

14. What is the principal-agent problem? Have you ever worked in a setting where this problem has arisen? If so, do you think increased monitoring would have eliminated the problem? Why don't firms simply hire more supervisors to eliminate shirking?

15. Professional baseball players are paid for only the first four games of the potential seven games of the World Series. Explain.

16. The notion of efficiency wages suggests that an above-equilibrium wage rate will elicit a more-than-offsetting increase in worker productivity. By what specific means might the higher wage cause worker productivity to rise? Why might young workers accept a seniority pay under which they are initially paid less than their MRPs?

17. *Key Question* *"There is an inherent cost to society that accompanies any union wage gain. That cost is the diminished efficiency with which labour resources are allocated." Explain this contention.*

18. Describe the various avenues through which unions might alter the distribution of earnings. Evaluate: "Unions purport to be egalitarian institutions, but their effect is to increase earnings inequality among Canadian workers."

19. *Key Question* *Use supply-and-demand analysis to explain the impact of occupational segregation or "crowding" on the relative wage rates and earnings of men and women. Who gains and who loses as a consequence of eliminating occupational segregation? Is there a net gain or loss to society as a whole? "Wage differences between men and women do not reflect discrimination, but rather differences in job continuity and rational decisions with respect to education and training." Do you agree?*

20. (Applying the Theory, Box 16-2). Use your understanding of competitive and monopsonistic labour markets to explain the changes in professional baseball players' salaries caused by free agency.

21. (Applying the Theory, Box 16-4) Black players numerically dominate the National Basketball Association and receive higher average salaries than white players. How can researchers argue there is wage discrimination against black players? What is the source of this discrimination?

CHAPTER 17

THE PRICING AND EMPLOYMENT OF RESOURCES: RENT, INTEREST, AND PROFITS

Emphasis in the previous two chapters was on labour markets because wages and salaries account for about three-fourths of our domestic income. In the present chapter we focus on three other sources of income — rent, interest, and profits — comprising the remaining one-fourth of domestic income.

In urban areas such as Tokyo, an acre of land may sell for more than $100 million. An acre of desert may cost $780 million along the Las Vegas casino strip; meanwhile, an acre of desert just 50 km away can be bought for about $72. *How are land prices and rents determined?*

If you put money in a one-year Guaranteed Investment Certificate (GIC) in 1994, you probably received an annual interest rate of about 8%. One year later the same GIC paid only about 6%. *What factors determine interest rates and explain changes in rates?*

The news media document the profit and loss performance of various firms and industries. The maker of Nintendo video games has reaped large profits. And the firm producing AZT, a drug that prolongs the life of AIDS patients, doubled its profits over a three-year period. Meanwhile, automakers have experienced wide swings in their earnings and airlines have recently suffered record losses. *What are the sources and functions of profits and losses?*

BOX 17-1   THE BIG PICTURE

This chapter looks at the employment and pricing of the remaining factors of production: land, capital, and entrepreneurial talent. The main principles set out in Chapter 15 about demand still apply. Supply factors are now introduced; they, along with demand factors, determine the "price" of land, capital, and entrepreneurship, and the amounts employed.

As you read this chapter, keep the following points in mind:

- Land rents are determined by specific supply and demand conditions. Differential rents allocate land among alternative uses.
- Interest is the price paid for the use of money (capital). The interest rate is determined by the supply and demand of loanable funds. The interest rate allocates capital among alternative uses.
- The "price" paid for entrepreneurship is profit; economic profit results from (a) the bearing of uninsurable risk, (b) innovation, and (c) monopoly power. Profit allocates entrepreneurship among alternative industries.

ECONOMIC RENT

To most people "rent" means the money one must pay for a two-bedroom apartment or a dormitory room. To the business executive, "rent" is a payment made for use of a factory building, machinery, or warehouse facilities. These common-sense definitions of rent can be confusing and ambiguous. Dormitory room rent, for example, includes interest on the money capital the university has borrowed to finance the dormitory's construction, wages for custodial service, utility payments, and so forth.

Economists use "rent" in a narrower, but less ambiguous, sense. **Economic rent** *is the price paid for the use of land and other natural resources that are completely fixed in total supply.* The unique supply conditions of land and other natural resources — their fixed supply — make rental payments distinguishable from wage, interest, and profit payments.

Let's examine this feature and some of its implications through supply and demand analysis. We'll assume first that all land is of the same grade or equally productive. Suppose too that all land has just one use, being capable of producing just one product — say, wheat. And assume that land is being rented in a competitive market.

In Figure 17-1, S indicates the supply of arable farmland available in the economy as a whole and D_1 the demand of farmers for use of that land. As with all economic resources, demand is a derived demand. It is downsloping because of the law of diminishing returns and because that product price must be reduced to sell additional units of output.

PERFECTLY INELASTIC SUPPLY

The unique feature of our analysis is on the supply side. For all practical purposes, the supply of land is perfectly inelastic, as reflected in S. Land has no production cost; it is a "free and nonreproducible gift of nature." The economy has only a limited amount of land. Within limits, any parcel of land can be made more usable by clearing, drainage, and irrigation. But these are capital improvements and not changes in the amount of land. Furthermore, such variations in the usability of land are a very small fraction of the total amount of land and do not undermine the basic argument that land and other natural resources are in virtually fixed supply.

CHANGES IN DEMAND

The fixed nature of the supply of land means demand is the only active determinant of land rent; supply is passive. And what determines the demand for land? Those factors discussed in Chapter 15 — the price of the product grown on the land, the productivity of land (which depends, in part, on the quantity and quality of the resources with which land is combined), and the prices of those other resources that are combined with land.

If in Figure 17-1, the demand for land should increase from D_2 to D_1 or decline from D_2 to D_3, land rent would change from R_2 to R_1 or R_3. But the amount of land supplied would remain unchanged at 0S. Changes in economic rent will have no impact on the amount of land available. In techni-

FIGURE 17-1   The determination of land rent

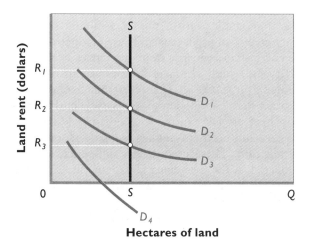

Hectares of land

Because the supply of land and other natural resources is perfectly inelastic (S), demand is the sole active determinant of land rent. An increase (D_2 to D_1) or decrease (D_2 to D_3) in demand will cause considerable changes in rent (R_2 to R_1 and R_2 to R_3). If demand is very small (D_4) relative to supply, land will be a "free good."

cal terms, there is a large price effect and no quantity effect when the demand for land changes. If the demand for land is only D_4, land rent will be zero — land will be a "free good," because it is not scarce enough in relation to the demand for it to command a price.

LAND RENT IS A SURPLUS

The completely inelastic supply of land must be contrasted with the relative elasticity of such property resources as apartment buildings, machinery, and warehouses. These resources are not fixed in total supply. A higher price will give entrepreneurs the incentive to construct and offer larger quantities of these resources. Conversely, a decline in their prices will induce suppliers to allow existing facilities to depreciate and not be replaced. The same reasoning applies to the total supply of labour. Within limits, a higher average level of wages will induce more workers to enter the labour force and lower wages will cause them to drop out. The supplies of non-land resources are upsloping, which means the prices paid to such resources perform an **incentive function**. A high price provides an incentive to offer more; a low price, to offer less.

Not so with land. Rent serves no incentive function, because the total supply of land is fixed. If rent is $10,000, $500, $1, or $0 a hectare, the same amount of land will be available to society. Rent could be eliminated without affecting the productive potential of the economy. For this reason, economists consider rent to be a *surplus* — a payment that is not necessary to ensure that land will be available to the economy as a whole.[1]

A SINGLE TAX ON LAND?

If land is a free gift of nature, costs nothing to produce, and would be available even without rental payments, why should rent be paid to those who, by historical accident or inheritance, happen to be landowners? Socialists have long argued that all land rents are unearned incomes. Land should be nationalized — owned by the state — so that any payments for its use can be used by the state to further the well-being of the entire population rather than being utilized by a landowning minority.

HENRY GEORGE'S PROPOSAL   In the United States, criticism of rental payments took the form of a **single-tax movement**, which gained much support in the late 1800s. Spearheaded by Henry George's provocative book *Progress and Poverty* (1879), this reform movement maintained that economic rent could be completely taxed away without impairing the available supply of land or, therefore, the productive potential of the economy as a whole.

George observed that as population grew and the geographic frontier closed, landowners enjoyed larger and larger rents from their landholdings. These increments in rent were the result of a growing demand for a resource whose supply was perfectly inelastic; some landlords were receiving high incomes, not through rendering any productive

---

[1] A portion — in some instances a major portion — of wage and salary incomes may be surplus, in that these incomes exceed the minimum amount necessary to keep individuals in their current line of work. For example, a hockey superstar may receive $1 million a year, while his next best occupational option, as, say, a high school coach, would earn him only $40,000 or $45,000 per year. Most of his current income is therefore a surplus. In the twilight of their careers, professional athletes sometimes accept sizable salary reductions rather than seek employment in alternative occupations.

effort, but solely from holding advantageously located land. George maintained that these increases in land rent belonged to the economy as a whole, and that land rents should be taxed away and spent for public uses.

Indeed, George held that there was no reason to tax away only 50% of the landowner's unearned rental income. Why not take 70% or 90% or 99%? In seeking popular support for his ideas on land taxation, Henry George proposed that taxes on rental incomes be the *only* tax levied by government.

George's case for taxing land was based not only on fairness, but also on efficiency grounds. Unlike virtually every other tax, a tax on land does *not* alter or distort the use or allocation of land. For example, a tax on wages will reduce after-tax wages and weaken incentives to work. But no such reallocations of resources occur when land is taxed. The most profitable use for land before it is taxed remains the most profitable use after the tax is imposed. Of course, a landlord could withdraw land from production when a tax is imposed, but this would mean no rental income at all.

CRITICISMS   Critics of the single tax on land say:

1. Current levels of government spending are such that a land tax alone would not bring in enough revenue; it cannot be considered realistically as a *single* tax.
2. Most income payments include elements of interest, rent, wages, and profits. Land is typically improved in some manner by productive effort, and economic rent cannot be readily disentangled from payments for capital improvements.
3. The question of unearned income goes beyond land and land ownership. Many people other than landowners benefit from receipt of "unearned" income associated with a growing economy. For example, consider the capital gains income received by someone who, 20 or 25 years ago, purchased (or inherited) stock in a firm that has experienced rapid growth. How is this income different from the rental income of the landowner?
4. A piece of land is likely to have changed ownership many times. *Former* owners may have been the beneficiaries of past increases in land rent. It is hardly fair to tax *current* owners who paid the repetitive market price for land.

PRODUCTIVITY DIFFERENCES

Thus far we have assumed all units of land are of the same grade. This is not so. Different hectares vary greatly in productivity. These productivity differences stem primarily from differences in soil fertility and such climatic factors as rainfall and temperature. It is these factors that explain why southeastern Saskatchewan soil is excellently suited to wheat production, the Palliser Triangle is much less so, and northern muskeg is incapable of wheat production. These productivity differences will be reflected in resource demand. Competitive bidding by farmers will establish a high rent for the very productive Saskatchewan land. The less-productive Palliser Triangle will command a lower rent, and northern muskeg no rent at all.

Location is equally important in explaining differences in land rent. Other things equal, renters will pay more for a unit of land strategically located with respect to materials, labour, and customers than for a unit of land whose location is remote from these markets. Witness the high land rents in large metropolitan areas.

The rent differentials arising from quality differences in land can be seen by looking at Figure 17-1 from a slightly different perspective. Suppose, as before, that only wheat can be produced on four grades of land, *each* of which is available in the fixed amount, $0S$. When combined with identical amounts of capital, labour, and other co-operating resources, the productivity of each grade of land is reflected in demand curves D_1, D_2, D_3, and D_4. Grade 1 land is the most productive, as reflected in D_1, whereas D_4 represents grade 4, the least productive. The resulting rents for grades 1, 2, and 3 land will be R_1, R_2, and R_3 respectively, rent differentials mirroring the differences in the productivity of the three grades of land. Grade 4 land is so poor in quality that it would not pay farmers to bring it fully into production; it would be a "free" and only partially used resource.

ALTERNATIVE USES AND COSTS

We have also supposed that land has only one use. Actually, we know land normally has alternative uses. A hectare of southeast Saskatchewan farmland may be useful in raising not only wheat, but also canola, barley, oats, and cattle, or it may be useful as a house or a factory site.

This indicates that although land is a free gift of nature and has no production cost from the viewpoint of society as a whole, the rental payments of individual producers are *costs*. The total supply of land will be available to society even if no rent is paid for its use, but from the standpoint of individual firms and industries, land has alternative uses, and therefore payment must be made by firms and industries to attract that land from those other uses. Such payments by definition are costs. Again, the fallacy of composition (Chapter 1) has entered our discussion. From society's standpoint, there is no alternative but for land to be used by society. Therefore, to society, rents are a surplus, not a cost. But because land has alternative uses, the rental payments of wheat farmers or any other individual user are a cost; such payments are required to attract land from alternative uses. (**Key Question 2**)

INTEREST

T*he interest rate is the price paid for the use of money.* It is the amount of money that must be paid for the use of one dollar for a year.

1. STATED AS PERCENTAGE Interest is stated as a percentage of the amount of money borrowed rather than as an absolute amount. Stating interest as a percentage facilitates comparison of interest paid on loans of much different absolute amounts. We can immediately compare an interest payment of, say, $432 per year per $2880 and one of $1800 per year per $12,000. In this case, both interest payments are 15% — which is not obvious from the absolute figures. Provincial laws call for the uniform statement of interest costs so that borrowers will understand the interest rate they are paying.

2. MONEY NOT A RESOURCE Money is *not* an economic resource. Coin, paper currency, or chequing accounts cannot produce goods and services. However, money can be used to acquire capital goods — factory buildings, machinery, warehouses, and so forth. These facilities do contribute to production. Thus, in hiring the use of money capital, businesses are ultimately buying the use of real capital goods.

LOANABLE FUNDS THEORY OF INTEREST

The **loanable funds theory of interest** explains the interest rate in terms of the demand for and supply of loanable funds. The equilibrium interest rate equates the quantities of loanable funds demanded and supplied.

SUPPLY OF LOANABLE FUNDS Let's first consider the loanable funds theory in a simplified form. Assume households are the sole suppliers and businesses are the only demanders of loanable funds. In Figure 17-2 the supply of loanable funds is shown as an upsloping curve; a larger quantity of funds will be made available at high interest rates than at low interest rates.

FIGURE 17-2 The loanable funds theory of interest

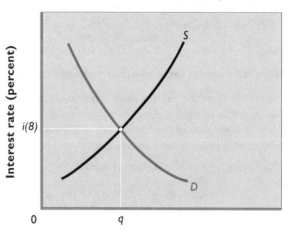

Quantity of loanable funds

The loanable funds theory of interest envisions the equilibrium interest rate as being determined by the intersection of the demand for, and the supply of, loanable funds. The supply curve is upsloping because, the higher the interest rate, the more willing households are to save. The demand curve is downsloping because businesses are more willing to borrow and invest loanable funds the lower the interest rate.

The explanation of this is that most individuals prefer present consumption to future consumption because, given the uncertainties of life, present consumption seems more tangible and therefore more valuable. It follows that a consumer must be compensated by an interest payment to defer consumption or, in other words, to save. The upsloping supply of loanable funds curve indicates that, the larger the interest rate, the more households are willing to save (or the less of their incomes they consume).

DEMAND FOR LOANABLE FUNDS   Demand for loanable funds comes from businesses that want to replace or add to their stocks of capital goods. Firms demand loanable funds to build new plants or warehouses and to purchase machinery and equipment.

Consider the character of such investment decisions. Suppose a firm is contemplating the purchase of a machine that will increase its output and sales to the extent that its total revenue will rise by $110 for the year. Also assume the machine costs $100 and has a useful life of just one year. Comparing the $10 earned above the cost of the machine with that cost, we find the **rate of return** on this investment is 10% (= $10/$100).

GLOBAL PERSPECTIVE 17-1

Nominal interest rates of banks, selected nations

These data show the interest rates which banks in various countries charged their prime customers in 1992. Because these are nominal rates, much of the variation reflects differences in rates of inflation.

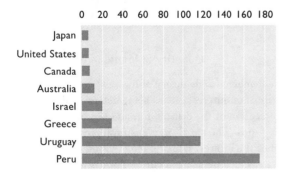

Source: *World Development Report*, 1994, pp. 184–185.

The firm must compare the interest rate — the price of loanable funds — with the 10% rate of return to determine whether the investment is profitable and therefore should be made. If funds can be borrowed at some rate less than the rate of return, say 6%, then the investment is profitable and should be undertaken. But if funds are available at a 14% rate of interest, this investment is unprofitable and should not be made.

Why is the demand for loanable funds downsloping, as in Figure 17-2? At higher interest rates, fewer investment projects will be profitable to businesses and hence a small quantity of loanable funds will be demanded. At lower interest rates, more investment projects will be profitable and therefore more loanable funds will be demanded. Indeed, we have just seen in our example that it is profitable to purchase the $100 machine if funds can be borrowed at 6%, but it is not profitable if the firm must borrow at 14%.

EXTENDING THE MODEL   We now want to make our portrayal of the loanable funds market more realistic in two different ways. In our first extension of the model, we consider factors that might cause the supply and demand curves of loanable funds to shift and thereby change the equilibrium interest rate.

CHANGES IN SUPPLY   Consider the supply side. Anything that causes households to be more thrifty will prompt them to save more at each interest rate, shifting the supply curve rightward. For example, if the tax laws were changed to exempt interest earned on savings from taxation, we would expect the supply of loanable funds to increase and the equilibrium interest rate to decrease. Conversely, a decline in thriftiness would shift the curve leftward and increase the equilibrium interest rate.

CHANGES IN DEMAND   On the demand side, anything that increases the rates of return on potential investments will increase the demand for loanable funds. Let's return to our earlier example, wherein a firm would receive additional revenues of $110 by purchasing a $100 machine and, hence, realize a 10% return on the investment. What factors might increase or decrease that rate of return? Suppose a technological advance raises the productivity of the machine so that it produces still more output and increases the firm's total revenue by $120 rather than $110. The rate of return will now be 20%, not 10%. Before the technological advance the firm would demand no loanable funds at, say, a 14% interest rate. But now it would demand $100, implying a rightward shift of the demand for loanable funds curve.

Similarly, an increase in consumer demand for the firm's product — reflecting perhaps the movement of the economy from recession to prosperity — will increase product price. Even though we assume the productivity of the machine is unchanged, the firm's additional total revenue might again rise from $110 to $120, which increases the rate of return to 20%. This implies that the demand for loanable funds has shifted rightward. Conversely, we would expect a decline in the price of the firm's product to decrease the demand for loanable funds.

OTHER PARTICIPANTS We must also recognize that there are more participants on both the demand and supply side of the loanable funds market. For example, while households are suppliers of loanable funds, many also demand those same funds. Households borrow to finance large purchases such as housing, automobiles, and furniture and household appliances. Governments are also on the demand side when they borrow to finance budgetary deficits. On the supply side, businesses that have revenues in excess of their current costs or expenditures may make the consequent business saving available in the market for loanable funds. Note that households and businesses are on both the supply and demand sides of the market.

In studying macroeconomics you will find that chartered banks and other financial institutions not only gather and make available the savings of households and businesses, but also create loanable funds when they lend. Thus, financial institutions are another source of loanable funds. (**Key Question 4**)

RANGE OF RATES

Although it is convenient to think in terms of a single interest rate, there is a cluster or range of interest rates. Table 17-1 lists many interest rates frequently referred to in the media. These rates range from 6.58% to 18.5%. Why the differences?

1. RISK The greater the chance the borrower will not repay the loan, the more interest the lender will charge to compensate for this risk.

TABLE 17-1 Selected interest rates, July, 1995

Type of interest rate	Annual percentage
10-year Government of Canada bond	8.22
8-year New Brunswick bond	7.50
30-year B.C. Telephone bond	9.65
9-year Thompson Corporation bond	9.15
5-year closed mortgage	8.50
91-day Treasury bill (Government of Canada)	6.58
Prime rate (rate charged by banks to their best corporate customers)	8.25
Visa interest rate	18.50

2. MATURITY Other things equal, long-term loans usually command higher rates of interest than do short-term loans, because the long-term lender suffers the inconvenience and possible financial sacrifice of forgoing alternative uses for his or her money for a greater period of time.

3. LOAN SIZE Given two loans of equal length and risk, the interest rate usually will be somewhat higher on the smaller of the two loans. This is because administrative costs of a large and a small loan are about the same.

4. MARKET IMPERFECTIONS Market imperfections also explain some interest rate differentials. The small-town bank branch that monopolizes the local money market may charge high interest rates on loans to consumers because households find it inconvenient to "shop around" at bank branches in somewhat distant cities, where they might have been able to negotiate a demand loan at a lower interest rate than a consumer loan. The large corporation, on the other hand, can survey a number of rival investment houses in floating a new bond issue, securing the lowest obtainable rate.

PURE RATE OF INTEREST

To circumvent the difficulties in discussing the whole structure of interest rates, economists talk of "the" interest rate or the **pure rate of interest**. This pure rate is best approximated by the interest paid on long-term, virtually riskless bonds, such as the long-term bonds of the Government of Canada. This interest payment can be thought of as being made solely for the use of money over an extended time period, because the risk factor and administrative costs are negligible and the interest on such securities is not distorted by market imperfections. The pure interest rate in the fall of 1995 was about 8.0%.

ROLE OF THE INTEREST RATE

The interest rate is an important price since it simultaneously affects both the *level* and *composition* of investment goods production.

BOX 17-2   APPLYING THE THEORY

DETERMINING THE PRICE OF CREDIT

There are a variety of lending practices that can cause the effective interest rate to be quite different than what it appears to be.

Borrowing and lending — receiving and granting credit — are a way of life. Individuals receive credit when they negotiate a mortgage loan and when they use their credit cards. Individuals make loans when they open a savings account at a chartered bank or buy a government saving bond.

It sometimes is difficult to determine exactly how much interest we pay and receive in borrowing and lending. Let's suppose that you borrow $10,000 that you agree to repay plus $1000 of interest at the end of the year. In this instance the interest rate is 10% per year. To determine the interest rate (r) we compare interest paid with the amount borrowed:

$$r = \frac{\$1000}{\$10,000} = 10\%$$

But in some cases a lender, say, a chartered bank, will *discount* the interest payment at the time the loan is made. Thus, instead of giving the borrower $10,000, the bank discounts the $1000 interest payment in advance, giving the borrower only $9000. This increases the interest rate:

$$r = \frac{\$1000}{\$9000} = 11\%$$

While the absolute amount of interest paid is the same, in this second case the borrower has only $9000 available for the year.

An even more subtle point is that, in order to simplify their calculations, many financial institutions assume a 360-day year (twelve 30-day months). This means the borrower has the use of the lender's funds for five days less than the normal year. This use of a "short year" also increases the interest rate paid by the borrower.

The interest rate paid can change dramatically if a loan is repaid in instalments. Suppose a chartered bank lends you $10,000 and charges interest in the amount of $1000 to be paid at the end of the year. But the loan contract requires you to repay the $10,000 loan in 12 equal monthly instalments. The effect of this is that the *average* amount of the loan outstanding during the year is only $5000. Hence:

$$r = \frac{\$1000}{\$5000} = 20\%$$

Here interest is paid on the total amount of the loan ($10,000) rather than the outstanding balance (which averages $5000 for the year), making for a much higher interest rate.

Another fact that influences the effective interest rate is whether interest is *compounded*. Suppose you deposit $10,000 in a savings account that pays a 10% interest rate compounded semiannually. In other words, interest is paid on your "loan" to the bank twice a year. At the end of the first six months, $500 of interest (10% of $10,000 for one-half a year) is added to your account. At the end of the year, interest is calculated on $10,500 so that the second interest payment is $525 (10% of $10,500 for one-half a year). Hence:

$$r = \frac{\$1025}{\$10,000} = 10.25\%$$

This means that a bank advertising a 10% interest rate compounded semiannually is actually paying more interest to its customers than a competitor paying a simple (noncompounded) interest rate of 10.20%.

"Let the borrower beware" is a fitting motto in the world of credit.

INTEREST AND DOMESTIC OUTPUT The level of the interest rate affects the aggregate levels of domestic output and employment in the economy. Other things equal, a high interest rate depresses, while a low interest rate stimulates domestic output and employment. When businesses can borrow at low interest rates, a larger volume of investments in capital equipment and plant facilities will be profitable. This means a higher volume of economic activity and, consequently, more output and more jobs. Low interest rates stimulate interest-sensitive expenditures by consumers in such goods as automobiles and housing. High interest rates depress investment and consumer spending and reduce both domestic output and employment.

INTEREST AND THE ALLOCATION OF CAPITAL
Prices are rationing devices. The interest rate is no exception; it performs the function of allocating money capital, and therefore physical capital, to various firms and investment projects. It rations the available supply of money or liquidity to investment projects whose expected profitability is sufficiently high to warrant payment of the going interest rate.

If the expected rate of net profits of additional physical capital in the computer industry is 12% and the required funds can be secured at an interest rate of 8%, the computer industry will be able to borrow and expand its capital facilities. If the rate of net profits of capital in the steel industry is expected to be only 6%, it may be unprofitable for this industry to accumulate more capital goods at the 8% interest rate. *The interest rate allocates money, and ultimately physical capital, to those industries in which it will be most productive and therefore most profitable. Such an allocation of capital goods is in the interest of society as a whole.*

APPLICATION: USURY LAWS

A number of states in the United States have passed *usury laws*, which specify the maximum interest rate at which loans can be made. The purpose is to make credit more widely available to borrowers, particularly those with low incomes.

We can assess the impact of such legislation with the help of Figure 17-2. The equilibrium interest rate is 8%, but now a usury law specifies that lenders cannot charge more than, say, 6%. The effects are:

1. NONMARKET RATIONING At 6% the quantity of loanable funds demanded exceeds the quantity supplied — there is a shortage of credit. The market no longer rations loanable funds to borrowers, so lenders (banks) will. We can expect them to make loans to the most credit-worthy borrowers (wealthy, high-income people), which defeats the goal of usury law. Low-income people excluded from the market may be forced to turn to unscrupulous loan-sharks who charge interest rates several times above the market rate.

2. GAINERS AND LOSERS Credit-worthy borrowers will gain from usury laws because they will pay below-market interest rates. Lenders (ultimately bank stockholders) will be losers, receiving 6 rather than 8% on each dollar loaned.

3. INEFFICIENCY We have just discussed how the equilibrium interest rate allocates money to those investments where the expected rate of return (productivity) is greatest. The rationing of credit under usury laws is less likely to provide financing for the most productive projects. Suppose Holly has a project so promising she would pay 8% for funds to finance it. Ben has a less promising investment and would be willing to pay only 6% for financing. If the market rationed funds, Holly's highly productive project would receive funds and Ben's would not. This allocation of funds is in the interest of both Holly and society. But with a 6% usury rate, there is a 50-50 chance Ben will be funded and Holly will not. Legal maximum interest rates may ration funds to less-productive uses.

QUICK REVIEW 17-2

1. Interest is the price paid for the use of money.

2. The equilibrium interest rate is determined by the demand for and the supply of loanable funds.

3. There exists a range of interest rates that is influenced by risk, maturity, loan size, taxability, and market imperfections.

4. The equilibrium real interest rate affects the aggregate level of investment and therefore the level of domestic output; it also allocates money and real capital to specific industries and firms.

5. Usury laws that establish an interest rate ceiling below the market rate **a** deny credit to low-income people; **b** subsidize high-income borrowers and penalize lenders; and **c** diminish the efficiency with which investment funds are allocated.

ECONOMIC PROFITS

As with rent, economists define profits more narrowly than accountants do. To accountants, "profit" is what remains of a firm's total revenue after it has paid individuals and other firms for materials, capital, and labour supplied to the firm. To the economist, this is too broad and ambiguous. The difficulty is that the accountant's view of profits takes into account only **explicit costs**: payments made by the firm to outsiders. It ignores **implicit costs**: payments to similar resources owned and self-employed by a firm. In other words, the accountant's concept of profits fails to allow for implicit wage, rent, and interest costs. **Economic**, or **pure, profits** are what remain after *all* opportunity costs — both explicit and implicit wage, rent, and interest costs and a normal profit — have been subtracted from a firm's total revenue (Chapter 9). Economic profits may be either positive or negative (losses).

For example, farmers who own their land and equipment and provide all their own labour grossly overstate their economic profits if they subtract only their payments to outsiders for seed, insecticides, fertilizer, and gasoline, from their total receipts. Actually, much or possibly all of what remains is the implicit rent, interest, and wage costs that the farmers forgo in deciding to self-employ the resources they own rather than make them available in alternative employments. Interest on the capital or wages for the labour contributed by the farmers are no more profits than are the payments that would be made if outsiders had supplied these resources. Economic profits are a residual — the total revenue remaining after *all* costs are taken into account.

ROLE OF THE ENTREPRENEUR

The economist views profits as the return to a very special type of resource — entrepreneurial ability. The entrepreneur (1) takes the initiative to combine other resources in producing a good or service; (2) makes basic, nonroutine policy decisions for the firm; (3) introduces innovations in the form of new products or production processes; (4) bears the economic risks associated with all these functions.

Part of the entrepreneur's return is called a **normal profit**. This is the minimum return or payment necessary to keep the entrepreneur in some specific line of business activity. This normal profit payment is a cost (Chapter 9). However, we know that a firm's total revenue may exceed its total costs (explicit and implicit, the latter inclusive of a normal profit). This extra or excess revenue above all costs is an economic profit. This residual — which is *not* a cost, because it is in excess of the normal profit required to retain the entrepreneur in the industry — accrues to the entrepreneur. The entrepreneur is the residual claimant.

There are several theories to explain why this residual of economic profit might occur. As we will see in a moment, these explanations relate to:

1. The *risks* the entrepreneur bears by functioning in a dynamic and uncertain environment, or by being innovative.
2. The possibility of attaining *monopoly power*.

SOURCES OF ECONOMIC PROFIT

To understand economic profits and the entrepreneur's functions, let's examine an artificial economic environment where pure profits would be zero. Then by noting real-world deviations from this environment, we can find the sources of economic profit.

In a purely competitive, static economy, pure profits would be zero. By a **static economy** we mean one in which all the basic data — resource supplies, technological knowledge, and consumer tastes — are constant and unchanging. A static economy is one in which all determinants of cost and supply, and demand and revenue, are constant.

In such an economic environment economic uncertainty is nonexistent. The outcome of price and production policies is accurately predictable. Furthermore, the static nature of such a society precludes innovation. Under pure competition, any pure profits (positive or negative) that might have existed initially in various industries will disappear with the entry or exodus of firms in the long run. All costs — both explicit and implicit — will therefore be precisely covered in the long run, leaving no residual in the form of economic profits (Figure 10-12).

The notion of zero economic profits in a static, competitive economy enhances our understanding of profits by suggesting that profits are linked to the dynamic nature of market economy and its accompanying uncertainty. Furthermore, it indicates that economic profits may arise from a source apart from the directing, innovating, risk-bearing functions of the entrepreneur. And that source is the presence of some degree of monopoly power.

UNCERTAINTY, RISK, AND PROFITS   In a dynamic economy, the future is always uncertain. This means the entrepreneur must assume risks. Profits can be thought of, in part, as a reward for taking risks.

In linking pure profits with uncertainty and risk-bearing, we must distinguish between risks that are insurable and those that are not. Some types of risks — fires, floods, theft, and accidents to employees — are measurable, in that actuaries can accurately estimate their average occurrence. As a result, these are insurable risks. Firms can avoid or at least provide for them by incurring a known cost in the form of an insurance premium. It is the bearing of **uninsurable risks** that is a potential source of economic profits.

Uninsurable risks are uncontrollable and unpredictable changes in demand (revenue) and supply (cost) conditions facing the firm. Some of these uninsurable risks stem from unpredictable changes in the general economic environment or, more specifically, from the business cycle. Prosperity brings substantial windfall profits to most firms; recessions result in widespread losses. In addition, changes are constantly taking place in the structure of the domestic and world economy.

Even in a full-employment, noninflationary economy, changes are always occurring in consumer tastes, technology, and resource supplies. Example: Technological change has been such that vinyl long-play records have given way to cassettes and these have lost their market to compact discs.

Such changes continually alter the revenue and cost data faced by individual firms and industries, leading to structural changes as favourably affected industries expand and adversely affected industries contract. The point is that profits and losses can be associated with taking on uninsurable risks stemming from both cyclical and structural changes in the economy.

UNCERTAINTY, INNOVATIONS, AND PROFITS
The uncertainties just discussed are external to the firm; they are beyond the control of the individual firm or industry. One other dynamic feature of a market economy — innovation — occurs at the initiative of the entrepreneur. Firms deliberately introduce new methods of production and distribution to reduce costs, introduce new products, and increase their revenue. The entrepreneur purposely undertakes to upset existing cost and revenue data in a way that is hoped will be profitable.

But again, uncertainty enters the picture. Despite exhaustive market surveys, new products may be economic failures. Three-dimensional movies come readily to mind as a product failure. Similarly, of the many new novels, textbooks, records, and tapes that appear every year, only a handful garner large profits. Nor is it known with certainty whether a new machine will actually provide the cost economies predicted for it while it is still in the blueprint stage. Innovations purposely undertaken by entrepreneurs bring with them uncertainty, just as do those changes in the economic environment over which an individual enterprise has no control. In a sense, innovation as a source of profits is merely a special case of risk-bearing.

Under competition and in the absence of patent laws, profits from innovations will be temporary. Rival firms will imitate successful (profitable) innovations, competing away all economic profits. Nevertheless, such profits may always exist in a progressive economy as new successful innovations replace older ones whose associated profits have been competed away.

MONOPOLY PROFITS   The existence of monopoly in some form or another is a final source of economic profits. Because of its ability to restrict output and deter entry, a monopolist may persistently enjoy economic profits, provided demand is strong relative to cost (Figure 11-4).

There are both a causal relationship and a distinction between uncertainty and monopoly as sources of profits. The causal relationship involves the fact that an entrepreneur can reduce uncertainty by achieving monopoly power. The competitive firm is exposed to the vagaries of the market; the monopolist, however, can partially control the market and minimize the adverse effects of uncertainty.

Furthermore, innovation is a source of monopoly power; the short-run uncertainty associated with the introduction of new techniques or products may have been carried out for the purpose of achieving a measure of monopoly power. (**Key Question 7**)

FUNCTIONS OF PROFITS

Profit is the prime mover of a market economy. As such, profits influence both the level of resource utilization and the allocation of resources among alternative uses.

INVESTMENT AND DOMESTIC OUTPUT It is profit — or the *expectation* of profit — that induces firms to innovate. Innovation stimulates investment, total output, and employment. Innovation is a fundamental aspect of economic growth, and it is the pursuit of profit that underlies most innovation. However, profit expectations are volatile, with the result that investment, employment, and the rate of growth have been unstable.

PROFITS AND RESOURCE ALLOCATION Entrepreneurs seek profits and shun losses. Economic profits are a signal that society wants that particular industry to expand. Profit rewards are more than an inducement for an industry to expand; they also are the financial means by which firms in such industries can add to their productive capacities.

Losses signal society's desire for the afflicted industries to contract; losses penalize firms that fail to adjust their productive efforts to those goods and services most preferred by consumers.

QUICK REVIEW 17-3

1. Pure or economic profits are determined by subtracting all explicit and implicit costs (including a normal profit) from a firm's total revenue.

2. Economic profits result from **a** the bearing of uninsurable risks, **b** innovation, and **c** monopoly power.

3. Profits and profit expectations affect the levels of investment and domestic output and also allocate resources among alternative uses.

INCOME SHARES

Our discussion in this and the previous chapter would be incomplete without a brief empirical summary as to the importance of wages, rent, interest, and profits as proportions or relative shares of the domestic income. Table 17-2 sets out income shares in terms of the income categories since 1926. Although these accounting conceptions of income do not neatly fit the economist's definitions of wages, rent, interest, and profits, they do yield some usable insights about the relative size and trends of income shares.

CURRENT SHARES

The most recent figures in the table reveal the dominant role of labour income. Defining labour income as "wages, salaries and supplementary labour income" (fringe benefits), labour currently receives about 75% of the domestic income. But some economists argue that since proprietors' income (the sum of columns 5 and 6) is largely made up of wages and salaries, it should be added to the official "wages and salaries" category to determine labour income. When we use this broad definition, labour's share rises to over 80% of domestic income. Interestingly, although we label our system a "capitalist economy," the capitalist share of domestic income — which we will define as the sum of "corporation profits" and "interest and miscellaneous investment income," less "inventory valuation adjustment" — is less than 20% of the domestic income.

HISTORICAL TRENDS

What historical trends can be deduced from Table 17-2? Let's concentrate on the dominant wage share. Using the narrow definition of labour's share as simply "wages and salaries," we see increase from about 60% in the late 1920s to over 70% in the past decade.

STRUCTURAL CHANGE Although there are several tentative explanations of these data, one prominent theory is based on the structural changes that have occurred in our economy.

1. CORPORATE GROWTH Noting the constancy of the capitalist share (the sum of columns 3 and 4) — which was roughly 17% in both the late 1920s and

TABLE 17-2 Relative shares of domestic income, 1926-1994 (*selected years or period averages of shares for individual years*)

(1)	(2)	(3)	(4)	(5)	(6)	(7)	(8)
Year or period	Wages, salaries, and supplementary labour income	Corporation profits before taxes	Interest and miscellaneous investment income	Accrued net income of farmers from farm production	Net income of nonfarm unincorporated business including rent	Inventory valuation adjustment	Net domestic income at factor cost
1926	55.3%	11.4%	3.2%	14.1%	14.9%	1.1%	100%
1927–28	55.5	12.5	3.4	13.1	15.2	0.3	100
1929	60.0	12.9	3.7	8.0	15.7	-0.3	100
1932	69.3	4.1	4.5	3.6	14.7	3.8	100
1933	70.2	9.7	4.3	2.6	14.1	-0.9	100
1937	62.6	15.6	3.1	6.9	13.9	-2.1	100
1941	61.9	18.1	2.8	7.0	12.6	-2.4	100
1945	63.4	13.1	2.7	9.2	12.0	-0.4	100
1951	60.7	17.9	2.5	10.5	12.0	-3.6	100
1952	60.5	15.4	2.5	9.4	11.6	0.6	100
1957–60	67.0	13.7	3.9	3.6	12.0	-0.2	100
1961–65	67.7	14.2	4.3	3.6	10.6	-0.3	100
1966–70	70.9	13.5	4.7	2.7	8.8	-0.6	100
1971	73.0	12.2	5.5	2.0	8.2	-0.9	100
1973	70.6	16.0	5.7	3.0	7.2	-2.5	100
1975	71.2	14.8	7.1	2.9	6.0	-2.0	100
1976	71.9	13.4	8.0	2.2	5.9	-1.4	100
1979	69.3	16.4	10.7	1.7	5.4	-3.5	100
1982	72.7	9.2	12.2	1.2	5.8	-1.1	100
1990	72.6	8.7	11.1	0.6	7.0	-0.0	100
1994	73.5	10.0	10.1	0.4	6.9	-0.9	100

Source: 1926-1986: Statistics Canada, *National Income and Expenditure Accounts.*

in the past decade — we find that the expansion of labour's share of the economy has come at the expense of the share going to proprietors (columns 5 and 6). This suggests that the evolution of the corporation as the dominant form of business enterprise may be an important explanatory factor. Individuals who would have operated their own corner grocery in the 1920s are the hired managers of corporate supermarkets in the 1980s or 1990s.

2. Changing Industry Mix The changing output mix, and therefore the industry mix, that

has occurred, has tended to increase labour's share. Overall, there has been a long-term change in the composition of output and industry. There has been a reallocation of labour from agriculture to both manufacturing and service sectors. These shifts account for much of the growth of labour's share, reflected in column 2 of Table 17-2.

Unions? It is tempting to explain an expanding wage share by the growth of labour unions. But there are difficulties with this approach.

1. The growth of the labour movement in Canada does not fit well chronologically with the growth of labour's share of domestic income. Most of the growth of "wages and salaries" occurred after 1952, while much of the growth in the labour movement came between 1900 and 1950.

2. Wage increases for union members may come at the expense of the wages of unorganized workers. In obtaining higher wages, unions restrict employment opportunities (Figures 16-6 and 16-7) in organized industries. Unemployed workers and new entrants to the labour force therefore seek jobs in the nonunion sectors. The resulting increases in labour supply tend to depress wage rates in nonunion jobs. If this scenario is correct, then higher wages for union workers may be achieved not at the expense of the capitalist share, but rather at the expense of the nonunion wage share. Overall, the total labour share — union plus nonunion — could well be unaffected by unions.

3. If domestic income is disaggregated into industry sectors and the historical trend of the wage share in each sector is examined, we reach a curious conclusion. Generally, labour's share has grown more rapidly in those sectors where unions are weak than in sectors that are highly unionized.

CHAPTER SUMMARY

1. Economic rent is the price paid for the use of land and other natural resources whose total supplies are fixed.

2. Rent is a surplus since land would be available to the economy as a whole even in the absence of all rental payments. The notion of land rent as a surplus gave rise to the single-tax movement of the late 1800s.

3. Differences in land rent are explainable in terms of differences in productivity due to the fertility and climatic features of land and in its location.

4. Land rent is a surplus rather than a cost to the economy as a whole; however, because land has alternative uses from the standpoint of individual firms and industries, rental payments of firms and industries are correctly regarded as costs.

5. Interest is the price paid for the use of money. The equilibrium interest rate is determined by the demand for and supply of loanable funds.

6. The equilibrium interest rate influences the level of investment and helps ration financial and physical capital to specific firms and industries. The real interest rate, not the nominal rate, is critical to investment decisions.

7. Economic, or pure, profits are the difference between a firm's total revenue and its total costs, the latter defined to include implicit costs, which include a normal profit. Profits accrue to entrepreneurs for assuming the uninsurable risks associated with organizing and directing economic resources and innovating. Profits also result from monopoly power.

8. Profit expectations influence innovating and investment activities, and therefore the level of employment. The basic function of profits and losses, however, is to induce that allocation of resources that is in general accord with the tastes of consumers.

9. The largest share of domestic income goes to labour. Narrowly defined as "wages and salaries," labour's relative share has increased through time. When more broadly defined to include "proprietor's income," labour's share has been about 80% and the capitalist share about 20% of domestic income since 1926.

TERMS AND CONCEPTS

economic or pure profit (p. 370)

economic rent (p. 362)

explicit and implicit costs (p. 370)

incentive function (p. 363)

loanable funds theory of interest (p. 365)

normal profit (p. 370)

pure rate of interest (p. 367)

rate of return (p.366)

single-tax movement (p. 363)

static economy (p. 370)

uninsurable risks (p. 371)

QUESTIONS AND STUDY SUGGESTIONS

1. How does the economist's usage of the term "rent" differ from everyday usage? "Though rent need not be paid by society to make land available, rental payments are very useful in guiding land into the most productive uses." Explain.

2. *Key Question   Explain why economic rent is a surplus to the economy as a whole but a cost of production from the standpoint of individual firms and industries. Explain: "Rent performs no 'incentive function' in the economy."*

3. If money capital is not an economic resource, why is interest paid and received for its use? What considerations account for the fact that interest rates differ greatly on various types of loans? Use these considerations to explain the relative size of the interest rates charged on the following:

   a. ten-year, $1000 government bond;

   b. a $20 pawnshop loan;

   c. a CMHA mortgage loan on a $120,000 house;

   d. a 36-month, $12,000 charted bank loan to finance an automobile;

   e. a 60-day, $100 loan from a personal finance company.

4. *Key Question   Why is the supply of loanable funds upsloping? Why is the demand for loanable funds downsloping? Explain the equilibrium interest rate and indicate factors that might cause it to change.*

5. What are the major economic functions of the interest rate? How might the fact that many firms are financing their investment activities internally affect the efficiency with which the interest rate performs its functions?

6. *Key Question   Distinguish between nominal and real interest rates. Which is more relevant in making investment decisions? If the nominal interest rate is 12% and the inflation rate is 8%, what is the real rate of interest? At various times during the 1970s, savers earned nominal rates of interest on their savings accounts that were less than the rate of inflation so that their savings earned negative real interest. Why, then, did they save?*

7. *Key Question   How do the concepts of accounting profits and economic profits differ? Why are economic profits smaller than accounting profits? What are the three basic sources of economic profits? Classify each of the following in accordance with these sources: a. a firm's profit from developing and patenting a ballpoint pen containing a permanent ink cartridge; b. a restaurant's profit that results from construction of a new highway past its door; c. the profit received by a firm benefiting from an unanticipated change in consumer tastes.*

8. Why is the distinction between insurable and uninsurable risks significant for the theory of profits? Carefully evaluate: "All economic profits can be traced to either uncertainty or the desire to avoid it." What are the major functions of profits?

9. Explain the absence of economic profit in a purely competitive, static economy. Realizing that the major function of profits is to allocate resources in accordance with consumer preferences, evaluate the allocation of resources in such an economy.

10. What has happened to wage, profit, interest, and rent shares of domestic income over time? Explain the alleged growth of labour's share in terms of structural changes in the economy. Have unions affected the size of labour's share?

11. (Applying the Theory)   Assume you borrow $5000 and pay back the $5000 plus $250 in interest at the end of the year. What is the interest rate? What would the interest rate be if the $250 of interest had been discounted at the time the loan was made? What would the interest rate be if you were required to repay the loan in equal monthly instalments?

CHAPTER 18

INCOME INEQUALITY AND POVERTY

T here is significant income inequality in Canada, and the incidence of poverty rose in the first half of the 1990s as a deep recession persisted in many parts of the country.

The issue of income inequality has come to the fore as the after-tax real family income stagnated over the course of the 1980s, having increased a meagre 0.5% compared with a 22% increase during the 1970s, 34% in the 1960s, and 27% in the 1950s.

Even more troubling is the fact that child poverty is on the rise, particularly in the "have" provinces of Ontario and British Columbia. Statistics Canada estimated that in 1993 30% of the nation's children under 18 were poor, or almost 1.5 million children.

How income should be distributed has a long and controversial history in both economics and philosophy. Should our national income and wealth be more, or less, equally distributed than is now the case? Or, is society making the proper response to the question "For whom?"

We begin by surveying some basic facts about the distribution of income in Canada. Next, the major causes of income inequality are considered. We then examine the trade-off between equality and efficiency. We will look at the poverty problem and consider existing income-maintenance programs, and the possibility of introducing a negative income tax to alleviate poverty.

BOX 18-1 THE BIG PICTURE

A persistent problem afflicting all market economies is unequal distribution of income. For example, some people command very high wages while others earn a wage that can barely pay for the absolute necessities of life. This chapter explains why there is such unequal distribution of the fruits of society's output of goods and services. Unfortunately, there are signs that income inequality is growing in Canada in the last decade of the twentieth century.

You may well ask why not simply legislate that everyone have an equal weekly or monthly income. The problem has to do with incentive to work and take on risk. We will discuss the trade-off between equality of income and getting the most out of scarce resources.

As you read this chapter, keep the following points in mind:
- Income inequality is caused by a variety of factors.
- A more equal distribution of income after a certain point can be accompanied by a reduction in the incentive to get the most out of limited resources.
- Poverty has both social and economic cost. It greatly increases suffering and impedes those who are poor from making an economic contribution to society because they cannot find work or do not have the required skills to get existing jobs.

INCOME INEQUALITY: SOME FACTS

How equally — or unequally — is income distributed in Canada? How wide is the gulf between rich and poor? Has the degree of income inequality increased or lessened over time?

PERSONAL INCOME DISTRIBUTION

Average income in Canada is among the highest in the world. The average income for all families was about $53,459 in 1993. In Table 18-1 we find that 2.1% of all families received less than $10,000 a year in 1993; 6.6% of all families received less than $20,000 per year. At the top of the income pyramid, we find that 20.5% of the families had incomes of $75,000 or more per year. These figures suggest *considerable* **income inequality** *in Canada*.

TRENDS IN INCOME INEQUALITY

Over time economic growth has raised incomes. In *absolute* terms, the entire distribution of income has been moving upward over time. Has this changed the *relative* distribution of income — that is, the income of one group compared to another? Incomes can move up in absolute terms and the degree of relative inequality may or may not be affected. Table 18-2 shows the relative distribution of income. Here we divide the total number of income receivers into five numerically equal groups, or *quintiles*, and show

the percentage of total personal (before tax) income received by each in selected years.

The relative distribution of income has been basically stable since 1951, when Statistics Canada began its detailed family-income surveys. Note that since 1951 the richest fifth of all families has received nine or ten times as much income as the poorest fifth.

CAUSES OF GROWING INEQUALITY

Growing income inequality in the last decade has attracted the attention of many scholars. A number of interrelated hypotheses have been suggested.

1. DEMOGRAPHIC CHANGES The entrance of large numbers of less experienced and less skilled "baby boomers" into the labour force in the 1970s and 1980s may have contributed to greater income inequality. As large numbers of younger people entered the labour force, the median age of the average worker fell. Since younger workers generally earn less than older workers, overall income inequality rose. In addition, the labour force participation of the wives of high-income husbands increased at a faster rate than for low-income husbands, adding to family income disparity. Finally, the number of unmarried or divorced women with children — who are very likely to be low income — has increased greatly.

2. IMPORT COMPETITION More competition from imports in the 1970s and 1980s severely reduced

TABLE 18-1 **The distribution of personal income by families and unattached individuals, 1993**

(a) (1) Personal income class	(2) Percent of all families in this class	(3) Percent of all unattached individuals in this class	(4) Percent of all families and unattached individuals in this class	(5) Percent of all families in this class and all lower classes	(6) Percent of all unattached individuals in this class and all lower classes	(7) Percent of all families and unattached individuals in this class and all lower classes
Under $10,000	2.1	18.4	7.3	2.1	18.4	7.3
$10,000 to $14,999	4.1	21.2	10.5	6.2	39.6	17.8
$15,000 to $19,999	6.6	12.0	8.4	12.8	51.6	26.2
$20,000 to $29,999	14.2	19.2	15.4	27.0	70.8	41.6
$30,000 to $49,999	26.9	20.9	24.5	53.5	91.7	66.1
$50,000 to $74,999	25.7	} 8.3	19.4	79.6	} 100.0	85.5
$75,000 and over	20.5		14.5	100.0		100.0
	100.0	100.0	100.0			

(b)	Families	Unattached individuals	Families & unattached individuals
Average 1993 income	$ 53,459	$ 24,386	$ 43,880
Median 1993 income	$ 47,069	$ 19,166	$ 36,109
1993 population	7,561,000	2,347,000	11,076,000

Source: Statistics Canada, *Income Distributions by Size in Canada, 1993* (Ottawa, December 1994), Tables 1, 24, and 34.

TABLE 18-2 **Percentage of total before-tax and after-tax income received by each one-fifth of families and unattached individuals**

	Before tax				After tax
Quintile	1951	1965	1989	1993	1993
Lowest 20%	4.4	4.4	4.8	4.7	5.7
Second 20%	11.2	11.8	10.5	10.2	11.4
Third 20%	18.3	18.0	16.9	16.5	17.2
Fourth 20%	23.3	24.5	24.6	24.8	24.7
Highest 20%	42.8	41.4	43.2	43.9	41.1
	100.0	100.0	100.0	100.0	100.0

Source: Statistics Canada, *Income Distributions: Incomes of Non-Farm Families and Individuals in Canada, 1951-1965* (Ottawa, 1969); *Income Distributions by Size in Canada, 1993* (Ottawa, 1994); and *Income After Taxes, Distributions by Size in Canada, 1993* (Ottawa, 1995), Table 26.

the demand for and employment of less skilled but highly paid workers in such industries as automobiles and steel. The decline in such jobs reduced the average wage for less skilled workers. It also swelled the ranks of workers in already low-paying industries, placing further downward pressure on wages in such industries. Similarly, the farming out of jobs of unskilled workers to lower-wage workers in less developed countries has exerted downward wage pressure in Canada.

3. DEMAND FOR HIGHLY SKILLED WORKERS Perhaps the most significant contributor to growing income inequality has been an increasing demand for workers with high levels of education and skills. Many companies have restructured their production techniques in ways that require more highly skilled, better-educated workers. Also, several industries requiring high-skilled workers have newly emerged or expanded greatly. Examples include computer software development, business consulting, biotechnology, health care, and advanced communications

GLOBAL PERSPECTIVE 18-1

Percentage of total income received by top one-fifth of income receivers, selected nations

The share of income going to the top fifth of income receivers varies among nations. Frequently income is less equally shared in poor nations than in rich ones.

Percent of total income earned by top fifth

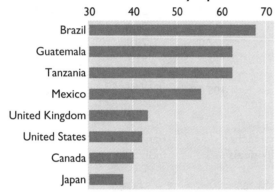

Source: *World Development Report, 1994*, pp. 220–221.

systems. Because skilled workers remain relatively scarce, their wages have been bid up so that the wage gap between them and less-educated workers has increased. The average male university graduate was paid about 70% more than a high school graduate in 1990, up from 45% in 1980. One study estimates that workers who use computers earn 10 to 15% more than otherwise similar workers who do not.

Caution: When we note growing income inequality we are *not* saying that "the rich are getting richer and the poor are getting poorer" in an absolute sense. Rather, what has happened is that, while incomes grew absolutely in all quintiles, growth was fastest in the top quintile.

THE LORENZ CURVE

The degree of income inequality can be seen through a **Lorenz curve**, as shown in Figure 18-1. Here we *cumulate* the "percent of families" on the horizontal axis and the "percent of income" on the vertical axis. The possibility of a completely equal distribution of income is represented by the diagonal line because such a line indicates that any given percentage of

families receives that same percentage of income. That is, if 20% of all families receives 20% of total income, 40% receives 40%, 60% receives 60%, and so on, all these points will fall on the diagonal line.

By plotting the 1993 data from Table 18-2, we locate the Lorenz curve to visualize the actual distribution of income. Observe that the bottom 20% of all families received 4.7% of the income, shown by point *a*; the bottom 40% received 14.9% (= 4.7 + 10.2), shown by point *b*; and so forth. The area between the diagonal line and the Lorenz curve, determined by the extent to which the Lorenz curve deviates from the line of perfect equality, indicates the degree of income inequality. The larger this area, the greater the degree of income inequality.

If the actual income distribution were perfectly equal, the Lorenz curve and the diagonal would coincide and the gap would disappear. At the opposite extreme is the situation of complete inequality, where 1% of families has 100% of the income and the rest have none. In that case, the Lorenz curve would coincide with the horizontal and right vertical axes of the graph, forming a right angle at point *f* as indicated by the heavy reverse "L" lines. This extreme degree of inequality would

FIGURE 18-1   The Lorenz curve

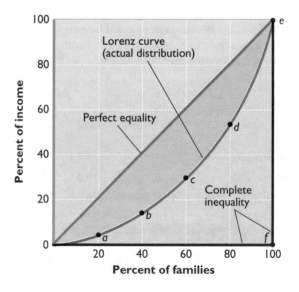

The Lorenz curve is a convenient means of visualizing the degree of income inequality. Specifically, the shaded area between the line of perfect equality and the Lorenz curve reflects the degree of income inequality.

be indicated by the entire area southeast of the diagonal (area 0*ef*).

The Lorenz curve can be used to contrast the distribution of income at different points in time, among different groups (for example, native-born and recent immigrants), before and after taxes and transfer payments are taken into account, or between different countries. The Lorenz curve has not shifted significantly since World War II. Comparisons with other countries suggest that the distribution of income in Canada is quite similar to most other industrially advanced countries. (**Key Question 2**)

TWO ADJUSTMENTS

There are two major criticisms of the data presented thus far. First, the income concept is too narrow. Second, the income accounting period of one year is too short.

BROADENED INCOME CONCEPT

The figures of Tables 18-1 and 18-2 show the distribution of *nominal* income and include not only wages, salaries, dividends, and interest but also all *cash transfer payments* such as unemployment insurance benefits and welfare payments to families with dependent children. The data are *before taxes* and therefore do not account for the effects of personal income and payroll taxes that are levied directly on income receivers. Nor do they include in-kind or **noncash transfers** that provide specified goods or services rather than cash. Noncash transfers include such things as subsidized public housing and dental care.

What impact would the use of a broader income concept — one that included both taxes and non-cash transfers — have on income distribution data? Because our overall tax system is only modestly progressive, after-tax data would reveal only slightly less inequality. Noncash transfers, however, are significant for the poorest quintile and their inclusion would diminish the degree of inequality.

INCOME MOBILITY: THE TIME DIMENSION

Another objection to the census data is that they portray the distribution of income in a single year and conceal the possibility that over a period of time — a few years, a decade, or even a lifetime — earnings might be more equal. If Ben earns $1000 in year 1 and $100,000 in year 2, while Holly earns $100,000 in year 1 and only $1000 in year 2, do we have income inequality? The answer depends on the period of measurement. Annual data would reveal great income inequality; but for the two-year period we have complete equality.

This is important because there is evidence to suggest that there is considerable "churning around" in the distribution of income over time. In fact most income receivers follow an age-earnings profile where their income starts at relatively low levels, reaches a peak during middle age, and then declines. A glance back at Figure 16-11 reveals this general pattern. It follows that even if people received the same stream of income over their lifetimes, considerable income inequality would still exist in any given year because of age differences. In any year the young and old would receive low incomes while the middle-aged received high incomes. This would occur despite complete equality of lifetime incomes.

What happens if we move from a "snapshot" view of income distribution in a single year to a "time exposure" view portraying the mobility of people between income classes over time? The answer is that we find considerable mobility both up and down, suggesting that income is more equally distributed over a 5-, 10-, or 20-year period than in a single year.

A recent U.S. study measures income mobility by tracing the movement of people from their quintile location in 1979 to their quintile status in 1988. It was found that slightly over two-thirds of those in the poorest quintile in 1979 had moved somewhere into the top three quintiles by 1988. Almost 18% of the lowest quintile jumped to the richest quintile during this decade. Undoubtedly this group included many who were in college or university in 1979, but who graduated and became high-income technicians, doctors, lawyers, and accountants by 1988. Two-thirds of the people in the middle quintile changed to another quintile in the ten-year period, approximately 20% becoming poorer and 47% becoming richer. For the richest quintile in 1979, one-third fell to a lower quintile by 1988.

The point of the study is that (a) there exists "significant household income mobility over time" and (b) the longer the time period considered, the more equal the distribution of income.

CAUSES OF INCOME INEQUALITY

The market economy is permissive of a high degree of income inequality. Factors contributing to income inequality include:

1. ABILITY DIFFERENCES People have different intellectual and physical abilities. Some are equipped to enter the highly paid fields of medicine and law. Others have the talent and drive to become great artists or musicians. On the other hand, some people can get only menial, low-paying jobs or are unable to work at all. Some are blessed with the physical ability and co-ordination to become highly paid professional athletes. Differences in ability mean that some individuals can make contributions to total output that command very high incomes, others cannot.

2. EDUCATION AND TRAINING Individuals differ significantly in the amounts of education and training they have obtained and, therefore, in their capacities to earn income. In part, these differences are a matter of voluntary choice. Smith chooses to enter the labour force upon high school graduation, while Jones decides to attend college or university. On the other hand, such differences may be involuntary: Smith's family may be unable to finance a college or university education or even to provide the necessary nutrition, shelter, or study conditions for Smith to do well in primary school.

3. JOB TASTES AND RISK Incomes differ because of differences in "job tastes." Those willing to take arduous, unpleasant jobs — for example, underground mining and automobile assembly — and work long hours with great intensity will tend to earn more. Some people boost their income by "moonlighting" — by holding two jobs. Individuals also differ in their willingness to assume risk. We refer here not only to the racing car driver, but to a person who takes an entrepreneurial risk. Though most fail, the fortunate few who gamble successfully on the introduction of a new product or service may realize very substantial incomes. Also, firms provide much on-the-job training. They tend to select workers with the most formal education for advanced and extensive on-the-job training.

4. DISTRIBUTION OF WEALTH How do income and wealth differ? Income is a *flow* concept; it represents a stream of wage and salary earnings, along with rents, interest, and profits, as portrayed in Chapter 5's circular flow. Wealth is a *stock* concept, reflecting at a particular moment the financial and real assets an individual has accumulated over time. A retired person may have very little income, but hold considerable wealth as a home, in savings accounts, and in a pension plan. A new college or university graduate may be earning a substantial income as an accountant, middle manager, or engineer, but has yet to accumulate significant wealth.

In fact, the ownership of wealth is very unequal and therefore the earnings from the wealth contribute to income inequality. Those who own more machinery, real estate, farmland, stocks and bonds, and savings accounts receive more income.

BOX 18-2 IN THE MEDIA

POVERTY GREW SHARPLY IN 1993: HALF MILLION MORE COUNTED AS POOR

BY EDWARD GREENSPON
Parliamentary Bureau

OTTAWA — Calling it a sombre year for poor people, the National Council of Welfare reported yesterday that poverty rates in Canada grew dramatically in 1993 despite the beginnings of an economic recovery.

The number of people living in poverty, as defined by the Council, grew to 4.8 million in 1993 from 4.3 million in 1992, the government advisory body reported in its annual profile. Addition of a half-million Canadians to the ranks of the poor brought the poverty rate to 17.4 per cent from 16.1 per cent in 1992.

The council says it is somewhat mystified by the sharp postrecession increase in poverty, although its figures show that the same pattern emerged after the 1981-82 recession. Council members concede that strong job growth in 1994 may have alleviated the situation somewhat.

The report uses a Statistics Canada definition of poverty as an income level at which at least 56.2 per cent of income goes to pay for food, shelter and housing. These cost the average Canadian family 36.2 per cent of its income.

Statscan's poverty line (the official term is the low-income cut off) in a large urban centre in 1993 was $15,452 for a single person, $20,945 for a couple and $30,655 for a family of four. The rate declines in smaller communities.

The high incidence of poverty, especially among children, and its stubbornness in the face of years of government programs provides a real-life backdrop to talk of social-security reform and welfare cutbacks.

"We are worried that another half million people are poor and we worry about the future," said Lucie Blais, the council's acting chairwoman.

One of the striking findings of the report is the high percentage of poor people who rely on wages rather than government cheques to get by. For most categories of poor people under 65 — with the notable exception of single mothers — government assistance makes up just about half of their total income, with the rest earned in the labour market.

"The myth is that most poor people are people that rely solely on welfare and UI and have no attachment to the labour force," said Kerstetter, the council's acting director. "But a huge proportion of poor families and individuals under 65 get significant amounts of their income from wages and salaries. They are working poor people."

The council has been among those who have counselled the government to redesign its programs to take these so-called working poor more into account.

Ms. Blais said it is unacceptable that people who are working should be in as dire straits as those on welfare. "We need to implement the social-security reform to give a revenue supplement to people who are working," she stated....

The disparities between those who are poor and those who are not is striking. Whereas an average working couple with children in Canada earns a pretax income of nearly $60,000 a year, the figure for those below the poverty line is just under $20,000. No group is

further behind the eight ball than poor single mothers, who on average are $8,500 below the poverty line.

The report documents the continued increase of children living in poverty, a number that has moved steadily upward since 1980. More than 1.4 million Canadian children — representing 20.8 per cent of all those under 18 — fall below the low-income cutoffs, the highest rate ever recorded....

The situation is most alarming among families headed by single mothers under 25 — 90 per cent of these family units fall below the poverty line. The figure falls to 58 per cent for single mothers aged 25 to 44 and is far lower for couples with children.

In general, family poverty is more pronounced when children are under seven. Once the youngest is in school, mothers are more likely to take jobs outside the home and improve their standard of living.

Source: Globe and Mail, April 6, 1995, pp. A1 and A2. Reprinted with permission.

The Story in Brief

Poverty in Canada is increasing. Many of those who are poor work but do not earn a sufficient wage to move them out of poverty. Poverty is rising most rapidly among children and families headed by single mothers under 25 years of age.

The Economics Behind the Story

• The growth of poverty has been most rapid among families headed by single mothers under 25. Many of these young mothers are unable to work because they have to raise their children. They do not have access to day-care facilities to allow them to participate in the work force.

• Many who are poor lack either the education or skills to acquire jobs that pay sufficiently high wages to get them out of poverty.

• What can the government do to help the poor acquire marketable skills that will raise their income potential?

5. MARKET POWER   Ability to "rig the market" on your own behalf is undoubtedly a factor in accounting for income inequality. Certain unions and professional groups have adopted policies that limit the supplies of their productive services, thereby boosting the incomes of their members. Legislation that provides for occupational licensing, as in the case of lawyers, doctors, and accountants, can exert market power favouring the licensed group.

6. DISCRIMINATION   Simple supply and demand analysis suggests how discrimination — in this case labour market discrimination — generates income inequality. Suppose gender discrimination restricts women to a few "female" occupations (secretaries and teachers). This means that the supplies of female workers will be great relative to demand in these few occupations so that wages and incomes will be low. Conversely, discrimination means males do not have to compete with women in "male" occupations. Supply is artificially limited relative to demand in these occupations with the result that wages and incomes are high.

7. LUCK, CONNECTIONS, MISFORTUNE   Luck, chance, and being in the right place at the right time have all caused individuals to stumble into fortunes. Discovering oil on a run-down farm or meeting the right press agent have accounted for some high incomes. Nor can personal contacts and political influence be discounted as means of attaining the higher income brackets. On the other hand, a host of misfortunes, such as prolonged illness, serious accident, death of the family breadwinner, and unemployment may plunge a family into relative poverty. The burden of such misfortunes is borne very unevenly by the population and contributes to the degree of income inequality. **(Key Question 4)**

QUICK REVIEW 18-1

1. Income inequality has remained largely unchanged in the last decade; currently the top fifth of all families receives about 43% of before-tax income and the bottom fifth receives under 5%.

2. The Lorenz curve portrays income inequality graphically.

3. Broadening the income concept and recognition of "churning" within the income distribution over time both lessen perceived income inequality.

4. Government taxes and transfer payments reduce income inequality.

5. Differences in ability, education, job tastes, property ownership, and market power — along with discrimination and luck — help explain income inequality.

EQUALITY VERSUS EFFICIENCY

Society ought to strive to eliminate, or at least minimize, income inequality. Unfortunately, there is a trade-off between equality and efficiency. Let's explore the case for and against greater equality to understand the nature of the trade-off.

THE CASE FOR EQUALITY: MAXIMIZING UTILITY

The basic argument for an equal distribution of income is that income equality is necessary if consumer satisfaction (utility) is to be maximized. The rationale for this argument is shown in Figure 18-2, where it is assumed that the money incomes of two individuals, Anderson and Brooks, are subject to diminishing marginal utility (Chapter 7). In any time period, income receivers spend the first dollars received on those products they value most — on products whose marginal utility is high. As their most pressing wants become satisfied, consumers then spend additional dollars of income on less important, lower marginal utility, goods. The identical diminishing "marginal utility from income" curves reflect the assumption that Anderson and Brooks have the same capacity to derive utility from income.

Now suppose there is $10,000 worth of income (output) to be distributed between Anderson and Brooks. The best or optimal distribution would be an equal distribution, which causes the marginal utility of the last dollar spent to be the same for both persons. We can prove this by demonstrating that for an initially unequal distribution of income, the combined total utility of the two individuals can be increased by distributing income more equally.

For example, suppose initially the $10,000 of income is distributed unequally so Anderson gets $2500 and Brooks receives $7500. We observe that the marginal utility from the last dollar received by Anderson is high (0a) and the marginal utility from Brooks's last dollar of income is low (0b). The redistribution of a dollar's worth of income from Brooks to Anderson — that is, towards greater equality —

would increase (by 0a – 0b) the combined total utility of the two consumers. Anderson's utility gain [area G in Figure 18-2(a)] exceeds Brooks's loss [area L in Figure 18-2(b)]. This will continue until income is equally distributed with each person receiving $5000. At this point, the marginal utility of the last dollar is identical for Anderson and Brooks (0a' = 0b') and hence further redistribution cannot increase total utility.

THE CASE FOR INEQUALITY: INCENTIVES AND EFFICIENCY

Although the logic of the argument for equality is sound, critics attack its fundamental assumption that there exists some fixed amount of income to be distributed. Critics of income equality argue that *the way in which income is distributed is an important determinant of economic growth — the amount of income produced and available for distribution.*

Suppose once again in Figure 18-2 that Anderson earns $2500 and Brooks $7500. In moving towards equality, society (government) must *tax* away some of Brooks's income and *transfer* it to Anderson. This tax-transfer process will diminish the income rewards of high-income Brooks and raise the income rewards of low-income Anderson and, in so doing, reduce the incentives of both to *earn* high incomes. Why should high-income Brooks work hard, save and invest, or undertake entrepreneurial risks, when the rewards from such activities will be reduced by taxation? And why should low-income Anderson be motivated to increase his income when government stands ready to transfer income to him? Taxes are a reduction in the rewards from increased productive effort; redistribution is a reward for diminished effort.

In the extreme, imagine a situation in which government levies a 100% tax on income and distributes the tax revenue equally to its citizens. Why

FIGURE 18-2 The utility-maximizing distribution of a given income

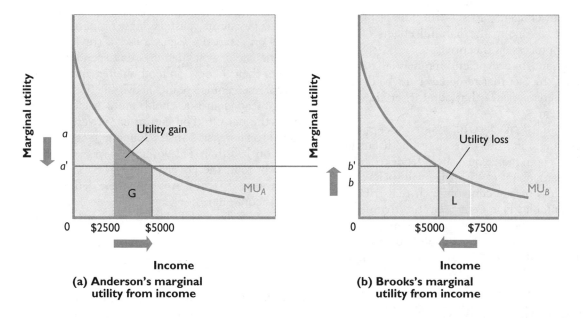

Proponents of income equality argue that, given identical "marginal utility from income" curves, Anderson and Brooks will maximize their combined utility when any given income (say, $10,000) is equally distributed. If income is unequally distributed ($2500 to Anderson and $7500 to Brooks), the marginal utility derived from the last dollar would be greater for Anderson (0a) than for Brooks (0b) and, thus, a redistribution towards equality will result in a net increase in total utility. The utility gain shown by area G in panel (a) exceeds the utility loss indicated by area L in panel (b). When equality is achieved, the marginal utility derived from the last dollar of income will be equal for both consumers (0a' = 0b'); therefore, there is no further redistribution of income that will increase total utility.

work hard? Why work at all? Why assume business risks? Why save — forgo current consumption — to invest? The economic incentives to get ahead will have been removed and the productive efficiency of the economy — and hence the amount of income to be distributed — will diminish. The way the income pie is distributed affects the size of that pie! *The basic argument for income inequality is that inequality is essential to maintain incentives to produce output and income.*

THE EQUALITY-EFFICIENCY TRADE-OFF

The essence of the income (in)equality debate is that there exists a fundamental **trade-off between equality and efficiency**. The problem for a society inclined towards social economic justice is how to achieve a more equal redistribution of income so as to minimize the adverse effects on economic efficiency. Consider this *leaky-bucket analogy*. Assume society agrees to shift income from the rich to the poor. But the money must be transferred from affluent to indigent in a leaky bucket. The leak represents an efficiency loss — the loss of output and income — due to the harmful effects of the tax-transfer process on incentives to work, to save and invest, and to accept entrepreneurial risk. It also reflects the fact that resources must be diverted to the bureaucracies that administer the tax-transfer system.

How much leakage will society accept and continue to endorse the redistribution? If cutting the income pie in more equal slices tends to shrink the pie, what amount of shrinkage will society tolerate? is a loss of one cent on each redistributed dollar acceptable? Five cents? Twenty-five cents? Forty cents? This is a critical, value-laden question that permeates future political debates over extensions and modifications of our income maintenance programs.

THE DISMAL ECONOMICS OF POVERTY

Many people are less concerned with the larger question of income distribution than they are with the more specific issue of inadequate income. Armed with some background information on income inequality, let's now turn to the poverty problem. How exten-

sive is poverty in Canada? What are the characteristics of the poor? And what is the best strategy to lessen poverty?

DEFINING POVERTY

Poverty does not lend itself to precise definition. But it helps to distinguish between absolute and relative poverty. **Absolute poverty** occurs when the basic material needs — food, clothing, and shelter — of an individual or family are not met. **Relative poverty** refers to an individual's or family's low income relative to others in society. While a family's basic material needs may be met, it would still be considered poor if its income relative to others is much lower.

While it is possible to eradicate absolute poverty, relative poverty will probably always be around, at least in a market economy, where some individuals are able to earn much more than others.

A family's needs have many determinants: its size, its health, the ages of its members, and so forth. Its means include currently earned income, transfer payments, past savings, property owned, and so on. Statistics Canada uses a (revised 1992) "low income cut-off": families that spend 54.7% or more of their income on food, shelter, and clothing (over 20 percentage points above the 32.5% of the average Canadian household) are considered to be below the cut-off. The cut-off or "poverty line" is related to family size. In 1993 an unattached person living on less than $11,967 a year was poor. For a family of four, the poverty line was $23,934; for a family of six, $31,114. Applying these definitions to 1993 income data for Canada, it was found that *14.5% of families and 40.8% of unattached individuals live in poverty.*

WHO ARE THE POOR?

Unfortunately for purposes of public policy, the poor are heterogeneous: they can be found in all geographic regions; they are whites, non-whites, and native peoples; they include large numbers of both rural and urban people; they are both old and young.

Yet, despite this pervasiveness, poverty is far from randomly distributed, as Table 18-3 demonstrates. An aging widow with four years of schooling living in an Atlantic town and prevented from seeking paid work by her four under-16 children

TABLE 18-3 **Incidence of low income by selected characteristics, 1993**

		ESTIMATED PERCENTAGE BELOW LOW INCOME CUT-OFF*	
		Families	**Unattached individuals**
All families and unattached individuals		14.5%	40.8%
By region	—Atlantic provinces	13.5	41.5
	— Quebec	16.8	48.7
By age of household head	— 24 and under	42.0	61.6
	— 25 to 34 years	21.6	30.6
	— 65 and over	9.4	51.1
By sex of household head — female		41.4	46.7
By marital status of household head — neither married nor single**		33.4	43.4
By weeks worked	— none	28.4	62.3
	— 1–9 weeks	39.3	71.9
	— 10–19 weeks	32.4	67.6
	— 20–29 weeks	23.3	53.0
	— 30–39 weeks	21.1	46.3
	— 40–48 weeks	11.7	28.8
	— 49–52 weeks	6.0	14.4
By education of household head — 0–8 years of school		19.2	64.7
	— some secondary	19.1	49.6
By origin of household head — Canadian born		13.3	39.4
	— non-Canadian born	19.3	48.7
By number of children younger than 16 years — none		9.6	40.8
	— 1	17.0	—
	— 2	21.5	—
	— 3 or more	26.6	—

*As defined on p. 44 of the source, families that on average spent 54.7% or more of their income on food, shelter, and clothing were considered to be in straitened circumstances and, therefore, below the 1992 low income cut-off. According to this criterion, it is estimated that 4.9 million persons — 3,470,000 in families and 1,433,000 unattached individuals — were below the low income cut-off in 1993. These represent 17.9% of the covered population, of whom 1,447,000 were children under 18 years of age.

**Divorced, separated, widowed.

Source: Statistics Canada, *Income Distribution by Size in Canada*, 1993 (Ottawa, 1994), Table 67 and Appendix Table 2.

still at home — well, she is likely to be poor. And when her children have left home and, she is over 70, her fortunes look no brighter. The strong correlation shown in Table 18-3 between working few weeks in the year and being poor is expected. However, note that 6% of families and 14.4% of unattached individuals who worked 49 to 52 weeks were still poor.

The high poverty rates for children are especially disturbing because in a very real sense poverty breeds poverty. Poor children are at greater risk for a range of long-term problems, including poor health and inadequate education, crime, drugs, and teenage pregnancy. Many of today's impoverished will reach adulthood unhealthy, illiterate, and unemployable. The increased concentration of poverty among children bodes poorly for reducing poverty in the future.

Recalling our previous discussion of movement or "churning" within the income distribution, we also note that there is considerable movement in and out of poverty. Just over half of those who are in poverty one year will remain below the poverty line the next year. On the other hand, poverty is much more persistent for some groups, in particular families headed by women, those with little education and few labour market skills, and those who are dysfunctional because of drugs, alcoholism, or mental illness.

THE "INVISIBLE" POOR

These facts and figures on the extent and character of poverty may be difficult to accept. After all, ours is an affluent society. How do we square the depressing statistics on poverty with everyday observations of abundance? The answer lies mainly in the fact that much Canadian poverty is hidden; it is largely invisible.

There are three reasons for this invisibility. First, a sizable proportion of the people in the poverty pool change from year to year. Research has shown that as many as one-half of those in poverty are poor for only one or two years before successfully climbing out of poverty. Many of these people are not visible as permanently downtrodden and needy. Second, the "permanently poor" are increasingly isolated. Poverty persists in the slums and ghettos of large cities and is not readily visible from the expressway or commuter train. Similarly, rural poverty and the chronically depressed areas of eastern Quebec and the Atlantic provinces are also off the beaten path. Third, and perhaps most important, the poor are politically invisible. They often do not have interest groups fighting the various levels of governments for their rights.

THE INCOME MAINTENANCE SYSTEM

The existence of a wide variety of income-maintenance programs is evidence that alleviation of poverty has been accepted as a legitimate goal of public policy. In recent years, income-maintenance programs have involved substantial monetary outlays and large numbers of beneficiaries. About one-half of the federal government's 1994–5 expenditures were transfer payments. The government estimated these $84 billion of expenditures would be disbursed as shown in Table 18-4. It should be noted, however, that the bulk of these transfers go to the non-poor, and only a few of these programs are specifically targeted at the poor.

In addition to all these programs, there is the **Canada Pension Plan (CPP)** — funded by obliga-

tory employee and employer contributions.[1] The maximum pension payable in 1992 was $636.11 a month. It increases each year, in January, by the percentage increase in the cost of living in the previous year.

The **Old Age Security (OAS)** pension is paid on application at age 65 to everyone resident in Canada for 40 years or for at least 10 years immediately before attaining the age of 65. The **Guaranteed Income Supplement (GIS)** is paid on application, subject to a means test, to those receiving the OAS pension but who have an income below a certain level. Considerably more than half of Canadians over 65 draw the GIS. Both the OAS pension and the GIS are increased every three months by the percentage increase in the cost of living in the previous three months.

Unemployment insurance (UI) was started in 1940 to insure *workers* against the hazards of losing their jobs. Certainly it has lessened the misery of the very large number of involuntarily unemployed during recessionary periods. In the early 1970s, unemployment insurance benefits were greatly increased so that there was created a positive incentive for *marginal* workers to enter the labour force, not to work, but to qualify for benefits. In 1977, benefits were decreased slightly while qualifying for them was made more difficult. By the early 1990s the federal government tightened the rules to qualify for UI, as it coped with mounting deficits. By mid-1995 the number of persons paid UI had fallen from two years earlier.

"THE WELFARE MESS"

There is no doubt the social insurance system — as well as local welfare, public housing, rent subsidies, minimum-wage legislation, agricultural subsidies, free dental treatment and drugs for those on welfare, private transfers through charities, veterans' benefits, and pensions — provides important means of alleviating poverty. Nevertheless, the system, broadly defined, has been subject to a wide variety of criticisms.

1. Work Incentives It is argued that many programs impair incentives to work. For example,

---

[1] The Quebec Pension Plan, for residents of that province, is similar.

TABLE 18-4 **Federal government transfer payments**

Program	Estimated expenditures, fiscal year ending March 31, 1995, millions of dollars
Unemployment insurance	$19,013
Old age security, guaranteed income supplement, and spouses' allowances	20,621
Established Programs Financing to support provision by the provinces of:	
health services	6,713
post-secondary education	2,119
Canada Assistance Plan to bear 50% of cost to provinces of such welfare as child and family support services, as well as payments under the Vocational Rehabilitation of Disabled Persons Act	7,411
Veterans' pensions and allowances	3,146
Transfers to other governments for Human Resource Development Programs	482
Indian and Inuit affairs: improved housing, social and medical services, education and training, economic and employment development, and community infrastructures	3,303
Transfers to the territorial governments	1,193
Other transfers (mostly to the provinces)	20,226
Total	84,227

Source: Government of Canada, *1994–1995 Estimates, Part I: The Government Expenditure Plan and Part II: The Main Estimates* (Ottawa: Supply and Services Canada, 1995).

many people on welfare would actually lose money by going to work. Since $1 of benefits is often lost for every $1 earned, there is no incentive to become a productive member of society. Moreover, a family going off welfare loses its right to free dental care and free medicine. Thus, the individual or family can be worse off by working.

Similarly, unemployment insurance benefits allow unemployed workers to seek a new job at a more leisurely pace, contributing to both the volume and duration of unemployment. Also, growing welfare benefits are financed by higher and higher taxes on the more productive, higher-income members of society, thereby weakening their incentives to work, take risks, and invest.

2. ABUSES AND INEQUITIES Many income-maintenance programs often benefit those who are *not* needy. This is particularly the case with unemployment insurance. The extension of coverage has induced many secondary income earners — those not primarily responsible for the family's income — to enter the labour force. Some of these people, as men-

tioned above, work barely long enough to qualify for unemployment insurance benefits. Other secondary income earners, while having an honest attachment to the labour force, on losing their jobs involuntarily, have no need of unemployment insurance benefits because of the continuing high income of the primary income earner. However, it is true that there are many families where the earnings of each spouse are so low that both must work to have a decent living standard for the family. But it is precisely those people who work, pay taxes, and make unemployment insurance contributions on their minimum wage incomes who are most victimized by someone's spouse drawing more in unneeded benefits than these working poor make in their unpleasant jobs.

3. ADMINISTRATIVE COSTS AND PROBLEMS Critics charge that the growth of our welfare programs has created a clumsy and inefficient system, characterized by red tape and dependent on a huge bureaucracy for its administration. As such, administration costs account for large portions of the total budget of many programs.

QUICK REVIEW 18-2

1. The fundamental argument for income equality is that it maximizes consumer utility; the basic argument for income inequality is that it is necessary to stimulate economic incentives.

2. Absolute poverty occurs when the basic material needs are not met. Relative poverty refers to an individual or family's low income relative to the rest of society.

3. By government standards some 4.9 million people or 17.9% of the population live in poverty.

4. Our income maintenance system is composed of both social insurance programs and public assistance ("welfare") programs.

REFORM PROPOSALS

NEGATIVE INCOME TAX (NIT)

This criticism has led to support for a new approach to income maintenance. The contention is that the entire patchwork of existing income maintenance programs should be replaced by a **negative income tax (NIT)**. The term NIT suggests that the government should subsidize households with NIT payments when household incomes fall *below* a certain level.

COMPARING PLANS Let's examine the two critical elements of any NIT plan. First, a NIT plan specifies a **guaranteed annual income** below which family incomes would not be allowed to fall. Second, the plan embodies a **benefit-reduction rate** (sometimes called a **marginal transfer rate**), which indicates the rate at which subsidy benefits — transfer payments — are reduced or "lost" as a consequence of earned income.

Consider Plan One of the three plans shown in Table 18-5. In Plan One, guaranteed annual income is $8000 and the benefit reduction loss rate is 50%. If the family earns no income, it will receive a NIT subsidy of $8000. If it earns $4000, it will lose $2000 ($4000 of earnings *times* the 50% benefit-reduction rate) of subsidy benefits and total income will be $10,000 (= $4000 of earnings *plus* $6000 of subsidy). If $8000 is earned, the subsidy will fall to $4000, and so on. Note that at $16,000 the NIT subsidy becomes zero. The level of earned income at which the subsidy disappears and at which normal (positive) income tax applies on *further* increases in earned income is called the **break-even income**.

We might criticize Plan One on the grounds that a 50% benefit-reduction rate is too high and therefore does not provide sufficient incentives to work. Thus, in Plan Two the $8000 guaranteed income is retained, but the benefit-reduction rate is reduced to 25%. But note that the break-even level of income increases to $32,000 and many more families would now qualify for NIT subsidies. Furthermore, a family with any given earned income will now receive a larger NIT subsidy. For

TABLE 18-5   The negative income tax: three plans for a family of four

Plan One ($8000 guaranteed annual income and 50% benefit-reduction rate)			Plan Two ($8000 guaranteed annual income and 25% benefit-reduction rate)			Plan Three ($16,000 guaranteed annual income and 50% benefit-reduction rate)		
(1) Earned income	(2) NIT subsidy	(3) Total income	(1) Earned income	(2) NIT subsidy	(3) Total income	(1) Earned income	(2) NIT subsidy	(3) Total income
$0	$8,000	$ 8,000	$0	$8,000	$ 8,000	$0	$16,000	$16,000
4,0000	6,000	10,000	8,000	6,000	14,000	8,000	12,000	20,000
8,000	4,000	12,000	16,000	4,000	20,000	16,000	8,000	24,000
12,0000	2,000	14,000	24,000	2,000	26,000	24,000	4,000	28,000
16,000*	0	16,000	32,000*	0	32,000	32,000*	0	32,000

*Indicates break-even income. Determined by dividing the guaranteed income by the benefit-reduction rate.

both of these reasons, a reduction of the benefit-reduction rate to enhance work incentives will raise the cost of a NIT plan.

Examining Plans One and Two, still another critic might argue that the guaranteed income is too low, in that it does not get families out of poverty. Plan Three raises the guaranteed income to $16,000 and retains the 50% benefit-reduction rate of Plan One. While Plan Three does a better job of raising the incomes of the poor, it too yields a higher break-even income and would therefore be more costly than Plan One. Furthermore, if the $16,000 income guarantee of Plan Three were coupled with Plan Two's 25% benefit-reduction rate to strengthen work incentives, the break-even income level would shoot up to $64,000 and add even more to NIT costs.[2]

_____

[2] You may have sensed the generalization that, given the guaranteed income, the break-even level of income varies *inversely* with the benefit-reduction rate. Specifically, the break-even income can be found by dividing the guaranteed income by the benefit-reduction rate. Hence for Plan One, $8,000/0.50 = $16,000. Can you also demonstrate that given the benefit-reduction rate, the break-even level of income varies *directly* with the guaranteed income?

GOALS AND CONFLICTS By comparing these three plans, we find there are trade-offs among the goals of an "ideal" income maintenance plan. First, a plan should be effective in getting families out of poverty. Second, it should provide adequate incentives to work. Third, the plan's costs must not be high. Table 18-5 tells us that these three objectives conflict with one another and that compromises or trade-offs are necessary.

Plan One, with a low guaranteed income and a high benefit-reduction rate, keeps costs down. But the low-income guarantee means it is not very effective in eliminating poverty and the high benefit-reduction rate weakens work incentives. In comparison, Plan Two has a lower benefit-reduction rate and therefore stronger work incentives. But it is more costly, because it involves a higher break-even income and therefore pays benefits to more families.

Compared to Plan One, Plan Three entails a higher guaranteed income and is more effective in eliminating poverty. While work incentives are the same as with Plan One, the higher guaranteed income makes the plan more costly. The problem is to find the magic numbers that will provide a "decent" guaranteed income, maintain "reasonable" incentives to work, and entail "acceptable" costs. (**Key Question 10**)

CHAPTER SUMMARY

1. The distribution of personal income in Canada reflects considerable inequality. Little change has occurred in the postwar period. The Lorenz curve shows the degree of income inequality graphically.

2. The use of a broadened concept of income that includes noncash transfers and taxes *and* recognition that the positions of individual families in the distribution of income change over time would reveal less income inequality than do standard census data.

3. Government taxes and transfers — particularly transfers — lessen the degree of income inequality significantly.

4. Causes of income inequality include discrimination and differences in abilities, education and training, job tastes, property ownership, and market power.

5. The basic argument for income equality is that it maximizes consumer satisfaction from a given income. The main argument against income equality is that equality undermines incentives to work, invest, and assume risks, thereby tending to reduce the amount of income available for distribution.

6. Absolute poverty occurs when the basic material needs are not met. Relative poverty refers to an individual or family's low income relative to the rest of society. Absolute poverty can be eradicated, but relative poverty is much more difficult to resolve.

7. Current statistics suggest that about 18% of the country lives in poverty. Poverty is concentrated among the poorly educated, the aged, and families headed by women.

8. Our present income maintenance system is made up of social insurance programs (Canada Pension Plan and unemployment insurance benefits), universal programs (Old Age Security Pension), and public assistance or welfare programs. The present welfare programs have been criticized as being administratively inefficient, fraught with inequities, and detrimental to work incentives. Some economists believe that a negative income tax would provide a superior income maintenance system.

TERMS AND CONCEPTS

absolute poverty (p. 386)
benefit-reduction rate (marginal transfer rate) (p. 390)
break-even income (p. 390)
Canada Pension Plan (p. 388)
equality–efficiency trade-off (p. 386)
guaranteed annual income (p. 390)
Guaranteed Income Supplement (p. 388)

income inequality (p. 378)
Lorenz curve (p. 380)
negative income tax (p. 390)
noncash transfers (p. 381)
Old Age Security (p. 388)
relative poverty (p. 386)
unemployment insurance benefits (p. 388)

QUESTIONS AND STUDY SUGGESTIONS

1. Using quintiles, briefly summarize the degree of income inequality in Canada.

2. *Key Qestion*   *Assume Al, Beth, Carol, David, and Ed receive incomes of $500, $250, $125, $75, and $50 respectively. Construct and interpret a Lorenz curve for this five-person economy. What percentage of total income is received by the richest and by the poorest quintiles?*

3. Why is the lifetime distribution of income more equal than the distribution in any specific year?

4. *Key Question*   *Briefly discuss the major causes of income inequality. With respect to income inequality, is there any difference between inheriting property and inheriting a high IQ? Explain.*

5. Use the "leaky-bucket analogy" to discuss the equality-efficiency trade-off. Compared to our present income maintenance system, do you believe that a negative income tax would reduce the leak?

6. Should a nation's income be distributed to its members according to their contributions to the production of that total income or to the members' needs? Should society attempt to equalize income or economic opportunities? Are the issues of "equity" and "equality" in the distribution of income synonymous? To what degree, if any, is income inequality equitable?

7. Analyze in detail: "There need be no trade-off between equality and efficiency. An 'efficient' economy that yields an income distribution that many regard as unfair may cause those with meagre income rewards to become discouraged and stop trying. Hence, efficiency is undermined. A fairer distribution of rewards may generate a higher average productive effort on the part of the population, thereby enhancing efficiency. If people think they are playing a fair economic game and this belief causes them to try harder, an economy with an equitable income distribution may be efficient as well."

8. Comment on or explain:

a. "To endow everyone with equal income will certainly make for very unequal enjoyment and satisfaction."

b. "Equality is a 'superior good': the richer we become, the more of it we can afford."

c. "The mob goes in search of bread, and the means it employs is generally to wreck the bakeries."

d. "Under our welfare system we have foolishly clung to the notion that employment and receipt of assistance must be mutually exclusive."

e. "Some freedoms may be more important in the long run than freedom from want on the part of every individual."

f. "Capitalism and democracy are really a most improbable mixture. Maybe that is why they need each other — to put some rationality into equality and some humanity into efficiency."

g. "The incentives created by the attempt to bring about a more equal distribution of income are in conflict with the incentives needed to generate increased income."

9. What are the major criticisms of our present income maintenance system?

10. *Key Question* *The following table contains three illustrative negative income tax (NIT) plans.*

Plan One			Plan Two			Plan Three		
Earned income	NIT subsidy	Total income	Earned income	NIT subsidy	Total income	Earned income	NIT subsidy	Total income
$0	$4,000	$4,000	$0	$4,000	$4,000	$0	$8,000	$ 8,000
2,000	3,000	5,000	4,000	3,000	7,000	4,000	6,000	10,000
4,000	2,000	6,000	8,000	2,000	10,000	8,000	4,000	12,000
6,000	1,000	7,000	12,000	1,000	13,000	12,000	2,000	14,000

a. *Determine the basic benefit, the benefit-reduction rate, and the break-even income for each plan.*

b. *Which plan is the most costly? The least costly? Which plan is the most effective in reducing poverty? The least effective? Which plan embodies the strongest disincentive to work? The weakest disincentive to work?*

c. *Use your answers in part b to explain the following statement: "The dilemma of the negative income tax is that you cannot bring families up to the poverty level and simultaneously preserve work incentives and minimize program costs."*

11. "The father of a child has a responsibility to help support that child, irrespective of whether he is married to the mother. In addition, the able-bodied single mother has a responsibility to help support her child by working." Do you agree? How might these "principles" be incorporated into a welfare program? What problems might arise in implementing this program in the real world?

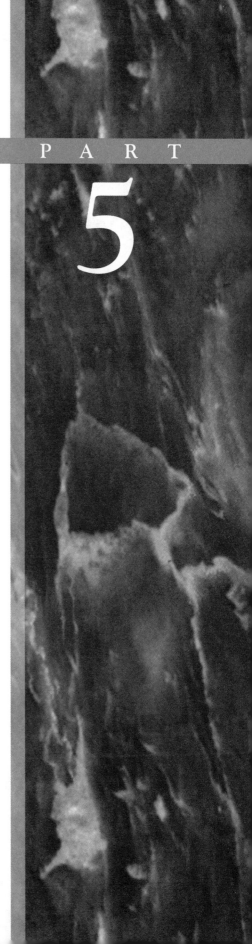

GOVERNMENT AND CURRENT ECONOMIC PROBLEMS

GOVERNMENT AND MARKET FAILURE: PUBLIC GOODS, THE ENVIRONMENT, AND INFORMATION PROBLEMS

The economic activities of government affect your well-being every day. If you attend a college or university, taxpayers heavily subsidize your education. When you receive a cheque from your part-time or summer job, you see deductions for income and payroll taxes. The beef in your Big Mac has been examined by government inspectors to prevent contamination and to ensure quality. Laws requiring seat belts and motorcycle helmets — and the sprinkler system government mandates in your dormitory — are all intended to enhance your safety. If you are a woman, a member of a minority group, or disabled, an array of legislation is designed to enhance your education and employment opportunities.

In this chapter and in Chapter 20 we will identify some of the problems government faces in carrying out its economic activities. We begin by returning to the topic of *market failure* introduced in Chapter 5. Our tools of marginal analysis permit us to provide a fuller discussion of public goods and externalities. Next, the pervasive externality — pollution — is discussed in some detail. Finally, we examine *information failures* in the private sector to determine their implication for government participation in the economy.

In Chapter 20 our discussion of government continues with an analysis of *government failure* and the microeconomics of taxation. Chapter 21 probes the farm problem. The analysis in this present chapter and in Chapter 20 will enhance your understanding of government's involvement in the economy.

BOX 19-1 THE BIG PICTURE

Throughout this book we have extolled the great virtues of markets in getting the most out of the available limited resources and producing those goods and services society wants most. But while markets have these wonderful virtues, they sometimes fail to do their job. As noted in Chapter 5, markets fail in the case of public goods; it is impossible to exclude those not paying for a public good from consuming it. Some people will consume a public good and try to avoid paying for it. Markets also fail when there are third party effects — a firm producing product X but polluting the air in the process will impose a cost on those living in the vicinity. The market price of product X, moreover, will not reflect the cost the pollution inflicts on those who suffer its effect. Another case of market failure discussed in this chapter is information

failures. The pure competitive market model assumes perfect information. In the absence of such an ideal state, markets will not bring about productive and allocative efficiency.

As you read this chapter, keep the following points in mind:

- It will be helpful to re-read the parts of Chapter 5 dealing with public good and externalities to refresh your memory of their definitions.
- The function of markets is to co-ordinate production and consumption decisions in a world of limited resources and unlimited wants. You will better appreciate the notion of "market failure" — instances when it fails to fulfil this function — if you remind yourself of the function of markets.

PUBLIC GOODS: EXTENDING THE ANALYSIS

A *private* good is divisible — it comes in small enough units to be afforded by individual buyers. It is also subject to the exclusion principle — those unable or unwilling to pay are excluded from the product's benefits.

A market demand curve for a private good is the *horizontal* summation of demand curves representing each buyer (review Table 4-2 and Figure 4-2). If Adams wants to buy three hot dogs at $1 each; Benson, one hot dog; and Conrad, two hot dogs; the market demand will reflect that six hot dogs (= 3 + 1 + 2) are demanded at a $1 price. The market demand resulting from the sum of the desires of each potential buyer creates a possibility for sellers to gain revenue and garner a profit. The equilibrium amount of a private good produced and purchased is dictated by product price, jointly determined by market demand and supply. This equilibrium output is optimal — it maximizes the combined well-being of the buyers and sellers, the only people affected by the transactions.

A snag develops, however, if we try to apply this same line of thinking to a public good. A *public good* is indivisible and does not fit the exclusion principle. Once the good is provided, the producer cannot exclude nonpayers from receiving its indivisible

benefits. Because potential buyers will obtain the benefit from a public good whether or not they pay for it, they will *not* reveal their true preferences for it. They will become *free riders* who will *not* voluntarily pay for the public good in the marketplace. *The market demand curve for a public good will be nonexistent or significantly understated.* The demand for the product expressed in the marketplace will not generate enough revenue to cover the costs of production, even though the collective benefits of the good may exceed the economic costs.

DEMAND FOR PUBLIC GOODS

How might we determine society's optimal (economically efficient) amount of a public good, in view of this problem? Suppose Adams and Benson are the only people in the economy and their true demand schedules for a public good, say, national defence, are shown as columns 1 and 2 and columns 1 and 3 of Table 19-1.

These demand schedules are "phantom" demand curves since the two people will not actually reveal their preferences in the marketplace. Instead, we assume this information has been discovered through a survey indicating Adams's and Benson's willingness to pay for each added unit of the public good, rather than go without it.

TABLE 19-1 Demand for a public good, two individuals

(1) Quantity	(2) Adams's willingness to pay (price)		(3) Benson's willingness to pay (price)		(4) Collective willingness to pay (price)
1	$4	+	$5	=	$9
2	3	+	4	=	7
3	2	+	3	=	5
4	1	+	2	=	3
5	0	+	1	=	1

FIGURE 19-1 The optimal amount of a public good

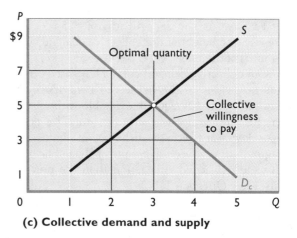

(c) Collective demand and supply

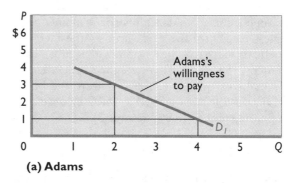

(b) Benson

(a) Adams

Suppose government produces 1 unit of this public good. Because the exclusion principle does not apply, neither Adams nor Benson will voluntarily offer to pay for this unit because each can consume it without paying. Adams's consumption of the good does not preclude Benson from also consuming it and vice-versa. But the combined amount of money these two citizens are willing to pay, rather than each not having this one unit of the good, can be determined through Table 19-1. Columns 1 and 2 show that Adams would be willing to pay $4 for the first unit of the public good; columns 1 and 3 show that Benson would be willing to pay $5 for it. The $9 price (column 4) these two are jointly willing to pay is the sum of the amounts *each* is willing to pay. For the second unit of the public good the collective price they are willing to pay is $7 (=$3 by Adams plus $4 by Benson).

We could then do the same for the third unit, and so on. Looking at the collective willingness to pay (column 4) for each additional unit, we construct a collective demand schedule for a public good. Rather than adding the *quantities demanded* at each price as when determining the market demand for a private good, we are adding the *prices* people collectively are willing to pay for the last unit of the public good at each quantity demanded.

Figure 19-1 shows the same summing procedure graphically, using data from Table 19-1 to illustrate the adding-up process. We are summing Adams's and Benson's demand curves for the public good *vertically* to derive the collective demand curve.

The collective demand curve D_c for the pubic good shown in (c) is found by summing vertically the individual demand curves D_1 and D_2 exhibited in (a) and (b). Government should provide 3 units of the public good because at that quantity the combined marginal benefit, as measured by the citizens' willingness to pay for the last unit (shown by D_c), equals the good's marginal cost (shown by S).

The height of the collective demand curve D_c at 2 units of output, for example, is $7 — the sum of the amount that Adams and Benson together are willing to pay for the second unit (= $3 + $4). Likewise, the height of the collective demand curve at 4 units of the public good is $3 (= $1 + $2).

Our collective demand curve D_c is based on the monetary value of the perceived benefits of the extra units that are equally available to both persons for simultaneous consumption. The curve slopes downward because of the law of diminishing marginal utility: Successive units of the public good will yield less added satisfaction than the previous units. (**Key Question 1**)

OPTIMAL QUANTITY OF A PUBLIC GOOD

We can now determine the optimal quantity of the specific public good alluded to in Figure 19-1. The collective demand curve D_c measures the marginal benefit of each unit of this particular good to society, whereas the supply curve S measures the marginal cost of each unit. The supply curve slopes upward because of the law of diminishing returns, which applies whether making missiles (public goods) or mufflers (private goods).

Optimal output occurs when marginal benefit equals marginal cost (MB = MC). In this case, the optimal quantity of the public good is 3 units — the intersection of the collective demand curve D_c and the supply curve S. At 3 units the combined willingness to pay for the extra unit — the marginal benefit to society — just matches that unit's marginal cost ($5 = $5). This "marginal benefit equals marginal cost" principle is analogous to the MR = MC output rule and the MRP = MRC input rule for maximizing profit. (**Key Question 2**)

BENEFIT-COST ANALYSIS

Economic theory thus provides guidance to efficient decision making in the public sector. This guidance can be helpful in understanding **benefit-cost analysis**.

CONCEPT Suppose government is contemplating a flood-control project. The economizing problem tells us that any decision to use more resources in the public sector will involve both a benefit and a cost. The benefit is the extra satisfaction resulting from the output of more public goods; the cost is the loss of satisfaction associated with the accompanying decline in the production of private goods (or some alternative public good). Should the resources be shifted from the private to the public sector? "Yes," *if* the benefits from the extra public goods exceed the cost resulting from having fewer private goods. "No," *if* the value or cost of the forgone private goods is greater than the benefits associated with the extra public goods.

But benefit-cost analysis can indicate more than whether a public program is worth doing. It can also help government decide the extent to which a specific project should be pursued. Economic questions are not questions to be answered simply by "Yes" or "No," but rather, matters of "how much" or "how little."

There is no doubt that a flood-control project is a public good since the exclusion principle is not readily applicable. Should government undertake a flood-control project in a particular river valley? If so, what is the proper size or scope for the project?

ILLUSTRATION Table 19-2 lists a series of increasingly ambitious and increasingly costly flood-control plans. To what extent, if at all, should government undertake flood control? The answers depend on costs and benefits. Costs in this case are largely the capital costs of constructing and maintaining levees and reservoirs; benefits are reduced flood damage.

A glance at all the plans shows that for each plan total benefits (column 4) exceed total costs (column 2), indicating that a flood-control project on this river is economically justifiable. We can see this directly in column 6 where total annual costs (column 2) are subtracted from total annual benefits (column 4).

But the question of the optimal size or scope for this project remains. This answer is determined by comparing the additional, or *marginal*, cost and the additional, or *marginal*, benefit associated with each plan. The guideline is the one we just established: Pursue an activity or project as long as the marginal benefit (column 5) exceeds the marginal cost (column 3). Stop the activity or project at, or as close as possible to, that point at which the marginal benefit equals the marginal cost.

In this case Plan C — the medium-sized reservoir — is the best plan. Plans A and B are too

TABLE 19-2   Benefit-cost analysis for a flood-control project

(1) Plan	(2) Total annual cost of project	(3) Marginal cost	(4) Total annual benefit (reduction in damage)	(5) Marginal benefit	(6) Net benefit or (4) - (2)
Without protection	$ 0		$ 0		$ 0
A: Levees	3,000	$ 3,000	6,000	6,000	3,000
B: Small reservoir	10,000	7,000	16,000	10,000	6,000
C: Medium reservoir	18,000	8,000	25,000	9,000	7,000
D: Large reservoir	30,000	12,000	32,000	7,000	2,000

Source: Adapted from Otto Eckstein, *Public Finance*, 3d ed. (Englewood Cliffs, N.J.: Prentice-Hall, Inc., 1973), p. 23. Used with permission.

modest; in both cases the marginal benefit exceeds the marginal cost. Plan D's marginal cost ($12,000) exceeds the marginal benefit ($7000) and therefore cannot be justified. Plan D isn't economically justifiable; it overallocates resources to this project. Plan C is closest to the optimum; it expands flood control so long as marginal benefits exceed marginal costs.

Seen slightly differently, the **marginal benefit = marginal cost rule** will determine which plan provides the maximum excess of total benefits (column 4) over total costs (column 2) or, in other words, the plan that yields the maximum *net* gain or benefit to society. We confirm directly in column 6 that the maximum net benefit (of $7000) is associated with Plan C.

Benefit-cost analysis shatters the myth that "economy in government" and "reduced government spending" are synonymous. "Economy" is concerned with using scarce resources efficiently. If a government program yields a lower marginal benefit than the marginal benefit attainable from the best alternative private use — that is, if costs exceed benefits — then the proposed public program should *not* be undertaken. But if benefits exceed cost, then it would be uneconomical or "wasteful" *not* to spend on that government program. Economy in government does *not* mean minimizing public spending; it means allocating resources between the private and public sectors until no net benefits can be had from further reallocations. (**Key Question 3**)

QUICK REVIEW 19-1

1. The demand for a public good is found by vertically adding the prices that members of the society are willing to pay for each unit of output at various output levels.

2. The optimal social amount of a public good is the amount when the marginal benefit and marginal cost of the good are equal.

3. Benefit-cost analysis is the method of evaluating alternative projects or sizes of projects by comparing marginal benefits and marginal costs.

EXTERNALITIES REVISITED

We can now better understand Chapter 5's discussion of government policies designed to correct the market failure we call externalities or spillovers. Recall that a spillover is a cost or benefit accruing to an individual or group — a third party — that is *external* to the market transaction. An example of a spillover cost is pollution; an example of a spillover benefit, inoculations. When there are spillover costs, an overproduction of the product occurs and there is an overallocation of resources to this use. Underproduction and underallocation of resources result from spillover benefits. Let's demonstrate both graphically.

SPILLOVER COSTS

Figure 19-2(a) illustrates how spillover or external costs affect the allocation of resources. When spillover costs occur — when producers shift some of their costs onto the community — their marginal costs are lower. The supply curve does not include or "capture" all the costs legitimately associated with production of the good. Therefore, the producer's supply curve, S, understates total costs of production; it lies to the right of the supply curve, which would include all costs, S_t. By polluting — by creating spillover costs — the firm enjoys lower production costs and the supply curve S.

The result, shown in Figure 19-2(a), is that equilibrium output Q_e is larger than optimal output Q_o. This means resources are *overallocated* to the production of this commodity, and too many units of the product are produced.

SPILLOVER BENEFITS

Figure 19-2(b) shows the impacts of spillover benefits on resource allocation. Spillover benefits mean the market demand curve, which reflects only private benefits, understates total benefits. The market demand curve does not capture all the benefits associated with the provision and consumption of goods and services entailing spillover benefits. Thus D in Figure 19-2(b) indicates the benefits private individuals derive from, say, inoculations against communicable diseases. Watson and Wienberg privately benefit when they get vaccinated, but so too do

associates Alvarez and Anderson who are less likely to contract the disease from them. Magnified to the entire population, inoculations mean a healthier and more productive workforce, yielding widespread output and income benefits to society. D_t is drawn to include the private benefits (D) from inoculations *plus* the additional benefits accruing to society at large.

While market demand D and supply S_t would yield an equilibrium output of Q_e, this output would be less than the optimal output Q_o, shown by the intersection of D_t and S_t. The market would not produce enough vaccinations; resources would be underallocated to this use.

Economists have explored several approaches to solving the problems of spillover costs and spillover benefits. We know from Chapter 6 that many of these remedies involve government. But let's first look at circumstances where government intervention is not needed.

INDIVIDUAL BARGAINING

In some situations externalities can be solved through individual bargaining.

COASE THEOREM   According to the **Coase theorem**, conceived by Ronald Coase, negative or positive spillovers do *not* require government intervention where (1) property ownership is clearly defined, (2) the number of people involved is small, and (3) bargaining costs are negligible.

FIGURE 19-2   **Spillover costs and spillover benefits**

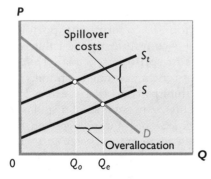

(a) The case of spillover costs

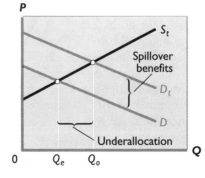

(b) The case of spillover benefits

With spillover costs in (a) we find that the lower costs borne by businesses, as reflected in S, fail to reflect all costs, as embodied in S_t. Consequently, the equilibrium output Q_e is greater than the efficient or optimal output Q_o. Spillover benefits in (a) cause society's total benefits from a product, as shown by D_t, to be understated by the market demand curve, D. As a result, the equilibrium output Q_e is less than the optimal output Q_o.

Government should confine its role under these circumstances to encouraging bargaining between affected individuals or groups. Because the economic self-interests of the parties are at stake, bargaining with one another will enable them to find an acceptable solution to the problem. Property rights place a price tag on an externality, creating an opportunity cost for both sides. A compelling incentive emerges for the parties to find ways to solve the externality problem.

EXTENDED EXAMPLE   Suppose the owner of a large parcel of forest land is considering contracting with a logging company to clear-cut (totally cut) thousands of hectares of mature fir trees. The complication is that the forest surrounds a lake with a popular resort on its shore. The resort is on land owned by the resort owner. The unspoiled beauty of the general area attracts vacationers from all over the nation to the resort. Should provincial or local government intervene to prevent the tree cutting?

According to the Coase theorem, the forest owner and the resort owner can resolve this situation without government intervention. As long as *one* of the parties to the dispute has property rights to what is at issue, an incentive will exist for *both* parties to negotiate a solution acceptable to each. In our example, the owner of the timberland holds the property rights to the land to be logged. The owner of the resort therefore has an incentive to negotiate with the forest owner to reduce the logging impact. Excessive logging of the forest surrounding the resort will reduce tourism and revenues to the resort owner.

But what is the economic incentive of the forest owner to explore the possibility of an agreement with the resort owner? The answer draws directly on the idea of opportunity cost. One cost incurred by the owner in logging the forest is the forgone payment which the forest owner could obtain from the resort owner for agreeing *not* to clear-cut the fir trees. The resort owner should be willing to make a lump-sum or annual payment to the owner of the forest to avoid or minimize the spillover cost. Or, perhaps the resort owner will be willing to buy the forested land at a high price to prevent the logging. As viewed by the forest owner, a payment to preclude logging or a purchase price above the value of the land as a tree farm are *opportunity costs* of logging the land.

We would predict a negotiated agreement that both parties would regard as better than clear-cutting the firs. The Coase theorem suggests government intervention would not be needed to correct this potential externality.

LIMITATIONS   Unfortunately, many negative externalities involve large numbers of affected parties, high bargaining costs, and community property such as air and water. Private bargaining in these situations will not remedy the spillover costs. For example, the acid-rain problem in Canada and the United States affects millions of people spread out over two nations. The vast number of affected parties could not independently negotiate an agreement to remedy this problem. In this example, we must rely on both governments to find acceptable solutions.

Nevertheless, the Coase theorem reminds us that clearly defined property rights can be a positive factor in remedying some spillover costs and spillover benefits.

LIABILITY RULES AND LAWSUITS

Although private negotiation may not be a realistic solution to most externality problems, clearly established property rights may be helpful in another way. Government has established a framework of laws that define private property and protect it from damage done by other parties. These laws — and the legal tort (wrongful act) system to which they give rise — permit those suffering spillover costs to sue for damages.

Consider the following case. Suppose the Ajax Degreaser Company regularly dumps leaky barrels containing solvents into a nearby canyon owned by Bar Q ranch. Bar Q eventually discovers this dump site, and, after tracing the drums to Ajax, immediately contacts its lawyer. Ajax gets sued! Not only will Ajax have to pay for the cleanup, it may well have to pay Bar Q additional damages for despoiling its property.

Clearly defined property rights and government specified liability rules provide an avenue for remedying some externality problems. They do so directly by forcing the perpetrator of the harmful externality to pay damages to those injured. They do so indirectly by discouraging firms and individuals from generating negative externalities, for fear of being sued. It is not surprising that many externalities do *not* involve private property, but rather property held in common. It is the *public* bodies of water, the *public* lands, and the *public* air, where ownership is less clear, that often bear the brunt of negative externalities.

Caveat: Like private negotiations, private lawsuits to resolve externalities have their own limitations. Lawsuits are expensive, time-consuming, and have uncertain outcomes. Large legal fees and major time delays in the court system are commonplace. Also, the uncertainty associated with the court outcome reduces the effectiveness of this approach. Will the court accept your claim that your emphysema has resulted from the smoke emitted by the factory next door, or will it conclude that your ailment is unrelated to the plant's pollution? Can you prove that a specific firm in the area is the

source of the contamination of your well? What are Bar Q's options if Ajax Degreaser goes out of business during the litigation?

GOVERNMENT INTERVENTION

Other approaches to achieving economic efficiency may be needed when externalities affect large numbers of people or when community interests are at stake. Specifically, direct controls and taxes can be used to counter spillover costs; subsidies and government provision are available for dealing with spillover benefits.

DIRECT CONTROLS   The most direct approach to reducing negative externalities is legislation placing limits on the amount of the activity taking place. To date, this approach has dominated public

BOX 19-2   IN THE MEDIA

PROPERTY RIGHTS ONLY ANSWER FOR FISHERY

TERENCE CORCORAN

The monumental failure of government management of the Canadian fishery is now a well-known national scandal. Decades of destructive policies — subsidies, massive income support, generous licencing arrangements and forced overcapacity — produced wild expansion of fishing and ultimately the decimation of a large part of the industry and most of the fish. Less well known is what actions are needed to turn the industry into a healthy, market-driven, profit-making segment of the economy. The best option, now in place in a few pioneering nations and parts of Canada, is to expand private property rights into the oceans.

The thought of applying property rights to fish brings howls of protest from those who believe that the oceans are a common resource that must forever remain in the public domain. The fear is that owners of property rights would plunder the

fish to extinction — a strange worry given the global experience with the free-for-all of common ownership.

The largest applications of property rights principles to ocean fishing have occurred in Iceland and New Zealand, where the commercial fisheries have been allocated to private interests. Under the system, generically known as individual transferable quotas or ITQs, the rights to fish are acquired and remain the property of the owner. The rights can be bought and sold, their prices fluctuating with market demand and supply conditions. They are long-term (essentially permanent) rights to fish based on species and areas.

Iceland and New Zealand have different regulations on quota ownership. New Zealand, for example, discourages foreign ownership of ITQs but has allowed heavy concentration of ownership in the hands of about half a dozen major companies. In Iceland,

ITQs are widely owned, reflecting the structure of the country's fishery. In both countries, however, the ITQs are divisible and transferable, which means that the owner can sell, swap or lease all or part of his quota.

In principle, ownership regulations should be kept to a minimum, allowing the market to set the value of fishing rights. The freer the rights to trade and set prices, the more accurate the signals and the more efficient the market will be.

ITQs do not remove government from the process, at least not initially, although the opportunity exists to eventually get government out of the business altogether. In the meantime, governments still seem to be needed to determine the total amount of fish that can be removed under quota. Setting the total allowable catch (TAC), however, is really a technical matter to be decided by biologists.

Determining the allowable catch is roughly equivalent to defining the boundaries of a land property, or delineating mineral rights. If the allowable catch is 20,000 tonnes, and the quota owner is entitled to 10 per cent of the catch, the property is defined and its value can be I based on the value of 2,000 tonnes of fish. The market price of a quota, however, would incorporate many complex and longer-term considerations. For example, if the outlook for stocks in coming years appeared to be improving, then the current value of the quota would rise.

ITQs help bring the discipline of property rights to the fishery. The owners of the quotas have a vested interest in conservation. Professor Peter Pearse of the University of British Columbia, a leading advocate of tradeable quotas, wrote recently that "fishers who find themselves with secure, defined shares of the productive capacity of a fish stock soon realize they have a common interest in protecting and enhancing it, and begin to co-operate in management, regulation and enforcement."

Ownership responsibility is the real benefit from the introduction of property rights principles. Quota owners have a direct financial and investment incentive to preserve and increase the long-term supply of fish. Under the common property system, the incentive is for a free-for-all rush to see who can get the most fish out of the fishery in the shortest period of time before they are all gone.

There are no government subsidies to the Iceland and New Zealand fisheries, which are self-supporting, market driven and profitable. Fishermen have an incentive to minimize their costs, and reports are that for the most part, fish quality has improved and overfishing has been eliminated.

Introducing property rights to the fishery is not without its own conflicts: Who should be given ITQs? Should they be sold or distributed to people who have historically fished a species in an area? How should the system be enforced? But these are essentially technical issues. In the past, for example, it would have been impossible to monitor fishing fleets to enforce property rights, but with satellite technology, poachers are easily detected.

When the fish were abundant, the need for property rights never seemed relevant. But as the global scarcity of fish grows, and the common property approach collapses, the application of property rights becomes the only solution.

SOURCE: *Globe and Mail*, March 16, 1995, p. B2. Reprinted with permission.

The Story in Brief

The writer advocates the application of property rights to Canadian ocean fishing to resolve the problem of over-fishing. The property right would be transferable through a market in which one could purchase and sell the right to fish a specific quantity of fish.

The Economics Behind the Story

• Common property rights to fishing the ocean lead to over-fishing, threatening the very survival of the fish stock. This occurs because there is no incentive for those fishing to co-operate in regulating and enforcing fishing quotas. Each person fishing figures that what he or she won't take from the fishing ground, the next person will. Why not take as much as possible? If everyone follows this behaviour, eventually the fish stock will be decimated.

• With the assignment of property rights, through individual transferable quotas (ITQ), a person has to purchase the right to take a specific amount of fish per time period, say, one year. If everyone holding those rights depletes the stock of fish, their ITQ will be worthless. Thus there is an incentive to protect the fishing ground as if it were your own.

• In the seventeenth and eighteenth centuries, Canadian beaver pelts became a precious commodity because of the high price they could fetch in Europe, where they were used in the making of felt hats. The beaver population in Canada soon dwindled as trapping of beavers increased in intensity. Some scholars attribute the dwindling of the beaver population to the absence of property rights. If this is so, explain how ITQs could have helped to stop the dwindling Canadian beaver population.

FIGURE 19-3   **Correcting for spillover costs (negative externalities)**

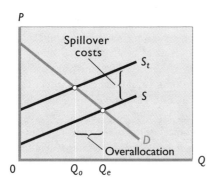

(a) The case of spillover costs

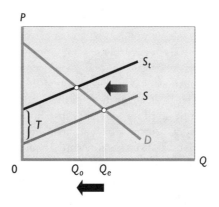

(b) Correcting the overallocation of resources via a tax

Spillover costs (a) result in an overallocation of resources. This overallocation can be corrected by direct controls or, as shown in (b), by imposing a specific tax T, which raises the firm's marginal costs and shifts its supply curve from S to S_t.

policy in Canada. Clean air legislation limits the amounts of nitrogen oxide, particulates, and other substances plants can emit into the air. Clean water legislation specifies the amount of heavy metals, detergents, and other pollutants firms can place into rivers and bays. Toxic-waste laws dictate special procedures and dump sites for disposing of contaminated soil and solvents. Violation of these laws means fines and, occasionally, imprisonment.

Direct controls force offending firms to incur costs associated with pollution control. Thus, the private marginal costs of producing these goods rise. The supply curve S of Figure 19-3(a) — which we know reflects only private marginal costs — shifts leftward from S to S_t, as shown in Figure 19-3(b). Product price increases, equilibrium output falls from Q_e to Q_o, and the initial Q_eQ_o overallocation of resources shown in Figure 19-3(a) is corrected.

SPECIFIC TAXES   A second policy approach to spillover costs is to levy specific taxes or emission charges on the perpetrators. For example, the federal government has placed an excise tax on manufacturers of chlorofluorocarbons (CFCs), which deplete the stratospheric ozone layer protecting the earth from excessive solar ultraviolet radiation. This substance is used widely as a coolant in refrigeration, a blowing agent for foam, and a solvent for electronics. Facing such a tax, manufacturers must decide whether to pay it or expend additional funds to purchase or develop substitute products. In either case, the tax will increase the marginal cost of pro-

ducing CFCs, shifting the private supply curve for this product leftward.

Look closely at Figure 19-3. A specific tax equal to T per unit in Figure 19-3(b) will increase the firm's marginal costs, shifting the supply curve from S to S_t. Equilibrium price will therefore increase and equilibrium output will decline from Q_e to the economically efficient level Q_o. The overallocation of resources shown in Figure 19-3(a) will be eliminated.

SUBSIDIES AND GOVERNMENT PROVISION
Where spillover benefits or positive externalities are large and diffuse — as with inoculations — government has three options for correcting the underallocation of resources.

1. SUBSIDIES TO BUYERS   Figure 19-4(a) repeats the case of spillover benefits described earlier. Government could correct the underallocation of resources — in this case, to inoculations — by subsidizing consumers of the product. It could give each new mother in Canada a discount coupon to be used to obtain a series of inoculations for her child. These coupons would reduce the "price" to the mother by, say, 50%. In terms of Figure 19-4(b), this program would increase the demand for inoculations from D to D_t. The number of vaccinations would rise from Q_e to Q_o, eliminating the underallocation of resources shown in Figure 19-4(a).

2. SUBSIDIES TO PRODUCERS   As it relates to supply, a subsidy is a specific tax in reverse; taxes

FIGURE 19-4 Correcting for spillover benefits (positive externalities)

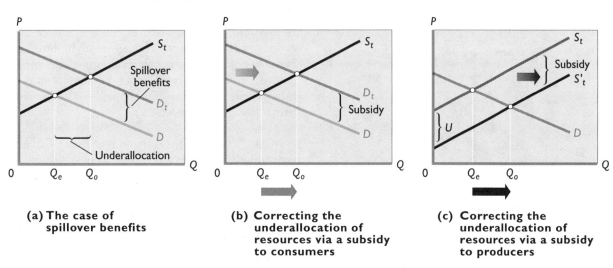

(a) The case of spillover benefits

(b) Correcting the underallocation of resources via a subsidy to consumers

(c) Correcting the underallocation of resources via a subsidy to producers

Spillover benefits (a) result in an underallocation of resources. This underallocation can be corrected by a subsidy to consumers, as shown in (b), which increases market demand from D to D_t. Alternatively, the underallocation can be eliminated by providing producers with a subsidy of U, which increases their supply curve from S_t to S'_t, as shown in (c).

impose an extra cost on producers, while subsidies reduce their costs. In Figure 19-4(c) a subsidy of U per inoculation to physicians and medical clinics will reduce marginal costs and shift the supply curve rightward from S_t to S'_t. Output will increase from Q_e to the optimal level Q_o and thus the underallocation of resources shown in Figure 19-4(a) will be corrected.

3. GOVERNMENT PROVISION Finally, where spillover benefits are extremely large, government may decide to provide the product as a public good. The Canadian government largely eradicated the crippling disease polio by administering free vaccines to all children. India ended smallpox by paying people in rural areas to come to public clinics to have their children vaccinated. **(Key Question 4)**

A MARKET FOR EXTERNALITY RIGHTS

One novel policy approach suggested to remedy spillover costs involves only limited government action. The idea is for government to create a **market for externality rights**. We confine our discussion to pollution, although other externalities might also lend themselves to this approach.

The air, rivers, lakes, oceans, and public lands, such as parks and streets, are all objects for pollution because the *rights* to use these resources are either held "in common" by society or are unspecified by law. As a result, no specific private individual or institution has an incentive to restrict the use or maintain the purity or quality of these resources because no one has the right to realize a monetary return from doing so.

We maintain the property we own — we paint and repair our homes periodically — in part because we will gain the value of these improvements at the time of resale. But, as long as "rights" to air, water, and certain land resources are commonly held and these resources are freely available, there will be no incentive to maintain them or restrict their use. The result? These natural resources are "overconsumed" and thereby polluted. But would they be consumed to this extent if there were a cost to pollute them — a market for the right to pollute?

CREATING A MARKET In this approach, an appropriate pollution-control agency would determine the amount of pollutants that can be discharged into the water or air of a specific region annually and still maintain the quality of the water

FIGURE 19-5 **The market for pollution rights**

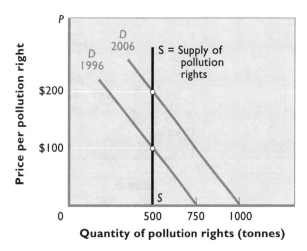

Quantity of pollution rights (tonnes)

Pollution can be controlled by having a public body determine the amount of pollution the atmosphere or a body of water can safely recycle, and then sell these limited rights to polluters. The effect is to make the environment a scarce resource with a positive price. Economic and population growth will increase the demand for pollution rights over time, but the consequence will be an increase in the price of pollution rights rather than more pollution.

or air at some acceptable standard. The agency may determine that 500 tonnes of pollutants can be discharged into Metropolitan Lake and "recycled" by Nature. Thus, 500 pollution rights, each entitling the owner to dump 1 tonne of pollutants into the lake in the particular year, are made available for sale each year. The resulting supply of pollution rights is fixed and therefore perfectly inelastic, as shown in Figure 19-5.

The demand for pollution rights — in this case D_{1996} — will take the same downsloping form as the demand for any other input. At high prices, polluters either will stop polluting or will pollute less by acquiring pollution-abatement equipment. An equilibrium market price for pollution rights of $100 will be determined at which an environment-preserving quantity of pollution rights will be rationed to polluters. Without this market — that is, if the use of the lake as a dump site for pollutants were free — 750 tonnes of pollutants would be discharged into the lake and it would be "overconsumed," or polluted, in the amount of 250 tonnes.

Over time, as human and business populations expand, demand will increase, as from D_{1996} to D_{2006}. *Without* a market for pollution rights, pollution would occur in 2006 in the amount of 500 tonnes beyond that which can be assimilated by Nature. *With* the market for pollution rights, price will rise from $100 to $200 and the amount of pollutants will remain at 500 tonnes — the amount which the lake can recycle.

ADVANTAGES   This scheme has several advantages relative to direct controls. Most importantly, it reduces society's costs because pollution rights can be bought and sold. Suppose it costs Acme Pulp Mill $20 a year to reduce a specific noxious waterborne discharge by 1 tonne while it costs Zemo Chemicals $8000 a year to accomplish this same 1-tonne reduction. Also assume that Zemo wants to expand its production of chemicals, but doing so will increase its pollution discharge by 1 tonne.

Without a market for pollution rights, Zemo will have to use $8000 of society's scarce resources to keep the 1-tonne pollution discharge from occurring. But with a market for pollution rights, Zemo has another option: It can buy 1 tonne of pollution rights for the $100 price shown in Figure 19-5. Acme would be willing to sell Zemo 1 tonne of pollution rights for $100, because that amount is more than Acme's $20 costs of reducing pollution by 1 tonne. Zemo increases its discharge by 1 tonne; Acme reduces its discharge by 1 tonne. Zemo benefits ($8000 – $100), Acme benefits ($100 – $20), and society benefits ($8000 – $20). Rather than using $8000 of its resources to hold the discharge at the specified level, society uses $20 of its resources.

Market-based plans have other advantages. Potential polluters are confronted with an explicit monetary incentive not to pollute: They must buy rights to pollute. Conservation groups can fight pollution by buying up and withholding pollution rights, reducing actual pollution below governmentally determined standards. As the demand for pollution rights increases over time, the growing revenue from the sale of the specific quantity of pollution rights could be devoted to environment improvement. Similarly, with time the rising price of pollution rights should stimulate the search for improved techniques to control pollution.

Administrative and political problems have dissuaded government from abandoning direct controls — uniform emission standards — for a full-scale market for pollution rights. But, as we will soon discuss, such markets *have* emerged for air pollution rights. Also, legislation has established a system of pollution rights, or "tradeable emission allowances," as part of a plan to reduce sulphur dioxide emitted by coal-burning public utilities. These firms are the major source of acid rain.

Table 19-3 reviews the methods for correcting externalities.

SOCIETY'S OPTIMAL AMOUNT OF EXTERNALITY REDUCTION

Negative externalities such as pollution reduce the recipient's utility rather than increase it. If something is bad, shouldn't society eliminate it? Why should society allow firms or municipalities to discharge *any* impure waste into public waterways or emit *any* pollution into our air?

Reducing a negative spillover has a "price." Society must decide how much of a reduction it wants to "buy." Totally eliminating pollution may not be desirable, even if it were technologically feasible. Because of the law of diminishing returns, cleaning up the last 1% of effluents from an industrial smokestack normally is far more costly than cleaning up the previous 10%. Eliminating that 10% is likely more costly than cleaning up the prior 10%, and so on.

The marginal cost (MC) to the firm and hence to society — the opportunity cost of the extra resources used — rises as more and more pollution is reduced. At some point MC may rise so high that it exceeds society's marginal benefit (MB) of further pollution abatement (reduction). Additional actions to reduce pollution will therefore lower society's well-being; total cost will rise by more than total benefit.

MC, MB, AND EQUILIBRIUM QUANTITY Observe in Figure 19-6 the rising marginal cost curve MC and the downsloping marginal benefit curve, MB. Society's marginal benefits of pollution abatement decline because of the law of diminishing marginal utility. The benefits from reducing pollution are a reflection of utility, and marginal utility (not total utility) falls as greater amounts of pollution abatement are achieved.

The **optimal reduction of an externality** occurs when society's marginal benefit and marginal cost of reducing that externality are equal (MB = MC). In Figure 19-6 this optimal amount of pollution abatement is Q_0. When MB exceeds MC, additional abatement moves society towards economic efficiency; the added benefit of cleaner air or water exceeds the benefit of any alternative use of the required resources. When MC exceeds MB, further abatement reduces economic efficiency; there would be greater benefits from using resources in some other way than using them to further reduce pollution.

In reality, it is difficult to measure the marginal costs and benefits of pollution control. Nevertheless, Figure 19-6 is useful in demonstrating that some pollution may be socially efficient. This is so, not because pollution is desirable, but because

TABLE 19-3 Methods for dealing with externalities

Problem	Resource allocation outcome	Ways to correct
Spillover costs (negative externalities)	Overallocation of resources	1. Individual bargaining 2. Liability rules and lawsuits 3. Tax on producers 4. Direct controls 5. Market for externality fights
Spillover benefits (positive externalities)	Underallocation of resources	1. Individual bargaining 2. Subsidy to consumers 3. Subsidy to producers 4. Government provision

FIGURE 19-6 **Society's optimal amount of pollution abatement**

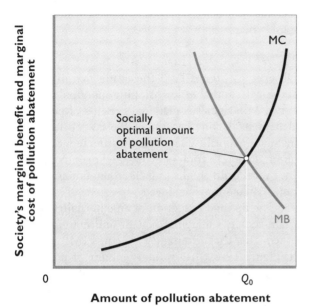

The optimal amount of externality reduction — in this case pollution abatement — occurs at Q_0 where society's marginal cost and marginal benefit of reducing the externality are equal. Reductions of pollution beyond Q_0 will reduce allocative efficiency by overallocating resources to pollution control.

beyond some level of control, further abatement may reduce our net well-being.

SHIFTS IN LOCATIONS OF CURVES   The locations of the marginal cost and marginal benefit curves in Figure 19-6 are not forever fixed; they can, and probably do, shift over time. For example, suppose the technology of pollution control equipment improves noticeably. We would expect the cost of pollution abatement to fall, society's MC curve to shift rightward, and the optimal level of abatement to rise. As another example, suppose society wants cleaner air and water because of new information about adverse health effects of pollution. The MB curve in Figure 19-6 would shift rightward, and the optimal level of pollution control would increase beyond Q_0. Test your understanding of these statements by drawing new MC and MB curves in Figure 19-6. (**Key Question 7**)

POLLUTION: A CLOSER LOOK

Pollution, the most acute negative externality facing industrial society, provides a relevant illustration of several of the concepts and public policies just discussed. This spillover takes several forms, including air, water, and solid-waste (garbage) pollution. How big are these problems? What are their causes? What public policies are in place to reduce them?

DIMENSIONS OF THE PROBLEM

We know some rivers, lakes, and bays have turned into municipal and industrial sewers. Almost half our population drinks water of dubious quality. There are an estimated 27,000 major industrial and utility sources of air pollution in North America; these contribute to lung cancer, emphysema, pneumonia, and other respiratory diseases. Over 1 billion kilograms of toxic chemicals, some of them carcinogens, are released into the air each year. Solid-waste disposal has become an acute problem for many cities as the most readily available dump sites have been filled and citizens resist the establishment of new dumps or incinerators near them.

The nations of Eastern Europe are so polluted that it will take several decades, at best, for them to be cleaned up. Government has identified hundreds of dangerous toxic-waste disposal sites in Canada. Within the past decade, giant oil spills in Alaska and the Persian Gulf seriously damaged those two ecosystems. Passive cigarette smoke has been found to cause cancer in nonsmokers.

Global consequences of environmental pollution are equally disturbing. Some scientists contend that the concentrations of industry, people, structures, and concrete that constitute cities might create air and heat pollution sufficient to cause irreversible and potentially disastrous global warming through the so-called greenhouse effect. Headlines warn us that our continued use of CFCs has contributed to a rising rate of skin cancer by depleting the earth's stratospheric ozone layer.

CAUSES: THE LAW OF CONSERVATION OF MATTER AND ENERGY

The root of the pollution problem can best be envisioned through the **law of conservation of matter and energy**. This law holds that matter can be transformed to other matter or into energy but can never vanish. All inputs (fuels, raw materials, water, and so forth) used in the economy's production processes will ultimately result in an equivalent residual of waste. For example, unless it is continuously recycled, the cotton found in a T-shirt ultimately will be abandoned in a closet, buried in a dump, or burned in an incinerator. Even if burned it will not truly vanish; instead, it will be transformed into heat and smoke.

Fortunately, the ecological system — Nature, if you are over 50 — has the self-regenerating capacity that allows it, within limits, to absorb or recycle such wastes. But the volume of such residuals has tended to outrun this absorptive capacity.

Why has this happened? Why do we have a pollution problem? There are lots of reasons, but four of them contribute a disproportionate share.

1. POPULATION DENSITY

One reason is population growth. An ecological system that can accommodate 50 or 100 million people may begin to break down under the pressures of 200 or 300 million.

2. RISING INCOMES

Economic growth means that each person consumes and disposes of more output. Paradoxically, a rising GDP (gross domestic product) means a rising GDG (gross domestic garbage). A high standard of living permits Canadians to own millions of motor vehicles. But autos and trucks pollute the air and give rise to the problem of disposing of hundreds of thousands of junked vehicles annually. Additionally, millions of tires hit the nation's scrap heap each year.

But we must not overgeneralize. While solid waste increases with GDP, this is not case with all pollutants. For example, concentrations of smoke (fine suspended particles), heavier suspended particles, and sulphur dioxide on average decrease when a nation's per capita GDP rises above $5000 per year. Expanded national income enables countries to "buy" cleaner air and water through enacting pollution control measures. Nevertheless, there is no doubt that industrialization itself — and the resulting increase in GDP — has brought with it serious pollution problems.

3. TECHNOLOGY

Technological change may also contribute to pollution. For example, the addition of lead to gasoline posed a serious threat to human health, leading to the government requirement of unleaded fuel. The development and widespread use of "throw-away" containers made of virtually indestructible aluminum or plastic add to the solid-waste crisis. Some detergent soap products have been highly resistant to sanitary treatment and recycling.

4. INCENTIVES

Profit-seeking manufacturers will choose the least-cost combination of inputs and will bear only unavoidable costs. If they can dump waste chemicals into rivers and lakes rather than pay for expensive treatment and proper disposal, businesses may be inclined to do so. Manufacturers that can will discharge smoke rather than purchase expensive abatement facilities. The result is air pollution — and, in the economist's jargon — the shifting of certain costs to the community at large as external or spillover costs. Enjoying lower "internal" costs than if they had not polluted the environment, the producers can sell their products more cheaply, expand their production, and obtain larger profits.

But it is neither just nor accurate to lay the entire blame for pollution at the door of industry. A well-intentioned firm wanting to operate in a socially responsible way with respect to pollution may find itself in an untenable position. If an individual firm "internalizes" all its external or spillover costs by installing, say, water-treatment and smoke-abatement equipment, the firm will have a cost disadvantage compared to its polluting competitors. The socially responsible firm will have higher costs and will be forced to raise its product price. The "reward" for the pollution-conscious firm is a declining market for its product, diminished profits, and, in the extreme, bankruptcy. This means effective action to combat pollution must be undertaken collectively through government.

Also, even though an important function of government is to correct the misallocation of resources that accompanies spillover costs, most major cities are heavy contributors to the pollution problem. Municipal power plants are contributors to air pollution; many cities discharge inadequately treated sewage into rivers or lakes because it is cheap and convenient to do so.

Many individuals avoid the costs of proper refuse pickup and disposal by burning their garbage or illegally dumping it in the woods. We also find it easier to use throw-away containers rather than recycle "return" containers. Most families with babies opt for the convenience of disposable diapers, which glut landfills, rather than reusable cloth diapers. Emissions from woodstoves, fireplaces, outdoor grills, and even lawn mowers have become pollution problems in some towns and cities.

TRADING OF POLLUTION RIGHTS

In Canada antipollution policies have been a mixture of direct controls and specific taxes levied by the federal and provincial governments. Although not yet tried in Canada, in the United States legislation in the last decade has allowed for trading of air pollution rights. The Clean Air Act of 1990 strengthened and extended such provisions. The American Environmental Protection Agency (EPA) now permits firms to exchange pollution rights internally and externally.

Polluters are allowed to transfer air pollution rights internally between individual sources within their plants. That is, as long as they meet the overall pollution standard assigned to them, firms may increase one source of pollution by offsetting it with reduced pollution from another part of their operations.

The EPA also permits external trading of pollution rights. It has set targets for reducing air pollution in regions where the minimum standards are not being met. Previously, new pollution sources could not enter these regions unless existing polluters went out of business. In the last decade or so, the EPA has allowed firms that reduce their pollution below set standards to sell pollution rights to new or existing firms. Thus, a new firm desiring to locate in a particular urban area might be able to buy rights to emit 20 tonnes of nitrous oxide annually from an existing firm that has reduced its emissions below its allowable limit. The price of these emission rights will depend on their supply and demand.

A small but growing market for such rights has recently emerged and appears to be working well. The acid rain provisions of the U.S. Clean Air Act of 1990 will greatly expand this market.

SOLID-WASTE DISPOSAL AND RECYCLING

Nowhere is the law of conservation of matter and energy more apparent than in solid-waste disposal

GLOBAL PERSPECTIVE 19-1

Solid waste per capita, selected nations

Industrially advanced nations generate large amounts of solid waste each day, including by-products from mining, manufacturing, and other industries, as well as household trash. Solid waste per capita varies among industrial nations largely because of the different mixes of products produced and consumed.

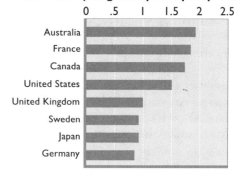

Solid waste (kilograms per capita per day)

Source: OECD estimates

(Global Perspective 19-1). The million tonnes of garbage that accumulate annually in our landfills have become a growing externality problem. Landfills in southern Ontario are either completely full or rapidly filling up.

On the receiving end, people in rural areas near newly expanding dumps are understandably upset about the increased truck traffic on their highways and growing mounds of smelly garbage in local dumps. Also, some landfills are producing serious groundwater pollution.

The high opportunity cost of urban and suburban land, and the negative externalities created by dumps, make the landfill solution to solid waste increasingly expensive. An alternative garbage policy is to incinerate it in plants that produce electricity. But people object to having garbage incinerators — a source of truck traffic and air pollution — close to their homes. What's the solution to the growing problem of solid waste?

Although garbage dumps and incinerators remain the main ways of garbage disposal, recycling is receiving increased attention.

FIGURE 19-7 **The economics of recycling**

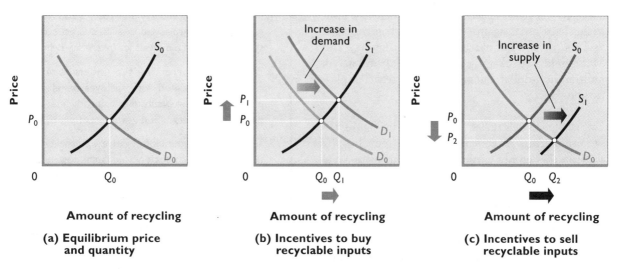

| (a) Equilibrium price and quantity | (b) Incentives to buy recyclable inputs | (c) Incentives to sell recyclable inputs |

The equilibrium price and amount of materials recycled are determined by supply and demand, as shown in (a). In (b), policies that increase the incentives for producers to buy recyclable items shift the demand curve rightward and raise both equilibrium price and the amount of recycling. In (c), policies that encourage households to recycle expand the equilibrium amount of recycling but also reduce the equilibrium price of recyclable items.

MARKET FOR RECYCLABLE INPUTS The incentives for recycling can be shown through Figure 19-7(a) where we have drawn a demand and supply curve for some recyclable product, say, glass.

The demand for recyclable glass derives from manufacturers of glass who use it as a resource in producing new glass. The demand curve for recyclable glass slopes downward, telling us the manufacturers will increase their purchases of recyclable glass as its price falls.

The location of the resource demand curve in Figure 19-7(a) depends partly on the demand for the product using the recycled glass. The greater the demand for the product, the greater is the demand for the recyclable input. The location of the curve also depends on the technology and thus the cost of using original raw materials rather than recycled glass production process. The more costly it is to use original materials relative to recycled glass, the further to the right will be the demand curve for recyclable glass.

The supply curve for recyclable glass slopes upward in the typical fashion because higher prices increase the incentive for households to recycle. The location of the supply curve depends on such factors as the attitudes of households towards recycling and the cost to them of alternative disposal.

The equilibrium price P_0 and quantity Q_0 in Figure 19-7(a) are determined at the intersection of the supply and demand curves. At price P_0 the market clears; there is neither a shortage nor a surplus of recyclable glass.

POLICY Suppose government wants to encourage recycling as an alternative to land dumps or incineration. It could do this in one of two ways.

1. DEMAND INCENTIVES Government could increase recycling by increasing the demand for recycled inputs. If the demand curve in Figure 19-7(b) shifts from D_0 rightward to D_1, equilibrium price and quantity will increase to P_1 and Q_1. A policy that might accomplish this goal would be to place specific taxes on the inputs that are substitutable for recycled glass in the production process. Such taxes would encourage firms to use more of the untaxed recycled glass and less of the original taxed inputs. Or government could shift its purchases towards goods produced with recycled inputs and require that its contractors do the same.

Also, environmental awareness by the public can contribute to rightward shifts of the demand curve for recycled resources. Fearing negative consumer backlashes against their products, firms such as Procter & Gamble (disposable diapers) and McDonald's (packaging of fast foods) undertook multimillion-dollar campaigns to use recycled plastic and paper.

2. SUPPLY INCENTIVES As shown in Figure 19-7(c), government can also increase recycling by shifting the supply curve rightward, as from S_0 to S_1. Equilibrium price would fall from P_0 to P_2 and equilibrium quantity — in this case, recyclable glass — would rise from Q_0 to Q_2. Many local governments have implemented specific policies that fit within this framework. For example, they encourage recycling by providing curbside pickup of recyclable goods such as glass, aluminum cans, and newspaper, at a lower monthly fee than for pickup of normal garbage.

In a few cases, supply incentives for recyclables have been so effective that the prices of some recycled items have fallen to zero. You can envision this outcome by shifting the supply curve in Figure 19-7(c) further and further rightward. Some cities now are *paying* manufacturers to truck away certain recyclable products such as mixed paper (negative price) rather than charging them a price. This may or may not promote economic efficiency. The cost of paying firms to take away recyclable products may be lower than the cost of alternative disposal, particularly in view of the negative externalities of dumps and incinerators. If so, recycling will promote economic efficiency.

However, a policy of paying firms to take away recyclable items need not always be economical. In some cases it may be more costly to recycle goods than to bury or incinerate them, even when externalities are considered. If so, recycling will *reduce* efficiency rather than increase it.

Government's task is to find the optimal amount of recycling compared to alternative disposal of garbage. It can do this by estimating and comparing the marginal benefit and marginal cost of recycling. And, incidentally, consumers as a group can reduce the initial accumulation of garbage by not buying products with excessive packaging.

QUICK REVIEW 19-2

1. Policies for coping with spillover costs are **a** private bargaining, **b** liability rules and lawsuits, **c** direct controls, **d** specific taxes, and **e** markets for externality rights.

2. Policies for correcting the underallocation of resources associated with spillover benefits are **a** private bargaining, **b** subsidies to producers, **c** subsidies to consumers, and **d** government provision.

3. The optimal amount of negative externality reduction occurs when society's marginal cost and marginal benefit of reducing the externality are equal.

4. The ultimate cause of pollution is the law of conservation of matter and energy, which holds that matter can be transformed into other matter or into energy, but cannot vanish.

INFORMATION FAILURES

Thus far we have added new detail and insights concerning two types of market failure: public goods and externalities. There is another, more subtle, market failure. This inefficiency results when either buyers or sellers have incomplete or inaccurate information and their cost of obtaining better information is prohibitive. Technically stated, this form of market failure occurs because of **asymmetric information** — unequal knowledge possessed by the parties to a market transaction. Buyers and sellers do not have identical information about price, quality, or some other aspect of the good or service.

Market information normally is sufficient to ensure that goods and services are produced and purchased in economically efficient quantities. But in some cases, inadequate information makes it difficult to distinguish legitimate from illegitimate sellers, or legitimate from illegitimate buyers. In these markets, society's scarce resources will not be used efficiently, implying that government should intervene by increasing the information available to the market participants. Under rarer circumstances government may itself supply a good for which information problems have prohibited profitable production.

INADEQUATE INFORMATION ABOUT SELLERS

We begin by asking how inadequate information about *sellers* and their products can cause market failure. Examining the market for gasoline and the services of surgeons will give us an answer.

GASOLINE MARKET   Assume an absurd situation. Suppose there is no system of weights and measures established by law, no government inspection of gasoline pumps, and no laws against false advertising. Each gas station can use whatever measure it chooses; it can define a litre of gas as it pleases. A station can advertise that its gas is 87 octane when in fact it is only 75. It can rig its pumps to indicate it is providing more gas than the amount being delivered.

The consumer's cost of obtaining reliable information under these conditions is exceptionally high, if not prohibitive. Each consumer will have to buy samples of gas from various gas stations, have them tested for octane level, and pour gas into a measuring device to see how the station has calibrated the pump. Also, the consumer will need to use a hand calculator to ascertain if the machine is correctly multiplying the price per litre by the number of litres. And these activities will need to be repeated regularly, since the station owner can alter the product quality and the accuracy of the pump at will.

Because of the high costs of obtaining information about the seller, many customers will opt out of this chaotic market. One tankful of a 50% solution of gasoline and water will be enough to discourage motorists from further driving. More realistically, the conditions described in this market will encourage consumers to vote for political candidates who promise to provide a governmental solution. The oil companies and honest gasoline suppliers will not object to this government intervention. They will realize that, by enabling this market to work, accurate information will expand their total sales.

Government has intervened in the market for gasoline and other markets having similar information difficulties. It has established a system of weights and measures, employed inspectors to check the accuracy of gasoline pumps, and passed laws against fraudulent claims and misleading advertising. There can be no doubt that these government activities have produced net benefits for society.

LICENSING OF SURGEONS   Let's look at another example of how inadequate information about sellers can create market failure. Suppose that anyone can hang out a shingle and claim to be a surgeon in much the same way that anyone can become a house painter. The market will eventually sort out the true surgeons from those who are learning by doing or are fly-by-night operators who move into and out of an area. As people die from unsuccessful surgery, lawsuits for malpractice eventually will eliminate the medical imposters. People needing surgery for themselves or their loved ones can glean information from newspaper reports and solicit information from people — or their relatives — who have undergone similar operations.

But this process of generating information for those needing surgery will take considerable time and will impose unacceptably high human and economic costs. There is a fundamental difference between an amateurish paint job on one's house and being on the receiving end of heart surgery by a bogus physician. The marginal cost of obtaining information about sellers in this market is excessively high. The risk of proceeding without good information will result in an underallocation of resources to surgery.

Government has remedied this market failure through a system of qualifying tests and licensing. This licensing enables consumers to obtain inexpensive information about a service they only infrequently buy. Government has taken a similar role in several other areas of the economy. For example, it approves new medicines, regulates the securities industry, and requires warnings on containers of potentially hazardous substances. It also requires warning labels on cigarette packages and disseminates information about communicable diseases. It issues warnings about unsafe toys and inspects restaurants for health-related violations.

INADEQUATE INFORMATION ABOUT BUYERS

Just as inadequate information about sellers can keep markets from achieving economic efficiency, so can inadequate information about *buyers*. These buyers can be consumers buying products or firms buying resources.

MORAL HAZARD PROBLEM   Private markets may underallocate resources to a particular good or service for which there is a severe **moral hazard problem**. *The moral hazard problem is the tendency of one party to a contract to alter her or his behaviour in ways that are costly to the other party.*

BOX 19-3   APPLYING THE THEORY

USED CARS: THE MARKET FOR "LEMONS"

Inadequate product information can result in markets where sellers offer only defective goods.

A new car loses much of its market value as the buyer drives it off the sales lot. Physical depreciation alone cannot explain this large loss of value. The same new car can sit on the dealer's lot for weeks, or even months, and retain its value.

One explanation of this paradox rests on the idea of asymmetric information about *used* cars.[*] Auto owners have much more knowledge about the mechanical conditions of their vehicles than do potential buyers of used cars. At the time of the purchase, individual buyers of used cars find it difficult to distinguish between so-called "lemons" — defective cars — and vehicles of the same car make and model that operate perfectly. Therefore, a single price emerges for used cars of the same year, make, and model whether they are lemons or high-quality vehicles. This price roughly reflects the average quality of the vehicles, influenced by the proportion of lemons to high-quality cars. The higher the proportion of lemons, the lower are prices of used cars.

An adverse selection problem now becomes evident. Owners of lemons have an incentive to sell their cars to unsuspecting buyers, while owners of high-quality autos will wish to keep their cars. Therefore, most used cars on the market will be of lower quality than the same car models that are *not* for sale. As people become aware of this, the demand for used cars will decline and prices of used cars will fall. These lower prices will further reduce the incentive of owners of high-quality used cars to offer them for sale. At the extreme, only lemons will appear on the market; *poor-quality products will drive out high-quality products.*

[*]The classical article on this topic is George A. Akerlof, "The Market for 'Lemons': Qualitative Uncertainty and the Market Mechanism," *Quarterly Journal of Economics*, August 1970, pp. 488–500.

We thus have a solution to our paradox. Once a buyer drives a new car away from the dealership, the auto's value becomes the value set in the lemons' market. This is true even though the probability is high that the new car is of high quality.

The instantaneous loss of new car value would be even greater were it not for several factors. Because new-car warranties are transferable to used-car buyers, purchasers of low-mileage late-model cars are protected against costly repairs. Thus, the demand for these vehicles rises. Also, prospective buyers can distinguish good cars from lemons by hiring mechanics to perform inspections. Moreover, sellers can signal potential buyers that their cars are not lemons through ads such as "Must sell, transferred abroad," "Divorce forces sale." Of course, the buyer must determine the truth of these claims. Additionally, auto rental companies routinely sell high-quality, late-model cars, increasing the ratio of good cars to lemons in the used-car market.

Government also plays a role in solving the market failure evident in the lemons' market. Many states in the United States have "lemon laws" that force auto dealers to take back defective new cars. Supposedly, dealers do not offer these lemons for sale in the used-car market until completing all needed repairs. Also, some American states require dealers to either offer warranties on used cars or explicitly state that a car is offered "as is." The latter designation gives the buyer a good clue that the car may be defective.

In brief, both private and governmental initiatives temper the lemons' problem. Nevertheless, this principle is applicable to a wide variety of used products such as autos, computers, and cameras, which are complex and occasionally defective. Buying any of these used products remains a somewhat risky transaction.

To understand this point, suppose a firm offers an insurance policy that pays a set amount of money per month to people who suffer divorces. The attraction of this insurance is that it pools the economic risk of divorce among thousands of people and, in particular, protects spouses and children from the economic hardship that divorce often brings. Unfortunately, the moral hazard problem reduces the likelihood that insurance companies can profitably provide this type of insurance contract.

After taking out this insurance, some people will alter their behaviour in ways that impose heavy costs on the insurer. Married couples will have less of an incentive to get along and to iron out marital difficulties. At the extreme, some people might be motivated to obtain a divorce, collect the insurance, and then live together. The insurance promotes *more* divorces, the very outcome it protects against. The moral hazard difficulty will force the insurer to charge such high premiums for this insurance that few policies will be bought. If the insurer could identify in advance those people most prone to alter their behaviour, the firm could exclude them from buying it. But the firm's marginal cost of getting this information is too high compared to the marginal benefit. Thus, this market fails.

Divorce insurance is not available in the marketplace, but society recognizes the benefits of insuring against the hardships of divorce. It has corrected for this underallocation of "hardship insurance" through child-support laws that dictate payments — when the economic circumstances warrant — to the spouse who retains the children. Alimony laws also play a role.

Government provides "divorce insurance" of sorts through the Mother's Allowance payments. If a divorce leaves a spouse with children destitute, the family is eligible for Mother's Allowance payments. Government intervention does not eliminate the moral hazard problem; instead, it offsets its adverse effects. Unlike private firms, government need not earn a profit to continue the insurance.

The moral hazard concept has numerous applications. We mention them to reinforce your understanding of the basic principle.

1. Drivers may be less cautious because they have insurance.
2. Medical malpractice insurance may increase the amount of malpractice.
3. Guaranteed contracts for professional athletes may reduce their performance.
4. Unemployment insurance may lead some workers to shirk.
5. Government insurance on bank deposits may encourage banks to make risky loans.

ADVERSE SELECTION PROBLEM   Another information problem resulting from inadequate information about buyers is the **adverse selection problem**. *The adverse selection problem arises when information known by the first party to a contract is not known by the second, and, as a result, the second party incurs major costs.* Unlike the moral hazard problem, which arises *after* a person signs a contract the adverse selection problem arises *at the time* a person signs the contract.

In insurance, the adverse selection problem is that people most likely to receive insurance payouts are those who will buy insurance. For example, those in poorest health will seek to buy the most generous health insurance policies. Or, at the extreme, a person planning to hire an arsonist to "torch" his failing business has an incentive to buy fire insurance.

Our hypothetical divorce insurance sheds further light on the adverse selection problem. If the insurance firm sets the premiums on the basis of the average rate of divorce, many of the married couples about to get a divorce will buy insurance. An insurance premium based on average probabilities will make for a great insurance buy for those about to get divorced. Meanwhile, those in highly stable marriages will opt against buying it.

The adverse selection problem will eliminate the pooling of risk that is the basis for profitable insurance. The insurance rates needed to cover payouts will be so high that few people will wish or be able to buy this insurance.

Where private firms underprovide insurance because of information problems, government often establishes some type of social insurance. Government can require everyone in a particular group to enter the insurance pool and therefore can overcome the adverse selection problem. Although the social insurance system in Canada is partly an insurance and partly a welfare program, in its broadest sense it is insurance against poverty during old age. The social insurance program overcomes the adverse selection problem by requiring nearly universal participation. People who are most likely to need the minimum benefits that social security provides automatically are participants in the program. So, too, are those not likely to need the benefits.

WORKPLACE SAFETY The labour market also provides an example of how inadequate information about buyers (employers) can produce market failures.

For several reasons employers have an economic incentive to provide safe workplaces. A safe workplace reduces the amount of disruption of the production process created by job accidents and lowers the costs of recruiting, screening, training, and retaining new workers. It also reduces a firm's worker compensation insurance premiums (legally required insurance against job injuries).

But a safe workplace has an expense. Safe equipment, protective gear, and slower paces of work all entail costs. The firm will compare its marginal cost and marginal benefit of providing a safer workplace in deciding how much safety to provide. Will this amount of job safety achieve social efficiency, as well as maximize the firm's profits?

The answer is "yes" if the labour and product markets are competitive and workers are fully aware of job risks at various places of employment. With full information, workers will avoid employers having unsafe workplaces. The supply of labour to these establishments will be greatly restricted, forcing them to boost their wages to attract a work force. These higher wages give the employer an incentive to provide socially desirable levels of workplace safety; safer workplaces will reduce wage expenses. Only firms that find it very costly to provide safer workplaces will choose to pay high compensating wage differentials, rather than reduce workplace hazards.

But a serious problem arises when workers *do not know* that particular occupations or workplaces are unsafe. Because information about the buyer is inadequate — that is, about the employer and the workplace — the firm may *not* need to pay a wage premium to attract its work force. Its incentive to remove safety hazards therefore is diminished and its profit-maximizing level of workplace safety will be less than socially desirable. In brief, the labour market will fail because of asymmetric information — specifically sellers (workers) having less information than buyers (employers.)

Government has several options for remedying this information problem.

1. It can directly provide information to workers about the injury experience of various employers, much like it publishes the on-time performance of the various airlines.

2. It can mandate that firms provide information to workers about known workplace hazards.
3. It can establish standards of workplace safety and enforce them through inspection and penalties.

The federal government has mainly employed the "standards and enforcement" approach to improve workplace safety, but some contend that an "information" strategy might be less costly and more effective. (**Key Question 11**)

QUICK REVIEW 19-3

1. Asymmetric information can cause markets to fail, causing society's scarce resources to be allocated inefficiently.

2. The moral hazard problem is the tendency of some parties to a contract to alter their behaviour in ways that are costly to the other party; for example, a person who buys insurance may incur added risk.

3. As it relates to insurance, the adverse selection problem is the tendency of people who are most likely to collect insurance benefits to buy large amounts of insurance.

QUALIFICATION

People have found many ingenious ways to overcome information difficulties short of government intervention. For example, many firms offer product warranties to overcome the lack of information about themselves and their products. Franchising also helps overcome this problem. When you visit McDonald's or Holiday Inn, you know precisely what you are going to get, as opposed to Sam's Hamburger Shop or the Bates Motel.

Also, some private firms and organizations have specialized in providing information to buyers and sellers. *Consumer Reports* provides product information, labour unions collect and disseminate information about job safety, and credit bureaus provide information to insurance companies. Brokers, bonding agencies, and intermediaries also provide information to clients.

However, economists agree that the private sector cannot remedy all information problems. In some situations government intervention is desirable to promote an efficient allocation of society's scarce resources.

CHAPTER SUMMARY

1. Graphically, the collective demand curve for a particular public good can be found by summing *vertically* each of the individual demand curves for that good. The demand curve resulting from this process indicates the collective willingness to pay for the last unit of any given amount of the public good.

2. The optimal quantity of a public good occurs when the combined willingness to pay for the last unit — the marginal benefit of the good — equals the good's marginal cost.

3. Benefit-cost analysis can provide guidance as to the economic desirability and most efficient scope of public goods output.

4. Spillovers or externalities cause the equilibrium output of certain goods to vary from the optimal output. Spillover costs result in an overallocation of resources that can be corrected by legislation or specific taxes. Spillover benefits are accompanied by an underallocation of resources that can be corrected by subsidies to consumers, subsidies to producers, or government provision.

5. According to the Coase theorem, private bargaining is capable of solving potential externality problems when **a** the property rights are clearly defined, **b** the number of people involved is small, and **c** bargaining costs are negligible.

6. Clearly established property rights and liability rules permit some spillover costs to be prevented or remedied through private lawsuits. Lawsuits, however, are costly, time-consuming, and uncertain as to their results.

7. Direct controls and specific taxes can improve resource allocation in situations where externalities affect many people and community resources. Both direct controls (smokestack emission standards) and specific taxes (taxes on firms producing toxic chemicals) increase production costs and thus product price. As product price rises, the externality is reduced since less of the output is bought and sold.

8. Markets for pollution rights, where people can buy and sell the rights to a fixed amount of pollution, put a price on pollution and encourage firms to reduce or eliminate it.

9. The optimal social amount of externality abatement occurs when society's marginal cost and marginal benefit of reducing the externality are equal. This optimal amount of pollution abatement is likely to be less than a 100% reduction. Changes in technology or changes in society's attitudes about pollution can affect the optimal amount of pollution abatement.

10. The law of conservation of matter and energy is at the heart of the pollution problem. Matter can be transformed into other matter or into energy, but does not disappear. If not recycled, all production will ultimately end up as waste. Recycling is a recent response to the growing garbage disposal problem. The equilibrium price and quantity of recyclable inputs depend on their demand and supply. Government can encourage recycling through either demand or supply incentives.

11. Asymmetric information about sellers or buyers can cause markets to fail. The moral hazard problem occurs when people alter their behaviour after they sign a contract, imposing costs on the other party. As it relates to insurance, the adverse selection problem occurs when people who are of above-average risk buy large amounts of insurance.

TERMS AND CONCEPTS

adverse selection problem (p. 417)
asymmetric information (p. 414)
benefit-cost analysis (p. 400)
Coase theorem (p. 402)
law of conservation of matter and energy (p. 410)

marginal benefit = marginal cost rule (p. 401)
market for externality rights (p. 407)
moral hazard problem (p. 415)
optimal reduction of an externality (p. 409)

QUESTIONS AND STUDY SUGGESTIONS

1. *Key Question* *Based on the following three individual demand schedules for a particular good, and assuming these three people are the only ones in the society, determine a. the market demand schedule on the assumption that the good is a private good, and b. the collective demand schedule on the assumption that the good is a public good. Explain the differences, if any, in your schedules.*

Individual 1		Individual 2		Individual 3	
P	**Q_d**	**P**	**Q_d**	**P**	**Q_d**
$8	0	$8	1	$8	0
7	0	7	2	7	0
6	0	6	3	6	1
5	1	5	4	5	2
4	2	4	5	4	3
3	3	3	6	3	4
2	4	2	7	2	5
1	5	1	8	1	6

2. *Key Question* *Use your demand schedule for a public good determined in question 1 and the following supply schedule to ascertain the optimal quantity of this public good. Why is this the optimal quantity?*

P	**Q_s**
$19	10
16	8
13	6
10	4
7	2
4	1

3. *Key Question* *The following table shows the total costs and total benefits in billions for four different antipollution programs of increasing scope. Which program should be undertaken? Why?*

Program	**Total cost**	**Total benefit**
A	$ 3	$ 7
B	7	12
C	12	16
D	18	19

4. *Key Question* *Why are spillover costs and spillover benefits also called negative and positive "externalities"? Show graphically how a tax can correct for a spillover cost and a subsidy to producers can correct for a spillover benefit. How does a subsidy to consumers differ from a subsidy to producers in correcting for a spillover benefit?*

5. An apple grower's orchard provides nectar to a neighbour's bees, while a beekeeper's bees help the apple grower by pollinating the apple blossoms. Use Figure 19-2(b) to explain why this situation might lead to an underallocation of resources to apple growing and to beekeeping. How might this underallocation get resolved via the means suggested by the Coase theorem?

6. Explain: "Without a market for pollution rights, dumping pollutants into the air or water is costless; in the presence of the right to buy and sell pollution rights, dumping pollution creates an opportunity cost for the polluter." What is the significance of this fact to the search for better technology to reduce pollution?

7. *Key Question* *Manipulate the MB curve in Figure 19-6 to explain the following statement: "The optimal amount of pollution abatement for some substances, say, water from storm drains, is very low; the optimal amount of abatement for other substances, say, cyanide poison, is close to 100 per cent." Explain.*

8. Relate the law of conservation of matter and energy to: a. the air pollution problem; and b. the solid-waste disposal problem.

9. Explain why there may be insufficient recycling of products when the externalities associated with landfills and garbage incinerators are not considered. What demand and supply incentives might government provide to promote more recycling?

10. Why is it in the interest of new home buyers *and* builders of new homes to have government building codes and building inspectors?

11. *Key Question* *Place an M beside items in the following list that describe a moral hazard problem; place an A beside those that describe an adverse selection problem.*

   a. *A person with a terminal illness buys several life insurance policies through the mail.*

   b. *A person drives carelessly because he or she has insurance.*

   c. *A person who intends to "torch" his warehouse takes out a large fire insurance policy.*

   d. *A professional athlete who has a guaranteed contract fails to stay in shape during the off-season.*

   e. *A woman anticipating having a large family takes a job with a firm that offers exceptional child-care benefits.*

12. (Applying the Theory) Relate the prices of used cars to the following two problems: a. asymmetric information; and b. adverse selection.

CHAPTER 20

PUBLIC CHOICE THEORY AND TAXATION

Why does government elicit so much public disenchantment and distrust? One reason is the apparent failure of costly government programs to resolve socioeconomic ills. For example, it is argued that foreign aid programs have contributed little or nothing to the economic growth of the less developed nations. We hear reports that well-financed school enrichment programs have had no perceptible impact on the educational attainment of students. Some programs have fostered the very problems they were designed to solve: Our farm programs were originally designed to save the small family farm, but instead have subsidized larger farms.

There are charges that government agencies have become mired in a blizzard of paperwork. It is alleged that the public bureaucracy has developed trivial regulations and created great duplication of effort; that obsolete programs persist; that various agencies work at cross purposes; and so on.

Just as there are certain limitations or failures in the private sector's market system, there are inherent deficiencies in the political processes, bureaucratic agencies, and tax systems within the public sector.

BOX 20-1 THE BIG PICTURE

This chapter is about public choice theory, the economic analysis of how governments make decisions. We know how decisions are made by firms and consumers in a market economy, but government decisions are based on different criteria. Democratic governments have to make decisions reflecting majority wants. Because these decisions fail to incorporate the preferences of each individual voter, majority voting may produce inefficient economic outcomes. Moreover, majority voting may not be able consistently to rank society's preferences for public goods and services. Finally, there may be significant divergence between "sound economics" and "good politics"; rather than getting the most out of limited resources and giving the public what it wants most, the public sector may fail to do so because of the power of special interest groups, opportunism by politicians, and simple bureaucratic inefficiency.

As you read this chapter, keep the following points in mind:

- We live in a world of limited resources but unlimited wants. The theory of public choice must be understood within these two fundamental facts.
- By definition, democratic governments have to make decisions that reflect the wishes of the majority. But gauging the wishes of millions of people is not easy, and since utility is a subjective criterion, decisions will never please everyone.
- The difficulty of gauging the desires of millions of people can lead to some group trying to exert its choice on the rest by claiming that its wishes are those of the rest of society.

This chapter will examine some of these difficulties. Specifically, we scrutinize the problems that society has in revealing its true preferences through majority voting. This is followed by a discussion of *government failure* — the contention that certain characteristics of the public sector hinder government's ability to assist the market system in achieving an efficient allocation of resources. Next, we turn towards an analytical examination of taxes and tax incidence. We want to learn how taxes are apportioned in Canada and who bears the burden. After examining the Goods and Services Tax (GST) introduced in 1991, we briefly discuss the conservative and liberal stances on government and economic freedom.

This is a chapter on **public choice theory** — the economic analysis of government decision making; and on selected topics and problems of **public finance** — the study of public expenditures and revenues.

REVEALING PREFERENCES THROUGH MAJORITY VOTING

Which public goods should government produce and in what amounts? In what circumstances and through what methods should government intervene to correct for externalities? How should the tax burden of financing government be apportioned?

Decisions like these concern government and are made collectively in Canada through a democratic process relying heavily on majority voting. Political parties offer voters alternative policy packages, and we elect people who we think will make the best decisions on our collective behalf. Voters "retire" officials who do not adequately represent their collective wishes and elect persons who convince them they will better reflect the collective wants of the electorate. Also, citizens periodically have opportunities at the provincial and municipal levels to vote directly on ballot issues involving public expenditures or new legislation.

Although this democratic process generally works well at revealing society's true preferences, it has shortcomings. Just as the market fails in some cases to allocate resources efficiently, our system of voting sometimes produces inefficiencies and inconsistencies.

INEFFICIENT VOTING OUTCOMES

Providing a public good having a total benefit greater than its total cost will add to society's well-being. Unfortunately, majority voting raises the possibility of economically inefficient outcomes. Voters may defeat a proposal to provide a public good even though it may yield total benefits exceeding its total cost. And it's possible that majority voting could result in provision of a public good costing more than the benefits it yields.

ILLUSTRATION: INEFFICIENT "NO" VOTE

Suppose a public good, say, national defence, can be provided at a total expense of $900. Also, assume there are only three individuals — Adams, Benson, and Conrad — in the society and they will equally share the $900 tax expense; each will be taxed $300. Suppose, as illustrated in Figure 20-1(a), that Adams is willing to pay $700 to have this good; Benson, $250; and Conrad, $200.

What might be the result if a majority vote is determined on whether this good will be provided? Although people do not always vote strictly on the basis of their own economic interest, it is likely Benson and Conrad will vote "No" because they will incur tax expenses of $300 each while gaining benefits of only $250 and $200, respectively. The majority vote in this case will defeat the proposal even though the total benefit of $1150 (= $700 for Adams + $250 for Benson + $200 for Conrad) exceeds the total cost of $900. More resources should be devoted to this good, but they are not.

ILLUSTRATION: INEFFICIENT "YES" VOTE

We can construct an example illustrating the converse — the majority favouring the provision of a public good even though its total cost exceeds its total benefit. Figure 20-1(b) shows the details. Again, Adams, Benson, and Conrad will equally share the $900 cost of the public good; they each will be taxed $300. But, now Adams is willing to pay only $100 for the public good, rather than forgo it. Meanwhile, Benson and Conrad are willing to pay $350 each. They will vote for the public good; Adams will vote against it. The election will result in provision of a public good costing $900 that produces total benefits of $800 (= $100 for Adams + $350 for Benson + $350 for Conrad). Society's resources will be inefficiently allocated to this public good.

CONCLUSION

The point of our examples is that an inefficiency may occur as either an overproduction or underproduction of a specific public good, and therefore an overallocation or underallocation of resources for that particular use. In Chapter 19 we saw that government might improve economic efficiency by providing public goods that the market system would not make available. Now we have extended that analysis to reveal that government might fail to provide some public goods whose production is economically justifiable while providing other goods not economically warranted.

Our examples illustrate that people have only a single vote no matter how much they might gain or lose from a public good. In both examples shown in Figure 20-1, if buying votes were legal, Adams would be willing to purchase a vote from either Benson or Conrad, paying for it out of prospective personal gain. In the marketplace the consumer can decide *not* to buy a good, even though it is popular with others. Also, specific goods are normally available to

---

FIGURE 20-1 Inefficient voting outcomes

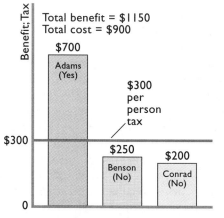

(a) Inefficient "no" vote

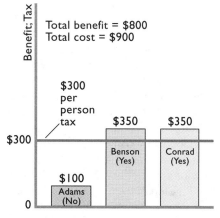

(b) Inefficient "yes" vote

Majority voting can produce inefficient decisions. In (a), majority voting leads to rejection of a public good that would entail a greater total benefit than total cost. In (b), majority voting results in provisions of a public good having a higher total cost than total benefit.

people with strong preferences for them even though most consumers conclude that product prices exceed the marginal utilities of these goods. A consumer can buy beef tongues and fresh squid in some supermarkets, but it is doubtful these products would be available under a system using majority voting to stock the shelves. On the other hand, you cannot easily "buy" national defence once the majority has decided it is not worth buying.

Because it fails to incorporate the preferences of the individual voter, majority voting may produce inefficient economic outcomes.

INTEREST GROUPS AND LOGROLLING Ways exist through which inefficiencies associated with majority voting *may* get resolved. Two examples:

1. INTEREST GROUPS Those who have strong preference for a public good may band together into an interest group and use advertisements, mailings, and the like to try to convince others of the merits of a public good. In our first example [Figure 20-1(a)], Adams might try to convince Benson and Conrad national defence is actually worth more than the $250 and $200 values they place on it.

2. POLITICAL LOGROLLING Logrolling — *the trading of votes to secure favourable outcomes on decisions that otherwise would be adverse* — can turn an inefficient outcome into an efficient one. In our first example [Figure 20-1(a)], perhaps Benson has a strong preference for a different public good, say, a new road, which Adams and Conrad do not think is worth the tax expense. Now, an opportunity has developed for Adams and Benson to trade votes to ensure provision of *both* national defence and the new road. The majority vote (Adams and Benson) in our three-person society will result in a positive vote for both national defence and the road. Without the logrolling, each would have been rejected. This logrolling will add to society's well-being if, as was true for national defence, the road creates a positive overall net benefit.

Logrolling need not increase economic efficiency. We could construct a scenario in which both national defence and the road individually cost more than the total benefits they each provide, and yet both would be provided because of vote trading. All that is necessary for the road and national defence to be provided is that Adams and Benson each secure net gains from their favoured public good.

The tax cost imposed on Conrad by the expenditures for national defence and the road could exceed Conrad's benefits so much that it swamped the combined net benefit received by Adams and Benson from the public goods. Under majority voting and logrolling, government will provide each of the public goods and shift a large net burden to Conrad. Political scientists call this practice "pork-barrel politics" (getting public goods for constituents from the public barrel).

Logrolling can either increase or diminish economic efficiency depending on the circumstances.

THE PARADOX OF VOTING

Another difficulty with majority voting is the **paradox of voting**, *a situation where society may not be able to rank its preferences consistently through majority voting.*

PREFERENCES Consider Table 20-1 where we again assume a community of three voters: Adams, Benson, and Conrad. Suppose the community has three alternative public goods from which to choose: national defence, a road, and a weather warning system. We would expect each member of the community to arrange the order of the three alternatives according to her or his preferences and then select the one preferred. This implies each voter will state that he or she prefers national defence to a road, next, a road to a weather warning system, or whatever. We can then attempt to determine the collective preference scale of the community using a majority voting procedure. Specifically, a vote can be held between any two of the public goods and the winner of the contest matched against the third public good.

The three goods and the assumed individual preferences of the three voters are listed at the top of Table 20-1. In the lower part, outcomes of various elections are listed. The upper portion indicates that Adams prefers national defence to the road and the road to the weather warning system. This implies Adams prefers national defence to the weather warning system. Benson values the road more than the weather warning system and the warning system more than national defence. Benson therefore prefers the road to national defence. Conrad's first choice is the weather warning system, second choice is national defence, and third choice is the road.

TABLE 20-1 Paradox of voting

	PREFERENCES		
Public good	Adams	Benson	Conrad
National defence	1st choice	3rd choice	2nd choice
Road	2nd choice	1st choice	3rd choice
Weather warning system	3rd choice	2nd choice	1st choice

	VOTING OUTCOMES
Election	Winner
(1) National defence vs. road	National defence (preferred by Adams and Conrad)
(2) Road vs. weather warning system	Road (preferred by Adams and Benson)
(3) National defence vs. weather warning system	Weather warning system (preferred by Benson and Conrad)

VOTING OUTCOMES Consider the outcomes of three hypothetical elections decided through majority vote. First, let us match national defence against the road in an election. In Table 20-1 national defence will win this contest because a majority of voters, Adams and Conrad, prefer national defence to a road. This outcome is reported in row (1) of the lower part of the table, where election outcomes are summarized. Next we hold an election to see whether this community wants a road or a weather warning system. A majority of voters, Adams and Benson, prefer the road to the weather warning system, as shown in row (2).

We have determined that the majority in this community prefer national defence to a road *and* prefer a road to a weather warning system. It seems logical to conclude the community prefers national defence to a weather warning system. But it does not!

To demonstrate this, consider a direct election between national defence and the weather warning system. In row (3) a majority of voters, Benson and Conrad, prefer the weather warning system to national defence. As indicated in Table 20-1, majority voting falsely implies that this community is irrational: it seems to prefer national defence to a road *and* a road to a weather warning system, but would rather have a weather warning system than national defence.

The problem is not irrational preferences, but rather a flawed procedure for determining those preferences. Majority voting can yield opposing outcomes depending on how the vote on public expenditures or other public issues is ordered. Majority voting fails under some circumstances to make *consistent* choices that reflect the community's underlying preferences. As a consequence, government might find it difficult to provide the "correct" public goods by acting in accordance with majority voting. (**Key Question 2**)

MEDIAN-VOTER MODEL

One final aspect of majority voting reveals insights into real-world phenomena. The **median-voter model** suggests that *under majority rule the median voter will in a sense determine the outcomes of elections.* The median voter is the person holding the middle position on an issue: One-half of the other voters have stronger preferences for an expenditure on a public good, amount of taxation, or the degree of government regulation; the other one-half have weaker — or negative — preferences. The extreme voters on each side of an issue prefer the median choice rather than the other extreme position, so the median voter's choice will predominate.

EXAMPLE Suppose a society composed of Adams, Benson, and Conrad have reached agreement that as a society they need a weather warning system. Each independently is to submit a total dollar amount he or she thinks should be spent on the warning system, assuming each will be taxed one-third of that amount. An election will determine the size of the system. Because each person can be expected to vote for his or her own proposal, no majority will occur if all the proposals are placed on the ballot at the same time. Thus, the group decides they will first vote between two of the proposals and then match the winner of that vote against the remaining proposal.

The three proposals are as follows: Adams desires a $400 system; Benson wants an $800 system; Conrad opts for a $300 system. Which proposal will win? The median-voter model suggests it will be the $400 proposal submitted by the median voter, Adams. One-half of the other voters favours a more costly system; one-half favours a less costly system. To understand why the $400 system will be the outcome we need to conduct two elections.

First, suppose that the $400 proposal is matched against the $800 proposal. Adams naturally will vote for her $400 proposal, but how will Benson and Conrad vote? Conrad — who proposed a $300 expenditure for the warning system — will vote for the $400 proposal rather than the one for $800. Adams's $400 proposal is selected by a 2-to-1 majority vote.

Next, we match the $400 proposal against the $300 proposal. Again the $400 proposal wins, because it gets a vote from Adams and one from Benson, who proposed the $800 expenditure and for that reason prefers a $400 expenditure to a $300 one. Adams — the median voter in this case — in a sense is the person who has decided the level of expenditure on a weather warning system for this society.

REAL-WORLD APPLICABILITY   Although a simple illustration, this idea explains much. We *do* note a tendency for public choices to match up closely with the median view. We observe political candidates appealing to the median voter *within the party* to get the nomination. They then shift their views more closely to the political centre when they square off against their opponent from the opposite political party. In effect, they redirect their appeal towards the median voter *within the total population.* They also try to label their opponents as being too liberal, or too conservative, and out of touch with the "mainstream." And they conduct polls and adjust their positions accordingly.

IMPLICATIONS   Two implications of the median voter model arise.

1. Many people will be dissatisfied by the extent of government involvement in the economy. The size of government will largely be determined by the median preference, leaving many people desiring a much larger, or a much smaller, public sector. In the marketplace you can buy 0 zucchinis, 2 zucchinis, or 200 zucchinis, depending on how much you enjoy them. In the public sector you get the number of hospital and provincial highways the median voter prefers.

2. Some people may "vote with their feet" by moving into political jurisdictions where the median voter's preferences are closer to their own. Someone may move from the city to a suburb where the level of government services and therefore taxes are lower. Or they may move into an area known for its excellent, but expensive, school system. Demographic changes within political jurisdictions also occur that change the median preference.

For these reasons, and because our personal preferences for government activity are not static, the median preference within political jurisdictions shifts over time. Also, information about people's preference is imperfect, leaving much room for politicians to mistake the true median position. **(Key Question 3)**

PUBLIC SECTOR FAILURE

It is clear that the economic functions of government are not always performed effectively and efficiently. Just because the economic results of the market are not entirely satisfactory, it does not necessarily follow that the political process will do better.

We might agree that government has a legitimate role in dealing with instances of market failure; government should make adjustments for spillover costs and benefits, provide public goods and services, provide information, and so forth. We might also accept benefit-cost analysis as a guide to efficient decision making in the public sector. But a fundamental question remains: Are there inherent problems or shortcomings within the public sector that constrain governmental decision making as a mechanism for promoting economic efficiency?

Casual reflection suggests there may be significant divergence between "sound economics" and "good politics." Sound economics calls for the public sector to pursue various programs so long as marginal benefits exceed marginal costs. Good politics, however, suggests that politicians support those programs and policies that will maximize their chances of getting elected and retained in office.

Let's briefly consider some reasons for **public sector failure** — why the public sector may function inefficiently.

SPECIAL INTERESTS AND "RENT SEEKING"

Ideally, public decisions promote the general welfare or, at least, the interests of the vast majority of the citizenry. But, instead, government often promotes the goals of small special-interest groups to the detriment of the larger public.

SPECIAL-INTEREST EFFECT Efficient public decision making is often impaired by a **special-interest effect**. A special-interest issue is a program or policy from which a small number of people individually will receive *large* gains at the expense of a vastly larger number of persons who individually suffer *small* losses.

The small group of potential beneficiaries will be well informed and highly vocal on this issue, pressing politicians for approval. The large numbers who face very small losses will generally be uninformed and indifferent on this issue; they have little at stake. Politicians feel they will lose the support of the small special-interest group that supports the program if they vote against it. But politicians will *not* lose the support of the large group of uninformed voters who will evaluate them on other issues in which these voters have a stronger interest. Furthermore, the politicians' inclination to support special-interest legislation is enhanced by the fact that such groups are often more than willing to help finance the campaigns of "right-minded" politicians. The result is that the politician will support the special-interest program, even though it may *not* be economically desirable from a social point of view.

RENT-SEEKING BEHAVIOUR This pursuit through government of a transfer of wealth at someone else's or society's expense is called **rent-seeking behaviour**. Used here, "rent" means any payment to a resource supplier, business, or other organization

above the amount that would accrue under competitive market conditions. Corporations, trade associations, labour unions, and professional organizations employ vast resources to secure "rent" directly or indirectly dispensed by government. Government provides this "rent" through legislation and policies that increase payments to some groups, leaving others or society less well-off.

There are many examples of special-interest or rent-seeking groups realizing legislation and policies unjustified on the basis of efficiency or equity tariffs on foreign products that limit competition and raise prices to consumers; tax loopholes that benefit only the wealthy; public work projects that cost more than the benefits they yield; occupational licensing that goes beyond what's needed to protect consumers; and large subsidies to farmers by taxpayers.

CLEAR BENEFITS, HIDDEN COSTS

Some say vote-seeking politicians will not *objectively* weigh all costs and benefits of various programs, as economic rationality demands, in deciding which to support and which to reject. Because political officeholders must seek voter support every few years, politicians favour programs with immediate and clear-cut benefits, on the one hand, and vague, difficult-to-identify, or deferred, costs, on the other. Conversely, politicians will shun programs that have easily identifiable costs along with future benefits that are diffuse and vague.

Such biases in the area of public choice can lead politicians to reject economically justifiable programs and to accept programs that are economically irrational. Example: A proposal to construct and expand mass-transit systems in large metropolitan areas may be economically rational on the basis of objective benefit-cost analysis as illustrated in Table 19-2. But if (1) the program is to be financed by immediate increases in highly visible income or sales taxes *and* (2) benefits will accrue only a decade hence when the project is completed, the vote-seeking politician may oppose the program.

Assume, on the other hand, that a proposed program of increased federal aid to housing is *not* justifiable on the basis of objective benefit-cost analysis. But if costs are concealed and deferred through deficit financing, the program's modest benefits may loom so large that it gains political approval.

LIMITED AND BUNDLED CHOICES

Public choice theorists also argue the political process is such that citizens and their elected MPs are forced to be less selective in the choice of public goods and services than they are in the choice of private goods and services.

In the private sector, the citizen *as consumer* can reflect personal preferences precisely by buying certain goods and forgoing others. However, in the public sector the citizen *as voter* is confronted with two or more candidates for office, each of whom represents different "bundles" of programs (public goods and services). In no case is the bundle of public goods represented by any particular candidate likely to fit precisely the wants of the particular voter. Voter Smith's favoured candidate for office may endorse national dental insurance, the development of nuclear energy, subsidies to tobacco farmers, and tariffs on imported automobiles. Citizen Smith votes for this candidate because the bundle of programs she endorses comes closest to matching Smith's preferences, even though Smith may oppose tobacco subsidies and tariffs on foreign cars.

The voter must take the bad with the good; in the public sector, we are forced to "buy" goods and services we do not want. It is as though, in going to a sporting goods store, you were forced to buy an unwanted pool cue to get a wanted pair of running shoes. This is clearly a situation where resources are *not* being used efficiently to satisfy consumer wants best. In this sense, the provision of public goods and services is inherently inefficient.

Similarly, the limited-choice, bundling problem confronts Parliament. Legislation often combines hundreds, or even thousands, of spending items into a single bill. These bills may even contain spending items unrelated to the main purpose of the legislation. Members of Parliament must vote on the entire package — yea or nay. Unlike consumers in the marketplace, they cannot be selective. (**Key Question 6**)

BUREAUCRACY AND INEFFICIENCY

It is contended that private businesses are innately more efficient than public agencies. The reason is *not* that lazy and incompetent workers somehow end up in the public sector, while the ambitious and capable gravitate to the private sector. Rather, it is held that the market system creates incentives and pressures for internal efficiency that are absent in the public sector. The managers of private enterprises have a strong personal incentive — increased profits — to be efficient in their operation. Whether a private firm is in a competitive or monopolistic environment, lower costs through efficient management contribute to enlarged profits. There is no tangible personal gain — a counterpart to profits — for the government bureau chief who achieves efficiency within his or her domain.

There is simply less incentive to be cost-conscious in the public sector. In a larger sense the market system imposes an explicit test of performance on private firms — the test of profits and losses. An efficient firm is profitable and therefore successful; it survives, prospers, and grows. An inefficient enterprise is unprofitable and unsuccessful; it declines and in time goes bankrupt and ceases to exist. But there is no similar, clear-cut test for us to assess efficiency or inefficiency of public agencies. How can anyone determine whether the Canadian Broadcasting Corporation, a university, a local fire department, or the Ministry of Agriculture, is operating efficiently?

Cynics argue that a public agency that uses its resources inefficiently may be in line for a budget increase! In the private sector, inefficiency and monetary losses lead to abandonment of certain activities — the discontinuing of certain products and services. But government, it is contended, is loath to abandon activities in which it has failed. Some suggest the typical response of government to failure of a program is to double its budget and staff. This means public sector inefficiency may be sustained on a larger scale.

Furthermore, returning to our earlier comments on special-interest and rent-seeking groups, public programs spawn new constituencies of bureaucrats and beneficiaries whose political clout causes programs to be sustained or expanded after they have fulfilled their goals — even if they have failed miserably in their mission. Relevant bureaucrats, school administrators, and teachers may band together to become a highly effective special-interest group for sustaining inefficient programs of provincial funding of education or for causing these programs to be expanded beyond the point at which marginal benefits equal marginal costs.

Some specific suggestions have been offered recently to deal with the problems of bureaucratic inefficiency. Benefit-cost analysis is one approach. It has also been proposed that all legislation establishing new programs contain well-defined performance standards so the public can better judge efficiency. Further, the suggestion has been made that expiration dates — so called "sunset laws" — be written into all new programs, forcing a thorough periodic evaluation that might indicate the need to abandon the program.

QUICK REVIEW 20-1

1. Majority voting can produce voting outcomes that are inefficient; projects having greater total benefits than costs can be defeated and projects having greater total costs than total benefits can win.

2. The paradox of voting occurs where voting by majority rule fails to provide a consistent ranking of society's preferences for public goods and services.

3. The median-voter model suggests that under majority rule the voter having the middle preference will determine the outcome of an election.

4. Public-sector failure allegedly occurs because of rent-seeking by special-interest groups, shortsighted political behaviour, limited and bundled choices, and bureaucratic inefficiency.

IMPERFECT INSTITUTIONS

It is possible to argue these criticisms of public sector efficiency are overdrawn and too cynical. Perhaps. Nevertheless, they are sufficiently persuasive to shake our faith in a simplistic concept of a benevolent government responding with precision and efficiency to the wants of its citizenry. The private sector is by no means perfectly efficient. Government's economic functions are attempts to correct the market system's shortcomings. But the public sector may also be subject to deficiencies in fulfilling its economic functions.

One implication of the fact that the market system and public agencies are both imperfect institutions is that, in practice, it can be difficult to determine whether some particular activity can be performed with greater success in the private or the public sector. It is easy to reach agreement on opposite extremes: National defence must lie in the public sector, whereas wheat production can best be accomplished in the private sector. But what about dental insurance? The provision of parks and recreation areas? Fire protection? Garbage collection? Housing? Education? Postal services? It is very hard to assess each type of good or service and to say unequivocally that its provision should be assigned to either the public or the private sector. Evidence? All the goods and services just mentioned are provided in part by both private enterprises and public agencies.

APPORTIONING THE TAX BURDEN

We now turn from the difficulties of making collective decisions on the types and amounts of public goods to the difficulties in deciding how those goods should be financed.

The characteristics of public goods and services make it hard to measure precisely how their benefits are apportioned among individuals and institutions. It is virtually impossible to determine accurately how much John Doe benefits from military installations, a network of highways, a public school system, the national weather bureau, and local police and fire protection.

The situation is a bit different on the taxation side of the picture. Studies reveal with somewhat greater clarity the way the overall tax burden is apportioned. This is a question affecting each of us. Although the average citizen is concerned with the overall level of taxes, chances are he or she is even more interested in exactly how the tax burden is allocated among individual taxpayers.

BENEFITS RECEIVED VERSUS ABILITY TO PAY

There are two basic philosophies on how the economy's tax burden should be apportioned.

BENEFITS-RECEIVED PRINCIPLE The **benefits-received principle** of taxation asserts that households and businesses should purchase the goods and services of government in the same way other commodities are bought. Those who benefit most from government-supplied goods or services should pay the taxes necessary for financing them. A few public goods are financed on this basis. Gasoline taxes are typically earmarked for financing highway construction and repairs. People who benefit from good roads pay the cost of those roads.

Difficulties immediately arise, however, when an accurate and widespread application of the benefits principle is considered:

1. How does government determine the benefits individual households and businesses receive from national defence, education, and police and fire protection? Recall that public goods provide widespread spillover benefits and that the exclusion principle is inapplicable. Even in the seemingly tangible case of highway finance we find it difficult to measure benefits. Individual car owners benefit in different degrees from good roads. And those who do not own cars also benefit. Businesses certainly benefit greatly from the widening of their markets that good roads encourage.

2. Government efforts to redistribute income would be self-defeating if financed on the basis of the benefits principle. It would be absurd and self-defeating to ask poor families to pay the taxes needed to finance their welfare payments! It would be ridiculous to think of taxing only unemployed workers to finance the unemployment insurance payments that they receive.

ABILITY-TO-PAY PRINCIPLE   The **ability-to-pay principle** rests on the idea that the tax burden should be geared directly to a taxpayer's income and wealth. In Canada the ability-to-pay principle means that individuals and businesses with larger incomes should pay more taxes — both absolutely and relatively — than those with modest incomes.

What is the rationale of ability-to-pay taxation? Proponents argue that each additional dollar of income received by a household will yield smaller and smaller increments of satisfaction, or marginal utility. Because consumers act rationally, the first dollars of income received in any period of time will be spent on high-urgency goods that yield the greatest marginal utility. Successive dollars of income will go for less urgently needed goods and finally for trivial goods and services. This means a dollar taken through taxes from a poor person who has few dollars is a greater sacrifice than is a dollar taken by taxes from the rich person. To balance the sacrifices that taxes impose on income-earners, taxes should be apportioned according to the amount of income one receives.

This argument is appealing, but problems of application exist. Although we might agree that the household earning $100,000 per year has a greater ability to pay taxes than the household receiving $10,000, exactly *how much more* ability to pay does the first family have as compared with the second? Should the rich person pay the *same percentage* of his or her larger income — and hence a larger absolute amount — as taxes? Or should the rich person be made to pay a *larger fraction* of this income as taxes?

The problem is there is no scientific way of measuring someone's ability to pay taxes. In practice, the answer hinges on guesswork, the tax views of the political party in power, expediency, and how urgently the government needs revenue.

PROGRESSIVE, PROPORTIONAL, AND REGRESSIVE TAXES

Any discussion of the ability-to-pay and the benefits-received principles of taxation ultimately leads to the question of tax rates and the manner in which tax rates change as income increases.

DEFINITIONS   Taxes are classified as progressive, proportional, or regressive. These designations focus on the relationship between tax rates and *income* simply because all taxes — regardless of whether they are on income or on a product or building or parcel of land — are ultimately paid out of someone's income.

1. A tax is **progressive** if its average rate *increases* as income increases. Such a tax claims not only a larger absolute amount, but also a larger fraction or percentage of income as income increases.
2. A **regressive** tax has an average rate that *declines* as income increases. Such a tax takes a smaller and smaller proportion of income as income increases. A regressive tax may or may not take a larger absolute amount of income as income expands.
3. A tax is **proportional** when its average rate *remains the same*, regardless of the size of income.

We can illustrate these ideas with the personal income tax. Suppose tax rates are such that a household pays 10% of its income in taxes, regardless of the size of its income. This is a proportional income tax.

Now suppose the rate structure is such that the household with an annual taxable income of less than $10,000 pays 5% in income taxes, the household realizing an income of $10,000 to $20,000 pays 10%, $20,000 to $30,000 pays 15%, and so forth. This would be a *progressive* income tax.

Now for the case where the rates decline as taxable income rises: You pay 15% if you earn less than $10,000; 10% if you earn $10,000 to $20,000; 5% if you earn $20,000 to $30,000; and so forth. This a *regressive* income tax.

In general, progressive taxes are those that weigh most heavily on the rich; regressive taxes are those that hit the poor relatively hardest. (**Key Question 9**)

APPLICATIONS   What can we say about the progressivity, proportionality, or regressivity of the kinds of taxes in Canada?

1. PERSONAL INCOME TAX   The federal *personal income tax* can be said to be reasonably progressive with marginal tax rates ranging from 15 to 49%.

2. SALES TAXES   At first glance a *general sales tax* with, say, a 3% rate would seem to be proportional. But in fact it is regressive with respect to income. A larger portion of a poor person's income is exposed to the tax than is true for a rich person; the rich avoid the tax on the part of income that is saved, whereas the poor are unable to save. Example: "Poor" Smith has an income of $15,000 and spends it all. "Rich" Jones has an income of $300,000 but spends only $200,000 of it. Assuming a 3% sales tax applies to the expenditures of each individual, we find Smith will pay $450 (3% of $15,000) in sales taxes, and Jones will pay $6000 (3% of $200,000). While *all* of Smith's $15,000 income is subject to the sales tax, only two-thirds of Jones's $300,000 income is taxed. Thus, while Smith pays $450, or 3%, of a $15,000 income as sales taxes, Jones pays $6000, or just 2%, of a $300,000 income. We conclude that the general sales tax is regressive. In Canada, sales taxes are levied for the most part by provincial governments. They vary from no sales tax in Alberta to a 12% sales tax in Newfoundland.

3. CORPORATE INCOME TAX   The *corporate income tax* is a flat-rate proportional tax levied by the federal government with a 28% tax rate. But this assumes that corporation owners (shareholders) bear the tax. Some tax experts argue that at least a part of the tax is passed through to consumers in the form of higher product prices. To the extent that this occurs, the tax tends to be regressive, like a sales tax.

4. PROPERTY TAXES   Most economists conclude that *property taxes* on buildings are regressive for the same reasons as sales taxes. First, property owners add the tax to the rents that tenants are charged. Second, property taxes, as a percentage of income, are higher for poor families than for rich families because the poor must spend a larger proportion of their incomes for housing.[1] The alleged regressivity of the property tax may be reinforced because property-tax rates are not likely to be uniform.

---

[1] Controversy arises in part because empirical research that compares the value of housing to lifetime (rather than a single year's) income suggests that this ratio is approximately the same for all income groups.

GLOBAL PERSPECTIVE 20-I

Taxes on goods and services as a percentage of total tax revenues, selected nations

Compared to its major trading partner, the United States, Canada relies more heavily on goods and services taxes (sales taxes, value-added taxes, and specific excise taxes). Canada's rates are closer to European Union countries.

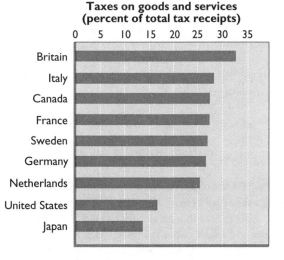

Taxes on goods and services (percent of total tax receipts)

Britain, Italy, Canada, France, Sweden, Germany, Netherlands, United States, Japan

Source: *Statistical Abstract of the United States 1994*, p. 867.

TAX INCIDENCE AND EFFICIENCY LOSS

Determining whether a particular tax is progressive, proportional, or regressive is complicated because the taxes do not always stick where they are levied. We therefore need to locate as best we can the final resting place of a tax, or, more technically, the **tax incidence**. The tools of elasticity of supply and demand are of considerable help in this endeavour. Let's focus on a hypothetical excise tax levied on producers of wine. Do producers pay this tax, or do they shift it to wine consumers? This analysis will provide a logical bridge to a discussion of other aspects of the economic burden of a tax.

ELASTICITY AND TAX INCIDENCE

Figure 20-2 shows the market for a certain domestic wine and the no-tax equilibrium price and quantity of

---

FIGURE 20-2   **The incidence of an excise tax**

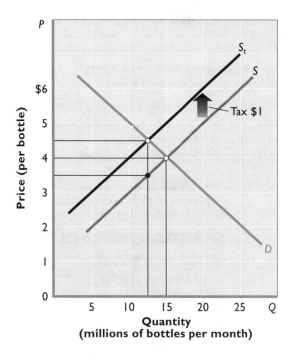

An excise tax of a specified amount, say $1 per unit, shifts the supply curve upward by the amount of the tax. This results in a higher price ($4.50) to the consumer and a lower after-tax price ($3.50) to the producer. In this particular case, consumers and producers equally share the burden of the tax.

$4 per bottle and 15 million bottles. Assume that government levies a specific sales or excise tax of $1 per bottle on this wine. What is the incidence of this tax?

DIVISION OF BURDEN   Assuming that government places the tax on sellers (suppliers), the tax can be viewed as an addition to the supply price of the product. While sellers were willing to offer, for example, 5 million bottles of untaxed wine at $2 per bottle, they must now receive $3 per bottle — $2 plus the $1 tax — to offer the same 5 million bottles. Sellers must get $1 more for each quantity supplied to receive the same per unit price they were getting before the tax. The tax shifts the supply curve upward as shown in Figure 20-2, where S is the "no-tax" supply curve and S_t is the "after-tax" supply curve.

Careful comparison of after-tax supply and demand with the pretax equilibrium reveals that with the tax the new equilibrium price is $4.50 per bottle, compared with the before-tax price of $4. In this case, one-half of the tax is paid by consumers as a higher price and the other half by producers as a lower after-tax price. Consumers pay 50¢ more per bottle and, after remitting the $1 tax per unit to government, producers receive $3.50, or 50¢ less than the $4 before-tax price. In this instance, consumers and producers share the burden of the tax equally.

ELASTICITIES   If the elasticities of demand and supply were different from those shown in Figure 20-2, the incidence of the tax would also be different. Two generalizations are relevant.

1. *With a specific supply, the more inelastic the demand for the product, the larger the portion of the tax shifted to consumers.* To verify this, sketch graphically the extreme cases where demand is perfectly elastic and perfectly inelastic. In the first case the incidence of the tax is entirely on sellers; in the second, the tax shifts entirely to consumers.
   Figure 20-3 contrasts the more likely cases where demand might be relatively elastic (D_e) or relatively inelastic (D_i) in the relevant price range. In the elastic demand case of Figure 20-3(a) a small portion of the tax (PP_e) is shifted to consumers and most of the tax (PP_a) is borne by producers. In the inelastic demand case of Figure 20-3(b), most of the tax (PP_i) is shifted to consumers and only a small amount (PP_b) is paid by producers.

FIGURE 20-3   Demand elasticity and the incidence of an excise tax

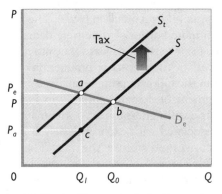

(a) Tax incidence and elastic demand

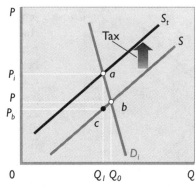

(b) Tax incidence and inelastic demand

In (a) we find that if demand is elastic in the relevant price range, price will rise modestly (P to P_e) when an excise tax is levied. Hence the producer bears most of the tax burden. But if demand is inelastic, as in (b), the price to the buyer will increase substantially (P to P_i), and most of the tax is thereby shifted to consumers.

The decline in equilibrium quantity is smaller, the more inelastic the demand. This recalls one of our previous applications of the elasticity concept: Revenue-seeking legislatures place heavy excise taxes on liquor, cigarettes, automobile tires, and other products whose demand is thought to be inelastic.

2. *With a specific demand, the more inelastic the supply, the larger the portion of the tax borne by producers.* While the demand curves are identical, the supply curve is elastic in Figure 20-4(a) and inelastic in Figure 20-4(b). For the elastic supply curve most of the tax (PP_e) is shifted to consumers and only a small portion (PP_a) is borne by producers or sellers. But where supply is inelastic, the reverse is

true. The major portion of the tax (PP_b) falls on sellers and a relatively small amount (PP_i) is shifted to buyers. Quantity also declines less with an inelastic supply than it does with an elastic supply.

Gold is an example of a product with an inelastic supply and therefore one where the burden of an excise tax would fall mainly on producers. On the other hand, because the supply of baseballs is elastic, much of an excise tax on baseballs would get passed on to consumers.

EFFICIENCY LOSS OF A TAX

We have just observed that an excise tax on producers in a market characterized by typical supply

FIGURE 20-4   Supply elasticity and the incidence of an excise tax

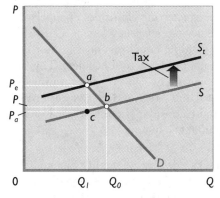

(a) Tax incidence and elastic supply

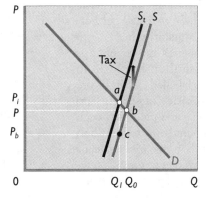

(b) Tax incidence and inelastic supply

Figure (a) indicates that with an elastic supply, an excise tax results in a large price increase (P to P_e), and the tax is paid largely by consumers. But if supply is inelastic, as in (b), the price rise will be small (P to P_i) and sellers will have to bear most of the tax.

FIGURE 20-5 **Efficiency loss of a tax**

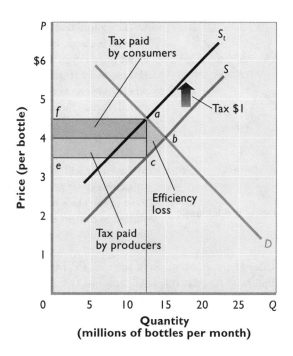

The levy of a $1 excise tax per bottle of wine increases the price per bottle to $4.50 and reduces the equilibrium quantity by 2.5 million bottles. Government's tax revenue is $12.5 million (area *efac*). The efficiency loss of the tax is the amount shown as triangle *abc*.

and demand curves is borne partly by producers and partly by consumers. Let's look more closely at the burden of an excise tax. Figure 20-5 is identical to Figure 20-2 but contains additional detail needed for our discussion.

TAX REVENUE   The $1 excise tax on wine increases the market price from $4 to $4.50 per bottle and reduces the equilibrium quantity from 15 to 12.5 million bottles. Government's tax revenue is $12.5 million (= $1 × 12.5 million bottles), an amount shown as the rectangle labelled *efac* in Figure 20-5. In this case, the elasticities of supply and demand are such that consumers and producers each pay one-half of this total amount, or $6.25 million apiece (= $.50 × 12.5 million bottles). Government uses this $12.5 million of tax revenue to provide public goods and services. There is no loss of well-being to society as a whole from this transfer from consumers and producers to government.

EFFICIENCY LOSS   The $1 tax on wine requires consumers and producers to pay $12.5 million of taxes, but also *reduces the equilibrium amount of wine produced and consumed by 2.5 million bottles.* The fact that 2.5 million more bottles of wine were demanded and supplied prior to the tax means they provided benefits in excess of their costs of production. We can see this from the following simple analysis.

The *ab* segment of demand curve *D* in Figure 20-5 indicates the willingness to pay — the marginal benefit — associated with each of these 2.5 million bottles consumed before the tax. The *cb* segment of supply curve *S* reflects the marginal cost of each of the bottles of wine. For all but the very last one of these 2.5 million bottles, the marginal benefit (shown by *ab*) exceeds the marginal cost (shown by *cb*). The reduction of well-being because these 2.5 million bottles are not produced is indicated by the triangle *abc*. This triangle shows the **efficiency loss of the tax.** *This loss is the sacrifice of net benefit accruing to society because consumption and production of the taxed product are reduced below their allocatively efficient levels.*

ROLE OF ELASTICITIES   Most taxes create some degree of efficiency loss. The amount depends on supply and demand elasticities. Glancing back to Figure 20-3, we observe that the efficiency loss triangle *abc* is greater in Figure 20-3(a), where demand is relatively elastic, than in Figure 20-3(b), where demand is relatively inelastic. Similarly, the area *abc* is greater in Figure 20-4(a) than in Figure 20-4(b), indicating a large efficiency loss where supply is more elastic.

The principle our analysis establishes is that the amount of efficiency loss of an excise tax or sales tax varies from market to market depending on the elasticities of supply and demand. *Other things equal, the greater the elasticities of supply and demand, the greater the efficiency loss of a particular tax.* Two taxes yielding equal revenues do not necessarily have equal tax burdens for society. This fact complicates government's job of determining the best way to collect its needed tax revenues. Government must consider the efficiency losses of taxes in an optimal tax system.

QUALIFICATION   We must qualify our analysis. Other tax goals in many instances may be more important than the goal of minimizing efficiency losses from taxes. Two examples:

1. REDISTRIBUTIVE GOALS Government may wish to impose progressive taxes as a way to redistribute income. A 10% excise tax placed on selected luxuries would be a case in point. Because the demand for luxuries is elastic, efficiency losses from this tax could be substantial. However, if the benefits from the redistribution effects of this tax would exceed these efficiency losses then a government would go ahead with such a tax.

2. REDUCING NEGATIVE EXTERNALITIES Government may have intended the $1 tax on wine in Figure 20-2 to reduce consumption of wine by 2.5 million bottles. It may have concluded that consumption of alcoholic beverages produces certain negative externalities. Therefore, it might have levied this tax to adjust the market supply curve for these costs to reduce the amount of resources allocated to wine. (**Key Question 11**)

QUICK REVIEW 20-2

1. The benefits-received principle holds that government should assess taxes on individuals according to the amount of benefits they receive, regardless of their income; the ability-to-pay tax principle holds that people should be taxed according to their income, regardless of the benefits they receive from government.

2. As income increases, the average tax rate rises for a progressive tax, remains the same for a proportional tax, and falls for a regressive tax.

3. For a product having an excise tax, the more inelastic the demand the more the tax borne by consumers; the more inelastic the supply, the larger the portion borne by producers.

4. The efficiency loss of a tax results from the loss of output for which marginal benefits exceed marginal costs.

RECENT CANADIAN TAX REFORM

The Canadian tax system has undergone two major changes in the last several years. These are (a) the 1987 Tax Reform and (b) the **Goods and Services Tax** (GST). It must be kept in mind that we refer to the federal government only; each province also levies a number of taxes, some in conjunction with the federal government.

THE 1987 TAX REFORM

Spurred on by the recent tax reform in the United States that significantly lowered marginal tax rates, the Canadian government simplified the personal income tax from 11 categories to only 3. The general implication is to lower the marginal tax rate, which combined with provincial levies was as high as 64%, and at the same time to eliminate tax deductions in favour of tax credits. The top federal marginal tax rate has come down to about 45%.

Subsequent to these reforms the federal surtax was increased and a "claw back" provision that in effect took back part of the social insurance benefits, primarily unemployment insurance and family allowance, paid to higher income Canadians. Both of these provisions made the income tax system more progressive.

THE GST

The controversy surrounding the introduction of the GST was unprecedented. Much of the dispute arose because of misunderstandings and a concerted and highly publicized effort by the official opposition in Parliament, the Liberal Party, to defeat the legislation.

The GST is similar to a **value-added tax** (VAT). It is much like a sales tax, except that it applies only to the difference between the value of a firm's sales and the value of its purchases from other firms. This is done by allowing firms a tax credit equal to the taxes paid on their inputs.

The GST replaced the federal sales tax, which was levied primarily on manufactured goods and was as high as 13% on some products. The GST at present stands at 7% and is levied on a much broader base that includes both goods and services. The only exemptions are agricultural and fish products, prescription drugs, and medical devices.

An important feature of the GST is that exports are in fact exempt since producers can claim a credit equal to the taxes paid on the inputs used to produce the product. Moreover, imported goods are subject to the GST, so they are at no particular advantage compared to domestically produced goods.

The GST's implementation on January 1, 1991, coincided with the country slipping into a recession. Many quickly jumped to the conclusion that the GST at least aggravated, if it was not the cause of, the recession. The government claims the GST will be revenue neutral: it will raise revenues just offset by the elimination of the federal sales tax.

There appears to be a consensus among economists that the GST is an improvement over the old federal sales tax since it introduces fewer distortions to the price of goods and services. For our exporters it is a definite advantage. Moreover, those in the lower income brackets receive a tax credit. Thus, it is not as regressive as some critics claim.

THE ISSUE OF FREEDOM

We end our discussion of government decision making by considering an elusive question: What is the relationship between the role and size of the public sector and individual freedom? Although no attempt is made here to explore this issue in depth, let's outline two divergent views.

THE CONSERVATIVE POSITION

Many conservative economists believe that, in addition to the economic costs of any expansion of the public sector, there is also a cost in the form of diminished individual freedom. Here's why.

First, there is the "power corrupts" argument.[2] "Freedom is a rare and delicate plant ... history confirms that the great threat to freedom is the concentration of power ... by concentrating power in political hands, [government] is ... a threat to freedom."

Second, we can be selective in the market system of the private sector, using our income to buy precisely what we choose and rejecting unwanted commodities. But, as noted, in the public sector — even assuming a high level of political democracy — conformity and coercion are inherent. If the majority decides in favour of certain governmental actions — to build a reservoir, to establish dental insurance, to provide a guaranteed annual income — the minority must conform. The "use of political channels, while inevitable, tends to strain the social cohesion essential for a stable society."[3] Because decisions can be rendered selectively by individuals through markets, the need for conformity and coercion is lessened and this "strain" reduced. The

scope of government should be strictly limited. Finally, the power and activities of government should be dispersed and decentralized.

THE LIBERAL STANCE

But liberal economists are sceptical of the conservative position. They say the conservative view is based on the **fallacy of limited decisions**. Conservatives implicitly assume that during any particular period there is a limited, or fixed, number of decisions to be made in the operation of the economy. If government makes more of these decisions in performing its stated functions, the private sector of the economy will necessarily have fewer "free" decisions or choices to make. This is considered to be flawed reasoning. By sponsoring the production of public goods, government is *extending* the range of free choice by permitting society to enjoy goods and services that would not be available without governmental provision.

We can argue it is largely through the economic functions of government that we have freed ourselves in some measure from ignorance, unemployment, poverty, disease, crime, discrimination, and other ills. In providing most public goods, government does not typically undertake production itself, but rather purchases these goods through private enterprise. When government decides to build a highway, private firms are given the responsibility of making many specific decisions and choices in connection with carrying out this decision.

A noted economist has summarized the liberal view in these pointed words:

> Traffic lights coerce me and limit my freedom. Yet in the midst of a traffic jam on the unopen road, was I really "free" before there were lights? And has the algebraic total of freedom, for me or the representative motorist or the group as a whole, been increased or decreased by the introduction of well-engineered stop lights? Stop lights, you know, are also go lights.... When we introduce the traffic light, we have, although the arch individualist may not like the new order, by cooperation and coercion created by ourselves greater freedom.[4]

---

[2] Milton Friedman, *Capitalism and Freedom* (Chicago: The University of Chicago Press, 1962), p. 2.

[3] Ibid., p. 23.

[4] Paul A. Samuelson, "Personal Freedoms and Economic Freedoms in the Mixed Economy," in Earl F. Cheit (ed.), *The Business Establishment* (New York: John Wiley & Sons, Inc., 1964), p. 219.

CHAPTER SUMMARY

1. Majority voting creates a possibility of **a** an underallocation or overallocation of resources to a particular public good, and **b** inconsistent voting outcomes. The median-voter model predicts that, under majority rule, the person holding the middle position on an issue will in a sense determine the election outcome.

2. Public choice theorists cite a number of reasons that government might be inefficient in providing public goods and services. **a** There are strong reasons for politicians to support special-interest legislation. **b** Public choice may be biased in favour of programs with immediate and clear-cut benefits and difficult-to-identify costs *and* against programs with immediate and easily identified costs and vague or deferred benefits. **c** Citizens as voters and government representatives face limited bundle choices as to public goods and services; whereas consumers in the private sector can be highly selective. **d** Government bureaucracies have less incentive to operate efficiently than do private businesses.

3. The benefits-received principle of taxation is that those who receive the benefits of goods and services provided by government should pay the taxes required to finance them. The ability-to-pay principle is that those who have greater income should be taxed absolutely and relatively more than those who have less income.

4. The federal personal income tax is progressive. The flat-rate federal corporate income tax is regressive. General sales and property taxes are regressive.

5. Excise taxes affect supply and therefore equilibrium price and quantity. The more inelastic the demand for a product, the greater the proportion of the tax shifted to consumers. The greater the inelasticity of supply, the larger the proportion of tax borne by the seller.

6. Taxation involves loss of some output whose marginal benefit exceeds its marginal cost. The more elastic the supply and demand curves, the greater is this efficiency loss of a particular tax.

7. Sales taxes are likely to be shifted; personal income taxes are not. Specific excise taxes may or may not be shifted to consumers, depending on the elasticities of demand and supply. There is disagreement as to whether corporate income taxes are shifted. The incidence of property taxes depends primarily on whether the property is owner- or tenant-occupied.

8. The 1987 federal tax reform simplified income taxes and lowered the marginal tax rate.

9. The GST is similar to a value-added tax. It is more favourable than the federal sales tax it replaced because it introduces fewer distortions, exports are exempt, and imports will compete on equal footing with domestic goods.

10. Conservatives and liberals disagree as to the relationship between the size of the public sector and individual freedom in a society.

TERMS AND CONCEPTS

ability-to-pay principle (p. 432)
benefits-received principle (p. 432)
efficiency loss of a tax (p. 436)
fallacy of limited decisions (p. 438)
Goods and Services Tax (p. 437)
logrolling (p. 426)
median-voter model (p. 427)
paradox of voting (p. 426)
progressive tax (p. 432)

proportional tax (p. 432)
public choice theory (p. 424)
public finance (p. 424)
public sector failure (p. 429)
regressive tax (p. 432)
rent-seeking behaviour (p. 429)
special-interest effect (p. 429)
tax incidence (p. 434)
value-added tax (p. 437)

QUESTIONS AND STUDY SUGGESTIONS

1. Explain how affirmative and negative majority votes can sometimes lead to inefficient allocations of resources to public goods. Is this problem likely to be greater under a benefits-received or an ability-to-pay tax system? Use the information in Figures 20-1(a) and 20-1(b) to show how society might be better off if Adams were allowed to buy votes.

2. *Key Question* *Explain the paradox of voting through reference to the accompanying table that shows the ranking of three public goods by voters Larry, Curley, and Moe.*

Public good	Larry	Curley	Moe
Courthouse	2nd choice	1st choice	3rd choice
School	3rd choice	2nd choice	1st choice
Park	1st choice	3rd choice	2nd choice

3. *Key Question* *Suppose that there are only five people in a society and that each favours one of the five flood-control options shown in Table 19-2 (include no protection as one of the options). Explain which of these flood-control options will be selected using a majority rule. Will this option be the optimal size of the project from an economic perspective?*

4. Carefully evaluate this statement: "The public, as a general rule, gets less production in return for a dollar spent by government than from a dollar spent by private enterprise."

5. "To show that a perfectly functioning government can correct some problem in a free economy is not enough to justify governmental intervention, for government itself does not function perfectly." Discuss in detail.

6. *Key Question* *How does the problem of limited and bundled choices in the public sector relate to economic efficiency? Why are public bureaucracies alleged to be less efficient than private enterprises?*

7. Explain: "Politicians would make more rational economic decisions if they weren't running for re-election every few years." Do you think this statement has a bearing on the growth of our public debt?

8. Distinguish between the benefits-received and the ability-to-pay principles of taxation. Which philosophy is more evident in our present tax structure? Justify your answer. To which principle of taxation do you subscribe? Why?

9. *Key Question* *Suppose a tax is such that an individual with an income of $10,000 pays $2000 of tax; a person with an income of $20,000 pays $3000 of tax; a person with an income of $30,000 pays $4000 of tax, and so forth. What is each person's average tax rate? Is this tax regressive, proportional, or progressive?*

10. What is meant by a progressive tax? A regressive tax? A proportional tax? Comment on the progressivity or regressivity of each of the following taxes, indicating in each case your assumption concerning tax incidence:

   a. The federal personal income tax

   b. A 7% general sales tax

   c. A federal excise tax on automobile tires

   d. A municipal property tax on real estate

   e. The federal corporate income tax

11. *Key Question* *What is the incidence of an excise tax when demand is highly inelastic? Elastic? What effect does the elasticity of supply have on the incidence of an excise tax? What is the efficiency loss of a tax and how does it relate to elasticity of demand and supply?*

12. Suppose you are heading a tax commission responsible for establishing a program to raise new revenue through excise taxes. Would elasticity of demand be important to you in determining those products on which excises should be levied? Explain.

13. Briefly explain the federal tax reforms of 1987 and the GST. What are the main advantages of the GST?

14. "The market economy is the only system compatible with political freedom. We therefore should greatly restrain the economic scope of government." Do you agree?

15. **Advanced Analysis:** Suppose that the equation for the demand curve for some product X is $P = 8 - .6Q$ and the supply curve is $P = 2 + .4Q$. What is the equilibrium price and quantity? Now suppose that an excise tax is imposed on X such that the new supply equation is $P = 4 + .4Q$. How much tax revenue will this excise tax yield the government? Graph the curves and label the area of the graph that represents the tax collection TC and the area that represents the efficiency loss of the tax EL. Briefly explain why area EL is the efficiency loss of the tax.

CHAPTER 21

AGRICULTURE: ECONOMICS AND POLICY

An economic analysis of Canadian agriculture can be justified on a number of grounds. Including the processing, wholesale, and retail sectors, agriculture accounts for approximately 20% of Canada's GDP. Moreover, agriculture employs about 3% of the nation's labour force.

It is a sector that, in the absence of government farm programs, is a real-world example of Chapter 10's purely competitive model. The sector is composed of many firms selling virtually standardized products. Agriculture can be understood by applying the demand and supply tools of competitive markets. As such, agricultural markets can reveal the intended and unintended effects of government policies that interfere with the forces of supply and demand.

Agriculture reflects the increasing globalization of markets. In recent decades the economic ups and downs of Canadian agriculture have been closely tied to its ability to gain access to world markets. Farm policies also provide an excellent illustration of Chapter 20's special-interest effect and rent-seeking behaviour.

BOX 21-1 THE BIG PICTURE

This chapter is the application of microeconomic theory to analyze the problems of the agricultural sector. Given that without food we would certainly perish, agriculture has always held our intense interest. The very necessity of agriculture to the sustaining of life has also often led to policies that have not served the interest of consumers. We have witnessed continual government intervention in agriculture through efforts to keep agricultural commodity prices from falling below certain levels, and heavy subsidization of certain crops. While the intentions of these policies were honourable, the outcome has often been inefficiencies, waste, and price distortions.

As you read this chapter, keep the following points in mind:

• Some of agriculture's problems are short-run, others are irreversible and long-run phenomenon.

• Historically, the major problem has been to produce more agricultural commodities. Ironically, in the late twentieth century, the main problem is an overabundance of agricultural output.

• Technological improvements have greatly increased the productivity of agriculture.

ECONOMICS OF AGRICULTURE

Farmers in the past have frequently faced severe problems of fluctuating prices and relatively low incomes. We distinguish between (1) the **short-run farm problem** of year-to-year fluctuations in farm prices and incomes, and (2) the **long-run farm problem** relating to forces causing agriculture to be a declining industry.

SHORT-RUN PROBLEM: PRICE AND INCOME INSTABILITY

The short-run farm problem is the result of (1) an inelastic demand for agriculture products; (2) fluctuations in farm output; and (3) shifts in the demand curve.

INELASTIC DEMAND FOR AGRICULTURAL PRODUCTS   In most developed societies, the price elasticity of demand for agricultural products is low. For farm products in the aggregate, the elasticity coefficient is estimated to be from .20 to .25. These figures suggest the prices of agricultural products would have to fall by 40 to 50% for consumers to increase their purchases by a mere 10%. Consumers apparently put a low value on additional agricultural output compared with alternative goods.

Why is this so? Recall that the basic determinant of elasticity of demand is substitutability. When the price of a product falls, the consumer will substitute *that* product for other products whose prices have not fallen. But in wealthy societies this

"substitution effect" is very modest for food. People do not switch from three to five or six meals each day in response to declines in the relative prices of agricultural products. An individual's capacity to substitute food for other products is subject to very real biological constraints.

The inelastic demand for agricultural products can also be explained in terms of diminishing marginal utility. In a wealthy society, the population by and large is well fed and well clothed; it is relatively saturated with the food and fibre of agriculture. Therefore, additional agricultural output entails rapidly diminishing marginal utility. Thus it takes very large price cuts to induce small increases in consumption. Curve D in Figure 21-1 portrays the inelastic demand for agricultural products.

FLUCTUATIONS IN OUTPUT   The inelastic demand for farm products magnifies small changes in agricultural production into relatively larger changes in farm prices and incomes. Farmers have limited control over their production. Floods, droughts, an unexpected frost, insect damage, rust and smut fungi, and similar disasters can mean poor crops while an excellent growing season may mean bumper crops. Weather and related factors are beyond the control of farmers, yet they exert an important influence on production.

The highly competitive nature of agriculture makes it impossible for farmers to control production unless governments authorize and assist in the setting-up of marketing boards, as has happened in

FIGURE 21-1 The effect of output changes on farm prices and incomes

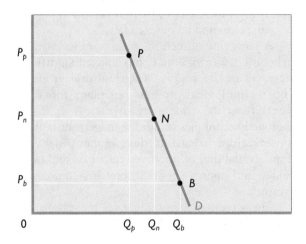

Because of the inelasticity of demand for farm products, a relatively small change in output (Q_n to Q_p or Q_b) will cause relatively large changes in farm prices (P_n to P_p or P_b) and incomes $0P_nNQ_n$ to $0P_pPQ_p$ or $0P_bBQ_b$).

Canada. In the absence of such boards, if hundreds of thousands of widely scattered and independent producers should by chance plant an unusually large or abnormally small portion of their land, very large or small outputs would result, even if the growing season were normal.

Combining the instability of farm production with the inelastic demand for farm products in Figure 21-1, we can see why farm prices and incomes are unstable. Even if we assume that the market demand for agriculture products is stable at D, the price inelastic demand will magnify small changes in output into relatively large changes in farm prices and income. For example, assume that a "normal" crop of Q_n results in a "normal" price of P_n and a "normal" farm income represented by $0P_nNQ_n$. But a bumper crop or a poor crop will cause large deviations from these normal prices and incomes.

If a good growing season occurs, the resulting bumper crop of Q_b will reduce farm incomes from $0P_nNQ_n$ to $0P_bBQ_b$. When demand is inelastic, an increase in the quantity sold will be accompanied by a *more than* proportionate decline in price. The net result is that total revenue (total farm income) will decline.

Similarly, for farmers as a group, a poor crop caused by drought may boost farm incomes. A poor crop of Q_p will raise total farm income from $0P_nNQ_n$ to $0P_pPQ_p$ because a decline in output will cause a *more than* proportionate increase in price when demand is inelastic. Ironically, for farmers as a group, a poor crop may be a blessing and a bumper crop a hardship. Conclusion: *Given a stable market demand for farm products, inelastic demand will turn relatively small changes in output into relatively larger changes in farm prices and incomes.*

FLUCTUATIONS IN DOMESTIC DEMAND The other aspect of the short-run instability of farm incomes has to do with shifts in the demand curve for agricultural products. Suppose that somehow agricultural output is stabilized at the "normal" level of Q_n in Figure 21-2. Now, because of the inelastic demand for farm products, short-run fluctuations in the demand for these products will cause markedly different prices and incomes to be associated with this level of production that we assume to be constant.

A slight drop in demand from D_0 to D_1 will reduce farm incomes from $0P_0aQ_n$ to $0P_1bQ_n$. A relatively small decline in demand gives farmers a

FIGURE 21-2 The effect of demand changes on farm prices and incomes

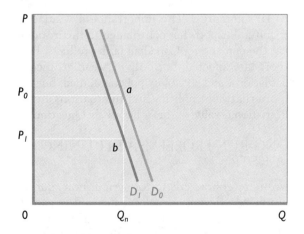

Because of the highly inelastic demand for agricultural products, a small shift in demand (D_0 to D_1) will cause drastically different levels of farm prices (P_0 to P_1) and farm incomes ($0 P_0aQ_n$ to $0P_1bQ_n$) to be associated with a given level of production Q_n.

drastically reduced money reward for the same amount of production. Conversely, a slight increase in demand — as from D_1 to D_0 — will bring an equally sharp increase in farm incomes for the same volume of output. These large price-income changes occur because demand is inelastic.

UNSTABLE FOREIGN DEMAND   The cause of farm prosperity in the 1970s was booming agricultural exports, while the collapse of export markets caused the farm crisis of the early 1980s. This turnabout shows Canadian agriculture is heavily dependent on world markets, which can be a source of demand volatility.

Changes in weather and crop production *in other countries* can affect the demand and, thus, the income of Canadian farmers. Similarly, cyclical fluctuations in incomes in Europe or Japan, for example, can shift the demand for Canadian farm products. So can changes in foreign economic policies. If the nations of western Europe decide to provide their farmers with greater protection from foreign (Canadian) competition, Canadian farmers will have less access to those markets and export demand will fall. International politics can also add to demand instability. Changes in the international value of the dollar can be critical. The depreciation of the dollar in the 1970s increased the demand for Canadian farm products, while appreciation of the dollar against overseas currencies decreased foreign demand in the early 1980s.

To summarize: The importance of Canadian agricultural exports has contributed to the instability of the demand for Canadian farm products. Farm exports are affected, not only by weather, income fluctuations, and economic policies abroad, but also by international politics and fluctuations in the international value of the dollar. **(Key Question 1)**

LONG-RUN PROBLEM: A DECLINING INDUSTRY

Two more characteristics of agricultural markets must be added to price inelastic demand to explain why agriculture has been a declining industry:

1. Over time the supply of agricultural products has increased rapidly because of technological progress.
2. Demand for agricultural products has increased slowly over time because demand for them is inelastic with respect to income.

TECHNOLOGY AND SUPPLY INCREASES
When a price inelastic and slowly increasing demand for farm products is accompanied by a rapidly increasing supply, there is persistent pressure for farm prices and incomes to fall.

A rapid rate of technological advance, particularly since World War I, has caused significant increases in the supply of agricultural products. This technological progress has many roots: the electrification and mechanization of farms; improved techniques of land management and soil conservation; irrigation; development of hybrid crops; availability of improved fertilizers and insecticides; and improvements in breeding and care of livestock.

These technological advances have been very significant. The amount of capital used per worker increased tremendously over the 1930–1995 period, permitting approximately a five-fold increase in the amount of land cultivated per farmer. The simplest general index is the increasing number of people a single farmer's output will support. Ninety years ago many Canadian farms were of the subsistence type: the farm kept the family alive and that was about all. By 1946, one farm worker produced enough food and fibre to support 15 people. By 1995 the number had risen to over 80! This gives some indication of the extent to which productivity in agriculture has risen. Since World War II productivity in agriculture has increased almost twice as fast as in the non-farm economy.

It is worth noting that most technological advances have *not* been initiated by farmers but are rather the result of government-sponsored programs of research and education and the work of farm machinery producers. Experimental farms, provincial agricultural representatives, educational pamphlets issued by the federal and provincial departments of agriculture, and the research departments of farm machinery, pesticide, and fertilizer producers are the primary sources of technological advance in Canadian agriculture.

LAGGING DEMAND   Increases in demand for agricultural commodities have failed to keep pace with technologically inspired increases in their supply. The reason lies in the two major determinants of agricultural demand — incomes and population.

INCOME INELASTIC DEMAND In less-developed countries, consumers must devote the bulk of their meagre incomes to sustain themselves. But as income expands beyond subsistence, consumers will increase their outlays on food at ever-declining rates. Once the stomach is filled, the consumer's thoughts turn to the amenities of life that industry — not agriculture — provides. Economic growth in Canada has boosted average per capita income far beyond the level of subsistence. As a result, *increases in the incomes of Canadian consumers lead to less-than-proportionate increases in expenditures on farm products.*

In technical terms, the demand for farm products is *income-inelastic*; it is quite insensitive to increases in income. Estimates indicate that a 10% increase in real per capita disposable income entails at most an increase in the consumption of farm products of only 2%. Certain specific farm products — for example, potatoes and lard — may be inferior goods; that is, as incomes increase, purchases of these products may actually decrease (Chapter 4).

POPULATION GROWTH Despite the fact that after a minimum income level is reached, each individual consumer's intake of food and fibre will become relatively fixed, more consumers increase the demand for farm products. In most advanced nations, the demand for farm products increases at a rate roughly corresponding to the rate of population growth. But population increases, added to the relatively small increase in the purchase of farm products that occurs as incomes rise, have not been great enough to match accompanying increases in farm output. Indeed, it is pertinent to note that population growth in Canada has slowed in recent decades.

GRAPHIC PORTRAYAL Coupled with the inelastic demand for agricultural products, these shifts in supply and demand have reduced farm incomes. This is illustrated in Figure 21-3, where a large increase in supply is shown against a modest increase in demand. Because of the inelastic demand for farm products, these shifts have resulted in a sharp decline in farm prices accompanied by relatively small increases in sales. Farm incomes therefore tend to decline. Graphically, income before the increase in supply occurs (measured by rectangle $0P_0aQ_0$) will exceed farm income after

FIGURE 21-3 A graphical summary of the long-run farm problem

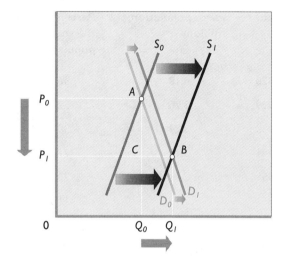

In the long run, increases in the demand for agricultural products (D_0 to D_1) have not kept pace with the increases in supply (S_0 to S_1) that technological advances have permitted. Coupled with the fact that agricultural demand is inelastic, these shifts have tended to depress farm prices (as from P_0 to P_1) and incomes (as from $0P_0aQ_0$ to $0P_1bQ_1$).

supply increases ($0P_1bQ_1$). The income "loss" of P_1P_0AC is not fully offset by the income "gain" of Q_0CBQ_1. *Given an inelastic demand for farm products, an increase in the supply of farm products relative to the demand for them has created persistent tendencies for farm incomes to be low in comparison to non-farm incomes.*

CONSEQUENCES The consequences have been essentially those predicted by the purely competitive model. Because of the demand and supply conditions just outlined, farm incomes were substantially less than nonfarm incomes during most of the post-World War II period. But this income differential triggered a massive exodus of labour from agriculture to other sectors of the economy as shown by Table 22-1. Consequently, farm incomes have risen relative to nonfarm incomes so that rough equality was realized by the mid-1980s. In the late 1980s and early 1990s average incomes of farm households have been 10 to 30% *higher* than average incomes of nonfarm households. (**Key Question 3**)

TABLE 21-1 The declining farm population, selected years, 1920-1991

Year	Farm population, millions	Percentage of the total population
1920	3.18	36.6
1929	3.26	32.2
1933	3.24	30.3
1941	3.15	27.4
1951	2.91	20.8
1961	2.13	11.7
1971	1.49	6.9
1981	1.08	4.4
1991	0.88[*]	3.2

[*]Estimate based on size of agricultural labour force.

Source: O.J. Firestone, *Canada's Economic Development 1867-1953* (London: Bowes & Bowes, 1958), p. 60, and Statistics Canada, *Census of Canada, 1931-1991.*

QUICK REVIEW 22-1

1. Agricultural prices and incomes are volatile in the short run because an inelastic demand translates small changes in farm output and demand into relatively larger price and income changes.

2. Technological progress has generated large increases in supplies of farm products over time.

3. Increases in demand for farm products have been modest because demand is inelastic with respect to income.

4. The combination of large supply increases and small demand increases has made agriculture a declining industry.

ECONOMICS OF FARM POLICY

Governments, both federal and provincial, have been increasingly involved in farm policy since World War I. Land clearing, drainage, production extension, farm management,

GLOBAL PERSPECTIVE 21-1

Percentage of labour force in agriculture, selected nations

Rich nations have much smaller percentages of their labour forces in agriculture than do poor nations. Because their work forces are so heavily committed to producing the food and fibre needed for their populations, poor nations have relatively little labour available to produce housing, schools, autos, and the other goods and services that contribute to a high standard of living.

Percentage of labour force in agriculture

Ethiopia	
Mozambique	
China	
India	
Brazil	
Japan	
France	
Canada	
United States	

Source: United Nations, *Human Development Report, 1994,* pp. 162–163, 194. Data are for 1990–1992.

pest and weed control, research, grading, and inspection services have long been fields for government involvement. But since the 1930s, detailed "farm programs" dealing with (1) farm prices, incomes, and output, (2) farm credit, and (3) crop insurance have been implemented. There is now more government involvement in agriculture than in any other goods-producing sector. The aim of farm policy is to both increase and stabilize farm prices and incomes. Those goals have been achieved through a combination of subsidies, price floors, and marketing boards.

A variety of arguments have been made to justify government involvement in the agricultural sector.

1. Farmers are comparatively poor and should therefore receive higher prices and incomes through public help.

2. Farmers are subject to certain extraordinary hazards — floods, droughts, and invasion by hordes of insects — to which other industries are not exposed and which cannot be fully insured.
3. While farmers are faced with highly competitive markets for their outputs, they buy inputs from industries that have considerable market power. Most firms from which farmers buy fertilizer, farm machinery, and gasoline have some capacity to control their prices. Farmers, in contrast, are at the "mercy of the market" in selling their outputs. Agriculture is the last stronghold of pure competition in an otherwise imperfectly competitive economy; it warrants public aid to offset the disadvantageous terms of trade that result.

FARM PRODUCTS MARKETING BOARDS

Government involvement in the farm produce marketplace began before the 1930s. With the Great Depression and with farm produce prices and incomes depressed, the federal government appointed a Royal Commission on Price Spreads. The commission reported that the hundreds of thousands of farm producers were no match for the concentrated agribusiness with which they dealt. With competitive farmers producing and selling and oligopolies buying and processing, market power was one-sided. Faced with a low offer-to-buy price, farmers could not successfully withhold their produce to force up the price.

The political pressure of farmers led to the federally enacted Natural Products Marketing Act in 1934, which set up a Federal Marketing Board. This board could delegate its power to local producers' boards, its most important power being to control the sales of a product.

By the end of 1935, about 20 marketing boards were functioning across Canada, but the federal law was declared *ultra vires* by the courts on the grounds that under the BNA Act, regulation of trade *within* a province was reserved exclusively to the provinces.

Several provinces, starting with British Columbia in 1936 and Ontario in 1937, passed laws to allow the already functioning marketing boards to continue under provincial authority. By 1940, all the provinces had farm marketing legislation in force except for Quebec, which brought in such legislation in 1956.

The following is an overview of the major legislation passed with regards to marketing boards and some of the boards and commissions created.

THE CANADIAN WHEAT BOARD The Canadian Wheat Board Act was passed in 1935. The Wheat Board is still with us, though under revised legislation. This Crown corporation has complete control over the price and marketing of western wheat.

When farmers deliver their wheat to the Wheat Board, they get an initial payment per bushel. This is in effect a floor price and is set low enough that the Wheat Board is confident of being able to meet it out of sales. There may be an interim payment, but almost always a final payment when the wheat is sold. The producers get the full selling price, less transportation and storage costs, and Wheat Board expenses.

AGRICULTURAL PRODUCTS MARKETING ACT This Act was passed by Parliament in 1949. It is the counterpart of the provincial legislation, for this federal law "permits extension of the powers of provincial marketing boards into interprovincial and export trade."

PROVINCIAL FARM PRODUCTS MARKETING ACTS Under these provincial umbrella Acts there now exist in Canada about 150 provincial marketing boards for farm commodities ranging from asparagus to wool. Under these provincial Acts, once a marketing board has been authorized to act at the request of the majority of producers of a specified primary or processed agricultural commodity, then all producers of that commodity are required by law to comply with the marketing board's regulations. The boards go beyond merely negotiating with agribusiness on behalf of the producers. The boards also have the power to allocate quotas, set prices, issue licences, collect fees, and require that the commodity be marketed through them. In a word, the boards create a monopoly. Since the federal government usually prevents the import of food in such quantities as would depress domestic farm prices, the agribusiness pays a marketing board's price or does not buy at all. More than half of the total cash receipts of our farmers are received through marketing boards.

But this does not mean that all farmers make a good living. There are still too many producers of any given commodity, and for many commodities — such as beef, pork, cereals and much of horticulture — no marketing boards exist.

AGRICULTURAL STABILIZATION BOARD
This is a federal agency established under the Agricultural Stabilization Act in 1958. By law it must support the following commodities at not less than 90% of their average price over the previous five years, with adjustments according to production costs: cattle, hogs, and sheep; industrial milk and cream; and oats and barley not produced on the Prairies (where the Canadian Wheat Board has jurisdiction). The Agricultural Stabilization Board supports prices by buying products outright at the minimum prices set by the law, by granting deficiency payments (see below), or by making direct payments to producers at a fixed rate.

AGRICULTURAL PRODUCTS BOARD This federal board — which has the same staff as the Agricultural Stabilization Board — buys, sells, or imports agricultural products and administers food contracts and other commodity operations. It may purchase and hold stocks of agricultural products for later sale, emergency relief in Canada, or assistance programs abroad.

CANADIAN DAIRY COMMISSION This important federal commission, established in 1966, works with the provincial milk marketing boards to ensure (1) a "fair" return to producers of cream and industrial milk — used in the manufacture of cheese, butter, and powdered milk — and (2) an adequate supply to consumers. The commission supports the market price of major processed products by buying and selling dairy products. In addition, the commission supplements returns from the market by making direct payments of government funds to individual producers under a quota system.

CANADIAN LIVESTOCK FEED BOARD Established as a Crown corporation in 1966, this board subsidizes part of the cost of moving feed grains to Eastern Canada and British Columbia to attain, generally, a "fair" equalization of feed grain prices in those parts of Canada. The board may buy, ship, store, handle, and sell feed grains.

NATIONAL FARM PRODUCTS MARKETING COUNCIL The Act setting up this council in 1972 provided for federal marketing agencies to regulate in interprovincial and export trade any farm product with the exception of those regulated by

the Canadian Wheat Board and the Canadian Dairy Commission. Thus, the Canadian Egg Marketing Agency was set up in December 1972, the Canadian Turkey Marketing Agency in 1973, and the Canadian Chicken Marketing Agency in 1978. The Canadian Broiler Hatching Egg Agency completes the list of federal marketing agencies.

THE ECONOMICS OF PRICE SUPPORTS

Marketing boards aim to stabilize agricultural prices at a level that insures higher incomes to farmers. This can be accomplished through price supports.

There are two basic methods of supporting prices above their market equilibrium values: (1) offers to purchase and (2) deficiency payments.

OFFERS TO PURCHASE

A marketing board can help to increase farm income by ensuring that the price farmers get for their produce does not fall below a specified minimum. Suppose, in Figure 21-4(a) that the *floor price* — or, as it is commonly called, the **support price** — is P_s as compared with the equilibrium price, P_e. What will be the effect of government making offers to purchase at P_s?

1. SURPLUS OUTPUT The most obvious result is product surpluses. Private consumers will be willing to purchase only $0Q_o$ units at the supported price, while farmers will supply $0Q_s$ units. What happens to the Q_oQ_s surplus that results? The government must buy it to make the above-equilibrium support price effective. Because of such purchases, for example, huge surpluses of butter, skim milk powder, eggs, and pork accumulated in the late 1950s. These large accumulated surpluses were undesirable on two counts. First, their very existence indicated a misallocation of the economy's resources. Government-held surpluses reflected that the economy was devoting large amounts of resources to the production of commodities that, *at existing supported prices*, were not wanted by consumers. Second, the storing of surplus products was expensive, adding to the cost of the farm program and, ultimately, to the consumer's tax bill. By the time the government acted to dispose of its excess butter, it had over 100 million pounds (45 million

FIGURE 21-4 **Price supports and crop restriction**

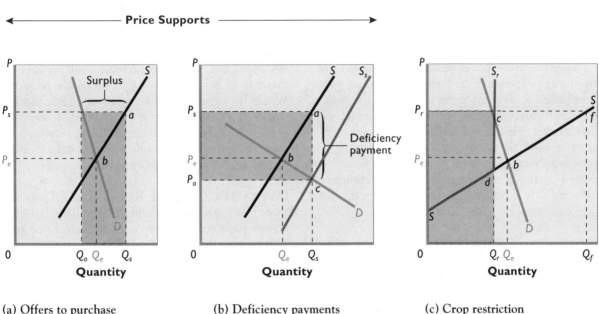

(a) Offers to purchase
Offers to purchase result in surpluses. This method should not be used if demand is elastic.

(b) Deficiency payments
Deficiency payments or subsidies do not result in surpluses. This method should not be used if demand is elastic.

(c) Crop restriction
Crop restriction is the only method with an elastic supply. This method should not be used if demand is elastic. Crop restriction results in neither surpluses nor government payments. All costs (the higher price) are borne by consumers.

kilograms) in storage — much of it rancid. The solution was to convert the butter into butter oil, which was then sold abroad at half the butter price.

2. CONSUMERS LOSS   Consumers "lose" in two ways. First, they will pay a higher price (P_s rather than P_e) and consume less (Q_0 rather than Q_e) of the product. Second, they will be paying higher taxes to finance the government's purchase of the surplus. In Figure 21-4(a), this added tax burden will amount to the surplus output $Q_0 Q_s$, multiplied by its price, P_s. Storage costs add to this tax burden. It is worth noting that the burden of higher food prices falls disproportionately on the poor because they spend a larger portion of their incomes on food.

3. FARMERS GAIN   Farmers gain from price supports. In Figure 21-4(a), gross receipts rise from the free market level of $0P_e bQ_e$ to the supported level of $0P_s aQ_s$.

4. SOCIETAL LOSS   Society at large loses in two important ways. First, taxpayers will pay higher taxes to finance the government's purchase of surplus. In Figure 21-4(a), this added burden will amount to the surplus output $Q_0 Q_s$ multiplied by its price P_s — as shown by the shaded area. Storage costs add to this tax burden as do costs of maintaining the elaborate bureaucracy that administers the various farm programs.

DEFICIENCY PAYMENTS

Deficiency payments are subsidies that make up the difference between the market price and the government supported price; they work as follows: Suppose, in Figure 21-4(b), just as in Figure 21-4(a), that the support price is P_s as compared with the equilibrium price P_e. Also, as before, at price P_s farmers expand production from Q_e to Q_s. However, with demand as shown by D, consumers will only buy Q_s if the price is P_o. The government arranges for this to be the market price by simply subsidizing production by the amount P_oP_s — the government makes a deficiency payment to each producer equal to P_oP_s times the quantity sold.

The total consumer expenditure is $0P_ocQ_s$, total government expenditure is P_oP_sac = deficiency payment times Q_s. The producers are still on the original supply curve S; that is why they produce Q_s when market demand and deficiency payments combine to present them with a price of P_s. However, S_s is the supply curve as seen by the consumer and is created by the government subsidy or deficiency payment. When we analyze the economic effect of these payments, two considerations arise.

ELASTICITY OF SUPPLY AND DEMAND   The incidence of the subsidy, like the sales tax, is related to the elasticity of the supply and demand curves. In Figure 21-4(b), the combined effects of the elastic demand curve in the price range P_oP_s and the inelastic supply curve result in the incidence of the subsidy being heavily in favour of the producer: the producer gets P_eS_s of the deficiency payment, the consumer only P_eP_o. The effect of elasticity on the incidence of a subsidy is precisely the same as that of a sales tax.

The question of price elasticity of demand does have relevance to Canada's programs. Among agricultural commodities, the demand for butter is relatively elastic — which is why the offer-to-purchase program of 1958–59 led to such a mountain of it spoiling in storage. Under the subsidies program that replaced it, Canada no longer has butter in storage.

COMPARING OFFERS TO PURCHASE AND DEFICIENCY PAYMENTS

Assuming, as we have done, that P_s is the same in both Figures 21-4(a) and (b), farmers will benefit equally from the two programs: their total income will be $0P_saQ_s$ in each case. In their role as consumers, the public will prefer **deficiency payments** whereby they receive a large amount of output, Q_s, at a low price, P_0. This compares with a high price, P_s, and small quantity, Q_0, under a program of offers to purchase. But, in addition to being consumers, the public also has a role as taxpayers. Thus when the subsidies of taxpayers to farmers (the shaded

areas) are taken into account, we find that total payments by the public (consumption expenditures plus tax-financed subsidies) to farmers are identical under both programs: $0P_saQ_s$.

Offers to purchase and deficiency payments do entail one rather important difference. As we have already noted, offers to purchase result in government-held surpluses that can be costly to store. While it might be desirable to have some reserve stocks as a buffer against a year or two of crop failures, it is quite another matter for government to spend hundreds of millions a year simply to store large surpluses of farm commodities.

OVERALLOCATION OF RESOURCES   There is a more subtle cost in *both* offers to purchase and deficiency payments. Society loses because price supports contribute to economic inefficiency by encouraging an overallocation of resources to agriculture. A price floor or support (P_s) gives more resources to the agricultural sector than would be generated by the free market (P_e). In terms of Chapter 10's purely competitive model, the market supply curve in Figure 21-4 represents the aggregated marginal costs of all farmers producing this product. An efficient allocation of resources occurs where market price (P_e) is equal to marginal cost at point b. The resulting output of Q_e reflects an efficient allocation of resources. In contrast, the Q_s output associated with the P_s price support represents an overallocation of resources. A misallocation of resources between agriculture and the rest of the economy imposes a cost on society.

ENVIRONMENTAL COSTS   We know from Figure 21-4 that price supports stimulate additional production. Although some of this extra output may require additional land, much of the added production comes from greater use of fertilizer and pesticides. Unfortunately, pesticides and fertilizers are also poisons that may pollute the environment (for example, groundwater) and pose health risks to farmworkers and to consumers as residues in food. Research shows a positive relationship between the level of price-support subsidies and the use of agrichemicals.

Farm policy may cause environmental problems in less obvious ways. First, farmers receive price supports only on land that is consistently used for a specific product such as corn or wheat. This creates a disincentive to practise crop rotation, a nonchemical technique for controlling pests. Farm policy thus encourages the substitution of chemical for non-chemical pest control.

Second, we know from the concept of derived demand that an increase in the price of a product will increase the demand for relevant inputs. Price supports increase the demand for land, therefore tending to bring more land into farm production. This land is often lower-quality "marginal" land. Similarly, price supports induce the use of more water for irrigation and the resulting runoff may contribute to soil erosion.

INTERNATIONAL COSTS   The costs of farm price supports go beyond those implicit in Figure 21-4. Price supports generate economic distortions that transcend national boundaries. For example, above-equilibrium price supports make the Canadian market attractive to foreign producers. But inflows of foreign agricultural products would increase supplies in Canada, aggravating our problem of agricultural surpluses. To prevent this from happening, Canada is likely to impose import barri-

ers in the form of tariffs or quotas. These barriers often restrict the production of more efficient foreign producers, while simultaneously encouraging more production from less efficient Canadian producers. The result is a less efficient use of world agricultural resources.

Similarly, as Canada and other industrially advanced countries with similar agricultural programs dump surplus farm products on world markets, the prices of such products are depressed. Less-developed countries — heavily dependent on world commodity markets — are hurt because their export earnings are reduced. Thus, Canadian price supports for wheat production have imposed significant costs on Argentina, a major wheat exporter. **(Key Question 8)**

COPING WITH SURPLUSES: CROP RESTRICTIONS

Another method for increasing prices to farmers is to manage the amount of land devoted to a given crop.

Suppose in Figure 21-4(c), that the government wishes to assure the producers price P_r. Neither offers to purchase nor deficiency payments would be appropriate because of the *elastic supply* with which we are now faced. An offer to purchase at price P_r would result in a surplus of Q_rQ_f, a greater amount than is bought for domestic consumption. A deficiency payment program makes even less sense, for there is simply no demand for quantity $0Q_f$ at any price.

The only sensible way for the government to ensure price P_r in these circumstances is to impose **crop restriction**. With production restricted to Q_r and with the inelastic demand as shown, price will rise to P_r. The supply curve, in effect, is no longer S, but SdS_r.

Crop or supply restriction is always in effect when marketing boards have the power to allot quotas. Quotas are imposed by the provincial milk marketing boards and the Ontario Flue-Cured Tobacco Growers' Marketing Plan — tobacco being an excellent product both for taxes and crop restriction because of the inelastic demand for it in its present price range.

Operation LIFT (Lower Inventory for Tomorrow) is an example of federal effort at crop restriction. Canada started the 1970–71 crop year with a billion bushels of wheat in storage — some of it still on the farms because of a lack of elevator

GLOBAL PERSPECTIVE 20-2

Agricultural subsidies, selected nations

Canadian farmers receive about 45% of their income as government subsidies; farmers in other nations receive as much as 80% and as little as 4%.

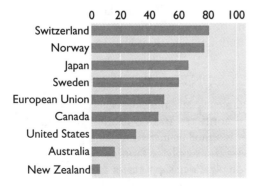

Government subsidies as a
percentage of farmers' income

Source: Organization for Economic Cooperation and Development.

space — and little prospect of selling it at $1.75 a bushel, let alone the $2 figure promised by the federal government in its 1968 election campaign. Under Operation LIFT, a Prairie wheat farmer got $10 for every acre (0.4 hectare) taken out of grain production and put into perennial forage such as hay, or $6 an acre for switching to summer fallow. With up to 1000 acres (400 hectares) eligible, the maximum a farmer could receive was $10,000. The program cost some $140 million and reduced both the wheat acreage and the crop in the 1970–71 crop year by half. The program was successful though, ironically, crop failures elsewhere — especially in what used to be the USSR — were to give farmers within three years not the long-promised $2 wheat but $5 wheat.

CRITICISM OF FARM POLICY

After more than a half century of experience with government policies designed to stabilize and enhance farm incomes, there is considerable evidence to suggest these programs are not working well. There is growing belief among economists and political leaders that the goals and techniques of farm policy must be re-examined and revised. Some of the more important criticisms of agricultural policy follow.

SYMPTOMS AND CAUSES

Our farm programs have failed to get at the causes of the farm problem. Public policy towards agriculture is designed to treat symptoms, not causes. The root *cause* of the farm problem has been a misallocation of resources between agriculture and the rest of the economy. Historically, the problem has been one of too many farmers. The effect or symptom of this misallocation of resources was relatively low farm incomes. *For the most part, public policy in agriculture has been oriented towards supporting farm prices and incomes rather than towards alleviating the resource allocation problem that is the fundamental cause of these relatively low farm incomes.*

Some critics argue further that price-income supports have encouraged people to stay in agriculture when they otherwise would have migrated to some nonfarm occupation. Thus, the price-income orientation of the farm programs have deterred the reallocation of resources that is necessary to resolve the long-run farm problem.

MISGUIDED SUBSIDIES

Price-income support programs have most benefited those farmers who least need government assistance. Assuming the goal of our farm program is bolstering low farm incomes, it follows that any program of government aid should be aimed at farmers at the bottom of the farm income distribution scale. But the poor, small-output farmer does not produce and sell enough in the market to get much aid from price supports. It is the large farm that reaps the benefits by virtue of its large output. If public policy must be designed to supplement farm incomes, a strong case can be made for targeting those benefits to those farmers in most need.

An income-support program should be geared to *people*, not *commodities*. Many economists contend that, on equity grounds, direct income subsidies to poor farmers are highly preferable to indirect price support subsidies, which go mainly to large and prosperous farmers.

A related point concerns land values. The price and income benefits that various farm programs provide are eventually capitalized into higher farmland values. By making crops more valuable, price supports have made the land itself more valuable. Sometimes this is helpful to farmers, but often it is not. To the extent that farmers rent their farmland, price supports become a subsidy to people who are *not* actively engaged in farming.

The quota system has a similar effect with regard to young would-be farmers. Before they may become dairy farmers, for example, they must buy milk quotas from retiring farmers. An adequate quota can easily cost $100,000. The interest payments on this become a permanent fixed cost that for the young farmer may very well eliminate the benefit of the higher price for milk brought about by the quota system. This applies with even greater force in the poultry business: the average value of an egg quota in Ontario is about $250,000.

POLICY CONTRADICTIONS

The complexity and multiple objectives of farm policy yield conflicts and contradictions. Subsidized research is aimed at increasing farm productivity and increasing the supply of farm products, while quotas reduce supply. Price supports for crops mean increased feed costs for ranchers and high prices for animal products to consumers. Tobacco farmers have been subsidized in the past even though serious health problems are associated with tobacco consumption. Conservation programs call for the retirement of vulnerable land, while price supports give incentives to bring additional acreage into production.

DECLINING EFFECTIVENESS

There is also reason to believe that farm policy has become less effective in accomplishing its goals. In the 1930s many farms were small, semi-isolated units that employed modest amounts of machinery and equipment and provided most of their own inputs. Now farms are large, highly capital-intensive, and closely integrated with both the domestic and international economies.

Farmers now depend on others for such inputs as seed, fertilizers, and insecticides. Agriculture uses more than twice as much physical capital (machinery and buildings) per worker as does the economy as a whole. Farmers now need to borrow large amounts of money to finance the purchases of capital equipment and land *and* for operating capital. Despite an elaborate farm policy designed to enhance farm incomes, high interest rates can easily precipitate losses or bankruptcy for many farmers. Dependence on export markets can also undermine farm policy. A fall in foreign incomes or an increase in the international value of the dollar (which makes Canadian farm products more expensive to foreigners) can unexpectedly reduce Canadian farm exports and wipe out any positive effects of agricultural programs on farm incomes. In short, a much wider range of variables may now alter farm incomes and thereby diminish the effectiveness of farm programs.

The difficult issue being brought into focus by these and similar criticisms is whether an increasingly expensive farm program is economically justifiable. Farm programs entail huge and increasing budgetary costs. The subsidies involved do not benefit the most needy farmers. Farm price supports distort economic incentives, which cause overproduction to persist. Farm programs impose substantial costs on consumers and complicate our international economic policies. Against this web of criticism, a number of economists believe that our farm policy is an example of public sector failure (Chapter 20). They suggest that public policy has not resolved the problems of Canadian agriculture, but rather has become a part of those problems.

THE POLITICS OF FARM POLICY

In view of these criticisms, we may ask why we have an extensive and costly farm program. Why not abandon price supports and return to free markets? Why do farm programs persist although the farm population — and the farm vote — has declined historically?

PUBLIC CHOICE THEORY REVISITED

We can respond to these questions largely in terms of Chapter 20's public choice theory concepts. Recall that *rent-seeking behaviour* involves a group — a labour union, firms in a particular industry, or farmers producing a particular product — pursuing political means to transfer income or wealth to themselves at the expense of another group or society as a whole. The *special-interest effect* refers to a program or policy from which a small group receives *large* benefits at the expense of a much larger group who *individually* suffer *small* losses.

Suppose a specific group of farmers — egg producers or dairy farmers — organize themselves and establish a well-financed political action committee (PAC). The PAC's job is to promote the establishment and perpetuation of government programs that will transfer income to the group (rent-seeking behaviour). The PAC vigorously lobbies Members of Parliament to enact or perpetuate price supports and establish import quotas for eggs or milk. They do this by making political contributions to sympathetic Members of Parliament or political parties. Although egg production is heavily concentrated in a few provinces, the PAC will make contributions to Members of Parliament from other provinces through the political parties to gain support.

But if an interest group is small in number, how can they successfully line their own pockets at the expense of society as a whole? The answer is that, although the aggregate costs of their program might be considerable, the cost imposed on *each individual* taxpayer is small (the special-interest effect). Citizen-taxpayers at large are likely uninformed about, and indifferent to, the issue at hand because they have little at stake. Civil rights, educational reform, and peace in the Middle East may seem to be much more urgent political issues than a program for a handful of egg producers.

Public choice theory also tells us that politicians are more likely to favour programs having hidden costs. As we have seen, this is often true of farm programs. In discussing Figure 21-4 we found that price supports involve, not simply an explicit transfer from taxpayer to farmer, but also the costs hidden in higher food prices, storage costs for surplus output, bureaucratic costs of administering farm programs, and costs associated with both domestic and international misallocations of resources. While the explicit or direct cost of an egg subsidy program to taxpayers may be small, the price increase provided by such a program carries a hidden subsidy (cost) that is much larger. Because the cost of the subsidy program is largely indirect and hidden, the program is much more acceptable to politicians and the public than if all costs were explicit.

NEW DIRECTIONS?

Farm subsidies may decline in the future.

1. DECLINING FARM POPULATION   As farm population has declined, its political clout has also diminished. The farm population was about 30% of the total in the 1930s when many of our farm programs were established. That population now is only about 3% of the total. Legislators are critically examining farm programs from the vantage point of their effect on consumers' grocery bills rather than farm incomes.

2. BUDGET DEFICITS   Continued pressures to bring under control the federal budget deficit have brought farm subsidies under increased political scrutiny.

3. POLICY CONFLICTS   It is increasingly apparent that domestic farm programs are seriously at odds with the objective of free world trade. This conflict merits more detailed consideration.

WORLD TRADE AND FARM POLICY

A more critical attitude towards farm subsidies is reflected in the Canadian government's desire to reduce world trade barriers to agricultural products.

POLICY IMPACTS

Consider the impacts of current farm programs on world trade. Virtually every industrialized country — Canada, the United States, Japan, and so forth — intervenes in agriculture by subsidizing and providing protective trade barriers. For example, the European Union (EU) — made up of 15 Western European nations — has established high prices for its domestic agricultural products. These price supports have a number of consequences.

1. To maintain high domestic prices the EU must restrict imports (supplies) of foreign farm products. It does this by imposing import tariffs (excise taxes) and quotas (specific quantitative limits on foreign goods).
2. Although the EU was once an importer of food, high price supports have induced European farmers to produce much more output than European consumers want to purchase.
3. To rid itself of these agricultural surpluses the EU has heavily subsidized their export into world markets.

The effects on Canada are that (1) our farmers have great difficulty in selling to EU nations because of their trade barriers; and (2) subsidized exports from the EU depress world prices for agricultural products, making these markets less attractive to our farmers.

Perhaps most important, from an international perspective farm programs such as those of the EU, Canada, and the United States distort world agricultural trade and thereby the international allocation of agricultural resources. Encouraged by artificially high prices, farmers in industrially advanced nations produce more agricultural output than they would otherwise. The resulting surpluses flow into world markets where they depress prices. This means farmers in countries with no farm programs — often developing countries — face artificially low prices for their exports, which signals them to produce less. In this way farm price distortions alter production away from that based on productive efficiency. For example, price supports cause agricultural resources to be allocated to wheat production, although wheat can perhaps be produced at a lower cost in a developing country.

One estimate suggests that the benefits of free, undistorted agricultural trade to the industrially advanced economies alone would be about $42 billion per year, with Canada, the United States, the EU, and Japan as the major beneficiaries.

Accompanying benefits are (1) increased Canadian farm exports; and (2) reduced expenditures on our domestic farm programs, which would help reduce the federal budget deficit. Thus, Canada has compelling economic reasons to favour the liberalization of international agricultural trade.

QUICK REVIEW 21-2

1. The main impacts of price supports are to cause surplus production that government must buy and store; raise both farmer incomes and food prices to consumers; and generate an overallocation of resources to agriculture.

2. Farm policy has been criticized for delaying the exodus of resources from farming; allocating most subsidies to wealthier farmers; conflicting with other policies such as freer world trade; and being very costly.

3. The persistence of farm programs is largely explainable in terms of rent-seeking behaviour, the special-interest effect, political logrolling, and other aspects of public choice theory.

4. The farm programs of Canada, the United States, the European Union, and other industrialized nations have contributed to a misallocation of the world's agricultural resources.

GATT NEGOTIATIONS

In fact, Canada — along with a number of food exporting nations known as the Cairns Group (including the United States, Australia, New Zealand, and Argentina) — has been a leading advocate for elimination of trade barriers on agricultural products and, by implication, the dismantling of price-support programs. Under the aegis of the General Agreement on Tariffs and Trade (GATT) — an international association of over 100 nations dedicated to the promotion of free world trade — Canada, along with the United States, has proposed (1) a ten-year phase out of all agricultural tariffs, (2) elimination of agricultural export subsidies over a five-year period, and (3) a phase out of all domestic farm supports that distort world agricultural trade. Unfortunately, under pressure from their politically powerful farm groups, the EU and Japan have rejected these proposals and negotiations have stalled.

MARKET-ORIENTED INCOME STABILIZATION

From a long-term perspective, it seems increasingly likely that farm policy will shift from the goal of enhancing to that of stabilizing farm incomes. The goal of *stabilization* is to reduce the sharp year-to-year fluctuations in farm incomes and prices, but to accept the long-run average of farm prices and incomes that free markets would provide. This contrasts with income *enhancement*, which seeks to provide farmers with commodity prices and incomes higher than free markets would yield. Government might moderate the boom and bust character of agricultural markets by supporting prices and accumulating surplus stocks when prices fell significantly below the long-run trend of prices. Conversely, government would augment supply by selling from these stocks when prices rose significantly above the long-run trend.

Proponents believe that the **market-oriented income stabilization policy** has a number of advantages. First, government involvement in agriculture would diminish in that programs of supply management through quotas would be abandoned. Second, prices would reflect long-run equilibrium levels and therefore be conducive to an efficient allocation of resources between agriculture and the rest of the economy. Third, taxpayer costs would be significantly reduced. And, fourth, the lower average level of farm prices would stimulate agricultural exports.

GLOBAL VIEW: FEAST OR FAMINE?

The Canadian (and American) farm problem — supply outrunning demand and farm policies that foster surplus production — is not common to most other countries. Many less-developed nations must persistently import food. We frequently read of malnutrition, chronic food shortages, and occasionally famine in the nations of Africa and elsewhere. In the future — say, four or five decades from now — will the world be able to feed itself?

PESSIMISM

While there is no simple answer to this question, it is of interest to summarize some of the pertinent pros and cons.

Pessimists, envisioning impending famine as demand increases ahead of supply, make these arguments.

1. The quantity of arable land is finite and its quality is being seriously impaired by wind and water erosion.
2. Urban sprawl and industrial expansion continue to convert agricultural land to nonagricultural uses.
3. Underground water systems, on which farmers depend for irrigation, are being mined so fast that farmlands in some areas will have to be abandoned.
4. World population continues to grow; every day there are hundreds of thousands of new mouths to feed.
5. Some environmentalists suggest that unfavourable long-run climatic changes will undermine future agricultural production.

OPTIMISM

Optimists offer these counterarguments.

1. The number of hectares planted to crops has been increasing and the world is far from bringing all its arable land into production.
2. Agricultural productivity continues to rise and the possibility of dramatic productivity breakthroughs lies ahead as we enter the age of genetic engineering. There is also room for substantial productivity increases in the agricultural sectors of the less-developed countries. For example, improved economic incentives for farm workers in China helped expand agricultural output by about one-third between 1980 and 1985. Indeed, food production could be greatly increased in many poor nations by removing existing government price controls that establish below-equilibrium prices.
3. The rate of growth of world population has been diminishing.
4. We must reckon with the adjustment processes elicited by the market system. If food shortages were to develop, food prices would rise. Higher prices would simultaneously induce more production, constrain the amount demanded, and head off the shortages.
5. The real price for food on international markets has been falling for many decades, suggesting that food supply has increased more rapidly than food demand.

The "feast or famine" debate is highly speculative; a clear picture of the world's future production capabilities and consumption needs is not easily discerned. The main point is that Canadian agricultural policies should take global considerations into account.

CHAPTER SUMMARY

1. In the short run, the highly inelastic nature of agricultural demand translates small changes in output and small shifts in domestic or foreign demand into large fluctuations in prices and incomes.

2. Rapid technological advance, coupled with a highly inelastic and relatively constant demand for agricultural output, has caused agriculture to be a declining industry.

3. Historically, agricultural policy has been price-centred and based on the parity concept that suggests that the relationship between prices received and paid by farmers should remain constant

4. The use of price floors or supports has a number of economic effects: **a** surplus production occurs; **b** the incomes of farmers are increased; **c** consumers pay higher prices for farm products; **d** an overallocation of resources to agriculture occurs; **e** society pays higher taxes to finance the purchase and storage of surplus output or to finance deficiency payments; **f** pollution increases because of the greater use of agrichemicals and vulnerable land; and **g** other nations bear the costs associated with import barriers and depressed world farm commodity prices.

5. Government has pursued with limited success programs to reduce the supply of, and increase the demand for, agricultural products in order to reduce the surpluses associated with price supports.

6. Farm policy has been criticized for **a** confusing symptoms (low farm incomes) with causes (excess capacity); **b** providing the largest subsidies to high-income farmers; **c** contradictions among specific farm programs; **d** declining effectiveness.

7. The persistence of agricultural subsidies can be explained in terms of public choice theory and, in particular, in terms of rent-seeking behaviour, and the special-interest effect.

8. Recent GATT provisions call for reduced export subsidies for agricultural products.

9. Canada may be moving towards a policy of stabilizing, but not enhancing, farm incomes.

TERMS AND CONCEPTS

Agricultural Products Board (p. 450)
Agricultural Products Marketing Act (p. 449)
Agricultural Stabilization Board (p. 450)
Canadian Dairy Commission (p. 450)
Canadian Wheat Board (p. 449)
crop restrictions (p. 453)

deficiency payments (p. 452)
long-run farm problem (p. 444)
market-oriented income stabilization (p. 457)
offers to purchase (p. 450)
short-run farm problem (p. 444)

QUESTIONS AND STUDY SUGGESTIONS

1. *Key Question* *"The supply and demand for agricultural products are such that small changes in agricultural supply will result in drastic changes in prices. However, large changes in farm prices have modest effects on agricultural output." Carefully evaluate. (Hint: A brief review of the distinction between supply and quantity supplied may be of assistance.) Do exports increase or reduce the instability of demand for farm products?*

2. What relationship, if any, can you detect between the fact that the farmer's fixed costs of production are large and the fact that the supply of most agricultural products is generally inelastic? Be specific in your answer.

3. *Key Question* *Explain how each of the following contributes to the farm problem: a. inelastic demand for farm products; b. rapid technological progress in farming; c. the modest long-run growth in demand for farm commodities; and d. the competitiveness of agriculture.*

4. The key to efficient resource allocation is shifting resources from low-productivity to high-productivity uses. Given the high and expanding physical productivity of agricultural resources, explain why many economists want to divert resources from farming in the interest of greater allocative efficiency.

5. "Industry complains of the higher taxes it must pay to finance subsidies to agriculture. Yet the trend of agricultural prices has been downward while industrial prices have been moving upward, suggesting that on balance agriculture is actually subsidizing industry." Explain and evaluate.

6. "Because consumers as a whole must ultimately pay the total incomes received by farmers, it makes no real difference whether this income is paid through free farm markets or through supported prices supplemented by subsidies financed out of tax revenues." Do you agree?

7. Suppose you are the president of a local district of one of the major farm organizations. You are directed by the district's membership to formulate policy statements for the district that cover the following topics: a. anti-combines (competition) policy; b. monetary policy; c. fiscal policy; and d. tariff policy. Briefly outline the policy statements that will best serve the interests of farmers. What is the rationale underlying each statement? Do you see any conflicts or inconsistencies in your policy statements?

8. *Key Question*   *Carefully demonstrate the economic effects of price supports. Explicitly include environmental and global impact in your answer. On what grounds do economists contend that price supports cause a misallocation of resources?*

9. Reconcile these two statements: "The farm problem is one of overproduction." "Despite the great productive capacity of Canadian agriculture, plenty of Canadians are going hungry." What assumptions about the price system are implied in your answer?

10. Compare the economic consequences of a. offers to purchase and b. deficiency payments for farmers, consumers, taxpayers, and the government. On what grounds do economists contend that offers to purchase and deficiency payments cause a misallocation of resources?

11. Use public choice theory to explain the size and persistence of subsidies to agriculture.

12. What are the effects of farm programs such as those of Canada, the United States, and the European Union on a. domestic agricultural prices; b. world agricultural prices; and c. the international allocation of agricultural resources.

13. What are the major criticisms of farm policy? Do you feel that government should attempt to enhance farm incomes, stabilize farm incomes, or allow farm incomes to be determined by free markets? Justify your position.

ANSWERS TO KEY QUESTIONS

CHAPTER 1

1-1 Effective policy must be based on sound theory — factually supported generalizations about behaviour. Two methods are used to obtain sound economic theory: deduction and induction.

In *deduction*, the economist starts directly with an untested hypothesis. The hypothesis or theory is tested for accuracy by gathering and examining all relevant facts. If the facts support the hypothesis, the theory can be used for policy. The other approach is *induction*, in which the economist starts by gathering facts and then notes their relationship to each other. Eventually, the data may reveal a cause and effect pattern from which a theory results. From this theory, economic policy relevant to the real world can be formulated. Deduction and induction are complementary and often used simultaneously.

As for the quotation, the opposite is true; any theory not supported by facts is not a good theory. Good economics is empirically grounded; it is based on facts and highly practical.

1-5 (a), (d), and (f) are macro; (b), (c), and (e) are micro.

1-6 (a) and (c) are positive; (b) and (d) are normative.

1-9 (a) The fallacy of composition is the mistake of believing that something true for an individual part is necessarily true for the whole. Example: A single auto producer can increase its profits by lowering its price and taking business away from its competitors. But matched price cuts by all auto manufacturers will not necessarily yield higher industry profits.

(b) The "after this, therefore because of this" fallacy is incorrectly reasoning that when one event precedes another, the first event *necessarily* caused the second. Example: Interest rates rise, followed by an increase in the rate of inflation, leading to the erroneous conclusion the rise in interest rates caused the inflation. Higher interest rates slow inflation.

Cause and effect relationships are difficult to isolate because "other things" are continually changing.

1-13 This behaviour can be explained in terms of marginal costs and marginal benefits. At a standard restaurant, items are priced individually — they have a positive marginal cost. If you order more, it will cost you more. You order until the marginal benefit from the extra food no longer exceeds the positive marginal cost. At a buffet you pay a flat fee no matter how much you eat. Once the fee is paid, additional food items have a zero marginal cost. You therefore continue to eat until your marginal benefit is also zero.

Appendix 1-2 (a) More tickets are bought at each price; the line plots to the right of the previous line. (b) and (c) Fewer tickets are bought at each price; the line plots to the left of the previous line.

Appendix 1-3 Income column: $0; $5,000; $10,000, $15,000; $20,000. Saving column: $–500; 0; $500; $1,000; $1,500. Slope = 0.1 (= $1,000 – $500)/($15,000 – $10,000). Vertical intercept = $–500. The slope shows how much saving will go up for every $1 increase in income; the intercept shows the amount of saving (dissaving) occurring when income is zero. Equation: $S = \${-}500 + 0.1Y$ (where S is saving and Y is income). Saving will be $750 at the $12,500 income level.

Appendix 1-6 Slopes: at $A = +4$; at $B = 0$; at $C = -4$.

CHAPTER 2

2-5 Economics deals with the "limited resources-unlimited wants" problem. Unemployment represents valuable resources that could have been used to produce more goods and services — to meet more wants and ease the economizing problem.

Allocative efficiency means that resources are being used to produce the goods and services most wanted by society. Society is located at the optimal point on its production possibilities curve where marginal benefit equals marginal cost for each good. *Productive efficiency* means the least costly production techniques are being used to produce wanted goods and services.

Example: manual typewriters produced using the least-cost techniques but for which there is no demand.

2-6 (a) See curve *EDCBA* in the accompanying figure. The assumptions are full employment and productive efficiency, fixed supplies of resources, and fixed technology.

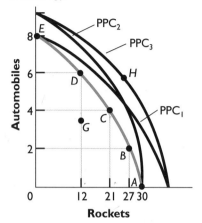

Rockets

(b) 4.5 rockets [=(21–12)/(6–4)]; .33 automobiles [=(4–2)/(27–21)], as determined from the table. Increasing opportunity costs are reflected in the concave-from-the-origin shape of the curve. This means the economy must give up larger and larger amounts of rockets to get constant added amounts of automobiles — and vice versa.

(c) It must obtain full employment and productive efficiency.

2-9 The marginal benefit (MB) curve is downsloping; MB falls as more of a product is consumed. The first units of a good consumed yield greater additional satisfaction than subsequent units. The marginal cost (MC) curve is upsloping; MC increases as more of a product is produced. The opportunity cost of producing good A rises as resources increasingly better suited to other uses are used to produce A. The optimal amount of a particular product occurs where MB equals MC. If MC exceeds MB, fewer resources should be allocated to this use. The resources have more value in some alternative use (as reflected in MC) than in this use (as reflected in MB).

2-10 See the figure accompanying the answer to question 2-6. G indicates unemployment, productive inefficiency, or both. *H* is at present unattainable. Economic growth — through more inputs, better inputs, improved technology — must be achieved to attain *H*.

2-11 See question 2-6 figure. PPC₁ shows improved rocket technology. PPC₂ shows improved auto technology. PPC₃ shows improved technology in producing both products.

CHAPTER 3

3-2 "Roundabout" production means using capital goods in the production process, enabling producers to obtain more output than through direct production. The direct way to produce a corn crop is to scatter seed about in an unploughed field. The roundabout way is to plough, fertilize, harrow, and till the field using machinery and then use a seed drill to sow the seeds in rows at the correct depth. The higher yield per acre will more than compensate the farmer for the cost of using the roundabout techniques.

To increase the capital stock at full employment, the current production of consumer goods must decrease. Moving along the production possibilities curve towards more capital goods comes at the expense of current consumption.

No, it can use its previously unemployed resources to produce more capital goods, without sacrificing consumption goods. It can move from a point inside to a point on the curve, thus obtaining more capital goods.

CHAPTER 4

4-2 Demand increases in (a), (c), (e), and (f); decreases in (b) and (d).

4-5 Supply increases in (a), (d), (e), and (g); decreases in (b), (c), and (f).

4-7 Data, from top to bottom: –13; –7; 0; +7; +14; and +21.

(a) P_e = $1.35; Q_e = 75,000. Equilibrium occurs where there is neither a shortage nor surplus of eggs. At the immediately lower price of $1.30, there is a shortage of 7000 dozen. At the immediately higher price of $1.40, there is a surplus of 7000 dozen.

(b)

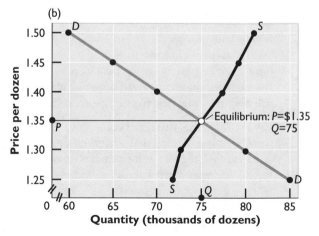

Quantity (thousands of dozens)

(c) Because at $1.25 there will be a 13,000 dozen eggs shortage, which will drive price up. Because at $1.50

there will be a 21,000 surplus, which will drive the price down. Quotation is incorrect; just the opposite is true.

(d) A $1.30 ceiling causes a persistent shortage. Also, a black market (illegal sales above $1.30) might occur. Government might want to suppress inflation.

(e) Once the government sets the price, that price cannot move towards an equilibrium where quantity demanded equals quantity supplied. The ceiling price removes any inducement for farmers to produce more, and the excess demand of buyers at this ceiling price remains unmet. Thus, there is no price movement upward to ration some buyers out of the market so that the quantity the remaining buyers want equals the quantity farmers bring to market.

4-8 (a) Price up; quantity down; (b) Price down; quantity down; (c) Price down; quantity up; (d) Price indeterminate; quantity up; (e) Price up; quantity up; (f) Price down; quantity indeterminate; (g) Price up; quantity indeterminate; (h) Price indeterminate and quantity down.

CHAPTER 5

5-3 Public goods (a) are indivisible — they are produced in such large units that they cannot be sold to individuals and (b) the exclusion principle does not apply; once the goods are produced nobody — including free riders — can be excluded from the goods' benefits. The free-rider problem explains the significance of the exclusion principle. The government must provide public goods such as the judicial system, national defence, police protection, and weather warning systems since people can obtain the benefits without paying. Government must levy taxes to get revenues to pay for public goods.

5-4 If on the curve, the only way to obtain more public goods is to reduce the production of private goods (from C to B).

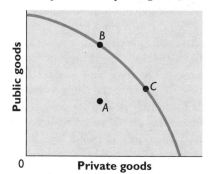

If operating inside the curve, it can expand the production of public goods without sacrificing private goods (from A to B).

CHAPTER 6

6-3 An export increases domestic output and revenues to domestic export firms. Because these firms would employ more resources, household income would rise. Households would then use part of their greater income to buy more imported goods.

Canadian exports in 1994 were $219.4 billion (flow 13) and imports were $202.3 billion (flow 16).

Flow 14 must equal flow 13. Flow 15 must equal flow 16.

6-4 (a) Yes, because the opportunity cost of radios is less (1R = 1C) in South Korea than in Canada (1R = 2C). South Korea should produce radios and Canada, chemicals.

(b) If they specialize, Canada can produce 20 tonnes of chemicals and South Korea can produce 30,000 radios. Before specialization South Korea produced alternative B and Canada alternative D for a total of 28,000 radios (24,000 + 4,000) and 18 tonnes of chemicals (6 tonnes + 12 tonnes). The gain is 2,000 radios and 2 tonnes of chemicals.

(c) The limits of the terms of trade are determined by the comparative cost conditions in each country before trade: 1R = 1C in South Korea and 1R = 2C in Canada. The terms of trade must be somewhere between these two ratios for trade to occur.

If the terms of trade are 1R = 1 1/2 C, South Korea would end up with 26,000 radios (= 30,000 – 4,000) and 6 tonnes of chemicals. Canada would have 4,000 radios and 14 tonnes of chemicals (= 20 – 6). South Korea has gained 2,000 radios. Canada has gained 2 tonnes of chemicals.

(d) Yes, the world js obtaining more output from its fixed resources.

6-6 The first part of this statement is incorrect. Our exports create a domestic *supply* of foreign currencies, not a domestic demand for them. The second part of the statement is accurate. The foreign demand for dollars (from our exports) generates a supply of foreign currencies to Canadians.

A decline in Canadian incomes or a weakening of Canadian preferences for foreign goods would reduce our imports, reducing our demand for foreign currencies. These currencies would depreciate (the dollar would appreciate). Dollar appreciation means our exports will decline and our imports will rise.

6-10 GATT is the General Agreement on Tariffs and Trade. Its provisions apply to more than 120 nations, affecting people around the globe. The Uruguay Round of GATT negotiations produced an agreement that will reduce tariffs, liberalize trade in services, cut agricultural subsidies, protect intellectual property, reduce import quotas, and create the World Trade Organization.

The EU and NAFTA are free-trade blocs. GATT reduces tariffs and liberalizes trade for nearly *all* nations, not just countries in these blocs. The ascendancy of the EU and the passage of NAFTA encouraged nations to reach a new GATT agreement. No nation wanted to be disadvantaged by the formation of the trade blocs.

CHAPTER 7

7-2 Elasticities, top to bottom: 3; 1.4; .714; .333. Slope does not measure elasticity. This demand curve has a constant slope of –1 (= –1/1), but elasticity declines as we move down the curve. When the initial price is high and initial quantity is low, a unit change in price is a *low* percentage change while a unit change in quantity is a *high* percentage change. The percentage change in quantity exceeds the percentage change in price, making demand elastic. When the initial price is low and initial quantity is high, a unit change in price is a *high* percentage change while a unit change in quantity is a *low* percentage change. The percentage change in quantity is less than the percentage change in price, making demand inelastic.

7-4 Total revenue data, top to bottom: $5; $8; $9; $8; $5. When demand is elastic, price and total revenue move in the opposite direction. When demand is inelastic, price and total revenue move in the same direction.

7-5 Total revenue will increase in (c), (d), (e), and (f); decrease in (a) and (b); and remain the same in (g).

7-9 Substitutability; proportion of income; luxury versus necessity; and time. Elastic: (a), (c), (e), (g), (h), and (i). Inelastic: (b), (d), (f), and (j).

7-14 Supply would be perfectly inelastic — vertical — at a quantity of 1 unit. The $82.5 million price was determined where the demand curve intersected this supply curve.

7-16 A and B are substitutes; C and D are complements.

7-17 All are normal goods — income and quantity demanded move in the same direction. These coefficients reveal that a 1% increase in income will increase the quantity of movies demanded by 3.4%, of dental services by 1.0%, and of clothing by 0.5%. A negative coefficient indicates an inferior good — income and quantity demanded move in the opposite direction.

7-18 The incidence of an excise tax is likely to be primarily on consumers when demand is highly inelastic and primarily on producers when demand is elastic. The more elastic the supply, the greater the incidence of tax on consumers.

CHAPTER 8

8-2 Missing total utility data, top to bottom: 18; 33. Missing marginal utility data, top to bottom: 7; 5; 1.

8-4 (a) 4 units of A; 3 units of B; 3 units of C, and 0 units of D. (b) Save $4. (c) 36/$18 = 12/$6 = 8/$4 = 2/$1. The marginal utility per dollar of the last unit of each is 2.

8-5 2 units of X and 5 units of Y. Marginal utility per dollar will be equal at 4 (= 8/$2 for X and 4/$1 for Y) and the $9 income will be spent. Total utility = 48 (= 10 + 8 for X and 8 + 7 + 6 + 5 + 4 for Y). When the price of X falls to $1, the quantity of X demanded increases from 2 to 4. Total utility is now 58 (= 10 + 8 + 6 + 4 for X and 8 + 7 + 6 + 5 + 4 for Y).

Demand schedule: $P = \$2; Q = 2. P = \$1; Q = 4.$

Appendix 8-3 The tangency point places the consumer on the highest attainable indifference curve; it identifies the combination of goods yielding the highest total utility. All intersection points place the consumer on a lower indifference curve. MRS is the slope of the indifference curve; P_B/P_A is the slope of the budget line. Only at the tangency point are these two slopes equal. If MRS > P_B/P_A or MRS < P_B/P_A, adjustments in the combination of products can be made to increase total utility (get to a higher indifference curve).

CHAPTER 9

9-2 Sole proprietorship, partnership, and corporation.

Proprietorship advantages: easy to open and provides maximum freedom for the proprietor to do what she or he thinks best. Proprietorship disadvantages: limited financial resources; the owner must be a "Jack-or-Jill-of-all-trades"; and unlimited liability.

Partnership advantages: easy to organize; greater specialization of management; and greater financial resources. Disadvantages: financial resources are still limited; unlimited liability; possibility of disagreement among the partners; and precarious continuity.

Corporation advantages: can raise large amounts of money by issuing stocks and bonds; limited liability; and continuity.

Corporation disadvantages: red tape and expense in incorporating; potential for abuse of stockholder and bondholder funds; double taxation of profits; and separation of ownership and control.

The dominant role of corporations stems from the advantages cited, particularly unlimited liability and superior ability to raise money capital.

9-5 Explicit costs: $37,000 (= $12,000 for the helper + $5,000 of rent + $20,000 of materials). Implicit costs: $22,000 (= $4,000 of forgone interest + $15,000 of forgone salary + $3,000 of entrepreneurship).

Accounting profits = $35,000 (= $72,000 of revenue – $37,000 of explicit costs); Economic profit = $13,000 [= $72,000 – ($37,000 of explicit cost + $22,000 of implicit costs)].

9-7 Marginal product data, top to bottom: 15; 19; 17; 14; 9; 6; 3; –1. Average product data, top to bottom: 15; 17; 17; 16.25; 14.8; 13.33; 11.86; 10.25.

MP is the slope — the rate of change — of the TP curve. When TP is rising at an increasing rate, MP is positive and rising. When TP is rising at a diminishing rate, MP is positive but falling. When TP is falling, MP is negative and falling. AP rises when MP is above it; AP falls when MP is below it.

MP first rises because the fixed capital gets used more productively as added workers are employed. Each added worker contributes more to output than the previous worker because the firm will be better able to use its fixed plant and equipment. As still more labour is added, the law of diminishing returns takes hold. Labour becomes so abundant relative to the fixed capital that congestion occurs and marginal product falls. At the extreme, the addition of labour will so overcrowd the plant that the marginal product of still more labour will be negative — total output will fall.

Because labour is the only variable input and its price (its wage rate) is constant, MC is found by dividing the wage rate by MP. When MP is rising, MC is falling; when MP reaches its maximum, MC is at its minimum; when MP is diminishing, MC is rising.

Illustrate: See Figure 9-7.

9-10 See Question 4 in Chapter 10 for the completed table.

(a) Over the 0 to 4 range of output, the TVC and TC curves slope upward at a decreasing rate because of increasing marginal returns. The slopes of the curves then increase at an increasing rate as diminishing marginal returns occur.

(b) AFC (= TFC/Q) falls continuously since a fixed amount of capital cost is spread over more units of output. The MC (= change in TC/change in Q), AVC (= TVC/Q), and ATC (= TC/Q) curves are U-shaped, reflecting the influence of increasing and diminishing returns. The ATC curve sums AFC and AVC vertically. The ATC curve falls when the MC curve is below it; the ATC curve rises when the MC curve is above it. This means the MC curve must intersect the ATC curve at its lowest point. The same logic holds for the minimum point of the AVC curve.

(c1) If TFC had been $100 instead of $60, the AFC and ATC curves would be higher — by an amount equal to $40 divided by the specific output. Example: at 4 units, AVC = $25.00 [= ($60 + $40/4)/4]; and ATC = $62.50 [= ($210 + $40)/4]. The AVC and MC curves are not affected by changes in fixed costs.

(c2) If TVC had been $10 less at each output, the MC curve would not be affected, except that it would be $10 lower at the first unit of output. The AVC and ATC curves would also be lower — by an amount equal to $10 divided by the specific output. Example: at 4 units of output AVC = $35.00 [= ($150 – $10)/4], ATC = $50 [= ($210 – $10)/4]. The AFC curve would not be affected by the change in variable cost.

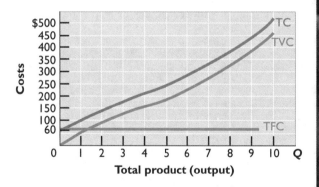

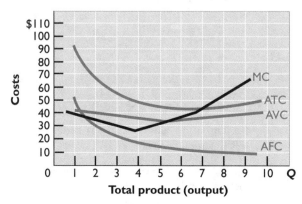

9-13   The long-run cost curve is U-shaped. The long-run ATC curve falls as the firm expands and realizes economies of scale from labour and managerial specialization, the use of more efficient capital, and the use of by-products. The long-run ATC curve turns upward when the firm experiences diseconomies of scale, usually resulting from managerial inefficiencies.

The MES (minimum efficient scale) is the smallest level of output needed to attain all economics of scale and minimum long-run ATC.

If the long-run ATC curve drops quickly to its minimum point which extends over a long range of output, the industry will be composed of both large and small firms. If the long-run ATC descends slowly to its minimum point over a long range of output, the industry will be composed of oligopolistic or monopolistic firms. If the long-run ATC curve drops quickly to its minimum point and then rises abruptly, the industry will be composed of many small firms.

CHAPTER 10

10-3   Total revenue, top to bottom: 0; $2; $4; $6; $8; $10. Marginal revenue, top to bottom: $2, throughout.

(a) The industry is purely competitive — this firm is a "price taker." The firm is so small relative to the size of the market that it can change its level of output without affecting the market price.

(b)

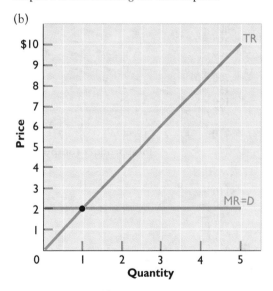

(c) The firm's demand curve is perfectly elastic; MR is constant and equal to P.

(d) Yes. Table: When output (quantity demanded) increases by 1 unit, total revenue increases by $2.

This $2 increase is the marginal revenue. Figure: The change in TR is measured by the slope of the TR line, 2 (= $2/1). MR is a perfectly horizontal line at $2.

10-4   (a) No, $32 is less than AVC. If it did produce, its output would be 4 — found by expanding output until MR no longer exceeds or is equal to MC. By producing 4 units, it would lose $82 [= 4($32 – $52.50)]. By not producing, it would lose only its total fixed cost of $60.

(b) Yes, $41 exceeds AVC. Using the MR = MC rule it will produce 6 units. Loss per unit of output is $6.50 (= $41 – $47.50). Total loss = $39 (= 6 × $6.50), which is less than its total fixed cost of $60.

(c) Yes, $56 exceeds AVC (and ATC). Using the MR = MC rule it will produce 8 units. Profit per unit = $7.87 (= $56 – $48.13); total profit = $62.96.

(d) Column (2) data, top to bottom: 0; 0; 5; 6; 7; 8; 9. Column (3) data, top to bottom, in dollars: –60; –60; –55; –39; – 8; +63; +144.

(e) The firm will not produce if P < AVC. When P > AVC, the firm will produce in the short run at the quantity where P (= MR) is equal to its increasing MC. Therefore, the MC above the AVC curve is the firm's short-run supply curve. It shows the quantity of output the firm will supply at each price level. See Figure 10-6 for a graphical illustration.

(f) Column (4) data, top to bottom: 0; 0; 7,500; 9,000; 10,500; 12,000, 13,500.

(g) Equilibrium price = $46; equilibrium output = 10,500. Each firm will produce 7 units. Loss per unit = $1.14, or $8 per firm. The industry will contract in the long run.

10-8   See Figures 10-8 and 10-9 and their legends. See Figure 10-11 for the supply curve for an increasing cost industry. The supply curve for a decreasing cost industry is below.

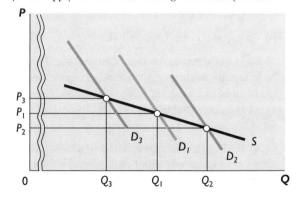

10-10 The equality of P and minimum ATC means the firm is achieving *productive efficiency*. It's using the most efficient technology and employing the least-costly combination of resources. The equality of P and MC means the firm is achieving *allocative efficiency*. It's producing the right product in the right amount based on society's valuation of marginal cost and marginal benefit.

CHAPTER 11

11-4 The TR curve is derived at each output level by multiplying $P \times Q$. Because TR is increasing at a diminishing rate, MR is declining. When TR turns downward, MR becomes negative. Four units sell for $5 each, but three of these four could have been sold for $5.50 had the monopolist been satisfied to sell only three. Having decided to sell four, the monopolist had to lower the price of the first three from $5.50 to $5, sacrificing $.50 on each for a total of $1.50. This "loss" of $1.50 explains the difference between the $5 price obtained on the fourth unit of output and its marginal revenue of $3.50. The demand curve is elastic from $P = \$6.50$ to $P = \$3.50$, a range where TR is rising. The curve is of unitary elasticity at $P = \$3.50$, where TR is at its maximum. The curve is inelastic from then on as the price continues to decrease and TR is falling. When MR is positive, demand is elastic. When MR is zero, demand is of unitary elasticity. When MR is negative, demand is inelastic. If MC is zero, the monopolist should produce 7 units where MR is also zero. It would never produce where demand is inelastic because MR is negative while MC is positive.

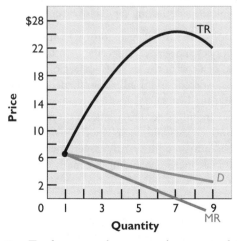

11-5 Total revenue data, top to bottom, in dollars: 0; 100; 166; 213; 252; 275; 288; 294; 296; 297; 290. Marginal revenue data, top to bottom, in dollars: 100; 66; 47; 39; 23; 13; 6; 2; 1; –7.

Price = $63; output = 4; profit = $42 [= 4($63 – 52.50)]. Your graph should have the same general appearance as Figure 11-4. At $Q = 4$, TR = $252 and TC = $210 [= 4($52.50)].

11-6 Perfect price discrimination: Output = 6. TR would be $420 (= $100 + $83 + $71 + $63 + $55 + $48). TC would be $285 [= 6($47.50)]. Profit = $135 (= $420 – $285).

Your single diagram should combine Figures 11-7(a) and 11-7(b) in the chapter. The discriminating monopolist faces a demand curve that is also its MR curve. It will sell the first unit at f in Figure 11-7(b) and then sell each successive unit at lower prices (as shown on the demand curve) as it moves to Q_2 units, where D (= MR) = MC. Discriminating monopolist: Greater output; total revenue, and profits. Some consumers will pay a higher price under discriminating monopoly than with nondiscriminating monopoly; others, a lower price. Good features: greater output and improved allocative efficiency. Bad feature: more income is transferred from consumers to the monopolist.

11-14 No, the proposal doesn't consider that the output of the natural monopolist would still be at the suboptimal level where $P > \text{MC}$. Too little would be produced and an underallocation of resources would result. Theoretically, it would be more desirable to force the natural monopolist to charge a price equal to marginal cost and subsidize any losses. Even setting price equal to ATC would be an improvement over this proposal. This fair-return pricing would allow for a normal profit and ensure a larger production than in the proposal.

CHAPTER 12

12-2 (a) Less elastic than a pure competitor; (b) more elastic than a pure monopolist. Price is higher and output lower for the monopolistic competitor. Pure competition: $P = \text{MC}$ (allocative efficiency); $P = \text{minimum ATC}$ (productive efficiency). Monopolistic competition: $P > \text{MC}$ (allocative inefficiency) and $P > \text{minimum ATC}$ (productive inefficiency). Monopolistic competitors have excess capacity, meaning that fewer firms operating at capacity (where $P = \text{minimum ATC}$) could supply the industry output.

12-6 Traditional view: Advertising is persuasive rather than informative; it enhances monopoly power (makes firms' demand curves less elastic); it creates an entry barrier; and it is the source of waste and inefficiency. New perspective: Advertising is a low-cost source of information for consumers; it increases competition by adding to consumer awareness of substitutes (makes firms' demand curves more elastic); makes entry of new firms easier; and improves economic efficiency.

12-9 Effect (1): Advertising may increase demand, allowing the firm to expand output and achieve economies of scale, meaning a lower ATC. Effect (2): Advertising is a business expense, implying a higher ATC. If (1) > (2), ATC will fall and consumers may benefit through lower prices. If (1) < (2), per unit cost will rise and consumers will likely face higher prices.

CHAPTER 13

13-3 A concentration ratio of 60% means the largest four firms in the industry account for 60% of sales; a concentration ratio of 90% means the largest four firms account for 90% of sales. Shortcomings: (1) they pertain to the nation as a whole, although relevant markets may be localized; (2) they do not account for interindustry competition; (3) the data are for Canadian products — imports are excluded; and (4) they don't reveal the dispersion of size among the top four firms.

13-4 Herfindahl index for A: 2400 (= 900 + 900 + 400 + 100 + 100). For B: 4300 (= 3600 + 625 + 25 + 25 + 25). We would expect Industry A to be more competitive than Industry B, where one firm dominates and two firms control 85% of the market.

13-5 The matrix shows the four possible profit outcomes for each of two firms, depending on which of two price strategies each follows. Example: If C sets price at $35 and D at $40, C's profits will be $59,000, and D's $55,000.

(a) C and D are interdependent because their profits depend not just on their own price, but also on the other firm's price.

(b) Likely outcome: Both firms will set price at $35. If either charged $40, they would be concerned the other would undercut the price by charging $35. At $35, C's profit would be $55,000; D's, $58,000.

(c) Through price collusion — agreeing to charge $40 — each firm would achieve higher profits (C = $57,000; D = $60,000). But once both firms agree on $40, each sees it can increase its profits even more by secretly charging $35 while its rival charges $40.

13-6 Assumptions: (1) Rivals will match price cuts; (2) Rivals will ignore price increases. The gap in the MR curve results from the abrupt change in the slope of the

demand curve at the going price. Firms will not change their price because if they do their total revenue and profits will fall. Shortcomings of the model: (1) It does not explain how the going price evolved in the first place; (2) it does not allow for price leadership and other forms of collusion.

CHAPTER 14

14-3 (a) They would block this horizontal merger.

(b) They would charge these firms with price fixing.

(c) They would allow this vertical merger, unless both firms had very large market share.

(d) They would allow this conglomerate merger.

14-7 Industries composed of natural monopolies subject to significant economies of scale. Regulation based on "fair-return" prices creates disincentives for firms to minimize costs, since cost reductions lead regulators to force firms to charge a lower price. Regulated firms may also use "creative" accounting to boost costs and hide profits. Because regulatory commissions depend on information provided by the firms themselves and commission members are often recruited from the industry, the agencies may in effect be controlled by the firms they are supposed to oversee. Also, industrial regulation sometimes is applied to industries that are not natural monopolies. Because the calculation of a fair return is based on the value of the firm's capital, there is an incentive for regulated natural monopolies to increase allowable profits by uneconomically substituting capital for labour.

14-9 Unlike industrial regulation — which concentrates on prices and service in specific industries — social regulation deals with the broader impact of business on consumers, workers, and third parties. Benefits: increased worker and product safety; less environmental damage; reduced economic discrimination. Two types of costs: administrative costs and compliance costs. Regulations must be administered by costly government agencies. The firms must increase spending to comply with the regulatory rules.

14-10 Industrial policy consists of direct government actions to promote technological advance and economic growth through subsidies to specific firms or industries. Anticombines, industrial, and social regulation restrict the conduct of firms, often increasing their costs or reducing their revenues. In contrast, industrial policy enhances profits — targeted firms view it favourably. Proponents contend industrial policy strengthens critical industries, speeds development of new technologies, increases labour productivity, and strengthens international competitiveness. Opponents charge that industrial policy substitutes the whims of politicians and bureaucrats for the hard scrutiny of entrepreneurs and business executives. They also point to failures of past industrial policies.

CHAPTER 15

15-2   Marginal product data, top to bottom: 17; 14; 12, 10; 7; 5. Total revenue data, top to bottom: $34; $62; $86; $106; $120; $130. Marginal revenue product data, top to bottom: $34; $28; $24; $20; $14; $10.

(a) Two workers. Because the MRP of the first worker is $34 and MRP of second worker is $28, each MRP exceeding the $27.95 wage. Four workers. Because the MRP of workers 1 through 4 have MRPs exceeding the $19.95 wage. But the fifth worker's MRP is only $14, and he will not be hired.

(b) The demand schedule consists of the first and last columns of the table in the question.

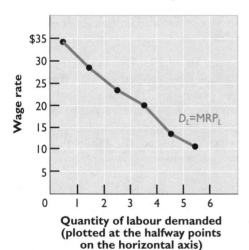

Quantity of labour demanded
(plotted at the halfway points
on the horizontal axis)

(c) Reconstruct the table. New product price data, top to bottom: $2.20; $2.15; $2.10; $2.05; $2.00; $1.95. New total revenue data, top to bottom: $37.40; $66.65; $90.30; $108.65; $120.00; $126.75. New marginal revenue product data, top to bottom: $37.40; $29.25; $23.65; $18.35; $11.35; $6.75. The second demand curve is less elastic. Here, MRP falls because of diminishing returns *and* because product price declines as output (and

inputs of labour) increase. A decrease in the wage rate will produce less of an increase in the quantity of labour demanded, because the output from the added labour will reduce product price.

15-4   Four factors: the rate at which MP declines; the ease of resource substitutability; elasticity of product demand; and labour cost to total ratio.

(a) Increases the demand for C. (b) The price increase for D will increase the demand for C through the *substitution effect*, but decrease the demand for all resources — including C — through the *output effect*. The net effect is uncertain; it depends on which effect outweighs the other. (c) Increases the elasticity of demand for C. (d) Increases the demand for C. (e) Increases the demand for C through the output effect. There is no substitution effect. (f) Reduces the elasticity of demand for C.

15-5   (a) 2 capital; 4 labour. $MP_L/P_L = 7/1$; $MP_C/P_C = 21/3 = 7/1$.

(b) 7 capital and 7 labour. $MRP_L/L = 1 (= 1/1) = MRP_C/P_C = 1 (= 3/3)$. Output is 142 (= 96 from capital + 46 from labour). Economic profit is $114 (= $142 – $28).

(c) Yes, least-cost production is part of maximizing profits — the profit-maximizing rule includes the least-cost rule.

15-7   (a) More of both; (b) less labour and more capital; (c) maximum profits obtained; (d) less of both.

CHAPTER 16

16-3   See Figure 16-3 and its legend.

16-4   Total labour cost data, top to bottom: $0; $14; $28; $42; $56; $70; $84. Marginal resource cost data: $14, throughout.

(a) The labour supply curve and MRC curve are shown as a single horizontal line at the market wage rate of $14. The firm can employ as much labour as it wants, each unit costing $14.

(b) The labour demand data of question 2 in Chapter 15 has been added to the graph. MRP intersects MRC at $14 when the fifth worker is hired. Thus, $14 is the equilibrium wage rate and 5 is the equilibrium level of employment. Economic profit is $50 (=$120–70). It would also be $50 at an employment level of 4, because the fifth worker adds $14 both to cost (the wage) and to total revenue. (MRP is plotted halfway between each unit of labour)

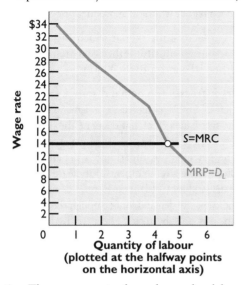

16-6 The monopsonist faces the market labour supply curve S — it is the only firm hiring this labour. MRC lies above S and rises more rapidly than S because all workers get the higher wage rate which is needed to attract the added worker. Equilibrium wage = $12; equilibrium employment = 3. The monopsonist can pay a below-competitive wage rate by restricting its employment.

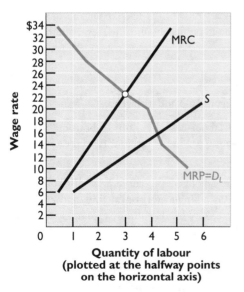

16-8 The union wage rate becomes the firm's MRC, which we would show as a horizontal line from W_c to S. Each unit of labour now adds only its own wage rate to the firm's costs. The firm will employ Q_c workers, where MRP = MRC (= W_c), an increase from the Q_m workers it would employ if there were no union.

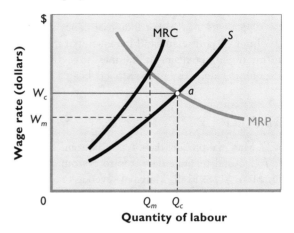

16-17 The higher wages that unions achieve reduce employment, displace workers, and increase the marginal revenue product in the union sector. Labour supply will increase in the nonunionized sector, reducing wages and decreasing marginal revenue product there. Because of the lower marginal revenue product, the workers added in the nonunion sector will contribute less to GDP than they would have in the unionized sector. The gain of GDP in the nonunionized sector will not offset the loss of GDP in the unionized sector, causing an efficiency loss.

16-19 See Figure 16-3. Discrimination against women in two of the three occupations will crowd women into the third occupation. The labour supply curve in the "men's occupations" (X and Y) shift to the left, making them high-wage occupations. The labour supply curve in the "women's occupation" (Z) shifts to the right, creating a low-wage occupation.

Eliminating occupational segregation would entice women into the high-wage occupations, increasing labour supply there and reducing it in the low-wage occupation. The wage rates in the three occupations would converge to B. Women would gain, men would lose. Society would gain, because the increase in GDP in the expanding occupations would exceed the loss of GDP in the contracting occupation.

Decisions relating to education and job duration have differed for men and women because of the larger role women traditionally have played in child-rearing. On average, men have higher levels of education and more years of work experience than women. Therefore, part of the pay gap between men and women reflects different choices.

CHAPTER 17

17-2 Land is completely fixed in total supply. As population expands and the demand for land increases, rent arises and grows. From society's perspective this rent is a surplus — a payment unnecessary for ensuring the land is available to the economy as a whole. If rent declined or disappeared, the same amount of land would be available. If it increased, no more land would be forthcoming. Thus, rent has no incentive function.

But land does have alternative uses. To get it to its most productive use, individuals and firms compete and the winners are those who pay the highest rent. To the high bidders, rent is a cost of production that must be covered by the revenue gained through the sale of the commodities produced on that land.

17-4 Supply is upsloping because households prefer present consumption to future consumption and must be enticed through higher interest rates to save more (consume less). The higher the interest rate, the greater the saving and the money made available in the loanable funds market. Demand is downsloping because more business investment projects become profitable as the cost of borrowing (the interest rate) falls. The equilibrium interest rate equates the quantity of funds supplied and demanded in the loanable funds market. Sources of changes: changes in the supply of loanable funds, changes in the demand for loanable funds, or changes in both.

17-6 The nominal interest rate is the interest rate stated in dollars of current value (unadjusted for inflation). The real interest rate is the nominal interest rate adjusted for inflation (or deflation). The real interest rate is relevant for making investment decisions — it reflects the true cost of borrowing money. It is compared to the expected return on the investment in the decision process. Real interest rate = 4% (= 12% – 8%). They saved because if they simply kept their money out of savings accounts, they would have earned no nominal interest at all and the value of their savings would have declined at the full rate of inflation. With inflation at 12% and the interest on their savings at, say, 7%, these people were losing 5% a year. Not good, but better than losing the full 12%.

17-7 Business profits (accounting profits) are what remains of a firm's total revenues after it has paid all its explicit costs, these being payments to the factors of production employed by the firm, but not to the resources owned by the business itself. Economists also take into consideration implicit costs — what the owners could have received using the resources they own in some other way. The economist adds these implicit costs to the accountant's explicit costs to arrive at total costs. Subtracting these total costs from total revenue results in a smaller profit (economic profit) than the accountant's business profit.

Sources of economic profits: (1) uncertainty and risk; (2) uncertainty and innovations; and (3) monopoly.

(a) Profits from assuming the risks and uncertainties of innovation, as well as the monopoly profits from the patent. (b) Monopoly profits arising from its locational advantage. (c) Profits from bearing the uninsurable risk of a change in demand (the change could have been unfavourable).

CHAPTER 18

18-2 In this simple economy each person represents a complete income quintile — 20% of the total population. The richest quintile (Al) receives 50% of total income; the poorest quintile (Ed) receives 5%.

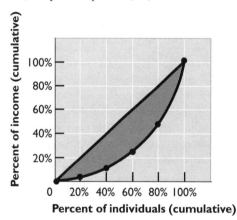

18-4 There are three broad reasons for income inequality; unequal personal endowments; differences in individual character; and external social factors. The first is largely a matter of luck — some people possess high intelligence, particular talents, or physical dexterity that allow them to earn high incomes. Also, they may inherit property or be aided by the social status and financial resources of their parents. The second reason involves personal initiative — individuals may be willing to undergo costly training, accept risk, or tolerate unpleasant working conditions in the expectation of higher pay. They may also show high personal initiative on the job. The third factor relates to society as a whole. Market power and discrimination are two important social determinants of income inequality.

A high IQ normally does not lead to high income unless it is combined with personal initiative and favourable social circumstances. Inherited property — as long as it is competently managed — provides income irrespective of one's character and personal attributes. Both factors are largely a matter of luck to the recipient.

18-10 (a) Plan 1: Basic benefit = $4,000; benefit-reduction rate = 50%; break-even income = $8,000 (= $4,000/.5). Plan 2: Basic benefit = $4,000; benefit-reduction rate = 25%; break-even income = $16,000 (= $4,000/.25). Plan 3: Basic benefit = $8,000; benefit-reduction rate = 50%; break-even income = $16,000 (= $8,000/.5).

(b) Plan 3 is the most costly. Plan 1 is the least costly. Plan 3 is most effective in reducing poverty (although it has a higher benefit-reduction rate than Plan 2, its basic benefit is higher). Plan 1 is least effective in reducing poverty. Plan 3 has the strongest disincentive to work (although it has the same benefit-reduction rate as Plan 1, its higher basic benefit discourages work). Plan 2 has the weakest disincentives to work (its basic benefit level and benefit-reduction rate are low).

(c) The only way to eliminate poverty is to provide a basic benefit high enough to lift everyone from poverty, including people who cannot work or choose not to work. But this large basic benefit reduces the incentive to work, expands the number of people receiving income supplements, and substantially boosts the overall program costs.

CHAPTER 19

19-1 (a) Private good, top to bottom: $P = \$8, Q = 1$; $P = \$7, Q = 2$; $P = \$6, Q = 4$; $P = \$5, Q = 7$; $P = \$4, Q = 10$; $P = \$3, Q = 13$; $P = \$2, Q = 16$; $P = \$1, Q = 19$. (b) Public good, top to bottom: $P = \$19, Q = 1$; $P = \$16, Q = 2$; $P = \$13, Q = 3$; $P = \$10, Q = 4$; $P = \$7, Q = 5$; $P = \$4, Q = 6$; $P = \$2, Q = 7$; $P = \$1, Q = 8$. The first schedule represents a horizontal summation of the individual demand curves; the second schedule represents a vertical summation of these curves. The market demand curve for the private good will determine — in combination with market supply — an actual price-quantity outcome in the marketplace. Because individual preferences are not revealed in the market by potential buyers of public

goods, the collective demand curve for the public good is hypothetical or needs to be determined through "willingness to pay" studies.

19-2 Optimal quantity = 4. Because at price $10 the collective willingness to pay for the final unit of the good (= $10) matches the marginal cost of production (= $10).

19-3 Program B, since the marginal benefit no longer exceeds marginal cost for programs which are larger in scope. Plan B is where net benefits — the excess of total benefits over total costs — are maximized.

19-4 Spillover costs are called negative externalities because they are *external* to the participants in the transaction and *reduce* the utility of affected third parties (thus "negative"). Spillover benefits are called positive externalities because they are *external* to the participants in the transaction and *increase* the utility of affected third parties (thus "positive"). See Figures 19-3 and 19-4. Compare (b) and (c) in Figure 19-4.

19-7 The low marginal benefit from reducing water flow from storm drains would mean the MB curve would be located far to the left of where it is in the text diagram. It will intersect the MC curve at a low amount of pollution abatement, indicating the optimal amount of pollution abatement (where MB = MC) is low. Any cyanide in public water sources could be deadly. Therefore, the marginal benefit of reducing cyanide would be extremely high and the MB curve in the figure would be shifted to the extreme right where it would intersect the MC curve at or near 100%.

19-11 Moral hazard problem: (b) and (d). Adverse selection problem: (a), (c), and (e).

CHAPTER 20

20-2 The paradox is that majority voting does not always provide a clear and consistent picture of the public's preferences. Here the courthouse is preferred to the school and the park is preferred to the courthouse, so we would surmise that the park is preferred to the school. But in fact the school is preferred to the park.

20-3 Project B (small reservoir wins). There are no "vote order" problems here, and B is the preference of the median voter. The two voters favouring No reservoir and Levees, respectively, will prefer Small reservoir — project B — to Medium or Large reservoir. The two voters preferring Large reservoir or Medium reservoir will prefer

Small reservoir to Levees or No reservoir. The median voter's preference for B will prevail. However, the optimal size of the project from an economic perspective is C — it would provide greater net benefits to society than B.

20-6 The electorate is faced with a small number of candidates, each of whom offers a broad range or "bundle" of proposed policies. Voters are then forced to choose the individual candidate whose bundle of policies most resembles their own. The chances of a perfect identity between a particular candidate's preferences and those of any voter are quite slim. As a result, the voter must purchase some unwanted public goods and services. This represents an inefficient allocation of resources.

Government bureaucracies do not function on the basis of profit, reducing the incentive for public servants to hold down costs. Because there is no market test of profits and losses, it is difficult to determine whether public agencies are operating efficiently. Nor is there entry of competing entities to stimulate efficiency and develop improved public goods and services. Also, wasteful expenditures can be maintained through the self-seeking lobbying of bureaucrats themselves, and the public budgetary process can reward rather than penalize inefficiency.

20-9 Average tax rates: 20; 15; and 13.3%. Regressive tax.

20-11 The incidence of an excise tax is likely to be primarily on consumers when demand is highly inelastic and primarily on producers when demand is elastic. The more elastic the supply, the greater the incidence of tax on consumers.

The efficiency loss of a sales or excise tax is the net benefit society sacrifices because consumption and production of the taxed product are reduced below the allocatively efficient level that would occur without the tax. Other things equal, the greater the elasticities of demand and supply, the greater the efficiency loss of a particular tax.

CHAPTER 21

21-1 First sentence: the supply curve is shifting (*a change in supply*) along a relevant inelastic demand curve, producing a large change in equilibrium price and a modest change in equilibrium quantity. Second sentence: the

demand curve is shifting along a relevant inelastic short-run supply curve, causing a large change in price and a small change in *quantity supplied*.

Being volatile from one year to the next, exports increase the instability of demand for farm products.

21-3 (a) Because the demand for most farm products is inelastic, the frequent fluctuations in supply brought about by weather and other factors have relatively small effects on quantity demanded, but large effects on equilibrium prices of farm products. Farmers' sales revenues and incomes therefore are unstable. (b) Technological innovations have decreased production costs, increased long-run supply for most agricultural goods, and reduced the prices of farm output. These declines in prices have put a downward pressure on farm income. (c) The modest long-run growth in the demand for farm products has not been sufficient to offset the expansion of supply, resulting in stagnant farm income. (d) Because the number of producers in most agricultural markets is high, it is difficult if not impossible for producers to collude as a way to limit supply and lessen fluctuations in prices and incomes or halt their long-run declines.

21-8 Price supports benefit farmers, harm consumers, impose costs on society, and contribute to problems in world agriculture. Farmers benefit because the prices they receive and the output they produce will both increase, expanding their gross incomes. Consumers lose because prices they pay for agricultural goods rise and quantities purchased decline. Society as a whole bears several costs. Surpluses of farm products will have to be bought and stored, leading to a greater burden on taxpayers. Domestic economic efficiency is lessened as the artificially high prices of farm products leads to an overallocation of resources to agriculture. The environment suffers: the greater use of pesticides and fertilizers contributes to water pollution; farm policies discourage crop rotation; and price supports encourage farming of environmentally sensitive land. The efficient use of world resources is also distorted because of the import tariffs or quotas which such programs often require. Finally, domestic overproduction leads to supply increases in international markets, decreasing prices and causing a decline in the gross incomes of foreign producers.

GLOSSARY

Ability-to-pay principle — The belief that those who have the greater income (or wealth) should be taxed absolutely and relatively more than those who have less.

Abstraction — Elimination of irrelevant and non-economic facts to obtain an economic principle.

Actual budget — The amount spent by the federal government (to purchase goods and services and for transfer payments) less the amount of tax revenue collected by it in any (fiscal) year; and which can *not* reliably be used to determine whether it is pursuing an expansionary or contractionary fiscal policy. Compare with the Cyclically adjusted budget (*see*).

Actual deficit — The size of the federal government's Budget deficit (*see*) actually measured or recorded in any given year.

Actual investment — The amount that business Firms do invest; equal to Planned investment plus Unplanned investment.

Actual reserve — The amount a bank has as Vault cash and on deposit at the Bank of Canada.

Adaptive expectations theory — The idea that people determine their expectations about future events (for example, inflation) on the basis of past and present events (rates of inflation) and only change their expectations as events unfold.

Adjustable pegs — The device utilized in the Bretton Woods system (*see*) to change Exchange rates in an orderly way to eliminate persistent Payments deficits and surpluses; each nation defined its monetary unit in terms of (pegged it to) gold or the U.S. dollar, kept the Rate of exchange for its money stable in the short run, and changed (adjusted) it in the long run when faced with international disequilibrium.

Adverse selection problem — A problem arising when information known to one party to a contract is not known to the other party, causing the latter to incur major costs. Example: individuals who have the poorest health are more likely to buy health insurance.

Aggregate demand — A schedule or curve that shows the total quantity of goods and services demanded (purchased) at different price levels.

Aggregate demand–aggregate supply model — The macroeconomic model that uses Aggregate demand and Aggregate supply (*see both*) to determine and explain the Price level and the real Domestic output.

Aggregate expenditures — The total amount spent for final goods and services in the economy.

Aggregate expenditures–domestic output approach — Determination of the Equilibrium gross domestic product (*see*) by finding the real GDP at which Aggregate expenditures are equal to the real Domestic output.

Aggregate expenditures schedule — A schedule or curve showing the total amount spent for final goods and services at different levels of real GDP.

Aggregate supply — A schedule or curve showing the total quantity of goods and services supplied (produced) at different Price levels.

Aggregation — Treating individual units or data as one unit or number. For example, all prices of individual goods and services are combined into a Price level, or all units of output are aggregated into Real GDP.

Agricultural Stabilization Board — The federal agency established in 1958 to support the following commodities at not less than 90% of their average price over the previous five years, with adjustments according to production costs: cattle, hogs, and sheep; industrial milk and cream; and oats and barley not produced on the Prairies [where the Canadian Wheat Board (*see*) has jurisdiction].

Allocative efficiency — The apportionment of resources among firms and industries to obtain the production of the products most wanted by society (consumers): the output of each product at which its Marginal cost and Price are equal.

Allocative factor — The ability of an economy to reallocate resources to achieve the Economic growth that the Supply factors (*see*) make possible.

American Federation of Labor (AFL) — The American organization of affiliated Craft unions formed in 1886.

Annually balanced budget — The equality of government expenditures and tax collections during a year.

Anticipated inflation — Inflation (*see*) at a rate that was equal to the rate expected in that period of time.

Anti-combines — (*See* Combines Investigation Act.)

Anti-Inflation Board — The federal agency established in 1975 (and disbanded in 1979) to administer the government's inflation control program.

Applied economics — (*See* Policy economics.)

Appreciation — An increase in the international price of a currency caused by market forces; not caused by the central bank; the opposite of Depreciation.

Arbitration — The designation of a neutral third to render a decision in a dispute by which both parties (the employer and the labour union) agree in advance to abide.

Asian tigers — The newly industrialized and rapidly growing nations of Hong Kong, Singapore, South Korea, and Taiwan.

Asset — Anything with a monetary value owned by a firm or an individual.

Asset demand for money — The amount of money people want to hold as a Store of value (the amount of their financial assets they wish to have in the form of Money); and which varies inversely with the Rate of interest.

Authoritarian capitalism — An economic system in which property resources are privately owned and government extensively directs and controls the economy.

Authoritarian socialism — (*See* Command economy.)

Average fixed cost — The total Fixed cost (*see*) of a Firm divided by output (the quantity of product produced).

Average product — The total output produced per unit of a resource employed (total product divided by the quantity of a resource employed).

Average propensity to consume — Fraction of Disposable income that households spend for consumer goods and services; consumption divided by Disposable income.

Average propensity to save — Fraction of Disposable income that households save; Saving divided by Disposable income.

Average revenue — Total revenue from the sale of a product divided by the quantity of the product sold (demanded); equal to the price at which the product is sold so long as all units of the product are sold at the same price.

Average tax rate — Total tax paid divided by total (taxable) income; the tax rate on total (taxable) income.

Average total cost — The Total cost of a Firm divided by its output (the quantity of product produced); equal to Average fixed cost (*see*) plus Average variable cost (*see*).

Average variable cost — The total Variable cost (*see*) of a Firm divided by output (the quantity of product produced).

Balanced budget multiplier — The effect of equal increases (decreases) in government spending for goods and services and in taxes is to increase (decrease) the Equilibrium gross domestic product.

Balance of (international) payments — The annual statement of a nation's international economic dealings showing the Current account (*see*) balance and the Capital account (*see*) balance, the latter including the balance in Official international reserves (*see*).

Balance of payments deficit — When the balance in Official international reserves (*see*) is *positive*.

Balance of payments surplus — When the balance in Official international reserves (*see*) is *negative*.

Balance of trade — The addition of the balances on goods (merchandise) and services in the Current account (*see*) of the Balance of payments (*see*).

Balance on the capital account — The Capital inflows (*see*) of a nation less its Capital outflows (*see*), both of which include Official international reserves (*see*).

Balance on current account — The exports of goods (merchandise) and services of a nation less its imports of goods (merchandise) and services plus its Net investment income from nonresidents (*see*) and its Net transfers.

Balance on goods and services — The Balance of trade (*see*).

Balance sheet — A statement of the Assets (*see*), Liabilities (*see*), and Net worth (*see*) of a Firm or individual at some given time.

Bank rate — The interest rate that the Bank of Canada charges on advances (*normally* very short-term loans) made to the chartered banks.

Bankers' bank — The bank that accepts the deposits of and makes loans to chartered banks: the Bank of Canada.

Barrier to entry — Anything that artificially prevents the entry of Firms into an industry.

Barter — The exchange of one good or service for another good or service.

Base year — The year with which prices in other years are compared when a Price index (*see*) is constructed.

Benefit-cost analysis — Deciding whether to employ resources and the quantity of resources to employ for a project or program (for the production of a good or service) by comparing the marginal benefits with the marginal costs.

Benefit-reduction rate — The percentage of any increase in earned income by which subsidy benefits in a Negative income tax (*see*) plan are reduced.

Benefits-received principle — The belief that those who receive the benefits of goods and services provided by government should pay the taxes required to finance them.

Bid rigging — The illegal action of oligopolists who agree either that one or more will not bid on a request for bids or tenders or, alternatively, agree on what bids they will make, and forbidden under the Competition Act (*see*).

Big business — A business Firm that either produces a large percentage of the total output of an industry, is large (measured by number of employees or stockholders, sales, assets, or profits) compared with other Firms in the economy, or both.

Bilateral monopoly — A market in which there is a single seller (Monopoly) and a single buyer (Monopsony).

Brain drain — The emigration of highly educated, highly skilled workers from a country.

Break-even income — The level of Disposable income at which Households plan to consume (spend) all of their income (for consumer goods and services) and to save none of it; also denotes that level of earned income at which subsidy payments become zero in an income-maintenance program.

Break-even point — Any output that a (competitive) Firm might produce at which its Total cost and Total revenue would be equal; an output at which it has neither a profit nor a loss.

Bretton Woods system — The international monetary system developed after World War II in which Adjustable pegs (*see*) were employed, the International Monetary Fund (*see*) helped to stabilize exchange rates, and gold and the major currencies were used as Official international reserves (*see*).

Budget deficit — The amount by which the expenditures of the federal government exceed its revenues in any year.

Budget line — A curve that shows the different combinations of two products a consumer can purchase with a given money income.

Budget restraint — The limit imposed on the ability of an individual consumer to obtain goods and services by the size of the consumer's income (and by the prices that must be paid for the goods and services).

Budget surplus — The amount by which the revenues of the federal government exceed its expenditures in any year.

Built-in stability — The effect of Nondiscretionary fiscal policy (*see*) upon the economy; when Net taxes vary directly with the Gross domestic product, the fall (rise) in Net taxes during a recession (inflation) helps to eliminate unemployment (inflationary pressures).

Business cycle — Recurrent ups and downs over a period of years in the level of economic activity.

Canada Assistance Plan — The federal Act under which the federal government makes funds available to the provinces for their programs of assistance to disabled, handicapped, unemployed who are not entitled to unemployment insurance benefits, and other needy persons.

Canada Deposit Insurance Corporation — Federal Crown Corporation that, for a fee payable by the chartered banks and federally chartered trust companies, insures their customers' deposits up to a limit of $60,000 per customer per bank or trust company.

Canada Labour Code — The federal law of 1970 that consolidated previous legislation regulating employment practices, labour standards, and so on, in the federal jurisdiction.

Canada Pension Plan — The compulsory, contributory, earnings-related federal pension plan that covers most employed members of the labour force between the ages of 18 and 65, and payable at the latter age; it came into effect in 1965; there is transferability between the Plan and the Quebec Pension Plan, which applies to the people of that province.

Canada-United States Free Trade Agreement (FTA) — An accord that came into effect on January 1, 1989, to eliminate all Tariffs (*see*) between the two countries over the following ten years.

Canadian Congress of Labour (CCL) — The federation of Industrial unions (*see*) formed in 1940 and affiliated with the Congress of Industrial Organizations (*see*); amalgamated into Canadian Labour Congress (*see*) in 1956.

Canadian International Development Agency (CIDA) — The federal agency responsible for the operation and administration of Canada's international development assistance programs of approximately $2.5 billion a year.

Canadian Labour Congress (CLC) — The largest federation of Labour unions (*see*) in Canada, with 3 million members in international and national unions; founded in 1956 on the amalgamation of the Canadian Congress of Labour (*see*) and the Trades and Labour Congress of Canada (*see*).

Canadian Payments Association — The federal agency set up in 1982 to provide for Cheque clearing (*see*).

Canadian Wheat Board — Federal Crown Corporation established in 1935, which does not own or operate grain-handling facilities but has complete control over the way western wheat is marketed and the price at which it is sold. The Board also acquired complete control of the supplies of all Prairie coarse grains in 1949.

Capacity-creating aspect of investment — The effect of investment spending on the productive capacity (the ability to produce goods and services) of an economy.

Capital — Human-made resources (machinery and equipment) used to produce goods and services; goods that do not directly satisfy human wants; capital goods.

Capital account — That part of the Balance of payments (*see*) that records the net inflows and outflows of liquid capital (money) for direct and portfolio investments at home and abroad, and includes the balance in Official international reserves (*see*).

Capital account deficit — A negative Balance on the capital account (*see*).

Capital account surplus — A positive Balance on the capital account (*see*).

Capital consumption allowances — Estimate of the amount of Capital worn out or used up (consumed) in producing the Gross domestic product; Depreciation.

Capital flight — The transfer of Savings from less developed to industrially advanced countries to avoid government expropriation, taxation, and high rates of inflation or to realize better investment opportunities.

Capital gain — The gain realized when securities or properties are sold for a price greater than the price paid for them.

Capital goods — (*See* Capital.)

Capital inflow — The expenditures made by the residents of foreign nations to purchase equity, shares, and bonds from the residents of a nation.

Capital-intensive commodity — A product that requires a relatively large amount of Capital to produce.

Capital outflow — The expenditures made by the residents of a nation to purchase equity, shares, and bonds from the residents of foreign nations.

Capital-output ratio — The ratio of the stock of Capital to the productive (output) capacity of the economy; and the ratio of a change in the stock of Capital (net investment) to the resulting change in productive capacity.

Capital-saving technological advance — An improvement in technology that permits a greater quantity of a product to be produced with a specific amount of Capital (or the same amount of the product to be produced with a smaller amount of Capital).

Capital-using technological advance — An improvement in technology that requires the use of a greater amount of Capital to produce a specific quantity of a product.

Cartel — A formal written or oral agreement among Firms to set the price of the product and the outputs of the individual firms or to divide the market for the product geographically.

Causation — A cause-and-effect relationship; one or several events bring about or result in another event.

Ceiling price — (*See* Price ceiling.)

Central bank — The bank whose chief function is the control of the nation's money supply: the Bank of Canada.

Central economic planning — Determination of the objectives of the economy and the direction of its resources to the attainment of these objectives by the national government.

Ceteris paribus assumption — (*See* "Other things being equal" assumption.)

Change in amount consumed — increase or decrease in consumption spending that results from an increase or decrease in Disposable income, the Consumption schedule (curve) remaining unchanged; movement from one line (point) to another on the same Consumption schedule (curve).

Change in amount saved — Increase or decrease in Saving that results from an increase or decrease in Disposable income, the Saving schedule (curve) remaining unchanged; movement from one line (point) to another on the same Saving schedule (curve).

Change in the consumption schedule — An increase or decrease in consumption at each level of Disposable income caused by changes in the Nonincome determinants of consumption and saving (*see*); an upward or downward movement of the Consumption schedule.

Change in the saving schedule — An increase or decrease in Saving at each level of Disposable income caused by changes in the Nonincome determinants of consumption and saving (*see*); an upward or downward movement of the Saving schedule.

Chartered bank — One of the 66 multibranched, privately owned, commercial, financial intermediaries that have received charters by Act of Parliament and that alone, with Quebec Savings Banks, may call themselves "banks"; and which accept Demand deposits (*see*).

Chartered banking system — All Chartered banks as a group.

Checkoff — The deduction by an employer of union dues from the pay of workers and the transfer of the amount deducted to a Labour union.

Chequable deposit — Any deposit in a Chartered bank or other financial intermediary (trust company, credit union, etc.) against which a cheque may be written and which deposit, if it is in a bank, is thus part of the M1 (*see*) money supply.

Cheque clearing — The process by which funds are transferred from the Chequing accounts of the writers of cheques to the Chequing accounts of the recipients of the cheques; also called the "collection" of cheques.

Chequing account — A Demand deposit (*see*) in a chartered bank.

Circular flow of income — The flow of resources from Households to Firms and of products from Firms to Households accompanied in an economy using money by flows of money from Households to Firms and from Firms to Households.

Civilian labour force — Persons 15 years of age and older who are not residents of the Yukon or the Northwest Territories, who are not in institutions or the armed forces, and who are employed for a wage or salary, seeking such employment, or self-employed for gain.

Classical economics — The Macroeconomic generalizations accepted by most economists before the 1930s that led to the conclusion that a capitalistic economy would employ its resources fully.

Closed economy — An economy that neither exports nor imports goods and services.

Close-down case — The circumstance in which a Firm would experience a loss greater than its total fixed cost if it were to produce any output greater than zero; alternatively, a situation in which a firm would cease to operate when the price at which it can sell its product is less than its Average variable cost.

Coase theorem — The idea that Externality problems may be resolved through private negotiations of the affected parties.

Coincidence of wants — The item (good or service) that one trader wishes to obtain is the same as another trader desires to give up and the item the second trader wishes to acquire is the same as the first trader desires to surrender.

COLA — (*See* Cost-of-living adjustment.)

Collection of cheques — (*See* Cheque clearing.)

Collective bargaining — The negotiation of work agreements between Labour unions (*see*) and their employers.

Collective voice — The function a union performs for its members as a group when it communicates their problems and grievances to management and presses management for a satisfactory resolution.

Collusion — A situation in which Firms act together and in agreement (collude) to set the price of the product and the output each firm will produce or to determine the geographic area in which each firm will sell.

Collusive oligopoly — Occurs when the few firms composing an oligopolistic industry reach an explicit or unspoken agreement to fix prices, divide a market, or otherwise restrict competition; may be a Cartel (*see*), Gentleman's agreement (*see*), or Price leadership (*see*).

Combined tax-transfer system — The percentage of income collected as taxes less the percentage of income received as transfer payments in different income classes.

Combines Investigation Act — The federal Act, first passed in 1910, whose avowed aim is to prevent agreements to lessen competition unduly; amended and renamed the Competition Act in June 1986.

Command economy — An economic system (method of organization) in which property resources are publicly owned and Central economic planning (*see*) is used to direct and co-ordinate economic activities.

Commercial bank — (*See* Chartered bank.)

Communism — (*See* Command economy.)

Company union — An organization of employees that is dominated by the employer (the company) and does not engage in genuine collective bargaining with the employer.

Comparable worth doctrine — The belief that women should receive the same salaries (wages) as men when the levels of skill, effort, and responsibility in their different jobs are the same.

Comparative advantage — A lower relative or Comparative cost (*see*) than another producer.

Comparative cost — The amount the production of one product must be reduced to increase the production of another product; Opportunity cost (*see*).

Compensating differences — The differences in the Wages received by workers in different jobs which compensate for nonmonetary differences in the jobs.

Competing goods — (*See* Substitute goods.)

Competition — The presence in a market of a large number of independent buyers and sellers and the freedom of buyers and sellers to enter and to leave the market.

Competition Act — The Act that amended the Combines Investigation Act (*see*) in June 1986 and, in so doing, renamed it the Competition Act.

Competitive industry's short-run supply curve — The horizontal summation of the short-run supply curves of the Firms in a purely competitive industry (*see* Pure competition); a curve that shows the total quantities offered for sale at various prices by the Firms in an industry in the Short run (*see*).

Competitive industry's short-run supply schedule — The summation of the short-run supply schedules of the Firms in a purely competitive industry (*see* Pure competition); a schedule that shows the total quantities that will be offered for sale at various prices by the Firms in an industry in the Short run (*see*).

Competitive labour market — A market in which a large number of (noncolluding) firms demand a particular type of labour from a large number of nonunionized workers.

Complementary goods — Goods or services for which there is an inverse relationship between the price of one and the demand for the other; when the price of one falls (rises) the demand for the other increases (decreases).

Complex multiplier — The Multiplier (*see*) when changes in the Gross domestic product change Net taxes and Imports, as well as Saving.

Concentration ratio — The percentage of the total sales of an industry made by the four (or some other number) largest sellers (Firms) in the industry.

Conditional grant — A transfer to a province by the federal government for a Shared-cost program whereby the federal government undertakes to pay part of the costs (usually half) of programs run by the provinces in accordance with federally set standards; such grants are mostly for health, post-secondary education, and general welfare [mostly under the Canada Assistance Plan (*see*)].

Confederation of National Trade Unions (CNTU) — The Labour union (*see*) federation that represents approximately 20% of Quebec's union members; established in 1921 as the Federation of Catholic Workers of Canada, it was later renamed the Canadian and Catholic Confederation of Labour; it adopted its present name and became nonconfessional in 1956.

Conglomerate combination — A group of Plants (*see*) owned by a single Firm and engaged at one or more stages in the production of different products (of products that do not compete with each other).

Conglomerate merger — The merger of a Firm in one Industry with a Firm in another industry (with a Firm that is neither supplier, customer, nor competitor).

Congress of Industrial Organizations (CIO) — The organization of affiliated Industrial unions formed in the United States in 1936.

Constant-cost industry — An Industry in which the expansion of the Industry by the entry of new Firms has no effect upon the prices the Firms in the Industry pay for resources and no effect, therefore, on their cost curves.

Consumer goods — Goods and services that satisfy human wants directly.

Consumer price index (CPI) — An index that measures the prices of a fixed "market basket" of some 300 consumer goods bought by a "typical" consumer.

Consumer sovereignty — Determination by consumers of the types and quantities of goods and services produced from the scarce resources of the economy.

Consumption schedule — A schedule showing the amounts Households plan to spend for Consumer goods at different levels of Disposable income.

Contractionary fiscal policy — A decrease in Aggregate demand brought about by a decrease in government expenditures for goods and services, an increase in Net taxes, or some combination of the two.

Contractionary monetary policy — Contracting, or restricting the growth of, the nation's Money supply (*see*).

Corporate income tax — A tax levied on the net income (profit) of Corporations.

Corporation — A legal entity ("person") chartered by the federal or a provincial government, which is distinct and separate from the individuals who own it.

Correlation — Systematic and dependable association between two sets of data (two kinds of events); does not necessarily indicate causation.

Cost-of-living adjustment (COLA) — An increase in the incomes (wages) of workers that is automatically received by them when there is inflation and guaranteed by a clause in their labour contracts with their employer.

Cost-plus pricing — A procedure used by (oligopolistic) firms to determine the price they will charge for a product and in which a percentage markup is added to the estimated average total cost of producing the product.

Cost-push inflation — Inflation resulting from a decrease in Aggregate supply (from higher wage rates and raw material prices) and accompanied by decreases in real output and employment (by increases in the Unemployment rate).

Cost ratio — The ratio of the decrease in the production of one product to the increase in the production of another product when resources are shifted from the production of the first to the second product; the amount the production of one product decreases when the production of a second increases by one unit.

Craft union — A Labour union that limits its membership to workers with a particular skill (craft).

Credit — An accounting notation that the value of an asset (such as the foreign money owned by the residents of a nation) has increased.

Credit union — An association of persons who often have a common tie (such as being employees of the same Firm or members of the same Labour union) that sells shares to (accepts deposits from) its members and makes loans to them.

Creeping inflation — A slow rate of inflation; a 2 to 4% annual rise in the price level.

Crop restriction — A method of increasing farm revenue when demand for the product is inelastic. Usually done through a Farm products marketing board (*see*) allotting quotas.

Cross elasticity of demand — The ratio of the percentage change in Quantity demanded of one good to the percentage change in the price of some other good. A positive coefficient indicates the two products are Substitute goods; a negative coefficient indicates Complementary goods.

Crowding model of occupational discrimination — A model of labour markets that assumes Occupational discrimination (*see*) against women and minorities has kept them out of many occupations and forced them into a limited number of other occupations in which the large Supply of labour (relative to the Demand) results in lower wages and incomes.

Crowding-out effect — The rise in interest rates and the resulting decrease in planned investment spending in the economy caused by increased borrowing in the money market by the federal government.

Currency — Coins and Paper money.

Currency appreciation — (*See* Exchange rate appreciation.)

Currency depreciation — (*See* Exchange rate depreciation.)

Current account — That part of the Balance of payments (*see*) that records the total current receipts for merchandise exports, services, investment income from nonresidents, and transfers and the total current payments for merchandise imports, services, investment income to nonresidents, and transfers.

Current account deficit — A negative Balance on current account (*see*).

Current account surplus — A positive Balance on current account (*see*).

Customary economy — (*See* Traditional economy.)

Cyclical unemployment — Unemployment caused by insufficient Aggregate expenditures (or by insufficient Aggregate demand).

Cyclically adjusted budget — What the budget balance would be for the total government sector if the economy were operating at an average or cyclically adjusted level of activity.

Cyclically adjusted deficit — The budget deficit that would have occurred even though the economy was operating at an average or cyclically adjusted level of activity.

Cyclically balanced budget — The equality of Government expenditures for goods and services and Net taxes collections over the course of a Business cycle; deficits incurred during periods of recession are offset by surpluses obtained during periods of prosperity (inflation).

Debit — An accounting notation that the value of an asset (such as the foreign money owned by the residents of a nation) has decreased.

Debt-equity swaps — The transfer of stock in private or government-owned enterprises of Less developed countries (*see*) to foreign creditors.

Declining economy — An economy in which Net investment (*see*) is less than zero (Gross private domestic investment is less than Depreciation).

Declining industry — An industry in which Economic profits are negative (losses are incurred) and which will, therefore, decrease its output as Firms leave the industry.

Decrease in demand — A decrease in the Quantity demanded of a good or service at every price; a shift of the Demand curve to the left.

Decrease in supply — A decrease in the Quantity supplied of a good or service at every price; a shift of the Supply curve to the left.

Deduction — Reasoning from assumption to conclusions; a method of reasoning that tests a hypothesis (an assumption) by comparing the conclusions to which it leads with economic facts.

Deficiency payments — A method of Price support (*see*) whereby the government pays a subsidy to producers when the market price is below the minimum price demand suitable by the government.

Deflating — Finding the Real gross domestic product (*see*) by decreasing the dollar value of the Gross domestic product produced in a year in which prices were higher than in the Base year (*see*).

Deflation — A fall in the general (average) level of prices in the economy.

Demand — A Demand schedule or a Demand curve (*see* both).

Demand curve — A curve showing the amounts of a good or service buyers wish to purchase at various prices during some period of time.

Demand deposit — A deposit in a Chartered bank against which cheques may be written for immediate payment; bank-created money.

Demand factor — The increase in the level of Aggregate expenditures that brings about the Economic growth made possible by an increase in the productive potential of the economy.

Demand management — The use of Fiscal policy (*see*) and Monetary policy (*see*) to increase or decrease Aggregate expenditures.

Demand-pull inflation — Inflation resulting from an increase in Aggregate demand.

Demand schedule — A schedule showing the amounts of a good or service buyers will purchase at various prices during some period of time.

Dependent variable — A variable that changes as a consequence of a change in some other (independent) variable; the "effect" or outcome.

Deposit multiplier — (*See* Monetary multiplier.)

Depository institution — A Firm that accepts the deposits of Money of the public (businesses and persons); Chartered banks and other Financial intermediaries (*see*).

Depreciation (1) — (*See* Capital consumption allowances.)

Depreciation (2) — A decrease in the international price of a currency caused by market forces; not caused by the Central bank; the opposite of Appreciation.

Derived demand — The demand for a good or service that is dependent on or related to the demand for some other good or service; the demand for a resource that depends on the demand for the products it can be used to produce.

Descriptive economics — The gathering or collection of relevant economic facts (data).

Desired reserves — The amount of vault cash each chartered bank chooses to keep on hand for daily transaction. This amount includes reserves held at the Bank of Canada for cheque settlements among the chartered banks.

Determinants of aggregate demand — Factors such as consumption, investment, government, and net export spending that, if they change, will shift the Aggregate demand curve.

Determinants of aggregate supply — Factors such as input prices, productivity, and the legal-institutional environment that, if they change, will shift the Aggregate supply curve.

Determinants of demand — Factors other than its price that determine the quantities demanded of a good or service.

Determinants of supply — Factors other than its price that determine the quantities supplied of a good or service.

Devaluation — A decrease in the government-defined value of a currency brought about by the Central bank; the opposite of Revaluation.

DI — (*See* Disposable income.)

Differentiated oligopoly — An Oligopoly in which the firms produce a Differentiated product (*see*).

Differentiated product — A product that differs physically or in some other way from the similar products produced by other Firms; a product such that buyers are *not* indifferent to the seller from whom they purchase it when the price charged by all sellers is the same.

Dilemma of regulation — When a Regulatory agency (*see*) must establish the maximum price a monopolist may charge, it finds that if it sets the price at the Optimal social price (*see*), this price is below Average total cost (and either bankrupts the Firm or requires that it be subsidized); and if it sets the price at the Fair-return price (*see*), it has failed to eliminate the underallocation of resources that is the consequence of unregulated monopoly.

Direct investment — Investment by nonresidents in a firm they thereby establish or control or come to control through the investment. (*See also* Portfolio investment.)

Directing function of prices — (*See* Guiding function of prices.)

Directly related — Two sets of economic data that change in the same direction; when one variable increases (decreases) the other increases (decreases).

Direct relationship — The relationship between two variables that change in the same direction, for example, product price and quantity supplied.

Discouraged workers — Workers who have left the Civilian labour force (*see*) because they have not been able to find employment.

Discretionary fiscal policy — Deliberate changes in taxes (tax rates) and government spending (spending for goods and services and transfer payment programs) by Parliament for the purpose of achieving a full-employment, noninflationary Gross domestic product and economic growth.

Diseconomies of scale — The forces that increase the Average total cost of producing a product as the Firm expands the size of its Plant (its output) in the Long run (*see*).

Disinflation — A reduction in the rate of Inflation (*see*).

Disposable income — Personal income (*see*) less Personal taxes (*see*); income available for Personal consumption expenditures (*see*) and Personal saving (*see*).

Dissaving — Spending for consumer goods and services in excess of Disposable income; the amount by which Personal consumption expenditures (*see*) exceed Disposable income.

Dividend tax credit — A federal government method of reducing the Double taxation (*see*) of corporation income.

Division of labour — Dividing the work required to produce a product into a number of different tasks that are performed by different workers; Specialization (*see*) of workers.

Dollar votes — The "votes" consumers and entrepreneurs in effect cast for the production of the different kinds of consumer and capital goods, respectively, when they purchase them in the markets of the economy.

Domestic economic goal — Assumed to be full employment with little or no Inflation.

Domestic income — (*See* Net domestic income.)

Domestic output — Gross domestic product (*see*).

Domestic price — The price of a good or service within a country, determined by domestic demand and supply.

Doomsday models — Computer-based models that predict that continued growth of population and production will exhaust available resources and the environment, causing an economic collapse.

Double counting — Including the value of Intermediate goods (*see*) in the Gross domestic product; counting the same good or service more than once.

Double taxation — Taxation of both corporation net income (profits) and the dividends paid from this net income when they become the Personal income of households.

Dumping — The sale of products below cost in a foreign country.

Duopoly — A Market in which there are only two sellers; an industry in which there are two firms.

Durable good — A consumer good with an expected life (use) of three years or more.

Dynamic progress — The development over time of more efficient (less costly) techniques of producing existing products and of improved products; technological progress.

Earnings — The Money income received by a worker; equal to the Wage (rate) multiplied by the quantity of labour supplied (the amount of time worked) by the worker.

Easy money policy — Central bank expanding the Money supply in an effort to decrease interest rates.

EC — European Economic Community (*See* European Union).

Economic analysis — Deriving Economic principles (*see*) from relevant economic facts.

Economic cost — A payment that must be made to obtain and retain the services of a resource; the income a Firm must provide to a resource supplier to attract the resource away from an alternative use; equal to the quantity of other products that cannot be produced when resources are employed to produce a particular product.

Economic efficiency — The relationship between the input of scarce resources and the resulting output of a good or service; production of an output with a specific dollar-and-cents value with the smallest total expenditure for resources; obtaining the largest total production of a good or service with resources of a specific dollar-and-cents value.

Economic growth — (1) An increase in the Production possibilities schedule or curve that results from an increase in resource supplies or an improvement in Technology; (2) an increase either in real output (Gross domestic product) or in real output per capita.

Economic integration — Co-operation among and the complete or partial unification of the economies of different nations; the elimination of the barriers to trade among these nations; the bringing together of the markets in each of the separate economies to form one large (a common) market.

Economic law — (*See* Economic principle.)

Economic model — A simplified picture of reality; an abstract generalization.

Economic perspective — A viewpoint that sees individuals and institutions making rational or purposeful decisions based on a consideration of the Marginal benefits and Marginal costs associated with one's actions.

Economic policy — Course of action that will correct or avoid a problem.

Economic principle — Generalization of the economic behaviour of individuals and institutions.

Economic profit — The total receipts (revenue) of a firm less all its Economic costs; also called "pure profit" and "above normal profit."

Economic regulation — (*See* Industrial regulation.)

Economic rent — The price paid for the use of land and other natural resources, the supply of which is fixed (perfectly inelastic).

Economic resources — Land, labour, capital, and entrepreneurial ability, which are used in the production of goods and services.

Economics — Social science concerned with using scarce resources to obtain the maximum satisfaction of the unlimited human wants of society.

Economic theory — Deriving Economic principles (*see*) from relevant economic facts; an Economic principle (*see*).

Economies of scale — The forces that reduce the Average total cost of producing a product as the Firm expands the size of its Plant (its output) in the Long run (*see*); the economies of mass production.

Economizing problem — Society's material wants are unlimited but the resources available to produce the goods and services that satisfy wants are limited (scarce); the inability to produce unlimited quantities of goods and services.

Efficiency factors in growth — The capacity of an economy to combine resources effectively to achieve the growth of real output that the Supply factors (*see*) make possible.

Efficiency loss of a tax — The loss of net benefits to society because a tax reduces the production and consumption of a taxed good below the economically efficient level.

Efficiency wage — A wage that minimizes wage costs per unit of output.

Efficient allocation of resources — The allocation of the resources of an economy among the production of different products that leads to the maximum satisfaction of the wants of consumers; producing the optimal mix of output.

Elastic demand — The Elasticity coefficient (*see*) is greater than one; the percentage change in Quantity demanded is greater than the percentage change in price.

Elasticity coefficient — The number obtained when the percentage change in quantity demanded (or supplied) is divided by the percentage change in the price of the commodity.

Elasticity formula — The price elasticity of demand (supply) is equal to

$$\frac{\text{Percentage change in quantity demanded (supplied)}}{\text{percentage change in price}}$$

Elastic supply — The Elasticity coefficient (*see*) is greater than one; the percentage change in Quantity supplied is greater than the percentage change in price.

Emission fees — Special fees that might be levied against those who discharge pollutants into the environment.

Employment and training policy — Policies and programs involving vocational training, job information, and anti-discrimination that are designed to improve labour market efficiency and lower unemployment at any level of aggregate demand.

Employment rate — The percentage of the Civilian labour force (*see*) employed at any time.

End products — Finished commodities that have attained their final degree of processing, such as commodities used directly for consumption, and machinery.

Entrepreneurial ability — The human resource that combines the other resources to produce a product, makes nonroutine decisions, innovates, and bears risks.

Equality vs. efficiency trade-off — The decrease in Economic efficiency (*see*) that may accompany a decrease in Income inequality (*see*); the presumption that an increase in Income inequality is required to increase Economic efficiency.

Equalization payment — An Unconditional grant (*see*) made by the federal government to the seven less wealthy provinces in an attempt to equalize incomes and opportunities across Canada.

Equalizing differences — The differences in the Wages received by workers in different jobs that compensate for nonmonetary differences in the jobs.

Equation of exchange — $MV = PQ$; in which M is the Money supply (*see*), V is the Velocity of money (*see*), P is the Price level, and Q is the physical volume of final goods and services produced.

Equilibrium GDP — The Gross domestic product at which the total quantity of final goods and services produced (the Domestic output) is equal to the total quantity of final goods and services purchased (Aggregate expenditures); the real Domestic output at which the Aggregate demand curve intersects the Aggregate supply curve.

Equilibrium position — The point at which the Budget line (*see*) is tangent to an Indifference curve (*see*) in the indifference curve approach to the theory of consumer behaviour.

Equilibrium price — The price in a competitive market where the Quantity demanded (*see*) and the Quantity supplied (*see*) are equal; where there is neither a shortage nor a surplus; and where there is no tendency for price to rise or fall.

Equilibrium price level — The Price level at which the Aggregate demand curve intersects the Aggregate supply curve.

Equilibrium quantity — The Quantity demanded (*see*) and Quantity supplied (*see*) at the Equilibrium price (*see*) in a competitive market.

European Common Market — (*See* European Union.)

European Union (EU) — The association of European nations initiated in 1958 to abolish gradually the Tariffs and Import quotas that exist among them, to establish common Tariffs for goods imported from outside the member nations, to allow the eventual free movement of labour and capital among them, and to create other common economic policies. (Earlier known as "European Economic Community" and the "Common Market.")

Excess capacity — A situation where an imperfectly competitive firm produces an output less than the minimum Average total cost output, thereby necessitating a higher product price than a purely competitive firm would charge.

Excess reserve — The amount by which a Chartered bank's Actual reserves (*see*) exceeds its Desired cash reserve (*see*); Actual reserves minus Desired reserves.

Exchange control — (*See* Foreign exchange control.)

Exchange Fund Account — The account operated by the Bank of Canada on the government's behalf wherein are held Canada's Official international reserves (*see*).

Exchange rate — The Rate of exchange (*see*).

Exchange rate appreciation — An increase in the value of a nation's money in foreign exchange markets caused by free market forces; a decrease in the Rates of exchange for foreign monies.

Exchange rate depreciation — A decrease in the value of a nation's money in foreign exchange markets caused by free market forces; an increase in the Rates of exchange for foreign monies.

Exchange rate determinant — Any factor other than the Rate of exchange (*see*) that determines the demand for and the supply of a currency in the Foreign exchange market (*see*).

Excise tax — A tax levied on the expenditure for a specific product or on the quantity of the product purchased.

Exclusion principle — The exclusion of those who do not pay for a product from the benefits of the product.

Exclusive dealing and tied selling — The illegal action whereby a supplier sells a product only on condition that the buyer acquire other products from the same seller and not from competitors; and forbidden under the Competition Act (*see*).

Exclusive unionism — The policies employed by a Labour union to restrict the supply of labour by excluding potential members to increase the Wages received by its members; the policies typically employed by a Craft union (*see*).

Exhaustive expenditure — An expenditure by government resulting directly in the employment of economic resources and in the absorption by government of the goods and services these resources produce; Government purchase (*see*).

Exit mechanism — Leaving a job and searching for another one to improve the conditions under which a worker is employed.

Expanding economy — An economy in which Net investment (*see*) is greater than zero (Gross investment is greater than Depreciation).

Expanding industry — An industry in which Economic profits are obtained by the firms in the industry and which will, therefore, increase its output as new firms enter the industry.

Expansionary fiscal policy — An increase in Aggregate demand brought about by an increase in Government expenditures for goods and services, a decrease in Net taxes, or some combination of the two.

Expectations — What consumers, business Firms, and others believe will happen or what conditions will be in the future.

Expected rate of net profits — Annual profits a firm anticipates it will obtain by purchasing Capital (by investing) expressed as a percentage of the price (cost) of the Capital.

Expenditure approach — The method that adds all the expenditures made for Final goods and services to measure the Gross domestic product.

Expenditures-output approach — (*See* Aggregate expenditures-domestic output approach.)

Explicit cost — The monetary payment a Firm must make to an outsider to obtain a resource.

Export controls — The limitation or prohibition of the export of certain high-technology products on the basis of foreign policy or national security objectives.

Exports — Goods and services produced in a nation and sold to customers in other nations.

Export subsidies — Government payments that reduce the price of a product to foreign buyers.

Export supply curve — An upsloping curve showing the amount of a product domestic firms will export at each World price (*see*) above the Domestic price (*see*).

Export transaction — A sale of a good or service that increases the amount of foreign money (or of their own money) held by the citizens, firms, and governments of a nation.

External benefit — (*See* Spillover benefit.)

External cost — (*See* Spillover cost.)

External debt — Debt (*see*) owed to foreign citizens, firms, and institutions.

Externality — (*See* Spillover.)

Externally held public debt — Public debt (*see*) owed to (Canadian government securities owned by) foreign citizens, firms, and institutions.

Face value — The dollar or cents value stamped on a coin.

Factors of production — Economic resources: Land, Capital, Labour, and Entrepreneurial ability.

Fair-return price — The price of a product that enables its producer to obtain a Normal profit (*see*), and that is equal to the Average total cost of producing it.

Fallacy of composition — Incorrectly reasoning that what is true for the individual (or part) is therefore necessarily true for the group (or whole).

Fallacy of limited decisions — The false notion that there are a limited number of economic decisions to be made so that, if government makes more decisions, there will be fewer private decisions to render.

Farm problem — Technological advance, coupled with a price inelastic and relatively constant demand has made agriculture a Declining industry; also the tendency for the prices farmers receive and their incomes to fluctuate sharply from year to year.

Farm products and marketing boards — The federal and provincial boards, numbering more than 100, that set marketing regulations for commodities ranging from asparagus to turkeys. The boards have the power to allocate quotas, set prices, issue licences, collect fees, and require that the commodity be marketed through them.

Featherbedding — Payment by an employer to a worker for work not actually performed.

Feedback effects — The effects a change in the money supply will have (because it affects the Interest rate, Planned investment, and the Equilibrium GDP) on the demand for money, which is itself directly related to the GDP.

Female participation rate — The percentage of the female population of working age in the Civilian labour force (*see*).

Fewness — A relatively small number of sellers (or buyers) of a good or service.

Fiat money — Anything that is Money because government has decreed it to be Money.

Final goods — Goods that have been purchased for final use and not for resale or further processing or manufacturing (during the year).

Financial capital — (*See* Money capital.)

Financial intermediary — A Chartered bank or other financial institution (trust or mortgage loan company, credit union, *caisse populaire*), which uses the funds (savings) deposited with it to make loans (for consumption or investment).

Financing exports and imports — The use of Foreign exchange markets by exporters and importers to receive and make payments for goods and services they sell and buy in foreign nations.

Firm — An organization that employs Resources to produce a good or service for profit and owns and operates one or more Plants (*see*).

Fiscal policy — Changes in government spending and tax collections designed to achieve a full-employment and noninflationary domestic output.

Five fundamental economic questions — The five questions every economy must answer: what to produce, how to produce, how to divide the total output, how to maintain Full employment, and how to assure economic flexibility.

Fixed cost — Any cost that in total does not change when the Firm changes its output; the cost of Fixed resources (*see*).

Fixed exchange rate — A Rate of exchange that is prevented from rising or falling by the intervention of government.

Fixed resource — Any resource employed by a Firm in a quantity that the firm cannot change.

Flat-rate income tax — A tax that taxes all incomes at the same rate.

Flexible exchange rate — A Rate of exchange determined by the demand for and supply of the foreign money and is free to rise or fall without government interference.

Floating exchange rate — (*See* Flexible exchange rate.)

Floor price — A price set by government that is above the Equilibrium price.

Food and Drugs Act — The federal law enacted in 1920 as outgrowth of legislation dating back to 1875; subsequently amended, the Act and its Regulations now provide for controls over all foods, drugs, cosmetics, and medical devices sold in Canada.

Foreign competition — (*See* Import competition.)

Foreign exchange — (*See* Official international reserves.)

Foreign exchange control — The control a government may exercise over the quantity of foreign money demanded by its citizens and business firms and over the

Rates of exchange in order to limit its outpayments to its inpayments (to eliminate a Payments deficit) (*see*).

Foreign exchange market — A market in which the money (currency) used by one nation is used to purchase (is exchanged for) the money used by another nation.

Foreign exchange rate — (*See* Rate of exchange.)

Foreign-trade effect — The inverse relationship between the Net exports (*see*) of an economy and its Price level (*see*) relative to foreign Price levels.

Foreign investment — (*See* Direct investment and Portfolio investment.)

45° line — A curve along which the value of the GDP (measured horizontally) is equal to the value of Aggregate expenditures (measured vertically).

Fractional reserve — A Reserve ratio (*see*) that is less than 100% of the deposit liabilities of a Chartered bank.

Freedom of choice — Freedom of owners of property resources and money to employ or dispose of these resources as they see fit, of workers to enter any line of work for which they are qualified, and of consumers to spend their incomes in a manner they deem appropriate (best for them).

Freedom of enterprise — Freedom of business Firms to employ economic resources, to use these resources to produce products of the firm's own choosing, and to sell these products in markets of their choice.

Freely floating exchange rates — Rates of exchange (*see*) that are not controlled and that may, therefore, rise and fall; and that are determined by the demand for and the supply of foreign monies.

Free-rider problem — The inability of potential providers of an economically desirable and indivisible good or service to obtain payment from those who benefit because the Exclusion principle (*see*) is not applicable.

Free trade — The absence of artificial (government-imposed) barriers to trade among individuals and firms in different nations.

Frictional unemployment — Unemployment caused by workers voluntarily changing jobs and by temporary lay-offs; unemployed workers between jobs.

Fringe benefits — The rewards other than Wages that employees receive from their employers and that include pensions, medical and dental insurance, paid vacations, and sick leaves.

Full employment — (1) Using all available economic resources to produce goods and services; (2) when the Unemployment rate is equal to the Full-employment unemployment rate and there is Frictional and Structural but no Cyclical unemployment (and the real output of the economy is equal to its Potential real output).

Full-employment unemployment rate — The Unemployment rate (*see*) at which there is no Cyclical unemployment (*see*) of the Civilian labour force (*see*) and, because some Frictional and Structural unemployment is unavoidable, equal to about 7.5 to 8%.

Full production — The maximum amount of goods and services that can be produced from the employed resources of an economy; occurs when both Allocative efficiency and Productive efficiency are realized.

Functional distribution of income — The manner in which national income is divided among those who perform different functions (provide the economy with different kinds of resources); the division of Net domestic income (*see*) into wages and salaries, corporation profits, farmers' income, unincorporated business income, interest, and rent.

Functional finance — Use of Fiscal policy to achieve a full-employment, noninflationary Gross domestic product without regard to the effect on the Public debt (*see*).

G-7 nations — A group of seven major industrial powers that meet regularly to discuss common economic problems and try to co-ordinate economic policies; Canada, the United States, Japan, Germany, United Kingdom, France, and Italy.

Game theory — A theory that compares the behaviour of participants in games of strategy, such as poker and chess, with that of a small group of mutually interdependent firms (an Oligopoly).

GATT — (*See* General Agreement on Tariffs and Trade.)

GDP — (*See* Gross domestic product.)

GDP deflator — The Price index (*see*) for all final goods and services used to adjust nominal GDP to derive real GDP.

GDP gap — Potential Real gross domestic product less actual Real gross domestic product.

General Agreement on Tariffs and Trade — The international agreement reached in 1947 in which 23 nations agreed to give equal and nondiscriminatory treatment to the other nations, to reduce tariff rates by multinational negotiations, and to eliminate import quotas. Now includes 123 nations.

Generalization — Statistical or probability statement; statement of the nature of the relation between two or more sets of facts.

Gentlemen's agreement — An informal understanding on the price to be charged among the firms in an Oligopoly (*see*).

GNP — (*See* Gross national product.)

Gold export point — The Rate of exchange for a foreign money above which — when nations participate in the International gold standard (*see*) — the foreign money will not be purchased and gold will be sent (exported) to the foreign country to make payments there.

Gold flow — The movement of gold into or out of a nation.

Gold import point — The Rate of exchange for a foreign money below which — when nations participate in the International gold standard (*see*) — a nation's own money will not be purchased and gold will be sent (imported) into that country by foreigners to make payments there.

Gorbachev's reforms — A mid-1980s series of reforms designed to revitalize the Soviet economy. The reforms stressed the modernization of productive facilities, less centralized control, improved worker discipline and productivity, more emphasis on market prices, and an expansion of private economic activity.

Government purchases — Disbursements of money by government for which government receives a currently produced good or service in return; the expenditures of all governments in the economy for Final goods (*see*) and services.

Government transfer payment — The disbursement of money (or goods and services) by government for which government receives no currently produced good or service in return.

Grievance procedure — The methods used by a Labour union and the Firm to settle disputes that arise during the life of the collective bargaining agreement between them.

Gross domestic product (GDP) — The total market value of all Final goods (*see*) and services produced annually within the boundaries of Canada, whether by Canadian or foreign-supplied resources.

Gross national product (GNP) — The total market value of all Final goods (*see*) and services produced annually by land, labour, and capital, and entrepreneurial talent supplied by Canadian residents, whether these resources are located in Canada or abroad.

Gross private domestic investment — Expenditures for newly produced Capital goods (*see*) — machinery, equipment, tools, and buildings — and for additions to inventories.

Guaranteed annual income — The minimum income a family (or individual) would receive if a Negative income tax (*see*) were to be adopted.

Guaranteed Income Supplement — A 1966 amendment to the Old Age Security Act (*see*) provides for the payment of a full supplement to pensioners with no other income and a partial supplement to those with other, but still low, income.

Guiding function of prices — The ability of price changes to bring about changes in the quantities of products and resources demanded and supplied. (*See* Incentive function of price.)

Herfindahl index — A measure of the concentration and competitiveness of an industry; calculated as the sum of the squared market shares of the individual firms.

Homogeneous oligopoly — An Oligopoly in which the firms produce a Standardized product (*see*).

Horizontal axis — The "left–right" or "west–east" axis on a graph or grid.

Horizontal combination — A group of Plants (*see*) in the same stage of production owned by a single Firm (*see*).

Horizontal merger — The merger of one or more Firms producing the same product into a single Firm.

Horizontal range — The horizontal segment of the short-run Aggregate supply curve, indicating much slack in the economy.

Household — An economic unit (of one or more persons) that provides the economy with resources and uses the money paid to it for these resources to purchase goods and services to satisfy material wants.

Human capital investment — Any action taken to increase the productivity (by improving the skills and abilities) of workers; expenditures made to improve the education, health, or mobility of workers.

Hyperinflation — A very rapid rise in the price level.

IMF — (*See* International Monetary Fund.)

Immobility — The inability or unwillingness of a worker or another resource to move from one geographic area or occupation to another or from a lower-paying to a higher-paying job.

Imperfect competition — All markets except Pure competition (*see*); Monopoly, Monopolistic competition, Oligopoly (*see all*).

Implicit cost — The monetary income a Firm sacrifices when it employs a resource it owns to produce a product rather than supplying the resource in the market; equal to what the resource could have earned in the best-paying alternative employment.

Import competition — Competition that domestic firms encounter from the products and services of foreign suppliers.

Import demand curve — A downsloping curve showing the amount of a product that an economy will import at each World price (*see*) below the Domestic price (*see*).

Import quota — A limit imposed by a nation on the quantity of a good may be imported during some period of time.

Imports — Spending by individuals, Firms, and governments for goods and services produced in foreign nations.

Import transaction — The purchase of a good or service that decreases the amount of foreign money held by citizens, firms, and governments of a nation.

Incentive function of price The inducement that an increase (a decrease) in the price of a commodity offers to sellers of the commodity to make more (less) of it available; and the inducement that an increase (decrease) in price offers to buyers to purchase smaller (larger) quantities; the Guiding function of prices (*see*).

Incentive pay plan — A compensation scheme that ties worker pay directly to performance. Such plans include piece rates, bonuses, commissions, and profit sharing.

Inclusive unionism — A union that attempts to include all workers employed in an industry as members.

Income approach — The method that adds all the incomes generated by the production of Final goods and services to measure the Gross domestic product.

Income effect — The effect of a change in price of a product on a consumer's Real income (purchasing power) and thus on the quantity of the product purchased, after the Substitution effect (*see*) has been determined and eliminated.

Income elasticity of demand — The ratio of the percentage change in the Quantity demanded of a good to the percentage change in income; it measures the responsiveness of consumer purchases to income changes.

Income inequality — The unequal distribution of an economy's total income among persons or families.

Income-maintenance system — The programs designed to eliminate poverty and to reduce inequality in the distribution of income.

Incomes policy — Government policy that affects the Nominal incomes of individuals (the wages workers receive) and the prices they pay for goods and services and alters their Real incomes; (*see* Wage-price policy).

Income velocity of money — (*See* Velocity of money.)

Increase in demand — An increase in the Quantity demanded of a good or service at every price; a shift in the Demand curve to the right.

Increase in supply — An increase in the Quantity supplied of a good or service at every price; a shift in the Supply curve to the right.

Increasing-cost industry — An Industry in which expansion through the entry of new firms increases the prices the Firms in the Industry must pay for resources and, therefore, increases their cost schedules (shifts their cost curves upward).

Increasing returns — An increase in the Marginal product (*see*) of a resource as successive units of the resource are employed.

Independent goods — Goods or services for which there is no relationship between the price of one and the demand for the other; when the price of one rises or falls the demand for the other remains constant.

Independent variable — The variable causing a change in some other (dependent) variable.

Indifference curve — A curve showing the different combinations of two products that give a consumer the same satisfaction or Utility (*see*).

Indifference map — A series of indifference curves (*see*), each representing a different level of Utility; and which together are the preferences of the consumer.

Indirect taxes — Such taxes as Sales, Excise, and business Property taxes (*see all*), licence fees, and Tariffs (*see*), which Firms treat as costs of producing a product and pass on (in whole or in part) to buyers of the product by charging them higher prices.

Individual demand — The Demand schedule (*see*) or Demand curve (*see*) of a single buyer of a good or service.

Individual supply — The Supply schedule (*see*) or Supply curve (*see*) of a single seller of a good or service.

Induction — A method of reasoning that proceeds from facts to Generalization (*see*).

Industrial Disputes Investigation Act — The 1907 law that marked the beginning of federal labour legislation; it required disputes in the federal jurisdiction to be submitted to a Board of Conciliation and Investigation; replaced by Canada Labour Code (*see*).

Industrial policy — Any policy in which government takes a direct and active role in promoting firms or industries to expand output and achieve economic growth.

Industrial regulation — The older and more traditional type of regulation in which government is concerned with the prices charged and the services provided the public in specific industries; in contrast to Social regulation (*see*).

Industrial union — A Labour union that accepts as members all workers employed in a particular industry (or by a particular firm).

Industrially advanced countries (IACs) — Countries such as Canada, the United States, Japan, and the nations of western Europe that have developed Market economies based on large stocks of technologically advanced capital goods and skilled labour forces.

Industry — A group of (one or more) Firms that produce identical or similar products.

Inelastic demand — The Elasticity coefficient (*see*) is less than one; the percentage change in Quantity demanded is less than the percentage change in Price.

Inelastic supply — The Elasticity coefficient (*see*) is less than one; the percentage change in Quantity supplied is less than the percentage change in Price.

Inferior good — A good or service of which consumers purchase less (more) at every price when their incomes increase (decrease).

Inflating — Finding the Real gross domestic product (*see*) by increasing the dollar value of the Gross domestic product produced in a year in which prices are lower than in the Base year (*see*).

Inflation — A rise in the general (average) level of prices in the economy.

Inflation premium — The component of the nominal interest rate that reflects anticipated inflation.

Inflationary expectations — The belief of workers, business Firms, and consumers that there will be substantial inflation in the future.

Inflationary gap — The amount by which equilibrium GDP exceeds full employment GDP.

Inflationary recession — (*See* Stagflation.)

Infrastructure — The capital goods usually provided by the Public sector for the use of its citizens and Firms (e.g., highways, bridges, transit systems, waste-water treatment facilities, municipal water systems, and airports).

Injection — An addition of spending to the income-expenditure stream: Investment Government purchases, and Exports.

Injunction — A court order directing a person or organization not to perform a certain act because the act would do irreparable damage to some other person or persons; a restraining order.

In-kind investment — Nonfinancial investment (*see*).

In-kind transfer — The distribution by government of goods and services to individuals and for which the government receives no currently produced good or service in return; a Government transfer payment (*see*) made in goods or services rather than in money.

Innovation — The introduction of a new product, the use of a new method of production, or the employment of a new form of business organization.

Inpayments — The receipts of (its own or foreign) money that the individuals, Firms, and governments of one nation obtain from the sale of goods and services, investment income, Remittances, and Capital inflows from abroad.

Insurable risk — An event — the average occurrence of which can be estimated with considerable accuracy — that would result in a loss that can be avoided by purchasing insurance.

Interest — The payment made for the use of money (of borrowed funds).

Interest income — Income of those who supply the economy with Capital (*see*).

Interest rate — The Rate of interest (*see*).

Interest-rate effect — The tendency for increases (decreases) in the Price level to increase (decrease) the demand for money; raise (lower) interest rates; and, as a result, to reduce (expand) total spending in the economy.

Intergovernmental grant — A transfer payment from the federal government to a provincial government or from a provincial to a local government. (*See* Conditional grant and Unconditional grant.)

Interindustry competition — Competition or rivalry between the products of one industry (*see*) and the products of another Industry (or of other Industries).

Interlocking directorate — A situation where one or more members of the board of directors of a Corporation are also on the board of directors of a competing Corporation; and which is illegal in the United States — but not in Canada — when it tends to reduce competition among the Corporations.

Intermediate goods — Goods that are purchased for resale or further processing or manufacturing during the year.

Intermediate range — The upsloping segment of the Aggregate supply curve lying between the Horizontal range and the Vertical range (*see both*).

Internal economic goal — (*See* Domestic economic goal.)

Internal economies — The reduction in the unit cost of producing or marketing a product that results from an increase in output of the Firm [*see* Economies of (large) scale].

Internally held public debt — Public debt (*see*) owed to (Government of Canada securities owned by) Canadian residents, Firms, and institutions.

International Bank for Reconstruction and Development — (*See* World Bank.)

International economic goal — Assumed to be a current-account balance of zero.

International gold standard — An international monetary system employed in the nineteenth and early twentieth centuries in which each nation defined its money in terms of a quantity of gold, maintained a fixed relationship between its gold stock and money supply, and allowed the free importation and exportation of gold.

International Monetary Fund (IMF) — The international association of nations that was formed after World War II to make loans of foreign monies to nations with temporary Payments deficits (*see*) and to administer the Adjustable pegs (*see*); and which today creates Special Drawing Rights (*see*).

International monetary reserves — The foreign monies — in Canada mostly U.S. dollars — and such other assets as gold and Special Drawing Rights (*see*) that a nation may use to settle a Payments deficit (*see*).

International value of the dollar — The price that must be paid in foreign currency (money) to obtain one Canadian dollar.

Intrinsic value — The value in the market of the metal in a coin.

Inverse relationship — The relationship between two variables that change in opposite directions, for example, product price and quantity demanded.

Investment — Spending for (the production and accumulation of) Capital goods (*see*) and additions to inventories.

Investment curve (schedule) — A curve (schedule) that shows the amounts firms plan to invest (along the vertical axis) at different income (Gross domestic product) levels (along the horizontal axis).

Investment-demand curve (schedule) — A curve (schedule) that shows real Rates of interest (along the vertical axis) and the amount of Investment (along the horizontal axis) at each Rate of interest.

Investment in human capital — (*See* Human capital investment.)

Invisible hand — The tendency of Firms and resource suppliers seeking to further their self-interests in competitive markets that furthers the best interest of society as a whole (the maximum satisfaction of wants).

Jurisdictional strike — A Labour union's withholding of its labour from an employer because of the union's dispute with another Labour union over which is to perform a specific kind of work.

Keynesian economics — The macroeconomic generalizations that lead to the conclusion that a capitalist economy does not always employ its resources fully and that Fiscal policy (*see*) and Monetary policy (*see*) can be used to promote Full employment (*see*).

Keynesianism — The philosophical, ideological, and analytical views pertaining to Keynesian economics (*see*).

Kinked demand curve — The demand curve for a noncollusive oligopolist, based on the assumption that rivals will follow a price decrease and will ignore a price increase.

Labour — The physical and mental talents (efforts) of people that can be used to produce goods and services.

Labour force — (*See* Civilian labour force.)

Labour force participation rate — The percentage of the working-age population that is actually in the labour force.

Labour-intensive commodity — A product that requires much labour to produce.

Labour productivity — Total output divided by the quantity of labour employed to produce the output; the Average product (*see*) of labour or output per worker per hour or per year.

Labour theory of value — The Marxian notion that the economic value of any commodity is determined solely by the amount of labour required to produce it.

Labour union — A group of workers organized to advance the interests of the group (to increase wages, shorten the hours worked, improve working conditions, and so on).

Laffer curve — A curve showing the relationship between tax rates and the tax revenues of government and on which there is a tax rate (between 0 and 100%) where tax revenues are at a maximum.

Laissez-faire capitalism — (*See* Pure capitalism.)

Land — Natural resources ("free gifts of nature") used to produce goods and services.

Land-intensive commodity — A product requiring a relatively large amount of Land to produce.

Law of conservation of matter and energy — The notion that matter can be changed to other matter or into energy but cannot disappear; all production inputs are ultimately transformed into an equal amount of finished product, energy, and waste (potentially pollution).

Law of demand — The inverse relationship between the price and the Quantity demanded (*see*) of a good or service during some period of time.

Law of diminishing marginal utility — As a consumer increases the consumption of a good or service, the Marginal utility (*see*) obtained from each additional unit of the good or service decreases.

Law of diminishing returns — When successive equal increments of a Variable resource (*see*) are added to the Fixed resources (*see*), beyond some level of employment, the Marginal product (*see*) of the Variable resource will decrease.

Law of increasing opportunity cost — As the amount of a product produced is increased, the Opportunity cost (*see*) — the Marginal cost (*see*) — of producing an additional unit of the product increases.

Law of supply — The direct relationship between the price and the Quantity supplied (*see*) of a good or service during some period.

Leakage — (1) A withdrawal of potential spending from the income-expenditures stream: Saving (*see*), tax payment, and Imports (*see*); (2) a withdrawal that reduces the lending potential of the Chartered banking system.

Leakages-injections approach — Determination of the Equilibrium gross domestic product (*see*) by finding the GDP at which Leakages (*see*) are equal to Injections (*see*).

Least-cost combination rule (of resources) — The quantity of each resource a Firm must employ if it is to produce an output at the lowest total cost; the combination in which the ratio of the Marginal product (*see*) of a resource to its Marginal resource cost (*see*) (to its price if the resource is employed in a competitive market) is the same for all resources employed.

Legal cartel theory of regulation — The hypothesis that industries want to be regulated so that they may form legal Cartels (*see*) and that government officials (the government) provide the regulation in return for their political and financial support.

Legal tender — Anything that government has decreed must be accepted in payment of a debt.

Lending potential of an individual chartered bank — The amount by which a single Chartered bank can safely increase the Money supply by making new loans to (or buying securities from) the public; equal to the Chartered bank's Excess cash reserve (*see*).

Lending potential of the banking system — The amount the Chartered banking system (*see*) can increase the Money supply by making new loans to (or buying securities from) the public; equal to the Excess reserve (*see*) of the Chartered banking system multiplied by the Money multiplier (*see*).

Less-developed countries (LDCs) — Many countries of Africa, Asia, and Latin America that are characterized by a lack of capital goods, primitive production technologies, low literacy rates, high unemployment, rapid population growth, and labour forces heavily committed to agriculture.

Liability — A debt with a monetary value; an amount owed by a Firm or an individual.

Limited liability — Restriction of the maximum loss to a predetermined amount; for the owners (stockholders) of a Corporation, the maximum loss is the amount they paid for their shares of stock.

Limited-liability company — An unincorporated business whose owners are protected by Limited liability (*see*).

Liquidity — Money or things that can be quickly and easily converted into Money with little or no loss of purchasing power.

Loaded terminology — Terms that arouse emotions and elicit approval or disapproval.

Loanable funds theory of interest — The concept that the supply of and demand for loanable funds determines the equilibrium rate of interest.

Log-rolling — The trading of votes by legislators to secure favourable outcomes on decisions to provide public goods and services.

Long run — A period of time long enough to enable producers of a product to change the quantities of all the resources they employ; in which all resources and costs are variable and no resources or costs are fixed.

Long-run aggregate supply curve — The aggregate supply curve associated with a time period in which input prices (especially nominal wages) are fully responsive to changes in the price level.

Long-run competitive equilibrium — The price at which the Firms in Pure competition (*see*) neither obtain Economic profit nor suffer losses in the Long run and the total quantity demanded and supplied at that price are equal; a price equal to the minimum long-run average total cost of producing the product.

Long-run farm problem — The tendency for agriculture to be a declining industry as technological progress increases supply relative to an inelastic and relatively constant demand.

Long-run supply — A schedule or curve showing the prices at which a Purely competitive industry will make various quantities of the product available in the Long run.

Lorenz curve — A curve showing the distribution of income in an economy; and when used for this purpose, the cumulated percentage of families (income receivers) is measured along the horizontal axis and the cumulated percentage of income is measured along the vertical axis.

Loss-minimizing case — The circumstances where a firm loses less than its Total cost; when the price at which the firm can sell its product is less than Average total but greater than Average variable cost.

Lotteries — Games of chance where people buy numbered tickets and winners are drawn by lot; a source of provincial government revenue.

Lump-sum tax — A tax that is a constant amount (the tax revenue of government is the same) at all levels of GDP.

M1 — The narrowly defined Money supply; the Currency (coins and Paper money) and Demand deposits in chartered banks (*see*) not owned by the federal government or banks.

M2 — Includes, in addition to M1, Canadian dollar personal savings deposits and nonpersonal notice deposits at chartered banks.

M2+ — Includes, in addition to M2, deposits at trust and mortgage loan companies, and deposits and shares at *caisses populaires* and credit unions.

M3 — Includes, in addition to M2, Canadian dollar nonpersonal fixed term deposits plus all foreign currency deposits of Canadian residents booked at chartered banks in Canada.

Macroeconomics — The part of economics concerned with the economy as a whole; with such major aggregates as the households, business, international trade, and governmental sectors and with totals for the economy.

Managed floating exchange rate — An Exchange rate allowed to change (float) to eliminate Payments deficits and surpluses and is controlled (managed) to eliminate day-to-day fluctuations.

Marginal analysis — Decision making that involves a comparison or marginal ("extra" or "additional") benefits.

Marginal cost — The extra (additional) cost of producing one more unit of output; equal to the change in Total cost divided by the change in output (and in the short run to the change in total Variable cost divided by the change in output).

Marginal labour cost — The amount the total cost of employing Labour increases when a Firm employs one additional unit of Labour (the quantity of other resources employed remaining constant); equal to the change in the total cost of Labour divided by the change in the quantity of Labour employed.

Marginal product — The additional output produced when one additional unit of a resource is employed (the quantity of all other resources employed remaining constant); equal to the change in total product divided by the change in the quantity of a resource employed.

Marginal productivity theory of income distribution — The contention that the distribution of income is equitable when each unit of each resource receives a money payment equal to its marginal contribution to the firm's revenue (its Marginal revenue product).

Marginal propensity to consume — Fraction of any change in Disposable income spent for Consumer goods; equal to the change in consumption divided by the change in Disposable income.

Marginal propensity to import — The fraction of any change in income (Gross domestic product) spent for imported goods and services; equal to the change in Imports (*see*) divided by the change in income.

Marginal propensity to save — Fraction of any change in Disposable income that households save; equal to change in Saving (*see*) divided by the change in Disposable income.

Marginal rate of substitution — The rate (at the margin) at which a consumer is prepared to substitute one good or service for another and remain equally satisfied (have the same total Utility); and equal to the slope of an Indifference curve (*see*).

Marginal resource cost — The amount the total cost of employing a resource increases when a Firm employs one additional unit of the resource (the quantity of all other resources employed remaining constant); equal to the change in the total cost of the resource divided by the change in the quantity of the resource employed.

Marginal revenue — The change in the Total revenue of the Firm that results from the sale of one additional unit of its product; equal to the change in Total revenue divided by the change in the quantity of the product sold (demanded).

Marginal-revenue–marginal-cost approach — The method that finds the total output where Economic profit (*see*) is a maximum (or losses a minimum) by comparing the Marginal revenue (*see*) and the Marginal cost (*see*) of additional units of output.

Marginal revenue product — The change in the Total revenue of the Firm when it employs one additional unit of a resource (the quantity of all other resources employed remaining constant); equal to the change in

Total revenue divided by the change in the quantity of the resource employed.

Marginal tax rate — The fraction of additional (taxable) income that must be paid in taxes.

Marginal utility — The extra Utility (*see*) a consumer obtains from the consumption of one additional unit of a good or service; equal to the change in total Utility divided by the change in the quantity consumed.

Market — Any institution or mechanism that brings together the buyers (demanders) and sellers (suppliers) of a particular good or service.

Market demand — (*See* Total demand.)

Market economy — An economy in which only the private decisions of consumers, resource suppliers, and business Firms determine how resources are allocated; the Market system (*see*).

Market failure — The failure of a market to bring about the allocation of resources that best satisfies the wants of society (that maximizes the satisfaction of wants). In particular, the over- or underallocation of resources to the production of a particular good or service (because of Spillovers) and no allocation of resources to the production of Public (social) goods (*see*).

Market for externality rights — A market in which the Perfectly inelastic supply (*see*) of the right to pollute the environment and the demand for the right to pollute would determine the price a polluter would have to pay for the right.

Market period — A period in which producers of a product are unable to change the quantity produced in response to a change in its price; in which there is Perfect inelasticity of supply (*see*); and where all resources are Fixed resources (*see*).

Market policies — Government policies designed to reduce the market power of Labour unions and large business firms and to reduce or eliminate imbalances and bottlenecks in labour markets.

Market socialism — An economic system (method of organization) in which property resources are publicly owned and markets and prices are used to direct and co-ordinate economic activities.

Market system — All the product and resource markets of the economy and the relationships among them; a method that allows the prices determined in these markets to allocate the economy's Scarce resources and to communicate and co-ordinate the decisions made by consumers, business firms, and resource suppliers.

Median-voter model — The view that under majority rule the median (middle) voter will be in the dominant position to determine the outcome of an election.

Medium of exchange — Money (*see*); a convenient means of exchanging goods and services without engaging in Barter (*see*); what sellers generally accept and buyers generally use to pay for a good or service.

Microeconomics — The part of economics concerned with such individual units within the economy as Industries, Firms, and Households, and with individual markets, particular prices, and specific goods and services.

Minimum wage — The lowest Wage (rate) employers may legally pay for an hour of Labour.

Mixed capitalism — An economy in which both government and private decisions determine how resources are allocated.

Monetarism — An alternative to Keynesianism (*see*); the macroeconomic view that the main cause of changes in aggregate output and the price level are fluctuations in the money supply; advocates a Monetary rule (*see*).

Monetary control instruments — Techniques the Bank of Canada employs to change the size of the nation's Money supply (*see*); Open-market operations (*see*) and Switching Government of Canada deposits (*see*).

Monetary policy — Changing the Money supply (*see*) in order to assist the economy to achieve a full-employment, noninflationary level of total output.

Monetary rule — The rule suggested by the Monetarists (*see*): the Money supply should be expanded each year at the same annual rate as the potential rate of growth of the Real gross domestic product; the supply of money should be increased steadily at from 3 to 5% per year.

Money — Any item that is generally acceptable to sellers in exchange for goods and services.

Money capital — Money available to purchase Capital goods (*see*).

Money income — (*See* Nominal income.)

Money interest rate — The Nominal interest rate (*see*).

Money market — The Market in which the demand for and the supply of Money determine the Interest rate (or the level of interest rates) in the economy.

Money multiplier — The multiple of its Excess reserve (*see*) by which the Chartered banking system (*see*) can expand deposits and the Money supply by making new loans (or buying securities); equal to one divided by the Reserve ratio (*see*).

Money supply — Narrowly defined: M1 (*see*); more broadly defined: M2, M3, and M2+ (*see*).

Money wage — The amount of Money received by a worker per unit of time (hour, day, and so on).

Money wage rate — (*See* Money wage.)

Monopolistic competition — A Market in which many Firms sell a Differentiated product (*see*), into which entry is relatively easy, in which the Firm has some control over its product prices, and in which there is considerable Nonprice competition (*see*).

Monopoly — (1) A Market in which the number of sellers is so few that each seller is able to influence the total supply and the price of the good or service; (2) a major industry in which a small number of Firms control all or a large portion of its output. (*See also* Pure Monopoly.)

Monopsony — A Market in which there is only one buyer of a good or service.

Moral hazard problem — The possibility that individuals or institutions will change their behaviour as the result of a contract or agreement. Example: A bank whose deposits are insured against loss may make riskier loans and investments.

Moral suasion — The statements, pronouncements, and appeals made by the Bank of Canada that are intended to influence the lending policies of Chartered banks.

Most-favoured-nation (MFN) clause — A clause in a trade agreement between Canada and another nation that provides that the other nation's Imports into Canada will be subjected to the lowest tariff rates levied then or later on any other nation's Imports into Canada.

MR = MC rule — A Firm will maximize its Economic profit (or minimize its losses) by producing the output at which Marginal revenue (*see*) and Marginal cost (*see*) are equal — provided the price at which it can sell its product is equal to or greater than Average variable cost (*see*).

MRP = MRC rule — To maximize Economic profit (or minimize losses), a Firm should employ the quantity of a resource where its Marginal revenue product (*see*) is equal to its Marginal resource cost (*see*).

Multinational corporation — A Firm that owns production facilities in other countries and produces and sells its products abroad.

Multiplier — The ratio of the change in the Equilibrium GDP to the change in Investment (*see*), or to the change in any other component in the Aggregate-expenditures schedule or to the change in Net taxes; the number by which a change in any component in the Aggregate-expenditures schedule or in Net taxes must be multiplied to find the resulting change in the Equilibrium GDP.

Multiplier effect — The effect on the Equilibrium gross domestic product of a change in the Aggregate-expenditures schedule (caused by a change in the Consumption schedule, Investment, Net taxes, Government expenditures, or Net exports).

Mutual interdependence — Situation in which a change in price (or in some other policy) by one Firm will affect the sales and profits of another Firm (or other Firms) and any Firm that makes such a change can expect the other Firm(s) to react in an unpredictable (uncertain) way.

Mutually exclusive goals — Goals that conflict and cannot be achieved simultaneously.

National income — Total income earned by resource suppliers for their contributions to the production of the Gross national product (*see*); equal to the Gross national product minus the Nonincome charges (*see*).

National income accounting — The techniques employed to measure the overall production of the economy and other related totals for the nation as a whole.

National Policy — Sir John A. Macdonald's 1879 policy of high tariff protection for Canadian (Ontario and Quebec) secondary manufacturers.

Natural monopoly — An industry in which Economies of scale (*see*) are so great the product can be produced by one Firm at a lower average total cost than if the product were produced by more than one Firm.

Natural rate hypothesis — Contends that the economy is stable in the Long run at the natural rate of unemployment; views the long-run Phillips curve (*see*) as vertical at the natural rate of unemployment.

Natural rate of unemployment — (*See* Full-employment unemployment rate.)

Near-money — Financial assets, the most important of which are savings, term, and notice deposits in Chartered banks, trust companies, credit unions, and other savings institutions, that can be readily converted into Money.

Negative income tax — The proposal to subsidize families and individuals with money payments when their incomes fall below a Guaranteed (annual) income (*see*); the negative tax would decrease as earned income increases (*see* Benefit-reduction rate).

Negative relationship — (*See* Inverse relationship.)

Net capital movement — The difference between the real and financial investments and loans made by individuals and Firms of one nation in the other nations of the world and the investments and loans made by individuals and Firms from other nations in a nation.

Net domestic income — The sum of the incomes earned through the production of the Gross domestic product (*see*).

Net exports effect — The notion that the impact of a change in Monetary policy (fiscal policy) will be strengthened (weakened) by the consequent change in Net exports (*see*). For example, a contractionary (expansionary) monetary policy will increase (decrease) domestic interest rates, increasing (decreasing) the foreign demand for dollars. The dollar appreciates (depreciates) and causes Canadian Net exports to decrease (increase).

Net exports — Exports (*see*) minus Imports (*see*).

Net investment — Gross investment (*see*) less Capital consumption allowances (*see*); the addition to the nation's stock of Capital during a year.

Net investment income — The interest and dividend income received by the residents of a nation from residents of other nations less the interest and dividend payments made by the residents of that nation to the residents of other nations. In Canada, always a negative quantity.

Net national income — National income (*see*).

Net national product — Gross national product (*see*) less that part of the output needed to replace the Capital goods worn out in producing the output (Capital consumption allowances [*see*]).

Net taxes — The taxes collected by government less Government transfer payments (*see*).

Net transfers — The personal and government Transfer payments made to residents of foreign nations less the personal and government Transfer payments received from residents of foreign nations.

Net worth — The total Assets (*see*) less the total Liabilities (*see*) of a Firm or an individual; the claims of the owners of a firm against its total Assets.

New classical economics — The theory that, although unanticipated price level changes may create macroeconomic instability in the Short run, the economy is stable at the full-employment level of domestic output in the Long run because of price and wage flexibility.

New global compact — A reform agenda by which Less-developed countries (*see*) seek more foreign aid, debt relief, greater access to a world market, freer immigration, and an end to neocolonialism.

NIT — (*See* Negative income tax.)

New perspective view of advertising — Envisions advertising as a low-cost source of consumer information that increases competition by making consumers more aware of substitute products.

NNP — (*See* Net national product.)

Nominal gross domestic output (GDP) — The GDP (*see*) measured in terms of the price level at the time of measurement (unadjusted for changes in the price level).

Nominal income — The number of dollars received by an individual or group during some period of time; the money income.

Nominal interest rate — The rate of interest expressed in dollars of current value (not adjusted for inflation).

Nominal wage rate — The Money wage (*see*).

Noncollusive oligopoly — An Oligopoly (*see*) in which the Firms do not act together and in agreement to determine the price of the product and the output each Firm will produce or to determine the geographic area in which each Firm will sell.

Noncompeting groups — Groups of workers in the economy who do not compete with each other for employment because the skill and training of the workers in one group are substantially different from those in other groups.

Nondiscretionary fiscal policy — The increases (decreases) in Net taxes (*see*) that occur without Parliamentary action when the Gross domestic product rises (falls) and that tend to stabilize the economy; also called Built-in stability.

Nondurable good — A Consumer good (*see*) with an expected life (use) of less than three years.

Nonexhaustive expenditure — An expenditure by government that does not result directly in the employment of economic resources or the production of goods and services; *see* Government transfer payment.

Nonfinancial investment — An investment that does not require Households to save a part of their money incomes; but that uses Surplus (unproductive) labour to build Capital goods.

Nonincome charges — Capital consumption allowances (*see*) and Indirect-taxes (*see*).

Nonincome determinants of consumption and saving — All influences on consumption spending and saving other than the level of Disposable income.

Noninterest determinants of investment — All influences on the level of investment spending other than the Rate of interest.

Noninvestment transaction — An expenditure for stocks, bonds, or second-hand Capital goods.

Nonmarket transactions — The production of goods and services not included in the measurement of the Gross domestic product because the goods and services are not bought and sold.

Nonmerchandise balance — The addition of the balances on services, investment income, and transfers in the Current account (*see*) of the Balance of payments (*see*).

Nonprice competition — The means other than decreasing the prices of their products that Firms employ to increase the sale of their products; and that includes Product differentiation (*see*), advertising, and sales promotion activities.

Nonproduction transaction — The purchase and sale of any item that is not a currently produced good or service.

Nontariff barriers (NTBs) — All barriers other than Tariffs (*see*) that nations erect to impede international trade: Import quotas (*see*), licensing requirements, unreasonable product-quality standards, unnecessary red tape in customs procedures, and so on.

Nonunion shop — A place of employment at which none of the employees are members of a Labour union (and at which the employer attempts to hire only workers who are not apt to join a union).

Normal good — A good or service whose consumption increases (decreases) when income increases (decreases).

Normal profit — Payment that must be made by a Firm to obtain and retain Entrepreneurial ability (*see*); the minimum payment (income) Entrepreneurial ability must (expect to) receive to induce it to perform the entrepreneurial functions for a Firm; an Implicit cost (*see*).

Normative economics — That part of economics pertaining to value judgements about what the economy should be like; concerned with economic goals and policies.

North American Free Trade Agreement (NAFTA) — A 1993 agreement establishing a Trade bock (*see*) comprising Canada, Mexico, and the United States. The goal is to establish free trade between the three nations.

Notice, term, and savings deposit — A deposit in a Chartered bank against which cheques may or may not be written but for which the bank has the right to demand notice of withdrawal.

NTBs — (*See* Nontariff barriers.)

Occupational discrimination — The form of discrimination that excludes women from certain occupations and the higher wages paid workers in these occupations.

Occupational licensing — The laws of provincial governments that require a worker to obtain a licence from a provincial board (by satisfying certain specified requirements) before engaging in a particular occupation.

Offers to purchase — A method of Price support (*see*) whereby the government buys the Surplus created when it sets the minimum price above the Equilibrium price (*see*).

Official international reserves — The international monetary assets (*see*) owned by the federal government and held in its behalf by the Bank of Canada in the Exchange Fund Account.

Official reserves — Official international reserves (*see*).

Okun's Law — The generalization that any one percentage point rise in the Unemployment rate above the Full-employment unemployment rate will increase the GDP gap by 2.5% of the Potential output (GDP) of the economy.

Old Age Security Act — The 1951 federal Act, as subsequently amended, by which a pension is payable to every person aged 65 and older provided the person has resided in Canada for ten years immediately preceding the approval of an application for pension; in addition a Guaranteed Income Supplement (*see*) may be paid; the pension is payable in addition to the Canada Pension (*see*).

Oligopoly — A Market in which a few Firms sell either a Standardized or Differentiated product, into which entry is difficult, in which the Firm has limited control over product price because of Mutual interdependence (*see*) (except when there is Collusion among firms), and in which there is typically Nonprice Competition (*see*).

Oligopsony — A market in which there are a few buyers.

OPEC — An acronym for the Organization of Petroleum Exporting Countries (*see*).

Open economy — An economy that both exports and imports goods and services.

Open-economy multiplier — The Multiplier (*see*) in an economy in which some part of any increase in the income (Gross domestic product) of the economy is used to purchase additional goods and services from abroad; and which is equal to the reciprocal of the sum of the Marginal propensity to save (*see*) and the Marginal propensity to import (*see*).

Open-market operations — The buying and selling of Government of Canada securities by the Bank of Canada.

Open shop — A place of employment where the employer may hire either Labour union members or workers who are not (and need not become) members of the union.

Opportunity cost — The amount of other products that must be forgone or sacrificed to produce a unit of a product.

Optimal amount of externality reduction — That reduction of pollution or other negative externality where society's marginal benefit and marginal cost of reducing the externality are equal.

Optimal social price — The price of a product that results in the most efficient allocation of an economy's resources and that is equal to the Marginal cost (*see*) of the last unit of the product produced.

Organization of Petroleum Exporting Countries — The cartel formed in 1970 by 13 oil-producing countries to control the price and quantity of crude oil exported by its members, and which accounts for a large proportion of the world's export of oil.

"Other things being equal" assumption — Assuming that the factors other than those being considered are constant.

Outpayments — The expenditures of (its own or foreign) money that the individuals, Firms, and governments of one nation make to purchase goods, services, and investment income, for Remittances, for government loans and grants, and (liquid) capital outflows abroad.

Output effect — The change in labour input resulting from the effect of a change in the wage rate on a Firm's cost of production and the subsequent change in the desired level of output, after the Substitution effect (*see*) has been determined and eliminated.

Paper money — Pieces of paper used as a Medium of exchange (*see*); in Canada, Bank of Canada notes.

Paradox of voting — A situation wherein voting by majority rule fails to provide a consistent ranking of society's preferences for public goods or services.

Partnership — An unincorporated business Firm owned and operated by two or more persons.

Patent laws — The federal laws granting to inventors and innovators the exclusive right to produce and sell a new product or machine for a period of 17 years.

Payments deficit — (*See* Balance of payments deficit.)

Payments surplus — (*See* Balance of payments surplus.)

Perestroika — The essential feature of Mikhail Gorbachev's reform program to "restructure" the Soviet economy; includes modernization, decentralization, some privatization, and improved worker incentives.

Perfect elastic demand — A change in the Quantity demanded requires no change in the price of the product or resource; buyers will purchase as much of a product or resource as is available at a constant price.

Perfect elastic supply — A change in the Quantity supplied requires no change in the price of the product or resource; sellers will make available as much of the product or resource as buyers will purchase at a constant price.

Perfect inelastic demand — A change in price results in no change in the Quantity demanded of a product or resource; the Quantity demanded is the same at all prices.

Perfect inelastic supply — A change in price results in no change in the Quantity supplied of a product or resource; the Quantity supplied is the same at all prices.

Personal consumption expenditures — The expenditures of Households for Durable, semidurable, and nondurable consumer goods and for services.

Personal distribution of income — The manner in which the economy's Personal or Disposable income is divided among different income classes or different Households.

Personal income — The income earned and unearned, available to resource suppliers and others before the payment of Personal taxes (*see*).

Personal income tax — A tax levied on the taxable income of individuals (Households and unincorporated Firms).

Personal saving — The Personal income of Households less Personal taxes (*see*) and Personal consumption expenditures (*see*); Disposable income less Personal consumption expenditures; that part of Disposable income not spent for Consumer goods (*see*).

Phillips curve — A curve showing the relationship between the Unemployment rate (*see*) (on the horizontal axis) and the annual rate of increase in the Price level (on the vertical axis).

Planned economy — An economy in which government determines how resources are allocated.

Planned investment — The amount that business firms plan or intend to invest.

Plant — A physical establishment (Land and Capital) that performs one or more of the functions in the production (fabrication and distribution) of goods and services.

P = MC rule — A Firm in Pure competition (*see*) will maximize its Economic profit (*see*) or minimize its losses by producing the output at which the price of the product is equal to Marginal cost (*see*), provided that price is equal to or greater than Average variable cost (*see*) in the short run and equal to or greater than Average total cost (*see*) in the long run.

Policy economics — The formulation of courses of action to bring about desired results or to prevent undesired occurrences (to control economic events).

Political business cycle — The tendency of Parliament to destabilize the economy by reducing taxes and increasing government expenditures before elections and to raise taxes and lower expenditures after the elections.

Portfolio investment — The buying of bonds and shares by nonresidents, the number of shares bought being insufficient to attain control of the firm. (*See also* Direct Investment.)

Positive economics — The analysis of facts or data for the purpose of establishing scientific generalizations about economic behaviour; compare Normative economics.

Positive relationship — The relationship between two variables that change in the same direction, for example, product price and quantity supplied.

Post hoc, ergo propter hoc **fallacy** — Incorrectly reasoning that when one event precedes another, the first event necessarily is the cause of the second.

Potential competition — The possibility that new competitors will be induced to enter an industry if Firms at present in that industry are realizing large economic profits.

Potential output — The real output (GDP) an economy is able to produce when it fully employs its available resources.

Poverty — An existence in which the basic needs of an individual or family exceed the means available to satisfy them.

Poverty rate — The percentage of the population with incomes below the official poverty income levels established by Statistics Canada.

Predatory pricing — A general, illegal policy of selling at prices unreasonably low with a view to eliminating competition; forbidden under the Competition Act (*see*).

Premature inflation — Inflation (*see*) that occurs before the economy has reached Full employment (*see*).

Price — The quantity of Money (or of other goods and services) paid and received for a unit of a good or service.

Price ceiling — A government-fixed maximum price for a good or service.

Price-decreasing effect — The effect in a competitive market of a Decrease in Demand or an Increase in Supply upon the Equilibrium price (*see*).

Price discrimination — The selling of a product to different buyers at different prices when the price differences are not justified by differences in production costs; an illegal trade practice under the Competition Act (*see*) when it consists of giving a trade purchaser an unfair advantage over its competitors by selling to it at a lower price.

Price elasticity of demand — The ratio of the percentage change in Quantity demanded of a product or resource to the percentage change in its price, the responsiveness or sensitivity of the quantity of a product or resource buyers demand to a change in the price of the product or resource.

Price elasticity of supply — The ratio of the percentage change in the Quantity supplied of a product or resource to the percentage change in its price; the responsiveness or sensitivity of the quantity sellers of a product or resource supply to a change in the price of the product or resource.

Price guidepost — The price charged by an Industry for its product should increase by no more than the increase in the Unit labour cost (*see*) of producing the product.

Price-increasing effect — The effect in a competitive market of an Increase in Demand or a Decrease in Supply upon the Equilibrium price (*see*).

Price index — An index number that shows how the average price of a "market basket" of goods changes through time. A price index is used to change nominal output (income) into real output (income).

Price leadership — An informal method that Firms in an Oligopoly (*see*) may employ to set the price of their product: one firm (the leader) is the first to announce a change in price and the other firms (the followers) quickly announce identical (or similar) changes in price.

Price level — The weighted average of the Prices paid for the final goods and services produced in the economy.

Price level surprises — Unanticipated changes in the price level.

Price-maker — A seller (or buyer) of a product or resource that is able to affect the product or resource price by changing the amount it sells (buys).

Price support — The minimum price government allows sellers to receive for a good or service; a price that is the established or maintained minimum price.

Price-taker — A seller (or buyer) of a product or resource that is unable to affect the price at which a product or resource sells by changing the amount it sells (or buys).

Price-wage flexibility — Changes in the prices of products and in the Wages paid to workers; the ability of prices and Wages to rise or to fall.

Price war — Successive and continued decreases in the prices charged by the firms in an oligopolistic industry by which each firm hopes to increase its sales and revenues and from which firms seldom benefit.

Primary reserve — (*See* Cash reserve.)

Prime rate — The interest rate the Chartered banks (*see*) charge on demand note loans to their best corporate customers.

Principal-agent problem — A conflict of interest that occurs when agents (workers) pursue their own objectives to the detriment of the principal's (employer's) goals.

Private good — A good or service subject to the Exclusion principle (*see*) and which is provided by privately owned firms to those who are willing to pay for it.

Private property — The right of private persons and Firms to obtain, own, control, employ, dispose of, and bequeath Land, Capital, and other Assets.

Private sector — The Households and business Firms of the economy.

Product differentiation — Physical or other differences between the products of different Firms that result in individual buyers preferring (so long as the price charged by all sellers is the same) the product of one Firm to the products of the other Firms.

Production possibilities curve (table) — A curve (table) showing the different combinations of two goods or services that can be produced in a Full-employment (*see*), Full-production (*see*) economy where the available supplies of resources and technology are constant.

Productive efficiency — The production of a good in the least-costly way: employing the minimum quantity of resources needed to produce a given output and producing the output at which Average total cost is a minimum.

Productivity — A measure of average output or real output per unit of input. For example, the productivity of labour may be determined by dividing hours of work into real output.

Productivity slowdown — The recent decline in the rate at which Labour productivity (*see*) in Canada has increased.

Product market — A market in which Households buy and Firms sell the products they have produced.

Profit — (*See*) Economic profit and Normal profit; without an adjective preceding it, the income of those who supply the economy with Entrepreneurial ability (*see*) or Normal profit.

Profit-maximizing case — The circumstances that result in an Economic profit (*see*) for a (competitive) Firm when it produces the output at which Economic profit is a maximum: when the price at which the Firm can sell its product is greater than the Average total cost of producing it.

Profit-maximizing rule (combination of resources) — The quantity of each resource a Firm must employ if its Economic profit (*see*) is to be a maximum or its losses a minimum; the combination in which the Marginal revenue product (*see*) of each resource is equal to its Marginal resource cost (*see*) (to its price if the resource is employed in a competitive market).

Progressive tax — A tax such that the tax rate increases as the taxpayer's income increases and decreases as income decreases.

Property tax — A tax on the value of property (Capital, Land, stocks and bonds, and other Assets) owned by Firms and Households.

Proportional tax — A tax such that the tax rate remains constant as the taxpayer's income increases and decreases.

Proprietors' income — The net income of the owners of unincorporated Firms (proprietorships and partnerships); the sum of the accrued net income of farm operators from farm production plus the net income of nonfarm unincorporated business, including rent.

Prosperous industry — (*See* Expanding industry.)

Protective tariff — A Tariff (*see*) designed to protect domestic producers of a good from the competition of foreign producers.

Public assistance programs — Programs that pay benefits to those who are unable to earn income (because of permanent handicaps or because they are dependent children), that are financed by general tax revenues, and that are viewed as public charity (rather than earned rights).

Public choice theory — Generalizations that describe how government (the Public sector) makes decisions for the use of economic resources.

Public debt — The amount owed by the Government of Canada to the owners of its securities and equal to the sum of its past Budget deficits (less its Budget surpluses).

Public finance — The branch of economics that analyzes government revenues and expenditures.

Public good — A good or service to which the Exclusion principle (*see*) is not applicable; and that is provided by government if it yields substantial benefits to society.

Public interest theory of regulation — The presumption that the purpose of the regulation of an Industry is to protect the public (consumers) from the abuse of the power possessed by Natural monopolies (*see*).

Public sector — The part of the economy that contains all its governments; government.

Public-sector failure — The failure of the Public sector (government) to resolve socioeconomic problems because it performs its functions inefficiently.

Public utility — A Firm that produces an essential good or service, that has obtained from a government the right to be the sole supplier of the good or service in an area, and that is regulated by that government to prevent the abuse of its monopoly power.

Purchasing power parity — The idea that exchange rates between nations equate the purchasing power of various currencies; exchange rates between any two nations adjust to reflect the price level differences between the countries.

Pure capitalism — An economic system in which property resources are privately owned and Markets and Prices are used to direct and co-ordinate economic activities.

Pure competition — (1) A market in which a very large number of Firms sells a Standardized product (see), into which entry is very easy, in which the individual seller has no control over the price at which the product sells, and in which there is no Nonprice competition (see); (2) a Market in which there is a very large number of buyers.

Pure monopoly — A Market in which one Firm sells a unique product (one for which there are no close substitutes), into which entry is blocked, in which the Firm has considerable control over the price at which the product sells, and in which Nonprice competition (see) may or may not be found.

Pure profit — (See Economic profit.)

Pure rate of interest — (See The Rate of interest.)

Quantity-decreasing effect — The effect in a competitive market of a decrease in Demand or a decrease in Supply on the Equilibrium quantity (see).

Quantity demanded — The amount of a good or service buyers wish (or a buyer wishes) to purchase at a particular price during some period of time.

Quantity-increasing effect — The effect in a competitive market of an increase in Demand or an increase in Supply on the Equilibrium quantity (see).

Quantity supplied — The amount of a good or service sellers offer (or a seller offers) to sell at a particular price during some period of time.

Quasi-public good — A good or service to which the Exclusion principle (see) could be applied, but which has such a large Spillover benefit (see) that government sponsors its production to prevent an underallocation of resources.

R&D — Research and development; activities undertaken to bring about progress in Technology.

Rate of exchange — The price paid in one's own Money to acquire one unit of a foreign Money; the rate at which the money of one nation is exchanged for the Money of another nation.

Rate of interest — Price paid for the use of Money or for the use of Capital; interest rate.

Rational — An adjective that describes the behaviour of an individual who consistently does those things enabling the achievement of the declared objective of the individual; describes the behaviour of a consumer who uses money income to buy the collection of goods and services that yields the maximum amount of Utility (see).

Rational expectations theory — The hypothesis that business Firms and Households expect monetary and fiscal policies to have certain effects on the economy and, in pursuit of their own self-interests, take actions that make these policies ineffective.

Rationing function of price — The ability of Price in a competitive market to equalize Quantity demanded and Quantity supplied and to eliminate shortages and surpluses by rising or falling.

Reaganomics — The policies of the United States Reagan Administration based on Supply-side economics (see) and intended to reduce Inflation and the Unemployment rate (Stagflation).

Real-balances effect — (See Wealth effect.)

Real capital — (See Capital.)

Real gross domestic product — Gross domestic product (see) adjusted for changes in the price level; Gross domestic product in a year divided by the GDP deflator (see) for that year.

Real income — The amount of goods and services an individual or group can purchase with his, her, or its Nominal income during some period of time; Nominal income adjusted for changes in the Price level.

Real interest rate — The Rate of interest expressed in dollars of constant value (adjusted for Inflation); and equal to the Nominal interest rate (see) less the expected rate of Inflation.

Real rate of interest — The Real interest rate (*see*).

Real wage — The amount of goods and services a worker can purchase with his or her Money wage (*see*); the purchasing power of the Money wage; the Money wage adjusted for changes in the Price level.

Real wage rate — (*See* Real wage.)

Recessionary gap — The amount by which equilibrium GDP falls short of full employment GDP.

Reciprocal selling — The practice in which one Firm agrees to buy a product from a second Firm, and the second Firm agrees, in return, to buy another product from the first Firm.

Reciprocal Trade Agreements Act of 1934 (U.S.) — The federal Act that gave the U.S. president the authority to negotiate agreements with other nations and lower American tariff rates by up to 50% if the other nations would reduce tariff rates on American goods, and which incorporated Most-favoured-nation clauses (*see*) in the agreements reached with these nations.

Refinancing the public debt — Paying owners of maturing Government of Canada securities with Money obtained by selling new securities or with new securities.

Regional Development Incentives Act — The federal Act of 1970 designed to create jobs in Canada's slow-growth or "designated" areas.

Regressive tax — A tax such that the tax rate decreases (increases) as the taxpayer's income increases (decreases).

Regulatory agency — An agency (commission or board) established by the federal or a provincial government to control the prices charged and the services offered (output produced) by a Natural monopoly (*see*).

Remittance — A gift or grant; a payment for which no good or service is received in return; the funds sent by workers who have legally or illegally entered a foreign nation to their families in the nations from which they have migrated.

Rental income — Income received by those who supply the economy with Land (*see*).

Rent-seeking behaviour — The pursuit through government of a transfer of income or wealth to a resource supplier, business, or consumer at someone else's or society's expense.

Required reserve — The weighted average of demand deposit and notice deposit Chartered banks were required to keep as Vault cash (*see*) or on deposit with the Bank of Canada up to the end of 1994, when these were eliminated.

Reserve ratio — The ratio of a Chartered bank's desired reserves to its deposit liabilities.

Reserves — Cash in a Chartered bank's vault plus its deposit with the Bank of Canada.

Resource market — A market in which Households sell and Firms buy the services of resources.

Retiring the public debt — Reducing the size of the Public debt (*see*) by paying money to owners of maturing Government of Canada securities.

Revaluation — An increase in the government-defined currency brought about by the Central bank; the opposite of Devaluation.

Revenue sharing — The distribution by the federal government of some of its tax revenues to provincial governments.

Revenue tariff — A Tariff (*see*) designed to produce income for the (federal) government.

Ricardian equivalence theorem — The idea that an increase in the public debt will have little or no effect on real output and employment because taxpayers will save more in anticipation of future higher taxes to pay the higher interest expense on the debt.

Roundabout production — The construction and use of Capital (*see*) to aid in the production of Consumer goods (*see*).

Ruble overhang — The large amount of forced saving formerly held by Russian Households due to the scarcity of Consumer goods; these savings fuelled Inflation when Russian prices were decontrolled.

Rule of 70 — A method for determining the number of years it will take for the Price level to double; divide 70 by the annual rate of inflation (the rate of increase).

Sales tax — A tax levied on expenditures for a broad group of products.

Saving — Disposable income not spent for Consumer goods (*see*); equal to Disposable income minus Personal consumption expenditures (*see*).

Savings account — A deposit in a financial institution that is interest-earning and that can normally be withdrawn by the depositor at any time (though the institution may legally require notice for withdrawal).

Saving schedule — Schedule that shows the amounts Households plan to save (plan not to spend for Consumer goods, *see*) at different levels of Disposable income.

Say's Law — The (discredited) macroeconomic generalization that the production of goods and services (supply) creates an equal demand for these goods and services.

Scarce resources — The fixed (limited) quantities of Land, Capital, Labour, and Entrepreneurial ability (*see all*) that are never sufficient to satisfy the wants of human beings because their wants are unlimited.

Schumpeter-Galbraith view (of oligopoly) — The belief shared by these two economists that large oligopolistic firms are necessary for rapid technological progress (because only this kind of firm has both the means and the incentive to introduce technological changes).

SDRs — (*See* Special Drawing Rights.)

Seasonal variation — An increase or decrease during a single year in the level of economic activity caused by a change in the season.

Secular trend — The expansion or contraction in the level of economic activity over a long period of years.

Self-interest — What each Firm, property owner, worker, and consumer believes is best for itself and seeks to obtain.

Seniority — The length of time a worker has been employed by an employer relative to the lengths of time the employer's other workers have been employed; the principle that is used to determine which workers will be laid off when there is insufficient work for them all, and which will be rehired when more work becomes available.

Separation of ownership and control — Difference between the group that owns the Corporation (the stockholders) and the group that manages it (the directors and officers) and between the interests (goals) of the two groups.

Service — That which is intangible (invisible) and for which a consumer, Firm, or government is willing to exchange something of value.

Shared-cost programs — (*See* Conditional grant.)

Shirking — Attempts by workers to increase their utility or well-being by neglecting or evading work.

Shortage — The amount by which the Quantity demanded of a product exceeds the Quantity supplied at a particular (below-equilibrium) price.

Short run — A period of time in which producers of a product are able to change the quantity of some but not all of the resources they employ; in which some resources — the Plant (*see*) — are Fixed resources (*see*) and some are Variable resources (*see*); in which some costs are Fixed costs (*see*) and some are Variable costs (*see*); a period of time too brief to allow a Firm (*see*) to vary its plant capacity but long enough to permit it to change the level at which the plant capacity is utilized; a period of time not long enough to enable Firms to enter or to leave an Industry (*see*).

Short-run aggregate supply curve — The aggregate supply curve relevant to a time period in which input prices (particularly nominal wages) remain constant when the price level changes.

Short-run competitive equilibrium — The price at which the total quantity of a product supplied in the Short run (*see*) by a purely competitive industry and the total quantity of the product demanded are equal and which is equal to or greater than the Average variable cost (*see*) of producing the product; and the quantity of the product demanded and supplied at this price.

Short-run farm problem — The sharp year-to-year changes in the prices of agricultural products and in the incomes of farmers.

Short-run supply curve — A curve that shows the quantities of a product a Firm in a purely competitive industry (*see* Pure competition) will offer to sell at various prices in the Short run (*see*); the portion of the Firm's short-run Marginal cost (*see*) curve that lies above the Average variable cost curve.

Simple multiplier — The Multiplier (*see*) in an economy in which government collects no Net taxes (*see*), there are no Imports (*see*), and Investment (*see*) is independent of the level of income (Gross domestic product); equal to one divided by the Marginal propensity to save (*see*).

Single-tax movement — The attempt of a group that followed the teachings of Henry George to eliminate all taxes except one that would tax all Rental income (*see*) at a rate of 100%.

Slope of a line — The ratio of the vertical change (the rise or fall) to the horizontal change (the run) in moving between two points on a line. The slope of an upward sloping line is positive, reflecting a direct relationship between two variables; the slope of a downward sloping line is negative, reflecting an inverse relationship between two variables.

Smoot-Hawley Tariff Act — Passed in 1930, this legislation established some of the highest Tariffs in U.S. history. Its objective was to reduce imports and stimulate the American economy.

Social accounting — (*See* National income accounting.)

Social good — (*See* Public good.)

Social insurance programs — The programs that replace the earnings lost when people retire or are temporarily unemployed, that are financed by pay deductions, and that are viewed as earned rights (rather than charity).

Social regulation — The newer and different type of regulation in which government is concerned with the conditions under which goods and services are produced, their physical characteristics, and the impact of their production on society; in contrast to Industrial regulation (*see*).

Sole proprietorship — An unincorporated business Firm owned and operated by a single person.

Special Drawing Rights — Credit created by the International Monetary Fund (*see*), which a member of the IMF may borrow to finance a Payments deficit (*see*) or to increase its Official international reserves (*see*); "paper gold."

Special-interest effect — Effect on public decision making and the allocation of resources in the economy when government promotes the interests (goals) of small groups to the detriment of society as a whole.

Specialization — The use of the resources of an individual, a Firm, a region, or a nation to produce one or a few goods and services.

Speculation — The activity of buying or selling with the motive of then reselling or rebuying to make a profit.

Spillover — A benefit or cost from production or consumption, accruing without compensation to nonbuyers and nonsellers of the product (*see* Spillover benefit and Spillover cost).

Spillover benefit — A benefit obtained without compensation by third parties from the production or consumption of other parties. Example: A beekeeper benefits when the neighbouring farmer plants clover.

Spillover cost — A cost imposed without compensation on third parties by the production or consumption of other parties. Example: A manufacturer dumps toxic chemicals into a river, killing the fish sought by sport fishers.

Stabilization funds — International monetary reserves (*see*) and domestic monies used to augment the supply of,

or demand for, any Currency required to avoid or restrict fluctuations in the Rate of exchange; in Canada held in the Exchange Fund Account by the Bank of Canada on behalf of the government.

Stabilization policy dilemma — The use of monetary and fiscal policy to decrease the Unemployment rate increases the rate of Inflation, and the use of monetary and fiscal policy to decrease the rate of Inflation increases the Unemployment rate; *see* the Phillips curve.

Stagflation — Inflation accompanied by stagnation in the rate of growth of output and a high unemployment rate in the economy; simultaneous increases in both the price level and the Unemployment rate (*see*).

Standardized product — A product such that buyers are indifferent to the seller from whom they purchase it so long as the price charged by all sellers is the same; a product such that all units of the product are perfect substitutes for each other (are identical).

Staple — An exported raw material.

State ownership — The ownership of property (Land and Capital) by government (the state); in the former Soviet Union by the central government (the nation).

Static economy — (1) An economy in which Net investment (*see*) is zero — Gross investment (*see*) is equal to the Capital consumption allowances (*see*); (2) an economy in which the supplies of resources, technology, and the tastes of consumers do not change and in which, therefore, the economic future is perfectly predictable and there is no uncertainty.

Store of value — Any Asset (*see*) or wealth set aside for future use; functions of Money.

Strategic trade policy — The use of trade barriers to reduce the risk of product development by domestic firms, particularly products involving advanced technology.

Strike — The withholding of their labour services by an organized group of workers (a Labour union).

Structural deficit — The difference between federal tax revenues and expenditures when the economy is at Full employment.

Structural unemployment — Unemployment caused by changes in the structure of demand for Consumer goods and in technology; workers who are unemployed because their skills are not demanded by employers, they lack sufficient skills to obtain employment, or they cannot easily move to locations where jobs for which they have skills are available.

Subsidy — A payment of funds (or goods and services) by a government, business Firm, or Household for which it receives no good or service in return. When made by a government, it is a Government transfer payment (*see*) or the reverse of a tax.

Substitutability — The ability of consumers to use one good or service instead of another to satisfy their wants and of Firms to use one resource instead of another to produce products.

Substitute goods — Goods or services for which there is a direct relationship between the price of one and the Demand for the other; when the price of one falls (rises) the Demand for the other decreases (increases).

Substitution effect — (1) The effect a change in the price of a Consumer good would have on the relative expensiveness of that good and the resulting effect on the quantity of the good a consumer would purchase if the consumer's Real income (*see*) remained constant; (2) the effect a change in the price of a resource would have on the quantity of the resource employed by a firm if the firm did not change its output.

Superior good — (*See* Normal good.)

Supplementary labour income — The payments by employers into unemployment insurance, worker's compensation, and a variety of private and public pension and welfare funds for workers: "fringe benefits."

Supply — A Supply schedule or a Supply curve (*see both*).

Supply curve — A curve showing the amounts of a good or service sellers (a seller) will offer to sell at various prices during some period.

Supply factor — An increase in the available quantity of a resource, an improvement in its quality, or an expansion of technological knowledge, which makes it possible for an economy to produce a greater output of goods and services.

Supply schedule — A schedule showing the amounts of a good or service sellers (a seller) will offer to sell at various prices during some period.

Supply shock — One of several events of the 1970s and early 1980s that increased production costs, decreased Aggregate supply, and helped generate Stagflation in Canada.

Supply-side economics — The part of modern Macroeconomics that emphasizes the role of costs and Aggregate supply in explaining Inflation, unemployed labour, and Economic growth.

Supply-side view — The view of fiscal policy held by the advocates of Supply-side economics that emphasizes increasing Aggregate supply (*see*) as a means of reducing the Unemployment rate and Inflation and encouraging Economic growth.

Support price — (*See* Price support.)

Surplus — The amount by which the Quantity supplied of product exceeds the Quantity demanded at a specific (above-equilibrium) price.

Surplus value — A Marxian term; the amount by which the value of a worker's daily output exceeds his or her daily wage; the output of workers appropriated by capitalists as profit.

Switching Government of Canada deposits — Action of Bank of Canada to increase (decrease) backing for Money supply (*see*) by switching government deposits from (to) itself to (from) the Chartered banks (*see*).

Tacit collusion — Any method utilized in a Collusive oligopoly (*see*) to set prices and outputs that does not involve outright (or overt) collusion (formal agreements or secret meetings); and of which Price leadership (*see*) is a frequent example.

Tangent — The point where a line touches, but does not intersect, a curve.

Target dilemma — A problem arising because the central bank cannot simultaneously stabilize both the money supply and the level of interest rates.

Tariff — A tax imposed by a nation on an imported good.

Tax — A nonvoluntary payment of money (or goods and services) to a government by a Household or Firm for which the Household or Firm receives no good or service directly in return.

Tax-based incomes policies (TIP) — An Incomes policy (*see*) that would include special tax penalties for those who do not comply and tax rebates for those who do comply with the Wage-price guideposts (*see*).

Tax incidence — The income or purchasing power different persons and groups lose as a result of the imposition of a tax after Tax shifting (*see*) has occurred.

Tax shifting — The transfer to others of all or part of a tax by charging them a higher price or by paying them a lower price for a good or service.

Tax subsidy — The subsidization of individuals or industries through favourable tax treatment.

Tax-transfer disincentives — Decreases in the incentives to work, save, invest, innovate, and take risks that allegedly result from high Marginal tax rates and Transfer payment programs.

Tax "wedge" — Such taxes as Indirect taxes (*see*) and pay deductions for Social insurance programs (*see*), which are treated as a cost by business firms and reflected in the prices of their products; equal to the price of the product less the cost of the resources required to produce it.

Technology — The body of knowledge that can be used to produce goods and services from Economic resources.

Term deposit — A deposit in a Chartered bank or other Financial intermediary against which cheques may not be written; a form of savings account; part of M2, M3, and M2+ (*see all*).

Terms of trade — The rate at which units of one product can be exchanged for units of another product; the Price (*see*) of a good or service; the amount of one good or service given up to obtain one unit of another good or service.

Theory of human capital — Generalization that Wage differentials (*see*) are the result of differences in the amount of Human capital investment (*see*); and that the incomes of lower-paid workers are increased by increasing the amount of such investment.

***The* rate of interest** — The Rate of interest (*see*) that is paid solely for the use of Money over an extended period of time and that excludes the charges made for the riskiness of the loan and its administrative costs; and that is approximately equal to the rate of interest paid on the long-term and virtually riskless bonds of the Government of Canada.

Third World — The semideveloped and less-developed nations; nations other than the industrially advanced market economies and the centrally planned economies.

Tied selling — (*See* Exclusive dealing.)

Tight money policy — Contracting the nation's Money supply (*see*). See also Contractionary monetary policy.

Till money — (*See* Vault cash.)

TIP — (*See* Tax-based incomes policies.)

Token money — Coins having a Face value (*see*) greater than their Intrinsic value (*see*).

Total cost — The sum of Fixed cost (*see*) and Variable cost (*see*).

Total demand — The Demand schedule (*see*) or the Demand curve (*see*) of all buyers of a good or service.

Total demand for money — The sum of the Transactions demand for money (*see*) and Asset demand for money (*see*); the relationship between the total amount of money demanded and nominal GDP and the Rate of interest.

Total product — The total output of a particular good or service produced by a Firm, a group of Firms or the entire economy.

Total revenue — The total number of dollars received by a Firm (or Firms) from the sale of a product; equal to the total expenditures for the product produced by the Firm (or Firms); equal to the quantity sold (demanded) multiplied by the price at which it is sold — by the Average revenue (*see*) from its sale.

Total-revenue test — A test to determine whether Demand is Elastic (*see*), Inelastic (*see*), or of Unitary elasticity (*see*) between any two prices: demand is elastic (inelastic, unit elastic) if the Total revenue (*see*) of sellers of the commodity increases (decreases, remains constant) when the price of the commodity falls; or Total revenue decreases (increases, remains constant) when its price rises.

Total-revenue–total-cost approach — The method that finds the output at which Economic profit (*see*) is a maximum or losses a minimum by comparing the total receipts (revenue) and the total costs of a Firm at different outputs.

Total spending — The total amount buyers of goods and services spend or plan to spend. Also called Aggregate expenditure.

Total supply — The Supply schedule (*see*) or the Supply curve (*see*) of all sellers of a good or service.

Total utility — The total amount of satisfaction derived from the consumption of some particular amount of a product.

Trade balance — The export of merchandise (goods) of a nation less its imports of merchandise (goods).

Trade bloc — A group of nations that lowers or abolishes trade barriers among members. Examples include the European Union (*see*) and the North American Free Trade Agreement (*see*).

Trade controls — Tariffs (*see*), export subsidies, Import quotas (*see*), and other means a nation may employ to reduce Imports (*see*) and expand Exports (*see*).

Trade deficit — The amount a nation's imports of merchandise (goods) exceed its exports of merchandise (goods).

Trade-offs — The notion that one economic goal or objective must be sacrificed to achieve some other goal.

Trade surplus — The amount a nation's exports of merchandise (goods) and services exceed its imports of merchandise (goods) and services.

Trades and Labour Congress of Canada (TLC) — The federation of Craft unions (see) formed in 1886 and affiliated with the American Federation of Labor (see); amalgamated into the Canadian Labour Congress (see) in 1956.

Trading possibilities line — A line that shows the different combinations of two products an economy is able to obtain (consume) when it specializes in the production of one product and trades (exports) this product to obtain the other product.

Traditional economy — An economic system in which traditions and customs determine how the economy will use its scarce resources.

Traditional view of advertising — The position that advertising is persuasive rather than informative; promotes industrial concentration; and is essentially inefficient and wasteful.

Transactions demand for money — The amount of Money people want to hold to use as a Medium of exchange (to make payments); and which varies directly with the nominal GDP.

Transfer payment — A payment of Money (or goods and services) by a government or a Firm to a Household or Firm for which the payer receives no good or service directly in return.

Tying agreement — A promise made by a buyer when allowed to purchase a patented product from a seller that it will make all its purchases of certain other (unpatented) products from the same seller.

Unanticipated inflation — Inflation (see) at a rate greater than the rate expected in that period of time.

Unconditional grant — A transfer to a province by the federal government that goes into the general revenues of the province to be used as it sees fit; such grants are made for two reasons: (1) as an Equalization payment (see) and (2) to make up for the general inadequacy of provincial revenues in relation to provincial responsibilities.

Underemployment — Failure to produce the maximum amount of goods and services that can be produced from the resources employed; failure to achieve Full production (see).

Undistributed corporation profits — After-tax corporate profits not distributed as dividends to stockholders; corporate or business saving.

Unemployment — Failure to use all available Economic resources to produce goods and services; failure of the economy to employ fully its Civilian labour force (see).

Unemployment insurance — The insurance program that in Canada is financed by compulsory contributions from employers and employees and from the general tax revenues of the federal government with benefits (income) made available to insured workers who are unable to find jobs.

Unemployment rate — The percentage of the Civilian labour force (see) unemployed at any time.

Uninsurable risk — An event — the occurrence of which is uncontrollable and unpredictable — that would result in a loss that cannot be avoided by purchasing insurance and must be assumed by an entrepreneur (see Entrepreneurial ability); sometimes called "uncertainty."

Union shop — A place of employment where the employer may hire either Labour union members or nonmembers, but where nonmembers must become members within a specified period of time or lose their jobs.

Unitary elasticity — The Elasticity coefficient (see) is equal to one; the percentage change in the quantity (demanded or supplied) is equal to the percentage change in price.

Unit labour cost — Labour costs per unit of output; equal to the Money wage rate (see) divided by the Average product (see) of labour.

Unlimited liability — Absence of any limit on the maximum amount that may be lost by an individual and that the individual may become legally required to pay; the maximum amount that may be lost and that a sole proprietor or partner may be required to pay.

Unlimited wants — The insatiable desire of consumers (people) for goods and services that will give them pleasure or satisfaction.

Unplanned investment — Actual investment less Planned investment; increases or decreases in the inventories of business firms resulting from production greater than or less than sales.

Unprosperous industry — (*See* Declining industry.)

Uruguay Round — The eighth round of trade negotiations under GATT (*see*).

Utility — The want-satisfying power of a good or service; the satisfaction or pleasure a consumer obtains from the consumption of a good or service (or from the consumption of a collection of goods and services).

Utility-maximizing rule — To obtain the greatest Utility (*see*) the consumer should allocate Money income so that the last dollar spent on each good or service yields the same Marginal utility (*see*); so that the Marginal utility of each good or service divided by its price is the same for all goods and services.

Value added — The value of the product sold by a Firm less the value of the goods (materials) purchased and used by the Firm to produce the product; and equal to the revenue that can be used for Wages, rent, interest, and profits.

Value-added tax — A tax imposed upon the difference between the value of the goods sold by a firm and the value of the goods purchased by the firm from other firms.

Value judgement — Opinion of what is desirable or undesirable; belief regarding what ought or ought not to be (regarding what is right or just and wrong or unjust).

Value of money — The quantity of goods and services for which a unit of money (a dollar) can be exchanged; the purchasing power of a unit of money; the reciprocal of the Price level.

Variable cost — A cost that, in total, increases (decreases) when the firm increases (decreases) its output; the cost of Variable resources (*see*).

Variable resource — Any resource employed by a firm the quantity of which can be increased or decreased (varied) in quantity.

VAT — Value-added tax (*see*).

Vault cash — The Currency (*see*) a bank has in its safe (vault) and cash drawers; till money.

Velocity of money — The number of times per year the average dollar in the Money supply (*see*) is spent for Final goods and services (*see*).

VERs — (*See* Voluntary export restrictions.)

Vertical axis — The "up-down" or "north-south" axis on a graph or grid.

Vertical combination — A group of Plants (*see*) engaged in different stages of the production of a final product and owned by a single Firm (*see*).

Vertical intercept — The point at which a line meets the vertical axis of a graph.

Vertical merger — The merger of one or more Firms engaged in different stages of the production of a final product.

Vertical range — Vertical segment of the short-run Aggregate supply curve along which the economy is operating at full capacity.

Voluntary export restrictions — The limitation by firms of their exports to particular foreign nations in order to avoid the erection of other trade barriers by the foreign nations.

Wage — The price paid for Labour [for the use or services of Labour (*see*)] per unit of time (per hour, per day, and so on).

Wage differential — The difference between the Wage (*see*) received by one worker or group of workers and that received by another worker or group of workers.

Wage discrimination — The payment to women (or minority groups) of a wage lower than that paid to men (or established groups) for doing the same work.

Wage guidepost — Wages (*see*) in all industries in the economy should increase at an annual rate equal to the rate of increase in the Average product (*see*) of Labour in the economy.

Wage-price controls — A Wage-price policy (*see*) that legally fixes the maximum amounts Wages (*see*) and prices may be increased in any period of time.

Wage-price guideposts — A Wage-price policy (*see*) that depends upon the voluntary co-operation of Labour unions and business firms.

Wage-price inflationary spiral — Increases in wage rates that bring about increases in prices and in turn result in further increases in wage rates and in prices.

Wage-price policy — Government policy that attempts to alter the behaviour of Labour unions and business firms to make their Wage and price decisions more nearly compatible with the goals of Full employment and stable prices.

Wage rate — (*See* Wages.)

Wages — The income of those who supply the economy with Labour (*see*).

Wastes of monopolistic competition — The waste of economic resources that is the result of producing an output at which price is greater than marginal cost and average cost is greater than the minimum average cost.

Wealth effect — The tendency for increases (decreases) in the price level to lower (raise) the real value (or purchasing power) of financial assets with fixed money values; and, as a result, to reduce (expand) total spending in the economy.

Welfare programs — (*See* Public assistance programs.)

(The) "will to develop" — Wanting economic growth strongly enough to change from old to new ways of doing things.

World Bank — A bank supported by 151 nations, which lends (and guarantees loans) to less-developed nations to assist them to grow; formally, the International Bank for Reconstruction and Development.

World Price — The international price of a good or service, determined by world demand and supply.

World Trade Organization (WTO) — An organization established in 1994 by GATT (*see*) to oversee the provisions of the Uruguay Round (*see*) and resolve any disputes stemming therefrom.

X-inefficiency — Failure to produce any given output at the lowest average (and total) cost possible.

NATIONAL INCOME STATISTICS, 1926-1994

NATIONAL INCOME AND RELATED STATISTICS FOR SELECTED YEARS, 1926–1967

National income statistics are in billions of current dollars

			1926	1929	1933	1939	1940	1942	1945	1946	1949	1950	1951
THE	1	Personal consumption expenditure	$3.508	$4.583	$2.974	$3.972	$4.464	$5.466	$6.972	$8.012	$11.463	$12.576	$13.973
SUM	2	Government current purchases of goods and services	0.390	0.469	0.392	0.566	1.048	3.622	3.576	1.655	1.722	1.928	2.811
OF	3	Gross investment	0.949	1.413	0.208	0.969	1.097	1.200	0.890	1.877	3.676	4.596	5.515
	4	Net exports of goods and services	0.368	−0.016	0.234	0.391	0.460	0.273	0.855	0.702	0.506	0.091	−0.137
	5	Statistical discrepancy	0.139	−0.049	−0.085	−0.018	−0.082	−0.064	−0.230	−0.079	−0.020	−0.066	0.118
EQUALS	6	**GDP at market prices**	**5.354**	**6.400**	**3.723**	**5.880**	**6.987**	**10.497**	**12.063**	**12.167**	**$17.347**	**$19.125**	**$22.280**
	7	Net investment income from nonresidents	−0.208	−0.261	−0.231	−0.259	−0.274	−0.232	−0.200	−0.282	−0.355	−0.425	−0.391
EQUALS	8	**GNP at market prices**	**5.146**	**6.139**	**3.492**	**5.621**	**6.713**	**10.265**	**11.863**	**11.885**	**$16.992**	**$18.700**	**$21.889**
LESS	9	Indirect taxes less subsidies	0.627	0.711	0.547	0.759	0.859	1.133	1.084	1.371	1.878	2.065	2.548
	10	Capital consumption allowances	0.572	0.726	0.532	0.671	0.786	1.091	1.042	1.071	1.657	1.889	2.108
	11	Statistical discrepancy	−0.139	0.050	0.085	0.019	0.083	0.064	0.231	0.080	0.020	0.067	−0.119
EQUALS	12	**Net national income at factor cost**	**4.086**	**4.652**	**2.328**	**4.172**	**4.985**	**7.997**	**9.506**	**9.363**	**$13.437**	**$14.679**	**$17.352**
PLUS	13	Government transfer payments	0.074	0.092	0.180	0.226	0.204	0.218	0.542	1.102	0.944	1.025	1.026
	14	Transfers from nonresidents	0.017	0.015	0.013	0.014	0.013	0.014	0.036	0.026	0.017	0.015	0.018
	15	Interest on the public debt	0.231	0.235	0.283	0.275	0.273	0.310	0.512	0.554	0.572	0.544	0.609
	16	Interest on consumer debt (transfer portion)	0.005	0.006	0.004	0.007	0.008	0.007	0.005	0.007	0.021	0.029	0.038
LESS	17	Corporation income taxes	0.034	0.048	0.037	0.115	0.327	0.629	0.599	0.654	0.723	0.993	1.431
	18	Undistributed corporation profits	0.189	0.225	−0.045	0.271	0.168	0.360	0.367	0.480	0.738	0.869	1.031
	19	Government investment income	0.075	0.076	0.027	0.064	0.104	0.184	0.310	0.263	0.242	0.280	0.285
	20	Other earnings not paid out to persons	0.058	−0.014	−0.051	−0.106	−0.088	−0.169	0.033	−0.232	−0.222	−0.238	−0.648
EQUALS	21	**Personal income**	**4.057**	**4.665**	**2.840**	**4.350**	**4.972**	**7.522**	**9.292**	**9.887**	**$13.510**	**$14.388**	**$16.944**
LESS	22	Personal taxes	0.069	0.093	0.088	0.143	0.174	0.604	0.938	0.937	1.013	0.977	1.356
EQUALS	23	**Personal disposable income**	**3.988**	**4.572**	**2.752**	**4.207**	**4.798**	**6.918**	**8.354**	**8.950**	**$12.497**	**$13.411**	**$15.588**
LESS	24	Personal consumption expenditure	3.508	4.583	2.974	3.972	4.464	5.466	6.972	8.012	11.463	12.576	13.973
	25	Interest paid by consumers to corporations	0.005	0.006	0.004	0.007	0.008	0.007	0.005	0.007	0.021	0.029	0.038
	26	Current transfers to nonresidents	0.042	0.044	0.016	0.026	0.026	0.024	0.026	0.038	0.032	0.036	0.044
EQUALS	27	**Personal saving**	**0.433**	**−0.061**	**−0.242**	**0.202**	**0.300**	**1.421**	**1.351**	**0.893**	**$0.981**	**$0.770**	**$1.533**

RELATED STATISTICS			1926	1929	1933	1939	1940	1942	1945	1946	1949	1950	1951
	28	Real GDP (in 1986 dollars)	43.986	52.997	38.331	56.265	63.722	84.925	89.170	87.177	97.234	104.821	109.492
	29	Growth rate of real GDP (annual %)		0.9	−7.2	7.5	13.3	17.6	−2.4	−2.2	4.5	7.8	4.5
	30	Consumer price index (1986 = 100)	14.0	13.9	10.7	11.6	12.1	13.4	13.9	14.4	18.5	14.0	21.1
	31	CPI change (annual %)	1.6	−0.2	−7.1	0	3.9	5.5	0.5	3.3	3.4	2.7	11.1
	32	Money supply, M3 less foreign currency (in billions of dollars in December)	2.01	2.27	1.99	2.90	2.99	3.76	5.88	6.74	8.05	8.51	8.68
	33	Growth rate of money supply (M3) (annual %)	3.9	−2.1	−1.3	13.3	3.3	13.1	13.3	14.7	4.8	5.7	2.1
	34	3-month Treasury Bill yield-year's low	–	–	2.00	0.56	0.64	0.52	0.36	0.36	0.41	0.51	0.63
	35	3-month Treasury Bill yield-year's high	–	–	2.99	0.88	0.78	0.55	0.37	0.40	0.51	0.63	0.90
	36	Unemployment (in thousands)	108	116	826	529	423	135	73	163	153	186	1.26
	37	Unemployment as % of civilian labour force	3.0	2.9	19.3	11.4	9.2	3.0	1.6	3.4	3.0	3.6	2.4

NATIONAL INCOME AND RELATED STATISTICS FOR SELECTED YEARS, 1926–1967   (cont'd)

National income statistics are in billions of current dollars

1952	1953	1954	1955	1956	1957	1958	1959	1960	1961	1962	1963	1964	1965	1966	1967	
$15.282	$16.296	$17.078	$18.543	$20.273	$21.699	$23.064	$24.643	$25.780	$26.240	$27.985	$29.846	$32.042	$34.714	$37.952	$41.068	1
3.620	3.824	3.825	4.036	4.426	4.573	4.854	4.976	5.281	6.166	6.567	6.923	7.526	8.269	9.643	11.092	2
5.823	6.583	5.773	7.047	9.379	9.228	8.584	9.421	9.253	8.870	9.928	10.673	12.260	14.960	17.200	16.453	3
0.511	-0.137	-0.079	-0.268	-0.866	-0.838	-0.486	-0.765	-0.494	-0.154	-0.038	0.350	0.502	-0.113	-0.020	0.700	4
-0.066	-0.171	-0.066	-0.108	-0.310	-0.195	-0.327	-0.398	-0.372	-0.236	-0.034	-0.114	-0.139	-0.307	-0.387	-0.249	5
$25.170	$26.395	$26.531	$29.250	$32.902	$34.467	$35.689	$37.877	$39.448	40.886	44.408	47.678	52.191	57.523	64.388	69.064	6
-0.324	-0.301	-0.339	-0.385	-0.461	-0.563	-0.525	-0.609	-0.616	-0.722	-0.771	-0.848	-0.908	-0.992	-1.120	-1.240	7
$24.846	$26.094	$26.192	$28.865	$32.441	$33.904	$35.164	$37.268	$38.832	40.164	43.637	46.830	51.283	56.531	63.268	67.824	8
2.799	2.994	3.042	3.321	3.731	3.975	4.036	4.401	4.587	4.767	5.369	5.628	6.357	7.181	7.918	8.729	9
2.347	2.648	2.947	3.366	3.838	4.184	4.155	4.478	4.769	4.919	5.297	5.658	6.148	6.684	7.369	7.881	10
0.066	0.171	0.066	0.109	0.310	0.195	0.327	0.399	0.373	0.237	0.035	0.115	0.139	0.307	0.388	0.250	11
$19.634	$20.281	$20.137	$22.069	$24.562	$25.550	$26.646	$27.990	$29.103	30.241	32.936	35.429	38.639	42.359	47.593	50.964	12
1.347	1.452	1.628	1.723	1.760	2.072	2.619	2.732	3.099	2.732	2.934	3.007	3.220	3.452	3.781	4.683	13
0.032	0.034	0.034	0.036	0.039	0.039	0.045	0.050	0.052	0.076	0.075	0.082	0.089	0.098	0.098	0.109	14
0.651	0.620	0.650	0.664	0.718	0.774	0.826	1.023	1.093	1.184	1.316	1.431	1.546	1.676	1.862	2.080	15
0.045	0.058	0.065	0.075	0.087	0.088	0.100	0.110	0.123	0.136	0.146	0.147	0.166	0.198	0.224	0.256	16
1.403	1.244	1.115	1.310	1.443	1.378	1.350	1.615	1.588	1.649	1.753	1.891	2.101	2.197	2.355	2.396	17
1.009	1.136	1.089	1.531	1.680	1.346	1.511	1.445	1.373	1.440	1.658	1.894	2.419	2.711	2.802	2.769	18
0.368	0.378	0.373	0.420	0.537	0.490	0.542	0.604	0.649	0.721	0.795	0.899	0.982	1.080	1.226	1.479	19
0.159	-0.031	0.069	-0.132	-0.217	-0.068	-0.047	-0.120	-0.023	-0.004	-0.087	-0.021	-0.004	-0.323	-0.122	-0.429	20
$18.770	$19.718	$19.868	$21.438	$23.723	$25.377	$26.880	$28.361	$29.883	30.563	33.288	35.433	38.162	42.118	47.297	51.877	21
1.670	1.832	1.849	1.934	2.224	2.456	2.338	2.668	3.028	3.191	3.436	3.655	4.226	4.801	6.185	7.445	22
$17.100	$17.886	$18.019	$19.504	$21.499	$22.921	$24.542	$25.693	$26.855	27.372	29.852	31.778	33.936	37.317	41.112	44.432	23
15.282	16.296	17.078	18.543	20.273	21.699	23.064	24.643	25.780	26.240	27.985	29.846	32.042	34.714	37.952	41.068	24
0.045	0.058	0.065	0.075	0.087	0.088	0.100	0.110	0.123	0.136	0.146	0.147	0.166	0.198	0.224	0.256	25
0.050	0.056	0.065	0.071	0.079	0.087	0.090	0.096	0.098	0.105	0.101	0.110	0.109	0.124	0.128	0.157	26
$1.723	$1.476	$0.811	$0.815	$1.060	$1.047	$1.288	$0.844	$0.854	0.891	1.660	1.675	1.619	2.281	2.808	2.951	27
1952	1953	1954	1955	1956	1957	1958	1959	1960	1961	1962	1963	1964	1965	1966	1967	
118.627	124.526	123.163	134.889	146.523	150.179	153.439	159.484	164.126	169.271	181.264	190.672	203.382	216.802	231.519	238.306	28
8.3	5.0	-1.1	9.5	8.6	2.5	2.2	3.9	2.9	3.1	7.1	5.2	6.7	6.6	6.8	2.9	29
21.6	21.4	21.5	21.5	21.8	22.5	23.1	23.4	23.7	23.9	24.2	24.6	25.1	25.7	26.6	27.6	30
2.4	-.9	0.5	0.0	1.4	3.2	2.7	1.3	1.3	0.8	1.3	1.7	2.0	2.4	3.5	3.8	31
9.22	9.21	9.99	10.85	11.16	11.38	12.83	12.64	13.22	14.37	14.91	15.87	17.03	19.08	20.31	23.59	32
6.2	-0.2	8.5	8.6	2.9	1.9	12.8	-1.5	4.6	8.7	3.8	6.4	7.3	12.0	6.5	16.1	33
0.89	1.34	1.06	0.88	2.52	3.62	0.87	3.28	1.70	2.26	3.07	3.19	3.58	3.62	4.63	4.00	34
1.30	1.97	1.81	2.56	3.67	4.03	3.49	5.50	4.61	3.28	5.47	3.78	3.88	4.54	5.19	5.95	35
155	162	250	245	197	278	432	372	446	466	390	374	324	280	267	315	36
2.9	3.0	4.6	4.4	3.4	4.6	7.0	6.0	7.0	7.1	5.9	5.5	4.7	3.9	3.6	4.1	37

NATIONAL INCOME AND RELATED STATISTICS FOR SELECTED YEARS, 1968–1994

National income statistics are in billions of current dollars

			1968	1969	1970	1971	1972	1973	1974	1975	1976	1977	1978
THE	1	Personal consumption expenditure	$44.842	$49.093	$51.853	$56.271	$63.021	$72.069	$84.231	$97.566	$111.500	$123.555	$137.427
SUM	2	Government current purchases of goods and services	12.685	14.186	16.448	18.228	20.136	22.851	27.480	33.266	38.274	43.411	47.386
OF	3	Gross investment	17.229	19.621	19.250	21.941	24.660	30.722	39.371	43.213	49.037	52.090	55.632
	4	Net exports of goods and services	0.980	0.139	2.248	1.642	0.958	1.743	0.439	–2.408	–1.027	–0.069	1.100
	5	Statistical discrepancy	–0.318	–0.013	–0.683	–0.792	–0.146	–0.013	0.590	–0.097	0.140	–1.108	0.059
EQUALS	6	**GDP at market prices**	**75.418**	**83.026**	**89.116**	**97.290**	**108.629**	**127.372**	**152.111**	**171.540**	**197.924**	**217.879**	**241.604**
	7	Net investment income from nonresidents	–1.221	–1.207	–1.351	–1.506	–1.461	–1.730	–2.238	–2.538	–3.536	–4.571	–5.950
EQUALS	8	**GNP at market prices**	**74.197**	**81.819**	**87.765**	**95.784**	**107.168**	**125.642**	**149.873**	**169.002**	**194.388**	**213.308**	**235.654**
LESS	9	Indirect taxes less subsidies	9.520	10.544	11.095	12.053	13.627	15.311	17.867	17.087	20.992	23.188	24.819
	10	Capital consumption allowances	8.412	9.753	9.948	10.764	11.734	13.628	16.447	18.760	21.454	23.798	26.619
	11	Statistical discrepancy	0.318	0.013	0.684	0.792	0.147	0.014	–0.590	0.098	–0.141	1.109	–0.059
EQUALS	12	**Net national income at factor cost**	**55.947**	**62.109**	**66.038**	**72.175**	**81.660**	**96.689**	**116.149**	**133.057**	**152.083**	**165.213**	**184.275**
PLUS	13	Government transfer payments	5.465	6.123	6.991	8.294	9.981	11.272	13.929	17.259	19.656	22.356	25.185
	14	Transfers from nonresidents	0.110	0.109	0.123	0.171	0.182	0.215	0.229	0.258	0.279	0.331	0.394
	15	Interest on the public debt	2.390	2.767	3.252	3.622	4.137	4.788	5.425	6.538	8.101	9.268	11.589
	16	Interest on consumer debt (transfer portion)	0.364	0.466	0.538	0.553	0.625	0.812	1.176	1.351	1.570	1.670	1.918
LESS	17	Corporation income taxes	2.852	3.221	3.070	3.346	3.920	5.079	7.051	7.494	7.128	7.238	8.188
	18	corporation profits	3.310	3.396	2.960	3.544	4.449	6.983	8.978	8.019	9.863	10.333	12.384
	19	Government investment income	1.752	2.276	2.724	3.217	3.739	4.423	6.009	7.176	8.446	9.978	12.467
	20	Other earnings not paid out to persons	–0.626	–0.505	–0.034	–0.569	–1.026	–2.547	–3.898	–2.804	–1.875	–3.549	–4.841
EQUALS	21	**Personal income**	**56.988**	**63.186**	**68.222**	**75.277**	**85.503**	**99.838**	**118.768**	**138.578**	**158.127**	**174.838**	**195.163**
LESS	22	Personal taxes	8.844	10.881	12.606	14.130	15.647	18.091	22.364	25.257	29.888	33.464	35.697
EQUALS	23	**Personal Disposable income**	**48.144**	**52.305**	**55.616**	**61.147**	**69.856**	**81.747**	**96.404**	**113.321**	**128.239**	**141.374**	**159.466**
LESS	24	Personal consumption expenditure	44.842	49.093	51.853	56.271	63.021	72.069	84.231	97.566	111.500	123.550	137.427
	25	Interest paid by consumers to corporations	0.364	0.466	0.538	0.553	0.625	0.812	1.176	1.351	1.570	1.670	1.918
	26	Current transfers to nonresidents	0.130	0.185	0.176	0.181	0.215	0.237	0.247	0.258	0.269	0.292	0.294
EQUALS	27	**Personal saving**	**2.808**	**2.561**	**3.049**	**4.142**	**5.995**	**8.692**	**10.750**	**14.146**	**14.900**	**15.862**	**19.827**

RELATED STATISTICS			1968	1969	1970	1971	1972	1973	1974	1975	1976	1977	1978
	28	Real GDP (in 1986 dollars)	251.064	264.508	271.372	286.998	303.447	326.848	341.235	350.113	371.688	385.122	402.737
	29	Growth rate of real GDP (annual %)	5.4	5.4	2.6	5.8	5.7	7.7	4.4	2.6	6.2	3.6	4.6
	30	Consumer price index (1986 = 100)	28.7	30.0	31.0	31.9	33.4	36.0	39.9	44.2	47.5	51.3	55.9
	31	CP change (annual %)	4.0	4.5	3.3	2.9	4.7	7.8	10.8	10.8	7.5	8.0	9.0
	*32	Money supply, M3 (in billions of dollars in December)	26.72	27.72	34.60	37.72	43.31	52.68	64.09	73.66	88.57	101.04	118.87
	33	Growth rate of money supply (annual %)	13.3	3.8	10.9†	9.0	14.8	21.6	21.7	14.9	20.2	16.5	14.3
	34	3-month Treasury Bill yield-year's low	5.48	6.38	4.40	3.00	3.36	3.90	6.07	6.26	8.14	7.05	7.13
	35	3-month Treasury Bill yield-year's high	6.99	7.81	7.78	4.68	3.73	6.53	9.11	8.64	9.13	8.04	10.46
	36	Unemployment (in thousands)	382	382	495	552	562	520	514	690	727	850	911
	37	Unemployment as % of civilian labour force	4.8	4.7	5.9	6.4	6.3	5.6	5.3	6.9	7.1	8.1	8.4

* Prior to 1970, this series *excluded* foreign currency booked in Canada as well as the liabilities of the chartered banks' majority–owned subsidiaries. Thus there is a discontinuity between 1969 and 1970.

†Growth rate of discontinued series.

NATIONAL INCOME AND RELATED STATISTICS FOR SELECTED YEARS, 1968–1994 (cont'd)

National income statistics are in billions of current dollars

1979	1980	1981	1982	1983	1984	1985	1986	1987	1988	1989	1990	1991	1992	1993	1994	
$153.390	$172.416	$196.191	$210.509	$231.452	$251.645	$274.503	$296.810	$322.769	$349.937	$378.077	398.208	411.960	422.515	436.542	452.859	1
52.286	59.250	68.792	78.655	84.571	89.089	95.519	100.337	105.836	114.472	123.718	133.781	161.279	166.106	167.970	167.522	2
68.428	72.624	87.305	71.574	78.329	89.460	96.479	104.122	119.788	136.585	149.898	137.207	112.372	109.098	114.175	125.250	3
1.794	5.646	3.879	14.053	13.612	15.403	11.531	4.490	4.914	2.925	−1.692	−1.361	−7.956	−6.065	−3.164	5.615	4
0.198	−0.045	−0.173	−0.349	−2.247	−0.862	−0.044	−1.128	−1.710	1.987	−0.085	0.008	−1.178	−1.882	−2.668	−1.193	5
276.096	309.891	355.994	374.442	405.717	444.735	477.988	504.631	551.597	605.906	649.916	667.843	676.477	690.122	712.855	750.053	6
−7.155	−7.827	−11.337	−12.670	−11.603	−13.486	−14.332	−16.548	−16.444	−18.712	−21.503	−24.256	−21.869	−24.242	−23.991	−26.272	7
268.941	302.064	344.657	361.772	394.114	431.249	463.656	488.083	535.153	587.194	628.413	643.587	654.608	665.880	688.864	723.781	8
26.635	27.272	36.457	38.908	40.135	42.714	47.212	53.532	59.719	67.790	75.844	75.231	79.878	84.389	88.731	93.662	9
30.743	35.527	40.677	44.356	47.060	50.884	55.926	60.214	64.116	68.128	72.411	76.184	82.331	85.305	87.904	92.973	10
−0.199	0.045	0.173	0.350	2.247	0.863	0.045	1.128	1.710	−1.987	0.085	−0.009	1.179	1.883	2.668	1.193	11
211.762	239.220	267.350	278.158	304.672	336.788	360.473	373.209	409.608	453.263	480.073	492.181	491.220	494.303	509.561	535.953	12
26.697	30.864	35.307	44.453	51.253	54.180	58.515	62.221	66.438	71.415	77.096	85.260	98.551	107.531	112.972	113.346	13
0.450	0.519	0.545	0.600	0.610	0.629	0.681	0.774	0.821	0.849	0.853	0.935	1.102	1.194	1.303	1.426	14
13.810	16.790	22.268	27.072	29.419	34.752	40.183	42.916	45.903	50.410	58.075	63.596	40.978	39.490	39.240	40.126	15
2.855	3.713	5.362	5.132	3.785	3.791	4.233	4.624	5.268	6.205	8.244	9.036	7.854	5.933	4.834	4.432	16
10.038	12.078	12.796	11.755	12.320	14.984	15.563	14.383	16.990	17.586	18.518	16.851	15.010	14.423	14.475	16.890	17
18.522	18.825	11.418	−0.498	11.657	16.971	19.827	15.481	24.172	28.970	22.426	6.660	−.068	.340	9.220	20.120	18
14.932	17.940	20.934	22.309	25.267	28.182	29.656	28.833	29.573	32.527	36.208	37.677	12.665	12.876	12.487	13.179	19
−7.385	−6.627	−7.531	−2.988	−2.557	−2.236	−1.160	−1.351	−3.888	−2.983	−2.002	0.269	6.131	−.964	−1.651	−2.098	20
219.467	248.890	293.215	324.837	343.052	372.239	400.199	426.398	461.191	506.042	549.191	589.551	605.967	621.776	633.379	647.192	21
39.615	45.237	55.533	61.976	67.039	71.893	78.862	89.244	99.756	111.807	117.951	135.921	140.024	143.618	144.917	149.835	22
179.852	203.653	237.682	262.861	276.013	300.346	321.337	337.154	361.435	394.235	431.240	453.630	465.943	478.158	488.462	497.357	23
153.390	172.416	196.191	210.509	231.452	251.645	274.503	296.810	322.769	349.937	378.077	398.208	411.960	422.515	436.540	452.859	24
2.855	3.713	5.362	5.132	3.785	3.791	4.233	4.624	5.268	6.205	8.244	9.036	7.854	5.933	4.834	4.432	25
0.347	0.364	0.385	0.443	0.473	0.500	0.554	0.574	0.629	0.709	0.780	0.820	.777	.941	.990	1.048	26
23.260	27.160	35.744	46.777	40.303	44.410	42.047	35.146	32.769	37.384	44.139	45.566	45.352	48.769	46.096	39.018	27

1979	1980	1981	1982	1983	1984	1985	1986	1987	1988	1989	1990	1991	1992	1993	1994	
418.328	424.537	440.127	425.970	439.448	467.167	489.437	504.631	526.730	552.958	565.779	563.060	555.052	559.305	571.722	597.936	28
3.9	1.5	3.7	−3.2	3.2	6.3	4.8	3.3	4.2	5.0	2.4	−0.2	−1.8	0.8	2.2	4.6	29
61.0	67.2	75.5	83.7	88.5	92.4	96.0	100.0	104.4	108.6	114.0	119.5	126.2	128.1	130.4	130.7	30
9.1	10.2	12.4	10.9	5.7	4.4	3.9	4.2	4.4	4.0	5.0	4.8	5.6	1.5	1.8	0.2	31
141.99	162.13	181.5	181.28	178.77	191.03	200.97	218.83	233.637	257.899	291.315	314.243	383.265	408.447	419.684	442.022	32
19.8	16.3	13.2	4.5	1.6	3.1	6.6	7.7	11.0	8.7	11.9	10.3	6.5	5.1	4.9	3.9	33
10.78	10.06	14.41	9.80	9.12	9.73	8.53	8.09	6.8	8.29	10.94	11.47	7.48	5.17	3.91	3.63	34
13.66	17.01	20.82	16.33	9.71	12.73	11.27	11.55	9.58	10.95	12.37	13.80	10.64	8.56	6.56	7.14	35
838	867	898	1,305	1,436	1,399	1,328	1,236	1,150	1,031	1,018	1,109	1,417	1,640	1,649	1,541	36
7.5	7.5	7.6	11.0	11.9	11.3	10.5	9.6	8.8	7.8	7.5	8.1	10.3	11.3	11.2	10.4	37

Sources: Statistics Canada: National Income and Expenditure Accounts; Bank of Canada Review, Bank of Canada printouts.

INDEX

STUDENT REPLY CARD

In order to improve future editions, we are seeking your comments on
Microeconomics: Scarcity, Wants, and Choices, Seventh Canadian Edition
by McConnell, Brue, and Barbiero. After you have read this text, please answer the
following questions and return this form via Business Reply Mail. *Your opinions
matter! Thank you in advance for your feedback!*

Name of your college or university: _____

Major program of study: _____

Course title: _____

Were you required to buy this book? ———— yes ———— no

Did you buy this book new or used? ———— new ———— used ($ ————)

Do you plan to keep or sell this book? ———— keep———— sell

Is the order of topic coverage consistent with what was taught in your course?

Are there chapters or sections of this text that were not assigned for your course?
Please specify:

Were there topics covered in your course that are not included in this text?
Please specify:

What did you like most about this text?

What did you like least?

If you would like to say more, we'd love to hear from you. Please write to us at the
address shown on the reverse of this card.